ILLUSTRATIONS

OF THE

MANNERS AND EXPENCES OF ANTIENT TIMES

IN ENGLAND,

AMS PRESS
NEW YORK

KRAUS REPRINT CO.
MILLWOOD, N.Y.

ILLUSTRATIONS

OF THE

MANNERS AND EXPENCES OF ANTIENT TIMES IN ENGLAND,

IN THE FIFTEENTH, SIXTEENTH, AND SEVENTEENTH CENTURIES,

DEDUCED FROM

THE ACCOMPTS OF CHURCHWARDENS,

AND OTHER AUTHENTIC DOCUMENTS,

COLLECTED FROM VARIOUS PARTS OF THE KINGDOM,

WITH EXPLANATORY NOTES.

"Our enlightened age laughs at the rudeneſs of our anceſtors, and overlooks the manners of that "rank of men whoſe ſimplicity is the beſt guardian of antiquity. Innumerable lights may be "drawn from local cuſtoms and uſages, which are generally founded on ſome antient fact, and "ſerve to guide us back to truth." PREFACE TO BRITISH TOPOGRAPHY.

LONDON:

PRINTED BY AND FOR JOHN NICHOLS,
PRINTER TO THE SOCIETY OF ANTIQUARIES.

MDCCXCVII.

Library of Congress Cataloging in Publication Data

[Nichols, John] 1745-1826, comp.
Illustrations of the manners and expences of antient times in England, in the fifteenth, sixteenth, and seventeenth century.

Attributed by Cushing and Halkett to Samuel Pegge, the elder, who contributed Annotations on the preceding articles: p. 243-268.
1. England--Social life and customs. 2. Prices--Great Britain--History. I. Pegge, Samuel, 1704-1796. II. Title.
DA320.N42 1973 309.1'42 79-173078
ISBN 0-404-04688-6

Reprinted from the edition of 1797, London
First AMS/Kraus edition published in 1973
Manufactured in the United States of America

CONTENTS.

* P. 272. notes, l. 2. r. "the tabernacle, or *niche*, wherein," &c.

PREFACE.

P R E F A C E.

THE uſe of books of accompts for aſcertaining and exemplifying the prices of the ſeveral articles of life in different ages has always been acknowledged. At the ſame time that they ſhew how our anceſtors lived, they inform us how they could afford to live.

The few monuments of this kind that have been brought to light are confined to particular ſocieties, and in places diſtant from the capital. Such are the regiſters recited in Biſhop Fleetwood's Chronicon Precioſum; thoſe of Burceſter Priory, printed in Biſhop Kennet's Parochial Antiquities; and thoſe of Chriſt Church College, Oxford, by Mr. Hearne, in his Antiquities of Glaſtonbury [1]. Or to individuals of higher rank; as the bills of fare for Archbiſhop Neville's inthronization, that of the Prior of St. Auſtin, Canterbury, 1309 [2]; dinners of the Mayor of London [3]; and the Mayor of Norwich [4]; of the Company of Salters [5], and of the Stationers, to the latter of whom literary property is a perpetual feaſt [6]. And the circumſtances of ſocieties and ſolemnities had an influence on the expence of the articles.

But the accounts of a *Pariſh* or a *Family* for half a century are not liable to this inconvenience. They conſumed proviſion, burned candle, paid for labour and materials at the current price; to ſay nothing of many leſſer circumſtances of time, place, cuſtoms, or manners, of which they inform us. Such a ſtock of cattle and corn we have in the reign of King John [7]. The appraiſement of Serjeant Keble's goods, 1500 [8]; and of Sir Peter Frechevile's, in 1582 [9]. The expences of the barriers in Weſt Smithfield, 1524 [10]. The ſtock and furniture of a London tavern 1612 [11].

The Accompts of the Churchwardens of St. Helen's church at Abingdon, originally printed by the Society of Antiquaries [12], with illuſtrations by their late learned member Profeſſor Ward, are re-publiſhed in the preſent collection [13].

Thoſe of Wigtoft [14], in Lincolnſhire, though belonging to a country town and pariſh, may perhaps be conſidered as a record of ſuperſtitious practices, rather than of neceſſaries or ordinary occurrences of life.

Theſe laſt are ſupplied, without omitting the other, in the extracts ſubmitted to the Society of Antiquaries, from the accompts of the Churchwardens of *St. Mary Hill*, near Billingſgate, with the peruſal of which Mr. Gough had been indulged by his friend Dr. Griffith, late rector of the ſaid church; and of which it may be ſaid, that they are unparalleled in their kind, and alſo, in point of time (1427), beyond any we have yet heard of; while thoſe of St. Margaret's Weſtminſter, which begin almoſt as early (in 1460), come down to a much later period (1692); and both contain much hiſtorical matter, local and general.

[1] Appendix, Nº VIII. [2] Thorn. ap Fleetwood, Chronicon Precioſum.
[3] Stowe. [4] Blomefield. [5] See p. 269. [6] See p. 221.
[7] Hearne's Gul. Neubrigenſis, vol. III p. 785. [8] See p. 239.
[9] See p. 233. [10] See p. 213. [11] See p. 239.
[12] Archæologia, vol I. p. 11. [13] See p. 140. [14] Pp. 77—87; 195—290.

Thoſe

Thofe of St. Martin and St. Mary de Caftro at Leicefter, the one beginning in 1489, the other in 1493, abound in remarkable entries, and will foon appear in the Hiftory of that County.

The accompts from York, whilft they exhibit an interefting fpecimen of provincial phrafeology, are enriched with illuftrations by Mr. Pegge, which render them peculiarly valuable, and form an admirable fupplement to the notes before fuggefted by his learned and venerable father.

Inventories of church-furniture[1] may be found in the prefent collection, pp. 136. 275; in Gunton's Hiftory of Peterborough, p. 58; Dart's Antiquities of Canterbury, Appendix; Somner's Hiftory of Canterbury, by Batteley, Appendix, p. 34; Ducarel's Hiftory of St. Catharine's Hofpital by the Tower, Appendix, p. 40; and in the Hiftory of Leicefterfhire, vol. I. p. cxxxvii.

In the celebrated *Fleta*, fuppofed to be written in the reign of Edward II. amidft the moft important heads of government and law, the author introduces a plan of houfehold management, and gives the minuteft directions for regulating the moft petty domeftic concerns. In the fecond book he defcribes very minutely every thing that pertains to the office of almoft every kind of houfehold fervant, not only of the fenefchal (or fteward), bailiff, fwineherd, baker, mower, carter or waggoner, cowkeeper, dairyman, &c.[2] Their wages were appointed to labourers[3], by a ftatute 11 H. VII. c. 22. 1495.[4]

Bifhop Percy obferves, "that calculating the value of money by the price of wheat" is ftating the account as much as poffible in conformity to modern times; for, it appears pretty evidently, that wheat was not the moft general bread confumed in that age as indeed it is hardly yet in the Northern counties[5]; but that rye, barley, or oats, were the common food of the lower or middle ranks of people, who at prefent (in the Southern parts of England at leaft) difdain any but what is nice wheaten bread: the great difference, therefore, in the value of money is farther to be increafed by the difproportion of value between wheat and other inferior grain.

Mr. Benet, in the preface to his edition of Afcham's Schoolmafter, has an obfervation to account for the comparative lownefs of prices in different ages, that "in the reign of Henry VIII. moft of the elegance and expences of our prefent fafhions were unknown; commerce had not yet diftributed fuperfluity through

[1] In Mr. Baker's MS Collections, vol. XVII. (Harl. MSS. 7044) are 20 curious pages (175—194) of "Collectanea e Rationario, five Libro Cenfuali Ecclefiæ B. Mariæ, juxta Forum Cantabr. in cuftodiâ Gardianorum ejufdem Ecclefiæ."

[2] Preface to Northumberland Houfehold Book, p. vii.

[3] See fuch in Rutland, 1610, Archæologia, vol. XI. p. 200; and in Warwickfhire, 1683, p. 208.

[4] Sir Frederick Morton Eden's State of the Poor; vol. III. p. lxxxix. where fee alfo the wages in Yorkfhire, 35 Eliz.; in Chefhire, 5 Mary; prices of meat 1593.

[5] We have it on very good authority, that 30 years ago the bread of the labouring people in the ifle of Axholme was made of flour of horfebeans. Harrifon, in his Defcription of England, (Preface to Holinfhed's Chronicle, 1586,) fays, "*in time of dearth* manie were forced to content themfelves with bread made either of beans, peafon, or otes, or of altogether, and fome *acorns* among. I will not fay that this extremitie is oft fo well to be feene in time of plentie as of dearth, but if I fhould I could eafily bring my triall."

the

the lower classes of people;" and therefore the same revenue (though the different value of money were out of the case) would have gone a great way farther than it would at present. We cannot, however, help being of opinion, that the gorgeous and substantial finery of the reign of Henry VIII. and his daughter Elizabeth[1], was in its way as expensive as the lighter and more flippant elegance of modern times, which has reduced dress to an airy thinness scarcely to be confined within the authority of decency.

The first instance of the regular expences of a family presented to the publick, was that of Thomas Earl of Lancaster; the particulars of whose housekeeping for one whole year, made out by his cofferer in 1313, are given in the History of Leicestershire, vol. I. p. 223, from a manuscript belonging to this great Earl, which Mr. Strype calls "The Record of Pontefract;" a copy of which was in the hands of the late John-Watson Reed, esq. F. S. A. who had intended to publish it, and had actually printed off sixteen pages in quarto (a copy of which is now before us), the completion of which was prevented by his death, Jan. 30, 1790. The accompts of one week shall be given at the end of this Preface[2] as a specimen.

Twenty years before this (in 1770) a complete Household Book, that of Henry Algernon, fifth Earl of Northumberland of the noble family of Percy, from about 1497 to 1527, in which year he died, was printed at their expence, for private use, 1770, and illustrated with a commentary by the present Bishop of Dromore, who observes of it, that "it contains a complete system of *antient œconomies*[3]."

Several such accompts of the Norfolk family were in the hands of the late Sir John Fenn, kt.

"The steward's account of sir John Howard, knt. (afterwards first Duke of Norfolk) from the 2d to the 9th of Edward IV. 1462—1469, 4to. Sir John lived at Stoke by Neyland, when these accounts were written, which are very curious, as they contain the prices of almost every article at that time in use. This book was taken from Framlyngham castle in 1727, and in it are many articles in sir John's almost illegible hand-writing. A specimen of them for 1523, and of Sir Edward Coke's for 1599, from the same collection, may be seen in Sir Frederick Morton Eden's State of the Poor, vol. III. App. p. cxvii—cxxxvi.

"The cater's account of the household expences at Stoke by Neyland of Thomas Howard, Earl of Surrey, folio. Some leaves are wanting at the beginning and end of this MS. which contains an exact daily account of every meal, from April 17 to January 18 following; the provisions, number of persons, &c. and at the end of each week is a particular of all the provisions expended and remaining, with the prices of every article. It exhibits a true picture of the time, which was between the 15th and 16th of Henry VIII. 1513—1524; as in the former year Thomas Howard was created Earl of Surrey, and in the latter succeeded his father as Duke of Norfolk."

[1] See her Sumptuary Proclamation in 1579, at the end of this Collection. [2] See pp. ix. x.

[3] It is a little extraordinary that, among this earl's accompts, no traces should be found of the tombs erected most probably at his expence, and under or by his direction, to his father and mother in Beverley minster, engraved in Sepulchral Monuments of Great Britain, vol. II. Plate CIX. CX. CXIV. particularly the second, which is highly finished, and well preserved; and, but for a brief hint of Leland, would still have remained unascertained.

The

The Wardrobe account of the 28th year, or eſtabliſhment of Edward I. has been printed by the Society of Antiquaries, 1787; alſo, a collection of ordinances and regulations for the government of the royal houſehold, made in divers reigns from King Edward III. to King William and Queen Mary, 1790. See alſo a Wardrobe charge of Henry VIII. in Archæologia, vol. IX. p. 243; and that of Richard the Third's coronation 1483, vol. I. p. 361.

By "A booke of Fees and Offices, primo die Auguſti, anno primo Regine Marie[1]," preſerved in the Library of Dulwich College (which contains many treaſures well worth inveſtigation), epitomized in the "Bibliotheca Topographica Britannica," N° VII. p. 231—233; it appears that the total of all the public charges at that time amounted to 72,364*l.* 19*s.* 10¼*d.*

Mr. Gough has in MS. a later but ſmaller volume, ſomewhat of the ſame nature (which formerly was P. Le Neve's, and afterwards T. Martin's), intituled, "A generall Collection of all the Offices of England, with their Fees, in the Queene's Guifte;" not dated, except "Temp. Eliz. Reginæ."

The charges of the funeral of John Dudley, eſq. 1580, are printed in the Additions to the Hiſtory of Stoke Newington, in the XIVth number of the "Bibliotheca Topographica Britannica;" that of Archbiſhop Parker, in the Appendix to Batteley's Antiquities of Canterbury, p. 39.; the expence of wax at the funerals of King Richard II. and Queen Anne, in Sepulchral Monuments of Great Britain.

The expences of ſeveral public entertainments and ceremonious viſits during the ſplendid reign of Queen Elizabeth will be found in the Hiſtory of her Progreſſes. Among theſe may be particularly noticed, the Expences of the Queen's own table in 1576, and of her viſit at Gorhambury in 1577; the numerous preſents both given and taken by her Majeſty as New Year's Gifts; and the various feaſts, maſques, and revels, at the Temple and other inns of court.

The houſehold expences of Henry the ſeventh Earl of Kent, for ſeven weeks, ending April 6, 1593, are printed in the "Bibliotheca Topographica Britannica," N° XLIII. p. 276; and thoſe of Chriſtiana Counteſs of Devonſhire, from 1635 to 1655, in the Hiſtory of Leiceſterſhire, vol. I. p. 290.

The obſervations on Pariſh-Regiſters, Archdeacons, Endowments of Vicarages, &c. may not ſeem ſtrictly in connexion with the ſubject; but, by thoſe who value the authors of them, will not be thought unworthy to be preſerved.

Some articles of a miſcellaneous nature are added, illuſtrative of the general object, the manners and the expences of antient times.

St. Andrew's-day, 1797. J. N.

[1] Among the artificers of various kinds, are enumerated the following names: Prynter, Thomas Bartlet; Statoner, Reynold Woolf; Keper of Libraries, Bartholomew Traſeron; Serjant Paynter, Anthony Tetto; Paynturs, Bartholomew Penne and Levyn Tirling; Graver of Stones, Richard Atzele; Clockemaker, Nicholas Urfewe; Clockekeper, John de Moylym; Aſtronomer, Nicholas Cracher; Mole-taker, John Whatton; three Keepers of the Pheſauntes and Partriges; and two Takers of Pheſauntes and Partriges. Fees to the royal band of "Muſitions and Players," including "Trumpeters, Lutars, Harpers, Rebeck, Sagbuts, Vialls, Bagpiper, Minſtrells, Drumſlades, Players on the Fluyte, Players on the Virginalles, Muſitions Straungers (Venetians), Players of Enterludes (in nombre 8, every of them at 66*s.* by yeare), and Makers of Inſtruments," were 1728*l.* 5*s.*

LIBER HOSPICII DOMINI THOME COMITIS LANCASTRIE INCEPTUS PER DOMINUM HENRICUM DE LEICESTRE A CRASTINO SANCTI MICHAELIS ANNO XIJ° USQUE [FESTUM EJUSDEM SANCTI ANNO XIIJ° REGIS EDWARDI SECUNDI.]

DIE Sabati, in craſtino Sancti Michaelis, apud Pountfret. Diſpenſa. xxiij s̃. vij đ. Butelleria. preter xviij. ſexteria vini de ſtauro. xxvi s̃. v đ. Coquina. preter xl. ſtocfiſh xxx. lienges de providencia Sancti Botulphi & viij^{c}. alleces de precomputatis. xxvij s̃. x đ. q̃. Aula. nichil. Stabulum ad iiij. $^{xx}_{iiii}$xj. equos xxxv. hakeneios. iiij li. xv s. ix đ. Ferrura. ix s̃. viij đ. In vadiis l s̃. j đ. ob̃.
Summa. xj li. xiij s. iiij đ. ob̃. q̃.

Die Dominico proximè ſequente. Diſpenſa. xxvj s̃. xj đ. Butelleria. preter xx. ſexteria vini. xxx s̃. iiij đ. Coquina. preter iij. carcoſia boum de inſtauro. lxj s̃. ij đ. Aula xviij đ. Stabulum ad iiij^{c}. $^{xx}_{iiii}$. ij. equos xxxiiij. hakeneios. cv s̃. iij đ. ob̃. q̃. Ferrura. v s. In vadiis. l s̃. ix đ. q̃.
Summa xiiij li. xij đ. q̃.

Die Lune. Diſpenſa. xvj s̃. xj đ. Butelleria. preter xvj. ſexteria vini dimidium. xxv s̃. iij đ. Coquina. preter iij. carcoſia boum iiij. pernas baconis iij. perdices de precomputatis. liij s̃. ij đ. ob̃. q̃. Aula vj đ. Stabulum ad ccc.$^{xx}_{iiii}$.xvj. equos xxxiij. hakeneios. iiij li. xiij đ. q̃ Ferrura. xj s̃. In vadiis. xlj s̃. vij đ.
Summa xj l. ix s̃. vij đ.

Die Martis. Diſpenſa. xvj s̃. xj đ. Butelleria. preter xiiij. ſexteria vini xxiiij s̃. x đ. Coquina. preter iij. quarteria boum iij. pernas baconis. lxj s. vij đ. Aula. nichil. Stabulum ad iiij^{c}. $^{xx}_{iiii}$. xix. equos xxxiij. hakeneios. iiij li. xj s̃. v đ. ob̃. Ferrura. v s̃. x đ. In vadiis. xlj s̃. v đ. ob̃.
Summa. xij l. ij s̃. j đ.

Die Mercurii. Diſpenſa. xiij s̃. vij đ. Butelleria. preter xvij. ſexteria vini. xvij s̃. x đ. Coquina. preter j. cignum v^{c}. alleces xx. lienges xlviij. ſtocfiſh. xxxviij s̃. v đ. q̃. Aula. nichil. Stabulum ad iij^{c}. xxix. equos xxxiiij hakeneios. lxvij s̃. xj đ. Ferrura. nichil. In vadiis xxxij s̃. vj đ. ob̃.
Summa viij li. x s̃. iij đ. ob̃. q.

Die Jovis. Diſpenſa. xxijs̄. vijđ. Butelleria. preter xiiij. ſexteria vini. xixs̄. xjđ. ob̄. Coquina. preter iiij. quarteria boum j. pernam baconis. lxvijs̄. jđ. Aula. nichil. Stabulum ad iij^{c}. xix. equos xxxiiij. hakeneios. iiijli. xviijs̄. ob̄. Ferrura xxđ. In vadiis. xxxijs̄. vjđ. ob̄.

Summa. xijli. xxijđ. ob̄.

Die Veneris. Diſpenſa. xiijs̄. vijđ. Butelleria. preter x. ſexteria vini. xvjs̄. vđ. ob̄. Coquina. preter xij. lienges xxiiij. ſtocfiſh iii^{c}. $\overset{xx}{iiii}$. alleces. xxvs̄. xjđ. ob̄. Aula xviijđ. Stabulum ad iij^{c}. xj. equos xxxiiij. hakeneios. iiijli. iijs̄. xjđ. Ferrura. vjs̄. viijđ. In vadiis. xxxjs. ijđ. ob̄.

Summa. viijli. xixs̄. iijđ. ob̄.

Die Sabati. Diſpenſa. xvjs̄. xjđ. Butelleria. preter xj. ſexteria vini. xxvijs̄. iiijđ. ob̄. Coquina. preter xx. lienges xliiij. ſtocfiſh ij^{c}. alleces de precomputatis. xxxijs̄. iiijđ. ob̄. Aula. nichil. Stabulum ad iij^{c}. xxxj. equos xxxij. hakeneios. lvjs̄. viijđ. ob̄. Ferrura. nichil. In vadiis. xxxijs̄. vđ. ob̄.

Summa. viijli. vs̄. xđ.

Eodem die computat Robertus de Holdene in vj. quarteriis dimidio ſalis emptis de Willielmo de Cotes. xiijs̄. In vij. quarteriis ſalis emptis de Willielmo Monner. xiiijs̄. In v. quarteriis ſalis emptis de Johanne Balderker. xs. In iij. quarteriis ſalis de Roberto Muriel. vjs̄. In xlij. quarteriis ſalis de Gilberto Stote. lxxs̄. In cariagio ejuſdem de Sneith uſque Pountfret per xx bigas. xvjs̄. viijđ. In proſtracione x quercuum per Adam Olive. xiijs̄. In proſtracione viij quercuum per Pacwode xs̄. In amputacione ramorum iiij. quercuum per Adam Olive. iijs̄. In carriagio buſce per diverſas carectas per dominum Henricum de Athelaſtre cum aliis minutis expenſis factis circa dictam buſcam cariandam cum factura vj^{c}. dimidii faggottorum et cariagio eorundem. vijli. xvjs̄. vđ. ob̄. In iiij^{c}. diſcis iiij^{c}. ſalſariis iiij^{c}. platellis emptis per dictum Dominum Henricum. xijs̄. In xiiij^{m}. allecibus cxijs̄.

Summa. xxjli. xvjs̄. jđ. ob̄.

Summa ſeptimane. cviijli. xixs̄. vjđ. ob̄. q̄.

CHURCH-

CHURCHWARDENS ACCOMPTS.

1460-61. Comp̃us Joh̃is Meriden & Joh̃is Whitney, cuſtod' bonor' Eccleſie ꝑochiat St̃e Margarete Weſtm', anno xv° die menſo' Maii, anno St̃i Imp' Hen' Sexti Regis Angl' de facto et non de jure XXXVIII, uſque XVII diem ejuſdem menſ' Maii, anno ſecundo Regis Edwardi Quarti, ſcil' ꝑ duos annos integros.

		£.	s.	d.
	ITEM, rec' de Joh̃e Braddyns die ſepultur' Rob̃ti Thorp, gen', ꝑ IIII tor', — — —	0	6	8
	Item, rec' die ſepultur' de la Ancreſe pro III tapr', —	0	0	8
	Item, deliv'at Dño Cancellar' Dñi Regis, prædict' die Martii, per aſſen' totius ville, ꝑ guerris dict' Dñi Regis, —	10	0	0
1464.	Item, rec' de perſonar' Convict' die ſepult', — —	. . . . . .		
1465.	Item, rec' die obit' Joh̃is Gray militis, — —	. . . .		
	Item, rec' die ſepult' cujuſd' pauperis apud Chayryng,	. . . .		
1466.	Item, rec' pro ſepult' ejuſdem Agnetis in Capellâ beatæ Mariæ Virginis infra Eccleſiam prædict', —	0	6	8
	Item, rec' die obit' Richard Salkeld, gen'.			
	Item, rec' die ſepult' Heremitæ apud Charyng.			
	Item, pro ſepult' ejuſdem in Capellâ Sancti Georgii infra Eccleſ' prædict'.			
	Item, rec' de Dño Abbate Weſt' die ſepult' Will̃i Payn ſervientis ſui.			
	Item, rec' de Dña Graa die trigintal' Reginaldi patris ſui.			
	Item, rec' die ſepult' Dñi Johan' Germyn Anachorit' Weſtm'.			
	Item, rec' de Jacobo Pemberton, armigero, pro ſep' ſuâ infra eccleſiam.			
	Item, rec' die ſepult' Clerici Stapulæ.			
1467.	Item, rec' die ſepult' Magiſtri Joh̃is Preſton, nuper vicarii de Wakefield.			
	Item, rec' die ſepult' pueri unius com̃orantis in Sellyes Ally.			
	Item, rec' de Will̃o Whitney pro ſepult' uxoris ſuæ infra Capellâ Sanctæ Trin' in eccleſia prædict'.			
	Item, rec' de Thomâ More, die obit' Dñi Edwardi Kyrton nuper Abbatis Weſtm'.			
	Item, rec' de Cuſt' Convictor' die ſep' Joh̃is Hede priſonar'.			
	Item, rec' de Rob̃to Thorp, die ſep' Dioniſiæ Swandlond, generoſæ, pro ſep' ſuâ infra eccleſiam paroch' prædict'.			

Imprimis,

		£.	s.	d.
	Imprimis, in expenſ' ad tabernam intra parochianos in die comptacōis prædeceſſ' cuſt' prædict'; videlt' in pane,	0	0	5
	Item, in v mut. pyes ad idem temp̄' — — —	0	0	3
	Item, in vino rubeo, &c. ——— ———	0	3	0
	Item, at the day of burying a man of my Lord Dureſſe.			
1474.	Item, at the burying of Thomas Rookes, Gent.			
	Item, at the burying of John Harvy, Squier, in Randolfs.			
1475.	Item, at the day of burying of my Lady Grace.			
	Item, at the day of burying of Sir Thomas Grey, Knight, for IIII tapers.			
	Item, at the burying of Sir John Galter.			
	Item, for a reward for a boke and chales to Sir Richard Widevyle.			
	Item, for II great books, called Antiphoners, ——	22	0	0
	Item, received of the keeper or maſter of the New Works.			
	Item, of the monaſtre of Seint Peter of Weſtminſter.			
1476.	Alſo paid to Roger Fylpott, learned in the law, for his counſel-giving to the ſaid late maſters in ſaying of evidence of David Selly 3s. 8d. with 4d. for his dinner.			

Brethren and Siſtern in Arrears.

Of *Edmond Downe*, late pryor of Hurley; of Sir *Henry Ward*, Knight; of Dame *Agnes Haſely*; of *Robert Shordycke*, Squier; of my Lady *Graa*; of *Raynold Colyer*, pryor of St. Bartholomew's; of the Ducheſs of *Bed'*; *William Bartram*, Eſq; *Richard Ruſton*, pryor of Hurley; my Lady *Willoughby*; my Lady *Ankeraſſe*; Sir *John Mannear* of Batreſſey; *John Rokes*, Eſq; Sir *Thomas Knolle*, vicar of Dachet; *John Fogge*, Knight; my Lady *Harecourt*; Sir *Roger Ree*, Knight.

		£.	s.	d.
1478.	Item, the day of burying of *William Caxton*, for II torches and IIII tapers at a low maſs —— ——	0	1	8
1479.	Item, the day of burying of Sir *John Wra*, for IIII torches, IIII tapers, and the pitt ———	0	14	0
	Item, the day of burying of Dr. *Alyne*, for his pytte in the church	0	6	8
1478.	Item, for a pulpytte in the church-yard, againſt the preaching of Dr. *Penkey*, — — —	0	2	8
1479.	Item, paid to *Blandford* for paving before St. Eraſmus Auter, and for lime and ſand, ——— ———	0	1	6
1480.	Item, the day of burying a man that was ſlayne in St. James's field, II tapers —— ——	....		
1482.	Item, the day of burying of *Thomas* of the Convicte houſe.	....		
1483.	Item, the day of Sir *Thomas Cawey*, for IIII tapers.	....		

Year	Item	£.	s.	d.
	Item, the day of burying of Sir *William Hopton*, treaſurer of the King's houſe, for his pytte in the church,	0	6	8
1482.	Item, paid for the amending of the cloaths before St. Margaret and St. Kateryn, and for cord, —	0	1	0
1484.	Item, at the burying of Mr. *Harcourt*, for his pytte, —	0	6	8
1485.	Item, at the burying of *John Barnard*, Gent. for IIII torches,	0	13	4
	Item, at the burying of my Lady *Stoner*, for VI torches, —	0	10	0
	Item, at the burying of *John Langley*, for his pytte in the church,	0	6	8
	Item, at the burying of Mr. *John* the Queen's foole.	....		
	Item, at the burying of Mr. *Edmund Reynford*, for IIII torches at his dirige, — — — —	0	3	4
1488.	Item, at the burying of *Daniel Richard Alyn*, parſon of Fulham, for IIII tapers, —— ——	0	1	0
	Item, for the burying of Maſter *Tayſdale*, for the bell, —	0	0	6
1489.	Item, at the burying of my Lady *Ancreſſe*, for the bell —	0	0	6
	Item, at the burying of *John Randolfe*, for IIII torches, —	0	6	8
	Item, for my Lady *Jakis* for her grave, in the feretre iſle, —	0	7	4
1489.	Item, at the burying of the parſon of *Arondell*, for torches, tapers, &c. —— —— ——	0	6	8
Brotherhood Account.	Received for Dame *Sybill Lakynn*, ——	1	0	0
	Alſo for Mr. *Harry Sharp*, dean of St. Stephyn's,	1	0	0
	Alſo paid for two XVths granted to the King for the tenements in Kenſington ——	0	1	9
1491.	Item, at the burying of *William Caxton*, for IIII torches, —	0	6	8
	Item, Received of a box that was ſet before *St. Gregory Pytey* in Lent laſt paſt, — — —	0	10	0
	Item, received of the churchwardens of St. Sepulcre's for the Dragon, — — —	0	2	8
	Item, paid for dreſſing of the Dragon and for packthread.			
	Item, paid for a ſleyne cloth of *St. Gregory's Pety* —	0	1	8
1494.	Item, paid for wyne for Mr. *Harry Abington* at divers times,	0	0	4
	Item, at the burying of Sir *Thomas Hungerford*, Knight.	....		
	Item, of the brotherhood of Rynſyvale for the plow-gere,	0	4	0
	Item, for amending the beſt ſuit of veſtments for preſt, dekyn, and ſubdekyn, and for ribband for the ſame, ——	0	16	0
1496.	Item, paid to Mrs. *Tebbys* for III potels of tyre ſent in a botelle to Mrs. More, —— ——	0	2	0
	Item, II tapers for the man that died in Tothill-Street going to St. Armilles Ward, —— ——	0	0	2
	Item, *Henry Abyngdon* for the bell, — —	0	0	6
1497.	Item, *Richard Caſtell* for his pitte in the church, ——	0	6	8
	Item, of Mr. *Baugh*, for licence of the ground for St. Eraſmus.	....		
	Item, in books called Legend, of the bequeſt of *William Caxton*.	0	13	0
1498.	Item, for licence of St. Cornelius torches, ——	0	0	10

Year	Item	£.	s.	d.
1498.	Item, for the knell of *Jone Grey* of Wilton for the great belle,	0	0	6
1499.	Item, for the knell of my Lady *Billing* with the great bell,	0	0	6
1498.	Item, for the knelle of *Elizabeth de Word* with the great bell,	0	0	6
	Item, for the knell of Sir *Pascalle Bethforde* with the great bell.			
	Item, received of Mr. *Lacy*, of the gift of my Lord of Dudley.			
1499.	Item, for the knell of the Bishop of *St. Asse* * with the bell.			
	Some of the recytes of *Abyngdon* rent in the second yere of this accounr, — —	8	10	4
1500.	Item, for the knell of *Julian de Worde* with the great bell,	0	0	6
	Item, for licence for IIII torches of St. John, —	0	0	8
	Item, for licence of IIII torches of Seynt Anne, —	0	0	4
	Item, received of the gift of my Lord *Edmund* the King's son, to the behove of the church-works, — —	0	6	8
	Item, received of my Lady *Morland* for a stone to lay upon her husband, — — — —	0	13	4
	First, received of a sanctuary-man for a quarter's rent of the first tenement that he holdeth, for Midsummer quarter, &c.	0	8	4
1501.	Item, for the knell of Sir *James Morland* with the bell, —	0	0	6
	Item, for the knell of *Owen Tuder* with the bell, —	0	0	6
1500.	Item, paid for fetching of II tonne of stone over the water from Fauks Hall unto the King's Bridge, —	0	0	6
	Item, paid to *Thomas Wright* for a day journey, for mendyne a flouer, and a windowe in the same rents, —	0	0	8
1502.	Item, Dame *Elizabeth Younge* for IIII, — —	0	1	4
	Item, received of Mr. *Payne*, the Queen's amner, for the said Queen, — — — —	0	6	8
	Sum of the College money in the first year of this accompts,	30	1	10½
	Item, to *Michell Wosebyche* for making of VIII dragons, —	0	6	8
	First paid to Sir *John Kelby* for a hole year's wages —	6	13	4
1503.	Item, received of the Southeseyer for IV tapers, —	..	..	..
	Item, received of Sir *Umpfrey Standley* for his knyll, —	0	1	0
	Item, received XXVIII torches, — —	1	8	0
	Item, received of the first blancke for the best lott, —	0	3	4
	Item, received of the second blanck, — —	0	5	0
	Item, received of the third blanck, — —	0	10	0
	Item, received of Sir *John Connyers*, curate —	0	7	0
1504.	Item, received of the Lady *Sottell*, in part of payment for her part of a pew, — —	0	0	4
	Item, received of *Robert Pynson* for IIII tapers, —	0	0	4
1504. 1505. 1506.	Also with an acre of land in the tenure of *John Norwys*, at XVI d. by year within the time of this account, — — } Our Ladies Brethren.	0	4	0

* Michael Dyacon, bishop of St. Asaph 1495—1499.

1506.

		£.	s.	d.
1506.	*Geoffry Simcon*, dean of the King's chapell,	0	6	8
	Thomas Shordich, Gent.	0	6	8
	Jamys Lord *Hamylton*,	0	6	8
	Item, of Sir *Gerveys Clifton*, Knight,	0	13	4
	Firſt, the ſaid accountants aſketh allowance of money by them paid to the office of ſelerer of Weſtminſter, for certain quit-rents going out of the tenements in Lady *Hardwyk's* Alley, ſometime *John Hardwik*, at VI s. by yere,	0	18	0
	Alſo for a certain quit-rent out of a little tenement in the Wolſtaple, to the Maire of the ſtaple, at xxd. by yere.			
	For the rent of a tenement, called *Wyllys*, lying in Totehil-Street, in the hands of Sir *William Stoner*, Knight, at LXVI s. VIII d. by yere.			
	Item, IIII printed books, II of them the Lyfe of St. Kateryn, and other II of the Birth of our Lady, of the gift of the executors of *Caxton*.			
	Another of the gift of *John Bradding*, which book is now occupied at St. Nicholas auter.			
1508.	Item, received of *Thomas Hogan*, maſter of our Lady Brotherhood, of the gift of one Mr. *Willys*, deceaſed, one of the founders of the Brotherhood,	0	3	4
	Item, received of my Lord of *Dudley*, in the term of St. Mighell, the 24th yere of the reign of our Sovereign Lord King Henry VII. deceaſed, whoſe ſoul God pardon, for the lone of a veſtment chaleys, and other neceſſarys, to ſing with in his place,	1	0	0
Abyndon's Rents.	Item, received of Mr. *William Balard*, the phiſicion, for the tenement that he dwelleth in, of the ſame rents, for a hole yere, after the rate of .... by the quarter, &c.	2	0	0
1509.	Item, at the burying of my Lady *Anne Ancres* for her knell, repeated 9 weeks after,	0	0	6
	Item, *John* Lord *Barnes Stuard* for his knyll,	0	0	6
	Item, at the burying of my Lady *Anne Clynton* for VI torches,	0	6	0
	Item, at the burying of Mrs. *Jane Vaughan*, for her pit in the church,	0	6	8
	Item, at the burying of Mrs. *Copley* for IV torches	0	1	4
	Item, of Sir *Hugh Vaughan*, Knight, for his part of a pew,	0	6	8
	Item, received of certain land lying by *Brent-brigge*, in the pariſh of *Hendon*, given to the intent to find a lamp before the Sacrament in the ſaid church, by one *Richard Wiſe*, for a hole yere, &c.	0	15	0

	£.	s.	d.
1508. Firſt ſpent at the peruſing and overlooking of the account of the laſt wardens accomptes, at the curate's houſe, for bread and drink,	0	0	4
1509. Sir *John Syms* curate of the ſaid pariſh.			
1510. Item, at the burying of *Robert the Hermyt* IV tapers,	0	0	4
Item, at the burying of my Lady *Vampage* VIII torches,	0	8	0
Item, the ſaid wardens now accomptants received of Mrs. *Elizabeth Morley*, widow, towards the new making of a rood *Mary* and *John* in the roodeloft, at the time that the pariſh be of power and ſubſtance to build and make the ſame rood, left the ſum of,	10	0	0
1511. Item, for the knyll of my Lady *Morland* VId. and for her pit in the church,	0	6	8
Item, at the burying of Mr. *Legh* for VIII torches,	0	8	0
Item, the knyll of *Dane John Rongwell*, abbot of *Buckfaſt'*,	0	0	6
Item, received of *Knight* the Courtyer, for his wive's pewe,	0	2	0
Item, of the gift of my Lady *Clynton* I tabilcloth, ſore worn, now hallowed for the high awter by the hands of Mr. Curate.			
Item, of Sir *William Vampage*, Knight, a pax coper and gilt, a relict of St. Margaret finger, ſilver and gilt.			
A peice of the head of St. George cloſid in ſilver and gilt.			

1515. *Kenſyngton.*

Our Ladies Brethren. } Sir *William Ironmonger* pariſh preſt there.

Alſo of oblacions and offerings received upon the feſtfull days of our Bleſſed Lady.

Of New Brethren, &c.

	£.	s.	d.
Item, of Mr. Dr. *Aynſworth*,	0	6	8
Item, of Sir *Rys ap Thomas*, Knight,	0	6	8
Item, of Sir *Griffith Rys*, Knight,	0	6	8
Leaſe made to *Thomas Juxſon*, citizen and merchant of *London*.			
Alſo ſpent at communicacion had with Mr. *Hall*, and other of my Lord Cardinal's counſell, for the right of the green before my Lord's place.			
Firſt, paid to the King's collectors for the King's ſubſidy for our Lady lands,	0	4	0
Alſo paid to *John Pomffret* and his company, collectors of the King's ſilver for our Lady lands, XVS.; alſo paid to the ſame collectors for the XL marks in the treaſury-box XIIIs. for XII burden ruſhes for the White Hall,	0	2	3
Item, of *Johan* of the Boyling Alley, for II tapers,	0	0	2

1516.

	£.	s.	d.
1516. Item, received of the fame accomptants of the overplufs of the box-money for my Lord Abbot's part IIs. VIId. and for the church and parifhioners part IIs. VIId.			
Item, received of the Virger of *St. Stephyn's*, for part of pew for his wife,	0	3	3

Gifts and Bequefts to the Church and Steeple.

	£.	s.	d.
Item, given the 7th day of September, by Mr. Dr. *Aynfworth*, late refident of *St. Stephen's*,	5	0	0
Item, received of the gift of Mrs. *Morley*, by reafon of II filver cups, weying 26 ounces, and being fold by the faid accountants at 3s. 4d. the ounce, with 16d. of overplus, amounting to 4l. 11s. 4d. whereof repaid to the faid Mrs. *Morley*, at her defire, 1l. 6s. 8d. and fo remains of her plate gift,	3	2	8
Item, given by Mr. *Peter Carmylian*, refidentiary of *St. Stephen's*,	0	6	8
Some of all the box-money gadered this firft yere	53	6	11½
1517. Item, of Mr. *Hungerford*, for his knyll,	0	0	6
Item, of a convict man for II tapers,	0	0	2
Item, for the knyll of Mr. *Anthony Legh*,	0	0	6
Item, received of Mr. Dr. *Aynfworth* for his knyll,	0	0	6
Item, for the knyll of Mr. *Robert Byfshop*,	0	0	6
Item, received the 6th day of September, of *Elyfabeth Sneth*, *Robert Sydlyng*, and *John Knight*, of the gift of the fraternity of our Lady of *Rouncydevall*,	0	11	0
Item, received the 13th day of September, of the gift of the brethren of *St. John Baptift*,	1	0	0
Item, received the fame day, of the gift of the brotherhood of *St. Chriftopher*,	0	7	0
Item, received the 5th day of October, of the brotherhood of *St. Cornelius*,	2	0	0
Item, received the fame day, of the gift of the brotherhood of *St. George*,	0	10	0
Item, received of the gift of Mrs. *Morley*,	4	0	0
Item, received of the gift of *Watir Gardynar*, to the making of the rode-loft in the middle ifle within the church, as more plainly appeareth by acquittance made by the faid church-wardens, to the faid Mr. *Watir*, dated the .... day of October, the 9th yere of the reign of King Henry VII.	38	0	0
Item, received the laft day of February, of Mrs. *Elizabeth Legh* and *Robert Flegg*, executors of the laft will and teftament of Mr. *Anthony Legh*, Efq; of his bequeft to the fteeple,	6	13	6

1518.

		£.	s.	d.
1518.	Item, received the 2d day of May, of *Thomas Brightman* and *Johan* his wife, and *John Cooke*, Taillor, executors to Mr. *Robert Biſshop*, late reſidentiary of *St. Stephen's*, of his bequeſt to the ſteeple,	10	0	0
	Some of all the box-money gaderyd this preſent yere,	48	2	0
1516.	Item, given to the broker that did help us to the bargain of the barneſton,	0	0	4
	Item, paid in the Cuſtom-houſe of *London* for the cuſtom and ſubſide of the ſame ſtone,	1	3	0
	Item, paid the 27th day of May to *John Branſtrette*, for 24 ton of barneſtone, with the pylage, ankarage, ſtallage, cuſtom, and water carriage from *St. Katryn Port* to the *King's Bridge*, for all in grete,	11	0	0
1519.	Item, offered on *Criſpany* and *Criſpanyany-Day*,	0	0	11
	Item, to the keeper of Scala Celi in the Abby.	0	0	4
1518.	Item, of Mr. *Roger Lukenor*, for his pit,	0	6	8
	Item, given by the children of the May-game,	0	0	8
	Item, by my Lady *Borough*,	0	0	8
1519.	Item, of Mr. *William Balard*, for his knyll,	0	0	6
	Item, for his pitt,	0	17	4
	Item, of *William Lownds* for II tapers	0	0	2
	Item, of Mr. *Robert Sampſon* for XVI torches,	0	16	0
	Item, for torches and the beſt lights at the burying of Mr. *Ward*,	2	2	8
	Item, given by Dr. *Barwick*,	0	1	8
	Item, given to the ſteeple by my Lady *Slayn*,	0	10	0
	Item, given by the executors of my Lord *Rede*,	0	10	0
	Item, hath to pledge of the goods and jewels of the ſaid church, a monſtre of ſilver and gilt to bear in the Sacrament on *Corpus Chriſti Day*, the pondre thereof 31 ounces and dimid.			
	Item, Mr. *Hall*, the curate, for IV torches, and for the beſt lights, at the buryal of Mr. *Henry Vued*, my Lord Cardinal's ſervant,	0	6	6
	Item, Mrs. *Elizabeth Talbot*, for the knell of Mr. *Edmund Talbot*, Eſq; her late huſband,	0	0	6
1520.	Item, for the pit of Mr. *John Grove*,	0	6	8
	Item, for the knyll and lights at the burying of my Lady *Bedill*,	0	7	0
	Item, for the ſetting up of God's houſe, and for taking it down again,	0	0	4
	Item, at the burying of Mr. *Thomas Newton* for VIII torches,	......		
	Item, at Mr. *John Gryffyn*, preſt, and ſtuard to Sir *Ryſap Thomas*, knight, for IV torches,	0	4	0

1521.

		£.	s.	d.
1521.	Item, paid to *Symond Symonds*, for mending of the glaſs windows, and of the ymagery works, that were broken with the grete wynds before Chriſtmas,	2	0	0
	Item, paid to Mr. Archdeacon *Man*, for ſkavage for the whole year,	0	1	4

Sir *Robert Danby* Curett.

		£.	s.	d.
1522.	Item, of him, for his herſt-clothe	0	2	0
	Item, of Hermytis child for II tapers,	0	0	2
	Item, of Mr. *Rokyſby* for IV tapers,	0	1	4
1523.	Whiche church was hallowed the 9th day of April, in the fourteenth year of our Lord God MCCCCCXXIII, and in the fourteenth yere of the reign of our Sovereign Lord King Henry VIII.			
	Received by the hands of *John Wright*, of the gift of *Richard Rokeby*, Knight, towards the reparacion of the pariſh church	0	10	0
1524.	Item, of *Elizabeth Morley*, for the beſt lights 2s. 8d. for her grave 6s. 8d.	0	9	4
	Item, paid for twelve *Judacis* * to ſtand with the tapers,	0	2	0
1525.	Item, of *John Chok*, Knight, for IV tapers,	0	0	8
	Item, of *Johan* of *St. Cornelis-houſe*, for II tapers,	0	0	2
	Memorandum, that the King's charter for the Condett at the Pales-Gate remaineth in the cuſtody of the church-wardens.			
1526.	Item, of *Richard Smith*, Ermytt, for his grave,	0	6	4
	Item, of *Richard Cotton*, for his grave,	0	6	8
	Firſt, received of the Baron of *Burford*, for the lone of a veſtment, a mas-book, a chales, and other neceſſaries,	0	1	4

The Weight of the Bells.

1527.	Firſt, the firſt bell weith	CCCCC lb.
	Item, the ſecond bell weith	CCCCCCXXI lb.
	Item, the third bell weith	DCCCCVI lb.
	Item, the fourth bell weith,	MX lb.
	Item, the fifth bell weith,	MCCCCCCXIII lb.
	Sum of the weight of all the bellis,	MMMMDCCII lb.

		£.	s.	d.
1529.	Item, of Mr. *Skelton* for VIII tapers,	0	2	8
	Item, of *William* and *Henry*, my Lady of *Hungerford's* ſervants, for IV tapers,	0	2	8
	Item, paid for a matt of wykers for the quere,	0	3	0

* This is clearly wrong: but Q. what ſhould it be?

This

		£.	s.	d.
	This account ys allowed in the presence of Mr. *William Tenant*, Curett, &c.			
1530.	Item, received of a parden at *Chayring Crosse*, ——	0	0	2
1531.	Item, received of Mr. *Laocas*, for lysence of IV tapers, —	0	0	8
	Item, received of *Anthony Tresylyon*, for his grave, ——	0	6	8
	Item, received of *Old John*, that begged at *Hay Crose*, —	*nil.*		
	Item, paid for paving of *Michell Smith's* hencheman's grave,	0	0	4
	Item, for mette for the theff that stalle the pyx, ——	0	0	4
	First, paid to *Renaeever*, payntour, for paynting and gyldyng of the LX storys of *St. Margarett's* tabernacle, —	3	6	8
	Item, paid for guilding of XII small images for the small tabernacle, —— —— ——	2	8	0
1532.	Item, received for the licence of IIII torches of the black guard,	0	0	6
	Received of Mr. *Tenaunte*, Curate, —— ——	*nil.*		
	Item, received for IV tapers for Sir *Milles*, priest of the King's almshouse, —— —— ——	0	0	8
	Item, received for the knyll and peals of the buryal of Abbot *Isslype*, —— —— —— ——	0	1	6
	Item, received of my Lady *Wynkefeld*, —— ——	0	2	0
	Item, received of Mr. *Thomas Alverd* for his grave, ——	0	6	8
1534.	Item, paid for a surpless for the curate, —— ——	0	10	0
	———————— *John More*, the clerk, ——	0	3	0
	———————— *Thomas Adams*, the clerk, ——	0	3	0
	———————— the sexton, —— ——	0	3	0
1535.	Item, one that did cut his own throte was had to Totehill.			
	Item, paid for a new ladder of steps for the pulpit, ——	0	2	0
1536.	Item, of Dr. *Stanley*, for IV tapers, —— ——	0	0	4
	Item, of Sir *Hugh Vaughan*, Knight, for lysans, and lights and torches in the church, —— —— —	0	10	0
1537.	Item, at the monyth mynde of Lady *Elizabeth* Countess of *Oxford*, for IV tapers, —— —— ——	0	0	8
	Item, of Mr. Dr. *John Appowell*, for the bells, ——	0	1	6
1538.	Item, of Dane *Kateryn Vampage*, —— —— ——	*nil.*		
	Item, of Mr. *William Walgrave*, for IV tapers — ——	0	1	4
	Item, of *Dorothy Vampage*, for IV tapers, —— ——	0	0	4
	Item, atte obsequy of *Alys Lord*, for the bells, —— ——	0	1	6
	First, received of my Lord *Dawbnei's* chaplayns, for the hyer of a chalis by a whole year——sum. ——	0	3	4
	Item, paid for a book to registre in the names of the buryals, weddings, and christnings, —— —— ——	0	0	2
	Item, paid for matts for the parishioners to kneel upon when they reverenced their Maker——price, ——	0	4	4
	Item, paid to my Lady *Ancress*, for washing of all the corporas clothes, —— —— —— ——	0	0	8

1539.

		£.	s.	d.
1539.	Item, paid for the half-part of the Bybell, accordingly after the King's injunction, —— —— ——	o	9	9
	Item, paid to the glazier, in reward for the pariſh, towards the ſetting up of the King's arms, and of my Lord Prince's armes, and of my Lord Privy Seal's arms, in the Eaſt window in the Trinity Chapelle,—ſum — —	o	10	o
	Item, paid to *Freeman*, for a bill made to the viſitors in the name of the whole pariſh, —— —— ——	o	o	8
1540.	Item, of Sir *Thomas Denys*, Knight, when he lay in the King's Old Place, given by him to the church, —— —	o	1	8
	Item, paid to *Symon Symons*, glaſier, for making and ſetting up of divers arms in the Trinity Chapell, within the pariſh of *St. Margaret* in *Weſtminſter* aforeſaid, by the advice and commandment of Mr. *Lancaſter* Herrolt at arms, —— —— —— ——	o	10	o
	Firſt, paid to *Alice Lewis*, a goldſmith's wife of *London*, for a ſerclett to marry maydens in, the 26th day of Sept.	3	o	o
	Item, paid to Mr. *Chidley*, lerned man, for his counſell, and drawing of a bill to the King's Highneſs for the church-yard, and to his clerk for ingroſynge of the ſame, —	o	6	2
1541.	Item, given by the conſent of the Worſhipfulls of the pariſh, of the church-money, towards the repairing of the high-way towards the Eye Croſs, as by the gadering book of Mr. . . . . . ., &c. —— — ——	3	o	o
	Item, and in the yere of the reign of our Sovereign Henry VIII. by the grace of God, of *England*, *France*, and *Ireland*, Defender of the Faith, and in Earth Supreme Head of the Church of *England* and *Ireland*.			
	Item, paid to *Roger Weſton*, for taking down of our Ladies tabernacle at *Rouncyval*, and for ſetting up thereof in the Trinity iſle in *St. Margaret* of *Weſtminſter*, ——	o	13	4
Rouncyval fraternity.	Item, paid for repairing the chapel wall at *Rouncyvall*, where the tabernacle ſtood, as by bill apperith, —	o	3	3
	Firſt, received on Good Friday, for crepinge to the Croſs the ſame yere, —— —— ——	o	o	5
1540.	Alſo received in offerynge-money to the Sacrament of the autar, —— —— ——	o	o	2
	Firſt, paid the laſt day of December to a prieſt and a clerk, for a low maſs and dyrge for the Earl of *Pembroke* and the Duke of *Bedford*, founders, —— ——	o	1	1
	Firſt, paid to Mr. Dr. *Kitchin*, in reward for preaching on our Lady-day, a pyke price 2s. 4d. a galland of wine 8d. and his bote-hire 4d.——ſum in all, —— ——	o	3	4

 1540.

Year	Item	£.	s.	d.
1540.	Item, paid to Mr. *Asheton*, the auditore, for the copy of the surveyed lands, ——— ——— ———	0	3	4
	Item, paid in rewards of the chancellors of thaugmentacions,	0	1	8
	This accompt is allowed in the Excheker Chamber, on Sunday the 10th day of Oct. in the 32d yere of the reign, &c.			
1543.	First, received of Mr. *Smalwoode*, for certain silver that the relyckes were in, and for a little coffer, ——— ———	1	18	0
	Item, paid for cleansing of the church-yard wall, when the cage was taken away, ——— ——— ———	0	1	4
1544.	Also paid for rushes against the Dedicacion-day, which is always the first Sunday of October, ——— ———	0	1	5
	First, paid for two new keys, the one for the quyer door, and the other for the steeple door, ——— ———	0	1	4
	Also paid for a board for the side doore of the quyer, ———	0	0	2
	Also paid for six books of the Litany in English, ———	0	1	6
1545.	First, paid to Mr. *Barnard*, for the table of the Concepcion now standing on the high altar, ——— ———	16	10	0
	Also paid to the ringers of Christmas-evyn, when the King's Grace came to the Parliament-house, ———	0	0	3
1546.	Also paid on Ascencion-even, for bread, ale, beer, and wyne, for the prebendaries and quyer of the mynster, after mass was done, ——— ——— ———	0	1	2
1547.	Also paid for bread, ale, and wyne, on Ascencion-even, for Mr. Dean and the prebendaries, ———	0	0	9
	Also paid to the poor men that did bere the copis and other necessaries to Knightsbridge, when that King Henry the Eighth was brought to his burial to Wynsor, and to the man that did ryng the bells, ———	0	3	0
	Also paid to the ringers at King Henry the Eighth his dirige in the parish church, ——— ———	0	0	8
	Also paid in Christmas quarter to Goodman *Burton*, for making of the stone in the body of the church, for the priest to declare the 'Pistells and Gospells, ———	0	2	0
	Also paid for a honest dish of meat, and for wyne, for the King's visitours, ——— ———	0	12	8
	Also paid for making of a little coffer upon the hie altar, for to set in the Sacrament, with other necessaries, ———	0	1	4
	Also paid to *Thomas Stockdale*, for xxxv ells of cloth for the frunte of the rode-lofte, whereas the Commandments be written, price of the ell 8d. ——— ———	. . .	. . .	. . .
	Also paid to the purcyvaunte, when he brought the commission for the presentment of all the Brothered, ———	0	1	0
	Also paid for 11 waynscotte boards for the high alter, ———	0	1	0
	Also paid for the wryghtyng of the Scriptures upon the same boards, ——— ——— ———	0	5	0

1547.

Year	Entry	£.	s.	d.
1547.	Alſo the ſaid accomptant hath received for images and for curtens,	3	6	8
1548.	Alſo paid to the ſaid *John Ivery*, for the keeping of the v a clock and viii a clock, for half a yere and half a quarter ended at the ſame feaſt,	0	16	8
	Alſo paid to *Philip Lentall*, for making clene of xi payer of harneſſis, ix daggers, and viii bylls, price every harnes 1s. 4d.	0	14	0
	Alſo paid to xi men for weryng of the ſame harneſſis at the muſter-day, to every man 6d.	0	5	6
	Alſo paid when we were commanded to appear before the Archdeacon of Middleſex for the King's matters,	0	1	2
	Alſo paid to the King's amner, when he would have ſealed up the church-doors, at the departure of the King's Majeſty, the 2d day of July, becauſe the bells were not rong,	0	2	4
	Alſo paid for the half part of the Paraphraſe of Eraſmus, the 10th of Auguſt,	0	5	0
	Alſo paid for eight Salters in Engliſh,	0	13	4
	Alſo paid to *Handforth*, for the inventory that was delivered to the King's commiſſioners,	0	4	8
	Alſo paid for bread, ale, and wine, for the gentlemen and children of the King's Chapel, for their paynes in helping of the divine ſervice at the bleſſed communion on Our Lady's-day in Lent,	0	2	11
1549.	Alſo paid to *William Curlewe*, for mending of divers pews that were broken when Dr. Lattymer did preach,	0	1	6
	Firſt paid for iv books of the ſervice in the church,	0	16	0
1550.	Alſo the ſaid accomptants do charge themſelves for the receipt of the overpluſs of the ſilver that remained of $^{\text{xx}}_{\text{viii}}$ and x ounces, which was delivered to *Robert Tayleboys*, of London, goldſmith, for to make thereof iv communion cups, ii all gylt, and the other ii parcell gylt; whereof we have received ii cups all gylt, weighing $^{\text{xx}}_{\text{iii}}$ and xviii ounces, alſo ii other parcel gylt, wayeng lxii ounces iii quarters, &c.			
	Alſo paid to a carpenter for a day's working, for to ſet up the ſkaffold for him that did write the vi chapter of St. John's Goſpel in the quire,	0	0	8
	Alſo paid to him that did paint and write the vi chapter of St. John's Goſpell in the quire,	2	0	0
1551.	Alſo paid for making of our bill, to put it in at the Biſhop's viſitation,	0	0	4
	Alſo paid for a Book of Articles,	0	0	2
	A croſs, the overpluſs thereof being ſold after 5s. 8d. the oz. did amount, &c.	......		

Year	Item	£.	s.	d.
1552.	Alſo received of Mr. *Richard Sycell* for his grave,	0	3	0
	Alſo received by the gift of the Right Worſhipfull Sir *John Arundell*, Knight, towards the byenge of neceſſaries to the church, by the hands of Mr. *Brightman*, the 28th day of Auguſt,	2	10	0
	Alſo paid for a recreacion for the Queſt the 12th of July, when they came to view the inventory of the church goods,	0	6	8
	Alſo paid to Mr. Curat and *Nicholas Poole*, for making the book of the church goods, to be preſented to the King's commiſſioners, and for the pains they took about it, &c.	0	10	0
	Alſo paid to the Taylor, for making 11 clothes meet for the Communion-table,	0	0	10
	Alſo paid for 11 communion books,	0	7	4
1553.	Alſo paid for the pulpit, where the Curate and the Clark did read the chapters at ſervice-time,	0	13	4
	Alſo paid for a foot-ſtool for them that diſtribnted the charyte to the poor,	0	1	0
	Alſo paid for bread and drink, on Aſh-wedneſday, to the ringers at the victory and overthrow of Wyat and his adherents,	0	0	8
	Alſo paid for a ſupplicacion to the Queen's Majeſty for the church goods,	0	1	8
1554.	Alſo paid to a painter for waſhing out of the Scripture of the high altar table,	0	1	0
	Alſo paid for a lantern to be borne before the Sacrament in viſitacion	0	2	10
	Alſo paid for 111 capons for the biſhop's dinner at the reconciliacion of the church,	0	7	0
	Alſo for half a veil,	0	5	6
	Alſo for 1111 green geeſe,	0	2	4
	Alſo for a dozen of rabetts,	0	2	8
	Alſo for a dozen of pigions,	0	2	6
	Alſo a ſurloyn of beef,	0	6	8
	Alſo for 11 gallons of wine,	0	2	[illegible]
	Alſo paid for bread, wine, bear, and ale, for Mr. Deane, the prebendaries, and the quire, when they came in proceſſion to our church,	0	3	8
1555.	Item, paid for a key to the Sanctuary-wickatt,	0	0	6
	Item, paid to *Low*, fletcher, for fetherying of 1111 ſheffe of arrowſe, and new trimming of the heads,	0	4	0
	Item, paid for ſpiced bread on the Aſcencion-even, and on the Aſcencion-day,	0	1	0
1556.	Item, of the Yeorle of *Suſſex* in reward,	0	3	4
	Item, paid to *Nycholas Clarke*, for making thymag of St. Margaret,	0	11	0

1556.

		£.	s.	d.
1556.	Item, paid for bread. wine, ale and beer, upon the Afcencion-even and day, againft my Lord Abbott and his covent cam in proceffion, and for ftrewing herbs the famme day,	0	7	1
1557.	Alfo paid for fetting out of foldyers the 7th day of Jaunuary, as appeareth by a bill, — — —	3	8	8½
	Item, paid for making of III ferplys of the cloth that hung before the rode-loft written with the Commandments,	0	2	0
1558.	Item, paid to the tinker for mending the fecond bell, —	0	8	0
	Item, for fetting forth the five foldiers to Portifmathe the laft yere of Queen Mary, — ——	1	13	4
1559.	Firft, paid for a Bybyl and a Parafrawfe, — —	0	16	0
	Item, for a Communion-book bound in parchemyne, —	0	6	0
	Item, paid to *John Rial*, for his III days work to take down the roode Mary and John, — —	0	2	8
	Item, to *John Rial*, for taking down the tabil on the high altar, and taking down the holy-water ftock, ——	0	1	0
	Item, for cleaving and fawing of the rood Mary and John,	0	1	0
	Item, paid for a dinner made to the vifitors when they came in vifitation, — — —	3	13	10
	Item, paid for wine and bread for the communion, —	0	3	5
	Item, paid for a book of the names of all fuch perfons as were buried within this parifh, from Midfummer-day A. D. 1558, unto Midfummer-day in the yere 1559, delivered to the vifitors, — — —	0	2	0
	Item, to a labourer for removing the ftones out of the pew where the collectors for the poor fitteth, ——	......		
	Item, for bread, ale and beer, on Tewifday in the Rogacion-weeke, for the parifhioners that went in proceffion,	0	1	0
	Item, firft, the faid accomptants afkithe allowance for the cofts and chargis of a fupper, made to the new wardens and other the worfhipfull of the parifh, fitting and taking of this account, — — —	4	0	0
1560.	Item, at the buryal of my Lady *Jane Semer*, ——	0	10	0
	Item, for a new calender fet forth for thorder of our furvey in the church, — — —	0	0	4
	Item, for a paper with the X Commandements, ——	0	1	4
	Item, paid to *John Welby*, for a frame to fet on the faid paper with the X Commandements, — ——	0	1	4
	Item, for bread and drink for the parifhioners that went the circuit the Tuefday in the Rogation-week, —	0	3	4
	Item, for bread and drink the Wednefday in the Rogation-week, for Mr. Archdeacon and the quire of the Minfter,	0	3	4
	Item, for a dinner made to Mr. Archdeacon, and other of the parifh, at his vifitation, —— —	1	3	8

1561.

£. s. d.

1561. Item, for making our bill to the commiſſioners for the concealed lands, — — — 0 0 6

Item, paid to joyners and labourers about the taking down and new reforming of the roode-loft, as by a particular book thereof made doth and may appear, — 37 10 2

1562. Hereafter enſueth an inventory made by the ſaid wardens accomptants, of all the goods, jewels, and ornaments to the ſaid church of St. Margarett appurtaining, anno Domini 1562.

Firſt, one veſtment of blew cloath of tiſſue with the tunicles for Deacon and Subdeacon.

Item, one cope of crymſon cloth of tiſſue, and II coorſe copes of blew tiſſue.

Item, one cope of purple cloth of tiſſue, one other cope of crymſon velvet with ſkallop ſhells of ſilver, and one other cope of crymſon velvet with flowrs of gold.

Item, one altar cloth of crymſon velvet and gold, and two other altar clothes of blew and ruſſet velvet with flowrs of gold.

Item, two cusſhons of cloth of gold and crymſon velvet, two cusſhons of green velvet with ſkochyns of needle work, two cusſhons of cloth of bawdkyn, and one little cusſhon with a tree of green ſilk.

Item, VI herſe cloaths, and a cloth for the pulpit, of black and red bawdkyn with flowers of gold.

Item, VIII old altar cloaths of diaper, one great new altar cloth of diaper fine, and five plain.

Item, XVII towels and II ſmall towells.

Item, one challis with the patent all gilt, and II great communion cupps all gylt.

Item, *a paſt for bird* *, ſet with pearl and ſtone.

Item, a ſtreamer of white ſarcenet with a whight croſs.

Item, ten pair of allmen riveletts, and one harnis for a horſeman, VI blak billes, VI armyngehoordis, VII ſhefe of arrowſe, and VI daggers.

1562. Item, for IV books of Pſalms in metre for the quire, — 0 4 8

Item, paid more than was gathered by Mr. More towards the ſetting out of XII men to Newhaven, 15th of Auguſt, 1562.

Item, for the new fethering of two ſheaf of arrows for the ſoldiers aboveſaid, — — 0 2 0

* So the tranſcript. But Q.?

Item,

Year	Item	£.	s.	d.
1562.	Item, for the carriage away of certain ſoyl and duſt of the church-yard, againſt the Queen's Majeſty's comyng to the college the firſt day of the parliament, —	0	1	10
	Item, for a book of the Queen's Majeſty's Injunctions, —	0	0	6
	Item, for IV ſong books for the ſervice of God in the ſame church, — — —	0	5	0
	Item, to *John Royal*, for his pains taken at ſundry times in the church, in ſetting forth the XII ſoldiers towards the muſters into the mantells, and taking of their harneſs at their return, — — —	0	5	0
1563.	Item, received of Mr. *More*, as a remain of certain money called the privy purſe, — —	5	0	0
	Item, for the altar table which remained in the late court of thaugmentacion defaced, — —	0	5	0
	Item, for IV books of ſervice for the Wedneſdays, Fridays, and Sondays, for the ceſſing of warrs, —	0	1	4
	Item, paid to XII ſoldiers that went towards Newhaven by commandment of the commiſſioners, that is to wit, to every one of them 5s.; in the whole, — —	3	0	0
	Item, paid more, for their preſt money and bound wages, by the ſpace of one month more than was required, by Mr. Gibbs, Mr. Culwick, and William Staunton, as appeareth by thaccompt thereof, — —	7	9	7½
	Item, to *John Welch*, for the killing and carrying away of dogs during the plague, and for the putting of them into the ground, and covering of the ſame, —	0	3	2
	Item, to the painter of Totehil Street, for painting of certain blue croſſes, to be fixed upon ſundry houſes infected,	0	0	6
	Item, for a quier of paper, for the clerks to make weekly certificates unto the court of all buryals and chriſtenings,	0	0	4
1564.	Received of Sir *William Sentlow*, for the hyer of the herſe cloth,	0	6	8
	Item, paid for a bill delivered to Mr. Archdeacon concerning our verdyte, — — —	0	0	6
1565.	Item, paid to *John Barrowell*, for making of the turret in the church ſteeple, and for timber thereunto belonging, wherein the ſame bell now hangeth, as appeareth by his bill, — — —	3	6	8
	Item, paid to *John Puttendall*, for the vane, —	0	5	0
1566.	Item, paid for a book of Homilies, — —	0	3	0
	Item, paid to the ringers when the Queen's Majeſty went from St. James's to *Hendon* * upon Thamyes, — —	0	0	6

* Q. *Hampton*, *Henley*, or *Kingſton*?

Year	Item	£.	s.	d.
1566.	Item, paid for two books of Praifes, fet out by the Bifhop of Canterbury, to be read Sundays, Wednefdays, and Fridays, — — —	0	0	6
1567.	Item, of Sir *Richard Walwyn*, for his part of a pew, —	0	5	0
	Item, paid for the carriage of a pofte from Scotland to the parifh church, — — —	0	0	2
	Item, for mending and fetting up the coate armour in Our Lady chapel, — — —	0	0	6
	Item, paid for a certificate made of all the ftrangers within the parifh, — — —	0	0	6
	Item, paid for a dinner made to the vifitors when they came in vifitation, — — —	3	2	6
	Item, paid for a drinking made at the Bifhop's-head when the fidemen gave up their verdict, —	0	3	6
	Item, paid for one book of Homilies, and for another book, called A Proteftacion, — —	0	1	0
1568.	Item, paid to the ringers for ringing for the profperous reign of the eleventh year of Queen Elizabeth, —	0	0	6
	Item, paid for writing of a book to the Queen's Majefty's commiffioners for armer, — —	0	1	0
	Item, paid for fetting of two foldiers into the North parts, and for their coates, flops, and other things, as it appeareth by a bill thereof, — — —	3	12	10
1569.	Item, paid towards the harnefs that came from the Tower of London, — — —	5	0	0
1570.	Item, for a new book of the Queen's Injunctions, —	0	0	4
	Item, for a plott of the church drawn out in parchment,	0	1	8
	Item, for ringing when the Queen's Majefty went to the Burffe *,	0	0	4
	Item, for a dinner made to the vifitors when they came to the vifitacion, — — —	2	18	4
	Item, for altering and defacing of the aulter-ftone, and for laying down of the fame, — —	0	1	4
	Item, paid for ringing when the Queen's Majefty went to Sir *Thomas Grefham's* †, and came back again, —	0	0	8
1571.	Item, paid for ringing for joy of the great victory that the Chriftians hath gotten of the Turk, —	0	2	6
	Item, paid to the ringers for ringing for the moft profperous reign and long continuance of our moft gracious Sovereign Lady Queen Elizabeth, — —	0	2	6

* *The Royal Exchange*, which name was given to it, in the Queen's prefence, Jan. 23, 1570. See her "Progreffes," vol. II. under 1578, p. 108.

† This fixes the date of her vifit at *Ofterley* a few years earlier than it has been generally fuppofed; and, as the houfe was not completely finifhed till 1577, it ferves to account for the ftory of the wall in the middle of the court. Ibid. p. 107.

		£.	s.	d.
1571.	Item, paid for iv loads of gravel to lay in the church-yard at the Queen's coming to the ſermon at the Minſter, —	0	2	6
1572.	Item, for a fine of the burial of my Lord *Wharton*, being buried at the college, — — —	0	9	6
	Item, for a new regiſter book, for to write in the names of every burial, chriſtening, and marriage, that is in the pariſh, — — —	0	5	0
	Item, for ringing when the Queen's Majeſty went from Whitehall to Havering, — — —	0	0	6
	Item, for iv new books of the Common Prayer ſet out by the biſhops, — — —	0	0	6
1574.	Item, paid for a dinner made to the viſitors, and others of the pariſh, when they came in the viſitacion, —	3	2	7
	Item, paid for a copy of the Articles given by the viſitors to the ſworn men to enquire of, — —	0	2	0
	Item, paid for ringing for the moſt proſperous reign of our gracious Sovereign Lady Queen Elizabeth long to contynew, — — —	0	2	0
	Item, paid for ringing when the Queen's Majeſty came from St. James's to Whitehall to the Maundy, —	0	0	6
1575	Item, paid for netesfoot oil to liquor the belles, —	0	0	2
1576	Item, paid for a fine of my Lady *Barnes*' burial, —	0	9	4
	Item, paid for *Botcheir* to London, and from London, taking a leaſe of St. Ann's chapell of Mr. *Standley*, —	0	1	0
	Item, paid to Mr. *Bailey* towards the making up of a conduit at the palace, — — —	2	0	0
	Item, paid for making, writing, and drawing out of a leaſe of St. Anne's chapell, to lay wood in for the poor, —	0	5	8
	Item, delivered to Mr. *Savedge* and Mr. *Jennens* for the ſolders,	5	0	0
1577.	Item, paid to *Anthony Greſarde* for new ſtocking of five calyvers,	0	12	0
	Item, paid to *Harry Redford*, for mending of St. Anne's chapell, and covering the ſame, — —	5	13	4
1579.	Item, paid for ringing for the Queen's Majeſty's burthe, the 7th of September, — — —	0	1	0
	Item, paid for ſcowering of the armor and ſhott againſt the muſters in Totehil Fields, — —	1	6	0
	Item, paid for powder for the ſoldiers upon the muſtering day,	0	12	4
	Item, paid to the ſoiers, the anſyant-bearer, and to him that played upon the drome, — —	1	7	4
1580.	Item, received of my Lady *Anne Knevet*, for the funeral, being carryed to Gilford to bury, — —	0	15	0
1581.	Item, paid for ſix new ſword gyrdles, — —	0	6	2
	Item, paid for the charges of the viſitation, —	57	4	0
	Item, paid for a book of the Abridgment of Statutes, to remain in the church, — — —	0	9	0

		£.	s.	d.
1581.	Item, given to *John Clarke*, for taking up the post in the great gate for my Lady *Sussex*, when she came to the church to a sermon, — — —	0	0	6
	Item, paid him more for XII pieces of imagery glass, which he set in that payne, — — —	0	1	0
1582.	Item, received for the funeral of my Lady *Wormall*, —	0	11	0

Money received towards the Conduitt, &c.

		£.	s.	d.
1582.	Item, received of Sir *Thomas Tresham*, knight, —	0	6	8
	Item, received of Sir *John Goodwin*, knight, —	1	0	0
	Item, &c. paid, — — — —	. . .	. . .	. . .
	Item, for stuff for the conduitt, and for the new building and making thereof, as doth and may appear by certain bills,	43	7	1½
	Item, paid for a fine to the amners of the Queen's Majesty's house, — — — —	0	5	0
1583.	Item, paid for ringing when the Queen's Majesty went from Greenwich to Otelands, — —	0	0	6
	Item, paid to the ringers the 5th day of October, when the Queen's Majesty came from Otelands to St. James's,	0	1	8
	Item, to Mr *Wheeler*, for recording of our names in the commissary's court, when we did put in our presentment,	0	0	8
1585.	Received for the funeral of my Lord *Windsor*, —	0	10	0
	Item, paid for ringing when the Queen's Majesty came from Greenwich to Lambeth, on Friday, being the 26th day of March, — — —	0	0	6
	Item, paid the 29th day of March, for ringing for the Queen's Majesty when she came from Lambeth to the Parliament-house, — — —	0	0	6
	Item, paid the 30th day of March for ringing when the Queen's Majesty went from Lambeth to Greenwich, —	0	0	6
	Item, paid to *Robert Jones*, for copienge out of Mr. Cornellis's will, and for parchment, for writing the poor people's names which were placed in Mr. Cornellis's alms houses,	0	4	0
	Item, paid for going the perambulacion, for fish, butter, cream, milk, conger, bread and drink, and other necessaries,	0	4	8½
	Item, paid to the ringers for ringing on the 19th day of November, when the Queen's Majesty came to my Lord Admiral's house, and back again to Richmond, —	0	0	4
	Item, paid to the ringers for their offering at Christmas,	0	1	0
1586.	Item, received for the funeral of Sir *Edward Sutton*, chief baron, and Lord *Dudley*, for the cloth and bells,	0	9	0
	Item, received for the fine of the blacks in the coach, and about the hearse, — — —	2	0	0

1586.

		£.	s.	d.
1586.	Item, paid for a bord and a frame for a table for the veftry-men, of orders, — — —	0	0	8
	Item, paid to *Davis Evans*, painter, for wafhing the cloth that hangs over the communion table, and for working IV badges of the Queen's arms, — —	0	15	0
	Item, paid for three books of prayers for the Queen's Majefty,	0	0	6
	Item, paid for ringing the 16th day of Auguft for joy of taking the traytors, — — —	0	1	0
	Item, paid to *William Piercy*, painter, for painting the lector pulpitt, — — —	0	6	8
	Item, paid to *William Piercy*, for making of the Queen's Majefty's arms in coollers, — —	0	5	0
	Item, paid for a book of Injunctions, — —	0	0	4
	Item, paid for ringing for the Queen's Majefty when fhe came from Richmont to my Lord *Bourghes*, —	0	0	6
	Item, paid to Mr. *Price* for two books of prayer for the Queen's day, — — —	0	0	6
	Item, paid for two proclamations for the church and church-yard, — — —	0	0	4
	Item, paid for the dinner for the vifitation for the church-wardens and the fidefmen kept at the Sarrizone's head,	4	5	0
	Item, paid for ringing at the beheading of the Queen of Scotts,	0	1	0
	Item, paid for candles to burn in the church while the Lady *Stafford's* clofet was making, — —	0	0	2
	Item, paid to *Warren*, the fmith, for mending the iron which holdeth up the actor, — —	0	0	2
1587.	Item, paid to Mr. *Fifher*, for making the butts in Totehil Fields,	1	3	0
	Item, paid for ringing for the Queen's Majefty when fhe went from the Lord Admiral's houfe to Richmond, —	0	0	6
	Item, paid the 25th of January for ringing when the Queen's Majefty came from Kenfington to the Lord of Canterbury's,	0	0	6
	Item, paid to the joyner for making a table, wherein are fet the names of all fuch that paid in every ward towards the Statute of Weftminfter, and for writing of the fame table, — —	0	2	8
	Item, received for the funeral of Sir *Henry Gates*, for the blacks about the church, — —	1	0	0
1588.	Item, received of Mr. *Marmaduke Servante*, for the ufe of the poor, to buy coals, being the gift of the Right Hon. the Lord *Burleigh*, lord high treafurer of England, the fum of — —	10	0	0
	Item, paid the 5th day of July, for ringing when the Queen's Majefty came from Greenwich to my Lord of Canterbury's houfe to dinner, —	0	0	6

1588.

	£.	s.	d.
1588. Item, paid the 25th of July, for ringing when the Queen's Majesty came from Richmond to St. James's, —	0	1	0
Item, paid to the ringers the 8th of August, when the Queen's Majesty went from St. James's to the Camp *, —	0	1	0
Item, paid to the ringers the 10th of August, when the Queen's Majesty came from the Camp to St. James's,	0	1	0
Item, paid for two Prayer Books, when the Spanish fleet was upon the Narrow Seas, ——— ———	0	0	3
Item, paid the 15th of October, 1588, to the ringers, for ringing when the Queen's Majesty removed from St. James's to Greenwich, — —	0	1	0
Item, paid the 20th day of December, 1588, for ringing when the Queen's Majesty came from Greenwich to Lambeth,	0	1	0
Item, paid the 22d day of December, for ringing when the Queen's Majesty went from Lambeth to Richmond,	0	1	0
Item, paid the 21st of January, 1588, when the Queen came from Richmond to Westminster, ——	0	1	0
Item, paid the 4th of February, for ringing when the Queen came from Whitehall to the college church, and so to the parliament house, — —	0	1	0
Item, paid for making of the indentures between Baron *Southerton* and the church wardens, —	0	1	0
1589. Item, paid for ringing the 26th of May, when the Queen's Majesty went from Whitehall to Barn Ellmes to Mr. Secretary's, — — —	0	0	6
Item, paid the 28th of May, for ringing when the Queen's Majesty came from Barn Ellmes to Whitehall,	0	0	6
Item, paid to the ringers for ringing the 11th of June, 1589, when the Queen's Majesty came from Highgate, —	0	0	6
Item, paid the 18th day of June, 1589, for ringing for the Queen's Majesty when she went from Whitehall to Nonsuche, ——— ——— ———	0	0	8
Item, paid for ringing the 15th of November, when the Queen came to Somerset-house, ——— ———	0	0	6
Item, paid for ringing when the Queen went to Richmond from Somerset-house, ——— ———	0	0	6
Item, for ringing when the Queen's Majesty went to Lambeth,	0	0	6
Item, for ringing when the Queen's Majesty came to Whitehall,	0	0	6
Item, paid for ringing when the Queen's Majesty came from Whitehall to Greenwich, ——— ———	0	0	6

And the church-wardens aforesaid have delivered the sum of forty pounds in money, which was the money given by

* At *Tilbury*, on the appearance of the Spanish Armada.

		£.	s.	d.
	Mr. *Feckenam*, late abbot of Weſtminſter, to the uſe of the poor of the ſame pariſh, to buy wood; which ſum the ſaid church-wardens have delivered into the hands of the new church-wardens now appointed,	40	0	0
1589.	And alſo the ſaid church-wardens have delivered the ſum of ten pounds in money, which was the money given by the Right Honourable the Lord *Burleigh*, lord high treaſurer of England, to the uſe of the poor in Weſtminſter aforeſaid, to buy ſea coles; which ſum the ſaid church-wardens have delivered into the hands of Mr. *Marmaduke Servante*,	10	0	0
1590.	Item, paid the 28th day of May, 1590, to the ringers for ringing when the Queen's Majeſty came from Hackney to my Lord Chancellor's,	0	0	6
	Item, for ringing the 11th day of February, 1590, when the Queen's Majeſty came from Richmond to Lambeth,	0	0	6
	Item, paid for ringing the 13th of February, when the Queen's Majeſty went from Lambeth to Greenwich,	0	0	6
1591.	Item, given to the company of the colledge, and for their pains,	1	0	0
	Item, paid for a dinner for the viſitacion, as doth appear by a bill,	3	10	3
1592.	Item, paid for ringing the 7th of April, when the Queen went from Whitehall,	0	0	6
	Received of the Lord *Cromwell* and Mr. *Freak*, being carried into the countrey to be buryed,	2	1	8
	Item, paid to the dog-killer for killing dogs the firſt time of infection,	0	16	0
	Item, paid more to the dog-killer for killing more dogs,	0	10	10
	Item, paid for perfumes of francomſence, junyper, and packthrede,	0	1	0
	Item, paid more to the poor men for killing of dogs by Mr. Dean's appointment,	0	10	4
	Item, paid more to the poor men for killing of dogs,	0	17	6
1593.	Item, the removing a ſtone from the church-yard to the poors' well,	0	1	0
	Item, paid Mr. *Palmer* for 11 years rent for the chapell in Totehill-ſtreet,	1	0	0
	Item, the broken tennor waied MDCXXI lb. weight; the new tennor that came in hir place weid MCCC and a half.			
	Item, the weight of the greateſt bell ys MMC. and a half.			
	Item, the weit of the treble delivered was CCCC. III quarters, and XVII lb.			
	Item, the weit of the fourth bell laſt brought in ys MDCC. and a half and XIV lb. weight; the weight of the fourth bell			

		£.	s.	d.
	bell taken away, as is before expreffed, is MCCC and a half.			
1593.	Item, weight of the fecond bell carried away DCCC. III quarters. The new bell brought in her place, weid juft DCCC and a half.			
	Item, they alfo demand for buryal of 313 poor people, as a due accuftomed, ——— ———	2	6	2
1594.	Item, paid to *Jhon Dore* and *George Jhonfon*, by confent of the veftry, for cafting a ditch between my Lady Dacres and Mr. Lyne, thereby to content her Ladyfhip, fhe being then determined to found an hofpital in this parifh, —	1	8	0
	Item, given to Mr. *Fletcher*, a preacher, who preached the 4th of Auguft, being Sonday, in the afternoon, by confent of fuch of the veftry as were prefent at that fermon,	0	5	0
	Item, beftowed upon *Avice Clark*, widow, late wife of Mr. *Clark* our curate, for the charge of herfelf and her children, to carry them from hence to Litchfield, by confent of the veftry, ——— ———	1	0	0
1595.	Item, paid to Mr. *Dobleday*, for a dinner provided at his houfe at the vifitacion, as appears by a bill; being prefent at the fame dinner Mr. Dr. *Lloyde*, Mr. Dr. *Mountford*, Mr. Dr. *Morgan* the regiftrar, Mr. *Wheeler* the curate, church-wardens, and fidefmen, and other, and the fame vifitacion being holden on Monday the laft of March, 1595, ——— ——— ———	2	17	0
	Item, paid to Mr. *Dobleday*, high-conftable, for releif of maimed foldiers, according to the ftatute of IIII a week for one yere ended at our Lady-day, 1595, ———	0	17	4
	Item, paid for bread, drink, cheefe, fifh, cream, and other victuals, when the worfhipfull of the parifh, and very many others of the pooreft fort, went the perambulacion to Kenfington, in this hard and dere time of all things, as may appear by a bill of particulars, ———	7	10	0
	Item, given to *Jhon Creveune*, alias *Sote*, a poor fcholar born in this parifh, after a fermon by him made in this church, by confent of fuch of the veftry as were prefent at that fermon, ——— ——— ———	1	0	0
	Item, paid to Mr. *Dericke*, the high-conftable, for releif of maimed foldiers, for one quarter ended at Midfummer, 1595, ——— ——— ———	0	4	4
	Item, paid to Mr. *Dericke*, the high-conftable, for the maimed foldiers for Mighelmas quarter, ——— ———	0	4	4
	Item, given to the finging-men of the colledge at their dinner, as hath been of late ufed, ——— ———	1	0	0

1595.

	£.	s.	d.
1595. Item, paid to Mr. *Dericke*, the high-conſtable, for the lame ſoldiers, for a quarter of a yere ended at Chriſtmas, 1595,	0	4	4
1596. Item, paid the bell-ringers the 7, for joy of victory againſt the Spaniards, — — —	0	7	6
Item, paid for a Prayer Book, — —	0	0	1
Item, paid for ringers when her Majeſty came to the Lord *Burrowes*, — — —	0	0	8
Item, paid for maimed ſoldiers, — —	0	13	4
1597. Item, to the lieftenant of *Middleſex*, — —	0	5	0
Item, for the charges of diet at Kenſington for the perambulacion of the pariſh, being a yere of great ſcarcity and deerneſs, — — —	6	8	8
Item, paid by us *Samuell Haſilwood* and *Roger Darley*, churchwardens of the pariſh church of St. Margaret in Weſtminſter, for the uſe of the poor of Weſtminſter aforeſaid, unto *John Griffyn*, collector to the Dean and Chapter, for one whole yere's rent due unto the Dean and Chapter of Weſtminſter at the feaſt of the Annunciacion of Our Lady laſt paſt, for two tenements in Tuthil-ſtreet, 1l. 6s. 8d.; and for one other tenement in the Sanctuary 20s. All this given to the uſe of the poor by *John Varnam*, late deceaſed, as by an acquittance under the ſaid collector's hand appeareth, — —	2	6	8
Item, for drawing the firſt letter in the book, —	0	5	0
Item, the ſaid accomptants do charge themſelves with the ſum of ten pounds, which was paid unto them by Mr. *Marmaduke*, as the gift of the Right Honourable the Lady *Burghley*, deceaſed, to be given to the church-wardens, to be by them employed to the uſe of the poor,	10	0	0
Item, the ſaid accomptants do charge themſelves with the ſum of twenty-ſix pounds, of the gift of *William Bagnall*, deceaſed, which was received of divers tenements which he left to the uſe of the poor, and by us to be diſtributed to XII old poor men, — — —	26	0	0
Item, Imprimis, paid to *John Dore*, the 16th of May, 1597, for making of the butts in Tuthil, and for caſting of a ditch about the butts, — —	1	1	4
Item, paid for a cheaſte, covered with black leather, and barde with iron, with five locks and keys thereunto, —	4	10	0
Item, paid to Mr. *Moat*, the firſt of November, 1597, for new caſting of the fourth bell, weying MDC. III quarters; for a new bell-clapper weighing XLVIII lb. —	10	0	0
Item, paid by Mr. *Haſlewood*, the 26th day of October, 1597, to Mr. *Henry Wetherfeild*, for half a year's pay for maimed ſoldiers, as doth appear by an acquittance,	0	6	8

		£.	s.	d.
1597.	Item, paid the 4th of March, to *Goodman Chambers*, for mending of the alms-houſes in Petty France, that was blown down by the laſt great wind, —— ——	0	5	6
	Item, paid at the viſitation of the book of Articles, —	0	5	0
	Item, paid to the maſters of the pariſh out of the church-box for a plott for the common ſewers, ——	8	0	0
1598.	Item, paid unto the ſaid Mr. *Wetherfeild*, treaſurer, for the maimed ſoldiers, for half a year's contribution ending at the Annunciation of our Lady St. Mary the Virgin laſt, 1598, —— —— ——	0	13	4
	Item, paid for a parchment book for the regiſter, ——	0	12	0
1599.	Item, paid to the bell-ringers the 13th of November, when the Queen came from Richmond to Weſtminſter,	0	2	6
	Item, paid for a long diaper table cloth to make two towels for the communicants, —— ——	0	12	8
1600.	Item, for making a pair of butts and brigs, and for the carpenter's work, —— ——	1	5	2
	Item, paid to maimed ſoldiers, to the King's Bench, and other priſoners, —— —— ——	0	17	4
	Item, paid to maimed ſoldiers, and to the priſoners of the King's Bench, and other priſons, according to the ſtatute, due by us one quarter 8s. 8d. and paid by us for the laſt church-wardens, which was left unpaid XIII to	1	1	8
	The charge for the organs, in all, ——	17	2	7
	Item, paid the ringers when the Queen came to Weſtminſter the 13th of November, —— ——	0	2	6
	Item, paid to maimed ſoldiers, and to the King's Bench, and other priſoners, the 11th of January, 1600, ——	0	17	4
	Item, paid for the dinner at the viſitacion, as by a bill appeareth,	4	5	10
	Item, paid to Mr. *Danſon*, high-conſtable, for maimed ſoldiers, the King's Bench, and other priſons, the 26th of April, 1600, —— —— ——	0	8	8
1601.	Item, paid the 4th of October, 1601, to the high-conſtable, for maimed ſoldiers, and to the hoſpital, ——	0	15	2
	Item, paid to the bell-ringers for ringing when the Queen came from Richmond, the 26th of October, 1601,	0	2	6
	Item, paid to Mr. *Danſon*, high-conſtable, for maimed ſoldiers, and to the hoſpital, the 20th of December, 1601,	0	10	10
	Item, paid for torch lights againſt her Majeſty's coming to Whitehall, A. D. 1600, —— ——	1	13	2
1602.	Item, paid to maimed ſoldiers and the hoſpital for Our Lady's day quarter 1602, delivered to Mr. *Danſon*, high-conſtable, —— —— ——	0	10	10

1602.

		£.	s.	d.
1602.	Item, paid to Mr. *Danson* for maimed soldiers, and for the hospitals,	0	10	10
	Item, paid to two surgions, to search a coarse suspected to be of the plague,	0	6	8
	Item, paid the 29th of September, 1602, for maimed soldiers and to the hospital,	0	10	10
	Item, paid for mending the step to go to read the lessens,	0	0	6
	Item, paid to *Edward Prince* and *William Collins*, for three days attendance on a warrant from the councell about the poor of the parish,	0	11	8
	Item, paid for maimed soldiers and to the hospital, due at Christmas, 1602,	0	10	10
	Item, paid for ringing the 14th of March, 1602,	0	3	4
	Item, paid for ringing at the funeral of the Queen,	0	1	0
1603.	Item, paid to *Robert Wells* the 19th of June, 1603, for killing of fore-score dogs,	0	6	8
	[N. B. This *Wells* was paid for the killing of 422 more at diverse times the same summer at the price of one penny each dog.]			
	Item, paid the 5th of August for ringing for the king,	0	3	0
	Item, paid for a book of publique prayer for the king,	0	0	8
	Item, paid to the ringers the 13th of February, when the Queen came to town,	0	2	6
	Item, paid for the graves of 451 poor folks,	1	17	7
1604.	Item, paid to the ordinary for the church-warden's oath, and the sidesmens, and for the thirty-three articles,	0	10	10
	Item, paid for ringing the 12th of July, at the King's going from Westminster,	0	1	0
	Item, paid for ringing when the King came to town the 11th of July,	0	2	6
	Item, paid to the smith, for mending the utter lock of the door, and for four keys for the burges pews, and for mending the locks,	0	12	6
	Item, paid for a sermon on the 5th of August for the King,	0	6	8
	Item, paid for the book of Canons,	0	1	2
	Item, paid to the ringers the 16th of October, when the King came to town,	0	2	6
	Item, paid to the ringers the 28th of March,	0	5	0
1605.	Item, paid for ringing at the birth of the King's daughter the 9th of April,	0	2	6
	Item, paid for bread, drink, cheese, fish, cream, and other necessaries, when the Worshipfull and others of the parish went the perambulation to Kensington,	15	0	0

		£.	s.	d.
1605.	Item, paid the ringers for ringing at the time when the parliament-houſe ſhould have been blown up, ——	0	10	0
	Item, paid the ringers for ringing when the King came from Oking, —— —— ——	0	3	0
	Item, paid to *Thomas Collings*, ſcrivener, for drawing and engroſſing an abſtract to be delivered to the juſtices,	0	10	0
1606.	Item, paid for ringing the 16th day of May, when the King and Queen went to Greenwich, — ——	0	2	6
	Item, paid for ringing the 27th day of May, 1606, when the King came to the parliament-houſe, being the laſt day of the parliament, —— —— ——	0	2	6
	Item, paid for bellringers on the birth of the King's child,	0	2	6
	Item, paid for ringing when the King of *Denmark* came to the Abby the 4th of Auguſt, —— ——	0	2	6
	Item, paid for ringing when the King came from Hampton-Court, the 19th day of October, —— ——	0	2	6
	Item, paid for ringing when the King came to the parliament-houſe, the 28th day of November, —— ——	0	2	6
1607.	Item, paid for ringing the 3d of June, at the King's remove to Greenwich, —— —— ——	0	2	6
	Item, paid to the ringers when the King came to Whitehall the 4th of July, —— —— ——	0	2	6
	Item, paid for ringing when the King and Queen removed the 19th of July, —— —— ——	0	2	6
	Item, paid for ringing on the 10th day of September, when the King came to Weſtminſter, —— ——	0	2	6
	Item, paid to the ſomner, for proceſs ſerved upon the two churchwardens, for not making preſentments ſo often as the commiſſary requireth, —— ——	0	1	0
1608.	Item, paid the ringers the 1ſt of July, when the King came to Weſtminſter, —— —— —	0	1	0
	Item, paid to the ringers the 5th of Auguſt for Gowre's-day,	0	5	0
	Item, paid to Mr. *Blines*, the preacher, for a ſermon the 20th of Auguſt, —— —— ——	0	6	8
	Item, paid for ringing the 20th of December, when the King came from *Royſton*, —— —— ——	0	2	0
	Item, bought a cloth of gold and a cuſhion for the communion table, and a cuſhion for the pulpit, ——	20	0	0
1609.	Item, paid to *Wright*, the carpenter, for ſix days work, —	0	9	0
	Item, paid to four joyners more, for ſix days work, —	1	16	0
	Item, ſum of the whole charges diſburſed and laid out for and about the old and new pews in the church, —	78	15	0

1609.

		£.	s.	d.
1609.	Item, paid to the ringers, when the King came to town the 6th of July, ——— ——— ———	0	2	6
	Item, paid to the ringers, when the King, Queen, and Prince, came to Whitehall, the 30th of October, ———	0	2	6
	Item, paid for ringing for the King the 1ſt of February, —	0	2	6
	Item, paid for ringing the 24th of March, being the coronation day, ——— ——— ———	0	5	0
	Item, paid for making the new wall, containing twenty-nine rodds, at 10s. the rodd, ——— ———	14	10	0
	Item, paid for making a new pair of butts in Tuthil fields,	0	14	0
1610.	Received for the token-money for the whole year, ended the 11th day of May, 1611, ——— ———	6	5	0
	Item, paid for ringing when the citizens met the Prince, —	0	2	6
	Item, paid for ringing when he was created Prince of Wales, and for ringing when the fire-works were made, —	0	5	0
	Item, paid for ringing the 9th of June, when the Queen came from Greenwich, and the King came from Oatlards, the 8th of July, ——— ——— ———	0	5	0
	Item, paid for ringing the ſame 5th of Auguſt for his Majeſty's preſervation, &c. ——— ———	0	5	0
	Item, paid to *Stockedell*, *Gardener*, and *Clarkeſon*, for work done in the church-yard, and for digging up of ſtones in the new ground, ——— ——— ———	2	0	0
	Item, paid for ringing the 19th day of December, 1610, when the King came from Royſton, and for oyl, ———	0	2	8
	Item, paid for orders made againſt killing and eating of fleſh,	0	0	2
	Item, paid for ringing on the 19th day of February, being the Princeſs's birth-day, ——— ———	0	3	4
	Item, paid for turning of the map-roller, and for tacks to nayl the map, ——— ——— ———	0	0	7
	Item, paid to the ringers when the King and Queen came to Whitehall, the 14th and 15th days of March, 1610,	0	2	6
	Item, paid to the ringers on the 24th day of March, being the firſt day of his King's Majeſty's 9th yere then begun,	0	5	0
	Item, paid to *Goodwyfe Wells*, for ſalt to deſtroy the fleas in churchwardens pew, ——— ———	0	0	6
1611.	Item, paid on Monday the 8th day of April, A. D. 1611, for oyl, and for ringing at the dedicating and conſecrating of the new ground encloſed within the church-yard wall of St. Margaret's, in Weſtminſter, for the buryal of the dead, ——— ——— ———	0	2	2
	Item, paid to *Richard Gardener*, the ſame day, for cleanſing and ſweeping of the ſaid new ground, and all the church-			

		£.	s.	d.
	church-yard, in the morning before the Reverend Father in God *Richard* Biſhop of Lichfield and Coventry did come to dedicate and conſecrate the ground, —	0	1	0
1611.	Item, paid the 27th of April, 1611, for ringing at the King and Queen's remove from Whitehall to Greenwich,	0	2	6
	Item, paid to *John Gurland*, for keeping the boys from the church-yard walls at the funeral of the Earl of *Dunbar*,	....		
	Item, paid to *John Moulten*, for two days work done about the two north gates in the church-yard, and about the coffin-houſe being uncovered with the great wind, as by his bill appeareth, — — —	0	3	0
	Item, paid to *John Roade*, for writing the names of all ſuch perſons as were preſented for not receiving of the holy communion at Eaſter laſt paſt, 1611, —	0	0	4
	Item, paid for five vines and one apricock tree, and for the planting of them before the veſtry window, —	0	10	0
	Item, paid to the ringers on the 15th day of February, 1611, at the King and Queen's coming to Whitehall from Royſton and Greenwich, — —	0	2	6
	Item, paid for a pound of orris-powder to put among the church linen, — — —	0	0	10
	Item, pacements made for the weſt gate which was removed, and the wall taken down, and ſet up the 24th day of Auguſt, 1611, by the appointment of the Right Worſhipfull *George Mountaine*, now dean of Weſtminſter,	6	6	7
1612.	Item, paid to *Michael Stockdale*, for ringing when the Queen of *Scots* was buried in St. Peter's church, —	0	2	6
	Item, paid to the ringers at the Lady *Elizabeth* her Grace's marriage, — — —	0	2	6
	Item, paid for the making of a pair of new butts in Tothil fields,	1	16	4
	Item, paid for the viſitacion dinner the 14th of May, 1612,	6	0	0
1613.	Item, paid for ringing when the King removed to Whitehall, the 30th of November, 1613, — —	0	2	6
	Item, paid for ringing the 8th of January, 1613, when news came that the Lady *Elizabeth* was brought to bed,	0	2	6
	Item, paid to *William Turping*, for making a new pair of butts in Tothil fields for this pariſh, as appeareth by his bill,	1	1	0
1614.	Item, paid to Dr. *Maſters*, for the oaths of the churchwardens and of 16 ſideſmen, — — —	0	11	4
	Item, paid for ringing when the King of *Denmark* came to London, — — —	0	2	0
	Item, paid for ringing when the King came to Whitehall, the 19th of December, 1614, — —	0	2	6

1615.

		£.	s.	d.
1615.	Item, to Mr. *Matthew Head*, high-conftable, for maimed foldiers, for one half yere ending the 25th of March, 1615,	1	6	0
	Item, paid for mending the ftone where the minifter reads fervice, — — —	0	0	6
	Item, paid to Mr. *Baker*, the bailiffe, for a fine or amerciament, which was affeffed upon the parifh out of the Crown Office, — — —	1	13	4
	Item, paid for ringing when the King came to Whitehall the 22d of March, 1615, — — —	0	2	6
	Item, paid to the glafier for 30 foot of new glafs, at 5d. the foot, which was for two windows that have been heretofore ftopped up, — —	0	12	6
	Item, paid for covering the graves of *Thomas Buller*, *James Jales*, and the bowels of Mr. Serjeant *Primrofe*, —	0	4	0
1616.	Item, of Sir *Richard Wigmore*, knight, for his part of a pew,	0	13	4
	Item, paid for ringing at the King's coming to Whitehall, the 3d day of November, and at the Prince his creation on the 4th of November, 1616, — —	0	5	0
	Item, paid to Mr. *Baker*, the bailiff, for a prefentment out of the Crown Office, upon this parifh, for digging gravel in the highway, — — —	0	13	4
	Item, paid to fcaven-men for fower daies workes apeice in making and digging a large pitt of twelve foot deepe, thirty foot long, and about ten foot broad, to bury the bones in the church-yard, at 1s. 6d. a day apiece,	2	2	0
1617.	Item, paid for making a new pew for the midwives, —	2	5	0
	Item, paid for making another new pew for the midwives adjoining to the former, — —	. . .	. . .	. . .
	Item, paid for ringing when the King came out of Scotland,	0	6	8
	Item, paid for ringing at the King and Queen's coming to Whitehall, the laft day of October, 1617, —	0	2	6
	Item, paid for ringing at the news of the birth of the Lady *Elizabeth* her Grace's child, — —	0	2	6
	Item, paid for twenty yards of diaper towelling for the defks,	1	3	4
	Item, paid to *Leonard Tenant*, for a new clock and chimes, and twoe dyals, and for a barrel, and pricking thereof, and for wyers to the chimes, and for all the iron-work and workmanfhip in the fetting up, and finifhing of the fame, according to an agreement made with him in that behalf, being for the ufe of this church and parifh,	37	0	0
	Item, paid for the velvet cloath for the Lord *Oliver Lambert*, buried in St. Peter's church, — —	0	12	0

1618.

		£.	s.	d.
1618.	Item, paid for ringing on the King's birth-day, the 29th of July, 1618,	0	3	0
	Item, paid to a poor man who brought home the church-book, being loſt at Whitehall fire,	0	2	0
1619.	Item, paid to the maſon for a ſtone-door to the church,	1	19	5
	Item, paid for ringing at the King's coming to town in September, 1619,	0	2	6
1620.	Item, given to *Edward Weaver*, *John Batt*, *Robert Clarkeſon*, *Margaret Wells*, and *Alice Bradſhaw*, for carrying of formes, cuſhions, and haſſocks, into the new church-yard, at the conſecration thereof,	0	2	0
	Item, paid for ringing at the King's remove in Sept. 1620,	0	2	6
	Item, paid for ringing at the King's remove in Oct. 1620,	0	2	6
	Item, paid for 14 loads of gravel laid into the church-yard, by *John Langford*, againſt the communion of the lower houſe of parliament,	0	18	8
	Item, paid to *Moiſes Bollwell*, freemaſon, for making up the wall at theaſt end of Trinity chapell, as expreſſed by bill,	0	6	6
1621.	Item, paid for ringing on the King's remove in September,	0	2	6
	Item, to him more for making a cupboord in the ould reading place, and for other work, as appeareth by his bill,	0	8	8
1622.	Item, paid to the maſon for cutting of the new door-caſe on the ſouth ſide of the church, and for finiſhing thereof, as by his bill appeareth,	0	12	0
	Item, paid to *Walter Hall*, bricklayer, for bricks, tiles, &c. for and about the building and erecting of the correction-houſe in Tuttle fields for this city, &c. being alſo for a houſe to ſet the poor of the pariſh on work there,	156	4	1
	Item, paid to *Thomas Hammond*, carpenter, for timber, &c. for and about the ſaid correction-houſe, and for the mills and other neceſſarys,	83	13	0
Houſe of Correction.	Item, paid to ———, lockſmith, for iron work of all ſorts needfull in the new building of the ſaid houſe, &c.	12	8	9
	Item, paid to the joyner for wainſcotting, and a table, and formes, in and about the ſaid houſe,	4	12	2
	Item, paid to the painter, for colouring in oil the great gate, and all the windows, doors, and door-caſes, in the ſaid houſe, &c.	1	12	0
	Item, paid to the glaſier for 89 foot of new glaſs for the ſaid houſes, and repairing the old windows, which were much decayed,	1	3	10

1622.

		£.	s.	d.
1622. Houſe of Correction.	Item, paid to the maſon, for putting hooks into the gate, and to a labourer to carry the chimney-ſtones thither, —	0	2	0
	Item, paid the labourers to fill up the ditches, and for ramming the foundations of the brick wall, and for drains to paſs the water away, and for cleanſing and enlarging the ſewers, — — —	3	6	0
	Item, paid for twenty blocks to beat hemp on, 3 plain blocks, and 28 beetles, for the ſaid houſe of correction, —	7	7	6
	Item, for a green broad cloth carpet, and ſix cuſhions of the ſame, a pair of large creepers, fire ſhovel, and tongs, for the court-houſe in the ſaid houſe of correction,	2	5	1
	Item, paid for precedents and orders taken and tranſcribed out of other houſes of correction, in Middleſex and Surry, and out of Ould Bridewell in London, and Seſſions-houſe,	1	0	0
	Item, paid for a pewter ſtandiſh, penknife, pens, and paper,	0	3	2
	Item, paid for a regiſter-book 2s. 2d. for 400 printed paſſes 6s. 6d. — — — —	0	8	8
1623.	Item, paid for ringing when the King's Majeſty feaſted the Spaniſh ambaſſador in July, 1623, — —	0	2	6
	Item, paid for ringing at the King's coming to Whitehall in September, — — —	0	2	6
	Item, paid for a new Church Bible for the reading-place, —	2	0	0
	Item, paid for ringing at the Prince his Highneſs coming out of Spain, — — —	0	5	0
	Item, paid for ringing the 30th of October, when the Prince came from Royſton to St. James's, — —	0	2	6
	Item, paid for ringing at his Majeſty's coming to Whitehall in December, — — —	0	2	6
1623.	Item, to Mr. *Girten*, for certain iſſues impoſed upon the pariſh, levyed upon one *Smith*, for the robbery of one *Halfehead* within this hundred, — —	0	8	4
Houſe of Correction. 1624.	Item, paid for two pieces of broad cloth for childrens coats,	1	2	0
	Item, paid for two pieces of cotton, — —	9	14	0
	Item, paid for twenty flock beds and bolſters, and for twenty ruggs, and twenty blankets, — —	26	0	0
	Item, paid for one hundred of muckenders at 2d. apeice, and for tape, — — —	0	17	8
	Item, paid for one hundred and ſix ells and a quarter of canvas, at 15d. the ell, to make ſhirts for the children,	6	12	10
	Item, paid for making of an hundred ſhirts at 2d. the piece,	0	6	8
	Item, paid for an hundred and fifteen ells and half of canvas to make ſheets at 15d. the ell, — —	13	4	2
	Item, to making forty-eight pair of ſheets, at 6d. a pair, —	1	4	0
	Item, paid for ſeven dozen and four double bands, at 3d. a band,	1	2	0

		£.	s.	d.
House of Corr.	1624.			
	Item, paid for two dozen of single bands, at 3d. a band,	0	6	0
	Item, paid for twenty-four pair of shoes for the children,	1	4	0
	Item, paid for forty coyfes, at 4d. apeice, ——	0	10	6
	Item, paid for gartering for the children, — —	0	3	9
	Item, paid for making of four and forty coats for children,	1	2	0
	Item, paid for making of forty petticoats, —— —	0	10	0
	Item, paid to Mr. *Hollowaie*, for 18 pounds of brass, at 14d. the pound, —— —— ——	1	1	7
Work about Green Coat Hospital.	Item, paid to *Robert Bishop*, bricklayer, more at several times for workmanship by him, and his men, in building and finishing the said hospital with bricklayers work, plaisterers work, and tilers work, as appeareth by his bills, and the particular book, —— ——	14	18	0
	Item, paid to *John Middleton*, carpenter, more for workmanship by him and his men, about the hospital, as appeareth, &c. —— ——	24	3	10
	Item, paid to the smith, for iron works, casements, locks, keys, iron bars, and other work, about the hospital, as appeareth, &c. —— —— ——	7	10	0
	Item, paid to the painter, for work done about the hospital, as appeareth, &c. —— —— ——	5	14	8
	Item, paid to the plumber, for his work in the hospital, —	1	3	6
	Item, paid for a plank for a table, being 37 foot long, at 16d. the foot, —— —— ——	2	9	0
	Item, paid for the sawing and carriage thereof, ——	0	5	0
1625.	Received of the Right Honourable the Commons House of Parliament, when they took the communion in the parish church, on the 3d day of July, 1628, &c. ——	47	5	8
	Item, received of the Right Reverend Father in God *George* Lord Bishop of *London*, by the direction and appointment of the Right Honourable the Upper House of Parliament, being part of the moneys collected by virtue of his Majesty's letters patents, and allotted by their Lordships for the relief of the poor visited of this city of Westminster, the sum of — —	300	0	0
	Item, paid to the dog-killer for killing of dogs, ——	0	9	8
	Item, paid to —— —— more for killing 14 dozen and ten dogs in time of visitacion, —— ——	1	9	8
	Item, paid for cleaning and sweeping the Sanctuary gate at the King's Majesty's coming to the feast, ——	0	7	6
	Item, paid to Dr. *Bargrave*, for preaching, and attending the Parliament communion, 1618, —— ——	10	0	0

1625.

		£.	s.	d.
1625.	Item, paid to the dog-killer, for killing of 24 dozen of dogs,	1	8	0
	Item, paid for copying out of letters and directions which came from the Lords of the Council in the time of visitacion, ——— ——— ———	0	4	6
	Item, paid for 272 loads of gravel for the church-yard, —	13	12	0
1626.	Item, paid to the ringers on coronacion-day, 1626, by consent and allowance of the vestry, — ———	1	0	0
	Item, paid to Mr. *Elsing's* clerk, for a copy of the order of parliament, touching the collected money out of the country, to the poor of London and Westminster,	0	10	0
	Item, to the graves of 1447 poor people this year, —	1	0	0
	Item, paid to Mr. *John Seals*, for keeping and dieting the hospital children, being sometimes in number thirty two every month, and sometimes less, for 20 months now ended, as appeareth by particulars, and the several acquittances of the said *John Seals* in that behalf made,	84	12	4
	Item, paid to the bricklayer, for stuff and workmanship at the vault in Tuthill, ——— ———	1	10	8
	Item, memorandum, that we have received of Mr. *Edward Reynolds* and Mr. *Lancelot Reynolds*, for giving them leave to erect a monument in the church-wall, to the memory of *Edward Reynolds*, Esq; (their deceased uncle) late one of the clarks of the privy seal, and register of the court of Requests, ——— ———	5	0	0
	Item, they do also charge themselves with the sum of two hundred and seven pounds, seven shillings, and ten pence, which they received out of the vestry, towards the building of the new church-yard wall, and other buildings which they have made; one hundred pounds whereof was the gift of *Thomas Hays*, knight; and the rest were remainders of overseers accompts and of rents,	211	7	10
	Item, received also of the Right Honourable the Commons House of Parliament, at several times, when they received the communion in the parish church, anno 1 et 2 Reg. Caroli, ——— ——— ———	52	12	0½
	Item, paid for six new service-books for the fast appointed the fifth of July, 1626, — ——— ———	0	3	6
	Item, paid for the sluice-door in Kingstreet, and the carpenter's work, ——— ———	0	5	6
	Item, paid for the making a bond of £.50. which we borrowed towards making the new pews, — ———	0	2	0
1627.	Item, paid for ringing the 27th of March, being the day of the King's Majesty's coronation, — —	1	0	0

	£.	s.	d.
1627. Item, paid for bread and wine, when the Right Honourable the Commons House of Parliament (being 468 persons) received the communion in the parish church 1626,	5	17	0
Item, given to Mr. *Vincent Peris*, curate, by their appointment, for his pains in the administration of the Sacrament unto them, ——— ——— ———	5	0	0
Item, paid to *Walter Hall*, bricklayer, for making and building the new church-yard wall near Tutle-fields, containing in the whole compass thereof threescore and two roods, at 2l. 13s. 4d. the rodde, viz. for brick, lime, sand, and workmanship, ——— ——— ———	165	6	8
Item, paid to *George Butt*, for making a ditch about the new church-yard wall, containing 52 rods ½, at 1s. the rodd,	2	12	6
Item, paid for twelve bundles of rushes, to fit the church-yard for consecracion, — —— ——	0	1	0
Item, paid for carrying and re-carrying the tent and other things, ——— ——— ———	0	1	8
Item, paid to Dr. *Pope* for his fee at the said consecration,	2	10	0
Item, paid to Mr. *Walsall*, the register, for his fee and pains for drawing and ingrossing an instrument to consecrate the new church-yard, — — ——	3	10	0
Item, paid to *Twinnibo*, the apparitor, for his pains, —	0	10	0
Item, spent in a dinner, at the said consecration, for the said officers, and other worshipful company that attended the solemnity, ——— ——— ———	1	19	2
Item, paid to *Adam Browne*, joyner, at several times before-hand, for and towards the making and setting up of the new pews on the north side pillars, and on the north side wall of the church, as by, &c. ——	50	0	0
Item, paid to Mr. *John Scales*, for keeping and dicting the hospital children in the first yere of this accompt, being in number sometimes 20 a month, sometimes more, sometimes less, as by the particulars, and the several acquittances of the said *John Scales*, in that behalf made, appeareth, — — — —	33	17	0
Item, paid for herbes and spices to make diet-drink for the children in the spring, — — —	0	6	10
Item, received of Mr. *Samuel Clarke* and *William Goodacres*, churchwardens of the parish of St. Martin in the Fields, for admitting them and the parishoners there to joyn and make use with us in the house of correction in Tothil fields, the sum of forty pounds, ——	40	0	0

		£.	s.	d.
1627.	Item, to him (*Adam Brown*) more, in full payment and fatisfaction for all the faid pews, the whole fum for his work amounting to one hundred eighteen pounds ten fhillings, as by bill appeareth, —	40	10	0
1628.	Item, to the ringers for ringing the 27th day of March, 1628, being the King's Majeftie's coronation-day, —	1	0	0
	Item, for thirteen ells of Holland more, to make furpliffes for the two clarks and fextons, at 3s. 4d. the ell,	3	16	8
	Item, to Mr. *John Scales*, for keeping and dieting the hofpital children, in this fecond yere, being fometimes in number 20 a month, fometimes more, fometimes lefs, as by the receipts of the faid *John Scales* every month in that behalf appeareth. — — —	35	15	10
	Item, received of the Right Honourable *William* the now Earl of *Salifbury*, as an annuity of eight pounds *per annum*, which is paid yearly by his Lordfhip, in lewe and confideration of the fum of one hundred pounds yet remaining in his hands, which was given by the Right Honourable *Robert* late Earl of *Salifbury* his father, deceafed, for two years, — —	16	0	0
	Item, paid to *George Edgelie*, by confent of the veftry, towards his charge to proceed mafter of arts,	5	0	0
	Item, To *Richard Goodwin*, by confent of the veftry, towards proceeding bachelor of arts, — —	4	0	0
	Item, To Mr. *Hennam*, the hufband of William Bowyer's widow, for carrying fnow and ice out of King ftreet after a great froft, by confent of the veftry, —	6	0	0
	Memorandum, that there alfo remaineth in the veftry, which was given by the Right Honourable the Commons Houfe of Parliament, at their communicating and faft, in April, 1628, the fum of forty pounds, whereof their Honours have directed and appointed twenty pounds to be laid out for the poor children of the hofpitals; and the other twenty pounds they have left to the direction of the church-wardens and overfeers for the ufe of the poor of this parifh, —— ——	40	0	0

GIFTS and BENEVOLENCES, *viz.*

	£.	s.	d.
Item, of the Right Honourable the Commons Houfe of Parliament, collected at their faft, 18th of Feb. 1628,	47	19	7½
Item, of the Right Honourable the Lords of the Upper Houfe of Parliament, for the hofpital children and the poor, —— —— ——	10	0	0

1628. Item,

		£.	s.	d.
1628.	Item, of the Right Reverend Father in God the Lord Bishop of *Winchester*, as of his Lordship's collection for the poor, upon his Majesty's letters patents, —	7	8	3
	Item, of the Right Honourable the Lords of the Higher House of Parliament to the hospitall children, —	4	0	0

RECEAVED:

		£.	s.	d.
	Item, of divers persons the parishoners of this parish, for their fines for swearing, and being drunk, and for breach of the Sabaoth, and being otherwise presented according to the penal laws, as by a particular of their names and several fines appeareth, which hath been employed to the use of the hospitall children, the some of —	3	9	4
	Item, of *Thomas Powell*, high constable, which was repaid unto us by his Majesty's directions, in lieu of the coat and conduit-money, which the parish had formerly laid out to his Majesty's soldiers when they went to Cadez,	9	1	8
	Item, to *Richard Busby*, by consent of the vestry, towards enabling him to proceed bachelor of arts, —	5	0	0
	Item, to Mr. *Thomas Maurice*, by appointment of the Committee of the Honourable Commons House of Parliament, of the money collected at their fast the 18th of February, 1628, to be distributed by him according to their directions, — —	28	10	0
	Item, paid to the ringers when his Majesty granted the petition of right, — — —	0	5	0
	Item, for cleaning the streets at the Duke of *Buckingham's* funeral, — — —	0	4	5
	Item, to *Thomas Stile*, mason, for stone and workmanship in the building the two new windows, as appears by bill,			
	Item, for bringing and carrying back the formes to *Scotland Yard*, borrowed at the fast in February, 1628, —	0	1	0
	Item, to *Richard Price*, which he laid out, being high constable, for the pressing, conducting, and cloathing of soldiers for Cadez, — — —	3	3	0
	Item, to the ringers at the news of the Queen's Majesty being with child, — — —	0	5	0
	Item, Disbursed for the hospital this year —	106	14	4
1629.	Item, paid to the ringers on his Majesty's coronation-day, the 27th of March, 1629, — —	1	0	0
	Item, to Mr. *Henry Weatherfield*, for wine for the monthly communions this yere, as appeareth by bill, —	6	10	0
	Item, to a distressed minister driven out of the Palatinate,	0	3	0

1629.

	£.	s.	d.
1629. Item, to *Middleton*, for making the bridge over the ditch between the new church-yard and Mr. *Fowles* ground,	1	7	6
Item, to *Augustine Morgan*, a constable in the Great Sanctuary, being fined twenty shillings for suffering vagrants to wander in the streets, to him of his said fine being a poor man, ——— ———	0	18	0
Item, to a poor minister of the Voltelins in distress, ———	0	2	6

RECEAVED:

	£.	s.	d.
Item, of divers persons, parishioners of this parish, for their fines for swearing, and being drunk, and for the breach of the Sabaoth, and being otherwise presented and fined according to the law, as by a particular of their names and fines appeareth, ——— ———	4	12	0
Item, of *Jasper Beedon*, for stones taken out of the new-built window places in the north side isle, ———	0	8	0
Item, to a Grecian, one Grammaticus, ——— ———	0	1	0
Item, to a poor man that lost £.700 at sea by the Dunkerkers,	0	0	6
Item, spent at sundry times going to the Temple about *Brentford Bridge*, ——— ———	0	7	8
Item, for ringing the 19th of November, being his Majesty's birth-day, ——— ——— ———	0	2	6
Item, to *George Plucknett*, for writing the inventorys of the church goods, ——— ——— ———	0	11	0
N. B. Disbursements for the hospital this year, ———	81	13	$0\frac{1}{2}$
Item, receaved of the tenants in *Turmill-street*, near *Clarkenwell*, in the county of *Middlesex*, of which was heretofore purchased an annuity, or rent charge, of fifty pounds *per annum* for ever, the sum of one hundred and thirteen pounds, one shilling, and five pence, as appeareth by a particular of the receipts thereof, viz.	113	1	5
Memorandum, that the two hundred pounds, for the which there is mention in our receipts of benevolences and gifts in either yere, that we have received of Mr. *William Ireland* twelve pounds for the interest of two hundred pounds remaining in his hands, is the only gift and benevolence of the Right Honourable *William* Lord *Pagett*, deceased, towards maintenance of the said hospitall children, whereof his lordship desired he might not openly be known to be the author or giver till after his decease, and therefore now first recorded,	200	0	0
Item, receaved of divers inhabitants of this parish, being victuallers, whose names are hereunder written, the several soms			

	£.	s.	d.
ſoms and fines hereafter mentioned; they being preſented by the informer to his Majeſty's juſtices of the peace, for ſelling beer or ale by defected meaſures; to which victualiers, in regard to their poverty, we did return, or give back again, as alſo is hereafter expreſſed, *viz.*			
Received	7	0	0
Returned to them	6	0	0
To the informer per order,	1	0	0
1630. Item, of Mrs. *Anne Corbett*, widow, by her given to the children of the hoſpitall, for erecting a monument in our church, in memory of her ſon, Sir John Corbett, knight and baronett,	6	0	0
Item, of divers perſons, pariſhoners of this pariſh, for their fines for ſwearing, and being drunk, and for breach of the Sabaoth, and being otherwiſe preſented and fined for their miſdemeanors, as by the particular of their names and fines appeareth,	40	2	0
Item, received of *John Fennell* and *Ralph Atkinſon*, collectors of the eſtreats for repair of Brentford Bridge and Knightſbridge,	23	6	4
Item, of the churchwardens of St. Martin in the Fields and St. Clement Danes, towards the charge of the ſuit for Brentford Bridge,	1	14	4
Item, to Dr. *Vincent Peirs*, by appointment of the veſtry, and for his pains taken, and to be taken, about burials in the new church-yard,	20	0	0
Item, to *Walter Hall*, bricklayer, for his work in building the peſthouſe, as appeareth by his bill, and for materials,	48	4	0
Item, to the ringers for ringing on Prince *Charles* his birth-day and on his chriſtening-day,	0	9	0
Item, for three proclamations with directions to his Majeſtie's juſtices of the peace concerning the market, &c.	0	1	0
Item, to the ringers for ringing on the 6th of October, in memory of the King's happy return from Spain,	0	5	0
Item, to *John Martin*, having his Majeſty's privy ſeal to begg relief towards his travel to Perſia,	0	0	3
Item, for ringing the 5th of December, when there was proclamation made of the concluſion of the peace with the King of *Spain*,	0	2	6
Item, to *Barnard Cliffe*, for writing of books of aſſeſſment and warrants to collect coat and conduct-money, and for other buſineſs, as appeareth by his bill,	3	10	0

		£.	s.	d.
1631.	Item, to *Harmon Hurleſhurſt*, an interpreter, being in neceſſitie, at the requeſt of Dr. *Peirs*,	0	4	0
	Item, paid towards the repaire of Brentford Bridge and of Knightſbridge, and for the charge of the ſute to defend ourſelves from the ſame, and other expences touching the ſame, as by the particulars appeareth,	24	7	10
	Diſburſements for the hoſpital:			
	Item, to Mr. *Packer's* clarke, for drawing a petition to the King's Majeſtie for a licence in mortmaine,	0	2	6
	N. B. The whole ſum diſburſed this laſt year for the hoſpitall was	60	13	1½
	Item, paid for ringing on Prince *Charles* his birthdaie, being the 29th of May,	0	5	0
	Item, for billes for viſited howſes,	0	1	0
	Item, to *Richard Buſby*, a king's ſcholler of Weſtminſter, towards enabling him to proceed maſter of arts at Oxon, by conſent of the veſtrie,	6	13	4
	Item, paid for ringing at a remove to Whitehall, Oct. 15.	0	2	6
	Item, paid for ringing when wee heard that the Queene was delivered of her daughter the Lady *Marie*,	0	5	0
	Item, paid for ringing on the King's birth-day, November 19,	0	5	0
	The Rents in *Turnemill-Street*:			
	Item, receaved of *Henrie Darell*, Eſquier, for a year and a quarter's rent, ended at Midſomer, 1631, for the tenements in Turnemill-Street, after the rate of £.70. *per annum*.	87	10	0
	Item, receaved of *Henrie Smith*, Eſquier, and of Mr. *Hugh Trappes*, for three-quarters rent, ended at the Annunciation laſt, at £.50. *per annum*, (the old rent charge),	37	10	0
	Item, receaved of them more in part of the arrearages of the ſaid rent-charge,	200	0	0
1632.	Item, for ringing at his Majeſtie's remove from Theobalds to Whitehall, primo Novembris, 1632,	0	2	6
	Item, to the joyner, for mending the viſcounteſs *Dorcheſter's* pewe,	0	12	0
1633.	Item, for ringing on the King's Majeſty's coronation daie, 1633,	1	0	0
	Item, to *Adam Brown*, for making and ſetting upp of two and twenty new pewes on the ſouth ſide of the church, according to an agreement made with him in that behalfe, as by his bills appears,	24	16	0

	£.	s.	d.
1633. Item, to *Nichalaus George* earle of *Galetenſis*, authorized to aſke reliefe, and divers poor miniſters, and miniſters widowes, being in diſtreſs, — —	0	15	0
Item, laid out for making the high-way from my Lord *Goring's* howſe to Tothil-fieldes, (more than was collected upon th'affeſſment in that behalf), being by command from the King's Majeſtie, and letters from the Right Honourable the Lordes of his Majeſtie's privie councell, five pounds fourteen ſhillings and eleven pence, and to diſcharge a at the verge thirteen ſhillings and ſixpence, as appears by the bills, — —	6	8	5
Item, of the Right Honourable *Henry* earl of *Mancheſter*, lord privie ſeale, the pardon of his lordſhip's fees for paſſing our licence in mortmaine for King Charles's hoſpitall in Weſtminſter, which his lordſhip, as the prime benefactor to that good worke, hath moſt freelie and nobly remitted unto us; in like manner hath ſir *Sidney Montague*, knight, his lordſhip's brother, one of the maſters of the Requeſts, remitted to us his fees; and ſo likewiſe did Mr. *William Noye*, attorney general to his Majeſtie, not only reſtore to us twenty pounds, which we gave him for his pains therein, but of his owne bounty gave us more ten pounds.			
Item, Of the churchwardens of St. Martin's in the Fields, for theire part of charges about the correction howſe, laid out in the laſt churchwarden's time, —	0	7	0
Item, for ringing at the King's Majeſty's coming home out of Scotland, ... July, 1633, — —	0	5	0
Item, for ringing at the Duke of *Yorke* his Grace's buirth,	0	5	0
Item, for ringing on the King's Majeſty's buirth day, —	0	5	0
Item, for ringing on the Duke his Grace's chriſtening day,	0	5	0
Item, diſburſed and paid for fees to divers officers at the greate ſeale, privie ſeale, and ſignett, and for drawing the books, and to Mr. Attorney Generall his ſervants, and other neceſſary charges, in paſſing his Majeſty's grant of licence in mortmain for King Charles his hoſpitall Weſtminſter, as by ſeveral billes thereof appeareth,	35	1	5
Item, paid for our part of the charges towards th'obteyning of a corporation for this citie and liberties, wherein, neverthelefs, we loſt our endeavour, —	7	11	10
1634. Item, to the fower poor women to carry the almes baſkett for the poore of our pariſh in the correction howſe, from the 18th of Januarie laſt to this time, being XVII weeks, at VI s. the weeke; in toto, — —	5	2	0

Diſburſements

	£.	s.	d.
Difburfements for the hofpitall : Summa Pagine ——	90	7	2
Item, of the benevolence of the Right Honourable Earle *Keymoule*, lord high chancellor of Scotland, given to the children of the hofpitall at his deceafe, ——	5	0	0
Item, of Mr. *Gregory Baker*, of Windfore, as a legacy given by Mr. *Samuel Baker*, of Weftminfter, by his laft will,	100	0	0
Item, for a pair of fheetes for *Jane Clare*, when wee fent her to the Spittle at Knightfbridge, —— ——	0	3	6
Item, for ringing at the King's Majeftie's remove from Hampton Court, on the 30th of October, 1634, ——	0	5	0
Item, for drawing and writing out the names of the inhabitants to make the affeffment of the fhip-money by, and for the affeffment and bills, —— ——	1	3	4
Item, fpent upon the commiffioners at theire fitting in the parifh church to collect the benevolence towards repairing St. Paul's church, London, ——	1	1	0
1635. Item, for ringing on the 27th of March, 1635, being the King's Majefty's coronation daie, ——	1	0	0
Difburfements for the hofpitall : Summa Pagine ——	87	14	1
Item, of the wardmott inqueft for the fame ufe, and to the poore prifoners in the Gate-houfe out of theire boxe at delivering upp theire verdict, —— ——	4	19	6
Item, to the ringers for ringing at the Queene's Majeftie's happie deliverie in child-bedd, —— ——	0	5	0
Item, to *John Green*, for writing the books of affeffment upon the parifhoners towards releife of the vifited howfes,	0	10	0
Item, to *Anne Davis*, to teach the poor to thread bedes five fhillings, for getting them two fhillings and fixpence,	0	7	6
Item, to *Thomas Gaffaway*, carpenter, for a new building added to the houfe of correction, as by his bill appeareth,	27	12	0
Item, to *Allen Gilbert*, bricklaier, for his work about the fame building, as by his bill appeareth, — —	37	15	0
Item, for bread for the houfe of correction for the whole year,	11	19	6
Item, for beere for them, as appeares by feveral bills, —	24	2	0
Item, for falt fifh for them in Lent, and for the carriage,	2	17	6
Difburfements for the hofpitall : Summa Pagine ——	78	19	11
Item, to Mr. *Edward Smith*, counfellor, for advife, and for the making conveyances to new feoffees in truft of the rents in *Turmill-ftreete*, and for folliciting and expences to get in arrearages upon the ftatute, as alfo to be advifed by councell upon the commiffion for the furvey of the pal-			

 lace,

		£.	s.	d.
	lace, and going to Greenwich about the towne water being ſtopt; in toto,	7	13	0
1636.	Item, for ringing on the Lady *Maries* buirth daie,	0	5	0
	Item, for ringing on the Ladie *Annes* buirth daie,	0	5	0
	Item, for two coppies of the lords of the privie counſell's warrant, touching the warning in of ſuch as had built contrary to his Majeſty's proclamation,	0	2	0
	Item, to *Philip Johns*, for ſalte fiſh for the poore in the correction howſe this year, as by his three ſeveral bills appeareth,	6	13	4
	Item, to the ſaid Mr. *Glynne*, for his advice on the behalfe of this town concerning his Majeſtie's ſhip money, and for his paines otherwiſe, by appointment of the veſtrie,	5	0	0
	Item, paid to Mr. *Mutas*, clarke of the counſell, for his fee for an order of the board, touching Mr. *Holloway* and Mr. *Reaſon's* buildings in Longditch,	....		
	Diſburſements for the ſetting of the towne-poore to worke: Summa Pagine,	242	10	6
	Diſburſements for the hoſpitall: Summa	117	16	10½
1637.	Item, receaved as a legacy given to the poor of this pariſh by the laſt will of Mr. *Thomas Knevitt*, late clark of the parliament, deceaſed,	20	0	0
	Item, receaved of the conſtables of this pariſh, which they collected from the inhabitants of the ſame, upon an aſſeſſment made towards the repair of *Cherſey Bridge*, as by a particular thereof appeareth,	19	11	3
	Item, to Mrs. *Stone*, the wife of John Stone, for bad farthings which her huſband had receaved when he was overſeer for the poor, as part of the ſtock brought in by his predeceſſors,	1	7	0
	Item, for ringing on the 6th of October, being the day that the King's Majeſtie landed in England at his Highneſs's retourne from *Spaine*,	0	5	0
	Item, to *George Hare*, ſcrivener, for drawing a draught of a releaſe from the clerks of this pariſh church relinquiſhing their claime to the patent concerning clarks wages, and for ingroſſing the ſame in parchment,	0	4	6
	Item, paid for a paper book to take the names of the preachers that preach in this pariſh,	0	0	6
	Item, paid for ringing the 16th of March, 1637, when the King's Majeſtie came from Newmarkett to Whitehall,	0	2	6
	Item, paid for writing of eight letters to the lords of his Majeſty's privie counſell, for an abatement to be made			

	£.	s.	d.
unto the inhabitants of this pariſh of this year's aſſeſſment to his Majeſtie's ſhip money, —— ——	0	2	8
Item, to Mr. *Anthony Cliffe*, deputie clark of the peace, for renewing the commiſſion of ſewers for this citie and liberties, —— —— ——	1	10	0
Item, to Mr. *William Butcher* and Mr. *Michael Arnold*, high conſtables, towards the repair of Cherſey Bridge, and other bridges in the county of Middleſex, charged upon this pariſh, as by their receipts appeareth, ——	24	10	0
Item, to ſir *Dudley Charlton*, knight, one of the clerks of his Majeſty's privie counſell, as his fee for an order of the board, on the behalf of this town porters, —	2	12	0
Item, to the clarke of the counſell, for the coppie of an order touching the parſon's tythes of this pariſh, ——	0	10	0
Item, to Mr. *John Glynne* and Mr. *Maynard*, for their advice concerning the parſon's tythes of this pariſh, —	3	11	6
Memorandum, that theſe accomptants (out of this remaine) have diſburſed, for the reliefe of the poore viſited with the plague in their two years, the ſum of three hundred fourſcore and one pounds, ſixteen ſhillings, and eleaven pence farthing, as by their particular accompt thereof appeareth, —— ——	....		
1638. for ringing on the fifth of October, for joy of his Majeſty's ſafe returne from *Spaine*, —— ——	0	5	0
Item, for ringing on the third of November, for the Queene Mother her arrival, —— —— —	0	5	0
Item, for ringing on the Lady *Maries* buirth day, ——	0	5	0
Item, to Mr. *Marr*, one of Dr. Eden's officers, for drawing of ſeveral articles to be delivered to my lord of *Canterbury*, about Mrs. Shepheard's pew being in controverſie,	0	5	0
Item, to *Edward Rogers*, for ringing on the 20th of January, for the Queen's ſafe delivery, ——	0	5	0
Item, for a proclamation, being his Majeſty's declaration againſt the Scots, which was read in the church,	0	0	6
Item, for the book of his Majeſtie's declaration againſt the Scotts, and of their carriage towards his Majeſtie in Scotland, which remaineth in the veſtrie, ——	0	7	6
Item, to *Edward Rogers* and juſtice *Heywood's* clarke, for writing of eight ſeveral books to collect, conduct, and other moneys, —— —— ——	0	10	0
Item, to Mr. *Thomas Falconbridge*, by order of the veſtry, at four ſeveral payments, twoe hundred pounds towards the building of the new chapell in Tuttle-fields; which ſum of two hundred pounds was diſburſed by the ſaid Mr. *Thomas Falconbridge* as followeth, *viz.*			

		£.	s.	d.
1638.	Item, to Mr. *Winter*, keeper of the hoſpitall at Knightſbridge, for the keeping of the Three Innocents for one month,	0	16	0
	Item, to *Michael Arnold*, high conſtable, for the yearly allowance heretofore aſſigned to the muſter-maſter of this county, for his diviſion in this pariſh, as by his receipt appeareth, — — —	1	10	0
	Item, more to the ſaid Mr. *Thomas Kirke*, for writing of ſeveral warrants to eſtabliſh the provoſt marſhall, —	0	5	0
	Item, to *William Lynes*, for removing the ſtocks from the ſheds in Tuttle, — — —	0	12	0
	Item, paid to Mr. *Henry Calcott*, for coate and conduct-money, as by his receipt appeareth, — —	25	0	0
1639.	Item, of the Right Honourable the Lord *Pollett*, ſir *Robert Pye*, and others, the ſum of one hundred pounds, given by the laſt will and teſtament of the Right Honourable the Dutcheſs of *Richmond* her Grace, to be diſtributed to the poore of this pariſh, — —	100	0	0
	Item, of the ſeveral conſtables of this pariſh, which they collected from the inhabitants of the ſame, upon an aſſeſſment made for coate and conduct-money for ſoldiers ſent to *Barwicke*, — — —	25	4	6
	Item, received of Mr. *George Blennerhaſſett* and Mr. *Robert Flood*, churchwardens of the pariſh of St. Martin in the Fields, towards the repaire of the houſe of correction, — — — —	3	10	0
	Item, for ringing on the 1ſt and 2d days of Auguſt, 1639, being the time of his Majeſtie's returne to *Whitehall* from the North, — — — —	0	10	0
	Item, to *Bummer* the beadle, for watching a houſe all night in Gardiner's-Lane, which was ſhut up and ſuppoſed to be viſited, — — —	0	0	8
	Item, to *Walter Davies*, gardiner, for laying of ſeven loads of gravell upon the pavement by the church-yard wall againſt his Majeſtie's going to Parliament, —	0	7	0
	Item, to Mr. *Thomas Kirke*, high conſtable, for preſſe-money, for billetting of ſouldiers ſent to *Barwick*, and for coate and conduit-money, as by his ſeveral receipts appeareth,	6	17	2
	Item, to Mr. *Thomas Neale*, for three paire of ſhoes, two paire for the poore Innocents at the Spittle at Knightſbridge, &c. — — — —	0	6	6
1640.	Item, paid for *Twinihoe*, for books of the Faſt and Canons of the Church, — — —	0	4	0
	Item, for ringing at his Majeſtie's returne from *Yorke*, —	0	5	0
	Item, paid to *Edward Rogers*, for three ſervice-books for the Faſts, — — —	0	2	6

1640.

		£.	s.	d.
1640.	Item, paid to Juftice *Heywood's* clerke, for writing out the Recufants names,	0	2	6
	Item, for ringing on that day which the Triennial Parliament was agreed upon in the Howfe of Parliament,	0	5	0
	Item, paid to the Clark's man of the Parliament Howfe, for the proteftation made in the Howfe of Parliament, and for the articles,	0	2	6
1641.	Item, paid to Mr. *Richard Vefie*, carpenter, in part of payment, for his worke about the new gallery in the church, the fumme of one hundred pounds, as by his receipt appeareth, viz.	100	0	0
	Item, paid for eight books of the act made for the pole-money, with the proclamations to the fame, at ten-pence apeece, which were bought and provided for the veftrie,	0	6	8
	Item, paid for a paper-booke, to take the name of fuch of the parifhioners as tooke the proteftation,	....		
	Item, paid to *Joane Parkinfon* and *Mary Clarkfon*, for making cleane the church and pews againft the 7th day of September, 1641, when there was a Thankfgiving for our unity with the Scotts,	0	1	6
	Item, given to the ringers that day,	0	5	0
	Item, paid more unto *Richard Vefey*, carpenter, in part of payment of his worke about the new gallery, as by his receipt of the 6th of September, 1641, appeareth, fiftie pounds, viz.	50	0	0
	Item, paid for a pint of fack, for the minifter that preached September 5,	0	0	7
	Item, paid to the finging men of the Abbie towards their feaft at St. James's tide, according to auncient cuftome,	1	0	0
	Item, paid to *Edward Huckwell*, mafon, for faftening the grate of the monument that is next to the fkreene, and for mending the pillar where Mrs. *Webb's* monument did ftand, and for plaifter to do it,	0	3	6
	Item, paid for the hyer of a coach, and other charges, which thefe accomptants laid out when they and others of the veftrie went to *Barking*, to receive the rent from the Inne there called *The Bull*, which was the guift of Mr. *Thomas Gawen*,	1	1	0
	Item, paid for fearching the court-rolls there, where we found that the mortmaine was enrolled,	0	1	6
	Item, paid to the ringers for ringing the 5th of October, in commemoration of his Majeftie's happie returne from *Spaine* that day,	0	5	0

1641.

		£.	s.	d.
1641.	Item, paid more unto them (painters) for the fowre new windows in the gallery, and eight iron caſements being laid in oile and colours, as by their bills appeareth, —	1	11	2
	Item, paid to *John Sanford* and *John Titchborne*, deputies unto *George Harwood*, gent. farmer to his Majeſtie, for the rents of concealements, the ſumme of twentie ſhillings, for twoe years arrere of rent due unto his Majeſtie for the howſes in Newgate Markett, which were the guift of Mr. *Thomas Gawen*, as by their receipt appeareth, — — —	1	0	0
	Item, paid for ringing the 16th of November, being the Queen's Majeſtie's birth day, — —	0	5	0
	Item, paid for ringing the 19th of November, being the King's Majeſtie's birth-day, — —	0	5	0
	Item, paid for ringing at his Majeſtie's retourne from *Scotland*,	0	5	0
	Item, paid more to Mr. *Richard Veſey*, carpenter, in part of payment of his worke about the galleries, as by his receipt,	50	0	0
	Item, paid more to Mr. *Duckin*, the carver, for carving the ſhield that ſtands next to the ſcreene in the church,	0	14	0
	Item, paid more to *Richard Veſey*, in full, for the carpenters work about the galleries, as by his receipt appeareth,	20	0	0
1642.	Item, paid for twoe pints of ſack for the miniſters that preached the faſt-day, which was the 30th of March,	0	1	0
	Item, paid for ringing on the 27th of March, being the King's coronation-day, — —	1	0	0
	Item, paid to *Thomas Booker*, coroner of Weſtminſter, by order of veſtrie, for ſitting upon the death of ſir *Richard Wiſeman*, and of a poor man found dead in this pariſh, as by his receipt appeareth, — —	1	6	8
	Item, paid for the quit-rent of the Bull at Barking, being Mr. *Thomas Gawen's* guift, and for other duties at a court holden there, — —	0	9	10
	Memorandum, that theis accomptants in their twoe years have diſburſed out of the moneys ſoe remaining in their hands as aforeſaid, for the relief of ſuch poore of this pariſh as have been viſited of the plague, the ſumme of fowre ſcore and foure pounds and ſix ſhillings, which was, &c.			

Benevolences to the Church and Poor given by the Parliament and others on the Faſt-dayes, (viz.)

	£.	s.	d.
Item, June 29, 1642, received then in good money (beſides 3s. 6d. in counterfeit money) the ſome of —	26	4	1
Item, collected at the pariſh church of St. Margarett's, Weſtminſter,			

	£.	s.	d.
minſter, for the reliefe of the poor Proteſtants in *Ireland*, at a faſt in September, 1642, —— ——	26	9	0
1642. Item, collected more at a faſt in the ſame church in October, 1642, for the reliefe of the ſaid poore in *Ireland*, —	44	0	0
Item, collected at the ſaid pariſh church for the reliefe of the town of *Braintford*, —— —— ——	41	10	0
Item, collected at the pariſh church for the reliefe of maimed ſouldiers, upon a faſt-day, —— ——	20	7	1
Item, collected at the pariſh church, and at the new chappell to carrie children to *New England*, —— ——	26	12	6
Item, receipts of moneys collected towards the payment for the building of the courts of guard, making poſts and chains, and other works for the ſafety of this town, ſumma —— —— ——	50	0	0
Item, received out of the black cheſt at ſeveral tymes for the building of the new peſt howſes, — ——	200	0	0
Item, of Doctor *Wimberley*, out of the token-money, after the rate of ob. out of every 3d. towards bread and wyne,	10	0	0
Money received of the collectors for the viſited, totall,	10	19	0
Item, paid to *Richard Veſey*, Oct. 15, for the carpenters worke of the floore over the ſtairs, where the powder and bullets, and match lyeth, —— ——	1	15	0
Item, ſpent at *Knightſbridge*, when divers of the burgeſſes and veſtrie-men of this pariſh went the perambulation,	2	19	9
Item, paid for an order from the Howſe of Commons, for ſtaying the money gathered on the faſt-day in September,	0	7	0
Item, November 3, given to the officers of the Tower of London and labourers that delivered the powder, bullett, and matche, —— —— ——	0	14	0
Item, paid for boathyer, when wee carried the money and cloth to the Guildhall, which was given and lent by the inhabitants of this pariſh, for the releife of *Ireland*,	0	2	0
Item, to *Margaret May*, a very poore ſicke woman in Lincoln Yard, at ſeveral tymes for her releife, ——	0	6	0

Diſburſements to the ſinging-men of the Abbey, *viz.*

	£.	s.	d.
Item, for an yearly allowance given unto them for ſinging anthems in the parriſh church at *Chriſtmas*, *Eaſter*, and *Whitſontide*, and is towards their feaſt at St. *James tyde*,	1	0	0

To the Bell-ringers for ringing at ſeveral tymes, *viz.*

Item, on the Prince's birth-day, 5s.; on the day that the King came out of *Spain*, 5s.; on the 5th day of November,

5s.;

		£.	s.	d.
	5s ; on the 19th of November, being the King's birth-day, 5s.; on the coronation-day, 20s.	....		
1642.	Item, the total of the charge for building of the peſt howſes amounteth to twoe hundred fiftie-ſeaven pounds, ſeaven ſhillings and nine-pence, *viz.* —— ——	257	7	9
	Item, Diſburſements for the building and making of courts of guard and ſluces for the ſafetye of this towne, and for poſts and chains in *St. James Street*, and *King Streete*,	....		
	Item, paid to the labourers for ſeveral days worke about digging, trenching, and making breaſt-workes and ſluces, as by the particular bill appeareth, —— —	17	6	4
	Summa —— ——	156	1	11
1643.	Item, given to the ſinging-men of the Abby, towards their feaſt at *St. James-tyde*, —— —— —	1	0	0
	Item, paid to *Thomas Gaſſoway*, carpenter, for worke done to the north porch of the Abby-church, as by his bill appeareth, —— —— ——	0	6	1
	Item, paid for boat-hier to the Tower, when theiſe accomptants went to pay in money that was collected for poor captives taken by the *Turks*, which was paid to the commiſſioners for the navie, —— ——	0	1	0
	Item, paid more unto him for a booke of the names of all the inhabitants of this pariſh, that are aſſeſſed to the poore, that was delivered to the committee; and for, &c.	....		
	Item, paid for twoe paper books, that were provided for taking of the covenant, —— ——	....		
	Item, paid to *George Hare*, for writing of an aſſeſſment for the viſited; for another aſſeſſment for maimed ſouldiers, which was twice written; for drawing out the names of all ſuch perſons in this pariſh as have taken the covenant, and putting them into an alphabetical way; alſoe for the drawing up of the names as well of all ſuch as had taken the covenant here, as thoſe that had not, and putting them together in an alphabetical way, &c. —— —— ——	3	11	4

Diſburſements to bell-ringers:

Item, the 29th of May, 5s.—the 5th of October, 5s.—the 5th of November, 5s.—the 19th of November, 5s.

1644. Item, the 27th of March, 20s.—the 29th of May, 5s.

1643. Rents abated unto ſeveral Tenants according to ſeveral ordinances of Parliament:

		£.	s.	d.
Weſtminſter.	Abated unto *Thomas Pullen*, for the weekly payments and for the roiall ſubſedie, —— ——	0	8	8

1643.

		£.	s.	d.
1643.	Item, more abated unto him for the maggazeene, ——	0	4	6
Turnemill Street.	Abated out of *Melchisadeck Fritters'* rent, for weekly payments, and for the out-works, ——	0	2	6
	Item, paid for the releife of a child of *Anne Beard's*, that died of the plague in the Still Yard; and a poore woman that was shutt up in her house there at several tymes,	0	10	0
	Item, disbursements for the poore visited with the plague, this yeare's totall, —— —— ——	24	2	2
1644.	Item, of *Edward Tasker*, by the hands of his daughter *Aylett*, for the stuff and materialls of the court of guard erected upon his ground at the Horse-ferrie, ——	5	0	0
	Item, for 29 pound of fine brasse, at 4d. a pound, and 96 pound of coarse brasse, at 3d. a pound, taken off from sundrie toombe-stones in the church, ——	1	13	6
	Item, of *Arthur Condall*, in part of £.5. for the screene and organ-loft, —— —— ——	50	0	0
	Item, of *Edward Stanthwaite*, for having companie in his howse on a fast-day, 10s. and for swearing, 1s. —	0	11	0
Westminster Rent.	Item, of Mr. *Edward Gerrard*, for our Ladie-daie, Midsomer, and Michaelmas quarters, 1644, 3*l*. 7*s*. 6*d*. (whereof allowed for the Lord Generall's recruit, 1s. 8d.) rest received, — ——	3	5	10
	Item, more names of rent allowed or abated, for the magazine —for the four months weeklie tax—for the *British* army—for sir *Thomas Fairfax*, —— ——	....		
	Item, received on the fast-day, 26 Junii, 1644, as the moytie of the collection for the maimed souldiers, and widows of such as have lost their lives in the warrs; th'other moytie being appointed for the poore, ——	6	13	0
	Item, to Mr. *John Redwood*, for charges upon sundry indictments touching the bridge at the water-mill, as by bill appears, —— —— ——	2	16	11
	Item, for mending the service-book, —— ——	0	1	10
	Item, to them (ringers) for the 19th of November, the King's birth-day, —— —— ——	0	5	0
	Item, to Mr. *Vesey*, for a post, worke, and paving against King Henrie the Seaventh's chappell, —— ——	0	5	0
	Item, to Mr. *Eaton*, minister, upon the motion of Mr. Recorder, for his pains in preaching and reading for about four months, —— —— ——	5	0	0
	Item, engrossing an answeare of my Lord Maior's letter, and drawing it, —— —— ——	0	1	0
	Item, a petition, certificate, and bond to the governors of the Lady *Dacre's* almeshowses, upon the admittance of *Joane Head*, —— —— ——	0	2	6

1644.

		£.	s.	d.
1644.	Item, for a quire of printed warrants for putting the ſtatutes in execution concerning the Lord's Day, &c. ——	0	1	6
	Item, for a table with the Covenant to hang in the church,	0	3	0
	Item, for a doſen of ordinances for obſerving the Lord's Day,	0	0	9
	Diſburſements for the poore viſited with the plague this year: Sum total, ——	59	4	4
1645.	Received of Captain *White*, for the organ-pipes, ——	4	0	0
	Item, of the ſeveral perſons following, as their contribution towards raiſing a ſtock to ſett the poore on worke, *viz.* ſir *Edward Powell*, 5l.—Captain *Fauconberge*, 3l. 6s. 8d.—Mr. *Laurence Swetnam*, 2l.—Mr. *George Prynn*, 2l.—Mr. *Michael Arnold*, 2l.—Mr. *William Huntley*, 2l.—Mr. *Stephen Bornman*, 2l.—*George Pluckenett*, 1l.—Mr. *John Brigham*, —— —— ——	21	6	8
Rent.	Item, of Mr. *Edward Gerrard*, for this quarter, 1l. 2s. 6d. (inde allowed for royall ſubſidie, Scottiſh army, and 6 men, for ſir *Thomas Fairfax*, 6s. 4d.) reſt received, ——	0	16	2
	Item, to *Francis Conſtable*, for a Bible, and Directorie for the church, delivered to Mr. *Gibſon*, — ——	0	10	0
	Item, to the Lady *Spotſwood*, in great want, — ——	0	2	6
	Item, to Mr. *Coſens*, for the order for the ſlaughter-howſe to ſet the poore on worke, —— ——	0	5	0
	Item, a petition to Mr. *Recorder*, for the rent of the Horſe-ferrie, for the uſe of the poore, 2s.—a petition for the markett, 1s. 6d. —— ——	0	3	6
	Item, a petition and draught to the Lords in Parliament, in behalf of the collector and conſtable, committed for diſtrayning the goods of Mr. *Throckmorton*, ——	0	2	6
	Item, for writing and copying three times certen orders touching the ordering of the Markett, ——	0	6	8
	Item, three petitions to the committee for priſoners, for ſhrowds, &c. burying 32 priſoners which died in Tuttle-fields, —— —— —— ——	0	3	0
	Item, to *John Forbench* and *George Chandler*, for their charges in the cuſtody of the meſſenger, about the diſtrayning of Mr. *Throgmorton's* goods for the viſited people,	1	10	7
	Item, for ringing the 19th of November, the King's birth daie,	0	5	0
	Item, three petitions to the committee for the colledge, for the uſual benevolence for the poore, —— ——	0	3	0
	Item, to Mr. *Prynne*, for repairing the new ſluce to drain the Levell, as by bill appeareth, —— ——	0	7	0
	Item, for ſeaven lanthorns to hang in the ſtreets, ——	0	18	0
	Item, for a dozen of candles to ſett in the lanthornes, ——	0	0	9
	Item, to the beadles to drink while they watched the chaines,	0	1	0

1645.

		£.	s.	d.
1645.	Item, to Captain *White*, for a bason to baptize withall,	0	6	0
	Item, to the ringers for ringing the 5th of February, being a day of publick thankſgiving for *Dartmouth*, *Hereford*, and the Weſt, —— —— ——	0	5	0
	Item, for a barr of timber in the church-yard, and ſaber,	0	6	0
	Diſburſement for the poore people viſited with the plague this year: ſum total —— ——	81	1	5
1646.	received at the collection on the thankſgiving day on the 12th of Maie, 1646, being a moytie, —— ——	4	0	0
	Item, by a collection at the pariſh church, on the 26th day of Auguſt, 1646, being a faſt day, —— ——	17	2	9
	Item, received more for the releiſe of the poore viſited with the plague, by another collection at the pariſh church upon the 9th of September, 1646, being a day ſett apart for publique thankſgiving, —— ——	9	10	0
	Item, September 14, received of Mr. *Richard Shering*, by virtue of an ordinance of parliament, touching the viſited, the ſum of one hundred pounds, ——	100	0	0
	Item, to the ringers for ringing on the Prince's birth day,	0	5	0
	Item, to them for ringing on the King's birth daie, ——	0	5	0
	Item, to them for ringing on the King's coronation day,	1	0	0
	Item, paid for ſweeping and cleanſing of the broad ſanctuary againſt the funeral of the Earl of Eſſex, and for broomes,	0	4	10
	Item, to *Nicholas Weeks*, for taking off a fine ſett on this towne for not repairing the Mill-bridge, ——	1	0	0
	Diſburſements for the poore Innocents in the Spittle or Lazar-howſe, at Knightſbridge; ſum total, ——	4	2	11
	Diſburſements for the uſe of the poore viſited with the plague in this pariſh; ſumma, —— ——	154	13	9
1647.	Item, of *William Holliday*, for the timber and ſtuff of the boarded howſe that was made and built in the paſſage to the neat howſe for a court of gard in Tuthill-feilds,	6	0	0
	Item, to the ringers, for ringing on a thankſgiving day,	0	5	0
	Item, to the ringers, for ringing on the 5th of October,	0	5	0
	Item, to them more, for ringing on his Majeſty's birth day,	0	5	0
	Item, paid for roſemarie and baies, that was ſtuck about the church at Chriſtmas, —— —— ——	0	1	6
	Item, paid in fees unto Mr. *Freind* and Mr. *Denham*, twoe of the meſſengers unto the ſergeant att armes, attending the Commons Houſe of Parliament, when theis accomptants were committed for permitting miniſters to preach upon Chriſtmas-day, and for adorning the church,	3	0	0
1648.	Item, to the ringers, for ringing on the 27th of March, being the day of the King's Majeſty's inauguration, —	1	0	0

4 1648.

	£.	s.	d.
1648. Item, laid out in Expences, when (by order) wee ſent forth ſcouts to bring intelligence of the armies' approach towards the cittie, — — —	0	12	6
1647. Item, Diſburſements for the uſe of the poore viſited with the plague in this pariſh, — —	165	10	0
Memorandum, that the five hundred and fiftie pounds which Mr. *George Smith* paid in for the redemption of the howſes in Turnmill Streete, ſometimes the eſtate of Mr. *Hugh Trapps*, was lent, by conſent of the veſtrie and feoffees, to *Richard Willis*, Eſq; and others at £.8. *per cent.* upon their recognizance remaining in the black cheſt, — — —	....		
1648. Item, of Mr. Juſtice *Manley*, as a fyne by him taken of one *Thomas Parker*, for ſelling of unlicenſed books, —	0	5	0
Item, of *Robert Bradford*, victualler, as a fyne, for having company tipling in his howſe upon the Sabboth day,	0	3	4
Item, of the churchwardens of the pariſh of St. Martin in the Fields, for one third part of the charge of repairing the howſe of correction in Tuthill fields, —	8	12	11
Item, of *William Eaton* and *Charles Jones*, conſtables, as a fyne, by them received of twoe butchers for riding out of town upon the Sabboth day, — —	0	10	0
Item, moneys received by aſſeſments and otherwiſe, for the releife of the poore viſited with the plague, —	....		
From collectors for the viſited; ſum total, —	61	16	6

Item, by collections at this pariſh church at publick faſts, being the moyety of thoſe collections:

Item, June 1648, £.3.—July 26, £.3. 18*s.*—Auguſt 30, £.4.—September 26, £.3. 10*s.*—October 25, £.3. 8*s.*—November 29, £.3.

Item, theiſe accomptants doe alſo charge themſelves with the receipt of the ſumme of nine pounds and ten ſhillings, which they, upon the tenne ſeverall faſt-daies hereunder mentioned, did receive and take from the collections then made at the pariſh church of St. Margaret's, Weſtminſter, for the releife of the poore, *viz.*

The 31ſt of May, £.1.—the 29th of June, £.1.—the 27th of July, £.1.—the 30th of Auguſt, £.1.—the 27th of September, £.1.—the 25th of October, £.1.—the 29th of November, £.1.—the 27th of December, £.1.—the 28th of February, £.1.—and the 19th of April, 1649, 10*s.*

	£.	s.	d.
Item, paid to the ringers, for ringing on the 29th of May, being the Prince's birth daie, — —	0	5	0

1648.

	£.	s.	d.
1648. Item, paid to the ringers, for ringing on the King's Majefty's birth day, ——— ——— ———	0	5	0
Item, to *Thomas Bowker*, coroner, for attending with a jury, touching the death of *John Kirby* and *John Butterfeild*, who were both flain in this parifh when the Surrey-men came down with a petition to the Parliament, as by his receipt appeareth, ——— ——— ———	0	6	8
Item, paid to Mr. *Elfing's* clarke, for an order of the Howfe of Commons, touching the collections upon thankf-giving and humiliation days, that it might be diftri-buted to the poore, ——— ———	0	1	0
Item, paid to *Nicholas Edlyn*, for half a chaldron of coles and half an hundred of faggets, that by command were fent to a regiment of fouldiers at Goring howfe, ———	0	17	6
Item, paid to *William Newington*, tallow-chandler, for one dozen of candles, fent to the fame regiment at the fame time as, &c. ——— ——— ———	0	6	6
Item, paid to Mr. *Jackfon*, clerke of the peace, for an order of feffions to ferve upon the churchwardens of St. Martin's, touching the payment of their proportion towards the repaire of the howfe of correction, —	0	4	6
Item, paid to Mr. *Bynns*, our late reader, by order of veftry, to carry him, his wife and children, to Yorkfhire, where he was born, ——— ———	2	0	0
Item, paid to Mr. *Philip Greenwood*, high conftable, for half a year's affeffment of the 8*d*. a weeke laid upon this parifh towards the releife of maimed foldiers within the hundred of Ofoulfton, due at our Lady Day laft, 1649, as, &c. ——— ——— ———	0	17	4
Item, to the Lady *Spotfworth*, that loft all in Ireland, upon every faft-day 5*s*. for tenne faft-daies together, out of the moneys collected at church, in all, ———	2	10	0
Item, difburfements for the ufe of the poore vifited with the plague in this parifh; fum total, ———	73	0	0
1649. Item, of Mr. Dr. *Wimberley*, towards the payment of the wyne which was prepared for the communions, which he al-loweth out of the token money, ——— ———	....		
Item, of Mr. *Richard Bufby*, the fumme of eleaven pounds, thirteene fhillings and four-pence (it having been for-merly difburfed for his ufe by Mr. *William Bell* and Mr. *James Parcall*, churchwardens, in annis 1628 and 1631), which, fo foone as it was made knowne unto him, he immediately repaid it, viz. ——— ———	11	13	4

1649.

		£.	s.	d.
1649.	Item, paid to *George Hare*, for going over the whole towne, and taking the names of all the inhabitants in order,	0	12	0
	Item, paid for boat-hyer att feverall times when wee went to Gurney houfe, to fearche for the retourne of the furvey made of the tenements which this parifh held of the late dean and chapter of Weftminfter, ——	0	4	6
	Item, laid out in expences upon that day when the furveyors meafured the faid tenements, —— ——	0	1	4
	Item, paid to Mr. *Freeman*, for the coppie of an order touching the money given unto this parifh out of the lord-mayor's fine, —— —— ——	0	2	0
	Item, paid to *Maffey*, the fheriff's bailiffe, for delaying to ferve the execution upon us touching the £.24. fine, fet upon this parifh for not repairing the highway between the gates near Whitehall, —— —— ——	0	5	0
	Difburfements for the ufe of the poore vifited with the plague; fumma pagine, —— ——	1	16	0
1650.	Item, of colonel *Barkeftead*, as money which he had received of one *Troughton* and Mrs. *Twiddie*, for felling of unlicenfed books, —— —— ——	2	0	0
	Item, *Jane Powell*, for an oath which fhe fwore before the juftices at the quarter feffions, —— ——	0	3	4
	Item, there was given by the Honourable Houfe of Parliament, for to repaire St. Margarett's church, the fumme of two hundred pounds, payable out of Mr. *Brett's* compounding fyne att Goldfmiths' Hall; but the fame being after transferred to Gurney houfe, and made payable there out of deans and chapters lands, thefe accomptants, by order of veftry, fould the fame to Mr. *Nicholas Love*, at 11*s*. in the pound, ——	110	0	0
	Item, received out of the veftrie to purchafe the inheritance of the rents belonging to the poore of this parifh, held of the late dean and chapter of Weftminfter, of and from the contractors for fale of deans and chapters lands, —— —— ——	400	0	0
	Item, paid towards the repair of the grate at Broken Crofs, for that there is a draine from the parifh church to the fame grate, —— —— ——	0	6	8
	Item, paid for herbs that were ftrewed in the windows of the church, and about the fame, att two feverall daies of humiliation, —— —— ——	0	3	10
	Item, paid for herbs that were ftrewed in the church upon a daie of thankfgiving, —— ——	0	2	6

1650.

£. s. d.

1650. Item, expended when ſixe of the pariſhioners went to Egham, to treat with Mr. *Banbury*, touching the poores' rents which he purchaſed, in horſe-hire and other charges, 2 7 0

Item, paid to Mr. *William Wheeler*, for money he laid out in procuring of orders about the £.200. given by the Honourable Houſe of Parliament, for repaire of St. Margarett's church, ——— ——— 4 5 6

Item, the purchaſe of the inheritance of the tenements held of the late dean and chapter of Weſtminſter, belonging to the poor of this pariſh, was made ſome of them at three, and ſome at four years purchaſe, in manner as followeth; viz. the whole purchaſe money, which theſe accomptants agreed with the contractors for the purchaſe aforeſaid, amounted to five hundred three ſcore and eight pounds, three ſhillings, and tenne pence; which theſe accomptants paid and ſatisfied in this manner: they bought as many bills as amounted to five hundred thirty-nyne pounds, three ſhillings, and two-pence, at the rate of £.60. *per centum*; for which they paid in ready money £.333. 9*s*. 11*d*.; by the buying of which bills they ſaved the pariſh £.215. 13*s*. 3*d*. Paid more in ready money unto the ſaid contractors, towards ſatisfaction of the purchaſe money aforeſaid, as for their ſix-pences in the pound £.14. 4*s*.; and alſo in ready money to the treaſurers for their three-pences in the pound, £.7. 6*s*. 6*d*. abated for intereſt according to act of parliament, in regard they made preſent payment of their whole money. So that £.223. 3*s*. 5*d*. of the whole purchaſe money was ſatisfied by the profitt made of the bills before mentioned, and by the intereſt ſo allowed as aforeſaid; and the remainder thereof being £.345. 0*s*. 5*d*. theſe accomptants paid in ready money, in manner as is before expreſſed, viz. — 345 0 0

Item, paid to Mr. *Gabriell Clinkard*, bailiffe of the liberty of the late dean and chapter of Weſtminſter, in diſcharge of certain fynes and amercements, amounting to the ſum of nineteene pounds and tenne ſhillings, yſſuing out of the Crowne-office, for want of repairs in pavements of the ſtreets, and between the two gates at Whitehall, and other defaults, as by receipt appeareth, 8 0 0

1651. Item, of colonell *Barkſtead*, being money by him received of one that ſold unlicenced books, ——— ——— 1 0 0

Item, of colonell *Barkſtead*, as money by him received of two perſons that entertained company to tipple on the Sabbath-day, ——— ——— ——— 0 10 0

	£.	s.	d.
1651. Item, of the commiſſioners of the cuſtoms, according to an order of the committee for the navie of the 16th of December, 1651, grounded on an act of Parliament of the 28th of March, 1651, the ſumme of one hundred pounds, given to the uſe of the poore within the city and limitts of Weſtminſter, viz. — ——	100	0	0
Item, of the ſaid commiſſioners of the cuſtomes, upon another order of the committee of the navie of the 16th of February, 1651, as given alſo by the Parliament to the uſe of the poore within the ſaid cittie and limitts of Weſtminſter, ——— ——— ——	300	0	0
Item, received more of the commiſſioners of the cuſtomes, by virtue of an order of the committee of the navie of the 2d of April, 1652, according to act of Parliament, the ſumme of two hundred pounds, for the uſe of the poore within this cittie and limitts of Weſtminſter,	200	0	0
Item, of the churchwardens of the pariſh of St. Martin's in the Fields, as a third of what was expended in repairing the howſe of correction the laſt year 1651, —	26	19	5
Item, of the Right Honourable the Counſell of State, toward reparation and cleanſing of the new church and the new church yard, after the Scottiſh priſoners had much annoyed and ſpoiled the ſame, ——— ——	30	0	0
Item, rents received of Mr. *Lawrence Blomley*, for the fee farmes purchaſed of the Truſtees of Worceſter houſe, to the uſe of the poore almes people of the Long Woolſtaple and Lady Alley, Weſtminſter:——for halfe yeare of the ſaid fee farme rents, — —	30	0	0
Item, paid for hearbs that were ſtrewed in the church on the 24th day of May, being a day of humiliation, —	0	3	0
Item, paid to the ringers, for ringing on the fourth of September, upon intelligence of the overthrow of the Scottiſh armey at Worceſter, —— ——	0	6	0
Item, paid to the ringers, for ringing on the four and twentieth day of October, being a day of thankſgiving for the victorie over the Scotts at Worceſter, ———	0	7	0
Item, paid for hearbes and lawrell that were ſtrewed in the church the ſame day, —— ——	0	8	0
Item, paid to *John Gomerſall*, for painting and guilding of the States armes in ſeveral places of the church and veſtry, as by his receipt appeareth, ——— ———	50	0	0
Item, paid to *John Browne*, for an oval table for the veſtrey, and for poſtage of it which he laid out, as by his bill and receipt appeareth, ——— ———	5	3	0

1651.

		£.	s.	d.
1651.	Item, paid unto Mr. *Thomas Stevens*, for maſons and carpenters worke done by him and Mr. *Dodſon*, in building of the new veſtrey, and for other worke done by the ſmith, glazier, and others, towards the compleating of the ſaid veſtrey, as by Mr. *Stevens* his bill and receipt appeares, —— —— ——	133	0	0
	Item, paid to Mr. *George Collingridge*, for lyning the ſhields (that contain the arms of the Common-wealth of England) with ſlitt deale, and for putting ſtaples in them,	0	4	6
	Item, paid to *Robert Criſpe*, and ſundry other labourers, for digging, trenching, and cleanſing the new church yard, whereby the annoyance made by the Scottiſh priſoners there was deſtroyed, —— ——	1	19	4
	Item, paid unto ſeveral labourers (whoſe names are inſerted in theſe accomptants rough booke) for ſweeping and cleanſing the Sanctuary high-way, when the Parliament accompanied the corpſe of general *Ireton* to the grave, and for filling the holes of the ſame high-way with rubbiſh to levell it, —— ——	1	13	6
	Diſburſements concerning the purchaſe of ſeverall fee farme rents, amounting to £.60. yearly; wherewith the penſions payable to the almes-people of Long Woolſtaple and Lady Alley, Weſtminſter, are diſcharged.			
	Item, paid for the certificate of Auditor *Powell*, whereby it appeared that the almes-houſes were conſtantly repaired out of the late King's treaſury, —— ——	0	2	6
Committee for removing obſtructions in the ſale of the fee farme rents.	Item, paid for two orders of the ſaid committee, graunted upon the auditor's certificate; by which the truſtees of Worceſter howſe were enjoined to convey the fee farme rents (now purchaſed) to the uſe of the ſaid almes-people, ——	0	5	0
	Item, paid for one double publicke faithe bill to make the purchaſe compleate, £.60. *per annum*, ——	0	19	0
	Item, money paid to the almes people of Long Woolſtaple and Ladie Alley, Weſtminſter, for one year's penſion ending att our Ladie-day, 1652, —— —	....		
	Item, paid to .... ſixe of the almes-people of Long Woolſtaple, each of them £.2. 13s. being for halfe a year's penſion, &c. —— —— ——	15	18	0
	Item, paid to .... the foure almes-women of Ladie Alley, 13s. 4d. apeece, for the halfe year's penſion, &c.	2	13	4
	Item, moneys paid to the churchwardens of the ſeveral pariſhes of Martyn in the Fields, Paul's Covent Garden, and Clement Danes, out of £.600. ordered to be paid			

 to

	£. s. d.
to the poore within the cittie and limitts of Weftminfter:	
Item, to the churchwardens of St. Martyn's in the Fields, — — £.20.—£.60.—£.40.	
Item, paid unto churchwarden of St. Paul's, Covent Garden, — — £.5.—£.15.—£.10.	
Item, paid unto churchwarden of Clement Danes, — — £.15.—£.45.—£.30.	
Item, paid unto Dr. *Wimberley*, for all his right, title, and intereft in and to the Anchorift houfe near the veftry, according to order and agreement, and as in the deed may appear, — — —	62 0 0
Item, paid for a petition to the committee of prifoners, for a recompence for injurie done by the Scottifh prifoners in the new church and church yard, — —	0 1 0
Item, paid to Mr. *Bailey*, for an order of the commiffioners of compounding at Haberdafhers hall, whereby two thirds of the rent iffuing out of the mannor of *Albury*, (then feized there) is become payable to the ufe of the poore of this parifh, — — —	0 9 2
Item, to *Nicholas Edlyn*, woodmonger, for feaventeene chaldron and a halfe of fea coales (which were given and diftributed unto many very poore people of this parifhe againft Chriftmas laft, 1651, when there were great frofts) at the rate of £.1. 3*s*. the chaldron, as by his bill and receipt appeareth, — —	21 0 0
Item, paid to *Thomas Fauconberge*, Efquire, receiver generall of the publicke revenue, the fumme of five pounds, in full difcharge of divers yffues, amounting to the fumme of £.232. 6*s*. 8*d*. which arofe upon feveral indictments out of the capitall office of the upper bench, againft the inhabitants of this parifh; but by act of Parliament the fame yffues were reduced to £.5. as by Mr. *Fauconberge* his receipt appeareth, — —	5 0 0
Item, paid unto Mr. *William Cutbert*, receiver of the colledge rents, for one whole year's rent of divers tenements (appertaining to the poore) within the faid parifh, held of the faid colledge, due at Michaelmas, 1651, as by acquittances appeareth, — —	7 15 6
1652. Item, of Mr. *Clendall* and Mr. *Webfter*, churchwardens of Martyn's in the Fields, as one third part of three quarters wages due to the governor of the houfe of correction at Chriftmas, 1652, — —	5 0 0

1652.

		£.	s.	d.
1652.	Item, of the Honourable the Commiſſioners of the Cuſtomes, by virtue of an order from the honourable the committee of the navie of the 18th of January, 1652, the ſumme of two hundred and fiftie pounds (out of the moneys which aroſe by the new impoſt on coles) for the uſe of the poore within the ſeveral pariſhes of Margaret's, Weſtminſter, Martyn's in the Fields, Paul's, Covent Garden, and Clement Danes, viz. — —	250	0	0
	Item, Of Doctor *Wimberley*, by the hands of Mr. Rogers, out of the token money, ——— ———	4	0	0
	Item, of *Adam Brown*, joiner, for the poſts and railes which ſtood before that porch of the abbey, called by the name of Solomon's porch, —— ——	2	0	0
	Item, of the Honourable Commiſſioners of the Cuſtomes, according to an order of the honourable committee for the navie of the 19th of Aprill, 1653, for the uſe of the poore within the ſeveral pariſhes of Margaret's, Weſtminſter, Martyn in the Fields, Paul's, Covent Garden, and Clement Danes, —— ——	250	0	0
	Item, paid to Mr. *Hernden*, for a white marble font ſett up in the church for baptizing of infants, as by his bill and receipt appeareth, —— ——	5	0	0
	Item, paid for an order of Parliament, whereby the revenue of the royaltie of Weſtminſter is transferred upon the poore of this pariſh, —— ——	0	6	8
	Item, paid to Mrs. *White*, for fifteene tickets of pewter, for fifteene poore people to aſke almes, according to the order of the juſtices of peace, —— ——	1	0	0
	Item, paid to Mr. *Morris*, ironmonger, for fifteene yards of braſſe chaine for the ſaid poore peoples ticketts, as by his bill appeareth, —— —— ——	0	9	6
	Item, paid to Mr. *Hatton*, gardiner, for making the paire of ſhooting butts in Tuttle-fields, as by his bill and receipt appears, —— —— —— ——	2	10	0
	Item, paid to *Thomas Wright*, for 67 load of ſoyle laid on the graves in Tuthill-fields, wherein 1200 Scotch priſoners (taken at the fight at Worceſter) were buried, and for other pains taken with his teeme of horſe about mending the Sanctuary highway, when general *Ireton* was buried, as, &c. —— —— ——	1	10	0
	Item, paid for the committee of obſtructions order towards ſettlement of the late King's ſlaughter-houſe near the Mill Bank, for the uſe of the poore, — —	0	2	6
	Item, paid for a ſearch in Gurney howſe for the ſurvey of Lambeth ferry, and for a coppie of that ſurvey, —	0	3	6

1652.

		£.	s.	d.
1652.	Item, paid for an order of the counsell of state, whereby the late King's slaughter house and yard neere the Mill Bank is graunted to store upp coales for the use of the poore,	0	10	0
	Item, paid to two porters for carrying goods distreyned on refusers to pay the assessment towards setting the poore on worke, —— —— ——	0	0	4
	Memorandum, that one hundred pounds of the said remainder is (according to order of vestrie) to be from time to time laid out and returned perpetually by the successive churchwardens in coles, for the advantage of the poore of this parish, who are to have them at the same price the coles shall be laid in for, which are to be bought at the most advantage.			
1653.	Item, paid to the ringers for ringing on the 23d daie of June, 1653, being a daie of thanksgiving, ——	0	5	0
	Item, paid to the ringers, for ringing on that day when the Lord Protector was installed, —— ——	0	3	0
	Item, paid to *Edward Huckwell*, mason, for eleaven stones to sett out the bounds of the parish, at 7*s*. 6*d*. the stone, as by his bill appeareth, —— ——	4	2	6
	Item, paid more to the said *Edward Huckwell*, for laying and squaring 194 foot of old paving stone in the slaughter-house, at two-pence the foot, and for other work done by him there, as by bill appears, ——	1	14	4
	Item, paid to the porters for sweeping and cleansing the sanctuary high-way for the funeral of general *Deane*,	0	3	0
	Item, paid to Mr. *Scobell*, for an order touching the royaltie of Westminster made in behalf of the poore, ——	0	8	6
	Item, paid to the door-keeper of the college, for bringing us an order from the committee there, touching the poore,	0	1	0

Moneys distributed about the building of four new almes houses in Lady Alley, Westminster:

		£.	s.	d.
	Bricklayer's work, £.32. 10*s*.—Carpenter's work, £.39. 7*s*.—Smith's work, £.2. 11*s*.—Painter's worke, 15*s*.—Pavier's worke in the alley, 9*s*. 8*d*.—Glasier's worke, 14*s*. 6d.			
	Item, paid more to him * for a year's rent of the Anchorist house, (late Dr. *Wimberley's*) due at Lady day, 1654, as by, &c. —— —— ——	8	0	0
1654.	Item, of Sergeant *Birkhead*, by order of Parliament, being collected at their fast, £.16. 4*s*. 6*d*. whereof in brasse money, 6*s*. —— —— ——	15	18	6

* Receiver of the College rents.

1654.

		£.	s.	d.
1654.	Item, of his Highneſs the Lord Protector his gift, ——	20	0	0
	Item, paid to *Francis Day*, carpenter, for building the turrett upon the ſteeple, as by his bill and receipt, ——	7	15	0
	Item, paid to *Richard Parrock*, ſmith, for making the vane and other irone worke upon the church ſteeple, as by bill, —— —— ——	4	14	0
1655.	Item, of Mr. *Hamilton*, for ſix oaths in breach of the ordinance, by the hands of Mr. Juſtice Sherwin, ——	1	0	0
	Item, paid to Mr. *Talman*, for ingroſſing the rowle of the whole pariſh that contributed to the reliefe of the Waldenſes, and for parchment, —— ——	2	15	0
	Item, to *Douglas*, the bearer, for cleanſing the wayes in the church yard for the Primate of *Ireland's* funerall,	0	3	0
1656.	Item, of Mr. *Gabriel Goodman*, the ſumme of twentie ſhillings, being a legacy bequeathed by the late biſhop of *Gloceſter*, to adorne the front in this church, ——	1	0	0
	Item, to Mr. *John Stone*, for mending the font in the pariſh church, and for the twoe ſtones engraven with the name of Chapel-ſtreet, as by his receipt appeareth,	0	16	3
	Item, ſpent at ſeveral times and places when the inhabitants of this pariſh and thoſe of Paddington mett to reconcile the differences concerning the bounds, ——	1	10	0
	Item, to *George Hare*, clerke of the veſtrie, for writing all manner of books of accompt, aſſeſſments, and other writings, concerning the affairs of this pariſh, and other ſervices, according to his contract, — —	40	0	0
1657.	Item, ſpent upon the churchwardens of St. Martyn's, when they treated about the markett, — ——	0	2	6
1658.	Item, of *Thomas Hamond*, *Francis Daye*, *Thomas Chandler*, and *Stephen Harebottle*, for 240 foot of ground in the old church yard, lett unto them to build ſcaffolds at the Lord Protector's funerall, at the rate of 1*s.* the foot,	12	0	0
	Item, to Mr. *Edward Martyn* and Mr. *Emery Hill*, charges which they diſburſed about Mr. *Palmer's* buſineſs, and for recording the deed for the almes-houſes in the long Woolſtaple, as by their receipt appeareth, ——	33	15	10
	Item, to Mr. *Sutton*, glaſſe painter, for the dial in the ſouth window, as by his bill appeareth, — —	2	10	0
	Item, paid back to Mr. *Hammond*, Mr. *Day*, Mr. *Chandler*, and Mr. *Harebottell*, of the money that we received of them for the ground to build ſcaffolds on, by order of veſtry, —— —— ——	8	0	0
	Item, for a petition to the Parliament, to make collection for the poore at a private faſt, —— ——	0	1	0

1658.

	£.	s.	d.
1658. Item, to Mr. *Farmer*, for making of the new diall on the weſt end of the church, as by his bill appeareth, ——	14	10	0
Item, to Mr. *Farmer*, for a new dyall at the weſt end of the church on the church yard ſide, —— ——	7	0	0
Item, to ſeverall men, to ſhovell up the dirt, and to ſweepe at the Protector's funerall, and to ſpread gravell,	0	12	6
Item, to *Richard May*, for informing of one that played at trap-ball on the Lord's day, —— ——	0	18	0
1659. Item, to *Henry Richards*, joyner, for taking down the States arms, —— —— ——	0	0	6

Moneys paid to the almes-people of the long Woolſtaple and the Lady Alley, and to other almes-people in Weſtminſter:

	£.	s.	d.
Item, to .... the eight almes-people of the long Woolſtaple, the ſumme of five pounds and ſixe ſhillings apeece, for their twoe half year's penſions, due at, &c.	42	8	0
Item, paid to .... the fower almes-women of the Ladie Alley, the ſumme of twentie-ſixe ſhillings and eight-pence apeece, for their twoe half year's penſion, due at, &c. —— ——	5	6	8
Item, paid for drawing and engroſſing three ſeveral petitions to the governors of the colledge, —— ——	0	5	6
Item, ſpent at twoe ſeverall meetings with Mr. *Phelps* and Mr. *Farrington*, and ſeverall of the inhabitants of this pariſh, that mett about the impropriation, —— ——	0	6	4
Item, to *Moiſes Weathers*, for twice ſummoning the pariſhioners to appear touching the buſineſs of the impropriation,	0	1	0
Item, paid for drawing and engroſſing a petition to the truſtees ſitting at Mr. *Phelps* his houſe, ——	0	2	6
1660. Item, to the ringers, for ringing on the day that the King landed, and on the day that his Majeſty came to White-hall, —— —— ——	0	11	0
Item, of his Majeſtie King *Charles* the Second, as his royal gift to the poore of this pariſh, att the interring of his brother the Duke of *Glouceſter*, and his ſiſter the Princeſſe Royal, the ſumme of fiftie pounds, *viz.* ——	50	0	0
Item, of *Edward Rogers*, ſexton, for thirty foot of ground to build ſcaffolding on, at the coronation of the King's Majeſtie *Charles* the Second, at the rate of 1*s.* 8*d.* the foote, —— —— ——	2	10	0
Item, of *Francis Daye* and *Thomas Chandler*, for eighty foot of ground in the old church yard, to build ſcaffolds on againſt the King's coronation, at 1*s.* 8*d.* the foot,	6	13	0
Item, of *Edward Rogers*, ſexton, for thirtie foot of ground in			

		£.	s.	d.
	in the church yard, to build fcaffolds on when the King's Majeftie went to Parliament, at the rate of 1*s*. 8*d*. the foote, ——— ———	2	10	0
1660.	Item, paid for ringing, on a thankfgiving day, the 8th of June,	0	5	0
	Item, paid for ringing at the Queen's return, ———	0	3	6
	Item, paid for drawing and engroffing a petition to the juftices at the quarter feffions, for an order for the deane and chapter to pave the high ways before the weft end of the abby, ——— ——— ———	0	2	6
	Item, fpent upon the inhabitants in fetting out the ground in the old church yard, and in gaining of it, for the ufe of the poore, ——— ——— ———	0	10	10
	Item, paid for ringing on the coronation of King *Charles* the Second, ——— ——— ———	1	0	0
	Item, to the town waits, for playing on the day of the King's coronation, ——— ——— ———	2	10	0
	Item, delivered to them in bread and wine, ———	0	5	2
1661.	Item, to Dr. *Gifford*, for preaching of a fermon in this church upon Sabboth, the 14th of April, 1661, ———	1	0	0
	Item, to feverall porters which brought in the blew cloths into the veftrie, that the King walked upon at his coronation, ——— ——— ———	0	17	6
	Item, to *Henry Richards*, for making of a fcaffold in the engine-houfe, to fett the hoggfhead of wine uppon which rann at the King's coronation, as by his receipt appeareth, ——— ——— ———	0	5	0
	Item, paid for ringing on the day that the King's Majeftie rode to Parliament, ——— ——— ———	1	0	0
	Item, paid for a hoggfhead of French wine which rann at the coronation of King *Charles* the Second, ———	8	0	0
	Item, fpent upon a dinner on the bifhop's almner's gentlemen that brought in the blew cloth which his Majeftie trode upon at the day of his coronation, — —	0	16	0
	Item, paid for bringing back the engines from Whitehall, when the fire was there, ——— ———	0	6	0
	Item, to *Mofes Perkins*, meffenger, for fummoning us to appear before the Houfe of Lords, as by note appears,	0	5	0
1662.	Item, to the ringers, for ringing on the Queen's landing,	0	5	0
	Item, for building a new paire of butts in Tuttle-fields, —	5	0	0
	Item, to the ringers, for the Queen's firft coming to towne, ringing all day, ——— ——— ———	1	0	0
	Item, to the ringers, for ringing on the Queen's birth day,	0	7	0
	Item, to Dr. *Tucker*, which hee paid the ordinary for paffing the church fees for burialls under feale, ———	1	0	0

		£.	s.	d.
1663.	Item, for proclamations concerning debauchery heer, and for the chapell, — — —	0	2	0
	Item, for writing two papers publiſhed in the church, as to the duty of conſtables, — —	....		
	Item, att Dr. *Bolton's* firſt appearing at the veſtry, —	0	8	0
	Item, to Mr. *Brown's* clerke, for a copy of the act concerning veſtries, — — —	0	10	0
	Item, to Mr. *Sibley*, for drawing up reaſons and exceptions againſt the additional act for corporations, and his pains in that buſineſs, — —	0	0	0
	Item, to ſir *William Scrogg* and Mr. *Dalbyn*, to attend the committee, and a copy of the bill, and orders, and expences, and divers meetings on behalf of the pariſh concerning the ſaid corporation, — —	18	10	2
1664.	Item, of Dr. *Tucker*, for token money, — —	4	0	0
	Item, of the biſhop of *Wincheſter* *, to make good the damage done by coaches in the church yard, and the reſt to the poore, — — —	5	0	0
	Item, expended in going twice to Windſmore Hill, touching Mrs. *Hambden*, her purchaſe, — —	0	9	6
	Item, for wine one day for the lords and juſtices, being at the veſtry, — — —	0	2	0
	Item, expended in going to *Peckham*, touching Mr. *Hambden's* purchaſe, — — —	0	3	6
	Item, to ſir *William Playters*, treaſurer of the corporation for the poore, — — —	88	0	0
	Item, to him more £.90.—more £.100.—more £.100.			
	Item, to ſeveral poore people at the funeral of Mrs. *Hambden*,	5	0	0
	Item, for two petitions unto the King's Majeſtie, and the deſires of the pariſh to the ſecretarie, — —	0	2	0
	Item, for books at the pariſh church and new church, being faſt day, — — —	0	2	8
	Item, for painting and guilding of armes in the veſtrey, —	1	0	0
	Item, expended upon the inhabitants when wee went the perambulation, — — —	23	1	5
	Item, for carving the King's armes in the veſtrie, as per receipt,	3	0	0
	Item, of the executors of Mrs. *Hambden*, as her guift, over and above £.250. by her given, — —	20	0	0
1665.	Item, of the King's Moſt Excellent Majeſtie, as his benevolence,	100	0	0
	Item, of her Royall Highneſs the Dutcheſs of *Yorke*, as her benevolence, — — —	22	10	0
	Item, of the lord biſhop of *London* †, as his benevolence towards the releife of poore houſekeepers, —	35	0	0

* Dr. George Morley.

† Dr. Humphry Henchman.

	£.	s.	d.
1665. Item, ſpent in going three times by water for the archbiſhop of *Canterbury's* * benevolence, —— ——	0	2	0
Item, to the ringers, at the late victory obtained againſt the Dutch, —— —— ——	1	0	0
Item, to the ringers, at the Duke of *York's* return, ——	0	10	0
Item, to the ringers, upon the thankſgiving day for the late victory, —— —— ——	0	6	0
Item, ſpent ſeveral times at Hampton Court in obtaining the privy ſeale for £.100. for the poore, — —	0	10	0
Item, to Mr. *Joanes*, for ſix Prayer Books, on the monethly faſt,	0	6	0
Item, to the ringers, at the Queen's returne, ——	0	5	0
Item, to the ringers, on St. George's day, —— ——	0	15	0
Item, to the ringers, at the King's returne to Weſtminſter,	0	10	0
Item, to .... the Lord *Ruthen*, 10*s*.—Lord *Ruthen*, 2*s*. 6*d*. —Lord *Ruthen*, 5*s*.—Lord *Ruthen* being ſicke, 5*s*.			
Item, allowed to ourſelves, for the graves of 275 poore people buryed in this pariſh this yeare, called *Nills*, at a penny apeece, —— —— ——	1	2	11
Item, to the 118 poore houſekeepers, being the benevolence of the Right Honourable the lord biſhop of *London*,	35	0	0
Item, laid out at ſeveral times towards the releife of the viſited, and for neceſſaries for them, which is not in the viſited accompt, —— —— ——	80	0	0
1666. Item, received of the King's Moſt Excellent Majeſtie, as his benevolence, —— —— ——	100	0	0
Item, of ſir *William Wheeler*, as one year's annual due at Lady day, 1666, —— ——	10	0	0
Item, paid for ringing at a victory obtained againſt the Dutch,	0	15	0
Item, to the ringers, more at a victory obtained againſt the Dutch, —— —— ——	0	10	0
Item, for ringing the 14th of Auguſt, being a thankſgiving day, —— —— ——	0	10	0
Item, to his Grace the Duke of *Albemarle* (by order of the juſtices) for the poores coles, —— ——	45	14	9
Item, for two matts when the Parliament received the Sacrament, —— —— ——	0	6	0
Item, expended in two dinners, and other neceſſarie charges on the inhabitants when wee went the perambulation within and without the pariſh, —— ——	28	6	2
Item, to ſir *Robert Pye's* man, when the juſtices ſate there about the Quakers, —— ——	0	1	0
Item, Auguſt .... to Lord *Ruthen*, 1*s*.—September, to Lord *Ruthen*, 1*s*.			

* Dr. Gilbert Sheldon was then archbiſhop.

	£.	s.	d.
1666. Item, to Major *Oneale*, being paſſed away by the lord-mayor and ſir *John Robinſon*, —— ——	0	2	6
Item, to the Lady *Hurleſton*, to carry her into the country,	0	10	0
Item, to the . . . . Lady *Mordent*, —— ——	0	5	0
1667. Item, of Dr. *William Outrim*, by order of the veſtry, for token-money for the two forepaſt years, —— ——	1	0	0
Item, of the Lady *Wheeler*, being the benevolence of Mr. *Forreſt*, payable out of a tenement in Channon Row, due the 25th of March, 1667, —— ——	10	0	0
Item, of the King's Moſt Excellent Majeſtie, as his benevolence to the poore of this pariſh, ——	100	0	0
Item, of Mr. *Lamply*, for Mr. *Coleman*, the preſent tenant of the ſhooting houſe in Tuttle-fields, for this quarter rent,	11	0	0
Item, to *Edward Axtell*, for breaking the wall for the window out of the veſtrie, —— —— ——	0	3	6
Item, to the ringers, on the 24th of Auguſt, when the peace was here proclaimed, —— ——	0	5	0
Item, to Mr. *Bennett*, the head baylyffe, for the leaſe of a certain tenement in Tuttle-fields, commonly called the Shooting houſe, —— —— ——	25	0	0
Item, to *William Halborne* and others, for removing the ſheets and other bedding that belonged to the ſouldiers of the Generall's regiment in the time of the late viſitation,	0	3	6
Item, laid out by order of veſtry upon a preſent for Dr. *Exton*, in regard of his great kindneſſe to this pariſh, in takeing no fees in the tryall againſt *Samuel Baker* and *Thomas Edwards*, —— —— ——	6	0	0
Item, to Lady *Johnſon*, on being very ſicke, ——	0	5	0
Item, to 6 poore priſoners from Holland, ——	0	3	0
Diſburſements for ſuits in law:			
Summa ——	93	15	0

In the pariſh of St. Margaret's, Weſtminſter.

The churchwardens are choſen according to the antient cuſtome of the ſayde pariſh (tyme out of mind) the Thurſday immediately before Whitſunday, after this manner following:

There is a bell appointed to be tolled, by which the pariſhioners have notice, and thereupon do repair unto the church, to ſee the churchwardens which be going out of their office deliver up their accompts and ballance moneys; and alſo to underſtand who be choſen churchwardens for the yeare enſuing. Then they have a table ſett in the chancell, at which the doctor or miniſter of the pariſh, and the reſt of the veſtry-men do ſit, and thither the churchwardens in being bring their accompts fairly engroſſed, and bound up in vellam, together with the ballance moneys; the antient veſtry-menn at the upper end of the table receiving the ſame,

 and

and inſpecting at leaſt the totall ſummes of what hath been received, what paid, and what remains to adjuſt the ſayd churchwardens accoumpts. Then they order and appoint ſome that have already executed the ſame office of churchwardens to audit the ſayd accoumpt, and within one moneth to make report thereof unto them. This being done, the veſtrey men adjourne from thence into the veſtrey roome, and there take out of the records of the names of former overſeeres of the poore, the names of eight or tenne perſons, and ſett them downe after this manner:

A. B.
C. D.

always ſetting down the younger of the preſent churchwardens firſt: then they debate the fitteſt man for that office; and ſoe every one croſſing thoſe whom they judge the moſt meet, they that have the moſt croſſes carry it. As ſoon as this is done, they give the paper into the hands of the miniſter, who immediately goeth therewith into the reading-pew, and there in the open church, and in the audience of the pariſhioners preſent, publiſheth and declareth the names of the perſons elected churchwardens, to the end they may have notice of the ſame. After this the churchwardens expired doe uſe to invite the doctor or miniſter, together with the veſtrey men, and other antient inhabitants of the pariſh, to a ſupper at the charge of the ſaid churchwardens.

N. B The churchwardens choſen after this form were adjudged to be the right churchwardens, by a decree of the commiſſary Dr. Exton, and afterwards by a court of delegates, againſt *Baker* and *Edwards*, who were choſen by ſome of the inhabitants in the church-porch.

	£.	s.	d.
1668. Item, of *Samuel Baker* and *Thomas Edwards*, for coſts of ſuite taxed againſt them in the late tryall betweene them and Mr. *Michael Arnold* and Mr *John Tyſon*, touching the chooſeing of churchwardens in this pariſh, ——	20	6	8
Item, of Dr. *William Outram*, for token-money ——	4	0	0
Item, of *John Allen*, for breach of Sabbath, — ——	0	6	8
Item, of *Richard Wilſon*, for breach of Sabbath, ——	0	5	0
Item, by the hands of Mr. *Nicholas Upbman*, being the charitable benevolence of Mrs. *Hambden*, late of this pariſh, deceaſed, and borrowed by Mr. *Arnold* and Mr. *Upbman*, churchwardens in the year 1665, for the uſe of the poore viſited, of the executors of the ſaid Mrs. *Hambden*, and now to be diſpoſed of according to the will of the ſaid Donatrix, —— ——	250	0	0
Item, of ſir *William Doyly*, being the benevolence of his Majeſtie, —— —— ——	50	0	0
Item, of Mr. *Humphry Grinſell*, being the charitable benevolence of Mr. *Hanwell*, for a ſermon at the new-chapel, on Good Fryday, for ever, —— ——	25	0	0
Item, of ſir *William Doyly*, one of the tellers of the Exchequer, being			

		£.	s.	d.
	being the remaining moiety of £.100. yearly, given by his Majestie to the poor of this parish, ——	50	0	0
1668.	Item, to *Thomas Thwaite*, joyner, for making of 24 new pews at the west end of the church, together with the fount pew, and a pew for the green-coate hospitall boyes,	177	10	0
	Item, to *Christopher Davison*, wyreman, for covering the vestry windows with wyre, —— ——	3	4	0
	Item, to *Lawrence Gorall*, vintener, for wine for the Sacrament,	7	10	0
	Item, allowed to *Edmond Coleman*, by order of vestry of the 20th of May, 1668, towards the making of a new payr of butts, at the shooting-house in Tuttle-fields, —	2	0	0
	Item, expended at a perambulation this yeare at Knightsbridge,	26	13	4
	Item, expended at a perambulation in visiting the in-bounds,	8	1	3
	Item, ... of the legacy and charitable benevolence of Mr. *John Allen*, late of this parish, brewer, deceased, who gave the same only for the putting forth of poore boyes apprentices, and for no other use whatsoever.			
	Summa totall of the receipts on this accompt,	186	2	2
	Item, to Mr. *Arthur Baron*, who is employed for the parish of Warington, in the county of Lancaster, touching the moiety of Mr. *Allen's* benevolence, —— ——	20	0	0
1669.	Item, of the Lady *Wheeler*, being the yearly guift of Mr. *Forrest*, issuing out of a tenement in Channor Row, for setting forth children to be apprentices, ——	10	0	0
	Item, of *Francis Lucy*, Esq; for the use of the poore of this parish, according to an order of the court of corporation for the poore, —— ——	5	0	0
	Item, of Mr. *Edward Rogers*, for one third parte of the cleare money received for a scaffold at the Duke's funerall,	0	13	4
	Item, of Mr. *Pipes*, being soe much allowed by the Doctor for wine spent at the Sacrament, in liew of token-money, —— —— ——	4	0	0
	Item, to Mr. *John Goodchild*, for a purchase bought of him, lying in St. Martyn's, Lawrence Poultney, London, being a ground rent of £.95. *per annum*, as by his receipt appeareth, the summe of five hundred pounds; two hundred and fifty pounds, whereof was the benevolence of Mrs. *Hambden*: Twenty-five pounds more thereof was the benevolence of Mr. *Thomas Hanwell*; and the other two hundred and twenty-five pounds was part of the parish stocke, —— ——	500	0	0
	Being free land of inheritance leased out to *John Goodchilde*, from the 22d of March, 1669, for 61 years.			

1669.

	£.	s.	d.
1669. Item, to the ringers upon the day of Union of both Houſes of Parliament, ——— ——— ———	0	3	4
Item, to Dr. *Twiſſe*, for preaching a funerall ſermon upon Good Friday, according to Mr. *Hanwell's* will, —	1	0	0
Item, for redeeming of two pieces of plate, diſtreyned by the ſheriffe's officers for a robbery done at Elyn, in the hundred of Oſulſton, there being ſo much charged on the pariſh of St. Margaret's, Weſtminſter, for that robbery, ——— ——— ———	7	8	0
Item, to Mr. *Godfrey Lee*, proctor to the officiall of the ſpiritual court in Weſtminſter, £.14. for proceeding *ex officio* againſt 9 perſons for incontinency, by which means the pariſh was freed from the charge of keeping 4 baſtard children, ——— ——— ———	14	0	0
1670. Item, of the King's Majeſty, as his benevolence, *pro annis* 1669 and 1670, ——— ——— ———	100	0	0
Item, of the executors of Mr. *Nicholas Butler*, late of this pariſh, deceaſed, the ſumme of £.150. being his charitable benevolence; £.100. thereof to be imployed towards repairing the almeſhouſes in this pariſh; and the other £.50. towards the rayſeing of a ſtock to ſett the poore at worke, as by his laſt will at large appeareth,	150	0	0
Item, of Mr. *Pipes*, being ſoe much allowed by the Doctor for wine ſpent at the Sacrament, in leiew of token-money,	4	0	0
Item, of the churchwardens of St. Martin's in the Fields, £.15. of St. Clement's, £.8. of St. Marie le Savoy, £.2. towards defraying the charge of mainteyning the ſuite at lawe againſt the high-ſheriffe of the county of Middleſex, to try whether the city of Weſtminſter ought to be taxed as part of the hundred of Oſeſtry, towards robberies, &c. ——— ——— ———	25	0	0
Item, to Mr. *John Underwood*, for a new engine, as *per* acquit,	36	0	0
Item, to Mr. *Emott*, for the two mapps of the church, and one of the gallery, as by his acquitt appeareth,	3	0	0
Item, to Mr. *Darbie*, bell-founder, for two new bells, as by, &c.	47	10	0
Item, expended for a dinner for Mrs. *Barnett* *, and her friends and truſtees, when ſhe ſealed the deed,	2	9	0
N. B. The gift is expreſſed on her monument in the chancell.			
Item, for an order of ſeſſions to take off the Ladie *Johnſon* the allowance of 5*s*. to 3*s*. *per* weeke, and for one other order, &c. ——— ——— ———	0	5	0
Item, for making a new payer of butts in Tuttle-fields,	3	1	0
Item, for ringing when the Prince of *Orange* landed, ———	0	5	0

* Mrs. Joane Barnett, by her will, dated in 1670, gave 42l. 10s. to the pariſh.

1670.

		£.	s.	d.
1670.	Item, to Mr. *Dolben*, counsellor, as a fee for his advice upon the deed to be made by Mr. *Butler's* heire, being for eight pounds *per annum* for the poore of this parish, formerly settled upon them by the Right Honourable the Earl of *Salisburie* *, to issue out of the mannor of South Mymes and Barnett,	0	10	0
1671.	Item, of Dr. *Busby*, to pay Mrs. *Hooper*, for teaching the parish children three weeks, at 2*s*. 6*d*. the weeke,	0	7	6
	Item, to the ringers, at his Majesty's returne from Plymouth,	0	5	0
	Item, to —— *Pryor*, joyner, for making the new rayles before the communion table,	15	0	0
	Item, to the ringers, at his Majesty's returne from Norwich and Newmarket, the 20th of October,	0	5	0
	Item, to the ringers, on the 14th of November, being the Queen's birth day,	0	10	0
	Item, to Mr. *Moore*, of the Augmentation office, for a search and the copy of the act of Parliament concerning the bounds of Westminster,	0	9	0
	Item, to four aged men of this parish, for their attendance at his Majestie's court of Green cloth, to give their testimony touching the parish bounds,	0	4	0
	Item, to *Sanders*, for inscribing the Tenn Commandments, Lord's Prayer, and Creed, with letters of gould, in the chancell of the parish church, as by acquittance,	10	0	0
	Item, to the ringers, at the King's returne from the fleete, the 28th of April, 1672,	0	5	0
	Item, to Mr. *Moore*, by order of vestry, for recording the names of the benefactors to the church and poor of this parish, in two tables, with gould letters at the west end of the church, as by acquittance,	10	0	0
	Item, to the high constable, by order of the vestrie, being soe much imposed upon this parish, by warrant under the hands of nine of his Majestie's justices of the peace for the county of Middlesex, towards repayring the bridge over the river Brent at New Brainford,	10	0	0
1672.	Item, received of Dr. *Busby*, for teaching the parish children, 15*s*. and 10*s*. and £.1. and £.1. 10*s*. and £.1. 10*s*.	5	5	0
	Item, for the burial of Lord *Hume's* bowells in the old church yard	0	5	0
	Item, expended in enterteyneing of Mrs. *Barnett*, when thanks was returned for her charitable guift to the church poore, per order,	10	5	8
	Item, to Mr. *William Brewer*, for making a maze in Tuttle fields	2	0	0

* William Cecil, second earl of Salisbury of that family; he died in 1612.

1673.

		£.	s.	d.
1673.	Item, received of Dr. *Richard Buſby* his benevolence, for teaching the pariſh children (by four quarterlie payments of £.1. 10*s*. each),	6	0	0
	Item, paid to Mr. *Emery Hill*, towards the building of the new watch-houſe,	12	12	0
	Item, to Mr. *William Dodd*, for wine extraordinary upon account of perſons receiving the Sacrament by certificate between Eaſter-day and Trinity Sunday	3	5	0
	Item, expended in going to attend Dr. *Lloyd* at Doctors Commons, about ſettling the bearers fees,	0	1	6
	Item, to the ringers on the 28th of February, being the day that peace was proclaymed,	0	8	0
1674.	Item, to the ringers, on the 11th of Aprill, at his Majeſtie's returne from Newmarkett,	0	6	0
1673.	Item, for four prayer books uſed on the fourth of February, being a day of publique humiliation,	0	4	0
	Item, to Mr. *Sibley*, for faire copying the bill for a court of conſcience,	0	5	0
1674.	Item, of Dr. *Richard Buſby*, as his benevolence towards the teaching the poore children of this pariſh from the 25th of March, 1674, to the 25th of March, 1675,	6	0	0
	Item, to *John Ruſſell*, for making good the leather bucketts that were ſpoiled and loſt, when the earle of *Arlington's* houſe was burned,	4	17	0
	Item, for taking out the order of parliament for reading the bill for a court of conſcience,	0	7	0
	Item, for ſending to the churchwardens of the upper liberties touching the ſame,	0	1	0
	Item, to *John Tuffnell*, maſon, for ſtone, with other materialls and workmanſhip, in repayring the weſt end of the pariſh church and tower, being part of the money ariſing by fees for burialls in the ſaid church and church yard,	164	0	0
1675.	Item, of Mr. *Robert White*, by order of the court in Weſtminſter, being moneys ariſing by fynes in the ſaid court, and is in lieu of moneys paid by theſe accomptants, towards the charge of obtaining an act of parliament for a court of conſcience in Weſtminſter,	20	0	0
	Item, of Dr. *Buſby*, as his guift yearly towards maintenance of the pariſh ſchool,	6	0	0
	Item, of ſeveral perſons of honour and others (whoſe names are contained in particular liſt) towards erecting an organ in the pariſh church, as their benevolence thereunto,	174	13	0
	Item, to Mr. *Gundy*, for the leaſe of the chancell,	4	6	8

		£.	s.	d.
1675.	Item, to Mr. *Bernard Smith*, for the charge of the organ newly erected in the pariſh church, — —	200	0	0
	Item, for reading over a bill for a court of conſcience the ſecond time, — — —	25	0	0
	Item, to Mr. *Saton* and Dr. *Lloyd*, for the table of fees, as per acquittance, — — —	4	14	4
1676.	Item, of the worſhipfull Dr. *Richard Buſby*, as his free guift yearly, &c. — — — —	4	0	0
	Item, of the right worſhipfull Dr. *Richard Buſby*, as his free benevolence, — — —	1	5	0
	Item, to the gentlemen of the abby quire, their yearly guift from the pariſh, — — —	1	2	0
	Item, for reading the bill for a court of conſcience the ſecond time, — — —	25	0	0
	Item, for the copie of an order of parliament, for hearing the bill for a court of conſcience before a committee,	0	11	8
	Item, for the fees of two counſellors to attend at the hearing of the bill for a court of conſcience, —	3	0	0
	Item, for papers printed touching the court of conſcience, and given to Mr. *Sell* about the ſame, — —	1	9	0
1677.	Item, to the gentlemen belonging to the quire at the abby, being an antient cuſtome yearly, — —	1	0	0
	Item, to the ringers, on the day the Prince of *Orange* was contracted to the Lady *Mary*, and on the Queen's birth-day,	0	10	0
	Item, allowed to Mr. *Shaw* for the trophy-tax anno 1677,	0	0	6
	Item, for a petition to the Houſe of Commons, touching a bill for a court of conſcience 2s. 6d.; for an order upon the ſame, and for poſtage about the ſame 1s. 4d. —	0	10	6
1678.	Item, expended at a meeting with the burgeſſes of parliament for Weſtminſter, to conſider of carrying on the bill for a court of conſcience, — —	0	9	0
1679.	Item, for a bound-ſtone, and placing the ſame at Pimlico, to diſtinguiſh between this pariſh and St. Martin's in the Fields, — — —	0	7	0
1680.	Item, expended in going to Windſor with a petition to his Majeſtie, to pray leave for the pariſh to make perambulation through his Majeſty's park at St. James's, to viſit their pariſh bounds, which was granted, —	1	10	11
1682.	Item, the benevolences by ſubſcription of ſeveral noblemen and others, for and towards the alteration of the pews, organ, roof of the church, and other work therein :			
	Sum total — —	370	10	11
	Item, received for rectory tythes of arable and mowing ground,			
	Sum — —	4	9	8

Diſ-

		£.	s.	d.
	Difburfed out of the above-mentioned receipts for rectory tythes:			
1682.	Item, paid to Mr. *Needham*, receiver for the dean and chapter, one year's rent ending at Michaelmas, 1682, ——	2	13	4
	Item, to the bell-ringers, at the King's coming from fea,	0	5	0
1683.	Item, to the ringers, on the thankfgiving day, for difcovery of the plott, —— —— ——	0	10	0
	Item, to the ringers, on the happy arrivall of Prince *George*,	0	10	0
1684, or 1685.	Item, of *Henry Roberts* and *John Thompfon*, for the ufe of part of the church yard, viz. from the little gate next the Feathers Tavern, to the weft end of the engine-houfe, to build fcaffolds for the coronation day, which grounds was allotted by the deane of Weftminfter to the parifh for that purpofe, —— ——	30	0	0
	Item, to *John Thompfon*, for drawing and engroffing the leafe for the paffage into St. Margaret's Lane, ——	0	15	0
	Item, to *Emery Arguis*, carpenter, for building a gallery over the weft gate of the church yard, for the wine and mufick on the coronation-day, and other work, —	4	2	6
	Item, to Dr. *Onley* *, for his part or fee out of four great corps buried in the chancell, —— ——	2	13	4
	Item, to Dr. *Onley*, for his third part of the rents received of fir *Chriftopher Mufgrave* and Efquire *Heward*, for pews in the new gallery, —— ——	2	0	0
	Item, expended with the fheriff, and given to his officers, to gett off the time about Stanes Bridge, ——	0	15	0
	Item, to the clarke of the claimes for drawing the petition for the cloath, &c. —— —— ——	2	10	0
	Item, expended on the Lord of *Exeter's* gentleman, who was lord almoner for the coronation-day, at receiving the cloth the King trode upon, and for porters, waterage, and cartage, &c. —— —— ——	1	16	5
	Memorandum, thefe accomptants had of the Earl of *Exeter*, as his guift to the poore of this parifh, 200 yards of the cloth which his Majeftie walked upon on his coronation-day, which thefe accomptants did difpofe of to the poore.			
1685.	Item, of Mr. *Tench*, one of fir *Philip Warwick's* executors, as a legacy for the putting out fome poore boy to fea-fervice; which money was, by order of veftry, made ufe			

* Nicholas Onely, who had been a Weftminfter fcholar, was D. D. of Chrift Church, Oxford, 1664, prebendary of Weftminfter 1672, rector of St. Margaret's 1682, and for a long period mafter of the Savoy. He died at Ealing, Sept. 28, 1724, aged 84.

		£.	s.	d.
	of by this pariſh, and intereſt therefore to be allowed from the receipt thereof, being the 9th of March, 1685,	100	0	0
1686.	Item, to *Mary Booth*, for the entrance of 8 children into the Colledge of Infants, and to the regiſter, ———	8	9	0
1686.	Item, to *Mary Booth*, for keeping 8 children 8 weeks at Clerkenwell, at 3s. per weeke, — ———	9	12	0
	Item, to ſir *Thomas Rowe*, for keeping 8 children in the Colledge of Infants 17 weekes, at 3s. per weeke each,	20	8	0
	Item, to the Right Rev. Father in God *Thomas*, lord biſhop of *Rocheſter*, being the moneys collected on the breife for French Proteſtants, as per receipt, ———	868	12	1
	Item, diſburſements for the robbery of the hundred of Offelſtone, expended in law charges: ſum total —	26	0	8
1687.	Item, to Mr. *Wagſtaffe*, town-clerke of the city of London, for his pains in procuring the order about the Lady *Dacre's* almes-houſes, ——— ———	1	1	6
	Item, to ſir *Thomas Rowe*, for 8 children at the general nurſery to the 6th of October, 1687, ——— ———	15	12	0
1688.	Item, collected by virtue of a brief in this pariſh, for releife of French Proteſtants, ——— ———	663	14	11½
	Item, to ſir *Thomas Rowe*, for keeping five children in the College of Infants, clearing to the 4th of Aprill, 1689; and to *Mary Booth*, for one moneth for the ſame children more to the 2d of May, 1689, ———	12	15	0
1689.	Item, received of moneys paid in upon the breife for the Iriſh proteſtants, ——— ——— ———	796	7	6
1692.	Item, expended in waiting upon ſir *Thomas Row*, to deſire him to uphold the College of Infants, ———	0	2	6.

Extracts

Extracts from the Churchwardens Accompts of WIGTOFT, a Village near Boston, in Lincolnshire [a].

(Communicated by a Correspondent who signs M. F.)

THIS is the resceite of money that *John Brigge* yonger, and *John Barre*, chirche maisters of the p'yshe chirche of Wigtoft, hath resceyved, from the fest of Sayth Peter, called Cathedra Peter, in the year of our Lord God 1484, unto the same fest by two zerez next ensuyng:

	£.	s.	d.
In the first, resceyved of *Will'm Brigg* and *John Almonds*, late chirche-maisters of the said chirche, in mony, —— —	0	2	10
Item, r. of *John Gybon*, of Algarkirk, for a queythe [b] word of *Will'm Garrard*, —— —— ——	0	7	5
Item, r. of *John Pullintoft*, to the use of the said chirche,	0	3	0
Item, r. of *Peby Saltweller*, of rent of a salt-panne [c] for the time of three years last past afore the date herof, by yere 1*s*. 2*d*. ——	0	3	6
Item, r. for the witworde of *Lamberd Toller*, —— ——	0	0	3
Item, r. for the legacy of *John Houson*, —— ——	0	0	4
Item, r. for *Agnes Stork*, —— —— ——	0	0	4
Item, r. of *Margaret Waryngton*, — —— —	0	0	4
Item, r. for a queythe word of *Thom. Farand*, late vicar of Quadring [d], paid by the hands of *Ric. Ranlyn*, vicar of Satterton [e], one of his executors, —— —— ——	0	1	0
Item, r. for the saule of *John Thurk*, —— ——	0	0	6
Item, r. for the queithe word of *John Hall*, — —	0	0	3
Item, r. for *Jenett Illary*, —— —— ——	0	0	2
Item, r. of dyvers pisanes, alsowell of men as of women of the said toune, to the use of the same chirche, gadderd at dyvers tymes,	0	3	9½
Item, r. of *John Palmer*, for the kirk-house, ——	0	2	0
Item, r. of *John Brigge*, for a nold [f] chist, —— ——	0	0	8
Item, r. of gaddryng in the towne for the well of the said chirche, one quarter and two strik barley [g], pc' of all, —— ——	0	3	5

[a] See a specimen of the hand-writing of these accompts. Gent. Mag. vol. LIX. pl. III. p. 6.

[b] Or bequest; for which *queythe word* and *witworde* seemed to be used indifferently.

[c] The sea at that time came near Wigtoft; and this salt-pan seems part of the church revenue, at fourteen pence a year. It was probably situate on what is now called Wigtoft Marsh.

[d] The livings of Quadring and Wigtoft are united; distant about three miles.

[e] Now Sutterton; distant one mile.

[f] *i.* an old.

[g] It appears that the inhabitants sometimes contributed barley instead of money, which was malted, and sold for the use of the church.

Item,

	£.	s.	d.
Item, r. in latter yere in lyke forme, 6 ſtrike barly, for the whiche the ſaid chirche ſhall hafe 6 ſtryke malt and a ſtrik barly,	0	2	6
Item, r. in the ſame yere of gaddryng 5 ſtrik barly, p̃c' le ſtrik 3*d*.	0	1	3
Item, r. of *Rob't Hunne* one ſtrike malt, whiche was ſold for	0	0	6
Item, r. of *Will'm Hackford*, — — —	0	0	4
Item, of *John Tollar*, for two ſton [h], — —	0	1	0
Item, reſevyed for old tymber [i], of *Jon Brig*, — —	0	2	1
Item, of *Agnes Mor*, for old tymbyr, — —	0	0	10
Item, reſevyd of *Agnes Benet*, for malt [k], — —	0	10	3
Item, reſevyd of gaderyng in ye kyrk of ſtrangers, —	0	3	0
Item, reſevyd of *John Chater*, — — —	0	0	2
Item, reſevyd for old brd of *Will'm Lamſon*, — —	0	1	7
Item, reſevyd of *Frankech*, for old bord, — —	0	0	2
Item, reſevyd of *Jon Newman* a ſton leed, — —	0	0	6
Item, for old tymbyr of *Jon Pantre*, — —	0	0	4
Item, of *Symond Hakforth*, for old tymbyr, — —	0	0	0½
Item, reſ'd of *Will'm Bryckty*, of the chantr of Sen Nicholys,	0	3	4
Item, reſevyd of *Rob't Feld*, for ye ſame, — —	0	6	0
Item, reſ'd of *Rob't Croſs*, for *Jon Garrae*, for the ſame, —	0	5	0
Item, reſev'd of *Jon Frankech*, for the ſame, —	0	1	0
Item, reſevyd of *Tom Bale*, for the ſame, — —	0	3	4
Item, reſevyd of *Rob't Carvar*, for the witworde of *Rickard Tomlynſon*, — — — —	0	2	2
Total received, — —	3	14	2

h I am not clear as to the meaning of this 2 ſton. Perhaps 2 old ſtones ſold among the materials, or 2 ſtone weight of lead.

i It ſeems the church had been repaired, and ſome old materials ſold.

k I ſuppoſe Agnes Benet was an inn-keeper, and bought the church malt; or a brewer, and brewed the ale.

THEIS bene the payments and expences that *John Brigge* the yonger, and *John Barre*, chirche-maſters of the p'rſhe [a] chirche of Wigtoft, have paid from the feſt of Seynt Peter, called Cathedr ſa Peter, in the yere of our Lorde God 1484, unto the ſame feſt by 2 [b] yeres next enſuwyng yat aftr.

	£.	s.	d.
In the firſt paide to *John Cony*, for making of a newe belle chele,	0	4	10
Item, in expences done of the ſame *John* for his dyner, —	0	0	3
Item, paide for repacion [c] of irren wark, that is to ſay, gogeons, keys, and what ye warkman's hire to dreſſe the grete belle, —	0	1	8
Item, paide for femble [d], and for makyng that of in bell-ropes,	0	1	5
Item, paide for neweſhotyng [e] of the grete bell claper, —	0	3	3

a Pariſh.

b It appears the office continued 2 years, and the accompts are for that time.

c Reparation.

d Thimble, ſee p. 80, note u.

e I am unacquainted with the exact meaning of the term. Q. new caſting or ſhaping?

 Item,

	£.	s.	d.
Item, paide for ſhotyng of the middell bell claper, —	0	1	0
Item, paide to *Ric. Anngell*, for kepyng[f] of the clok, —	0	3	4
Item, paide to *John Inglysſhe* for his tyme — —	0	1	8
Item, paide for makyng of a pullpitt, and for waſſhyng of auter[g] clothes, — — — —	0	1	4
Item, paide to *Ric. Michell* and to *Ranlot Wright*, for mendyng of the tymbwark of all the bells, and for their bordyng, —	0	1	4
Item, paide for fechyng a tabull from Sutterton to Wigtoft, and home ayen by 2 tymes, and for ſhotyng of an irren bolte to the forbell whele, and for nayles to the ſame bell, — —	0	0	6
Item, paide for heſpes and ſtapulls to the bells, —	0	0	10
Item, paide for ſaudyng[h] of the beſt croſſe, — —	0	0	1
Item, paide for ſcowryng of 4 candelſticks afore ye hye auter, and ye candelſtyk afore Seynt Peter, and for ſaudryng of the holy-water fatte[i], — — — —	0	0	11
Item, paide to *Thomas Smyth*, wright, for mendyng of the kirke-ſtoles[k] by half a day, and for nailes, — — —	0	0	4½
Item, paide for dreſſyng of the clok, — —	0	0	10
Item, paide for truſſyng of the forbell, and for the ſanctus[l] bell, and for bordyng of ye wright, and for nailes to ye ſame, and for a nere[m] makyng to the ſame bell — — —	0	2	3
Item, paide to a plumer, for mendyng of the ledes and for ſauder,	0	3	5
Item, paide to his man for a day and di. — —	0	0	4½
Item, paide to a bell-rope to the forbell, — —	0	0	5
Item, in expences for takyng downe of the bell, —	0	0	2
Item, paide to *Agnes Grymſton*, for 11 lb.[n] braſſe of hir boght to the bolſters to all ye belles, pr. of ye lb. 1½*d.* — —	0	1	2½
Paide to *John Tynkir* in arneſt[o] for to make the bolſters to the bells, and for his comyng hidder, and for fewell, —	0	1	0
Item, paide for 100 nailes to the bells, — —	0	0	2
Item, in expenſes in hiryng of *Thomas Tynkir*, of Goſberkirk[p], at 2 tymes for the makyng of the ſaid bolſters, —	0	0	8
Item, in expenſes for hiryng of 2 wrightes to mend ye belles, att Palmer's[q] houſe expent, — — —	0	0	4
Item[r], paide to *John Harby* and to *Will.* his broder, for 15 days wirkyng upon the bells in makyng of the croſſe triſtles[s], and ſettyng on a grete almery in the reveſtry, whiche *Water Dey*[t] gaf for his noble for liggyng in the chirche, takyng by the day they bothe 5*d.* with 4*d.* more, att alle, — — —	0	6	7

[f] Looking after or managing the clock. [g] Linen laid over the altar at the ſacrament. [h] Soldering. [i] Vatt, I imagine. [k] Stools to ſupport coffins during funerals, &c. [l] *Saints*, or little bell. [m] An ere or ear. [n] An abatement of 2d. in that quantity. [o] Erneſt. [p] Now called Goſberton, diſtant about 3 miles. [q] Probably a public-houſe. [r] The latter part of this Item is ſo obſcure, I cannot decypher its meaning, but have copied it exact. The ſum total denotes that the two men together had 5d. a day for 15 days, which is 6s. 3d.; and 4d. over makes 6s. 7d. [s] Truſſels. [t] *i.* Walter Dey or Day gave.

Item,

	£.	s.	d.
Item, paide to the faide *Thomas Tynkir*, for makyng of 6 bolfters of braffe to all ye belles,	0	5	8
Item, in expenfes made and done at *John Briggs*, of kirkhoufe, upon the wright aforefaid,	0	0	4
Item, paide to *John Almonds*, for a ftone femble [u] to the bell ftryngs,	0	0	3
Item, paide for makyng that of in ropes for the belles,	0	0	4
Item, paide to *Will'm Whelpdale*, fremafon, for makyng of the croffe in ye chirchrth [x],	0	5	0
Item, in expens done upon the fame *Will'm*,	0	0	2
Item, paide to the faid wright for mending of the forbell wirkyng y'opon [y] by 3 days, and for their borde by the fame tyme,	0	1	8
Item, paide to *Rob't Rudd*, for di. ftone femble [z],	0	0	2
Item, paide for the makyng of the fame in a bell rope,	0	0	2
Item, paide to *Alis Crigge*, for bordyng of 2 wrights wirkyng an oy' tyme upon the belles for 14 days, takyng for yem bothe and ye day 3*d*.	0	3	6
Item, paide to *Thomas Wright*, for makyng of the chirche yates in grete [a],	0	0	9
Item, paide to *Will'm Crigge*, for tymber for the fame,	0	0	6
Item, paid to *Rob't Wells*, fmyth, for makyng of two fquyer [b] gogeons, a bolt, and a ftapull to the forbell,	0	0	5
Item, paid for grete fpikyngs to all the treftles of all the belles,	0	0	4
Item, paide to *Will'm Cofton*, for tymber to the belles,	0	4	0
Item, paide to *John Norys*, for wasfhyng of 2 awbes [c] and 2 parres,	0	0	2
Item, paide for meltyng of 10 ftrike barly [d] into malte,	0	0	7
Item, paide for nailes to the faid forbell,	0	0	0½
Item, paide to *Rob't Panlyn*, for di. ftone femble for lynes to clocke plumes [e], and for makyng of the fame femble,	0	0	5
Item, paide for nailes to the faid clok,	0	0	1
Item, paide by the hands of the faid *John Carre*, for his aune [f] expenfes and cofts yat he didd and fpent in rydyng and goyng by dyvers tymes unto Bofton [g], to Donyngton [h], Swynfhed [i], and to Sutterton [k], for ye well [l] of the faid chirche and pisfhen' [m],	0	0	10
Item, paide for paup [n] to this newe boke, and for writing of the fame, and of our receits in or paupers [o] or yis boke was made newe,	0	0	8
Item, paide to *Edward Smyth*, of Sutterton, for makyng of all the clafpes of irren, and an ere to ye for bell,	0	0	8
Sum of all the payments, coft, and expens,	3	7	1

[u] See before, p. 78, note [d].

[x] Chirchgarth. Concerning the term Freemafon, fee Gov. Pownall, Archæol. vol. IX. p. 120.

[y] y'opon for thereupon.   [z] Dimidium, or half.

[a] I fuppofe agreed with him for the job for 9d. by the great.   [b] Square.

[c] Albes or furplices are meant.

[d] Barley given to the church, made into malt at the church's expence, and then fold. See before, p. 77.   [e] *Plumbs*, lead weights.   [f] Own.   [g] Diftant 7 miles.

[h] Diftant 4 miles.   [i] Diftant 3 miles.   [k] Diftant 1 mile.   Benefit.

[m] Parifhioners.   [n] Paper.   [o] Our papers ere, or before, the book was made.

Theife

THEISE bene the refceits of *John Shepherd* and *John Frankisfh*, the [a] cherch-maifters of the pifsh cherch of Wigtoft, frome the day and feft of Goode Fryday, in the yere of our Lorde God 1487, unto the fame feft next following aft' that by an hole yere:

	£.	s.	d.
In the firft refceyved of *John Brigg* and *John Barr*, chirche-maifters, in the yere next afore paft, in mony upon yeir arrerages,	0	1	1
Item, r. in barly 13 ftr. fold by the faid *John Shepherd* and *John Frankifh*, — — —	0	4	0
Item, refc' of gaddryng in the toune of divs pfans [b], as it arpeireth by a bill y'opon made, — — —	0	13	2½
Item, r. in gaddryng of chefe [c] of div's pfanes, —	0	4	0
Item, r. upon the executors of *John Conyn*, — —	0	3	4
Item, r. for the rent of a falt-panne — —	0	1	2
Item, r. *Rob't Carver* for a legacy of *Ric. Thomlynfon*, in part of payment of 20*s*. — — — —	0	6	8
Item, r. of the executos of *Kattine Baffe*, — —	0	6	8
Item, r. of *John Aleynfon* for a legacy of *Will'm Blakburne*,	0	6	8
Item, r. of *Ric. Alger*, — — — —	0	0	3
Item, r. *Will'm Hakford* hath giffen to the chirche a long ledder, pc'	0	2	0
Item, the fame *Will'm* hath giffen a white cloth to lappe ye beft croffe clothe in, and a cloth to hill the hye road with anoy'r to Saynt Mary's awtr.			
Sm̄ [d] to. — — — —	2	9	0½

[a] The fpelling varies confiderably in the different accounts: this in the former account was "chirche."

[b] Divers perfons.

[c] It appears the inhabitants contributed cheefe as well as barley.

[d] Total receipts in 1487.

THEIS bene the coft, expenfes, and payments, of *John Shepherd* and *John Frankysfh*, chirch-maifters aforefaide, done and paide in the yere aforefaid:

	£.	s.	d.
In the firft paide to *John Swafeld*, fmyth, for 4 pynnes of irren made to the belles, with the amendyng of a lok, — —	0	0	6
Item, paide to *Thomas Brigge*, for oke wod of hym bought for the repacion of the kirke yates 1*s*. and to *Ric. Bewne*, for oke of hym boght for the fame 1*d*. — — —	0	1	1
Item, paide for borde to the fame yates, and to the repacion of the northe dore of ye kirke, — — —	0	1	0

Item,

	£.	s.	d.
Item, paide for nayles to ye same warke, ———	0	0	7
Item, for makyng of the same yatts, and for mendyng of ye said chirche dore, — — — — —	0	2	8
Item, paide to *Edward Smyth*, of Sutton [a], for amendyng of the irren wark of the said church yates, and an newe claspe, —	0	0	3
Item, for an hangyng lok to ye same yat, — —	0	0	3
Item, paide to *Edward Smyth*, for turnyng of 2 bell claspes, and for laying upon yem 4 lb. irren, — — —	0	0	10
Item, paide for borde to the repacion of the church eleys [b] yopon ye north side of ye chirch, — — —	0	1	0
Item, paide for nayles and for warkmanship of the same,	0	1	0
Item, paide for paryng away of the erth from the chirche walles,	0	0	8
Item, paide for heynyng [c] of the chirche walls, and clensyng of the vestre, and makyng clene of the spoutes, ———	0	0	8
Item, paide for 2 trayes [d] of lyme for mendyng and stoppyng of the botrasses, and other defauts in the chirche walles rounde abowte the chirche, ——— ——— ———	0	2	8
Item, paide an other tyme for 3 trayes lyme for the same warke p ye traye 14*d*. ——— ——— ———	0	3	6
Item, paide for a traye of sande, p̃c' ——— ———	0	0	4
Item, paide for cariage of the said lyme and sand, with cariage of the aforesaid borde, ——— ——— ———	0	1	0
Item, to *Thomas Whelpedale*, mason, for mending of dyvers defauts withyn [e] the chirche and withouten rounde aboute, —	0	10	8
Item, paide to *John Norys*, for wesshyng and mendyng of alle the awbes [f] and õr necessar, ——— ———	0	1	10
Item, paid for a lok to a chist, ——— ———	0	0	2
Item, paide to *Herry Tiller*, for 7 days labor in whityng of the chirche, takyng by the day 5*d*. and paide to his man for 4 days eny day 4*d*. ——— ——— ———	0	4	3
Item, allowed unto *John*, for laboryng by ye forsaid 7 days aboute ye same warke, takyng by ye day 4*d*. at his awne borde, with one day pdone [g], — — — —	0	2	0
Item, to be allowed to *John Frankissh*, for 4 days at the same warke by ye day 4*d*. ——— ——— ———	0	1	4

[a] I suppose this to be an abbreviation of Sutterton, a neighbouring town.

[b] I think this obscurely written word is *isles*, which is here spelt *eleys*.

[c] What this word means I know not: it is wrote thus, *heynyg*.

[d] I frequently in these accounts meet with *tray* of lime and *tray* of sand: I am not acquainted with the exact quantity of the measure. It may mean a *hod*.

[e] Within and withouten.

[f] Albes or surplices, and other necessaries 22d.

[g] One day *pardoned*, or abated. The charge would otherwise have been 2s. 4d.

5 Item,

	£.	s.	d.
Item, paide for a lok to a cheſt in the reveſtr [h], ———	0	1	2
Item, paide for anoг lok to the ſame cheſt, ———	0	0	6
Item, paide for mendyng of ye chirche wall next unto the chirche yate, ——— ——— ——— ———	0	0	1
Item, paid for hokes and hengles unto the ſkolehouſe [i] dore, with a key, and for nailes to the ſame dore, ——— ———	0	0	4½
Item, for 2 ſtone of femble bought for the bell ropes, ———	0	0	10
Item, paide for makyng of the ſame, — ———	0	1	3
Item, paide to *E. Smith*, for a fyre-panne to feche fire into the chirch 4*d.* and for a chene [k] of irren with an holy water ſtik, at the fouth chirch dore 4*d.* ——— ——— ———	0	0	8
Item, paide for a ſhefe [l] of glaſs 8*d.* to 2 glaſyers for mendyng of divs glaſſe wyndowes rounde aboute ye chirch by 3 days warking, takyng by the day eny pece of yem 5*d.* ——— ———	0	2	6
Item, paide to *Agnes Bennett*, for bordyng of the ſaid 2 glaſiers, and for bordyng of the ſaid *Harry Tiller* and his man, whilſt they whited the chirche in grete, ——— ———	0	2	10
Item, in expenſes done upon the ſaid glaſiers, and in gaddryng in the toune for ye well [m] of ye ſaid chirche, ——— ———	0	0	4
Sm̄ tot. expenſ', ——— ———	2	8	3½

[h] The modern veſtry-room.

[i] It appears a ſchool was kept in the church at that time, as is the caſe at this day.

[k] An iron chain to faſten the *aſpergillum*, or ſprinkler of the holy water, to the holy water veſſel at the ſouth door of the church.

[l] What quantity or meaſure is this?

[m] Repair.

THEIS

	£.	s.	d.
THEIS bene the detts that bene owyng to ye chirche.			
Robert Carver oweth for a legacy of *Ric. Thomlynſon*, whiche the ſame *Ric.* bequeythed to the chirche of Wigtoft 20*s.* whereof is paide in the reſceyte next afore 6*s.* 8*d.* and ſo is yr in the hands of the ſaid *Robert Carver* yit remaynyng clere toward ye ſaid chirche,	0	13	4
Item, the executors of *Will'm Child* oweth for the pſon[a] of Weſt-myle, called *Robert Colleſon*, which he gaf to the ſaid chirche,	20	4	0
Item, the executors of the ſame *Will'm Child* oweth that .... *Baxſter* gave unto *Will'm Child* in his lyve[b] to the uſe of the ſaid chirche, — — — —	0	10	0
Item, of the executos of *John Palmer*, for the rent of the kirk-houſe for 3 yeres, — — —	0	6	0
Item, *Robert Peby* oweth for ferme[c] of a ſalt-panne of 16 ſtone of lede, — — —	0	1	2
Sm̄ of the detts dewe unto ye ſaid chirche of Wigtoft,	14	17	2

[a] This item is ſomewhat obſcure; it ſeems to mean *parſon*, i. e. rector of *Weſtmill* in Hertfordſhire, in Lincoln dioceſe.

[b] Life.

[c] The farm or uſe of this panne, which it here ſeems conſiſted of 16 ſtone of lead.

Continuation of the WIGTOFT Pariſh Book[1].

	£.	s.	d.
Fab eand[2] de wygtoft,			
Recept[3] p *Joh. Frankes.*			
Lawrenas brigge 1 ſtryke ordii[4].			
Alic mee, 1 frendyll[5] ord.			
Joh. grave, 1 frend . . . . ord.			
Rob. feld, 1 frendyll ord.			
hugo looke, 1 frendyll ord.			
Willm Biſhopwrith 1 frendyll ord.			
Cealid Frankes 1 frendyll ord.			
Mergerid[6] *lampſon* 1 frendyll ord. dim[7] qrt ord. xii *d.*	0	1	0
Rob. Ardnell, — — —	0	0	1
Joh. Woods, — —	0	0	1
Willm Carway, — —	0	0	1
Joh. ryppyngall, for 1 cwtt[8] of eſoh, — —	0	0	3
Willm brihty, for chantre mony (I imagine at twice) xvi *d.*	0	1	0
Joh. Newma', for leyde[9], — —	0	2	8
It. *dcs*[10] *Joh.* p plu'b[11], — — —	0	6	0
It. *dcs Joh.* p 1 wytte ſton, — —	0	0	1
Itm. recept. de *laurenas brige* p plu'b, — —	0	1	8
Itm. *xpina Carawer*[12], for tymb & bords Recept, —	0	0	10
It. recept. de *Willmo gudſon,* — — —	0	0	4

[1] In theſe accounts it may be proper to obſerve, there is a conſiderable chaſm as to time; that printed in p. 81—84, being dated 1487; the next date (ſee p. 195) is 1499, though there is the preſent intermediate account without a date. It does not appear that any leaves are torn out; but the hand-writing is now a different one, the accounts are not ſo clearly ſtated, and are in ſome places an imperfect Latinſed Engliſh. Perhaps we ought not much to wonder at theſe irregularities, when we reflect on the ſtate of literature three centuries ago, in ſo ſmall a pariſh as Wigtoft, when the number muſt be very few who were capable of writing at all, and might be nearly confined to the prieſts. Notwithſtanding this, we meet with articles in this Account that are curious and worthy preſervation.

[2] *Fabrica eccleſiæ* de Wygtoft. [3] Receptum. [4] Hordei.

[5] By the quantity at laſt it ſeems about two pecks are intended.

[6] Margaret. [7] The whole is half a quarter of barley.

[8] One hundred weight; but of what I cannot tell.

[9] Lead. [10] *dictus,* the ſaid.

[11] *pro plumbo.* [12] Chriſtina Carawer.

	£.	s.	d.
It. recept. de *Joh. brige*, fen^r, for 1 Peloree [1], ——	0	1	2
It. vendit. *Thome feld* plu'b [2], — —	0	8	0
It. Recept. de *necholas Smyth*, for 1 Salt pan ii anns [3], —	0	2	4
It. Recept. de *Joh. brige*, fen^r, — —	0	7	0
Om̃ 1l. 13s. 9d.			

Solutum p *Joh frankes*, a° d̃m [4] ut fup^a.

	£.	s.	d.
Inprimis, *Edwardo Smyth* de Kyrton, for yrren warke to fpowtys, and ii candylftykes, — — —	0	3	0
Itm. *Willmo bribty*, for fplynt wodde to the kyrk, —	0	1	4
It. fol. *laurenas brige*, ftranit [5] to the fayd kyrk, —	0	1	0
It. fol. *χpinæ caraver* [6], for tymb & borde, —	0	0	10
It. fol. for naylis, — — —	0	0	6
It. fol. *Joh. hervy*, p i die and bord, — —	0	0	6
It. fol. *Symon Wryth*, p uno die & bord, —	0	0	5
It. fol. *Joh. Franke*, p vii dieb' & bord, — —	0	2	8
It. fol. *thomæ howfon*, for walling ii dieb, — —	0	0	8
It. fol. *Alexand. tompfon*, for layng of fton, — —	0	0	3
It. fol. *Joh. Wadde*, ii dieb. for wallyng [7], ——	0	0	8
It. fol. *Willmo Carway*, for wallyng, — —	0	0	8
It. *Rob. malft.* fol. for makyng of wallyng erth, —	0	0	4
It. fol. *Willmo derott*, for erth makyng, — —	0	0	3
It. fol. *Rob. ardnell*, p ii dieb. & bord, — —	0	0	10
It. fol. *Joh. frankes*, p iii dieb. & bord, — —	0	1	0
It. fol. *Willmo frankes*, p ii dieb. & bord, — —	0	0	8
It. fol. for ii cresfhaffes [8] and paynting, — —	0	0	8
It. fol. for 1 ledd^r [9] fpyldyng & wodde therto, —	0	0	3
It. fol. in fawd^r to the clathers [10], — —	0	0	4
It. fol. *R. Brandon*, for labryng iii dieb. dim̃ & bord on the rode [11],	0	1	2
It. fol. *Willmo magelyn capel* [12] & *Joh. frales*, for rydyng to Lincol', for the townys matt^r, in expens hors mett and man mett [13], —	0	4	0
It. fol. *R. ftircroft*, for fmall yryns [14], — —	0	4	6
It. fol. expens' ad Donyngton p *Joh. brige*, *Joh. frankes*, *lambt worme*, *Joh. fnell*, — — — —	0	0	9

[1] or *Selorre*. [2] Lead fold to Thomas Feld.

[3] Two years. [4] Anno Domini. [5] Quære. [6] Chriftina Carawer, as in the preceding page.

[7] It appears fome part of the church walls were no better than ftud and mud, by the charge for fplintwood and walling earth; or thefe articles might be for the "kirk-houfe."

[8] Creffets or fockets for candles. See Gloffary to Wardrobe account of Edward I.

[9] I imagine a ladder is meant; fplitting or hewing the wood, and the wood itfelf.

[10] Solder for the glaziers.

[11] Board on the road, or travelling expences; *bord* (board) is always charged for workmen.

[12] *Capellanus*, chaplain. [13] Horfe meat and man meat.

[14] Irons. I meet with this word fpelt in every poffible manner.

It. fol.

	£.	s.	d.
It. sol. *edwarde Smythe*, for yryne warke to ye bellys, —	0	2	4
It. sol. *Joh. herwy*, for dreſſyng of the ſayd bellys, —	0	0	8
It. sol. *Alice brige*, for the bord of the ſayd *Joh. herwy*, —	0	0	4
It. sol. *Joh. Frankes*, p ii days mett and hyer [1], ———	0	0	9
It. sol. *Writh*, for h^s Lab^r & coſts to lincoln & in this toune,	0	1	8
It. sol. *Joh. writh*, on herlys [2] for ou^r warke xii d. of the condicyan that the ſayd ſhall take no nod warke, or we have dyñ w^t our lives [3],	0	1	0
It. sol. *edwardo Smyth* for dryſſyng [4] of the cheſts, —	0	7	8
It. sol. for one ſton [5] pyke, —— ——	0	0	6
It. sol. *edwardo Smyth*, for i platt to the Kyrk dor, and i ſtabull to the Reverſtre dore, — — —	0	0	2
It. sol. *Alic brige*, for the bord of the clazer, ——	0	1	6
It. sol. *Joh. brige*, ſen. for wodde, —— —	0	0	2
It. sol. for wyſſyng of awt^r clowth, — —	0	0	8
It. sol. for coſts & charges to abb' [6] of ſwynſhed, *W. magelyn*, *Joh. Newma'*, and *Joh. frankes*, — — —	0	0	3
It. sol. *Joh. frankes*, p i die for makyng of triſtylles [7], —	0	0	4
Sm tot. 2^l. 5^s. 1^d.			

[1] Meat and hire.

[2] I imagine this to mean earneſt.

[3] On condition that the ſaid workman ſhall take no other work till we have done without our leaves, or conſents. It appears the 12d. earneſt was to bind him to finiſh their buſineſs before any other.

[4] This appears a large ſum for repairing cheſts.

[5] Perhaps for a boundary ſtone.

[6] Abbey of Swineſhead, diſtant about 2 miles and a half, the place where king John is ſaid by hiſtorians to have been poiſoned. Not a veſtige of the abbey is now remaining, except the ſtone effigy of a knight in armour, in a niche in the back wall of the houſe, on the left hand of the door into the garden, which is by time much impaired and defaced. The houſe is an excellent farm-houſe built of ſtone from the old abbey. Speed, in his "Catalogue of the Religious "Houſes, Colledges, and Hoſpitals, ſometimes in England and Wales," ſays this abbey was dedicated to Saint Marie, was founded by Sir Robert Griſley, contained white monks, and its revenue was 175l. 19s. 10d. per annum.

[7] Treſſels.

Extracts from the Accompts of the Churchwardens of the Pariſh of ST. MARY HILL, London.

THESE Accompts are written in two large folio paper books, containing the Churchwardens' accompts, extracts from the wills of benefactors, and ſeveral other matters relating to the pariſh.

One of theſe books is of a ſmaller ſized paper, but vaſtly thicker than the other, and made up of many little parcels, which, being on paper of unequal ſizes, and written in different hands, were doubtleſs once ſeparate, and afterwards bound up in a rude manner with a thick parchment cover, lapping over like a pocket-book after the manner of our antient regiſter-books. This conſiſts wholly of Churchwardens' accompts, the firſt of which has the following title:

" Theſe ben the Parcellis of Paymentis made be William Gelam and John " Gretyng, Wardeyns of the Chirche of Seint Marie at the Hille, begynnyng at " the Feſte of Eſter, the Yer of the Regne of Kyng Henry the Sixte, after the " Conqueſt, v°." [1427].

Theſe payments are chiefly for repairs, &c. of the church; and no receipts are mentioned, nor any balance of the accompts, as is done regularly afterwards.

Then follows an inventory of the church-plate, veſtments, &c. 10 Hen. VI. the firſt article of which is " a cowpe of ſilver and golde to ber in Godde's body with " criſtall."

Item, " a cup of ſilver for Godde's body."

Then follows " the accompt of John Palmer and John Clerke, churchwardens, from Michaelmas, 17 Edw. IV. to Michaelmas, 19 Edw. IV. by two hoole yere;" in which, having firſt given a rental of the lands and tenements belonging to the chantries founded by *Weſton*, *Cauſton*, *Goſſelyne*, *Bedeham*, and *Cambridge*, they charge themſelves with the ſaid rents, and the increaſe and arrears of the ſame, bequeſts, caſuell receipts, and burials. They then ſet forth various payments and expences upon the church and chantries, under the head of *Quitrents* *, *Prieſts' wages*,

* viz.	£	s.	d.
for John Weſton's chantry to the Churchwardens of St. George, Botolph-lane,	1	0	0
Prior of Chriſt Church, Oxford,	0	3	0
Abbot of Waltham,	1	18	0
for Cambridge's chantry to the Abbot of Bermeſeye,	0	6	0
for Cawſton's to the Brotherhood of our Lady and St. Thomas of Canterbury of Salve Regina in St. Magnus church,	0	6	0
Prior of Chriſt Church without Aldgate, London,	0	5	0
Maſters of the Bridge-houſe,	0	13	4
Abbot of Barmoldſey,	0	13	4
for Goſlyn's to the abbeſs of Kilborn,	0	0	6
for John Naſyng's to the Abbot of Waltham-croſſe,	1	2	0
for the ſouth aile of the church to ditto,	0	10	0
	6	17	2
for the Bell at Tower-hill, purchaſed 1425, to Sir J. Cornwallis,	0	1	0
	6	18	2

wages *, *Vacations* (i. e. lofs of rent by empty houfes), *Obits*, *Reparacyons*, *Almes-money* (mifcellanies), *Cofts of the Wax-chandler* ‡, *Potations* §, *Rents*, &c. *due, but not paid*; and the balance is then drawn.

The account is followed by a fimilar one for two years, from Michaelmas 19, to 21 Edw. IV. of Mille and Merfh; to which fucceeds that of Vavafour and Baker, for two years alfo, from Michaelmas 1483 to 1485. After which fucceed regular feries of accounts for *one* year each, according to the prefent method obferved in the parifh, (by which the junior churchwarden of each year becomes fenior churchwarden the next year), down to Michaelmas 1538. The book being then turned, and beginning at the other end, there are accounts from Chriftmas 1556-7, and fo on upwards to 1539 in no regular feries. Then follows an inventory of houfhold goods and furniture; apparel male and female; debts pro and con; chattels and funeral expences; figned JOHN PORT, layt the Kyng's fervant. Here ends this book.

The other folio book, though not near fo thick as the former, is made of a much larger paper, very ftrong and good, the edges cut, and evidently bound before it was written. " This booke was made, and the moft part therein wryten, by the hands of John Halhed, grocer and pifhioner of the pyfhe of Seynte Mary at Hill, on whoes foule Allmyghttye God have m'cye. Amen for charyte, a° 1468. By me, Martin Stower." It contains large extracts from the wills of Rofe Wryttel, and the other founders of chantries, with rentals of all, except Wefton's and Bedeham's. The copy of a deed of releafe, 31 Hen. I. and of other deeds, proving Bedeham's right to difpofe of the tenements bequeathed by him. Copy of a leafe, dated March 13, 1507, from William Hatclyff, clerk, parfon, and churchwardens of St. Mary Hill, to Andrew Evyngar, his wife Ellyn, and their natural daughter Elizabeth, of a houfe in Thames-ftreet, for 50 years, if any of them live fo long, at 5 marks *per annum*: the faid Evyngar, &c. to rebuild it the firft year, to keep it in proper repair, the king's highway well paved before it, and the *fege* or *prevey* duly voided, for the firft twenty years; the landlords to do it the reft of the term: N. B. and if neither of them live to the end of the 50 years, the leffees are to enter on the premifes immediately on the death of the furvivor, the day of whofe demife is to

* The wages of the *chantry* priefts were fixed by their refpective founders, and were generally £6. 13*s*. 4*d*.; but about the reign of Edward VI. were raifed to £8. each. Befides thefe there was a *parifh* prieft (as he is fometimes called) to whom was paid annually 2*s*. for rehearfing in the bede-roll the founders' names. We find no payments to the rector, except fome tithes which he forgave towards the expences of the choir, which encreafed before their abolition under Edward VI. In the early accounts there are only *two* clerks at £2. 13*s*. 4*d*. each *per annum*; but in later years, when wages were encreafed and *conducts* hired to fing, the expence amounted to between £30. and £40. *per annum*; and in 1539 was £51. 19*s*. In 1547 the feveral organ-players employed had from £8. 10*s*. to £11.; the parifh-clark £6. 13*s*. 4*d*.; the fexton £4.

‡ The charge of the wax-chandler was at an average a little above 25*s*. *per annum*; fometimes 12*s*. fometimes 53*s*. according to the allowance for old wax.

§ Or money fpent on receiving rents, &c. was annually about 5*s*. Writing and endorfing the Church-wardens' accompts was at firft only 6*s*. 8*d*.; but afterwards, when the abftract was entered in the *broad-book*, it was doubled. The raker's or fcavenger's pay was at firft 8*d*. afterwards doubled.

be

be ſolemnly kept, at the expence of the leſſors, during the remainder of the ſaid 50 years, for the ſouls of the ſaid Andrew, Ellyn, and Elizabeth by name, and generally for all Chriſtian ſouls; the ſaid parſon and churchwardens being entitled to the premiſes immediately on the demiſe of the three parties.

Next comes an inventory of goods delivered to Marynn Conteryn *, Marchaunte of Venyſe, and to Powle Priour, his attorney, by J. Bedham, when he entered into the place in Botolph-lane, where now one Peter Conteryn dwellith, anno 1485. Another inventory of the church goods.

Then a very full and particular account of Willym Prewne and John Halhed, churchwardens, from Michaelmas 1 Hen. VII. 1485, to Michaelmas 2 Hen. VII.; a rental of all the *lyvelode*, or income from rents of tenements †, belonging to the church in their time, regularly made out according to the ſituation of the tenements. An abſtract of every ſucceeding churchwarden down to 1537.

A memorandum that, 27 March, 6 Edw. VI. it was agreed by the parſon of St. Mary Hill ‡, that Francis Semper and his wife, for certain conſiderations, ſhould have the houſe in the north church-yard for 20 years from next Lady-day, paying yearly for the ſame 30*s.*: the churchwardens to keep the houſe from *Wyndtide* and *Weithertide* during the ſaid term.

Commiſſion of Edward VI. to the Lord mayor and others, to make enquiry into the church goods, plate, ornaments, &c. dated Guildhall, July 13, 1552; ditto, April 15, 1553; ditto, about linnen, Jan. 6, 6 Edward VI.; and the Churchwardens' anſwer, inventory, &c. and an account of ornaments reſtored by Mary, and ſome others given by the pariſhioners.

Memorandum. Dec. 26, 1556. Sir Allyn Percy, parſon, with the moſt part of the worſhipful and awnſyent pariſhioners, granted unto John Fraute, bere-brewer, an annual rent of £4. for 40 years, from laſt Michaelmas, to be paid quarterly by the churchwardens.

Extracts from T. Clayton's will, 1554, bequeathing tenements for repairs of the church.——Memorandum of writings and leaſes 1577. The remaining half of the book is blank: but at the end reverſed, the names of the parſon and pariſhioners at the making of the book, Sept. 29, 1486.

The paper of this book is of a coarſe texture and yellowiſh; the mark a crown,

The ſand remains on ſome of the later writing.

* *Contarini* is a well known Venetian family name.

† Among the tenants are William Parys, *reynner*; J. Breuſter, *tornor*; Robert Eryche, *woolmonger*; William Reynnesforth, *poyntmaker*; Maiſter Lewes, the king's *feciſſian*; J. Mouce, *capper*; and other more common trades, &c. The ſituations are about the church and church-yard, St. Mary-Hill-lane, Temmyſtrete, Love lane, pariſhes of St. Andrew's Hubberd, St. Leonard Eaſtchepe, St. Chriſtopher at Stocks, St. Botolph beſyde the Menery, Fauſter-lane, and at the Tower-Hill beſide the Pyllerye beyond the new Abbey. The income this year amounted to £78. 19*s.* 2*d.*

‡ Allyn Percy.

Stowe's account of this church is very fuperficial *, confifting of one page of epitaphs. He fays indeed, that it was " a *faire* church, and hath been lately " builded, as may appere by this that followeth." This is only Fabian's account of the finding Alice Hackney's body intire after 175 years inhumation, as they were " digging the foundation of a wall *within* the church." This digging or reparation comes within the time of our regifters, which have preferved a receipt of 7*s*. 8*d*. from John Halhed, grocer, paid by Thomas Colyn, 1496, " for the obyt and fettyng upe of the tombe, and buryenge of Richard Hackney † " and Alys his wyff, the xx day of Marche;" which in the fecond book is charged " for lyme, fande, and for mafon's huyr and his laborer, makyng *ageyne* " of their tombe, and their dyrge and maffe and maffe-peny; and for drynkyng " to the priefts and to the parifhioners, and for al maner of charges."

The walls and tower of this church being all that efcaped the fire in 1666, we are not to expect the leaft traces of the parts of the building that occur in thefe accounts; nor is there a fingle brafs or antient mural monument now remaining here.

The church antiently appears to have had a crofs aile, and two ailes to the body: the north aile was begun 1487; finifhed 1489; the fouth aile about 1501, on the fite of the abbot of Waltham's kitchen. In a grand repair, 1490, Mr. Alderman Remington ‡, John Smarte, and William Prewne, granted each a fum of money to " make a whole arch;" as did Harry Kello for a large one, and John Suckling, and fir John Plumer (chantry prieft) united to make a whole arch, upon condition " that all the parifhioners will be contributing to the fame after their " power that may be." According 5 of them gave from 40*s*. to 20*s*. and 10*s*. apiece. " Thomas Hant will give as Mr. Alderman will fet him; and Mr. W. " Wilde, parfon, as his pleafur."

Robert Revett (one of the fheriffs 1490) gave liberally towards it §.

Different fums were collected for this work in 1496 to the amount of £13. 1*s*. 8*d*. including 8*d*. by " the bedyll's wyff at two times for two of her geefts."

My lady the King's grandam ⸸, gave to our church 20*s*.; Mr. Robert Ryvett, alderman and grocer of London, to the repairs of the church and fteeple 200 marks.

Here were feven chantries founded by the following perfons:

1. Rofe Wrytell, fometime wife of William Fairftede, clerk. She died 1328, and by will, dated 1323, 16th of king Edward, fon of king Edward, bequeathed a tenement of olde tyme callid the *Swanne on the Hope* ||, in Thames-ftreet, in this

* Survey of London, p. 227. Ed. 1633, fol.

† He was fheriff 1322, 15 Edward II. Fabian fays the corpfe was found April 1497. Some bodies of the Engaine family were difcovered in the fame ftate in repairing the family chapel near Upminfter.

‡ He was fheriff 1487; mayor 1500; and died 1510 or 1511. § Stowe.

⸸ Margaret, countefs of Richmond, grandmother to Henry VIII.

|| The Swan and Hoop, a corruption of Swan on or in Hoop. Q. has this fign any relation to the *Swan-hopping*, an annual ceremony obferved by fome of the livery companies of London; or, as *hoppet* is defined by Skinner a Lincolnfhire word for a *bafket*, is *hope* any inclofure of *wicker* in which the fwans had their nefts?—A *Hooper* is explained by Bailey to be *a wild fwan*; a *Hope* is the fide of a hill, or low ground among hills.

parifh,

parifh, to maintain a prieft at the altar of St. Edmund King and Martyr, for her foul, and thofe of her hufband, her father, and mother.

2. John Caufton, mercer, died 1353, buried in the church of St. Pancras, Soper-lane, left the rents of certain tenements here, and in other parifhes, for one prieft and 5 tapers before the image of Our Lady at the high-altar of the Salutation, St. Thomas the Martyr, and St. Nicholas, who had altars on the fouth fide of the high-altar. Alfo another prieft to fing for the foul of Henry Barnard, and all Chriftian fouls in this church.

3. John Nafyng, brewer, by will, dated 1356, 35 Edward III. requiring his body to be buried in this church, gave the rents of feveral tenements and fhops in this parifh, to the amount of £9. 3*s*. 4*d*. *per annum*, for one prieft. The abbot of Waltham had a quit-rent of 22*s*. out of thefe rents from 1493 to the diffolution.

4. John Wefton, merchant of London, fheriff in 1420, by will, dated 1407, 3 Henry IV. orders his body to be buried here, and appoints a prieft to fing for his foul. If the parfon and parifhioners neglect to perform his will, the money to go to the mayor or wardeyn and commonalty of the city of London, to the ufe and fuftentacion of the brigge of London, and to find a prieft, &c. to fyng in the chapel of London bridge.

5. William Cambridge, grocer, mayor 1420, by will, dated 1431, 10 Henry VI. orders his body to be buried in St. Stephen's chapel of his own making, on the north fide of this church, and bequeaths lands to the amount of £10. *per annum* to the rectors of this church; and the Grocers' company to find one prieft; and 6*s*. 8*d*. for an anniverfary; and 6*s*. 8*d*. for the poor on the fame. In cafe of failure of his executors, the money to go to the ufe of London bridge, as Wefton's.

6. Richard Goflyng, ironmonger, fheriff 1420, by will, dated 1428, 6 Henry VI. bequeaths his body to be buried here *, and five marks for a prieft; a taper on St. Catherine's altar; and 6*d*. a week for two poor men or women of this parifh each, &c.; and on failure of application by the parfon and churchwardens here, to thofe of St. Botolph, Bifhopfgate; and on their neglect, to the mayor and aldermen, to find a prieft in the chapel of London bridge, as the preceding ones.

7. John Bredham, fifhmonger, by will dated 1472, 12 Edward VI. appoints a prieft in St. Catharine's chapel, and leaves 4*d*. a week to three poor men of the parifh: in cafe of neglect, the whole to go to St. Botolph, Bifhopfgate.

Thomas Ryvett, grocer, by will dated 1496, left half the reverfion of his daughters' fortunes, in cafe of their deceafe under age and fingle, to maintain a prieft here: but this feems not to have taken place.

* He leaves to St. Clement's church, Rochefter, where he was born, 6*s*. 8*d*.; to his wife Alice his meffuage at Mepam, and lands at Luddifdon, Kent. The expence of his obit to be divided between the parfon (then William Hatclyff, D. D), if prefent, 8*d*. his curate 8*d*. eight priefts and two clerks 3*s*. 6*d*. wax 8*d*. clark for ryngyng 20*d*. a dozen of bread price 12*d*. a kilderkyn of ale 2*s*. for the priefts, clerks, and parifhioners affifting, to be paid by his wife, and after her death by the Fifhmongers' company; the remaining 20*s*. to go to the common box of the fellowfhip, to affift at the obit, and pay the faid fum, viz. 10*s*. to the quere, and 10*s*. to the wardens of the company; and in failure of this, the whole to go to the repairs of the church. If neceffary, his wife to fell the meffuage and garden at Rochefter, called the Bell.

John Yongeham, of Rocheſter, fiſhmonger, buried here, founded an obit.

Here was another for John Bradmer; and the pariſh prieſt had two-pence to remember in the pulpit the ſoule of Richard Bliet **, of Thurroc, Eſſex, who gave 6*s.* 8*d.* to the church works.

In this church were ſeven altars. The high altar or St. Mary's, or Our Lady's; St. Thomas's on the ſouth ſide of the church; St. Edmund's; St. Catharine's; St. John Baptiſt's; St. Stephen's in his chapel on the north ſide of the church; the ſouth altar between the images of St. Thomas the Martyr and St. Nicholas. This, if not the ſame with St. Thomas' abovementioned, might be dedicated to Becket and St. Nicholas jointly. The chapels of St. Chriſtopher and St. Anne had their altars.

Here were three brotherhoods of St. Catharine, St. Anne, and St. Chriſtopher.

The window of the Trinity is mentioned in the ſouth ſide of the church, and that of St. John on the north. Here was a charnell-houſe, and no leſs than ſix church-yards, unleſs ſome of them went by two names; viz. the Great and Little, north and ſouth; the Pardon church-yard *; and the Proceſſion church-yard, with it's gravelled cauſey. Perſons buried here, beſides Cambridge, Goſlin, Ryvett, and Remington, who occur in the regiſter, may be ſeen in Stowe.

From theſe regiſters we are enabled to correct Newcourt's Liſt of the Rectors: After H. Webb, 1400, we are to inſert Thomas Atherſton, who was rector † here 1407; William Sparke was rector 1428 ‡, undated in Newcourt; John Horne (Newcourt, alias Daventre) was rector ‡ 1431; William Hatclyffe, undated in Newcourt, was rector 1507.

Each year's accompt comprehends Quitrents, Charges, Receipts, and Expences of the Chantries; Payments for the Church Reparations, Ornaments, &c.; Burial Fees, or *Caſualties.*

The Quitrents were as follow annually:	£.	s.	d.
To the abbot of Waltham Croſſe, for *John Naſyng,* To ditto for *John Weſton,* out of a tenement ſometime *J. Weſton's,* ſette in the pariſh of	III	o	o
To ditto for the ſouth aile,	o	x	o
To the prior of Chriſt Church without Aldgate, out of a meſſuage in this pariſh, for *J. Cawſton* and *John Weſton,*	o	VIII	o
To ditto for a tenement in St. Botolph's pariſh without Aldgate, late *John Weſton's,*			
To the Maſter of the Bridge-houſe, for *Hugh Brounham,* for a tenement in the pariſh of St. Leonard's in Eaſtcheap,		XIII	IIII
To the brotherhood of Our Lady and St. Thomas the Martyr, in St. Magnus § church, for *Hugh Brownham,* for the *Salve* per ann.		XII	
To the brotherhood of Our Lady in ſame church, for *J. Cauſton,*		VI	
To the church of St. George in Pudding-lane ‖, out of a tenement in this pariſh,		XX	

** Q. Richard Butte, vicar of Greys Thurrock, 1395—1399. Newcourt, II. 589.

* See p. 92. and note.

† Weſton's will.

‡ Cambridge's will.

§ Elſewhere ſpelt Mangnus.

‖ Elſewhere called *Buttowe* [Botolph] lane.

To

	£.	s.	d.
To the prioreſs of Kilborn, for a tenement in Fauſter-lane, per annum,			XII
To the abbot of *Burmeſey* [Bermondſey] for Mr. *Cambrugs's* rents,		VI	
To the prioreſs of Kilborn, for *Coſlyn*,			VI
	VI	I	IX
To Sir *John Cornwallis*, for the bell at Tower Hill,			XII
	VI	III	X*

Burial Fees, or Caſwelties, 1492.

One of Loſpan of Colcheſter's men	0	1	0
A child	0	1	0
A man of Maldon	0	3	4
Peter Andrew's wife,	0	13	4
A ſtranger,	0	3	4
Young Thomas Semer	0	2	0
1493. A Bretaygne	0	3	4
In Reparacion and Vacacion of Mr. Cambrug's chantre	5	15	5
In potacionys and makyng up of this accompte	0	11	8

Repacions on Books.

Paide to a Stacioner, for byndyng of an olde Saulte', and for newe kewyng † of a grayle *, and for repeyryng and new kewyng † of viii proceſſionaryes: ſum	0	10	0

* The Quitrents 1494 are thus ſtated:

Abbot of Waltham, for *John Naſyng*,	0	27	0
In the other book 1517—1519, this quitrent is out of a tenement that was ſometyme *J. Weſton's*, ſette in the pariſh of......			
Prior of Chriſt Churche without Aldgate, for fower hilk for *John Fauſton*, out of a meſſuage in St. Mary Hill pariſh,	0	5	0
Maſter of the Breeghouſe for *Hugh Brounham*, for the quitrent of a tenement lying in St. Leonard, Eaſtcheap.	0	13	0
The bretherhed of our Lady, St. Thomas the Martyr, kept within the church of St. Magnus for the Salve 12*s. per annum.*	0	6	0
Abbot of Burmeſey, for Mr. *Cambrug's* rents,			
Prioreſs of Kilborne, for *Richard Goſſelyn*, in Foſter-lane, 12*d.* a year,	0	0	6
Prioreſs of Chriſt Church, for a tenement in Botolph's pariſh without Aldgate, late *J. Weſton's*,	0	3	0
The Seint George, in Pudding-lane, out of a tenement in St. Mary Hill pariſh,	1	0	0
The abbot of Waltham for *John Weſton*, out of a tenement ſette in the pariſh of.......	1	18	0
Summa Totalis,	5	13	10

† *Kevryng*, covering. * Gradual.

Coſtes

Coftes upon Bellis.	£.	s.	d.
Payde for mendyng of 3 clapers of the greate bells to a fmyth without Algate — — — —	3	2	6
Item, for a rope for the fecond bell, waying 9lb. ——	0	11	9
Item, for a rope for the fainte bell, —— ——	0	0	4
Item, for makyng of a whele to the faince bell, ——	0	1	0
Item, for makyng of a bolt to a bell-claper, ——	0	1	6

The plaifterer (called the *Dawber*) tyler, carpenter, plomer, and fmith, are the mechanics imployed.

	£.	s.	d.
A lode of lombe —— —	0	0	4
Laborers per day — —	0	0	10
Bufhell and ½ of tyle pynnes —	0	0	9
Dawber's laborer 3 days — —	0	1	3

	£.	s.	d.
Paide to *Chriftopher Bechen*, for a p̃ * of tymber, containing 11 feate	0	1	10
Item, to *William Pavys*, for werkmanfhipp and fettyng of the fepulcre, —— ——	0	3	8
Item, for a plannk's ende for the one ende ——	0	0	6
Item, for a fmall quart next the wall behynde the fepulcre,	0	0	2
Item, to the fmyth for 13 pynnes yryn, —— —	0	0	3
Summa, ——	0	6	6

1497.

It was agreed by Mr. Parfon †, Mr. Alderman ‡, and divers others of the parifhioners, that the clark and churchwardens from that time fhould take for any knyell of the grete bell 6*s*. 8*d*. i. e. to either of them 40*d*.; for the knyell of the fecond bell rynging only an hour the clark to take 12*d*.; and for ½ a day 40*d*. only to himfelf; and for the lyttle or firft bell, for a man 8*d*. for a child 4*d*.; for a pytt in the chirche 2*s*.; and for a pytt in the Pardon § church-yard, for a man 8*d*. for a child

* Piece. All this apparatus was to clofe the fepulcre on Eafter-eve; during which one or more men were hired to watch it, in allufion to the foldiers. From this and other accounts of the fepulchre in thefe regifters, it appears to have been here at leaft a temporary erection, perhaps a cheft of wood, and not fixt againft the north wall of the choir as part of the building, as in the churches of Northwold, Norfolk, and Hackington, Lincolnfhire. At Abyngdon fomething of this temporary kind was made of ftone 1559, and coft 17*s*. 6*d*.; whereas in this church it did not exceed 5*s*.

† Either William Wyld, or William Atclyff.

‡ William Remington, alderman of the ward of Billingfgate. See p. 88.

§ We have two more fuch places in London mentioned by Stowe: one the area of the great cloyfter on the north fide of St. Paul's (355); the other the cemitery inclofed by Bifhop Stratford near the Charter-houfe, for the perfons who died of the plague 1348. Both thefe places had chapels in them. Perhaps this regifter firft difcovers a third of the name diftinct from the other or Great church-yard. The burial-fees too feem to be different and lefs.

4*d*.;

4*d.*; and ſo likewiſe in the Grete church-yard.

1500	is expreſſed	m. v. c.
1501	—	m. v. ci.
1502	—	xvxii.
1503	—	xviii.

May fyſt, the yere of King Henry the Sixth, after the conqueſt x°.

Fyſt, a cowpe of ſilver and gold to lay in Goddes body with criſtall.

A cowpe of ſilver for Goddes body. [Theſe are plainly paxes wherein to keep the hoſt].

iii paxbredes of ſylver gilt.

ii ſheppis of ſylver *.

a lytill cofyr with relekys †.

Among the caſuell receiptes from 17 Edward IV. to 19 Edward IV. are,

For the bemelight ‡ in the ſaid ii yeres, —	2	2	0
Waſte of ii tapers at Cauſton's obit, — —	1	5	4
So of ditto at the other obits.			
An empty hoggiſhede ſold to *William Proyne*, —	0	0	6
An olde graveſtone § ſold to .... —	0	6	8
For ryngyng the grete bell for *Thomas Henllis*, —	0	3	4
Burying ditto in the church, — — —	0	13	4
Burying Syr *Thomas Wilkynſon*, preſte, in the church, —	0	13	4
Burying a ſtrange man in the church-yard, —	0	3	4
Of *John Jacob*, for the obſervaunce in the church for a Spaynarde that was ſlayne, — — — — —	0	5	0

Parcellis receyved for burying of 9 corſes in the Pardon church-yard at 2*s.* each: and for *John Clerke's* doghter 4*s.*

Among the Coſtes.

Paid to *William Paris*, for beryng of the grete boke to Sir *William Palmer's* chambre, to write another boke by yt, —	0	0	4
To a veſtment-maker, for the mendyng of the blake copes, and of all other copes that were fawty, by 14 days, taking by the day 9*d.*	0	10	6

* A ſhippe for frankincenſe. Abingdon Churchwardens' Accompts. Archæol. I. 12. In Catholic rituals this is now called *navicula*. William Bruges, by will 1449, bequeathed, among other plate, to the church of St. George in Stamford, "a ſhip of ſylver for frankincence, and 1 "ſpone in the ſame ſhype of ſylver." Peck's Annals, XIV. p. 25.

† See ſuch an one engraved in Vetuſta Monumenta of the Society of Antiquaries, II. pl. 51 and 52.

‡ The light before the *rood-beam.*

§ Wee ſee here graveſtones ſold long before the Reformation; conſequently all the ſacrilege of ſuch outrages is not to be charged on the ſpirit that then prevailed.

N Mendyng

	£.	s.	d.
Mendyng a chayne to a boke in the quere 2*d.*; makyng of a bawdryk and a nywe bokyll to the lytill bell 8*d.* ———	0	10	0
Scowryng, amendyng, and gyldyng of a crosse, —	0	5	0
Six dozen of talow candill spent in diverse servyse doon in the church withyn the tyme of the account, and in wacching the churche,	0	6	5
To *William Preyne*, for XVIII galons of oil spent in lampis in the churche, — — — —	0	16	0
1489, 19 gallons of sweete oyl, at 1*s.* 4*d.* per gallon, —	0	5	4
To *William Paris*, for watching in the church 16 nights in time of making the vestry, —— — —	0	1	4
For brede and ale bought of the *Wyfe of the Bell* *, —	0	1	1
For nywe wax for the use of the church as in beme-light tapers, prykkets, and candillis, weighing 92 lb. at 4½*d.* per lb. —	1	14	8
Paid the wax-chandlyr for making the whole in tapers, &c. and tenebre candils † at ½*d.* per lb. ——— ———	0	11	9
To ditto for the Pascall taper for 2 yeres, each yere weighing 30lb. at 1*d.* per lb. ——— ——— ———	0	5	0
And for the waste of the same in the 2 yeres, being 5lb. for every 4½*d.* —— ——— ——	0	1	10½
William Paris, for takyng down of the crosse upon the stepull,	0	0	2
For birch at Midsomer 8*d.*; box and palme on Palmesonday 1*s.*; polis on Estir-evyne 10*d.*; garlondes on Corpus Christi-day 10*d.*; to 10 men to bere the torches 9*d.*; for rose-garlondis and wodrove- ‡ garlondis on Saynt Barnebes day, 11*d.*			
For 3 mattis of wicker bought for prestis and clarkis, —	0	0	4
To *Wat. Pleasance*, for playing at the organ, ——	0	0	6
For mending the capis § of the organs, — —	0	0	8
To 4 children of St. Magnus, for ringing ———	0	0	4
For 4 cwts. of hertlaths **, the cwt. at 5*d.* ——	0	1	8
A lode of lome to ovircast the floore ‖ in *Levisham's* hows,	0	0	4
For 3 dozen *tukkyn* gyrdlis for the 2 yeres, — —	0	2	0

* The landlady of the Bell-alehouse before mentioned.

† Candles used at the service called *Tenebræ.* ‡ Q. Wood*bine.* § Q. caps.

** Laths of *heart* of oak.

‖ The floors of the upper rooms in the old part of the abbey-house at Waltham, built by Sir Edward Denny, were *overcast* in this manner with a coarse plaister of sand and pebbles, forming a crust of above an inch thick, coloured deep red like a bright brick-floor. The same rude rough-cast or stucco-floors are retained in some parts of Lincoln and Yorkshires. We have here, 1485, paid the dawber for *teryfing* [terrassing] *of floris*, per day 8*d.*

21 Edward

	£.	s.	d.
21 Edward IV. Reparacions of the Lumbardys Place *, and of other tenements in *Fawster Lane.*			
Twenty-three gallons of oyle spende in this church, and a potell of oyle, the gallon 1*s.* — — —	1	3	6
The churchwardens charge for expences, giving to the tenants at receiving the rents, in potacions among them, and wayting on the workmen one yere, ——— ——— ———	0	10	5
For attending the church-work one year, — —	0	6	8
Then comes the account for 1483; followed by that for 1487.			
For holme and yve anenst Crist †, ——— ———	0	0	1
Three dozen and ½ talugh candels for the quere, the dozen 1*s.* 3*d.*	0	3	4
Scouring the latten candelstycks, standards, branches, bolles ‡ upon the beame anenst Estir, ———	0	1	11
A quart' coles § ayenst Ester, ——— —	0	5	5
A dozen and ½ rose garlondes on St. Barnebes' day, ———	0	0	8½

The paper in this book is marked with a hand displayed erect, a quatrefoil on the point of the middle finger, a bull's head cabost, between the horns ☓: a unicorn trotting, is that of the year 1483; another walking, his horn horizontal 1491; a hand as before, with a rose of 6 leaves, or mullet of 5, pierced.

* Stowe [p. 217.) says, the Lombards or Florentine merchants met in a house abutting south on Lombard street, and north on Cornhill, confirmed to them by Edward II. May not this *Lumbardy's place* have been destined to the like use in the reign of Edward IV. in another part of the town.

Toward the end of the account of the same churchwardens is the following article:

" Item, paid to John Carpenter for his good wyll, to be shewed in the byldyng of the Lumbardis place, in *St. Botolph's Lane*, 6*s.* 8*d.*

1483—5. Gabriel de Urs, merchaunte de Venes, held the great Lombard's Place here at £13. 6*s.* 8*d.* *per annum.*

The last article in their account is the following:

" Delyvyd to Gabriel Lombarde, clerk, tenaunte in Botolf-lane, inn olde lede c. weyghte."

This same tenement was occupied by Lewis Lumbarde, in the accompts of the preceding churchwardens.

In 1496, received of Benet Tople, Lombarde, for the great place of Botolph-lane, £13. 6*s.* 8*d.*

† Holly and ivy against Christmas.

‡ These *Bolles* were probably the plates or bosses fastened against the rood loft, into which the candlesticks were fixed.

§ Bishop Fleetwood, Chron. Prec. p. 118, says coals are always to be understood *Charcoal*, which in 1551 was 12*s.* per load. If the measure here means a quarter of a load, it must have been almost as dear at this time. But 1529, here is a charge of 1*s.* 2*d.* for two quarters of *Charcole* for the fount. *Quarter* is the measure for coals in the Wardrobe Account of Edw. I. p. 119.

N 2 From

From the Broad Book.

Thefe ben the parcellis of paymentis made be *Wilham Gelam* and *John Gretyng*, wardeyns of the chirche of Seint Marie at the Hille, begynnyng at the fefte of Efter, the yer of the regne of Kyng Herry the Sixte after the Conqueft, v°.

	£.	s.	d.
Fyft, payd for the fepulcre for divers naylis and wires, and glu,	o	o	9½
Alfo payd to *Thomas Joynes* (Q. Joiner) for makyng of the fame fepulcre,	o	4	o
For a piece of tymbre to the newe Pafcall *,	o	2	o
For bokeram for the peñons, and for the makynge,	o	1	10
For betyng † and fteynynge of the fame peñons,	o	o	6
For a dysfh of peuter for the Pafcall,	o	o	8
For pynnes of iron for the fame Pafcall,	o	o	4
For a rolle and 2 gaioñs ‡ of iron, and a rope,	o	1	2
For a lode of ftone for the door of the rode lofte,	o	6	2
To 3 carpenters remoynge the ftallis of the quayr,	o	1	8
For vi peny nail and v peny nayl,	o	o	11
For crochyts and 3 iron pynnes and a ftaple,	o	1	1
For 2 yardes and a half of grene bokram,	o	3	3½
For lengthyng of 2 cheynes, and 6 yards of gret wyre,	o	1	2
To the Lavender ‖ for a whole yere wafhing and fowing,	o	o	2
Alfo payd to the rakar,	o	o	2
Alfo payd for carage to a carter,	o	o	3
Alfo paid for xx/xi pavyng tyle,	o	3	4
Alfo for making of a peire endentos § betwene *William Serle*, carpenter, and us, for the rode-lofte and the . . . . . clerk's chambre,	o	2	8
Alfo for cariage of 3 lode tymbre,	o	1	o
Alfo the xx day of May, 2 carpenters **,	o	1	5
Alfo the xxi day, 3 carpenters **,	o	2	1

The accompts of *John Prewne* and *John Halhed*, churchwardens, from Michaelmas, 1 Henry VII. to Michaelmas following; beginning with arrearages that *Herry Vavefour*, a former churchwarden, left in detturs hands.

N. B. *Harry Vavefour* and *John Baker* were churchwardens from Michaelmas 1483 to 1485.

* It is hard to fay what this *Pafcall* was: nor have we any parallel inftance whereby to illuftrate. The materials would make one conjecture it was a *rood* or *crofs* for that particular folemnity, perhaps made *new* this year after fome long ftanding.

† In the charges for Henry V's funeral (Rymer, X. 256.) is for *betyng* (vapulatione) efcocheons, vallans, &c. Sepulch. Mon. II. 91. This fenfe of *vapulatio* is not in the Gloffaries.

‡ *Gudgeons* is ftill a technical term for *hinges*.

‖ Launder, i. e. wafherwoman, who was alfo fempftrefs. § Pair of indentures.

** In Edward I's accompts, carpenters had 4*d*. a day; mafter carpenters had but 4*d*. a day, and others 3*d*. in Fleetwood's Chron. Prec. 156. Their pay doubled in a century.

Dettys

	£.	s.	d.
Dettys for bequefts, pyttys [graves], and knyllys [knolls].			
Maifter *Kives* oweth for the ground in St. Stephen's chapel for his fonn's wiff, — — — —	5	13	4
Johane Staverton, for the grounde in the Pardon chirch-yard,	5	2	0
John Baker's wif, for the grete bell, — —	8	13	4
Item, for the grounde in the chirche, — —	8	13	4
Thomas Hunte, for a knyll with the great bell, —	8	3	4
Alfo for tymbre and eftrich borde * for gynnes and wyndowes,	0	2	4½
Carriage of 2 lode ftone, — — —	0	0	11
Four munells † for windowes, — —	0	0	5
Alfo the Thorfday in the Whitfon weke, at the refynge of the fame chambre, in bred and ale, and 2 ribbes of beff ‡, and our coftes, — — — — —	0	1	4
A bufhell tyle pynnes, — — —	0	0	8
A tyler and his man, — — — —	0	1	2
m. m. m. tile and the carriage, — —	0	1	6
Four hundred long hert ‖ latthes per the hundred 7*d.* —	0	2	4
A dawber and his man, — — —	0	1	2
A goter betwene the church and the chambre, weyeng 126 lb.	0	10	6
A pavior and his man to pave in Love-lane at the weft-dore,	0	2	11
To fir *John* and ... for raluenge the auter clothis, —	0	0	4
Glymesford and his felowes, to make the fteyer § at a weke,	0	8	6
A pound pychor for lygt to the werkmen, —	0	0	1½
The ftone of fir *William Sparke* **, — —	1	3	4
Glymesford's table 9 days, every day 2*d.* — —	0	18	0
Certeyne pavynge and mendynge of pewes in the churche,	0	7	9
Bryngynge owte donge of the Pardon chirche-hawe to the raker,	0	0	2
For lodyng away of a cart-full of the fame donge, —	0	0	4
ix C. x of great pavyng tyle, per c. 5 or 6*d.* —	2	9	6
To the lauender for waffching of divers clothis, —	0	0	2
For buryinge the kerchiefe launder's †† doghter in the Pardon church-yard, — — —	0	2	0
For waffching of 2 aubis and amys, — —	0	0	3
Keyenge of a gate of fton 8 fote of heyghte withynne, boght of *William Gemet*, mafon, and the fote of thicknes clene appareled the geft III fote thicknes, alfo with the coynes withynne and withowte as many as be nedful to the fame gate, and alfo a bafe 6 fote, —	1	15	0

* *Eftrege bord*, wainfcot. Kennet, Par. Antiq. p. 575. Q. if the fame with *Eaftland bordæ*, in Edward the Firft's accompts, p. 119; or *bordæ de Eftland*. Rymer, IV. 730.

† Q. if mullions, or mu*n*ions?

‡ N. B. Ribs of beef are elfewhere charged.

‖ Q. if fo called becaufe fplit out of the *heart* of oak.

§ Stair.

** Parfon, 1420.

†† Q. was this a wafherwoman of finer linen, or a millener?

Whereof

	£.	s.	d.
Whereof I paid him in hande, 0 6 8 } Sum 1 15 0			
Alſo I paid him after that, 1 8 4 }			
Alſo for cariage of 2 lode from *Cambrigge's* * kay ladyng and unladyng, — — — — —	0	1	2
A lode from the Tour-wharf, ladyng and unladyng, —	0	0	8
A lode from Baynard's caſtel, ladyng and unladyng, —	0	0	8
A carpenter IIII dayes to amende the pewes ‡‡ where the olde font ſtode, takyng 6*d*. and his men a day, —	0	2	8
Makyng of IIII polefis of bras and iron work and lede that ſerved for the vayl, — — — —	0	5	8
Thirty-eight yards of liſte for the vayl, — —	0	1	1
For ſewynge and *trymming* [hem̄ynge] of the ſame vayl and rynges,	0	1	0
For echyng †† of the ſame veil 10 elnes of lynnen cloth, ꝑ the elne 8½*d*. — — — —	0	7	7
To *Richard Botelar*, for a lede ſten for the corbel † and the rode lofte, — — — —	0	6	2
For hewing of the ſame corbel, — — —	0	4	4
A maſon and his man 3 days, for ſettyng up of the ſame corbel ‡,	0	0	5
For 2 carpenters mendynge § the ſepulchre a day and more,	0	1	0
Makyng clene the churche and the aley, —	0	0	1
To *Apulby* for hewing the halywat' ſtop ‖, — —	0	0	4
Paid to *Serle* for the rode lofte, —	36	0	0
Serle, for ſtalles in the quer, — — —	12	0	0
Four garnetts to the quere dore with the nayles, —	0	14	4
A laborer a day **, — — —	0	0	5
Two ſtaplis and 2 lokes to the fonte ‡‡, — —	0	1	0
Eight ſtaplis, and 4 haſpis, and 3*d*. naill, — —	0	1	0
Pynnyng a wall and dawbing, — — —	0	2	0

* Probably the property of John Cambridge, who was buried, and had a chantry in this church.

‡‡ It was no uncommon thing to incloſe the fonts in caſes or tabernacles of wood curiouſly carved, as they are now in ſome old churches ſurrounded by a large pew, which is here mentioned in the preceding page.

†† Ekeing, lengthening, or piecing.

† A load of ſtone for making niches for images; *Corbels* are ſtones wherein images ſtand. Gloſſary to Urry's Chaucer. This was probably for the *ſcreen*.

‡ The daily pay of a maſter-maſon in 1351 was but 3d. and of a journeyman 2d. Fleetwood's Chron. Prec. 159. In Edward the Firſt's accompts a maſon had 4*d* a day.

§ By this it ſhould ſeem the ſepulchre was fixed, or at leaſt portable, and ſerved as long as it would hold together.

‖ *Stop* or *ſtoup* is the antient technical term for a ſtone veſſel for holy-water. See Blomefield's Norfolk.

** A labourer's daily pay with diet was 2d. without diet 3½d. in 1389, in the country. Fleetwood's Chron. Prec. 161. In London, in the ſpace of a century, it was almoſt double. For I preſume this pay is to be underſtood to exclude diet.

Three

	£.	s.	d.
Three sakkes of lyme, — — — —	0	0	6
Five roff* tyle, — — — —	0	0	4
Lodyng away of robys † in a lyghter, —	0	1	4
Washing and amendyng of aubys and surplys, ——	0	0	2
Paid for 4 Evangelists makyng and kervynge, ——	0	11	8
For makyng a childe's cope of cloth of golde and the orpharis ‡ of blue velvet, — — — —	0	1	0
Makyng a cope of grene bays, with an orpharas of chekered werke,	0	1	0
1491. 1492. Costis spent in the laws agenst the priores § of St. Elyn, for *John Cawston's* chauntrye, —— —	14	6	4½
Item, paid unto *Foux* of the geld halle ‖ for the testament of *J. Cawston*, — —	0	0	4
Item, paid to Mr. *Wode*, serjaunt **, ———	0	3	4
Item, paid to Mr. *Saull* and Mr. *Marow*, [each] —	0	3	4
Item, that *Mylton* and I spent to Lambeth, ———	0	3	0½
Item, to Mr. *Wode*, Mr. *Sawle*, and Mr. *Marow*, the 23d of November, [each] — —	0	10	0
Item, that was spent upon them, ——	0	0	11
Item, to Mr. *Morden*, for the same cawse, —	0	3	4
Item, to Mr. Master *Morden* and to Mr. *Marow*, [each]	0	6	8
Item, for copying out of the testament to Mr. *Marow's* clarke,	0	3	4
Item, paid to *John Purfoote*, clark of the mayor's court, for copying out of the testament of *J. Cawston*, —	0	6	8
Item, spent be Mr. *Plomere* and *John Mylton*, for going to Westminster, and to my Lourd Bryant's ††, and also at the King's Hed, and at the Sent Jone's hed, ——	0	2	3
Item, to Mr. *Wod*, ———	0	3	4
Item, to Mr. *Morden*, ———	0	3	4
Item, to my Lourd Cheff Justice §§ and to my Lourd *Bryant*, [each]	0	13	4
Item, to Mr. *Morden* and Mr. *Marowe*, —	0	6	8
1492, Item, spent for our part of the dyner when my Lourd *Hussy* ‡‡ and my Lourd Bryant was at the Cardnall's hall agenst the Priories of St. Olyv's, ——	0	18	11

* Roof or ridge tile. † Rubbish.

‡ Orfrays in Chaucer's Romaunt of the Rose, 562. 869. is explained in Speght's Glossary *Aurifrisium*, frizled cloth of gold. Du Cange explains it a *gold fringe*, particularly on ecclesiastical vestments. It seems here to mean a *fringe* in general.

§ Mr. Causton left the reversion of his lands, &c. to *the Prioress and Convent* of the honour of St. Elyn within Bishoppesgate, charged with the expence of finding a chauntry-priest, &c. in the church of St. Mary Hill. ‖ Guildhall.

** Thomas Wode was called to the degree of serjeant Nov. 20, 1486. Claus. 1 Henry VII. p. 1. Dugd. ubi supr. p. 75. He was King's serjeant 1488. Ib.

†† Sir Thomas *Bryant* was chief justice of the King's Bench, 1486. Ib.

§§ Q. Thomas Tremayle, chief justice of the Common Pleas. Dugd. Chron. ser. sub an.

‡‡ Sir William Huse was chief justice of the Common Pleas, 1486. Dugd. Ib.

1492. Item,

	£.	s.	d.
Item, for a dyn' was made laſt for my Lourd Cheff Juſtice and my Lord Bryant, for on thing and others that went thereto, ———	0	4	10
Item, for a ronlett of malmuſeyn * gevyn unto Mr. *Plomer*, and for the barell, ———	0	12	7
Sum tot. —	6	3	5½
1485. Received for hire of the garments for pageants †, —	0	1	8
Received of *John Ruſſel* ‡, in that we have appointed his abſenting from the dyvyne ſervice for a yere upon certain holydays, ——— ———	0	2	0
For two men workyng, &c. and *tranſlating* of St. Stephen's chapel-door, &c.			
For five *teyſe* of new pavement, at 7*d*. a *teyſe*, ———	0	2	11
For two gallons of wyne, red and claret, given to the abbot of Waltham, and to ſir Thomas Bowghſer §, for that they ſhould have been good benefactors to our church in divers things, ——— ———	0	1	8
Delivered to *Alexander Worſley*, clerk, for to ride to ſpeak with ſir William Palmer, for the antiphoner that he hath to write, — — —	0	6	8
1486. Nine ells of Hollande clothe for a ſurplyſe and rochet, at 7*d*. per ell, ——— ———	0	5	3
Makyng the ſame, ——— ———	0	2	0
1489. Ale and brede on our Lady-day the Aſſumption, ———	0	0	3
[This ſeems the grand feſtival here.]			
1489. For the halowing of a veſtment, ———	0	0	6
In coſtes for two children for three quarters of a yere: 1*s*. is allowed for 3 pair of ſhoes *for the time:* 3 pair for another child coſt 1*s*. 2*d*. In the former yere a new doublet for one of them coſt 1*s*. 4*d*.; clouting 3 pair of ſhoes 4*d*.; two ſhirts 1*s*. 3*d*.; a cap 10*d*.; one yard of black and one yard of blanket 1*s*.; ¾ of an ell of canvas for a doublet 2¼*d*.; 2 yards of blue 6*s*.; 4 yards of white freeze 2*s*. 3*d*.			
1491. For a quart of *baſtard* on Chriſtmas-day, ———	0	0	4½
For two pair of *pattens* for the prieſts —	....		

* Malmeſey was £4. per *Gallon* 1502; Somner's Canterb. App. p. 27, two quarts of it 8*d*. 1551; Stow in Fleetwood's Chron. Prec. p. 118, four gallons of this wine are charged 5*s*. 4*d*. 1529, i. e. 16*d*. per gallon.

† This is a pageant unnoticed by the hiſtorians in the ſecond year of Richard III.

‡ Perhaps ſome chantry prieſt.

§ Q. Fifth ſon of Henry Boorchier, firſt earl of Eſſex, who married Iſabel daughter and heir of ſir John Bane, knight, relict of Humphrey Stafford earl of Devon. Dugd. Bar. II. 130.

	£.	s.	d.
Thefe cofts are repeated the next year; and there is charged for 10 gallons of maumfey fent to the Lords Bryan and Huffey, at 10*d.* per gallon, £1. 6*s.* 8*d.*; and for two runletts of the fame wyn 2*s.* 8*d*; to the two porters to bear it 4*d.*; a gofe 2*d.*; and a dozen of larks fent to them to the bifhop of Elye his place 1*s.* 9*d.*			
For a pottel of Ranyfhe wyn, ditto of red wyn fent to them the fame time, — —	0	1	0
More cofts of law on the above fuit £3. 2*s.* 10*d.* have among other articles:			
Paid for our part of 4 difhes of mete that was fent to my Lords Huffey and Bryan, —	0	2	8
1493. For ditto of a mefs of meat fent to ditto on St. Mark's day,	0	2	5
For a reward for our part to ditto May, —	1	0	0
For bote hire *, and other expences at Weftminfter, weere we gede to fpeke with ditto, July 10, —	0	0	6
To the Suffragan of *London*, for halowyng St. Stephen's awter,	0	10	4
To the King's amener for ferzght † of *rynging off the belle agenft the Kynge*, — —	0	4	10
For makyng the croffys on the fup altarys, —	0	0	4
For a bokfkynne, —	0	3	4
For makyng the fpere ‡ at St. Thomas's altar,	0	0	2
For two Alywat' fprygs §, —	0	0	2
1496. Received of Mr. *Fabyan* for M. ‖ tyle, —	0	5	0
Paid to *Adrian*, glafyer in St. Thomas's fpital, for 5 windows of the clereftorye, and for a reft for the wyndoe at the high awter, and for 6 fmall ymages, —	1	11	8
1497. Cofts paid for peynting of the roodes, with karvyng and odir cofts alfo:			
Furft, paid at the note takyng of the endentures of cooñands,	0	0	2
Item, to Sir *John Plomer*, for makyng of the fyngyrrs of the roade, — —	0	1	8
Item, to the karvars for makỹg of III dyadems, and of oon of the Evangelifts, and for mendỹg the roode **, the croffe,			

* Boat hire to Weftminfter and back again in 1496 was 1*s.* † Q. forfeit.

‡ Spire. § Holywater fprinklers. ‖ 1000.

** Dr. Ward obferves that *rood* is applied to the *image* of faints, as of Mary and John, and even of St. Helen in the Abingdon accompts; and Dr. Morell appeals to Junius in confirmation hereof. But the words of the regifter are by no means capable of the fenfe affigned them by the firft of thefe able critics. "The roode, Mary and John, with the patron of the church," evidently mean diftinct images of the Crucifix, Mary, John, and Helen. With deference to fuch authority as Junius, the Saxon ufe of the word ꞃoꝺ confines it to the crofs or crucifix. But in this place of our accompts *rood* can mean only the rood-loft. In the Waltham accounts we have "Mary and John that ftand in the Rood-loft." Fuller's Hift. of Waltham Abbey, p. 17.

O the

		£.	s.	d.
	the Mary and John, the crown of thorn, with all odir fawts, — —	0	10	0
	Item, to *Undirwood*, for peynting and gyldyng of the roode, the croſſe, Mary and John, the IIII Evangeliſts, and the III dyadems, with the nobills that I owe to him in money £5. —— —	5	11	10
	For ſprigge * and lathe [among dauber's work],	0	0	5
	For 6 ells of Normandy clothe for the clark's ſurplice, and for whitning the ſame, ——	0	3	3
	For bred, ale, and a rybb of bief, ſpent at the Caſtell in Fiſh-ſtreet, on diverſe of the pariſhioners, at the viſitation of the biſhop in St. Magnus church, —	0	0	8
1498.	For mendyng of the monſtyr † for the ſacrament, —	0	1	4
1499.	For the waching of the ſepulchre and the chirche to III men,	0	1	0
	For brede and ale to them that wached, ——	0	0	6
	For a lampe and for tentyr hookes to the ſepulcre,	0	0	1½
	For two rybbs of bief, and for bred and ale, to the wyvys yn the pariſh that gathered on Hokmonday ‡, ——	0	1	1
	For a creſſet § to *Rooſe Wrytell's* chantry, ——	0	0	4
1500.	A pair of awngell wyngs and 3 diadems ‖ were ſold for	0	1	2
	The paſcalls [Eaſter offerings] for this year (the only one in which they are ſummed up) amounted to ——	9	14	11
	For II C. of ſarpe lathe, ——	0	0	8
	For XI ſpytt, —— ——	0	0	6
	For III C. of Spaniſh nailes, ——	0	1	3
	For II C. of 5*d*. nailes Engelyſh, ——	0	0	8
	For II plats for a whell berow, ——	0	0	2
	Paid to Mr. *Suklyng*, for coſts ſpent to the abbot of Waltham at the abbot's maner, ——	0	0	3
	Paid in coſts ſpent when Mr. *Suklyng*, *Thomas Hunt*, *Robert Hotyng*, *Thomas Tolynds*, at their rydyng to Waltham to ſpeke with the abbot for the kechen, —	0	8	7
	Spent at the abbott's inn on Mr. *Wryne*, Mr. *Sucklyng*, *R. Howtyng*, when we began to make a note for the ſeed-ground, —— ——	0	0	5
	To Mr. *Marow*, at my Lord-mayor's houſe, when the abbot's councell were there to over-run the note, ——	0	3	4
	To *Thomas Sharpe*, for writing the note that was devyſed by us at the abbott's inn, ——	0	0	8

* Q. if *ſprigge* means reeds or ruſhes.

† The Oſtenſorium.

‡ A like charge in the accompts of the churchwardens of Lambeth ſee in Archæol. VII. 251. ubi vide plura.

§ A ſocket for a candle.

‖ Probably made of metal, and gilt.

1500. To

	£.	s.	d.
1500. To ditto, for writing a new copy of the note after Mayfter *Marow* and Maifter *Grene* had enterlyned hit, —	0	0	4
Spent at the abbot's at dyvers tymes upon Maifter *Wren* and divers of the parifhioners, ——	. . .	. . .	. . .
Expences at Waltham, when the good [man] *Howtyng* and I rode for the convent feale, ——	0	0	9
To *George Nicholls*, for writing the note and the indenture, and two fingle obligacions betwyne the abbot and his convent and us, ——	0	5	0

N. B. This was on the purchafe of the abbot's kitchen here to build the fouth aile, at which time *Alice Hackney's* body came to light. The parifh paid an original quitrent of 10*s*. to Waltham abbey for ever. At the fame time was begun the fteeple at the weft end: and there is a charge of 4*d*. a night to certain men fet to watch the church 14 weeks, while the weft end was broken down for this purpofe, with 1*d*. for brede and ale, and 2 lb. of candle weekly.

	£.	s.	d.
1501. For paper ryal to pricke fonges in for the quere, —	0	0	7
For the fubfidy to the King for the chirche rents, — In 1503 it was £1. 18*s*. 10*d*.	15	3	11½
1502. To 6 pore men for beryng and holdyng of 6 torches in Faenchirche-ftreet, whan Quene Elizabeth * was karyn to Weftminfter, — — —	0	1	0
For ryngyng of our bellys whan the Kyng came from Baynard's caftle to Panelle †, ——	0	0	3
For two pair of indentures and two obligacions for *Hickeling* [the carpenter] for performing our new ifle, —	0	2	0
He had for the roof of this ifle, ——	11	3	4
For rydyng to Shoreham for to fee tymber, and hyryng three horfes, and horfe mete, and marys mete, —	0	6	7
For a pike fent to my Lord Abbot of Waltham to the abbot's inn, —— ——	0	2	8
For a turbot ditto, ——	0	1	8
To a fervant of ditto for a reward for bringing venifon,	0	1	8
For the baking ditto and pepper, ——	0	1	9
For weighing up the hye awter ftone hier, ——	0	5	0
1506. On a treat of the mayor, fheriffs, and fword-bearer, at Cambridge's obit, the total of which amounted to —	1	8	7

* Elizabeth, queen of Henry VII. died Feb. 11, 1503, in child-bed in the Tower, having been delivered of a daughter, Elizabeth, who died foon after her mother. She was buried at Weftminfter in Henry VII's chapel.

† Q. Paul's.

	£.	s.	d.
1506. Among other articles,			
For a dozen fpycyd bred, ——	o	1	6
For butter and eggs, fpyces, and good ale, ——	o	2	4
For two dozen de white bunnys for pore pepyll, —	o	2	6
For three gallons and a quart Gafkon wine, ——	o	2	2
For a quart of redd wyn, ——	o	o	3
For a kylderkyn good ale, ——	o	2	o
For 2 C. *Pers*, ——	o	o	8
For hyryng three gallon pots to bere drinke about the chirche for the pepyl of the parifh, ——	o	o	1
[which is the deceafed's wyll; and he that fpendyth more to pay it out of his own purfe without any allowance.]			

This year *Evyngar* was fenior churchwarden, as he had been junior 1502.

	£.	s.	d.
1503. For 5 C. of fprigg, ——	o	o	3
For 25 foote of Efer * borde, ——	o	o	8
For box at the hallowyng of the cherche to wafhe the auttyr [at Chriftmas] ——	o	o	1
For to the fuffragan's man for the barrellys and tubbys, [that contained the ale and wine fpent in hallowing the church.]	o	o	4
For 12 elles of bryffell to make creffoms for the ballys,	o	o	5
Spent at the abbot's in, at the ettyng of a bok † that my Lorde Abbot of Valttom gauf to the parifhe, ——	o	1	8
For three ellys and quarter of Normandy canvas to make large the lentty clothe for the hey auttyr, ——	o	1	5½
For making the pulpitt with nayles [2*d.*] and ftuffe [6*d.*]	o	13	8
1503. For veffels for the ftaynyng of the fam clothe, ——	o	3	4
Spent at etyng at Mr. Alderman's a bok given to the parifh by the Lord Abbot of Waltham, ——	o	9	8
For fettyng of the corttens heyyr to the hey auttyr, —	o	o	3
For menddyng of a nafk at Seynt Jonny's auttyr, —	o	o	1
To a marbler for fettyng of 4 emagys, ——	o	3	4
For bromys for the churche, ——	o	o	o½
Spent upon the workmen in the church on bred and ale,	o	o	4
For tynyng of a peyyer ef fmaull garnetts, ——	o	o	1
For mendyng and ftellyng ‡ of the mattock, ——	o	o	2
For a C. of reede for the wynddow, ——	o	o	10
For thred and for reddyng of the wynddow, ——	o	o	5
1504. Received of Mr. *Develyn* towards the makyng a *pentowes* § over his father's tombe, ——	o	2	o

* Q. *Eftrige* as before, p. 97. † Buck.
‡ Steeling. § Q. a canopy in the church, or a penthoufe out of it.

1509. For

		£.	s.	d.
1509.	For watyr for the funt on Wytfon-yevyn, ——	. . .	. . .	. . .
	Paid to fevyn men that rong the bellis when the Kingis' grace * went to Weftmyfter to be crownyd, ——	0	1	2
	For byrche for the chyrche at Mydefomer, ——	0	0	4
1504.	To the bokebynder at Ledon Halle, for covering, bynding, and pefyng 4 antiphors, a book, a manuell, a legend, 2 folomes, and 3 grayles, —	2	6	8
1510.	For 6 breke † for mendyng a chemeney, ——	0	0	8
	To Maifter *Darby*, for the bederolle for a yere, —	0	2	0
	For three dozen of coten candill for the quere and the morowe maffe for all the yere, —	0	3	6
	For a cruet for the morowe maffe, ——	0	0	4
	For watur of Mawndy Thurfday and Eftur ewe, —	0	0	1
	For diffeplynyng, roddis, and nayles, for the fepulchre,	0	0	2
1506.	Paid to *Nicholas Betnam*, mafon, of Ottam, in Kent, yn part of payment for the battlement of the fouth fide of the church, ——	3	0	0
1513.	he had £.26. for this and that of the middle ifle.			
1510.	For freight of a lode of coynes [ftones] from Maydefton,	0	1	2
	For two galons wyne gevyn to the fyngers of the King's chapell at Mr. Sidborought's at dynner, ——	0	1	4
	For a lode of breke fpent in the ufe of the vyfe on the fouth fide, ——	0	2	6
	[The church feems to have been repairing, and we read of fcaffolds on the fouth fide.]			
	Boathyre to Grenewich for *J. Althorpe* and *N. Betnaham* ‡ to fpeke with Mr. Hatclyff §, ——		0	0
	Paid the baker for a hole yere for the churche, ——	0	0	8
	Received of the gaderynge of Hobmonday and Tewifday ‖,	1	12	6
	Received for a rufty harnes ** that was fold, —	0	3	0
	For palme flowrys and cake on Palme-Sonday, —	0	0	10
	For brede and drynke on Goodfriday at dynner and at night 3*d*. and on Eftur-eve for dynner and at night 5*d*. fumma	0	0	8
	For naylis for the fepulcre, ——	0	0	1½
	For brede and drynk to hym that ftrake the bells, —	0	0	2
	For ftrekyng of the two bells to the grownde, ——	0	2	0
	For a C. of fmale ropis for to ftreke the bells —	0	10	0
	For drynke to the porters that hope to ftryke the bells,	0	0	2
	For the carriage of two belles to the founder's, —	0	2	0
	For fix porters to help them to the flede ††, ——	0	0	6
	For brede, ale, and wyne, at the Feft of Transfiguration,	0	0	4

* Henry VIII. † Bricks. ‡ The mafon. § The parfon.
‖ See before, p. 102. ** Q. ? Coat of mail hung up in the church. †† Sledge.

1510. For

	£.	s.	d.
1510. For brede, ale, and wyne, on Allhollowes day in the vestry,	0	0	6
For wyne at the Salutacyon * at the bargeyne makyng for the frame of the belle, —	0	0	7
For the obligacyon makyng for the bergeyne, —	0	0	4
For the goddis peny in hande †, —	2	0	0
To *William Howtyng*, for a waynscot, —	0	1	2
For sawing of the waynscot for the bell whelis, —	0	0	6
For IX C. fote of plauncke bourde, per Ct. the carriage,	1	0	5
Received for the burial of an armyte ‡, —	0	2	0

1509. For a soper to Mr. *Kyght* and Mr. *Sidborough*, for the arbitryng between the parish and *Bullisden* for the bells:

	£.	s.	d.
For mutton, a shoulder,	0	0	3
For three conys, —	0	0	5
For four chekyns, —	0	0	6
For a capon, —	0	1	8
For bred, ale, wyn, and bere, —	0	1	9
	0	4	0

1516. At Cambridge's obit, sugar 1 lb. —	0	0	7
Two oz. pepper, —	0	0	2
Half an oz. saffron, —	0	0	5
One oz. macis and cloves, —	0	0	5
Two great dishes of butter, —	0	0	5
	0	2	0

1511. To the glasier for mendyng all the holys of the wyndowes in the church, and for colys that he ocupyed, —	0	13	6
1511. For mendyng the ladder § and the pulpit, —	0	0	4
Paid Mr. *Kytis* and Mr. *Cornysh* dynner in Mr. Alderman's place; for a pyke XXII*d.*; for three playse XII*d.*; oysters I*d.*; brede, ale, wyne, and perys XIX*d.*	0	6	4
Paid for a pyke II*s.* VIII*d.*; rochis IIII*d.*; oysters I*d.*; buttur I*d.*; a pye of gruufis ‖ VI*d.*; brede, ale, wyne, erbys, and a side of lynge and flownders, notts, fyre, and sawce II*s.* VI*d.*; and for the coke's labour for dressyng this dynner at Mr. *Sudborough's*, for Mr. *Kyte* and *Harry Prentts*, of the King's chapell, IIII*d.* —	0	7	1
To *William Smyth*, founder, for makyng the Scripture abought the bell, — —	0	13	4

* Tavern.

† God's penny was Earnest money for any bargain or purchase, which by the canons was to be applied to pious uses. Du Cange, v. *Denarius Dei.*

‡ Hermit. See before, p. § Q. pulpit stairs? ‖ Q. growse.

1511. To

		£.	s.	d.
	To *Pargetour*, for half a C. of Polen * wax, ——	1	10	0
	Ten quarts oyle, —— ——	0	1	8
	Mem. that the *judas* of the paſtal, i. e. the tymbre that *the wax of the paſtel is driven upon*, weigheth 7lb.			
1513.	To a maſon and his man for hewyng the dore therewe the vyſe into the bellfray, ——	0	1	8
	For fresſhynge † the canopy at the high awter, and for fresſhyng a veſtment, &c. ——	....		
1516.	In part for a cheſt to lay the ſepulchre in, ——	0	13	4
1519.	Fresſhyng the tabernacle of our Lady Aſſumption,	....		
1517.	For a great holywater ſtopp ‡, weying lb. and di. the lb. vi*d.* and to the ſervaunt for his labour for bryngyng home, —— ——	0	7	4
	For two holywater ſprynkells, ——	0	0	2
	For mending *John Baker's* ſtone, and for leying thereof ayene,	0	1	1
	For two quarters of colis for the fire to be hallowed,	0	0	11

In 1518 *Stephen Sanderſon* was churchwarden; and his accounts are audited and ſigned that year.

		£.	s.	d.
1518.	For makyng the pcloſe § about the croſs in the great church-yard, —— ——	0	1	8
	For cleanſing of the Romeland ‖ and Billingeſgate 1518.			
	Paid Mrs. *Skerne* for the hyer of two lyghters for two weeks, (the week 10*s.*) —— ——	1	0	0
	For 12 men the ſame two weeks, every man the day and night 8*d.*	4	16	0
	For three more men in a ſmall lyghter that two weekes,	1	4	6
	The third week to three men in a ſmall lyghter ſix days,	0	12	0
	The fourth week to Mres. *Skerne* for a great lyghter,	0	5	0
	Six men to that lyghter, their work ſix days, —	1	4	0
	Three men to the ſmall lyghter ſix days, —	0	12	0
		9	13	0

For which £6. 16*s.* 10*d.* was received.

In 1519 *John Wolfe* was churchwarden.

1519. Received for owld laten at 2*d.* the lb.
pewter 2½*d.*
potbras 1½*d.*

* Q. *Poland.* † Repairing.

‡ See before, note, p. 98. It ſeems to have been of lead. "The *ſtock* of braſs for holy water "at Waltham was of marble or metal, and in no caſe of brick, by the canon." Fuller's Hiſtory of Waltham Abbey, p. 17. § *Percluſe.* Incloſure or fence.

‖ *Rome land* at Waltham was a ſpacious place in the town at the entrance of the abbey, built about with houſes, the rents whereof, it is generally believed, belonged to the church of Rome. Fuller's Hiſtory of Waltham Abbey, p. 8.

1519. For

		£.	s.	d.
1519.	For bringing the organs from St. Andrew's * church againſt St. Barnabas' eve, and carrying them back again, —	0	0	5
1520.	A ſum of money was given us by our executor towards buying a table for the high altar, "when and as ſone as God ſhall ſend money into the box of the ſaid church."			
1521.	For ſetting 23 new *quarrells* † in the window of the Trinite that was blown down, — —	0	1	8
	To the organ-maker, for a payre of new organs, and for bringing them home, —	0	10	8
	To ditto, 1*s.* *per ann.* for the overſight of them for certan years; the whole coſt of the organs ſeems —	16	5	7
1520.	For water § to be halowed on Maundy Thurſday for the alters and Eſtur-even for the fountain ‡, —	0	0	2
	For the coſt of *William Smyth*, condukte, for ſettyng ‖ a childe at Waltham, — —	0	1	0
1510.	For *Reve's* labur and his brekefaſt, for coming from Ludgate to Aldgate, to here the fourth bell in tewne, —	0	0	6½
	For wine and pers at *Skrafis* houſe at Aldgate for Mr. *Gentyll*, &c. and the clerks of St. Antony's **, to go to ſee whether Smythe's bell were tewne well or not, —	0	0	8
1523.	For milke and rattiſbane for the rats in the church,	0	0	1½
	Paid to *Northfolke* and his cōpenny †† and the children, when that Mr. Parſon gave to them a playing weke to make mery, — —	0	3	4
1527.	For workmanſhip of Mr. Rocke's ‡‡ mayden's pew, —	...	...	...
	A piece of Sandwych lyne for the church, —	0	0	4
	For xx ells of lynnen cloth for ſurplices, the ell 7½*d.* —	2	2	0
	At the Salutacyon at the hyryn of Petur the clarke,	0	0	6½
	Paid to hym by command of the veſtry for a godde's penny §§,	0	0	4
	Half a C. of new wax ‖‖ for the church, —	1	7	6
	Spent on the pariſhioners at the burying of two prieſts,	0	0	6
1524.	Ryngyng the belles at the triumphe for the takyng the French King *** and by the commandment of the mayor,	0	0	8
1531.	Workman plaiſterer, workman tyler †††, —	...	...	...
	A hard hewer for pavying the kechen, —	...	...	...

* Q. St. Andrew's Wardrobe, near Baynard's Caſtle, now united to St. Anne's, Blackfriars.

† Quarries or panes of glaſs.

§ The moſt extraordinary charge in theſe accounts ſeems to be this and others for *water*.

‡ Q. font. ‖ Hired for apprenticing. ** Q. St. Anthony's, Budgerow. †† Company.

‡‡ A pew for the maid-ſervants of William Rokes, chamberlain for the city 1513; ſheriff 1524; alderman 1529 or 30; knight and mayor, 1540. §§ See before, p. 106.

‖‖ Wax ſeems to have kept its price from 1380; when 300 lb. of it coſt £.8. or near 6½*d.* per lb.; which is the proportion here. Fleetwood's Chron. Prec. 85.

*** Francis I. ††† For journeymen.

1531. For

	£.	s.	d.
For two ftolys for the rectors in the quyre, and two greyes fkynnes, —— —	0	4	1
For water for the church for a yere *, —	0	0	4
For two quayres of paper rial to mend the prik fong boke,	0	1	2
For fettyng up the ymage about the quyre dore, —	0	0	4
1531. Three gallonds and fix pynts of malvefay †, for a yere for Lady's maffe, — ——	0	3	9
1524. Paid *Bright* for riding to the *Moore* to Mr. Parfon for to fpeke to my Lord Cardinall for the taking of the children,	0	4	4
Received at the maryage of *Caapel* the waterbearer, —	0	0	6
Received for the knyll and burial of Mr. *Port* in the chapell (St. Stephen's, where his wife was buried the preceding year), —— ——	1	0	0
[*Port*, late the King's fervant, the inventory of whofe goods is extracted, dedicated a chantry ‡, and was a benefactor towards building the church; and a memorandum is entered, to fearch for his will].			
Mem. given for the berying the croffes on Corpus Chrifti 3*d*. Mem. given for two pair of gloves to the churchwardens at Efter, — —	to be no precedent hereafter.		
1525. Money fpent in going to Weftminfter to fpeke with Mr. Parfon for hay to lay under the ledes of the church, —	0	0	5
[Three loades of old reyd were carted away from the top of the fteple, 1506.]			
Ringing None's courfew and day pele, and courfew and other pelis on our Lady's day the Affumption, —	0	1	0
1527. For a great iron to hang the veil of the chancel § againft Lent,	0	1	0
For painting and renewing the images in the fepulchre cloth,	0	5	0
For *drying* of the pix for the facrament againft Efter, —	0	0	4
For a pekrell ‖ given to the chancellor of London *for allowing our tolleration*, for Mr. Nafyng, —	0	2	8
1531. For the hyre of the rayment *pphets* 1*s*. and of cloth of arras 1*s*. 4*d*. for Palmfunday.			
1536. To a man for beryng the copes to Gracechurch-ftreet, and back again, when the King and Queen ** rode thoro' the city, — —	0	2	0
For rynging the grete bell fix hours for Queen Jane, and for ringing the bells divers peles to the fame, —	0	2	6

* See before, p. 108.

† Two quarts of malvefey coft 8*d*. in 1551. Stow in Fleetwood's Chron. Prec. p. 118. Here it is 3*d*. per quart.

‡ The prieft of which officiated only from 1527 to 1530, the expence exceeding the revenues.

§ Was this any allufion to the veil of the temple rent at the Crucifixion?

‖ Q. pikerell, a fifh fo called: a common fign in Suffolk.

** Jane Seymour, whom Henry VIII. married this year, and beheaded Anne Bullen.

	£.	s.	d.
To two men for beryng of the copes to Powlis and home agayn, at the birth of Prince *Edward*,	0	1	0
1539. For a caase for my Lord-mayor's sworde,	0	1	0
1547. Received of *Jasper*, the basket-maker, for 7½ lb. of alabaster sold to him at 2*s*. 4*d*. per lb. *	0	17	6
1547. Paid for takyng down the tabernacle over the vestry door, being all stone, and other stone works in the church, and for making up thereof, and lyme and sand,	0	13	4
Dinner and supper for Mr. *Clarke*, counsellor, for 12 days, for the view of the church evidence concerning the chantry lands, at 3*s*. 4*d*. per day,	2	0	0
For painting the rode lofte with scriptures,	4	0	0
[These were put out 1554 at the expence of 1*s*. 8*d*.]			
For a boke of the prayer from the Trotts,	0	0	2
For a boke called the paraphrase of Erasmus,	0	5	0
For four song bokes of Te Deum in Englyshe,	0	0	8
1548. Received for the buryal cloth when *Wyman* was buried,	0	0	4
Received for the gylt of two images,	0	12	0
Received for a painted cloth that remained to the quere 20 yards and an half, at 4*d*. per yard,	0	6	10
1549. They sold silver at 5*s*. 8*d*. and 5*s*. 11*d*. per oz. to the amount of	18	5	8
1553. They bought two antiphonars, a grayle, two symnolls, and four processionars, for £.6.; two antiphonars and a grale for £.1. 6*s*. 8*d*.; and three processionars, 1554, for 7*s*. The high altar cost taking down in 1549 £.1. 2*s*. 6*d*.; and in 1554 15*s*. 8*d*. was contributed towards making it; and in 1554 the suffragan's fee and dinner for hallowing it amounted to £.1. 16*s*. 11*d*.			
1554. Received for two maryages for that they were maryed in the newe house,	0	2	0
Paid for makyng the bishop's myter with stuff and lace that went to it,	0	3	0
Paid for a boke for St. Nicholas,	0	0	8
In 1555 we have expences on the rood, Mary and John, the patroness, the tabernacle of the patroness, painting the patroness, refreshing the tabernacle, and coloring the backside of the board of the cross.			
1555. Paid for sing brede [a charge frequently repeated],	0	0	2
1556. To five ryngers that ronge the same day that the King and the Queen's Highness came through London by command of the bishop to rynge †,	0	1	8

* Was this any tomb or image pulled down and sold? The following article increases the suspicion.

† Philip arrived in England May 30, 1556. (Rapin, VIII. 202.) and Mary died Nov. 17, 1558. Ib. 214.

1556. To

	£.	s.	d.
1556. To the carpenter for the crofs in the church yard, and the payles, and the *Lenten* crofs, &c. ———	2	8	4
1557. Paid for three fprings for *regalles*, ——	0	1	0
For 10 fprings and 4 fongs for the regalles *, and for his glew,	0	2	0
Spent upon Mr. *Philip* of Poles, for playing at organs, the 17th July, at the Salutation, Mr. *Lucas* and Mr. *Win* being there,	0	1	4
For bringing down the images to Romeland and other things to be burnt, ——— ———	0	1	0

The accounts of *William Prewne* and *John Halbed*, churchwardens, from Michael-1 Henry VII. 1485-6, to Michaelmas following.

	£.	s.	d.
Paide for three dofs' talough candell, fpent from Alhallowmas to Candilmas a° 1486, paid the dofs' 14½*d*. Summa	0	3	7
Item, for makyng clene of ftandards, candilfticks, braunches, with the bolls † of laten upon the beame of the rodeloft anenft the feft of Eft' a° 1486, ———	0	1	8
Item, for fcouryng of the ymage of the Trynyte befyde the hye altar, and of the table at the high altar of St. Thomas, with the ymage of Seynt Ladye and the Crucifix in St. Stephen's chapell of alablaft, ———	0	1	0
Item, for two dofs' di. bocfe ‡ garlonds for prefts and clerkes on St. Barnabe daye, ——— ———	0	1	10
Item, for wyne and ale fpente at the hye fefts of the yer amongft preftes and clerkes, ———	0	3	4
Item, for coles two quarters ayenft Eft' a° 1486, ———	0	1	0
Item, for flowrs obleyes, and for box and palme ayenft Palmfondaye, — —	0	0	6
Item, to *William Parys*, for wachyng of the fepulchre, and for brede and ale, ——— ———	0	0	6
Item, for birch bowes § ayenft Midfummer, ———	0	0	3
Item, to *William Parys*, for kepyng clene the chyrch, dreffyng up the veftrye, and fettyng up divers thyngs in the ftorehoufe by many tymes for his labor, ———	0	1	8
Summa tot. ——— ———	0	14	4

Coftes upon the ornaments.

Paid to *Thomas Pate*, browderer, for garnyfhing and repayring an old cheafible of blew velvent, and another of red faten broidered with flours, and makyng of a tunycle for the dekoy of rede faten in fewte to the fame, for his

* The organs were removed 1547.

† Ornaments of metal. See before, p. 95, n. and p. 112. n.

‡ Box. § boughs.

 workmanfhip

	£.	s.	d.
workmanſhip upon it, and the appareyle belonging thereto, ——— ———	0	0	10
Item, for four tacs of riban and a frenge of ſylke, waying 17 ounces di. per the ounce 1*s.* ſum, ———	0	17	6
Item, for the makyng of the brockets and mendyng of one vaket, ——— ———	0	0	4
Summa ——— ———	1	7	6

Coſtis uppon certen jewells.

	£.	s.	d.
Paid to *William Bonn*, goldſmith, for new makyng and geldyng * of the booſe † belongyng to the daylye croſs, and for mendyng and borneſhyng of the ſhipp ‡, with two ſpones of ſilver. Item, for mending and geldynge a pte of the cryſmatorye. Item, for makyng ayene of the haliwat' ſprenkle, for the gyldyng and workmanſhip; ſumma,	0	18	0
Item, for three ounces ſilvyr mor amongſt thys parcel than before paid, ——— ———	0	9	6
Item, for makyng and mendyng of three cheynes of ſilver to the three ſenſers, which weyed in the delivraunce 14 ounces 3 quarters; and in reſſeyvyng home ayene they wayed 29 ounces di; ſo the wayghte mor is 14 ounces di.; paid the ounce 3*s.* 2*d.* ſumma ———	2	5	5
Item, for workmanſhypp of the ſaide three cheynes, ———	0	10	0
Sum. ——— ——— ———	4	3	8

The Inventorye of Chyrch Goades, 1485-6, when *Prewne* and *Halhed* were Churchwardens.

The appareyle for the hyghe aulter.

Item, two awlter clothes of ruſſet cloth of golde, of the gyfte of Mr. *William Marowe*, and *William* and *Thomas* his two ſonnes, by the helpe of Mr. *John Smarte*, grocer.

Item, a corporas caaſe of the ſame.

Item, the curtens of ruſſet ſarſynett frenged with ſylke.

Item, a ſewte of rede ſatyn frynged with golde, of the gyfte of the ſaide Mr. *Wyll'm Marowe*, and of *John Smart*, grocer, conteyning 3 coopes, 2 chaſſubles, 2 aulbes, 2 amytts §, 2 ſtoles, 3 fanons, and 2 gyrdylls.

* Gilding. † Q. Boſs; ſee before, p 95, note.

‡ See before, p. 93; alſo the Inventory of the furniture of Peterborough Cathedral. Gunton, 58.

§ The amice (amictus) was the undermoſt of the garments that compoſed the habit of a prieſt, going over the head and tied over the breaſt with two ſtrings. Next was the albe or aube of linen, like a ſurplice. Over this the girdle; and laſt of all the ſtole. Spelm. Gloſſ. voc. Amictus. The fanon was a towel or linen cloth which the prieſt held in his hands when celebrating maſs, called alſo the maniple. Id. v. Fano.

Item,

Item, a chaasyble * of clothe of golde, that Mr. *Cambrugge* made with an albe, and amytts and albe, ftole and fanon, and a gyrdyll of fylke made like a call, with a corpas caafe of the fame.

Item, an ault of wyte damafke, with the frontel paled with pple clothe of golde and white; and a awlt cloth dyapre fewed to the fame.

Item, two curteynes of white fylke to the fame.

Item, an awlt clothe blewe velvent, powdred with flewrs of golde, and the frontell of the fame fewte.

Item, a frontell for the fchelffe ftandyng on the altar of blue farfenet, with brydds of golde, and two blew curteyns of fylke frenghed.

Item, a peyer altar cloths of grene bawdkyn † above and benethe, with 2 curteynes of grene farfenet, frenget with fylke, blue, grene, yelow, and rede.

Item, a fewte of whyte clothys of golde, of the gyfte of *John Yongeham* ‡, fifhmonger, conteyning 3 copes, 1 cheafible, 2 tonykles, 3 albes, 3 amyts, 3 ftoles, 3 fannones, and 3 girdells.

Item, two awter clothes of red cloth of gold and whyght panyd, and 2 curtens of red farfynet and whyght panyd, and fringed with filke.

Item, a corporas cafe, with the one fide of cloth of gold of tyfew al gold, and the other fyde grene faten barrid with taps of gold, of the gyft of *Elyz. Goofwell.*

Item, a fewte of reede clothe of lukis § golde, containing a coope, with a cheafible, 2 tonykles, 3 aulbes, 3 amyts, 3 ftoles, 3 fanons, and 3 gyrdills, of the gyfte of *William Baker*, peauterer.

Item, a rede veftment broudred with lyons of golde of reede faten; that is to faye, a chefible and a tonykle to the fame, with 2 albis, 2 amyts, 2 ftoles, 2 fannones, and 2 girdels, late amended, and a coope thereto of reede faten proudrid with lyons.

Item, a blacke veftment of velvet poudyrd with lambes, mones, and fterrs; the cheafible, the albe, the amys, the ftole, the fanon, and girdill.

Item, a canapye of blue clothe of baudkyn with birds of flour in golde.

Item, a canapye of rede fylke, with grene braunchys and white flours poudryd with fwannys of golde betweene the branches.

Item, a veftyment of the gyfte of Maift. *Wyll'm Wylde* ‖, late pfon of this chirch.

Item, a cheffyble of blew faten fringed with filk, with an albe and amys, and a gyrdill.

* Chefuble was a fmaller cope. Ib. v. Cafula.

† Bawdekyn, Baldicum, Baldichinum, Baldekinum, Pannus auro rigidus plumatoque opere intertextus. Baudekyn, cloth of filk. Spelman's Gloffary, in voce. Gold brocade, the richeft cloth. Hift. of Hawfted, p. 119, n. In Peterborough Inventory are altar cloths of bawdkyn. Gunton, 58.

‡ *John Yongeham*, fifhmonger, by will dated 1514, leaves £40. for a fuit of veftments, white or black, with 3 copes, &c. This and the two following articles are written with different ink, and in a different hand from the articles both before and after; fo that this gift of Mr. Yongeham's was inferted in a part of the regifter before left vacant.

§ Louvois, or Lovain, or Lucchefe.

‖ He appears to have died about 1504.

Item,

Item, two corporas cafes of white and golde, and 3 nedyl wyrke, and 6 other cafes of dyvers wyrke.

Item, fix copes for children of dyvers forts, and 8 fmall ftremers of the gyfte of Mr. *Remyngton* * and Mr. *Revett* †, and of fquare baner.

Item, a myter for a byfhop ‡ at Seint Nycholas tyde, garnyfhed with fylver and anelyd, and perle and counterfete ftone.

Item, two cheyres § of iron for Rectes copes.

Item, a pyx clothe for the hight aulter of fipers ‖ frenged with golde, with knoppes of golde, and fylke of Spaynefhe makyng, of the gyfte of Mr. Doctor *Hatclyff*, pfon.

Item, a pyx clothe of fipers frenged with grene fylke and red, with knoppes filver and gylt with corners goyng, of Mres. *Sucklyng's* gyfte.

Item, three croffe ftavys clothes gyldyd with ymages of golde.

Item, a canape for the pyx of whyte Baudekyn lyke thefe.

Item, a leefke of laton with a flakon.

Item, two ftandards of laton.

Item, on the hygh aulter 2 gret candelftyks, and 3 fmall, and on Sent Stephen's alter 2 candylftyks.

Item, 2 croffe ftaves laten gyldyd.

Item, two gylt feet for croffys, and oon copper gylt.

The Aulter Cloths.

Firft, an awlter diap. hole and found, conteyning in length 3 yards di.; in breede 1 ell, with 3 pt blew ftarres at the one ende.

Item, an awlt' cloth diap, conteyning in lengthe 3 yards di.; in breede 1 ell, with 3 blew kayes ** at each ende of the faide clothe.

Item, a clothe of fyne diaper, croffe worke, conteyning in lengthe 6 yards and qr.; in breede 1 ell, and the one ende forfid oute longe.

Item, a clothe whole diaper, conteyning in lengthe 4 yards; in brede a large yard, garnyfhed with blewe at both ends.

* William Remington, mayor, and buried here 1500. Stowe.

† Robert Revett, one of the fheriffs 1409, gave liberally towards the new building of this church and fteple, and was there buried. Stowe.

‡ It appears by this and the next article that the cuftom of boy-bifhops, or Epifcopi Puerorum, prevailed here, as well as at Salifbury and other places.

§ Q. chains or frames to hang the rector's copes on. Or was it fomething for the *Rectores chori*, mentioned at Peterborough. Gunton, 58.

‖ At Peterborough were 7 copes of fattin of *Cyprus*. Gunton, 60.

** In that cathedral were "a fuit of Peter keys;" and "3 tunicles with Peter keys;" which were part of the abbey arms, in honour of the patron faint. That inventory is one of the moft curious in its kind, and in many articles conformable to this.

Item,

Item, a clothe of crosse diap fyne, conteyning in lengthe 9 yards; and in brede a ell.

Item, an olde aulter clothe conteyning in length 3 yards di.; in brede 1 yard; imbed with the keyes at each ende.

Item, another broken pece diap conteyning in length 2 yards di.; in brede a yard; imbed with the blew keyes, in the myddl.

Item, another aulter clothe diap conteyning in length 3 in brede 3 yards di.; with 4 blywe keyes at either ende.

Item, an olde diap clothe of 3 p , conteyning in length 6 yards di.; in brede 1 yard; full of holis.

Item, a diap clothe wrack *, conteyning in length 3 di. in brede 1 ell.

Item, an olde diap clothe, conteyning in length 4 and di.; in brede 1 yard.

Item, an olde diap clothe, with losengis, conteyning 4 yards; in brede o yarde large, with a blew marke on the ende.

Item, an olde diap clothe, conteyning in length 4 yards di.; in brede a large yerd; with 3 brade keyes on the one ende.

Item, a playne clothe peced in the myddis, conteyning in length 3 yards qr.; in breede a large yarde, with an Antony crosse of rede on the one side.

Item, a broken awlter clothe pleyne, conteyning in length 3 yards qr.; in breede a yarde and di. or qr. with 3 blew keyes in midd.

Item, eight surplyces for the quere, of the which 2 have no slevys.

Item, three rochets for children, 7

Item, three albys for children, 6 and 6 ameses with parells, and 3 albys and amefes without parells.

Item, two peyre of old organs.

Item, five grete bells, and a sanctus bell, of the which 5 grete bells the fourth greate bell was clere of the gyfte of *John Sucklyng*, fishmonger, as is graved upon the bell.

Item, four holywater stoupes † of laton.

Item, four gret quysshons with downe, 2 of them with sylke, and 2 with fustean.

Item, three smale candelstyks of laton for tapers.

Item, four candelstyks of laton with 6 branches for talough candell.

Item, a gylt table of the Trynete for to sett on the high aulter.

Item, a corporas case of nedyll work, the bakside purpill velvett; and a fine corporas therein with semys of gold, of the gyfte of Mres. *Julian Roche*.

Item, more of the gyfte of the same *Julian*, a sylver bell parcell gylt.

Towells.

Item, a fyene diap towell hole, conteyning in length 6 yards 3 qrs.; in brede di.; an ell with a blewe laye at eyder ende.

* Ragged or worn, as in the next page.

† In the Peterborough Inventory this is called a *stock*, as here, p. 107.

Item, a diap towell hole, conteyning in length 5 yards and qt.; in brede di. a yard; with 6 ftrakes at eyder ende.

Item, a diap towell of croffe worke, fyne and hole, conteyning in length 10 yards; in brede 3 qrs. large.

Item, a fyne diap towell cheker worke, conteyning in length 6 yards di.; in brede di. a yard di. qr. chekred at both endes with blew and tawnny.

Item, a diap towell hole, conteyning in length 9 yards; in brede di. a yard.

Item, a diap towell cheker werks hole, conteyning in length 10 yards; in brede di. a ell, with blewe rayes at eyther ende.

Item, a diap towell, conteyning in length 7 yards 3 qrs.; in brede di. a yard; with 3 white keyes at eyder ender.

Item, a diap towell, conteyning in length 7 yards 3 qrs.; in brede di. a yard; ēbroudred at both endes.

Item, a fyne diap towell, conteyning in length 3 yards 3 qrs. di.; in brede 3 qrs.; with 3 blewe keyes at the one ende.

Item, a fyne diap towell, conteyning in length 4 yards di.; in brede di. a yard; broudred at both endes.

Item, a diap towell, conteynyng in length 3 yards di.; in brede 3 qrs.; keyed at both endes.

Wrackt { Item, an olde diap towell, conteynyng in length 7 yards 3 qrs.; in brede di. ell.
Item, an olde broken towell, conteynyng in length 5 yards 3 qrs.; in brede 3 qrs. }

Item, a courfe diap towell of the gyfte of *Patrick Wolf*, late yoman, conteyning in length ....; and in brede ....

Item, a pleyne towell, conteyning in length 3 yards 3 qrs. di.; in brede 19 di.

Item, a pleyne towell, conteyning in length 2 yards di.; in brede di. yard.

Item, a towell, conteyning in length 3 yards di.; in brede a qr.

Item, a towell, conteyning in length 3 yards; in brede di. yard.

Item, a towell, conteyning in length 4 yards; in brede di. yard.

Item, a towell, conteyning ....

Item, two aulter cloths canvas, conteyning a pece 4 yards; in brede a yard and di. qr.

Item, two dyapre table clothes for the high aulter of the gyfte of Meftres *Jentyll*.

Item, a towell, of the gyfte of Mother *Jenet*.

Item, a fyne ryben furplis in a lynnyn bag, of the gyfte of Sir *John Colyns*; this furples was geven unto Mr. Well'm Weld, perfon, be the afentt of the pyfh, in the yer a° 1492, be the handis of me, R° Cloos.

N. B. This laft paragraph has a line drawn through it.

Inventory

Inventory of the Church Goods about 1524.

Item, an alter clothe of fine dyapre, with a cros of ſylke in the middes, and at every ende inbed in 2 places emmings and crownys in the mid, and at every ende 5 blewe mylyngs, the length thereof 3 ells 3 quarters.

Item, a dyapre aulter cloth on marked, of the length 3 ells di.

Item, a playne aulter cloth marked with ſylke in the middis, and our Lorde beyng in the ſepulcre, in length 4 elles and quarter.

Item, a dyapre aulter onmarked, of the length of 2 ells di.

Item, a dyapre aulter clothe marked in the mydds with a cros of ſylke, of the length of 4 ells quarter.

Item, a dyapre alter cloth marked in the middes with M, and at the ende with  and , which is in length 4 ells quarter.

Item, a playne alter cloth marked with a croſe of ſylke in the middes, which is in length 3 ells di. and more.

Item, a peced alter cloth with a ſeme in the middes, of oon ell and di.

Item, a worne alt' cloth of dyapre, of 2 elles long and di. elle broode.

Item, old ſeer dyapry cloth, of an ell di.

Item, an olde ſeer diapry towell, of 3 ells quarter.

Item, five diapry hand towells, and woon playne towell.

Item, a holy-bred clothe of dyapre made doble, with a frenge at the ende, marked with rede ſylke with Xˢ. and b *.

Towells dyapre and playne.

Item, a newe towell of dyapre branched lyke damaſk, of the gyfte of Mres. *Roche*, marked W. † and R. of length 13 ells 39, of a yerd brood.

Item, a dyapre towell, marked with whight threde lyke 2 trew loves, in length 13 ells, in bredith 3 quarters.

Item, a towell of dyapre blewe, mylyd at both endes with an M. crowned ‡ of red ſylke, marked in the midds, in length 8 ells.

Item, a towell of dyapre towell marked in the myddes, with a crowned M of blake ſylke, in length 2 ells 3 quarters.

Item, a towell of dyapre, marked in the middes with a crowned M. of blake ſylke, containing in length 5 ells.

Item, an aulter clothe of fyne dyapre, marked with red ſylke in 2 places with Ihs, of the length of 4 ells.

Item, a towell of dyapre, marked with blake ſylke in the middes with M. crowned, which is in length 3 quarters.

Item, a playne towell, marked in the myddes with blake ſylke with an M. crowned, which is in length 2 ells di.

Item,   playne ſurplics for men aftir chappell gyſe.

Item,   reveld § ſurplics for men.

* Chriſt's bread, or the holy bread diſtributed in the church; or perhaps initials of ſome name.

† Perhaps Winefred Roche.

‡ The crowned M is the common emblem of the Virgin Mary, in carving, painting, and embroidery.

§ Ruffled.

Inventory of Goods delivered to *Marynn Conteryn* and to *Powle Priour*, attorney of *Agaryn Conteryn*, marchaunte of Venyse, by the hand of *John Bedham*, when he entyred into the place in Botolph-lane, wher now one *Peter Conteryn* dwellith, 1481. (See before, p. 87.)

In the cheffe * chaumbre.

A ftandyng bed made with eftrychborde †, having the hed on the fame wife.

In the chamber over the plour.

A ftandynge bed, a forme, and 3 barris of yryn for to hyng on curtynes.

Item, a chambre within the fame chambre.

A ftandyng bed covvey with eftricg borde of beyond-fee makyng, and a forme.

In the inner chamber.

A ftandyng bed and a forme, and 2 treftills.

In another chambre.

A bed without a botom.

In the ploure.

A fpear with 2 leves.

In the bottrye.

Four fhelves.

In the chambre over the gate.

A ftandyng bed.

In the chamber over the kechen.

A ftandyng bed, a forme, and a ftole.

In Antonye's chambre.

A ftandyng bedd, a grete new ftandyng almerye ‡ with 4 leves.

In the chambre next St. Botolph's chirch-yard.

A ftandyng bedd.

In the next chambre bye.

A ftandyng bedd; alfo a coumptour that *John de Ponnt* § had covered with grene clothe; a coumptour in the chambre of over the well covered with grene.

Two coumptours by Antonye's chambre covered with grene.

A comptour by the chambre *Peter Vatas* had covered with grene.

A newe coumptour in the higheft chambre on the ftrete covered with grene.

In the kechen.

Three fhelves, 2 dreffyng bordes, 2 great formes, a forme, and a great almarye with 2 leves.

* Chief.

† See before, p. 97.

‡ *Eleemofynaria*, *loculi* feu potius *arcula*, ubi reponuntur eleemofynæ. Du Cange. Whence it came to fignify any prefs or cheft.

§ Q. *Pourt*, or Port, of whom fee next page.

In

In the larder-hous.

Two ſhelves.

In the houſe next the gardyn.

Two ſhelves, and a grete bynn to laye in otes.

In the ſtable.

A racke and a maunger, and it was new planked.

For the well.

A bokett with a cheyne of yryn.

Alſo ther be 30 ſpryng lockes and keyes; and there be 22 ſtock locks and keys; alſo ther be 4 plate lockes for the greate almarye and keyes; alſo 5 plate locks and keyes, with 6 boltes yryn.

A poſtern gate unto the houſe, in which Mr. *Bayead* now dwelleth, of ould antiquity.

Alſo there is for the poſtern gate a plate locke, with a bolte yryn and 2 keyes; alſo 5 plate lockes with 5 *cleket* keyes.

Alſo all the glaſs wyndowes in the ſaide place, and in the comptors longyng to the ſaide place, bethe myne hole and ſufficiently amended, and made at the comyng in of the ſaide *Powle*; and ſo to leve them att the goyng owte of the ſaide *Agaryn*, and of his attorney, by covenant made by them, him, and me, the ſaid *J. Bedham*.

The Inventory of *John Port*, layt the King's ſervant, as after followeth. [He died in 1524 or 5.]

In the hall.	£.	s.	d.
Item, the hyngyng of the hall, 10 yeards at 2*d*. per yard, —	0	8	4
Item, the cortyn of the wendo, —— ——	0	0	4
Item, half a dozen coſhens, —— ——	0	8	0
Item, a nelde * pageant † of ihus, ——	0	0	9
Item, two cankers of corſe vardus ‡ of 9 yards, at 1½*d*. per yard,	0	9	0
Item, two peces of Kentyſhe carpet, —— —	0	0	8
Item, a dovell counter of dauſke §, —— ——	0	6	8
Item, a tabull with a pair of foulding tryſſels, ——	0	2	0
Item, four joynt ſtolls, at 4*d*. a pece, —— ——	0	1	4
Item, a nolde ‖ cobbord, —— ——	0	5	4
Item, a ſtakyd forme, —— —— ——	0	0	6

* An old, as in a variety of inſtances following.

† Q. if *pageant* here and in the next page does not mean *picture*, or rather a proceſſional banner with the figure of Jeſus Chriſt on it. *Ihus* is *Jeſus*.

‡ Q. the ſame with *Vador*, p. 119, 120. *Vardor* in Fermer's, *Verders*, in Foſkewe's inventory in Strutt's Horda Angla-cynnan III. 63. *Vardures* in others.

§ Damaſke. ‖ See note *.

	£.	s.	d.
Item, two tornyd * chares,	o	o	4
Item, lytell old ofter bord, and a peffe of Kent's kerpets †,	o	o	6
Item, a clofe chare,	o	o	10
Item, a chare of Spanyfhe makyng,	o	1	4
Item, a clofe chare of wainfkot,	....		
Item, a hyngyng beam of Laton with 4 fnoffs,	o	5	o
Item, a pair of andōrs ‡, and a pair of tongs, with a fyer rake, with a lytell fyer choffell,	o	o	8
In the Payrlor.			
Item, a hyngyng of grene fay with a border of 37 yards, at 2*d.* per yard,	....		
Item, fix paygents with a lytyll one,	o	2	8
Item, fix cofhens of gant § makyng,	o	3	o
Item, a carpet of autnold vardors ||,	o	3	4
Item, a nolde carpet of Kentefh make,	o	o	8
Item, a nolde meddle cowntor,	o	2	o
Item, four joyned ** formes of waynfkot,	o	4	o
Item, two torned chares and a jake,	o	o	4
Item, a rownd tabul of fypars †† with a fott,	o	1	4
Item, a rownd cobbord with a fayling haufe,	o	8	o
Item, a hanging with 4 noffes ‡‡, with a hangyng glaffe,	o	o	8
Item, a pair of awdorns §§ caft of yrne,	o	2	o
Item, four olde boks and a ftandyche,	o	o	4
Item, two halbards and a bell,	o	1	8
Item, two old polakes,	o	1	4
Item, two bokelers,	o	2	o
Item, two lytyll tabolls of emaige ||||,	o	o	4
Item, a payer of olde tabolls playng ***,	o	o	6
In the bottry.			
Item, a garnyfhe of veffel †††, 4 old chargers, 4 platers, 16 difhes, 8 fafers, 2 potyngars, weighing 152, at 2*d.* per lb.	2	7	10
Item, two bafons, 2 ewars,	o	3	4

* So in Mr. Fermer's inventory in Strutt, Horda Anglo-cynnan III. 63. *turnyde* chaires.

† A piece of Kentifh carpeting.

‡ Andirons, ufed to this day in the country, and called *cobb-irons*; they ftand on the hearth where they burn wood to lay it upon; their fronts are ufually curved with a large round nob at the top; fome of them are kept polifhed and bright. Antiently many of them were embellifhed with numerous ornaments. Strutt, Ib. 64.

§ Q. Ghent.

|| *Vador* occurs again in next page.

** Q. joint, as hereafter, joynt ftools, pp. 118. 120.

†† Cyprefs wood.

‡‡ Q. noffels.

§§ Andirons.

|||| Q. imagery.

*** Playing tables.

††† A *fervice* of any metal, pewter not excepted. See Hift. of Hawfted, p. 127, n. and Northumberland Houfhold-book.

Item,

	£.	s	d.
Item, five old bafens, great and fmall, 3 pottyl potts, two quarts and two pints for wyne, ditto for ayll, 2 holly water ftocks *, a bottel of tinne, weighing all 56 lb. at 2*d.* per lb. —— ——	0	11	8
Item, four barber's bafyngs, with broken candlefticks and latten bafyng, 4 ewars, weighing 53 lb. at 2*d.* per lb. ——	0	8	10
Item, five fmall candleftiks, —— ——	0	1	8
Item, a nolde cobbord, a nolde beme, with other old lumber,	0	3	4
Item, fix large candleftiks, —— —— ——	0	6	0
Item, fourteen brafs potts, great and fmall, and a fmall fyre chaffer, a brafen mortar, and a freter chafer, 7 fmall chafers with ftolls, 2 lytell poffetts †, weighing 342 lb. at 1*d.* per lb. —	2	7	3
Item, five barber's bafens and a collender, all weighing 14 lb. at 2*d.* per lb. —— —— —— ——	0	2	4
Item, thirteen payns ‡ great and fmall, 8 kettells bound and unbound, weighing 148 lb. at 2*d.* per lb. —— ——	2	6	8
Item, fix fpeytts and a burd fpett, —— ——	0	2	4
Item, a payre of cobb yrn, —— ——	0	1	0
Item, a payre of raks, —— —— ——	0	1	0
Item, a pott hangar and a pot hoke, —— ——	0	0	4
Item, a drepyng pan and a fyre pane, —— ——	0	1	0
Item, pair of tongs and a fyre fchoffell, and a fyer forke, and a chopping knyffe, —— —— ——	0	2	0
Item, two treyvetts, —— —— ——	0	0	4
Item, in lede 40 lb. —— —— ——	0	1	4
Item, a ftone morter and a fkemmer, —— ——	0	0	8
Item, two bowls, with other old lomer in the kechyng, —	0	1	0

In his chamber.

	£.	s	d.
Item, the hangings of the chamber, 50 yards, at 2*d.* per yard,	0	8	4
Item, a filer § paynted, with 3 cortens of grene bokerane,	....		
Item, two feather beds, with a bolfter, one 7 qrs. the other 8 qrs.	0	13	4
Item, a nolde matraffe, —— ——	0	0	8
Item, a pair of wollen blankets ||, — —	0	2	0
Item, a covering of vardor on his bed of 28 ftoks, at 18*d.* per yard,	0	18	8
Item, a bedftede, 2 fett chefts, and a ftalyd forme, ——	0	2	0
Item, a nolde coberd with a defke, —— ——	0	4	0

* See before, p. 107.

† Little bafons or porringers, Q. for *poffet*, as *porringers* for *pottage*. In Fermer's inventory they are porengers. ‡ Pans.

§ Called in next page *feler* and *foller*. Q. head of the bed, either of wood or linen. In Farmer's inventory *cellar*.

\|\| Sir J. Cullum explains *a pair of fufteans*, blankets. They are in Fermer's inventory befides blankets and mattrafs and *under* the bed.

Item,

	£.	s.	d.
Item, a ſkawer * cheſt of oke that the awter was on †, —	0	5	4
Item, a nater ‡ clothe and a front of whit damaſke and red velvet, frenged with white and rede, with a peſe of old valate, —	0	13	4
Item, a ſuper altare §, — — —	0	0	6
Item, two littel tabells of cypars, — —	0	1	8
Item, a crucefyxe, and a emage of Our Lady, and a paxe,	0	1	0
Item, two crewets ‖ and a pewter candleſtik, — —	0	0	8
Item, a nator clothe and linnen — — —	0	0	4
Item, a ſprewſe ** cheſt and 2 old ſkawer cheſts, —	0	2	8
Item, a ſhort ſtandard cheſt round, and another longer cheſt round, — — — — —	0	13	4
Item, two ſchope †† cheſts, — — —	0	1	4
Item, a nolde cloſe chare and a joynt ſtole, —	0	1	0
Item, a pair of ſmall andryons, — — —	0	0	6
Item, a coveryng of vardor fine 24 ſtokes, — —	1	6	8
Item, three peſes of Kenteſh carpets in mendo ‡‡, —	0	0	4
Item, another covering of olde emagery §§ with 30 ſtokes,	1	0	0

In the chamber over the hall.

	£.	s.	d.
Item, the hole hanging, — — —	0	4	0
Item, a nolde feather bed and bolſter, — —	0	8	8
Item, a nolde ſeler with a teſter, — —	0	2	0
Item, a nolde broken covering of tapeſtly, —	0	1	4
Item, a ſtanding bedſtede with 2 ſet banks, — —	0	1	4
Item, a nolde preſſe of wanſkot, — — —	0	8	0
Item, a tabull and a pair of ſtreſſels ‖‖, — —	0	2	0
Item, a nold counter and a nold ſettel, — —	0	1	4
Item, two old ſkewer cheſts, — —	0	2	0
Item, another ſkawer, cover of wainſkott, — —	0	4	0
Item, a garde vyanſe *** and a torſyng con', — —	0	1	0
Item, a nolde ſkawer cover low †††, and lytyll ſpreuſe and leſt,	0	2	0
Item, a nolde broken preſſe, — —	0	2	0
Item, a pyllo with a counter vallans, — —	0	2	8

In the lytyll chamber next.

	£.	s.	d.
Item, the hangings, 24 yards, at 2*d.* per yard, —	0	2	0

* Q. *ſquare.*

† See the portable altar deſcribed in the Hiſtory of Hawſted, p. 122, 123; which the oaken altar in the beautiful, but little known, old chapel at Lord Bute's ſeat at Luton, though of larger dimenſions, will ſerve to explain. ‡ An altar.

§ Cloth of ordinary ſtuff to cover the whole.

‖ Theſe ſtood on one ſide of the altar, and contained water and wine (Hiſt. of Hawſted, 113), and thence have been applied to the ſideboard.

** Q. Cypreſs, or ſpruce fir. †† Shop, or rather ſoap. ‡‡ Faulty.

§§ So in Fermer's inventory, "tapeſtry of imagery."

‖‖ Treſſels. *** A meat ſafe. ††† Coverlid.

Item,

	£.	s.	d.
Item, a teſter of the bede with a ſoller,	0	2	0
Item, a feather bed with a bolſter,	0	10	0
Item, a ſtanding bedeſtede, a ſtrō clothe with a forme,	0	1	4
Item, a lytell torneng cover,	0	2	0
Item, a nalmery * old with a deſk,	0	0	8
Item, a ſkawer cheſt,	0	1	8
Item, a ſmall cover,	0	1	0
Item, a lytyll tabole folding, with one treſſel of the Spanyards makyng,	0	4	0
Item, in the longe ſtandert cheſt: fyrſt, an olde jacket of crymſon velvet,	0	4	0
Item, a pair of ſleves of cremyſyng velvet inbroderet † with damaſke gold,	1	0	0
Item, a pair of ſleves of the ſame velvet,	0	8	0
Item, a lynyng of a robe of white ſarſnet, 2 peſes, without ſleffs,	0	13	4
Item, a peſe of old ſarſnet white,	0	0	6
Item, a remnant of tawny velvet moth eaten,	0	5	0
Item, a quarter and ½ of cremyſyng velvet,	0	3	4
Item, a lytyll jerkyn of cremyſyng velvet,	0	1	8
Item, three ſhreds of cloth, a tiſſew,	0	6	8
Item, three lytyll ſhreds of cloth, a ſilver,	0	1	4
Item, ten ditto of tenſyn ſatten,	0	3	4
Item, dyvers ſmall ſhreds of velvet,	0	1	4
Item, a quarter and ½ of white ſatten,	0	1	4
Item, a quarter red a quarter white of ſaten bur'ds,	0	0	8
Item, ſix yards ¾ of rare taſte,	...	...	...
Item, twenty-four corſe Romney boge ‡,	...	...	...
Item, a Spanyſhe ſkyn yellow,	0	0	8
Item, two yards of lenneng clothe naro,	0	0	8
The Napry.			
Item, a tabell clothe of dyapre, containing 7 yards, at *6d.* per yd.	0	3	6
Item, old ditto broken and corſe,	0	0	8
Item, a corſe diap̄ cloth, 9 yards ½, at *3d.* per yard,	0	2	5
Item, a tabull cloth of coſſe dyamonds, 4 yards, at *3d.*	0	1	0
Item, four ſhort playn tabell cloth, 8 ells, at *2d.*	0	1	4
Item, five old towells of diapre broken, 30 yards, at *2d.*	0	5	0
Item, two old hengen § towels,	0	0	4
Item, two dozen diapre napkins,	0	8	0
Item, a long towell of diap̄ of 14 yards,	0	2	4
Item, two towells of diap̄, 9 yards, at *2d.*	0	1	6
Item, two old table cloths broken,	0	0	4
Item, three ſhetts of 3 breds Holonde,	0	10	0
Item, a pair of two breds and ½,	0	5	0

* See note ‡, p. 118. † Embroidered. ‡ Fur. § Hanging.

Item,

	£.	s.	d.
Item, a beryinge ſheet * with a ſeme, ——	0	4	0
Item, a dozen broken napkins, —— ——	0	1	0
Item, a pair of ſhets of Holonde of 3 breds, ——	0	2	8
Item, two pair of flexen ſhets, — —	0	4	8
Item, five pair of ſhets, at 16*d.* a pair, — —	0	6	8
Item, ſix pyllobers † of Hollond, — —	0	2	0
Item, ſeven ditto of canvas, —— ——	0	1	2
Item, an old rayll ‡ of one yard ½, —— ——	0	2	0
Item, ſeven ſherts, at 12*d.* the peſe, —— —	0	7	0
Item, ſix old ſmoks and good, —— ——	0	4	0
Hes rayment.			
Item, a gowne, a tawny chamlet furrd with black bugge §,	1	6	0
Item, a nolde gowne of ſkerlet furrd with blak boge of Spain §,	0	16	0
Item, ditto of violet furryd with blak lawne, and faced with bugge,	1	0	0
Item, ditto furred with feches ‖, — —	1	0	0
Item, a roſſet old gowne furred with coney and faced with foxe,	0	13	4
Item, a nolde blak gowne with old blak conney, ——	0	10	0
Item, a gowne of pewke ** with blak ſarſenet, —	0	13	4
Item, ditto old lyned with ſatten of cypars ††, and faced with blak chamlet, — —— — —	0	8	0
Item, a gabarden ‡‡ of ſkayrlet garded with blak velvet, —	0	6	8
Jacketts.			
Item, a jakett old and playne of blak velvet, furred with laune and bugge §, — — —	0	13	4
Item, ditto of ruſſet ſatten furred with jenetts, — —	0	6	8
Item, ditto, the one part blak velvet, the neder part ſatten, furred with laune and boge whit, — — —	0	3	4
Item, ditto broken, of blak velvet furred with blak laune,	0	2	0
Item, a nolde jackett of blue chamlet furred with blak laune,	0	2	0
Item, two old jerkins of blue ſatten, — —	0	6	8
Item, a nolde jacket of tawne §§ lyned with yello cotton of chamlet, — — — —	0	1	4
Item, a cott of tawny chamlet lined with yello cotton, —	0	5	0
Item, ditto of ruſſet marull garded with velvet, ——	0	4	0
Item, a nolde green rydyng cott, —— ——	0	1	8
Item, a nolde gowne, lacking the ſleſſs, furred with broken foxe,	0	1	8
Item, a doblet of cremyſynt velvet ſlevyd with tawny velvet,	0	3	4
Item, a nolde ditto of blak ſatten, —— ——	0	0	8

* A ſhroud.

† Pillowbeirs.

‡ *Rail*, a woman's upper garment. Johnſon. Hence *night rail.*

§ Furr. See Sepulch. Mon. Introd. p. cxc.

‖ Can this be the ſkin of the polecat, frequently called *fitchet?* See Gent. Mag. LV. 534.

** *Puke*, an old word for yellow. Johnſon.

†† Cyprus. See before, p. 114.

‡‡ *Gavardina*, Ital. a coarſe frock. Johnſon, from Shakeſpeare.

§§ A ſhade of yellow.

Item,

	£.	s.	d.
Item, one ditto of white fatten, one blak, — —	o	1	8
Item, two cotts of fence *, one covered with fowks, the other with bokeram, — — — —	o	16	o
Item, two armyng dobletts, and a pair of fleffs of mayle, —	o	1	4
Item, a pair of fcarlet hofe, ditto blak, — —	o	4	o
Item, two old capps and two other caps, — —	o	o	10
Item, a pello of party filke, — — —	....		
The wyffe rayment.			
Item, a gowne of tawny chamlet furred with gray, —	1	16	8
Item, ditto of cremyfyng with bogge of Spayne, —	1	10	o
Item, ditto of violet with gray, — —	1	o	o
Item, ditto of ditto furred with callyvan and mynks, —	1	10	o
Item, ditto old of murre † furred with gray, — —	o	13	4
Item, ditto of blak furred with blak facks ‡, — —	o	13	4
Item, ditto, — — —	1	o	o
Item, ditto with old gray, — —	o	8	o
Item, a nolde gowne of cremyfyng lyned with farfnet, and purfelyd § with blak velvet, — — — —	1	6	8
Item, a gowne of pewke lyned with aveke, purfelyd with tawny velvet,	o	13	4
Item, a nold gown of murrey lined with bokram, and furred with blak velvet, — — —	o	13	4
Item, a kertell ‖ of damafk, the bodys of faten old, lined with yello cotton, — — — —	o	10	o
Item, a nolde ditto of fatten broken, — —	o	2	8
Item, ditto of blak chamlet, — — —	o	3	4
Item, ditto of tawny ditto, — — —	o	4	o
Item, ditto, — — —	o	1	8
Item, half a yard of cremyfyng cloth moth eaten, —	o	2	o
Item, two yards of white cotton, — —	o	1	8
Item, two old furrs of caleyvar, — — —	o	8	o
Her bonnetts.			
Item, a bonnet of black velvet garnifhed with damafke gold,	1	6	8
Item, a nolde ditto worn fore, — — —	o	4	o
Item, four old frontletts of dyvers colors of velvet, —	o	8	o
Item, four partelets of velvet of tawne and blak, 2 unfurred and 2 furred with conny, — — — —	o	4	o
Item, two old tepetts of farfnet, worne, — —	o	1	8
Item, a kerftenyng ** towell broken, — — —	o	o	2

* Coats of defence or armour. † Dark red. Johnfon. ‡ Q. *facks* for *fox*.

§ *Pourfilee*, French. A fort of antient trimming for women's gowns. Bailey.

‖ Jacket or fhort gown.

** *Chriftening* or *chrifm* cloth. *Chrifmalis* or *Chrifmatis pannus*. *Chrifmal* veftis candida quæ fuper caput baptizati ponitur. Durand. VI. Ration. c. 82. num. 16. c. 95. num. 3. See more in Du Cange in voc.

	£.	s.	d.
In the garret over the great chamber.			
Item, two peſſes of old painted hangyng, — —	0	0	8
Item, a nolde cols, and a cheſt paynted, — —	0	1	4
Item, a bedeſtede with pyllors *, — — —	0	1	8
Item, old torches broken, — — —	0	1	8
Item, a nold pair clavycords, — — —	0	0	8
Item, two pyllors of down covered with old broken ſarſnett, —	0	2	0
Item, ſix playn pyllors of down of dyvers ſorts, —	0	6	8
In the garrett next the ſtreet.			
Item, in dyvers lomber therefore a ſylke the women, —	0	0	4
In the chamber againſt the ſtrete.			
Item, three peſſes of hangyngs, — —	0	1	0
Item, two old fetherbeds without bolſters, — —	0	8	0
Item, a ſtanding bedeſtede, and a pair of blankets of wollen, and a Norwege coveryng, — — —	0	2	0
In the ſhop.			
Item, two lode of fawle † wode, — —	0	4	0
Item, in bellets, — — —	0	2	0
Item, in colls, — — —	....		
Item, three ſwords, a hanger, and a dagger, —	0	4	2
Item, a premer printed in parchment, with two claſpis of ſilver,	0	4	0
Item a demy portuos ‡ printed, — —	0	1	0
Item, a premmer lymmed with gold, and with imagery written honds, — — —	0	8	4
Item, an old purſe, and a pyncaſe of cloth of gold, —	0	2	0
Item, an image of Our Lady of mother perle, —	0	0	4
Item, a pair of ſmall ſilver bedes, — —	0	3	4
Item, a ſtandyſhe of cypreſs, — —	0	0	4
Item, two remnants of ſarſnet, — —	0	0	4
Item, three old doblets and ſhredys of velvet, —	0	8	0
Item, a lytell button of courſe gold, — —	0	1	0
Item, an olde lytell covering for a lytell trokell bed, —	0	2	0
Item, an old pelyon with the pelyon cloth of old chamlet,	0	0	6
Item, two dozen poynts § with other ends of ſylk, —	0	0	8

* Or as we now ſay a *four-poſt* bed. I cannot help thinking that this is a miſpelling for *fore* poſt, and that the tranſition was from heavy teaſters with vallance hung up to the cieling, and ſupported only behind by two poſts or the frame of the head-board to the teaſter intirely ſupported by 4 poſts or pillars. A *ſtanding* bedſtead is only oppoſed to a *truckle* or preſs bed, or one that folded up.

† Q. *large*, oppoſed to billets. ‡ Portiforium.

§ Point, a ſtring with a tag. Johnſon from Shakeſpeare.

Item,

	£.	s.	d.
Item, thirty-fix ells of browne lynnen cloth, the ell 4*d*. —	0	12	0
Item, other old gere found in the houfe, — —	0	1	4
Item, one oz and ½ of corall, — — —	0	2	6
Item, a carpet of jeen * makyng, — —	0	8	4
£.74. 15*s*. 1*d*.			

Certain ftuff at the George at Billingfgate, as appereth by the teftimony of Mr. *Porther*.

	£.	s.	d.
Sperat † detts.			
Item, fir Henry Wyatt, knyght, for his wages, —	1	0	0
Item, the prior of Amyfbury, — — —	3	9	8
Chattells.			
Item, for the recorde for the howfes at the ftoks by patent,	21	17	6
Item, for the lees of a houfe at Billingfgate, —	1	0	0
Defperat detts.			
Item, the abbot of Bewley ‡, — — —	3	0	0
Item, Mr. *Copynger*, — — —	16	0	0
Item, the abbot of Ramfey, — —	5	6	8
Item, the priory of Showerdreth §, — —	5	13	4
Item, *Robert Jonys*, — — —	1	0	0
Detts that the teftator oweth.			
Item, to the bere wyff ‖, — — —	2	0	0
Item, the wever for weving lynnen cloth, — —	0	5	0
Item, houfe-rent, — — —	2	15	10
Fynerall expences.			
Fynerall expences, with other neceffary charges, —	73	6	8
Item, the probate of the teftament, with other neceffary charges,	...	...	...
Playte and jewells.			
Item, a ftandyng cope gilt, with a cover chaffyd upright, and a woman in the bodame, poyze 41 oz. at 3*s*. 6*d*. —	7	3	6
Item, ditto playne with a cover gilt, with a rofe and a garlent in the bodom, weighing 18 oz. at 3*s*. 6*d*. — —	3	3	0
Item, three goblets gilt with a cover, and in the fnope ** a white fheld with a grene lyon graven, weighing 72 oz. at 3*s*. 6*d*. —	12	12	0
Item, a lytle playn ftondyng cope gylt, with a cover, with a broken flower of amell †† broken in the bodom, weighing			

* *Genoa*, as *Jane* in Chaucer. † Oppofed to *defperat*. ‡ Q. *Beaulieu*, Hants.
§ Q. St. Mary Spittle, an Auftin *priory* without Bifhopfgate, which had lands in Shoreditch. Tanner, N. M. 312.
‖ Ale wife. ** handle. See p. 126. †† *Emaille*, enamel.

	£.	s.	d.
Item, three goblets pſell gilt, with a cover, with a collombyne in the tope, weighing 56 oz. at 3*s*. 6*d*. — —	9	6	8
Item, a playne peyſe with a ſtere, and a man ſhering in the bodom, 10 oz. at 3*s*. 2*d*. — — —	1	11	8
Item, a peſſe pſell gilt with St. Gregory's pelly in the bodome, weighing 9 oz. at 3*s*. 2*d*. — — —	1	8	6
Item, two peſſes pſell gilt chaſſyd, with a cover, weighing 39 oz. at 3*s*. 2*d*. — — —	4	11	10
Item, two ſmall peſſes pſell gilt, with ſome ...... in the bodome, weighing 23 oz. at 3*s*. 4*d*. — —	3	16	8
Item, two rownde ſalts with a cover pſell gilt, chaſſyd, weighing 42 oz. at 3*s*. 4*d*. — — —	7	0	0
Item, ſeven ſpoons with apoſtles *, and on gilt ſpone, weighing 12 ox. at 3*s*. 2*d*. — — —	1	19	7
Item, ten ſpoons with dyamonds ſnops †, weighing 9 oz. at 3*s*.	1	7	0
Item, two flat maſſors ‡, one broken, weighing 17 oz. at 2*s*.	1	14	0
Item, two meddell maſſors with olde bones and boſſys, weighing			
Item, two ſkawere § ſalts, 8 ſkawere § with the covers pſell gilt, weighing 32 oz. at 3*s*. 4*d*. — — —	5	6	8
Item, thirteen ſpoons with the apoſtles gilt, weighing 22 oz. at 3*s*. 4*d*. — — — —	3	13	4
Item, two ſtanding maſſors with a broken cover, and 2 ſcops of maſors covers, weighing 28 oz. at 2*s*. 8*d*. — —	3	14	8
Item, a naylle ‖ pot pſell gilt, the cover broken, weighing 12½ oz. at 3*s*. 4*d*. — — — —	2	1	8
Item, a littel broken pott with a cover gilt, weighing 13 oz. at 2*s*. 8*d*.	1	14	8
£.94. 4*s*. 11*d*.			

Jewells for her body.

	£.	s.	d.
Item, a girdell of ſilver lyned with black velvet, with 32 roſſes, and another lyned with cremyſyne velvet, both weighing 19 oz. at 3*s*. 4*d*. — — —	3	3	4
Item, a broad gerdell of ſilver, with 12 ſtods of ſilver, weighing 12 oz. at 3*s*. 4*d*. — — —	2	0	0
Item, a gerdell of corne work, with a bokell and a pendent, the croſſe damaſke golde, weighing 7 oz. at 3*s*. 4*d*. —	1	3	4
Item, a demyſent with a chyne, and a pommander ** and a pendent, a freangell of ſilver and gelt, 7 oz. at 3*s*. 4*d*. —	1	3	4
Item, two pair of beds of ſilver gelt, 13 oz. at 3*s*. 4*d*. —	2	3	4
Item, a pair of coral beds gawdyd with gawdys of ſilver ††, and gelt, 10 oz. at 3*s*. 4*d*. — — — —	1	13	4

* Of them ſee Hiſt. of Hawſted, p. 209. n. † See the preceding page.
‡ Bowls. See Hiſt. of Hawſted, p. 119. n. § Square and eight ſquare. ‖ An ale-pot.
** Q. gems or jewels.

Item,

	£.	s.	d.
Item, a demeffent*, and 2 pair of hooks of filver and gelt, 5 oz. at 3*s*. 4*d*. — — — — —	0	16	8
Item, five gret ryngs of gold fyne, weighing 3½ oz. at £.1. 16*s*. per oz. — — — — —	6	12	6
Item, fifteen ryngs, and 2 fmall jomes †, and a littyll fmall chyne of gold, weighing 2 oz. at £.1. 13*s*. 4*d*. ——	4	11	8
Item, broken filver, 1¾ oz. at 3*s*. 2*d*. — —	0	5	6
Item, a lytell fhelde of gold, innamyled with whyt and grene, and with 3 perlls, weighig 1¼ oz. prayfed at —	0	8	0

£.23. 2*s*. 7½*d*.

From 1516 to 1530 the charges and difcharges confift of little more than rents, and quitrents, and expences of chantries. Under 1552 is inferted the King's commiffion, directed by the lord mayor and other commiffioners to Edmond Ca'difhe and Robert Young, churchwardens, for the trewe certificate of all the churche-goods and ornaments; alfo what, to whom, and when fold. The commiffioners order, figned George Barne ‡, knight, lord-mayor, Nicolas, boufshe § of London, fir Roger Chomle ||, knight, lord chief juftice, and others. Dated Guildhall, April 15, 1553.

The effect of the King's Majefty's letters to them, that all the linen of the churches in London and fuburbs, except what is neceffary for prefent ufe, be given to the ufe of the poor in Chrift Church hofpital. A letter to the churchwardens hereon, dated 24 Jan. 6 Edward VI. figned Nicolas London, Rowland Hill, Richard Dobo.

The churchwardens return of veftments, linen, and plate: among the former were three fuits of cloth of gold, with three copes of the fame to each fuit; four ditto ditto of velvet **, two ditto ditto of bodkin; feveral others of damafk, &c.; eight childrens' copes; three croffe clothes; a carnife cloth of red bodkyn with eight ftremers; a ftayned cloth which went about the fepulcre; 15 banner cloths; an ould veftment of fattyn and brydgis; a veftment of whitbuftyne with a red crofs; another of whit bufime for the high aulter whole *barnys* [hangings] of clothe of goulde, courtins of red and white farfnet; another of ruffet clothe of golde with courtins of ruffet fylke; two others of white fylke and grene bodkin; another of grene bodkyn for St. Chriftopher's altar; one of white for St. Catharine's; one of blewe for St. Anne's; and one of white for our Lady's. Thefe harnyfes are diftinguifhed into thofe "above and beneath with curtains."

* See p. 128. l. 35. † Q. gems or jewels.

‡ Haberdafher, fon to George Barne, citizen and haberdafher of London. Stowe, 584. He was buried in the church of Allhallows, Gracechurch-ftreet, 1586, Ib. 220; and was probably a benefactor to that of St. Bartholomew behind the Royal Exchange. Ib. 191.

§ Bifhop Ridley. || *Cholmeley*. Dugdale, Chron. Ser. fub anno. ** Baudekyn.

The plate conſiſted of . . . gilt chalice and pattyns of ſilver, and one ſilver criſmatory, two ſhipps with two ſpoons, two cruetts, two candelſtics, and a pyx; two paire of orgayns, the one paire gretter than the other; a ſilver croſs with a criſtoll in it bound with latice wire.

The churchwardens had ſold, 2 Edward VI. a chalice and pix of ſilver unaccounted for (at 5*s.* 5*d.* per oz.), and a deſke with other lattyn; alſo to *Jefres* the baſket-maker 7 lb. ½ of alliblaſter, at 2*s.* 4*d.* per lb. total 17*s.* 6*d.* To others the *gilt* of three images at 12*s.*; and 14 lb. of pewter at 4*s.* 8*d.*; to —— *Red*, goldſmith, 12 oz. of ſilver, being claſpes of bokes, and the plate of a rinter *, and other plate.

The parſelles of ornaments lately appertaying to this church are now reſtorede agayne by the Quene's Majeſtie's goodnes, 20 December, 1° of her reign, by the handes of Arthur Sturton, at the Quene's wardrop at Weſtminſter; viz. three copes of red clothe of gold, for the prieſt, deacon, and ſubdeacon; three ditto of white ditto for ditto; three ditto of blue ditto; one whole hangens of cloth of gold riſed with ruſſet velvet for the high altar; and one of ditto with white and grene velvet for St. Chriſtopher's. A liſt of the church-plate, &c. 1553, 1 Mary, precedes this.

The pariſhioners gave a croſs of copper gilt, a veſtment of grene bodkin, and two curtains of white ſilke and ſarſnet.

Then follows the churchwardens' accempt, 1554-5, 1 and 2 Philip and Mary, and their grant of an annual rent of £.4. to John Frank, bere-brewer, for 40 years, from 1556 to 1596; and extract from the will of Thomas Clayton, late citizen and white-baker, of London, giving a tenement for repairs of the church; and 46 oz. of ſilver plate, 20 *downewaight* * to be made into two chalices. Allyn Percy, parſon. Other leaſes, the laſt of which is dated 13 Jan. 1557, 20 Elizabeth, Thomas Fallerd, parſon.

The remaining half of this book is blank. The paper of a coarſe texture, and yellowiſh; the mark a crown.

The ſand remains on ſome of the late writing.

The other book is twice as thick.

* Q. rincer, or veſſel to *rince* or waſh others in?

† Q. *avoirdupoize?*

The

The Charge or Receipt 1516.	£.	s.	d.
Received of *John Nafing's* chantry, — —	9	2	0
John Cauflon's, — — —	18	13	4
Richard Goflyn's, — — —	8	19	4
William Cambryge's, — — —	10	6	8
John Bedham's, — — —	13	6	8
Rofe Wrytyll's, — — —	6	14	4
The rents of our chirche, — — —	18	3	6
In Cafueltys, — — — — —	3	13	8
In Clerk's wages and Pafchall Money, and in beme lights,	8	13	2
[£.104. 8*s.* 8*d.*] Summa totalis, —	80	12	8

Difcharge or Expence.			
Paid for charge of *J. Nafyng's* chantry, —	8	18	6
J. Cauflon's, — —	10	9	10
R. Goflyng's, — — —	8	2	9½
W. Cambryg's, — — —	6	4	2
J. Bedham's, — — —	14	3	8
R. Wrytyll's, — — —	7	3	8
Chirch rentys, — — —	15	17	6
To our clark conduct and our fextyns, for their wages in this yere,	11	14	0
Paid for the charge of the wax-chandler, — —	1	2	4
Indofing of this accompt, — — —	0	18	4
[£.90. 18*s.* 4½*d.*] Somma, —	83	13	4½

So ther reftyth of this account due to the chirche be me *Andrew Evyngar*, — — — —	13	14	3½
Item, money received of *John Ruffel*, the fame tyme beynge behynde for clarke's wages, — — — —	0	5	5
Received of *Robert Revell*, for beyng behynde of clarke's wages,	0	2	3
Received of *John Petyt*, for ftuff which remayned in hys handes,	0	6	4
Som̃ totalis put into the box as this day of accompt,	14	8	7½

* Q. if the fame as the other article to this priorefs?

Expences on St. Mary's Church, STAMFORD, 1427, ex Comput' Johis Leche, Goldſmyth, de Stamf', ppoſiti eccleſie ad pontem Stamf', anno ſexto Regis Henrici Sexti poſt Conqueſtum. Cotton MSS. Veſp. A. XXIV. fol. 3. b.

	£.	s.	d.
Expended in mending the bells,	0	6	0
Paid for timber and iron,	0	1	2
Wax bought to make two torches,	0	15	4
A chain,	0	0	7
Paid *Thomas Harpmaker*, for making the ſchafte *,	0	3	4
And for making two torches,	0	1	10
Glue,	0	0	11
Red lead,	0	0	2
In charges for bringing the ſchafte,	0	0	8
A bell rope,	0	0	8
Pro nerfis † for the ſchafte	0	0	1
A little rope,	0	0	2
For the plomber,	0	3	4
Cloth for the ſchafte,	0	0	11
Writing,	0	0	2
Given the players,	0	0	6
For hanging the towel ‡,	0	0	4
Thred for the canopy,	0	0	1
Mending the books,	0	0	10
For hanging the napary and towel,	0	0	5
Leather ‡ for the bell-ropes,	0	0	2
Victuals for *Richard Kerver*, and brother *Rowſby* ‖	0	0	5
Given to a certain carpenter, a carver, to inſpect the rood loft,	0	0	6
Paid to the carter *(bigario)* of *John Whitſide*,	0	0	9
Paid *Thomas* [the] glazier, for mending the church-windows,	0	5	0
Paid *John* [the] roper, for a bell-rope,	0	0	11
Paid him for another rope,	0	0	10
Thred bought for the veſtments,	0	0	1
Paid *Agnes Young* and others,	0	0	10
Paid *Thomas Baſſe*, for a bawdryck §,	0	0	6
Paid *Richard Kerver*,	1	10	0
For a little bow for a bell,	0	0	4
Wax for the common light,	0	4	0
Total	3	12	10

The two torches above were great wax candles, as I take it, made to carry in proceſſion, or to ſet on the high altar, or before the rood, or ſome other image.

The ſhaft, or ſpire, was an ornament made to adorn the image, or ſhrine, of ſome ſaint.

* Compare l. 11. 13. 16. and 39. † Perhaps *ſtrings*. ‡ See l. 22.

‡ To be put round the ropes, at the diſtance of *fallowing*, as they call it in ringing.

§ A belt. See p. 135. l. 25. p. 155. l. 16.

‖ Can this be the ſame perſon who is mentioned in the next page, l. 19, as dying 5 Edward VI.?

The money given the players, I guefs, was paid the wardens of the crafts or trades, who, every year, acted the play of Corpus Chrifti * upon Corpus Chrifti day, in the north-chancel of this church, called Corpus Chrifti chapel; or elfewhere in the town.

The canopy mentioned in the above account was a common ftate, fet up, in thefe times, in all churches over the high altar; under which in a pix †, or little box of gold, filver, ivory, or chryftal, hung the confecrated hoft, referved there to be carried to the fick upon any emergency; when it was taken down, and with the canopy over it, born by the clergy in proceffion to the houfes of fuch inhabitants as were dying, as they thought, and called for that facred *viaticum*. By the above account it fhould feem that many of the common fort of people had, as yet, no furnames, but were rather known by the names of their feveral trades, as Richard the Carver, Thomas the Glafier, John the Roper, &c.

Brother Rowfby abovementioned was not a frier, but a fecular prieft. He attended the carver, as it fhould feem, to overfee and direct him whilft he was defigning fome new image or piece of fculpture for the farther ornament of the church; and therefore the churchwarden fpent 5*d*. upon them; money enough, in thefe days, to entertain any two men either at dinner or fupper. This William Rowceby made a ftrange will, and died 5 Edward VI. being then parfon of St. Clement's ‡.

The rood-loft, infpected, as above, by the carver, was a gallery, in popifh times, fituate in every church between the nave and chancel. It was called the rood-loft, from a great rood, or image of the crucifixion fet up in the midft of it; befides which, there were two other images, a Mary and a John (as the common people then called them) ftanding by it, that of the bleffed Virgin on the right, that of the beloved difciple on the left, hand fide of the rood. In the fame place was likewife a figure of the particular faint to whom the church was dedicated. All thefe had generally a veil, or curtain, let down before them when fervice was done; but in fervice-time were lighted up with lamps and wax tapers.

In thofe days men were fond of fuch pageantries; but I now mention them, that my readers may better underftand what I treat of §.

* For further particulars of this play, fee Peck's Annals of Stamford, B. xiv. §. 4. p. 4, 5.

† The pix contained the confecrated hofts for communion, and for the ufe of the fick, called the *viaticum*. The repofitory for expofition and carrying in publick proceffions is called the Remonftrance; and in old inventories the *monftre*, or *mounftier*, from the French word *monftrer*, to fhew or exhibit to public view. In the Ely inventory it is called *monftral*.

‡ See Gentleman's Magazine, LIX. p. 900; or fir J. Cullum's Hift. of Hawfted, 18, 48; and p. 101 before, note.

§ Peck, ut fupra.

The

The will of William Bruges, Garter King at arms, 1449.

In the name of the Fader, Son, and Holy Goſt, III perſons in Trinite, and on ſole God, Y William Bruges, otherwiſe cleped Garter Kyng of Armes, in my right and in my freſh mynde thrugh the enſpiracion of the Holy Goſt, the Thurſday the XXVI day of Feverer, the yere of our Lord God $\text{MCCCC}^{\text{XLIX}}_{\text{L.}}$ and the yere of the Kyng Henry the Sexte the XXVI, make this my preſent teſtament and laſt will. As for the firſt and foremoſt, Y bequethe my ſoule to the gret mercy of oure Lord God Jhu, that ſuffred payne and paſſion of his gret mercy, to bring my wretched ſoule from the carnal peyne and dampnation to the eternal blyſſe and redempcion, and to that gret mercy Y to be brought, Y beſeech our bleſſed Lady, mayden and wyf, that, ſhe, of her gret grace and goodneſſe, like and pleaſe to be mean and immediatrice. And alſo Y beſeche al the glorious ſeyntes and ſeynteſſes in heaven, that they, for thaire glorious martirdoms and goodneſſes, ... to Almighty God, that ſo Y may finde, and have alſo, yf it be poſſible, my body to be brought and buryed in the church of Saynt George within Staunford, there to be buried, in the myddes of the quere of the ſaid chirch. To the whych ſaid chirch Y bequeth a gret holy-water ſcoppe* of ſilver, with a ſtaff benature †, the ſaid benature, and ſtaff weyng XX. nobles in plate and more. Item, to the ſaid chirch I bequethe a peyre of cenſours of ſylver, with a ſhip of ſylver for frankincenſe, and I ſpone in the ſame ſhip, of ſylver ‡. Item, I bequethe to the ſaid chirch a little handbell of ſylver, of the gretneſſe of a ſacryng-bell §. Item, I bequethe to the ſame chirche, a little round cofyn of ſylver, cloſed in ſyngyng bred, and not the hoſte. Item, Y bequethe to the ſaid chirch, for ther ſolempne feſte dayes, to ſtande upon the high awter, II grete baſyne of ſylver, and II high candleſticks of ſylver. Item, I bequethe to the ſaid chirch, I coupe of ſylver, in the whych is one litel box of yvory, to put in the bleſſid ſacrament; and to hang over the high awter. . . . . Item, Y bequethe to the ſaid chirch, one gret chalice, over-gilt; of the wight of C*s*. to ſerve for theyre ſolempne feſtes. Item, I bequethe to the ſaid chirch, ane hole ſute of veſtmytes of ruſſet velvet. One coope, cheſible diacones ‖, for decones; with the awbes and parures. And two caſe corporaſſes ** of the ſame ſute of veſtmyntes. Item, I bequethe to the ſaid chirch an other hole ſute of black velvet, I cheſible diacones, for decones, or frees of white clothe of gold powdred with garters, and two caſſe corporaſſes. Item, Y bequethe and ordeyne that the gret framd . . . . that Y have lying in the gret berne in my place at Kentiſhton [by London] to be ſold to the moſt value, and the mony riſing thereof to be beſtowed upon the compleſſhyng and endyng of the ſeyd chirch of Staunford; that is to be underſtand, in coveryng with lede, glaſyng, and makyng of pleyn deſques, and of a pleyn rodelofte, and in puyng of the ſeyd chirch,

* See before, p. 107   † *Benoiſtier*, *Benitier*, Fr. *Benedictarium*, a portable veſſel for holywater. Or Staff benature I take to be the ſprinkling bruſh with a ſilver handle, called by the Romaniſts at this day, *Aſperges*, borrowed from the old Roman *Aſpergillum* or ſprinkler.

‡ See before, p. 93.   § Maſs-bell.   ‖ Dalmatics.

** A caſe for the *corporas* or conſecrated hoſt. Caſe coporaſſes, a kind of burſe to preſerve the corporal cloth on which the hoſt is laid before and after conſecration, and made ſquare with guſſets to open and ſhut.

nourt curiouſly, but pleynly; and in paving of the hole chirch, body and quere, with broad Holand tyle. Item, I bequethe to the ſeyd chirch of Seynt George, a ſolempnitie of array for the feſt of Corpus Chriſti, oon partie wrought in the plate, of ſylver, and over-gilt; and that other in tymbre to be born between the decon and ſubdeacon: the tymbre is peynted, and over-gilt with fyne gold. And, for every ſign of the paſſion, an aungel berynge the ſign of the croſſe, and of the crowne of thorne; another aungel beryng the pillar and the ſcourges: another aungel beyryng the ſpere and the ſponges; another aungel beyryng the remnant of the ſigns of the paſſion; and, in the middle of the feretorye, a gret round blak corver; and one peynted with gold and aſure, and peynted with ſterres of gold, in the middel of that round blok, for a gret coupe of ſylver, and overgilt, to ſtande on, upon a pynne of tre*. And, in the ſeyd couple, a litel box of ſilver, and over-gilt; to put in the ſacrament. This gret coupe, and the litle together, firſt to be ſet upon the gret blok of tre*, with a gret croun of and over gilt, garniſhed with ſtones clepyd dublets, redde, blue, grene, and yellowe, garniſhed wyth counterfeyt perles made of ſilver; the croun of the wight of Cs. This croun fyrſt to be ſet upon the gret round blok of tre, and thanne upon the pynne ſtandyng in the ſeyd blok. The ſaid coupe to be crouned withoute wyth a ſmall croune, ordeyned redy therefore. Item, I bequethe to the ſeyd feretorye, a tabernacle wele ywrought of ſylver and over-gilt, of the wight of one marc, or thereabouts, goyng wyth a byll to be ſet high upon the coupe. And above, upon the poynt of the ſeyd tabernacle, a litel croſſe of ſilver and over-gilt, goyng alſo by a vyce †. All this plate that longeth to the feſte (that is to ſay of Corpus Chriſti) yf myn executors ſamyn that yt ſhould be in more ſure garde of the parisſhors of the chirch of oure Lady of Staunford; Y would yt ſhuld reſt and abyde in the garde of hem; and wythyn theire treſour. And atte daye of the feſt of Corpus Chriſti, hit to follow the ſacrement of the ſeyd chirch of our Lady, yf it pleſe the parysſhors of the ſeyd chirch of our Lady; onleſſe that they wol have yt ſerve for both. Item, Y ordeyn and bequethe that the II chapelles of our Lady and Seynt George ‡, wythyn the ſeyd chirch of Seynt George be cloſid wyth oſtrich boarde §, and clere ſtoried ||, after ſuch quantite as the cloſure of pleyn borde there now conteineth. And to the ſeyd chappel of our Lady, Y bequethe II images of our Lady and Seynt George, beyng in paynted ſtone, and in my chapel at Kentisſhton. And to the ſame chappel of our Lady of Staunford, Y bequethe my grete candleſtykes of laton, that ſtanden in my chapel at Kentiſhton. Item, Y bequethe to the ſeyd chappel of Seynt George of Staunford, the ymage of the Trinite of ſtoon, ſtandyng in my chapel at Ken-

* Pin and block of *wood*. † Screw.

‡ This church having neither north or ſouth chancels, theſe two chapels were therefore made of the upper parts of the north and ſouth iſles. The north chapel was parted from the reſt of the church by a ſcreen, which went from the north ſide of the chancel to the firſt pillar on the north ſide of the nave, and from that pillar by another ſcreen which ran acroſs to the wall of the ſaid north iſle. So that it took in a handſome ſquare corner, and two windows at the upper end of the ſaid north iſle. The ſouth chapel was exactly of the ſame compaſs and proportion. Theſe ſcreens were taken down in 1719, when the church was repaired.

§ See before, p. 97. 104.

|| Q. with an *upper* ſtory, as the *upper* windows of nave and chancel are called *clere-ſtory* windows.

tifhton, wyth the brannche of laton, for III lights, accordyng thereto; yt to be fett upon a foot of ftone, higher than the heddes of the ymages of our Lady and Seynt George. Item, I bequethe the feyd fmall candleftykkes ftandyng in my chapel at Kentifhton, to the new chapel of our Lady now in makyng in the fame town. And as for the feyd three ymages of ftoon (that is to fay, the ymages of the Trinite, our Lady, and Seynt George) Y woyl have made, for eiche of theym, a gret cofyn of elmyn borde; the feyd ymages to be nayled in faft, ftuffed with hey, and fo carryed, at my cofte, unto Staunford, and fet up in the feyd church of Seynt George. Item, the II lefs candleftyks to be fet upon the awter of our Lady, in the feyd town of Staunford; and there to ferve brennyng from the begynnyng of the Gofpel, unto the tyme that the preft have ufed, upon my coft, as my goods will fuffyce to contynue yt . . . every taper of halfe a pound wight; and every day a maffe to be feyd of our Lady. Item, I ordeyn and wol that the II greter candelftyks, beyng in my feyd chappel at Staunford, ferve in the chapel of our lady of Staunford; and that on ftand upon the ground, afore the ymage of Seynt George in the fame chapel. And for eiche of thefe candelftykkes to be ordeyned a taper of waxe of I pound wight, and, fo ferved, to be lighted atte dyvyne fervyce at pryncipal feft-days, and al other folempne feftes, as, at matyns, pryme, maffe, and the yeven fongs. Item, I bequethe and ordeyne to the feyd church of St. George of Staunford, a little coffre, ftandyng bounden wyth plate of yren, ful of veftments; except on veftment, yf yt be therein, and that ys of blak fatyn ground, figured wyth rede velvet; the orfreyes wrought wyth the nedel with ymages, the which faid veft-ment Y wol yt ferve for our Lady-chapel in Staunford only. Item, I ordeyne and bequethe to the chapel of our Lady in Seynt Mary chirch at Sandewich, an half long gown of purple velvett furred wyth martrons *, of that to be made a chefible wyth the parures †, and wyth the furre to be bouzt and ordeyned the orfreyes, lyke to the orfreyes of the fingel veftyment of blak fatyn, lyned with red velvet. And yf the feyd furre of matrones wol not fuffice to ordeyne the feyd orfreys, myn ex-ecutors to put to fuch mony as they may have of myne, to the percomplisfhing of the feyd orfreyes; and fo endid to be delyvered to the feyd chirch. Item, I be-quethe to the feyd chappel of our Lady in Seynt Mary chirch of Sandwich, the chalice of fylver and over-gilt, that my wyf hath; and myne executors to make for the fame chalice II fmall nets of fylver and over-gilt, of the price of XX*s*. and than my wyfe to fend yt to the feyd chirch. The refidue of all my goodes, after my dettes payd, Y geve and bequethe to Anneys my wyf principal execu-trice, Thomas Haddon, hir broder, co-executor to her, and Mafter Clement Den-fton, clerk, overfeer of the fame my teftament; and that they ordeyne and dyfpofe for my foule, as they fhall feem beft, to the plefire of God, and to the proffite of my foule. Geven at London, the day and yere abovementioned ‡.

* Martens. † Ornaments. Fr.

‡ E. MSS. Afhmoleanis ex regiftro Stafford, Archiepifc. Cantuarienfis, p. 187. Probatum coram domino archiepifcopo apud Lambith XII die Martii MCCCCXLIX. & commiffa fuit admi-niftratio executoribus in dicto teftamento nominatis. Peck's Account of Stamford, B. XIV. p. 25.

Extracts

Extracts from the Church Books belonging to the pariſh of Great Marlow, Bucks, beginning in 1593.

Year	Item	£.	s.	d.
	Item, received of the churchmen *William James* and *James Lynne*, for the profytt of the Whitſonale,	5	0	0
	Item, payde *John Blacke*, for mendynge the bells when the Queen came to Biſham,	0	1	1
	Item, payde for nayylls and drynke the ſame tyme,	0	1	0
	Item, payde to the ringers upon Saint Hughe's daye, anno 1592,	0	4	4
1595.	Item, received of players for playinge in the church leofte,	0	2	4
	Item, received of the profytt of the Mydſemer ale laſte paſte,	6	3	4
	Item, payde to one for the carrying of the morrys coats to Maydenhed,	0	0	4
1596.	Item, agred for the bells and ſallett oyle for the clocke,	0	0	4
1603.	Item, gayned by the Whyſſonale,	11	7	2
1605.	Item, payede to the parritor for our warninge,	0	0	6
	Item, for the booke of articles,	0	0	10
	Item, payde to the ryngers when the Kynge came to Byſſome,	0	5	0
	Item, payde for the booke of Cannons,	0	2	0
	Item, for payntinge the Kyng's armes in the churche,	1	3	4
1607.	Item, payde to the ryngers when the Kynge came to Buſtleham,	0	4	0
	Item, payde for beare when the loft was pulled downe and ſett up againe,	0	0	6

1608. Goods belonging to the church.

Item, fyve payr of garters of bells.
Item, fyve coats.
Item, fower fethrs.

Year	Item	£.	s.	d.
1609.	Item, cleared at our Whitſonale,	16	0	0
	Item, payde to Mr. *Robert Farmer* towards his charges in following of our ſuite for the churche and bridge lands,	1	0	0
	Item, delivered to the bridge wardens,	7	0	0
1610.	Item, payd to Dr. *Smyth*, for a lycenſe to place men in the churche,	0	2	6
	Item, payde to his clerke for writinge it,	0	1	0
	Item, payde for a quart of ſack gyven to Dr. *Smythe*,	0	1	0
1611.	Item, payde to the ryngers when the Kynge came to Byſham,	0	3	4
	Item, delivered to the bridge wardens of the money that was gotten at the Whitſonale,	7	3	0
1612.	Item, received of the churchwardens of Byſham Loane of our Morris's coats and bells,	0	2	6
	Item, payde for a booke of Biſhop *Jewel's* works,	1	4	0
	Item, payde to the Biſhop's apparitor for his fees for warninge us to the courte att Amtill, for not havinge a table of degrees of marriage, and a regiſter-booke in parchment,	0	2	4
1613.	Item, received for ſir *Rotheram Willoughby* his grave in the church,	0	6	8

An Inventory of the Plate, Jewels, and Ornaments of the Cathedral Church at Ely, which were left in the cuſtody of Mr. Robert Wells, Guardian there, after the Surrender of the Monaſtery into the King's Hands (made November 20, 31 Henry VIII.), excluſive of what had been taken away for the King's Uſe. From a MS. in the Library of Corpus Chriſti College, Cambridge, Miſcell. 20. p. 341.

In the Veſtrye, Jowells.

Gilt Plate.

Imprimis, a pair of gret candleſticks gilt weying 80 ounces.
Item, a pix gilt weying 17.
A ſtonding monſtral for the ſacrament, within a pynne of tre * in the bottom, 124.
A croſs gilt, with a fote of copper, 94.
One croſs with a ſtaff, weying 175 un.
Another croſs, without Mary and John, with a ſtaff, 88.
A gilt chalice, with a patent † enameled, 73.
Six other chalices with patents, 124.
Three pair of ſenſers with chaynes, white, 124.
Two gilt crewets, 13.
A cryſmatory of lether, with 3 boxes of ſilver not weyd.
A ball, ſilver and gilt, 14.
A chalice and two crewets gilt, 37.

Gilt and White.

A hole ‡ water-pot with a ſtick, weying 51.
A peyr of candleſticks, with a pece of wode on the foot of one of them, 71.
Two white baſons, 80.
Two crewets, 13.
A ſhip §, lacking a cover, 11.
In all, 1188 ounces.

Ornaments in the Veſtrie.

Imprimis, a ſute of red tiſſewe, with 3 coopes.
Item, a ſute of courſe tiſſewe, with thre coopes ſutable.
A ſute of rede velvet, imbrodred with flowers.
A ſute of rede velvet, with ſmall lyons of perle, with 2 coopes ſutable.
Four coopes of rede ſilke full of ymagerie.
A ſute of old bawdkyn, red and grene, with 8 coopes ſutable.
Four coopes of old bawdkyn.
A ſute of white damaſke imbrodred with angels, and 11 coopes ſutable.
A ſute of old white ſilke with garters, and two coopes ſuitable.

* A ſhaft of wood. † Paten. ‡ holy. § See before, p. 93.

A coope

A coope of white ſilke with jeſſy rooles * and prophetes.
A coope of white bawdkyn with birds of gold.
Two copes of old white bawdkin with offers of red tiſſewe.
A ſute of old white bawdkin mixt with flowers, and one cope ſutable.
A ſute of blue velvet imbrodred with flowers, and 3 copes ſutable.
A cope of blue bawdkin, with lyons of gold and unicorns white.
A ſute of old grene bawdkyn, with 2 copes ſutable.
A cheſable of blue.
A red pall for the ſepulture †.
Two veſtments of white damaſke with croſſes.
A ſute of black velvet with egles.
Twenty albes with their apparels.
Three corporaſſe caſes, with one corporaſſe.
One old cope of diaper ſilke.
Four copes of blue damaſke with flowers.
A ſute of blue bawdkyn, with birds and beaſts of gold.
An old cope of red velvet, with 2 tinnicles ‡.
A ſute of old yellow ſilke.
Two old copes.
A ſute of crymiſſen velvet, Biſhop Weſt's gift.
An altar-piece of blew velvet, imbrodred with archangels.
A front of white damaſke with roſes.
A front of crimiſſen velvet, white lyons of perle.
A front of yellow ſilke with golde.
Eight old ſtooles, and 5 phannans §.
An old veſtment of red tiſſew, imbrodred with gold.
A ſute of red velvet, with offers and ſpred egles.
Two white tinnicles of damaſke, with flowers of gold.
A ſingle veſtment of grene velvet.
Two tinnicles of bawdkyn, lyn'd with yellow ſilke.
Thirty-ſeven albes with th' apparels.
Twenty albes without apparels.
A grete tappytt of red to lye afore the altar, with white roſes and pomegarnetts.
Another old blew tapytt.
A front of red and grene bawdkyn, with ſwannes of gold.
Five old ſingle albes.
A tinnicle of blew ſarſenyt.
Five tinnicles, and a cheaſable of bawdkyn of divers colors with ſtrakes.
Seven grate cheſtes.

* Q. Jeſſe rootes. The root of Jeſſe, a genealogical tree of the genealogy of Chriſt iſſuing from Jeſſy, lying at the bottom, was a common ſubject in painted windows. In Dorcheſter church, Oxford, the mullions of ſtone form the tree, and the perſons repreſenting the deſcent, are painted in glaſs. The prophets are repreſented ſeparately.

† See pp. 92. 141. ‡ Tunicles. § Pennons or banners.

In

In Byſhope Weſt's Chaple.

Item, a ſingle veſtment of clothe of gold.
A veſtment of clothe of gold damaſke wurke.
A ſingle veſtment of clothe of tiſſewe.
An altar clothe, and a fronte of clothe of gold.
A corporaſſe, with 2 caſes of red and yellow bawdkyn.
An herſeclothe of black damaſke with a white croſſe.
A ſingle veſtment of blew ſilke.

In Byſhope Alcok's Chaple.

An altar clothe of bawdkyn.
A gilted table upon the altar.
A cheaſeable of purple ſatyn, with a croſs of rede velvet, and ſcalope ſhelles.
A ſingle veſtement of grene velvet with flowr de-luces.
A ſingle veſtement of blew tiſſew, with a red croſs of tiſſew.
A ſingle veſtement of white bawdkyn, with a croſs of blew.
An altar cloth of rede bawdkyn.
A ſingle veſtement of white damaſke imbroidrede with lilly potts.

In the Quyer.

Two paer of organs, and 6 lether ſtoles with iron to ſit upon the quyer.
Four great laten candleſticks before the baſe altar, and 2 other of iron.
Two altar frontes, one of the blew bawdkyn, the other of grene bawdkyn.

To the Highe Altare.

A fronte of bawdkyn imbrodred with ſwannes.
Thirteen altar clothes good and bad.
Two rede tappets to ly afore the altar, with roſes and flowers, and other of blew.
A pall of ſilke for an altar.
A ſtandyng lecture of latten with an egle.
Two grete candleſticks of laten, and 2 little candleſticks of laten.

In Byſhope Redmanne's Chaple.

A ſingle veſtment of grene damaſke, with an albe.
An old dyaper alter clothe.
A front of rede ſilke, with a little cheſte.

In the Lady Chaple.

A paer of organs, with 2 laten candleſticks.
An altar front of rede counterfete bawdkyn.
Two old tappetts, one rede, th'other white.
A paer of little laten candleſticks.
A veſtment of white bawdkyn.
An altar pillow of tinſon, and 2 old quyſhins.

In the Ladie Chaple Chambre.

A folding table, 2 forms, 3 cheſtes, one chair, 2 old quyſhins aundieron, and a paer of tongs.

2 Two

Two pullies of brafs, with 2 iren pynnes.
An old bafyn and ewer of pewter, and an hanginge laver of laten.
Two quyfhins of old filke.
A fingle veftment of blew velvet, with the offers of gold.
A veftmente of olde damafke with lylly potts, and an altar front of the fame.
A veftment of white bawdkyn with lilly potts.
Four cheafeables of white filke with an albe.
A veftment called the Lent Veftment.
Certeyn lynnen clothes for the Lent.
Five white altar clothes, 2 towels, one of diaper.
A fronte for the altar of white bawdkyn, with a frontlet of the fame.
Four albes with th' apparels.
Two corporaffes, with cafes imbrodred.
Certain fcroles and p .... ms.
A fawter-booke with clafpes of filver.
A paynted hanging for the altar with a fringe.
A grete chefte, and a hangeing lamp.

Extracts from the Churchwardens Accompts of the parish of St. Helen's, in Abington, Berkshire; from the first year of the reign of Philip and Mary, to the thirty-fourth of Q. Elizabeth; now in the possession of the Reverend Mr. G. Benson; with some observations upon them. By the late Professor *Ward*, of Gresham College. Printed in Archæologia, I. 11—23.

Anno 1555, 1 and 2 of Philip and Mary.

	£.	s.	d.
Payde for making the roode and peynting the same,	0	5	4
For making the herse lyghtes and paskal tapers	0	11	1
For making the roode lyghtes,	0	10	6
For a legend,	0	5	0
For a hollie water-pott,	0	6	0
Anno 1556 payde for a boke of articles,	0	0	2
For a shippe for frankincense,	0	1	8
For new wax and making the hetse lyghtes,	0	5	8
For the font taper and the paskal taper,	0	6	7
Received for the holye looft liyghtes,	1	13	4
For the rood lyghtes at Christmas,	1	3	2½
At the buryal and monethes mynde of *George Clynche*,	0	1	10
For twelve tapers at the yeres mynde of Maister *John Hide*,	0	1	9
At the buryal and monethes mynde of Mr. *Rede*,	0	13	0
At the buryal and monethes mynde of the good wiff,	0	12	4
Braunche,	0	12	4
Anno 1557, Received of the paryshe for the roode lyghtes at Christmas,	1	1	9
Of the clarke for the holye loft,	1	16	8
At the buryal of *Richard Ballerd*, for four tapers,	0	0	6
At the monethes mynde of *R. Ballerd*, for six tapers,	0	0	6
At the buryal of *Richard Frende* a stranger, for four tapers,	0	0	8
At the twelve monethes mynde of Maister *Rede*, for twelve tapers, and the best paule,	0	2	4
At the monethes mynde of *William Hide*, esquire, for ditto,	0	2	4
At the monethes mynde of *William Myles*, laborer, for four tapers,	0	0	4
At the twelve monethes mynde of *Elizabeth Branche*, widdow, for two tapers,	0	0	4
At the monethes mynde of *Thomas Cowles* wif, for two tapers,	0	0	2
At the monethes mynde of *Thomas Perkins*, for twelve tapers, two torches, and the best paule,	0	2	6
Of Mrs. *Tesdale's* daughter, for six tapers, and two tapers for quater dirges,	0	0	8
Payde for peynting the roode of Marie and John, and the patron of the churche,	0	6	8

To

	£.	s.	d.
To faſten the tabernacle where the patron of the churche now ſtandeth, —— ——	0	0	8
For the roode Marie and John, with the patron of the churche,	0	18	0
For making the herſe lyghtes, ——	0	3	8
For making the roode lyghtes, ——	0	15	5
For the roode Marie and John, and the patron of the churche,	0	7	0
To the ſextin for watching the ſepulter * two nyghtes, —	0	0	8
To the ſuffrigan for halowing the churche yarde, and other implements of the churche, —— ——	1	10	0
For waſt of the paſkall, and for holye yoyle, ——	0	5	10

Anno 1558, 1559, or 4 and 5 of Philip and Mary. And 1 and 2 of Elizabeth.

	£.	s.	d.
Received for roode lyghtes at Chriſtmas 1558, ——	0	18	6
For roode lyghtes at Chriſtmas 1559, —— ——	0	18	3½
At Eſter 1558, for the paſkall lyghte, ——	1	14	0
For wax to thenſe the church on Eſter day, ——	0	1	8
At Eſter 1559 for the paſkall lyghte, ——	1	15	0
For the holye loff 1558, —— ——	1	14	0
For the holye loff 1559, —— ——	1	14	0
At the burial of *Richard Crooſe*, ſkolemaſter, for ſix tapers,	0	0	6
At the monethes mynde of Maiſter *Crooſe*, for four tapers, —	0	0	4
At the burial of *Agnes Teſdale*, for eighteen tapers, two torches and the paule, —— ——	0	3	0
More for *Agnes Teſdale*, for two tapers every day and nyghte by all the monethe, —— ——	1	11	8
At the monethes mynde of *John Langley*, for twelve tapers, and *Richard Langley*, both under one, —— ——	0	1	6
At the obbit of Maiſter *Rede*, for twelve tapers, ——	0	1	6
At the monethes mynde of *Richard Large*, for twelve tapers,	0	2	0
At the twelve monethes mynde of *Elyn Mathew*, for twelve tapers,	0	1	6
At the monethes mynde of *Elyn Lynge*, for ſix tapers, ——	0	0	9
At the twelve monethes mynde of *Thomas Perkyns*, for four tapers,	0	0	4
At the twelve monethes mynde of *John Dowſying*, and the monethes mynde of *Agnes Borne*, for ten tapers, —— ——	0	0	10
At the monethes mynde of *Thomas Teſdale*, for twelve tapers,	0	3	0
At the two yers mynde of Mr. *Rede*, for twelve tapers, —	0	1	6
At the buryall and monethes mynde of *William Powell*, for ſix tapers,	0	1	0
Payde for making the ſepulture, —— ——	0	10	0

* Watching the ſepulter or ſepulchre. This happens in holy week, the week before Eaſter, Thurſday night and Friday night. The conſecrated hoſt being laid in a kind of monument either upon or under the altar from Thurſday noon till Saturday noon, and expoſed during the whole of that time; it was therefore uſual to watch and pray. See the firſt note in p. 145.

	£.	s.	d.
For peynting the ſame ſepulture, —— ——	0	3	0
For ſtones and other charges about it, —— —	0	4	6
To the ſexten for meat and drinck and watching the ſepulture according to cuſtom, —— ——	0	1	10
For gathering herſe lyghtes by the yere, —— ——	0	4	0
For making herſe lyghtes and roode lyghtes, ——	1	4	1
To the bellman for meat, drinck, and cooles, watching the ſepulture,	0	1	7
For the communyon boke, —— ——	0	5	0
For taking down the altere, —— —— ——	0	1	8
For four ſong bokes and a ſawter, —— ——	0	6	8

Anno 1559, or 3 of Elizabeth.

Received of *Thomas Hethe*, for the holye loft, ——	0	2	0
Of *William Dale*, for the holye loft, — ——	0	6	4
At the burial of *Robert Charilton*, for his grave and the paule, and other benevolence to the church, and for his monethes monument,	0	10	0
At the burial of *Thomas Jenens*, and alſo his wyf, for the paule and other benevolence, and at the monethes monument, ——	0	16	0
At the burial of *William Bakehouſe*, for the paule and other benevolence, and at his monethes monument, —— ——	0	2	4
At the burial and monument of *John Collyngs*, and *Jone* the wif of *Northecote*, —— —— —— ——	0	1	6
At the burial of *Richard Hill*, and at his monethes mynde, with the paule, — —	0	3	8
At the yeres mynde of *Agnes Walter*, —— ——	0	0	8
Payde for tymber and making the communyon table, —	0	6	0
For a carpet for the communyon table, —— ——	0	2	8
For mending and paving the place where the altere ſtoode,	0	2	8
For two doſſin of Morres belles —— ——	0	1	0
For fower new ſaulter bookes, —— ——	0	8	0
For gathering the herſe lyghtes, —— —— —	0	4	0

Anno 1561, or 4 of Elizabeth.

Payde for four pounde of candilles upon Chriſtmas in the morning for the maſſe, —— —— —— ——	0	1	0
For a table of commandments and kalender, or rewle to find out the leſſons and pſalmes, and for the frame, ——	0	2	0
To the ſomner for bringing the order for the roode lofte,	0	0	8
To the carpenter and others for taking down the roode lofte, and ſtopping the holes in the wall, where the joices ſtoode, ——	0	15	8
To the peynter, for writing the ſcripture, where the roode lofte ſtoode, and overthwarte the ſame iſle, —— —	0	3	4

To

	£.	s.	d.
To the clarkes for mayntaining and repayring the fong bokes in the quyer, ——	0	4	0
Anno 1562, or 5 of Eliz. payde for a bybill for the church,	0	10	0
Anno 1563, or 6 of Eliz. payde for one boke of Wednefdayes fafting, which contaynes omellies, —— ——	0	0	6
Anno 1564, or 7 of Eliz. payd for a communyon boke, —	0	4	0
For reparations of the crofs in the market-place, ——	0	5	2
Anno 1565, or 8 of Eliz. payde for two bokes of common prayer agaynfte invading the Turke, — —	0	0	6
For the repetition of the communyon boke —— —	0	4	0
Anno 1566, or 9 of Eliz. payde for fetting up *Robin Hoode's* bower,	0	1	6
Anno 1573, or 16 of Eliz. payde for a quire of paper to make four bokes of Geneva falmes, —— ——	0	0	4
For two bokes of common prayer new fett forth, —	0	0	4
Anno 1574, or 17 of Eliz. payde for candilles for the church at Chriftmas, ——	0	1	3
Anno 1576, 1577, or 19 and 20 of Eliz. payde for a new byble,	2	0	0
For a boke of prayer, —— —— —	0	7	0
For writing the commandments in the quire, and peynting the fame, —— ——	0	19	0
Anno 1578, or 21 of Eliz. payde for a boke of th'Articles,	0	1	6
Anno 1591, or 34 of Eliz. paid for an houre glafs for the pilpitt,	0	0	4

The churchwardens accompts of a particular parifh may in themfelves be juftly thought a matter of no great confequence, and not worthy of much regard. But thefe feem to deferve fome confideration, as they relate to a very remarkable period in our hiftory, and prove, by facts, the great alterations that were made in religious affairs under the fucceffive reigns of Queene Mary and Queen Elizabeth, together with the time and manner of putting them in execution; and may therefore ferve both to confirm and illuftrate feveral things related by our ecclefiaftical hiftorians.

1. We find mention made, in the extracts, of the roode and rood-loft. By the former of which was meant either a crucifix, or the image of fome faint, erected in popifh churches [a]. And here that name is given to the images of Mary and John; as

[a] The word *rood* is derived from the A. S. *rode*, crux. Skinn. In its primary fignification, as Junius obferves, it formerly denoted any fort of image, but was afterwards peculiarly adapted to our Saviour, as fixed on the crofs, or to the crofs itfelf. Hence *rood-beam*, *rood-tree*, in Chaucer.

"I lokynge up unto that rufull roode." Magd. 204.
"He lyethe in the grave under the roode beme." W. B. 496.
"That for us dyede on the roode tree." Cl. Ox. 558.
So Piers Plowman, p. 8.—"Mercie for Mary's love of heven,
"That bare the blisful barne, that bought us on the rood,"

Scot.

as alſo to that of St. Helen, the patroneſs of the church. Theſe images were ſet in ſhrines, or tabernacles, and the place where they ſtood was called the rood-loft; which was commonly over, or near the paſſage out of the body of the church into the chancel [*b*]. In the year 1548, the firſt of King Edward VI. ſuch images and their ſhrines were ordered to be taken down, as we are told by biſhop Burnet (Hiſt. of the Reformation, Vol. II. B. I. p. 61.); but they were reſtored again upon the acceſſion of Queen Mary, as we find here by the firſt article.

2. The ſhip for frankincenſe, mentioned in the year 1556, was a ſmall veſſel, in form of a ſhip or boat, in which the Roman Catholics burn frankincenſe; and uſed at the altar on greater ſolemnities.

3. The book of articles purchaſed in 1556, ſeems to be that which was printed, and ſent over the kingdom, by order of Queen Mary, at the end of the year 1554 [*c*], containing inſtructions to the biſhops for viſiting the clergy. See Burnet, Vol. III. B. ii. p. 254.

4. We find frequent mention made of lights and other expences at the *funeral*, "the monethes mind, the year's mind, the two years mind," and the *obit* of deceaſed perſons; which were maſſes performed at thoſe ſeaſons for the reſt of their ſouls; the word *mind* there ſignifying the ſame as memorial or remembrance. And ſo it is uſed in a ſermon yet extant by biſhop Fiſher, intitled, "A mornynge re-"membrance had at the monethes mynde of the noble princeſs Margarete, coun-"teſſe of Richmonde and Darbye, &c." As to the term *obits*, ſervices of that kind ſeem to have been ſo called, when annually performed [*d*]. The office of the maſs for each of theſe ſolemnities may be ſeen in the Roman-Miſſal, under the

Scot. *rude*. The good and learned biſhop Douglas, in the prologue to the tenth book of his anſlation of Virgil, ſays,

"Thou large ſtremys ſched upon the rude."

And in his prologue to the eleventh book,

"Think how the Lord for the on rude was rent."

[*b*] And, wot you what ſpiritual myſtery was couched in this poſition thereof? The church (forſooth) typified the church militant; the chancel repreſents ths church triumphant, and all who will paſs out of the former into the latter muſt go under the Rood-loft, *i. e.* carry the croſs, and be acquainted with affliction. Fuller, (Hiſt. of Waltham Abbey, p. 16.) who ſays, he adds this the rather, becauſe Harpsfield (Fox, Act. and Mar. p. 1690), confeſſeth himſelf ignorant of the Rood-ſituation. Anno 1554, or 1 of Mary, in the churchwardens account of Waltham abby, "payde for Mary and John that ſtand in the rood-loft 26*s.* 8*d.*" Chriſt on the croſs ſaw his "mother and the diſciple whom he loved ſtanding by." (John xix. 26.) "In apiſh imitation "whereof the Rood (when perfectly made, with all the appurtenances thereof) was attended "with theſe two images." (Fuller's Hiſt. p. 17.)

[*c*] Anno 1554, or 1 of Mary, "payde to the apparitor for the biſhop's boke of articles, at "the viſitation, 6*d.*" This biſhop was Bonner. His articles were in number thirty-ſeven. And John Bayle wrote a book againſt them. The biſhop's chief care herein was the ſetting up of compleat Roods, commonly called Bonner's Block-almightie. (Fuller's Hiſt. p. 18.)

[*d*] The common expence of an Obit (anno 1542, 34 of Henry VIII.) was 2*s.* and 2*d.* And, if any be curious to have the particulars thereof, it was thus expended. To the pariſh-prieſt 4*d.* to the charnel-prieſt 3*d.* to the two clarks 4*d.* to the children (choriſters) 3*d.* to the ſexton and bellman 2*d.* each; for two tapers 2*d.* for oblation 2*d.* (Fuller's Hiſt. of Waltham Abbey, p. 14.)

title

title of "Miſſæ pro Defunctis." And it appears, by the different ſums here charged on that account, that the expences were ſuited to perſons of all ranks, that none might be deprived of the benefit which was ſuppoſed to accrue from them.

5. It has been cuſtomary in popiſh countries, upon Good Friday, to erect a ſmall building, to repreſent the ſepulchre of our Saviour. In this they put the hoſt, and ſet a perſon to watch it, both that night and the next. And the morning following, very early, the hoſt being taken out, Chriſt is ſaid to be riſen [*e*]. This we find was done here in 1557, and the two following years, the laſt of which was in the reign of Queen Elizabeth. Du Freſne has given us a particular account of this ceremony, as performed at Rouen in France, where three perſons, in female habits, uſed to go to the ſepulchre, where two others were placed repreſenting angels, who told them Chriſt was riſen. (Latin Gloſſary, under the words Sepulchri Officium.) The building mentioned in theſe extracts muſt be but very ſlight, ſince the whole expence amounted to no more than ſeventeen ſhillings and ſix pence.

6. In the article of "wax to thenſe the church," under the year 1558, the word Thenſe is, I preſume, a miſtake for Cenſe; as they might uſe wax with the frankincenſe in perfuming the church.

7. In 1559, the Altar was taken down, and the year following the Communion Table was put in its place, agreeably to the injunctions then given by Queen Elizabeth. See Burnet, Vol. III. B. iii. p. 368.

8. We find maſſes for the dead continued to this time, though here, inſtead of Month's Mind, the expreſſion is a Month's Monument [*f*]. But as that office was performed at the altar, this being taken down that year, the other could no longer be continued. And yet we have the word Maſs applied to the ſervice performed upon Chriſtmas-day the year following. So difficult it is to drop the uſe of words to which one has been accuſtomed.

9. The morrice bells, mentioned under the year 1560, as purchaſed by the pariſh, were uſed in their morrice-dances, a diverſion then practiſed at their feſtivals;

[*e*] There is the like article in the churchwardens account of Waltham Abbey, anno 1542, or 34 of Henry VIII. "payde for watching the ſepulchre 4*d*." This, ſays Fuller, conſtantly returns in every yearly account, though what is meant thereby, I know not I could ſuſpect ſome ceremony on Eaſter Eve (in imitation of the ſoldiers watching Chriſt's grave), but am loth to charge that age with more ſuperſtition than it was clearly guilty of. (Hiſt. p. 14.)

Anno 1554, or 1 of Mary, "payde for watching the ſepulchre 8*d*." But we find none of the former Obits anniverſarily performed: The lands for whoſe maintenance were alienated in the reign of K. Edward VI. and the vicar not ſo charitably diſpoſed as to celebrate theſe Obits gratis. (Ibid. p. 17.)

[*f*] In the Injunctions of K. Edward VI. they are called Memories. "At even-ſong the "reſponds, with all the memories, ſhall be omitted." Injunct. 21. By Memories (ſays Fuller) we underſtand the Obſequia for the dead, which ſome ſay ſucceeded in the place of the Heathen Parentalia. (Church Hiſt. p. 375.) See Middleton's Letter from Rome.

in

in which the populace might be indulged, from a political view, to keep them in good humour [g].

10. In 1561, the Rood-loft was taken down; and the better to obliterate the remembrance of it (as had been doue before in the reign of King Edward VI.) ſome paſſages out of the Bible were painted in the place where it ſtood, which could then give little offence, ſince the images had been removed the preceding year by the Queen's injunction, upon a repreſentation of the biſhops. (See Burnet, Vol. II. B. III. p. 368, and Strype's Annals.)

11. In 1562, a Bible is ſaid to have been bought for the church, which coſt ten ſhillings. This, I ſuppoſe, was the Geneva Bible in quarto, both on account of the ſmall price, and that edition, having the diviſion of verſes, was beſt ſuited to public uſe. It was an Engliſh tranſlation, which had been reviſed and corrected by the Engliſh exiles at Geneva in Queen Mary's reign, and printed there in 1560, with a dedication to Queen Elizabeth. In the year 1576, we find another Bible was bought, which in the article is termed the New Bible, and ſaid to have coſt forty ſhillings; which muſt doubtleſs have been the folio, uſually called Archbiſhop Parker's Bible, printed at London 1568, by Richard Jugge the Queen's printer. They had prayer books, pſalters, and ſong-books, for the churches at the beginning of this reign, but the whole Bible was not then eaſily procured.

12. In 1565, there is a charge of ſix-pence for two common-prayer books "againſt invading of the Turke." It was thought the common cauſe of the Chriſtian ſtate in Europe to oppoſe the progreſs of the Turkiſh arms by all methods, both civil and religious. And this year the Turks had made a deſcent upon the iſle of Malta, where they beſieged the town and caſtle of St. Michael; when, the approach of the Chriſtian fleet, they broke up the ſiege, aud ſuffered a conſiderable loſs in the flight, as may be ſeen in Thuanus, lib. XXXVIII. And as the war was carried on between them and the Emperor Maximilian in Hungary, the like prayer books were annually purchaſed for the pariſh, till the year 1565 incluſive.

13. The year following there is an article of "eighteen pence for ſetting up "Robin Hood's bower [h]. This, I imagine, might be an arbor, or booth, erected by the pariſh at ſome feſtival ſeaſon, though for what reaſon it received that name I know not.

14. In 1573, mention is mode of "paper for four bookes of Geneva Pſalmes." It is well known that the vocal muſic in parochial chnrches received a great altera-

[g] Upon my aſking the late Mr. Handel, what he took to be the genuine and peculiar taſte in muſic of the ſeveral nations in Europe; to the French, he gave the Minuet; to the Spaniard, the Saraband; to the Italian, the Arietta; and to the Engliſh, the Hornpipe, or Morris-dance. Belg. *Mcriſchen dans*, *i e.* Tripudium Mauritanicum. (Skin.) "Nam faciem plerunque inficiunt fuligine, et peregrinum veſtium cultum aſſumunt, qui ludicris talibus indulgent, ut "Mauri eſſe videantur, aut e longius remotâ patriâ credantur advolâſſe, atque inſolens recreationis genus advexiſſe." (Jun. Etymol.) T. M. [Thomas Morell.]

[h] The ſtory of Robin Hood was in high vogue among the common people; as Sloth ſayth of himſelf in Piers Ploughman:

"I cannot Parfitly mi Pater noſter as the Prieſt it ſyngeth;
"But I can Rymes of Robenhode, and Randof earl of Cheſter."

tion

tion in the reign of Queen Elizabeth, being changed from antiphonies into metrical pfalmody, which is here called the Geneva Pfalms.

15. In the year 1578, ten-pence were paid for a book of the Articles. Thofe Articles were agreed to and fubfcribed by both houfes of Convocation in 1562, and printed the year following. But in 1571, being again revived, and ratified by act of parliament, they feem to have been placed in churches.

16. The laft article in thefe extracts is "four-pence for an hour-glafs for the "pulpit." How early the cuftom was of ufing hour-glaffes in the pulpit, I cannot fay; but this is the firft inftance of it which I remember to have met with.

It is not to be thought that the like regulations were all made within the fame time in all other places. That depended in a good meafure upon the care and vigilance of the bifhops in their feveral diocefes. And according to their affection and zeal for the Reformation, thefe things were managed with greater or lefs expedition. Abington lies in the diocefe of Salifbury; and as bifhop Jewel, who was firft nominated to that fee by Queen Elizabeth, continued in it till the year 1571, it is not to be doubted but every thing was there carried on with as much expedition as was judged confiftent with prudence [*i*].

Some further remarks might be made upon thefe accompts; but they feem fo obvious, as to render it unneceffary; and I fear, left thofe already offered fhould be thought too tedious [*k*]. T. M.

[*i*] It is wittily obferved by Fuller, that as careful mothers and nurfes, on condition they can get their children to part with Knives, are contented to let them play with Rattles: fo they permitted ignorant people ftill to retain fome of their fond and foolifh cuftoms, that they might remove from them the moft dangerous and deftructive fuperftitions. (Ch. Hift. p. 375.)

[*k*] It may not be improper however (as mention is here made of "a common prayer book "new fet forth," anno 1573, and a bible anno 1562) to remind, or inform fome readers, that, in the reign of King Henry VIII. the liturgy was faid or fung in Latin, fave only "the creed, the "Lord's prayer, and the ten commandments," anno 1536. But anno 1548, or 2 of K. Edward VI. the firft edition of the liturgy, or common prayer, was fet forth in print by authority. The 2d edition as reviewed, &c. by a Statute in Parliament, anno 1552. And the 3d edition anno 1559, or 1 of Q. Elizabeth, the prayer-book here mentioned.—And as to the Bible, the firft tranflation was made anno 1541, in the reign of K. Henry VIII. The fecond tranflation in the reign of K. Edward VI. anno 1549 and 1551. The third in 1559, or 2 of Q. Elizabeth, commonly called the Queen's Bible.

The title of this article put me in mind of a fort of prophecy in that antient poem, called, Piers Ploughman.

"And than fhull the Abbot of Abyngton, and all his iffue for ever,
"Have a knock of a king, and incurable the wound." T. M.

Extracts from the Churchwardens Accompts of GREAT WIGSTON, Leicestershire.

	£.	s.	d.
1591. New close-money paid to the churchwardens, *Robert Hall* and *John Simons*,	0	13	0
A bell new cast at Leicester.			
1593. Mr. *Law's* free gift to the new clock,	2	0	0
Paid *John West* for white-washing the church,	1	18	10
1594. Communion bread and wine,	1	7	0
Removing the pulpit, cover and door made,	6	8	0
Painting the pulpit,	0	2	4
Paid for the prisoners,	0	8	0
A new Psalter-book,	0	7	0
For a candle on the coronation-day of our gracious Queen. God long continue her in health and peace to raigne over us; so be it, Amen,	0	0	1
Received of Mr. *Law* for Holy Thursday dues,	0	6	8
John Barley gave a pewter flaggon for the communion wine.			
1596. Paid at the visitation,	0	4	8
Paid for registering Mr. *Law's* 3*l.* 6*s.* 8*d.* at sessions,	0	0	2
1597. Fore and great bell cast.			
Henry Chamberlayne gave to the church	1	0	0
William Herrick ditto	0	3	4
Simon Brett paid for burying his mother in the church *	0	3	4
1599. Eight yards of cloth for a surplis and table-cloth, and making,	1	11	6
For binding the service-book,	0	2	2
A cover for the font,	0	1	8
Spent at the Commissary's court,	0	4	0
1600. Paid for 12 communions,	1	12	1
Poors stock is now, beside 10 loads of coals,	6	18	7
1601. Two-penny levy a yard-land for catching moles,	1	12	0
1601. Paid for casting the third bell and metal,	5	19	0
Gave to a man that had great loss of his wares going to Lenton fair,	0	2	6
For the Hospital, King's Bench, and Marshalsea,	0	3	3
Mrs. *Heyrick* gave to the poor's stock,	1	0	0
1611. Communion cup and cover of silver, two pewter pottes, a flacket or box, a carpet, a table cloth, a surplice, the Custom-book.			
Gave the men coming from Jerusalem, having the admiral's licence to gather for the ransoming their seven sons.			
1613. Paid for *Jewel's* works,	1	0	0
Spent at Willoughby when the overseers gave their accompts,	0	2	8
Levy 3*d.* a yard land, 1*d.* a horse, and 1*d.* a cow,	7	7	10
John Lawe for bread and beer on Maunday Thursday,	0	8	4

* In 1614 the fee paid upon the same occasion was 6*s.* 8*d.*; perhaps the fee to the vicar was here included. This fee remained the same till very lately.

	£.	s.	d.
For Good Friday, — —	0	3	4
Paid ringers on St. James's day, —	0	0	8
1615. Paid Dr. *Chippendale* for a warrant when the church was robbed	0	0	8
New carpet-cloth for the communion-table, — —	0	7	6
1617. The following things belong to the pariſh; viz. two Bibles, one Communion-book, Jewel's Works, part of ditto, Homily-book, Whitaker's Works, Himminge's book upon the Goſpels, Eraſmus, Cuſtom-book, Book of Martyrs, 2 vols.			
Spent at three times before the juſtices about recuſants, —	0	3	8
1619. Paid the miniſter who preached at the biſhop's viſitation,	0	2	0
1620. Paid ringers on coronation day, — —	0	2	6
Paid for the New Bible, — — —	2	0	0
Sold the Old Bible, — — — —	0	10	0
Given to a brief from Greece, — — —	0	2	6
Paid for 16 dozen of ſparrows, — — —	0	1	4
1621. Received of *Simon Pawley*, for part of May-green tree,	0	4	0
Spent on Rogation Monday, — — —	0	2	0
Paid for three books, "God and the King," —	0	1	6
1622. Paid to a man earneſt to take 100 dozen ſparrows,	0	0	6
1623. Given to the poor on Good Friday out of poor's ſtock,	1	16	2
Given to a licenſed preacher, — — —	0	3	4
Paid for 3 loads of Enderby ſtone 3s. carriage 4s. —	0	7	0
For copying the King's and Council's letters, —	0	3	0
Paid for matting the chancel, — —	0	5	0
1624. Spent at Leiceſter, being called before the ordinary the 2d day of November, about them that went to ſermons, giving us our oaths, &c.	0	5	0
1625. Received of *Robert Hill* for the brooke-ruſhes, —	0	7	6
In the poor man's box, — — —	0	1	6
Given to *Jane* the wife of *William Whaley*, and other poor people of Lancaſter, who had a long law-ſuit with Sir Francis Howorth, —	0	1	6
Paid for *Robert Clarke* and *William Pinder's* coſts of ſuit with Sir William Faunt, for the willow on the back-ſide the water-mill, —	1	16	6
1626. Given to Waterleſs Burſtable, in the county of Devon, which town was burnt down with fire, which ſeemed to come from heaven, which burnt 400 houſes and above; therein was burnt 7 ſcore and 14 perſons, and 8 women in their beds, and 500 more women that loſt of goods, by eſtimation, amounting to 200,000 pounds, —	0	5	0
Paid for frankincenſe, — — —	0	0	2
Paid for the apparitor, for bringing a note to keep diſeaſed people* forth of the town, — — —	0	0	4
Given to a poor man, whoſe wife was burnt in bed, and 200 pounds loſs of goods, — — —	0	0	8

* Dr. Short, of Sheffield, in his Hiſtory of the Air, in two volumes, obſerves, that the ſweating ſickneſs began in 1485, continued to 1525; and, after ſeveral intervals, it quite ceaſed in 1626 at Malton in Yorkſhire. Scarce one in 600 recovered who had it; it was at laſt cured by much ſweating and hot cordials. He ſays, more died of the phyſicians than the diſeaſe.

	£.	s.	d.
Given to *Wm. Holmes*, for eating his grafs, by confent of neighbours,	0	3	0
Gave to a merchant, who had great lofs, and 3 men prifoners taken,	0	0	9
1627. Gave to *William Townfhend* for reftoring the accompt-book,	0	5	0
Given for fire to be burnt in the church, — —	0	0	1
Gave to two minifters of God's word, — —	0	1	1
1628. To a poor man, who had great lofs by the Spaniards,	0	1	0
1629. Given to *Jane Shore* and her company, —	0	1	0
1631. Given to the brief from Cambridge, —	0	3	4
1632. Taken out of the poor's box, — —	0	1	4½
Spent when we carried the money collected for the poor minifters in the Palatinate, — — —	0	0	2
Given to *Elizabeth Grey*, and others, of Baltimore, in the county of Corke, which town was invaded and fpoiled by the Turks; her hufband and 7 fcore perfons were taken prifoners in July laft *,	0	3	0
Given to Mr. *Wattes*, a fcholar, who offered himfelf to teach fchool with us, — — — —	0	1	0
Richard Boulter prefented at the court for his two pence a year; expences paid on this occafion, — — —	0	7	10
Church roof fell in. Affeffment — —	49	13	3
Paid apparitor for fummoning and unfummoning, —	0	0	8
Paid *John Ranford*, when he went to the training, —	1	0	0
1633. Given to *Jane Stanup*, of Abergane, having loft 800l. by fire,	0	2	0
Given to *Thomas Brown*, a fhipman, who was taken by the Turks, having loft 500l. — — — —	0	1	4
Mending the Weft loft, — — —	0	3	4
1634. Gave the ringers when the King and Queen came, —	0	1	8
1635. Given to Mr. *Scarborough*, minifter, — —	0	2	6
1636. Paid for rails round the communion-table, —	2	16	0
Paid to the court for receiving the Sacrament in the church,	0	16	0
1638. Paid to the minifter of Come, — —	0	5	0
Paid to Mr. *Major* and *Richard Freer*, for charge about St. Wifton (St. Wolfton) church, — — —	9	2	0
1640. This, and three preceding years, the church was greatly repaired.			
1641. Received of *John Davenport* for bun-bread, —	0	10	0
1659. Spent about Poland money, when paid to the fheriff's man,	0	1	6
1659. Spent when we gathered for the great lofs, —	0	0	6
1660. Paid the painter for the King's arms, —	2	0	0
Paid for boards for the King's arms, — —	1	2	6

* Strange as it may appear to the prefent generation, on June 20, 1631, in the dead of night, two Algerine rovers landed and plundered this place juft before fettled and incorporated with an Englifh colony, and carried off a number of the inhabitants and 100 Englifh to Algiers. Among others, William Gunter, a perfon of fome credit, had his wife and 7 children carried away. Two fhips of war at Kinfale received timely notice, but did not ftir to prevent this defcent. A fecond was intended next year, but timely precautions were taken againft it. Baltimore, however, never recovered itfelf fince that accident, and is now a poor decayed fifhing-town. Smith's Hift. of Cork, I. p. 278—289.

Church-

Churchwardens' Accompts * belonging to the Pariſh of HEYBRIDGE, near MALDEN, ESSEX.

Commencing towards the cloſe of the Reign of King Henry VII. or the beginning of the Reign of King Henry VIII.

Communicated by the Rev. JOHN PRIDDEN, M. A. F. S. A. Vicar of Heybridge.

Item, payde for the ſtrykynge for new and olde waxe,	0	0	8
Item, payde to *John Arthur*, for mendyng of the chirche porche,	0	1	4
Item, payde for frankyncenſe,	0	0	1
Item, payde agenſe Cryſtemaſſe for tallowe candyll,	0	0	3
Item, payde for halfe a calfe's ſkyne,	0	0	2
Item, payde for 8 pownde and 3 querteres of waxe agenſe Eſtur, prys of a pownde 5¼*d.*	0	3	9¾
Item, receyed of *Robard Chapman*, for a hole yere's rent of his howſe that he dwellythe in.			
Item, receyved of the vykare of *Annes Barnard's* bequeſte,	0	1	6
Item, receyved for ſelling of 3 pownde of halfpennye candills.			
Sum total of receipts this year,	0	18	7
Remaynynge in the handys of the ſaid chirchewardeyns, at theyr accownte made at the feſte of Seynt Mighell the Archangell, in the yere aforeſaid,	0	7	2¼
Item, payed for 2 powndes of waxe agenſe our Ladye.			
Item, payed for 8 powndes of waxe agenſe Eſtur.			
Item, payed for halfe a pownde of waxe lyhgte wantyd to the Paſchall,	0	0	3
Item, payed for frankyncence agenſe Eſtur,	0	0	1
Item, boughte 2 belle roppes, the pryce of bothe,	0	1	3
Item, boughte halfe a calffys ſkynne for	0	0	2
Item, payed for 1 pownd of waxe ageyn Seynt Jemy's daye, pryce theroff,	0	0	6
Item, payed for ſtrykvnge of the ſayde pownde of waxe,	0	0	1
Item, payed for ſtrykynge of the paſchall lyghte and for betynge lyghte,	0	0	1
Item, boughte 2 pownde of waxe ageyn Mighelmas, one pownde betynge lyghte, another pownde for halfpenny candill, pryce of bothe the powndes of wax,	0	1	0
Item, payed for ſtrykynge of the ſaid waxe,	0	0	2
Item, payed for 2 pound of tallowe candill ageyn Chryſtemaſſe,	0	0	2
Sum of this year's expences,	0	11	6¼

* Mem. When the ſum total agrees not with the receipts or expenditure, it proceeds from ſome of the articles being omitted, being impoſſible to be aſcertained from the decayed ſtate of the book.

	£.	s.	d.
Item, reſeyved of *Wyllyam Phillpott*, for rent of the chirche crofte.			
Item. reſeyved of *Wyllyam Barrett*, for a yere's ferme of Paſchalles crofte.			
Item, reſeyved of *Thomas Ruſſell*, for halfe a yeare's rent of the chirche crofte.			
Item, reſeyved of *Wyllyam Barrett*, halfe a yere's rente of paſchalle crofte, due at our Ladye-daye in Lente.			
Item, reſeyved of *John Barrett*, for the ferme of a cowe, —	0	1	0
Item, reſeyved of *John Samwell*, for halfe a yere's rente of the parcele of grounde, the whyche he holdythe, —	0	0	3
Item, reſeyved of *Wyllyam Phillpott*, for the ferme of a chirch cowe,	0	1	0
Sum total of this year's receipts, —	0	14	5
Item, payed for 6 pownde of waxe agenſe St. Thomas, —	0	3	0
Item, payed for ſtrykynge of the olde waxe and the new, —	0	0	8
Item, payd for the mendynge of a ſurples and 4 rocketts *,	0	0	4
Item, payed for 8 pownde of waxe agenſe Eſter, —	0	3	8
Item, payed for frankynſenſe, — — —	0	0	1
Item, payed for ſtrykynge the olde waxe agenſe Eſter, —	0	1	0
Item, payed for 2 pownde of tallowe candill ageyn Chryſtemaſſe,	0	0	2
Item, payed to *Andrew Elyott*, for the makynge of the ſeconde bell knepitt, — — — —	0	1	8
Item, payed to *Andrew Elyott*, for the makynge of the eaye of the great bell knepill, — — — —	0	2	4
Item, payed for frankyncenſe, — — —	0	0	1
Item, payed for a bell roppe, — —	0	0	9
Sum of this year's expences, —	0	15	5
Inprymis, receyed of the ferme of a hole yere of *Robard* ...... howſe, — — — —	0	2	0
Item, receyved of *John Barrett*, for the ferme of a cowe, —	0	1	0
Item, receyved of *John Samuell*, for a yere's rent of a parcelle of grownde, — — — — —	0	0	6
Item, receyved of *Wyllyam Barrett*, for a yere's rente of paſchallis croft, due at our Lady-day in Lente, — —	0	7	0
Item, reſeyved of *Herry Pedder*, for the rente of a crofte, ſumtyme Richarde Smythe, — — —	0	0	8
Item, reſeyved of *Herry Pedder*, for the rent of the chirche lande,	0	2	8
Item, reſeyved for the brekynge of the grownde in the chirche for the berryall of Myſtrys *Saye*, — —	0	3	4
Sum total, — — —	0	17	2
Inprimis, bought agenſe the feſte of Hallowemas, —	0	3	0
Item, payed for ſtrykynge the olde waxe and the newe, —	0	0	8

* Rochets.

	£.	s.	d.
Item, payd for frankyncence, ——— ———	0	0	1
Item, payed for 2 pownde of tollowe candill ageyn Cryftemaffe,	0	0	2
Item, payed for halfe a kalfys fkynne, ——— ———	0	0	2
Item, payed for 8 pownde and a halfe of waxe ageyn Eftur,	0	3	8¾
Item, payed for ftrykynge of the fame waxe and the old waxe,	0	1	0
Item, payed for ftrykynge of 3 pownde ageyn Mafter *Hillis* yere mynde, ——— ——— ——— ———	0	0	2
Item, payed to *Richard Barnard*, for naylynge downe of leede on the chyrche, ——— ——— ——— ———	0	0	3
Item, payed to *Richard Barnard*, for mendynge of the leede,	0	0	2
Item, payed to *Annes Gill*, for fkorynge * of the candillftykkes,	0	0	1
Item, payed to the fhynger in ernefte, ——— ———	0	0	4
Item, payed to the plomer in ernefte, ——— ———	0	1	0
Item, payed to *John Arther*, for mendynge of the chirche porche,	0	1	4
Sum total ——— ———	0	12	0¾

John Arthur hathe layde out of hys owne purfe 5*s.* 4*d.*

Three leaves have been cut out from this part of the book.

Receipts of this year impoffible to be made out, being fo much decayed in the writing.

Inprimis, payed for waxe agenfe Hollowmas.			
Item, payed for ftrykynge of the olde and new waxe.			
Item, payed for a fawdrye †, ——— ———	0	2	8
Item, payed for frankynfenfe, ——— ——— ———	.....	.....	.....
Item, payed for mendyng of the chirche-gate and ierne worke,	0	0	7
Item, payed to *Thomas Byrde*, for makynge of the bell napyll,	0	2	0
Item, payed to *Robebord*, for the yroyns, ——— ———	0	0	4
Item, payed to *Robebord*, for a ftapyll, ——— ———	0	0	2
Item, payed for mendyng of the bellys, ——— ———	0	0	4
Item, payed for a fmale lyne, ——— ——— ———	0	0	2
Item, payed for a bell roppe, ——— ———	.....	.....	.....
Item, payed for 8 pownde of waxe agenfe Efter, ———	0	0	4
Item, payed for ftrykynge of the faid waxe.			
Item, payed for frankyncenfe.			
Item, payed for ftrykynge agenfe Efter.			

Two blank leaves.

Item, for a pownde of halfpennye candill.

* Scouring. † Pfalter.

Thefe

£. s. d.

These being the rentes, the whyche be owyng to the paryshe chyrche of *Heybridge*, for the tyme of *Parretts* and *John Smythe*, then beyng chyrchewardeyns of the paryshe chyrche aforesayed, at the electyng the sayd chyrchewardens.

Owyng to the chyrche, — — 1 0 0

Item, *Henry Pedder* owythe to the sayde chyrche for halfe a yerys ferme of the lande, — — — 0 1 8

Item, *Wyllyam Allen* owythe to the sayde chyrche for a hole yerys ferme of a cowe, — — — 0 1 0

Item, *Wyllyam Barrett* owythe to the sayde chyrche for halfe a yerys ferme of paschall crofte, — - — 0 3 6

Item, *John Lynsey*, junior, owythe to the sayde chyrche for the ferm of paschall's crofte, — — — 0 4 0

A blank page.

The moneys receavyd and payed by *John Reynolds* and *John* ———, the chyrchewardens elect, and choosen by the hoole paryshe at the feste of St. Mighell the Archangell, in the yere of our Lorde Gode, 1516, unto the seyd feste then nexte followinge, that is to saye, for oone hole yere, ended the sayd feaste in the yere of our Lorde God 1517.

Heibredge.

Inprimis, receyved of *John Samwell*, for a hole yere's rent of the ferme of lande he holdythe, — — 0 0 6

Item, receyved of *Robert Chapman*, for a hole yere's rent of the ferme of a howse he holdythe, — — 0 2 0

Item, receyed of *John Pagett*, for a hole yere's rent of the ferme of land of John Bredge, — — — 0 1 0

Item, receyved of *John Lyndesey*, junior, for a hole yere's rent of the ferme of land he holdethe, — — 0 8 0

Item, receyved of *John Alleyn*, at Hotthellis, for a yere's ferme of a cowe, — — — — 0 1 0

Item, receyved of *Richard Bernarde*, for halfpenny waxe candill fellynge, — — — — 0 1 3

Item, receyved of *Edwarde Rande*, of Cokeshall *, for Phillpott's dett, owynge to the sayd chyrche, — — 0 10 0

Item, receyved of *Robard Cokshott*, for halfe a yere's farme of lande that he holdethe, — — — — 0 1 8

Inprimis, payed for frankyncence agense Hollowmasse, — 0 0 1

Item, payed to *Andrew Elyott*, of Maldon, for newe mendynge of the third bell knappell agense Hallowmasse, — — 0 1 8

Item, payed to *John Gidney*, of Maldon, for a new bell-rope agenste Hallowmasse, — — — 0 0 8

Item, payed to *Phillipp Goldborne*, of Maldon, for makynge a paire of indentures and 2 obligations for the rodelotte, — 0 1 8

* Coggeshall.

	£.	s.	d.
Item, payed to *Henry Downe*, of Colcheſtre, for makynge of another paire of indentures and 2 obligations for the rodelofte,	o	2	o
Item, payed to *Henry Downe*, for makynge of a quyttance of the receyte of £5.	o	o	1
Item, payed for my coſtes, for me *John Reynold*, to Colcheſtre, for me and my horſe,	o	o	6
Item, payed for the coſtes of me the ſeid *John Reynold* and *John Lyndeſey*, to Colcheſtre, another tyme, for us and our 2 horſes,	o	o	8
Item, payed to *Andrew Elyott*, of Maldon, for makynge of a newe eye to the great bell claper,	o	3	o
Item, payed to *Richard Landegore*, for ſtrykynge of waxe ageyn Hallowmas,	o	o	3
Item, payed to *John Robard*, of Maldon, for halfe a kalfys ſkyne,	o	o	3
Item, payed to ...... *Reve*, of Chelmesforde, for a lyne for the vaile clothe agenſe Lent,	o	o	2
Item, payed to *Richarde Barnard*, for mendynge of the bawdrick to the bellis,	o	o	2
Item, payed to the plomer, for mendynge the gret candilſtyk that ſtondeth in the chaunſell,	o	o	4
Item, payed for frankynſence,	o	o	1
Item, payed to *Richard Langore*, for ſtrykynge of waxe agaynſt Eſter,	o	o	3

For the Rodelofte.

	£.	s.	d.
Item, paied to *Cruſtill*, of Danbury, for halfe a ſeme of lyme,	o	1	o
Item, paied for the caryage of the ſame lyme,	o	o	1
Item, paied to *Wynterborne*, of Maldon, for a daye's work upon the chirche for hym and hys ladde,	o	1	1
Item, paied to *Richard Robard*, for a hundred of fourpenny nayle,	o	o	4
Item, paied to *Richard Robard*, for halfe a hundred of threepenny nayle,	o	o	1½
Item, paied for ſpykes to the bellis,	o	o	2½
Item, paied for 6 ſtapels for truſſynge of the bellis,	o	o	10
Item, paied for halfe a hundred of threepenny nayle,	o	o	1½
Item, paide to the carver for truſſynge of the bellis,	o	o	10
Item, paide for frankyncenſe againſte chirche holidaye,	o	o	1
Item, paide to *Doraunte*, of Maldon, for takynge downe the rodelofte,	o	o	6
Item, paide to *Richard Malſon*, for helpyng hym,	o	o	4
Item, paide to *Thruſtall*, of Danbury, for a ſeme and a halfe of lyme,	o	3	o
Item, paide to *Robert Cokſhott*, for the caryage of the ſame,	o	o	8
Item, paide for .... wort about	o	1	6

Item

	£.	s.	d.
Item, paide to 2 laborers to ſerve the bricklayers for 3 days,	1	0	0
Item, paide for a pennyworth of leed, — —	0	0	1
Item, paide to *Phillipp Goldborne*, for wrytyng of the premiſſes,	0	0	8
Sum of the paymentes for the ſaid year, —	1	8	3½

The coſtes and charges belongynge to the batilments of the ſeid chirche, paied by the handes of the ſeid chirchwardeyns within the ſeid yere.

	£.	s.	d.
Inprimis, paied to *Damyon*, the property player, for caryinge of his propertes home *, — — —	0	1	4
Item, paied to *Peter Roche*, for two hundred of ledd naile, —	0	1	0
Item, paied to *Peter Roche*, for 200 of fivepeny nayle to the ſteepill,	0	0	10
Item, paied to *Peter Roche*, for a locke and a keye to the weſte dore of the ſolare within the chirch, — —	0	0	7
Item, paied to *Richard Robard*, for a ſtapill to the ſaid locke,	0	0	1
Item, paied to —— *Bode*, of Danbury, for 5 ſeme of lyme,	0	10	0
Item, paied for the cariage of the ſame, — —	0	0	4
Item, paied to my Lord Abbot of *Bileigh*, for 2000 brickkes,	0	8	0
Item, paied for the cariage of the ſame, — —	0	2	8
Item, paied to *Richard Crote*, for a daies worke abowt the ſtepill,	0	0	5
Item, paied to *Wynterborne*, for 5 daies worke of hymſelfe and hys ladde, the one 7*d.* a daie, the other			
Item, paied to the carpenter for 2 daies werke abowte the ſtepill,	0	1	0
Item, paied to *John Barrett*, for the cariage of 12 lode of yertle †,	0	2	8
Item, paied to *Richard Langore*, for ſervynge of Winterborne 4 daies, 5*d.* the daie, — — —	0	1	8
Item, paied to *Roberd Cokſhott*, for a daies worke to ſerve the ſeide Winterborne, — — — — —	0	0	5
Item, paid to *John Stifted*, for 5 daies werke to ſerve the ſaide Wynterborne, every daye 5*d.* — — —	0	2	1
Item, paied the ſeid *Wynterborne*, at anothere tyme, for 3 daies werke for hym and hys ladde, — — —	0	3	3
Item, paied to *Richard Langore*, to ſerve the ſeid Wynterborne the ſaid 3 daies, 5*d.* the daie, — — — —	0	1	3
Item, paied to *John Stifted*, for 2 daies worke, 5*d.* the daie,	0	0	10
Item, paied the plomer for ſoderynge of the fonte, —	0	0	4
Item, paied to *Morecock*, for 3 daies werke and a halfe upon the chirche, 6*d.* the daye, — — —	0	1	9
Item, paied for a rope to the gret bell, — —	0	0	7
Item, paied for 30 fote of okyn borde, — —	0	1	0
Item, paied to *John Landſey*, the elder, for carryinge of 800 of olde lede from Heibredge to Bileigh, and for carring of 3 newe ſhets of lede from Bileigh to Heibredge, — —	0	0	6

* Q. a play for the benefit of the church, of which ſee the *grant* in the next page.
† Q. yerthe, earth.

Item,

	£.	s.	d.
Item, paied to *Morecocke*, for 5 daies werke upon the chirche, 6*d*. the daie,	0	2	6
Item, paied for 100 and a halfe of fourpeny naile,	0	0	6
Item, paied to *Richard Robard*, for gret naile,	0	0	1¼
Item, paied to *Morecocke*, for a daies werke and a halfe,	0	0	9
Item, paied to *John Irifhman*, for pynnynge of the fell of the rode-lofte, and pynnynge of the fell of the two awters,	0	0	9
Item, paied for a rope to the fore bell,	0	0	7
Item, paied to *Phillipp Goldborn*, of Maldon, for wrytynge of thefe two fides,	0	0	4
Sum of the charges of the battilments,	3	7	1¼

Heybredge.

	£.	s.	d.
Inprimis, receyved of ——— ———, for halfe a yere's ferme of land due at the fefte of	0	2	8
Item, receyved of *Alleyn*, of Brodeftrete, for a hole yere's ferme of a cowe,	0	1	0
Item, receyved of *Robard Frauncys*, for a hole yere's ferme of a cowe and 4 fhepe,	0	2	0
Item, receyved of *John Dredge*, for a hole yere's ferme of lande,	0	1	0
Item, receyved of *John Samwell*, for halfe a yere's ferme of lande,	0	0	3
Item, receyved of *Thomas Benfon*, for the graunte towarde our playe *,	0	1	0
Item, receyved of *Thomas Stowe*,	0	1	0
Item, receyved of *Robard Chapman*, for halfe a yere's ferme of his howfe,	0	1	0
Item, receyved of *Thomas Wedde*, of Maldon, for halfe a hundred of ledde,	0	1	3
Item, receyved of *John Lindfey*, junior, for halfe yere's ferme of lande,	0	4	0
Item, receyved of Sir *John Godday*, vicar, for halfe a hundred of leede,	0	2	2
Sum total,	0	17	4

	£.	s.	d.
Inprimis, paied to *Richarde*, for takynge upp the ..... of tymbre before the two awters,	0	0	2
Item, paied to *Richard Robard*, for 4 ftapils and hokes to fett upp the feynts,	0	0	4
Item, paied to *John Whighthede*, of Maldon, for tylynge of the two chirch porchis,	0	1	0
Item, paied for 300 of tile,	0	1	4
Item, paied to *Hugh Snell*, of Maldon, for 2000 of large naile,	0	1	6
Item, paide to *William Pinde*, of Langforde, for 500 of lathe, pryce the hundred 7*d*.	0	2	9

* See the preceding page.

Item,

	£.	s.	d.
Item, paied to *John Letyn*, junior, for carriage of bricke that was owyng of the olde,	0	1	0
Item, paide to *William Sponer*, of Maldon, for a bawdrikke for the litle bell,	0	0	8
Item, paide to *William Dode*, of Danbury, for 3 ſeme of lyme,	0	6	0
Item, paide to *William Dode*, of Danbury, for cariage of the ſame,	0	0	6
Item, paide to *John Meſſynge*, of Maldon, for 100 of lathe,	0	0	7
Item, paid to *Morecocke*, for gettynge upp of the ſeynts in the chirche,	0	0	4
Item, paid to *William Wade*, of Kelden, for ſetynge of the rode-lofte, and ſhuvynge home of the too botraſſes of the ſeid to rodelofte,	0	10	4
Item, paide to *William Wade*, of Kelden, for caſtyng and whityng of . . . . . chirche,	0	5	6
Item, paide to *Richarde G* . . . . for makynge clene of the chirche at Hallowmas,	0	0	1
Item, paide to *Richard Langoee*, for ſtrikyng of waxe againſte Hallowmas,	0	0	1½
Item, paide to *Thomas Benſon*, for ſkorynge of a diche *, called Paſchall diche,	0	2	0
Item, paide for a lyne before the baſen of our Ladye,	0	0	2
Item, paide to *Morecocke*, for ſettynge upp of a baſen and leyinge in a piece of tymbre on the north ſyde of the chirche,	0	0	6
Item, paide to *Richarde Gernarde*, for makynge clene of the chirche after the whitynge of it,	0	0	1
Item, paide for 3 buſhell of lyme,	0	0	9
Item, paide agenſt Criſtmaſs for a pownde of talow candell,	0	0	1¼
Item, paide to *Richard Gernarde*, for caryinge home of the leden wayts to the bailliffs,	0	0	1
Item, paide for ſkorynge of a baſen and a branche before our Ladye and Seynt John,	0	0	6
Item, paide to *Morecocke*, for ſettynge up of Seynt George, and naylynge of lede on the ſteeple,	0	0	2
Item, paide to *John Letyn*, junior, for caryage of the chirche tymbre,	0	0	2
Item, paide to *Richard Gernarde*, for mendynge of the chirche-gate,	0	0	1
Item, paide for 4 pownde of waxe,	0	2	0
Item, paide to *Andrewe Elyott*, of Maldon, for mendynge of the grete bell claper, and the third bell claper,	0	4	0
Item, paide to *William Sponer*, for a bawdrykke for the grete bell,	0	0	10
Item, paide for ſtrykynge of the waxe agenſt Eſter,	0	0	4
Item, paide to *Phillipp Goldborne*, for wrytynge of this halfe yere's accownte,	0	0	8
Sum	10	5	7¼

* The ditch round the Paſchal Croft.

Receyts resfeyved by the hands of *John Reynolde* and *John Lettyn*, the elder, chirchewardeyns, from the feste of Seynt Marke, unto the feste of Seynt Mighell, the 10th yere of Kynge Henrye the Eighth.

	£.	s.	d.
Inprimis, refeyved of *Robard Chapman*, for the halfe yere's ferme of his howse, — — —	0	1	0
Item, refeyved of *John Lyndesey*, junior, for the halfe yere's ferme of his lande, — — —	0	4	0
Item, refeyved of *Richard Cokshett*, for the halfe yere's ferme of his lande, — — — —	0	2	0
Item, refeyved of *John Samwell*, for halfe a yere's ferme of lande,	0	0	3
Item, refeyved of *John Hewett*, for John Pagett's dett, —	0	1	0
Item, refeyved of our vicar for John Sprott, —	0	1	8
Item, refeyved of our vicar for 2 busshell of lyme, —	0	0	6
Item, refeyved of *Stephen Gyll*, for 18 stykkes, —	0	0	1
Item, refeyved of *John Samwell*, for 2 ferthynge potts, —	0	0	0½
Item, refeyved of *John Herward*, for lythe * that were abowte his wyfe's beriall, — — — — —	0	0	4
Item, refeyved of *John Reynold*, chirchewarden, halfe a hundred of lede and 3 quarters, — — — —	0	3	3
Sum — — — —	0	14	1½

Payments paid by the seid wardeyns the seid halfe yere.

	£.	s.	d.
Inprimis, paid to *Dode*, of Danbury, for 2 seme and 2 busshell of lyme, — — — — — —	0	4	6
Item, paid for gettynge the same lyme, — —	0	0	0½
Item, paid for the cariage of the same lyme, — —	0	0	6
Item, paid for 10 pownde of rede oker to the bartillments of the chirche and the porche, — — —	0	0	5
Item, paid to *Langore's* wyfe, for drynke for the cartere that brought in the chirche tymbre, — —	0	0	1
Item, paid to *Sponer*, of Maldon, for a bell rope, —	0	0	9
Item, paid to *Wynterborne* .... of the bartillments of the chirche, — — — — —	0	6	10
Item, paid for frankynsence, — — —	0	0	1
Item, paid to *Winterborne*, for whytynge and rede skerynge of the chirche porche, — — — —	0	1	8
Item, paid to *Richard Gernard*, for haveynge in of the lyme and the sande into the chirche, — — —	0	0	1
Item, paid to *Richard Gernard*, for brounynge of 2 glase windowes on the south side of the chirch, — — —	0	0	1
Item, paid to *Sponer*, of Maldon, for a bell-rope, —	0	0	8
Item, paid to *Swyfte*, for caryinge of a ladd to the friers of Maldon,	0	0	1

* Lights.

	£.	s.	d.
Item, paid for frankynſence,	0	0	0½
Item, paid to *Phillipp Goldborn*, for wrytyng,	0	0	4
Sum	0	16	2

Detts that are owinge to the ſeid chirche at the ſeid feſte of Seynt Mighell, anno 10 Henry VIII.

	£.	s.	d.
Inprimis, *John Lyndſey*, junior, owethe for halfe a yere's farme,	0	4	0
Item, *Robard Cockſhett*, for halfe a yere's farme,	0	2	0
Item, *John Samwell*, owethe for half a yere's ferme,	0	0	3
Item, *John Dredge*, for 3 quarters of a yere's farme,	...	...	...
Item, *Robart Chapman*, for halfe a yere's ferme,	0	1	0
Item, *Robard Fraunceis*, for a hole yere's ferm of a cowe and 4 ſhepe,	0	2	0
Item, *John Alleyn*, for a yere's ferm of a cowe,	0	1	0
Item, *John Lettyn*, ſenior, owethe for tymbre,	0	1	0
Total	0	11	8

A reckynyng made betwene the chyrchwardeyns and the paryſhe on Mickelmas-day, the yere of the rayne of Kyng Henry the Eighth the 9th yere, and the chyrche owethe to the ſeyd wardens.

Detts that be owynge to the ſaide churche atte the feſte of Mychaelmas next enſuing, anno 11 Henry VIII.

	£.	s.	d.
Inprimis, *John Lyndſey*, the younger, owethe for halfe a yere's farme,	0	6	4
Item, *John Samwell*, for halfe a yere's ferme,	0	0	3
Item, *Robard Chapman*, for halfe a yere's ferme,	0	1	0
Item, *Robard Frauncis*, for a hole yere's ferme of a cowe and 4 ſheepe,	0	2	0
Item, *John Alleyn*, for a year's ferme of a cowe,	0	1	0
Item, *John Gregge*, owethe for a hole yere's ferme of his howſe,	0	0	3
Sum	0	10	10

	£.	s.	d.
Reſtyng in Mayſter *Bayly's* handys,	3	2	3
Whereofe he hath payd to *John Arthur*,	0	8	8
Item, payd to *Alyſander*, for drynkyng pottys,	0	0	6
Item, payd to *Willyam Pynd*, for 300 of pavyng tyles,	0	6	8
Item, payd to *Lettyn*,	0	6	0
Item, payd to *Thomas Gwyn*,	0	4	0
Item, payd to	0	1	0
Item, payd to	0	11	0

Item,

	£.	s.	d.
Item, payd to .... — — — —	0	17	0
Item, payd to Moder *Reynolds*, — —	0	6	8
Item, payd to .... — —	0	6	8
Item, payd to *Richard Lobber*, — —	0	12	0
Total ſum, — — —	3	9	2

Accountes the whyche wee *John Lettyn*, the elder, and *John Arthur*, churchwardens of the pariſhe of Seynt Andrewe's, in Heybregge, have receyved, from the feſt of Mychelmas, in the 10th yere of the rayne of Kyng Henry the Eighth, unto the feſt of Michelmas then next followynge, in the 11th yere of oure ſeyd Sovereigne Lorde the Kynge.

	£.	s.	d.
Inprimis, receyved of Mayſter *Hyllys*, of London, for hys gyfte,	0	6	8
Item, receyved the gyfte of Mayſter *Bayly*, —	0	2	0
Item, receyved the gyfte of Mayſter *Baker*, of London, —	0	1	8
Item, receyved of *Denby*, for the gyfte of John Sharpe, —	0	13	4
Item, receyved of the gyfte of *John Paget*, of Maldon, —	0	6	8
Item, receyved of *Denby*, for the gyfte of John Sharpe, —	0	6	8
Item, receyved for the campyng ſporte, — —	0	18	3
Item, receyved of *John Wykelin*, — —	0	3	4
Item, receyved of Maſter *Bayly*, for a potte of the churchys,	0	7	8
Item, receyved the gyfte of *John Kyngeſman*, — —	0	6	8
Item, receyved the gyfte of *Thomas Spratte*, — —	0	6	8
Item, receyved of *John Wykelin*, — — —	0	3	4
Item, receyved of Maſter *Bayly*, the gifte of John More, —	0	1	8
Item, receyved of *John Bregge*, for a hole yery's rent due at Michelmas laſt paſt, — — — —	0	1	0
Item, receyved of *Robert Fraunces*, for a ferm of a cowe and 13 ſheepe, — — — — —	0	2	0
Item, receyved of *Robert Chapman*, for a hole yere's rent dew at the ſeid feſte, — — — —	0	2	0
Item, receyved of *John Lyndſey*, junior, for a hole yere's rent,	0	8	0
Item, receyved of *Robert Cokſhotte*, for a halfe yere's rent, —	0	2	0
Item, receyved of *John Samwell*, for a hole yere's rent, —	0	0	3
Item, receyved for ſettyng of candell in the churche, —	0	0	8
Sum — — — —	5	1	4

Heybregge.

Thes be the paymentes payde by the ſeid churchewardens from the ſeid feſte.

	£.	s.	d.
Inprimis, paide to the ſawyers at too tymes, — —	0	11	4
Item, paide for two bell-roppys, — — —	0	1	8
Item, paide for a lanthorne, — —	0	0	4

Item,

	£.	s.	d.
Item, paide for an erneſt grote to *Foſter*, —— ——	0	0	4
Item, paide to the ſawyers ageyn, —— ——	0	6	0
Item, paide to the carpenters by the day, — —	0	10	8
Item, paide for the bordyng of the ſeid carpenters, ——	0	1	0
Item, paide for 100 of fourpeny nayle, — —	0	0	4
Item, paide for 3 pownde of candell, —— ——	0	0	4½
Item, paide to the carpenters for borde and wages, —	0	6	8
Item, paide to the carpenters for theyr wages, cheyz, and borde, the hole weeke before Candylmas, — — —	0	9	0
Item, paide for ſpyknayle, — — —	0	0	1
Itom, paide for two pownde of candell, —— —	0	0	3
Item, paide to the carpenters for theyr wages, cheyz, and borde, in Candylmas weke, — — — —	0	4	0
Item, paide for 3 pownde of candell, — —	0	0	4½
Item, paide to the carpenters a grette, — —	3	18	6
Item, paide to the ſawyers, — — —	0	5	6
Item, paide for halfe a calfe's ſkynne, — —	0	0	4
Item, paide to the ſawyers, — — —	0	3	4
Item, paide to *Willyam Alexander*, for nayle and ſpyke ageynſt the campyng, —— —— ——	0	1	4
Item, paide for two pownde of waxe, — —	0	1	6
Item, paide for mendynge of the cape, — —	0	0	8
Item, payde for 3 pownde of waxe, —— ——	0	2	4
Item, payde to the ſawyers, — — —	0	2	8
Item, payde for mendynge of the grete bell-claper, —	0	1	4
Item, payde for a bell-roppe, — — —	0	0	8
Item, payde for waxe, — — — —	0	1	8
Item, payde to the gerdatt *Somney*, — —	0	1	0
Item, payde to a plomer for mendynge of the church lede,	0	0	4
Item, payde for hys coſtes that bare upp oure vardyte, —	0	1	0
Item, payde to them that bare the pavynge tile into the churche,	0	0	1
Item, payde to *Richard Robard*, for ſpyke and nayle, —	0	1	0
Item, payde to *Richard Mathewſon*, for wrytyng of oure accounte,	0	0	8
Item, payde for ſtrykynge of our waxe for the hole yere, —	0	0	8
Item, payde for waſhyng of the churche gere, —	0	0	6
Item, payde for frankynſence, —— ——	0	0	2½
Sum — — —	8	17	8½

Heybregge.

Heybregge.

Memorandum.

That thefe be the receyts receyved by *John Arthur* and *John Tatott*, churchewardens of the pariyfche churche of Seynt Andrewe's, in Heybregge aforfeyde, from the fefte of Mighelmas, in the 11th yere of the reigne of Kynge Henrye the Eighth, unto the fefte of Mighelmas then nexte followyng, in the 12th yere of the reigne of Kynge Henrye the Eighth.

	£.	s.	d.
Inprimis, receyved from *John Lynfey*, the yonger, for a hole yere's ferme dew, — — —	0	1	0
Item, receyved of *Robard Fraunfeys*, for a hole yere's ferme of a cowe and 4 fhepe, — — — — —	0	2	0
Item, receyved of *Thomas Alleyn*, for a hole yere's ferme of a cowe,	0	1	0
Item, receyved of *John Samwell*, the elder, —	0	0	3
Item, receyved of *John Wyklyn*, — —	0	3	4
Item, receyved of *John Lynfey*, fenyor, for the halfe yere's ferme of his howfe, — — —	0	1	0
Item, receyved of *John Brygge*, for a hole yere's ferme, —	0	1	0
Item, receyved of *John Tattott*, for repayring of the founte,	0	2	0
Item, receyved of *John Tattott*, for makynge of the ftanding of the torches, — — —	0	1	0
Sum — — —	1	3	7

Thefe be the paymentes whyche the feid churchewardens have payed.

	£.	s.	d.
Inprimis, payed for makyng of the churche-gate, —	0	4	6
Item, payed for hokys and hynges to the feyd gate, —	0	0	8
Item, payed for nayles to the feid gate, — —	0	0	c½
Item, payde for waxe ageynft Alhallontide, — —	0	3	4
Item, payde for ftrykynge of the feyd waxe, —	0	0	2½
Item, payde for 2 bell-roppys, — —	0	1	8
Item, payde for mendyng of the awtys ageynfe the feyd fefte,	0	0	1
Item, payde to *John Letyn*, for a feme of lyme, —	0	2	3
Item, payde to *Wynterborne*, for layinge of the payment in the churche, — — —	0	3	0
Item, payde for 2 pownde of waxe agenfe Cryftemas, —	0	1	8
Item, payde for ftrykynge of the feyd waxe, —	0	0	1½
Item, payde for 2 pownde of talowr candell agenfe the fame fefte, — — — —	0	0	2½
Item, payde for mendyng of the grete herfe, —	0	0	3
Item, payde for a ladder and for the letyll herfe, —	0	0	8
Item, payde for frankencence, — —	0	0	1¼
Item, payde for mendyng of the churche rofe, and the bowdryng of the funte, — — — —	0	0	8

Item,

	£.	s.	d.
Item, payde for 8 pownde of waxe ageynſe Eſter, pryce the pownde 10*d*. — — — —	0	6	8
Item, payde for ſtrykynge of the ſeyd waxe agenſe Eſter, —	0	0	6
Item, payde for mendyng of the bellys, — —	0	0	5
Item, payde for neyles and frankincenſe, — —	0	0	3½
Item, payde to *Wynterborne*, for repairing the founte, —	0	3	8
Item, payde to the plomer, for ledyng the founte, —	0	3	0
Item, payde to *Hopkins*, for the lyme-ſtonys, — —	0	0	4
Item, payde for 5 yerds of lynnyn clothe, — —	0	3	4
Item, payde for makyng of a awter clothe of the ſame clothe,	0	0	3
Item, payde for mendynge of a albe, — —	0	0	1
Item, payde for 2 ſtremerys, — —	0	3	0
Item, payde for mendynge of 5 ſtremers beſydes, —	0	1	0
Item, payde for makynge of the canope, — —	0	2	4
Item, payde for a lytyll bell-rope, — —	0	0	1
Item, payde to the ſomner at the late viſytacion, —	0	1	0
Item, payde to *Willym Alexſander*, for a boſhell of oytys for the commeſſary's horſe, — — —	0	0	4
Item, payde for mendynge of the candylſtycke, — —	0	0	4
Item, payde for 2 pownde of waxe againſe Halowmas, —	0	1	8
Item, payde for ſtrykynge of it, — — —	0	0	1
Sum — — —	2	9	5

Detts that be owynge to the churche at Heybregge.

Inprimis, *John Lynſey* owyth for the churche lande, —	0	6	0
Item, *Robard Fraunceys*, for a hole yere's ferme of 4 ſhepe and one cowe, and hath no ſewertye, — — —	0	2	0
Item, *Thomas Allcyn*, for a hole yere's ferme of a cowe; ſewertye for hym *John Lynſey*, the elder, — — —	0	1	0
Item, *John Bregge*, owythe for a hole yerys ferme of churche lande,	0	0	6
Item, *John Samwell*, for a hole yere's ferme, —	0	0	3
Item, *John Totell*, or *Catell*, junior, for the gyfte of his father,	1	6	8
Item, *John Totell*, or *Catell*, junior, for the gyfte of his father, 4 ſhepe payable atte Wytſontyde, — —	...	...	...
Item, *John Lettyn*, the elder, for the bequeſte of hys ſyſter,	0	6	8
Item, Mayſtor *Baylye*, owythe — —	0	13	2
Item, *John Lynſey*, the elder, for a hole yere's ferme of his howſe rent, — — — —	0	2	0
Sum — — —	2	16	0

Heybredge.

Heybredge.

The receyts receyved by the handys of *John Reynolds* and *John Sprott*, churchwardeyns, from the feste of Michelmas, anno 12° of Kynge Henrye VIII. endeth at the feste of Michelmas, anno 13° of Kynge Henrye VIII.

	£.	s.	d.
Inprimis, receyved of *John Samwell*, for halfe a yere arrerages of land dew the seid feste of Seynt Mighell, anno 12° Henry VIII.	0	0	3
Item, receyved of *John Lyndsey*, for halfe yere's ferme of lande dew at the seid feste, — — —	0	6	0
Item, receyved of *John Dredge*, for ditto, — —	0	0	6
Item, receyved of *John Lyndsey*, for halfe yere's ferme of lande due at the feste of the Annunciation of our Ladye, anno 12° Henry VIII. — — —	0	6	0
Item, receyved of *John Samwell*, for ditto, due at the seid feste,	0	0	3
Item, receyved of *John Dredge*, for ditto, due at the seid feste,	0	0	6
Item, receyved of *John Harwarde*, for ditto, due at the seid feste,	0	1	0
Item, receyved of *John Lyndsey*, the elder, for a yere's ferme of a howse, due at the feste of Seynt Mighell, anno 12° Henry VIII.	0	2	0
Item, receyved of *John Alleyn*, of Moche Totham, for a yere's ferme of a cowe, dewe at the seid feste, — —	0	1	0
Item, receyved of *Robard Frauncys*, for a yere's ferme of a cowe, and 4 shepe, dew at the seid feste, — —	0	1	9
Item, receyved of *John Car.....* for arrerages of dett that he owythe to the churche, — — —	0	10	0
Sum of receyts — —	1	9	3

Paymentes payde by the handys of the seid churchwardeyns in the yere aforwrytyng.

	£.	s.	d.
Inprimis, payde for waxe for the rode-lofte light agenst Chystemas last paste, pryce the pownde 10*d*. — —	0	4	2
Item, payde to *Richard Langore*, for strykynge of the same waxe, and 2 pownde of olde waxe, — — — —	0	0	5
Item, payde to a bell-hanger for trussynge of the 3de belle and the great bell ageynse Crystemas, — —	0	1	10
Item, payde to *Richard Robards*, for spykes to the seid bellis,	0	0	2
Item, payde for 2 pownde of tallowe candell agense Crystemas,	0	0	3
Item, payde for frankynsence, — —	0	0	1
Item, payde for a bell-rope, — —	0	0	8
Item, payde for 6 pownde of waxe agense Ester, pryce the pownde 9½*d*. — — — — —	0	4	9

Item,

	£.	s.	d.
Item, payde for halfe a pownde of frankyncenſe agenſe Eſter,	0	0	4
Item, payde to *Richard Langore*, for ſtrykynge of the ſeid newe waxe and old waxe agenſe Eſter, — —	0	0	6
Item, payde for a locke to the Southe dore of the churche,	0	1	6
Item, payde for 2 keys, — — —	0	0	6
Item, payde to *William Wode*, ſmythe, for the flight of the gret bell knepill, — — — —	0	2	11
Item, payde to *Crow*, for dickynge of 8 rodd of diche agenſe the churchelande, — — — —	0	0	8
Item, payde to *William Wode*, for mendynge of another bell knepill,	0	1	3
Item, payde to *Henry Marney*, for the rent of Wallcroftes, —	0	1	8
Item, payde to the commiſſaries ſomner *, for arrerages of Peter-pence, beynge byhynde unpaide, — — —	0	4	0
Item, payde for ſtrykynge of the Paſkall-tapers into betynge light for the tapers, — — — —	0	0	1
Item, payde to *Philip Goldborne*, for wrytynge of thys accownt,	0	0	8
Sum — — —	1	6	1

Detts owynge to the churche of Herbredge att the feſte of St. Mighell, anno 13° Henry VIII.

	£.	s.	d.
Inprimis, *John Lyndſey*, junior, oweth for halfe yere's rent of the churchelande, — — — —	0	6	0
Item, *Robard Fraunceys*, for a yere's ferme of a cowe, and 4 ſhepe,	0	2	0
Item, *William Alleyn*, owethe for a yere's ferme of a cowe. He hathe ſewertee *John Lynſey*, ſenior, — — —	0	1	0
Item, *John Dredge*, for halfe a yere's ferme of churchelande,	0	0	6
Item, *John Samwell*, for halfe a yere's ferme of churchelande,	0	0	3
Item, *John Tatell*, for the bequeſt of his father, —	1	6	8
Item, *John Tatell*, for the gyfte of 4 ſhepe, —	......		
Item, *John Lettyn*, for the bequeſte of hys ſyſter, —	0	6	8
Item, *John Carrington*, owythe of 13*s.* 2*d.* — —	0	3	2
Item, *John Lynſey*, ſenior, for a hole yere's rent of his howſe,	0	2	0
Sum — — — —	......		

Receypts of the ſeyd Wardens, from the feſte of Seynt Mighell, anno 13° Henry VIII. unto the feſte of Criſtmas then next followynge,

	£.	s.	d.
Inprimis, receyved of *John Letten*, the elder, of hys ſyſter's bequeſte, — — — — — —	0	6	8
Item, receyved of *John Carryngton*, of olde arrerages, —	0	3	2
Item, receyved of *John Tatyll*, of hys father's bequeſte, —	0	6	8

* Summoner: an officer appointed to ſummon delinquents to appear in eccleſiaſtical courts, now called an Apparitor. See Chaucer's Canterb. Tales, l. 625—670.

Item,

	£.	s.	d.
Item, receyved of *John Tatyll*, of hys father's bequeſte, —	1	6	8
Item, receyved of the churche gaderynge, — —	0	5	8
Item, receyved of the carpentre that made the bell-frame, for a pece of tymbre that he gave to the churche, — —	0	1	5
Item, receyved of *John Lyndſey*, junior, for the halfe yere's ferme of lande, dew at the feſt of Seynt Mighell, anno 13° Henry VIII.	0	6	0
Item, receyved of *John Samwell*, for halfe a yere's ferme of lande, dew at the ſeyd feſte, — — —	0	0	3
Item, receyed of *John Dredge*, for halfe a yere's ferme of lande, dew at the ſeid feſte, — — —	0	0	6
Item, receyed of —— *Alleyn*, of Totham, for a year's ferme of a cowe, dew the ſeyd feſte, — — —	0	1	0
Item, receyved of *Robard Frauncеys*, for the hole yere's ferme of a cowe and 4 ſhepe, — — —	0	2	0
Item, receyved of Old *Lyndſey*, for the half yere's rent of his howſe, dew att the ſeyd feſte, — — —	0	1	0
Item, receyved of *John Tatell*, for a yere's ferme of 5 ſhepe, dew att the ſeid feſte, — — — —	0	1	3
Sum — — —	2	14	3

Paymentes payed by the ſeyd Churchwardeyns from the ſeid feſte of Seynt Mighell, unto the ſeyd feſte of Criſtemas.

	£.	s.	d.
Inprimis, paide to *Clarke*, of Thaxted, for 35 fote of tymbre to the bell-frame, — — — —	0	4	1
Item, paide for caryinge of a pece of tymbre to the ſeyd frame,	0	0	2
Item, paide for 2 pownde of tallowe candell for the werkemen to werke by, — — — —	0	0	2½
Item, paide to *Clarke*, of Thaxted, for 21 fote of tymbre to the ſame frame, — — — — —	0	2	2
Item, paide to the Maſter Carpenter, for 12 days werke, 6*d*. the daye, — — — —	0	6	0
Item, paide to 3 of hys men for 12 dayes werke abowte the ſeyd frame, 4*d*. apeece the daye, — —	0	12	0
Item, paide to the ſeyd Maſter Carpentre, and oon of hys men, for oon daye's werke abowte the ſame, — —	0	0	10
Item, paide for the bordynge of the ſeyd Maſtere Carpentre, and the ſeid 3 men, the ſeid 12 dayes, 13*d*. apece by the weke, —	0	8	8
Item, paide for halfe a pownde of .... to the ſocketts of the bellys, — — — —	0	0	1½
Item, paide for grece for the bellys, — —	0	0	0½
Item, paide for bordynge of the ſeyd Maſtere Carpentre, and hys 3 men, by the ſpace of 3 holydaies, — —	0	3	6
Item, paid for nayles and ſtapyls to the ſeyd frames, —	0	2	8

	£.	s.	d.
Item, paide to the carpentres and ſawyers for werkyng of the tymbre to the ſame frame, — — —	0	6	8
Item, paid for the bordynge of them, — —	0	3	6
Item, paide to the Maſter Carpenter, for hym and hys man, for a daie's werke and a halfe, — —	0	0	10
Item, paide more for 3 dayes werke and a halfe, 4*d.* the daye,	0	1	2
Item, paide to hys man for 5 daies werke and a halfe, —	0	1	10
Item, paide for theyr bordynge that tyme, —	0	2	0
Item, paide more to the ſeyd Maſter and hys 3 men, for a daye's werke and more, — — —	0	2	0
Item, paide for their bordynge, — —	0	1	1
Item, paide *John Tatell*, for caryinge of the tymbre, —	0	0	5
Item, paide for wax agenſt Hollowmas *, — —	0	3	3
Item, paide for ſtrykyng of the ſeid waxe, —	0	0	4
Item, paide for a bell-rope, — — —	0	0	8
Item, paide for halfe a calve's ſkin for mendyng of the bell-roppis,	0	0	3
Item, paide for 2 pownde of tallow candell agenſt Chriſtmas,	0	0	3
Item, paide to *Philip Goldborne*, for wrytynge of this accownt,	0	0	8
Sum — —	3	5	2½

Receyts receyved by the handys of *John Reynold* and *John Sprott*, wardeyns of the ſeid churche, from the feſte of Criſtemas, anno 13° Henry VIII. unto the feſt of Seynt Mighell then next followynge, anno 14° Henry VIII.

	£.	s.	d.
Inprimis, receyved of *John Lynſey* ...... for halfe a yere's ferme of Paſkall-crofte ...... and for another crofte 18*d.* due at the feſte of the Annunciation of oure Bleſſed Lady, anno 13° Henry VIII.	0	4	6
Item, receyved of *John Samwell*, for halfe a yere's ferme of lande, due at the ſeid feſte, — — —	0	0	3
Item, receyved of *John Dredge*, for halfe a yere's ferme of lande, due at the ſeid feſte, — — — —	0	0	6
Sum — — — —	0	5	3

Paymentes paide by the ſeid wardeyns from the ſeid feſte of Criſtemas unto the ſeid feſte of Seynt Mighell.

	£.	s.	d.
Item, paide for a pownde of frankynſence, —	0	0	4
Item, paide to *Richard Langore*, for ſtrykyng of wax ageynſt Eſter,	0	0	7
Item, paide to *Richard Langore* for waxe ageynſt the ſeid feſte,	0	1	0
Item, paide to *Richard Langore*, for ſtrykyng of a pownde and halfe of betynge lyght ageynſt the feſte of the Natyvyte of oure Bleſſed Lady, anno 14° Henry VIII. — —	0	0	1½
Item, for wrytyng of this accompte, — — —	0	0	4
Sum, — — —	0	2	4½

* Allhallows maſs.

The arreragye of the church lande due att the feſte of St. Mighell, anno 14° Henry VIII.

	£.	s.	d.
Inprimis, *John Lynſey*, the yonger, owethe for halfe yere's ferme of lande, due at the ſeid feſte, ——— ———	o	4	6
Item, *John Samwell* owethe for halfe a year's ferme of lande, due at the ſeide feſte, ——— ——— ———	o	o	3
Item, *John Dredge*, owethe for halfe a yere's ferme of lande, due at the ſeid feſte, —— —— —— ——	o	o	6
Item, *John Lindſey*, the elder, owethe for a hole yere's ferme of a howſe, due at the ſeid feſte, ——— ———	o	2	o
Item, *Wyllyam Aleyn*, owethe for a hole yere's ferme of a kowe, due at the ſeid feſte, ——— ——— ———	o	I	o
Item, *Robard Fraunceys*, for .... a kowe and 9 ſhepe,	....		
Item, *John Pagett*, of Maldon, ... premyſe when he was wardeyn.........			
Sum			

Receyts by the handys of *Wyllyam* .... and *Wyliyam Wodde*, the cherchewardeyns of Hebregg, from the feſte of Seynt .... to the feſte of Saynt Mighell, anno 1522.

	£.	s.	d.
Receyved of *John Lynſey*, the yonger, for a hole yere's	o	9	o
Item, receyved of *John Lynſey*, the elder, — —	o	2	o
Item, receyved of *Robard Fraunceys*, for a kowe and 9 ſhepe, a hole yere, — — — — —	o	3	3
Item, reſeyved of *John Samwell*, for a hole yere's rent of the chirche land, —— —— ——	o	o	6
Item, receyved of *John Dredge*, for a hole yere's rent of the churche land, — — — — —	o	I	o
Item, receyved of *Philip* ...... for the chirche dewe, —	o	3	4
Item, receyved of Maſter ....*ly*, for the poſtes in the ſtone,	o	o	6
Item, receyved in the cherche-box, ——— ———	o	o	I
Item, receyved of *Alleyn*, of Totham, for a cowe, ———	o	I	o
Item, receyved of *John Brege*, for woode, — —	o	7	4
Item, receyved of the gadryng of the white plowe *, ——	o	I	3
Item, receyved of the ſellyng of waxe in the cherche, —	o	4	I
Sum — — —	I	13	3

* Q. does this mean Plough Monday; on which the country people come and dance and make a gathering as on May-day?

Thes

	£.	s.	d.
Thes be the paymentes paide by the feid churchewardeyns.			
First, we payed to Mastere *Baly*			
Item, payed for mendyng the bellis			
Item, payed for Peter-pense,	0	1	2
Item, payed for hierne * werke for the bellis,	. . .	. . .	. . .
Item, payed for a bell-rope,	. . .	. . .	. . .
Item, payed for 6 pownds of waxe and a halfe,	. . .	. . .	. . .
Item, payed for strykyng of the feid waxe,	. . .	. . .	. . .
Item, payed for waxe at a nother tyme 6 ponds,	0	4	0
Item, payed for strykyng of the same waxe at Ester,	0	0	7
Item, payed for mendyng of the . . . . . paskall, and mendyng of the lampe,	. . .	. . .	. . .
Item, payed for frankyncense and 2 ponde of candell,	. . .	. . .	. . .
Item, payed to *Thomas Rowy*,	. . .	. . .	. . .
Item, payed for a rope for the sance † bell and halfe a calfe's skynne,	. . .	. . .	. . .
Item, payed for heaveyng down of the grett bell,	0	1	1
Sum	1	3	3½

Anno Domini 1523.

	£.	s.	d.
Accompte made betweene *Wyllyam Alexander* and *Willyam Wode*, wardeyns in the paryshe, the 8th daye of Novembre, remeynyng in hande, the Chirchewardyns handys,	0	10	0½
Receypts receyved by the handys of *Wyllyam* . . . . . . and *Wyllyam Halysander*, the Chirchwardeyns of Herbregge, from the feste of Seynt Mighell, to the feste of St. Mighell next ensuyng, anno Domini 1523.			
Receyved of *John Lynsey*, the yonger, for a yere's ferme of lands,	0	9	0
Item, receyved of *John Lynsey*, the elder,	0	2	0
Item, receyved of *Robard Franceys*, for the hole yere's ferme of a cowe and 9 shepe,	0	3	3
Item, receyved of *John Dredge*, for the chirche lande,	0	1	0
Item, receyved of *John Samwell*, for the chirche lande,	0	0	6
Item, receyved of *Alleyne*, for the ferme of a cowe,	0	1	0
Sum	0	16	9

These be the paymentes layed owte of the same monys by the handys of Cherchewardeyns.

	£.	s.	d.
Layed out for 5 pownd of waxe and a halfe agenst Hallowmas,	0	3	6
Item, layed out for strykyng of the same waxe,	0	0	6

* Iron.

† Saints or facring-bell.

Item,

	£.	s.	d.
Item, for Peter-pencye, — — —	0	0	6
Item, for two pownd of candell agenst Cristemas, —	0	0	3
Item, for 7 pownd and a half of waxe agenste Ester, —	0	5	0
Item, for strykyng of the same waxe, — —	0	0	8
Item, for skorynge * of the cherche gere, — —	0	0	10
Item, for frankynsense, — — —	0	0	2
Item, for sope to washe the cherche gere, —	0	0	2
Item, for frankynsence, — — —	0	0	2
Sum — — — —	0	11	10

Owynge to the cherche 5*s.*
Woodde.

The resayts of *Necolas Ord* and *Wyllyam Woodde*, the Chirchewardens of Heybreg, from the feste of Seynt Mighell to the feste of St. Mighell, anno Domini 1525.

	£.	s.	d.
Resayved of .... dewe at ...... last past			
Item, of my Lorde Abbott, for			
Item, of *Robard Frayncys*, for a whole yere's rent, dewe at Mikelmas last past, anno 1524. — — — —	....		
Item, of *Dredge*, for a yere's rent due at the sayd feste, —	....		
Item, of *John Lynsey*, for a yere's rent, — —	....		
Item, of *Alleyn*, of Totham, for a cowe, — —	0	1	0
Item, of *John Samwell*, for halfe a yere's rente, —	0	0	3
Item, of *John Samwell*, for another halfe yere's rente, —	0	0	4
Item, of *John Reynolds*			

Paymentes.

	£.	s.	d.
Payed for the makyng of an auter cloth, — —	0	0	4
Payed to the broiderer †, — — — —	0	4	2
Payed for candylls agense Cristemas, — —	0	0	3
Payed to *Wode*, of Maldon, for glazinge, — —	0	1	5
Payed to *Wynterborne*, for settyng a saynte, — —	0	0	6
Payed for Peter-moneye, — — —	0	0	6
Payed for 2 belle-ropes, — — —	0	1	6
Item, payd to the carpentres for theyr werke in settyng up of the Southdore of the churche, — — — —	0	1	4
Item, payd for 2 dayes werke for doyng of the churche werke for pale, — — — —	0	0	8
Item, payd for the burdyn ‡ of the said 2 dayes, —	0	0	5
Item, payd for caryyng of the saym times, — —	0	1	0
Item, payd for 3 dayes werke when he made the gate and the stylle,	0	1	0

* Scouring. † Embroiderer. ‡ Boarding.

Item,

	£.	s.	d.
Item, payd for the ſaym 3 dayes burde,	0	0	7½
Item, payd to the carpendres for 3 rod and a quartere of the cherche payle,	0	1	10
Item, payd for nayle,	0	0	7
Item, payd for carrying of the ſkreene in the cherche,	0	2	0
Item, payd for boards to the cherche gayte,	0	0	3
Item, payd for ſtrykyng of waxe agenſe Hallowontide,	0	0	6
Item, payd for waxe,	0	2	2
Item, payd for wax,	0	2	9
Item, payd for wax,	0	0	8
Item, payd for ſtrykyng of wax,	0	0	2
Item, payd for dreſſynge of the canope,	0	0	4
Item, payd for mendynge of the canope,	0	0	2
Item, payd for mendyng of the ſurplys,	0	0	1
Item, payd for ſkorynge of the baſons and the ewers,	0	0	1
Item, payd for waſhynge of the cherche gere,	0	0	2
Item, payd for makyng of 5000 ſhengyll,	0	1	8
Item, payd for carying of 5 loode of tymbre out of the comon,	0	2	0
Item, payd to *Bowelſhon*, for clevyng and fellyng of 3 treys,	0	0	10
Item, payd to *Hobberd*, for fellyng 4 treys,	0	0	9
Item, payd to *Roberte Ruſſell*, for felling of a tree at Langford Parke *,	0	0	4
Item, payd for carying of 2 loade of ſhengyll from Langford,	0	0	8
Item, payd for the tree that was bought of *Thomas Samys* in Langford Parke,	0	3	4
Item, payd to *Shangler* †, for makyng ...... 3900 ſhingle,	1	19	0
Item, payd for makyng of the			
Item, payd for ſettynge upp of the croſſe,	....		
Item, payd for nayle 2100 of them,	....		
Item, payd for ſettyng a rope at Maldon,	....		

Sum totall of paymentes by the handys of *Nycolas Thirke* and *Wyllyam Woode*, as is ſixe thys daye the 21ſt day of October, 1525.

	£.	s.	d.
Sum of paymentes,	5	13	8

The accownte of *Nicholas Trevey* and *Wyllyam Wode*, the cherchewardeyn of Heybreg, from the feſte of Seynt Mighell the Archangel, anno 1525, to the feſte of Seynt Mighell the Archangel next followynge, anno 1526.

	£.	s.	d.
Receyved the bequeſte of *John Tatell*,	6	13	4
Item, receyved of *Wyllyam Wode*, for 2 ſhepe of the ſaym John Tatell's bequeſte,	0	2	8

* In the adjoining pariſh of Langford, then belonging to Henry Earl of Eſſex. Morant I. 382.

† Q. The ſhingler?

Item,

	£.	s.	d.
Item, receyved of *John Lyndſey*, for a hole yere's rente, —	0	9	0
Item, receyved of *Aleyn* of the lofte for a churche kowe,	0	1	0
Item, receyved of *Dredge*, for a hole yere's rent, — —	0	1	2
Item, receyved of *John Samwell*, for a hole yere's rent, —	0	0	8
Item, receyved of *John Hopton*, for a yere's rent, — —	0	1	0
Sum — — — — —	7	8	10

Paymentes paide by the ſeide Churchwardeyns in the ſeide yere as hereafter followethe.

	£.	s.	d.
Paide to *John Sprott* and *John Reynolde*, for the newe croſſe,	1	5	0
Paide for 3000 of ſhengle, — — —	1	10	0
Paide to Maiſter *Carryngtons*, — —	0	10	0
Paide to *Fraunceys*, for tymbre, — —	0	1	0
Paide for 2000 nayle, — — —	0	4	2
Paide for nayle, — — —	0	1	0
Paide for 600 nayle, — — — —	0	1	8
Paide to *Wyllyam Sponer*, for roppis and for a bawdrikke, —	0	1	10
Paide to *Richard Langore*, for a daye's werke, —	0	0	4
Paide to *Kerwys*, for berynge of ſhyngle, — —	0	0	2
Paide to *Lely*, the carpendre, for workmanſhyppe, —	0	2	8
Paide to *Gooddayds* wyfe, for bordynge of the ſeid carpentres,	0	2	5
Paide to *Andrewe*, of Braxted, for a logge, — —	0	0	6
Paide to *Thomas Sammys*, for a lode of wode, — —	0	1	0
Paide the ſhyngelers for laying of 5000 ſhyngell, —	. . .	. . .	. . .
Paide the ſhyngelers for makynge of 800 ſhyngell, —	0	3	4
Paide the ſhyngelers for makynge of lathe, — —	0	2	4
Paide for 5 powndes of waxe, 7*d.* the pownde, —	0	2	11
Paide for ſtrykynge of the ſame waxe, — —	0	0	5
Paide for 2 powndes of candyll agenſte Criſtemas, —	0	0	3
Paide for Peter-penſe, — — — —	0	0	3
Paide for 8 pownde of waxe agenſte Eſter, — —	0	4	4
Item, for ſawynge of borde abowte the porche, — —	0	2	4
Item, for a calffe's ſkynne, — — —	0	0	4
Item, for 100 of 5 peny nayle, — — —	0	0	5
Item, for a bell-rope, — — —	0	0	8
Item, for carryinge the logge to the ſawe-pytt, — —	0	0	4
Item, to the bell-hanger, — — — —	0	1	0
Item, for a daye's borde, — — — —	0	0	5
Item, for making of hierne-werke to the great bell, —	0	1	8
Item, for a bawdrikke, — — —	0	0	4
Item, for ſtrykinge of waxe agenſte Eſter, —	0	0	6
Item, for waſhynge agenſte Eſter, — —	0	0	2

	£.	s.	d.
Item, for makynge of thys acowmpte, —— ——	0	1	0
Item, for ſkorynge of the baſſens agenſte Eſter, ——	0	0	2
Sum —— —— ——	7	10	4

Memorandum.

That the Sondays next before the feſte of Seynt Luke the Evangelyſt, in the 18th yere of Kynge Henry VIII. the ſeide Wardeyns hathe gyven upp theyr accownte for the foreſeid too yeres ended in the feſte of Seynt Mighell the Archangell laſte paſte, in the preſence of Mr. *John Godedaye*, vykare of Heybregge, *John Reynold*, *John Sprott*, *John Hoptone*, and *Nicholas Godedaye*, of the ſame pariſhe, with others; and all thyngs cownted, and to be cownted, allowed, and to be allowed; the ſame wardeyns hathe broughte in clere to the uſe of the ſame churche in ready money 11*s.* 10½*d.* and 4¾*d.* in farthynge waxe candell: the whyche 11*s.* 10½*d.* is putt into the churche-box, and delyvered unto *John Hoptone* and *Richard Langore*, whych *John* and *Richarde* are choſen Churchewardeyns of the ſame churche for this yere enſuinge.

	£.	s.	d.
Sum { 11*s.* 10½*d.* —— / 0 4¾*d.* in farthyne waxe candells } Total —	0	12	3¼

Heybredge.

The accowntes of *John Hoptone* and *Richarde Langore*, Churchewardeyns from the feſte of St. Mighell the Archangell, in the 18th yere of the reigne of Kynge Henry VIII. to the ſaide feſte then followinge, in the 19th yere of Kynge Henry VIII.

	£.	s.	d.
Firſt, they yelde acompte of what the have receyved from the late churchwardyns, as apperethe in the fote of theyr ſeid acownte,	0	12	3½
Item, receyved of *John Samwell*, for halfe yere's rent of the church land, dew at the Anunciacyon of our Bleſſed Lady laſt paſt, —	0	0	4
Item, receyved of *John Lyndſey*, for a hole yere's rent, dew at the ſeid feſt of St. Mighell the Archangell, anno 19 Henry VIII. —	0	9	0
Item, receyved of *Alcyn*, of the lofte for the yere's rent of a cowe, dew at the ſeid feſte, —— —— ——	0	1	0
Item, receyved of the Wedowe *Melner*, for a yere's rent of the churche howſe, dew at the ſeid feſte, — —	0	2	0
Item, receyved of *Dredge*, for a yere and a halfe's rent of churche land, dew at the ſeid feſte, —— —— —	0	1	9
Item, receyved of *John Hopton*, for a yere's rent, dew att the ſeid feſte, —— —— —— —— ——	0	1	0
Item, receyved of *John Arthere*, for ferme of ſhepe, ——	0	1	4

5

Item,

	£.	s.	d.
Item, receyved of *Nycolas Godebaye*, for olde tymbre, —	0	1	0
Item, receyved of my Lord Abbott of *Bilegh*, in exchange betwix olde lede and a olde bell whele, — —	0	0	8
Sum — — — — —	1	10	4¼

Heybredge.

Paymentes paide by the handes of the feide Churchewardeyns in the feid yere as hereafter followethe.

	£.	s.	d.
Paide for 8 pownde of waxe agenfte Hallowmas, 5½*d.* the pownde,	0	3	8
Item, for ftrykynge the feid waxe, — —	0	0	5
Item, for 6 pownde of waxe agenfte Efter, 6*d.* the pownde,	0	3	0
Item, for caryinge of the fame waxe from London to Heibredge,	0	0	2
Item, for ftrykynge of the feid waxe and for ftrykynge of the olde waxe, — — — — —	0	0	7
Item, for fodorynge of the churche roffe, — —	. . . .		
Item, to *Richard Otterley*, for fellynge and hewynge of a tre for the churche, — — — — —	. . . .		
Item, at too tymes for Peter-pence, — —	0	1	0
Item, for halfe a calfe's fkynne, — —	0	0	2
Item, to *Spencer*, for mendynge of the gret bell knepill, —	0	1	4
Item, to *Spencer*, for mendynge of the loke att the South dore,	0	1	0
Item, to *Spencer*, for mendynge a chefte in the chawncell, —	0	0	3
Item, to *Spencer*, for makynge of a new keye to the littelle boxe,	0	0	2
Item, paide for wafhynge of the churche ornaments for thys fame yere, — — — — —	0	0	6
Item, paide to *Wyllyam Wode*, for mendyng of the third bell knepill,	0	2	0
Item, paide for 2 pownde of talowe candell agenfte Criftemaffe,	0	0	2½
Item, paide for mendynge of the North wyndowe and for nayles to the fame, — — — —	0	0	10

In the yere of our Lorde Gode 15 . . . . *John Stocke* . . . . with the confente of all the faide made an Inventory of all the churche goodds, the 19th daye of December.

Inprimis, 3 maffe bowkes.
Item, 2 chalyffes, onne of fylver and anothere gilte.
Item, a antyfyphonar * and a grayll.
Item, a pixe of fylver, and another of coper the facram . . . .
Item, 2 proffofynerfe † and a . . . er with 2 fawters.
Item, a . . . . belongyng
Item, 2 fayre b . . . . s
Item, ...

* Antiphonar. † Proceffioners, or proceffionals.

Item, ... ſmale . . . . awter

Item, ...

Item, ... efter

Item, ...

Item, ...

Item, ... aw . . . .

Item, ... of . . . .

Item, ...

Item, ... and . . . .

Item, a cope of rede damaſke.

Item, a cope of blew ſatten wythe flowerys of golde, with a . . . . ſaide bawdkyng.

Item, a cope of rede ſatten.

Item, 2 clothes . . . .

Item, 3 ſhott

Item, 2 cowles of dyaper and . . . . . .

Item, a ſeconde pelowſe, alſo a clothe of aroſe for the ſepult . . . .*

Item, . . clothes of dyaper and 4 of playne clothe.

Item, 2 towell of dyaper.

Item, 2 . . . . . of ſilke for ende of awter.

Item, 2 ſecunde . . . .

Item, 2 canſtyks † for the grete awter.

Item, a croſe of cooper and geylte, with a ſtandyng fotte, and a ſtaffe with a clothe of grene ſarſenet thereto belongyng, with 2 ymages, one of our Lady, and another of Seynt Andrewe.

Item, another croſe of coper and clothe with the ſame, with the ymages of . . .

Item, ... for the croſe on Goode Fryday.

Item, oon . . . . . .

Item, ... l laten hangyng bey for the hey awter for . . . . .

Item, 2 . . . . . of laten, and . . . . . alſo 3 crewetts, and a . . . . . . of ty . . . . .

Item, ... of . . . . . . with a . . . . alſo the . . . . . with the lyde thereto.

Item, a ſaca . . . . the awter

Item, 2 . . . . with . . . . a awter clothe, be . . . . the ymage of Seynt Margarete.

Item, ... clothe with forowed, alſo a curten of . . . . . . tyng of . . . . upone yt.

Item, an awter clothe of whyte ſpremed ‡ with rede . . . . to the ſame.

Item, another awter clothe, the ſame with 2 curtaynſe at . . . . ende, and another curteyn above the awter of the ſame of whyt ſpremed with rede.

Item, a cotte of rede velvet for the rode, and a payer of bodds.

Item, another cotte of blacke ſaten for the ſame rode, alſo a payer of latten . . . . before the . . . . . .

Item, 3 hande-bells for proceſſion.

* A cloth of arras for the holy ſepulchre. † Candleſticks. ‡ Striped.

Item,

Item, for ſtandynge byfore the hey awter . . . . . with a . . . . ſtyk of . . . .
Item, 3 baner clothes, oon of rede and 2 of blewe.
Item, another baner clothe of grene with a gilte . . . .
Item, 3 cowlles.
Item, 2 clothes of blew with lambys . . . .
Item, 18 canſtyks of iron in the rodelofte.
Item, ... for to bere over the goode lorde.
Item, ... for the . . . . . .
Item, a clothe . . . . and another for the hey awter.
Item, a clothe for the . . . . ron.
Item, ... with ſtremers of grene ſilke.
Item, 2 coverynge of carpet worke.
Item, a ſherpolys.
Item, 2 awter clothys of the Paſſyon for the hey awter in Lent-tyme.
Item, 2 croſſe clothys of the Paſſyon with frynge.
Item, a clothe of the Paſſyon to hange in the rede-lofte in Lente.
Item, 3 awter clothys of rede ſeye and yellow.
Item, 2 curtenſe for the Quere of rede ſaye and yellow.
Item, 3 new awter clothys of fyne Holand to laye a ponne the awtyr.
Item, a olde matoke new layd with owte a ſtele.
Item, 4 newe ſtremeres, 2 of blew tonks, with an ymage of Seynt Andrewe, and another of Seynt George, and 2 of rede bokeram, with an ymage of owre Ladye, and another of St. Mighell.
Item, 3 awter clothys of . . . . . .
Item, a new ladder.

Memorandum.

Thatt in the 21ſt yere of Kynge Henrye VIII. the bachellers of the paryſhe of Heybryge have delyvarede the 9 tapers belongynge to the ſepulker, at the feſte of Eſter, each taper contaynynge 5 pownde of waxe.

Sum 45 pownde of waxe.

And they have in . . . . above all charchgys, 5*s.* 10*d.*

And ſo remaynethe in the ſtoke clerely above all chargys, 43 pounde of waxe, the whyche reſtyth in the handes of *Richard Langore*, wax-chandeleyr.

Memorandum.

Memorandum.

Alſo in the ſeid yere the maydens of the ſeid pariſhe have delyverede on to the 9 tapers belongynge to the ſeid ſepulkre, at the feſte of Eſter, every taper contaynynge 5 pownde of waxe.

Sum 45 pownde of waxe.

And they have . . . . above all chargys, 2*s.* 10*d.*

And ſo remaynethe clerely, beſyde the waſte in the ſtoke, 42 pownde, the whyche ryſtyth in the handes of the ſeid *Richard Langore.*

Memorandum.

That *John Fuller* and *Wyllyam Ruſhbroke* hath lett to farme 3 crofts, for one yere, unto *Richard Cuſts*, paying 3*s.* for the ſame; he *Richard Cuſts* fyndyng *Phillipp Fryer* for to be hys ſewertie for hys bryngyng in the ſame 3*s.* at Myghellmas.

Memorandum.

This laſt memorandum is ſtruck acroſs with a pen in the original.

Thys

Thys ys the ſume of monys of all the townſe the wyche was browgte in att the day of ower playe.

	£.	s.	d.
Maldon, — — —	1	3	4
Bylygh, — — —	0	8	1
Cockſhall, — — —	0	0	11
Bracſted Magna, — — — —	0	6	0
Inford, — — — —	0	1	1
Bracſted Parva, — — — —	0	4	3
Purly, — — — —	0	4	2
Woddam Mortymers, — — —	0	2	1½
Toleſbery, — — —	0	0	7
Woddam Wattere, — — —	0	2	4
Langforde, — — —	0	3	6
Owlde, — — — —	0	1	5
Tottam and Golde Angere, — — —	0	8	6
Terlynge, — — — —	0	12	2
Tolſonte Mag. — — — —	0	4	2
Wychcam, — — — — —	0	5	4
Woddam Ferys, — — — —	0	1	0
Felſtede, — — — —	0	6	8
Keldon, — — — —	0	1	1½
Ferynge, — — — —	0	1	0
Hatfield, — — —	0	6	8
Tolſonte Daſſys, — — —	0	3	6
Moche Tottam, — — —	0	10	0
Sum total	5	17	11

Thy

Thys ys the Cowafe * of the Playe made at Heybryygth, the Sonday byfore Whytenfundaye, in the yere of oure Lorde 1532, that tyme beyng Churche-wardeyns, *John Stock*, *Wyllyam Datte*.

Firſt, receyved and gathered of whett .... and 3 peckes.
Item, receyved and gathered of myſtelyne .... a busſhele.
Item, receyved and gathered in malte 3 ſemes and 2 busſheles.
Item, receyved and gathered of cheſe 700 and a halfe.
Item, receyved and gathered 12 lambys.
Item, receyved and gathered 3 ſhepe.
Item, receyved and gathered 2 cawvys †.

Thys ys the ſumm of the whett that was baked—3 ſeme.
Thys ys the ſumm of the malte that was brewde—3 ſeme.

Beſyde 8 kylderkyns of dobell bere.

Thys ys the ſumm of the expenſys of the mette atte the Playe.

Firſte, a qwartere of 2 beſſes.
Item, 6 cawvys.
Item, 6 ſhepe.
Item, 8 lambys.
As more playnly hereafter yt dothe appere.

	£.	s.	d.
Receyved and gathered in redy money —	1	15	7½

Reſayts.

	£.	s.	d.
Item, reſayved at the daye of owr dry ...... g — —	7	10	2½
Item, reſayved of the parſon the next daye, —	0	13	1
Item, delyvered to Maſter *Fryar* 3 peckes of whett, —	0	1	0
Item, reſayved for tallow, — — —	0	0	11
Item, reſayved for lycence, — — —	0	0	7
Item, reſayved for brede, — — — — —	0	1	1
Item, reſayved for cheſſe, — — — — —	0	1	1
Item, reſayved for a pecke of maltt, — — —	0	0	4
Item, reſayved for 6 ſhepe ſkynnys, — — —	0	0	4
Item, reſayved for 8 lambe ſkynnys, — — —	0	1	4
Item, reſayved of *Gooddays* wyffe for beſſe, — —	0	0	7
Item, reſayved of *Colben* for a lambe, — — —	0	0	8
Item, reſayved of *Arter's* wyffe for mett, — —	0	0	4
Item, reſayved of *Rycharde Alyng*, for a lambe, — —	0	0	10
Item, reſayved for a peſe of beve, — — —	0	0	4
Item, reſayved of Maſtere *Harrye*, for a lambe, — —	0	1	4
Item, reſayved of *Oſborne*, for a lambe, — —	0	1	2
Item, reſayved for 5 cawfys ſkynnys, — —	0	1	8
Item, reſayved for cawfe ...... — —	0	0	8
Sum — — —	10	13	2

* Q. Coſt. † Calves.

Paymentes.

Paymentes.	£.	s.	d.
Paide to fome of Maldon for . . . . . . quarter of beffe,	o	3	8
Item, for a quartere of whett,	o	9	8
Item, for 4 dofen potts,	o	2	2
Item, to the pagentt players,	o	13	4
Item, for goulde forrall,	o	o	3
Item, for baryng of the boke,	o	o	6
Item, to the pageyntt player for hys rewarde,	o	1	o
Item, to 5 payr of gloves,	o	o	7
Item, to the minftrell,	o	o	10
Item, to *John Wylford*, (Wylfon)	o	o	4
Item, towards the gyldeyng of the tabernikell,	o	6	8
Item, paide to *Colben*, for hys tabor,	o	o	2
Item, for payntyng of the cote-armes,	o	o	4
Item, for 7 kylderkyns of dobell bere, and nyne of fynggyll,	o	12	8
Item, for a locke,	o	o	3
Item, for gret lathe,	o	o	2
Item, a locke for the porche dore,	o	o	4
Item, for 2 payer of	o	1	6
Item, to *Hoowe* that played the folle,	o	1	8
Item, for 100 of 6 penny nayle,	o	o	6
Item, for 2	o	o	1
Item, for a calfe fkynne for the bell-ropes,	o	o	6
Item, for a pecke of whyte falte,	o	o	2
Item, for 4 cawfys	. . .	. . .	. . .
Item, for 3 fhepe,	o	o	9
Item, for halfe a pownde of pepper,	o	o	11
Item, for drynkynge in the towne,	o	o	2
Item, for tape,	o	o	1
Item, for paper,	o	o	2
Item, for 2 loode of wode,	o	2	o
Item, to the cookes,	o	1	o
Item, to fhe that turned the fpitt,	o	o	8
Item, to the bafteter,	o	o	4
Item, to *Goodday's* wyfe, for good alle,	o	1	4
Item, to *Goodday's* wyfe, for mett and drynke for the pagentt players, and 3 that holpe them,	o	o	4
Sum	3	5	11

And fo remayneth clere above all charge £7. 10*s*. befyde the . . . .
The wych £7. 10*s*. reftyth in the churchwardeyns handys.

	£.	s.	d.
Item, p . . . . for chefe,	o	13	4
Sum	8	4	5

Two leaves loft here.

£. s. d.

Thes be the ſureytes of the land and catell of the paryſhe of Heybredge.

Fyrſt, *John Lynſay*, for the land that he howlds of the chyrch. *John Reygnold* hys ſuertie.

Item, for *Hopton*, for the land that he howlds of the chyrch. *John Cattyl* hys ſuertie.

Memorandum. The ſame *Hopton* hathe alſo taken the chyrch land to keype in all maner of repayr, to uſe yt tenand lyke neider to loppe nor to fell trees, but for to gydde as if it had been hys, A. D. 1528.

	£.	s.	d.
Item, *John Samwell*, for land that he howldeth of the chyrch,	0	0	10
Item, *John Bryge*, for the land he howldeth of the chyrch,	0	1	2
Item, *Robard Frauncys*, for a cowe and 9 ſhepe, payed by the yere to the chyrch, — — —	0	3	3
the ſtoke of the ſaid cattel, —	1	0	0
Woolan's the ſuertye.			
Item, *Wyllyam*, of Loft, a cowe, 12*d.* the ferme payeth the ſtoke 8*s.* Suertye.			
Item, *Nycholas Trevy* hath reſayved of . . . . . . ſuertie for a cowe and 9 ſhepe of the chyrche of Heybregge, the wych *John Arty* is ſuertie for the ſeid ſtoke, the ſum of — — —	1	0	0

Memorandum.

The lower half of this page (in the original) on which is a continuation of the above account, and of the following one of the great bell is torn out.

Charges and Coſtes layde owte for the grete Belle.

	£.	s.	d.
Inprimis, payed for caſten of the belle, —	1	15	8
Item, for 24 pownde of newe metell, — —	0	8	4
Item, for makyng of the oblygacione, — —	0	0	5
Item, for 6 dayes werke to the bell-hanger, — —	0	3	0
Item, for 6 dayes bordynge, — — — —	0	1	9
Item, for the carpynters borde for 5 dayes, — —	0	1	2
Item, for the claper and yern worke of the gret bell, —	0	6	8
Item, for cranage, — — —	0	0	2
Item, for greſe, — — — —	0	0	0½
Item, for the water-carier, — — —	0	0	2
Item, for the freyt of yt, — — —	0	0	3

Memorandum.

The lower half of this page (in the original) is torn out.

The

The following are Tranfcripts from Church-Wardens Accompts of WALBERSWICK, in the County of Suffolk.

From GARDNER's Hiftory of DUNWICH, p. 145.

Here is remembruance, that *Harry Poty*, and *Thomas Pafchelewe*, churche mayfters of *Walburyfwyche*, have made a rechenynge of her acounfe to the parifshe, upon Sonynday next after the 12th day, the zere of Kynge Edwarde the IVth, after the Conquefte the 3d zer. And all thynges clene quitte, be clene rechanynge. M. whyffe Acounfe; left in the box 4 nobyllys, and 20*d*.

Anno Domini 1489, in this zer we make a conftitucon for the town Dolys by ower crecon and wyfdom, to the profeyth of the cherche, yt ys to feye, *Thomas Byrd*, *Kichard Poty*, *Thomas Brown*, *John Almyngham*, *Roberd Gardner*, *John Palmer*, *Roberd Goodyng*, *John Blybor*, *Harry Gybbys*, *William Nune*, *Cuthbert Eyer*, *John Co-Carnyfhe*, *John Greywe*, *Sawndyr Richardfon*, *Thomas Pegot*, wt o'her mooharn confent be ys prefent, yt 1 man, or 2 men fhall rec the town doollys of heryngs, and fperlings of the mafters of the fhyppys, and bots, and to tewe them to moft profyte of the town. And the fed 2 men to gef a rekenynge of the heryngs, and fperlinges un newer daye, unto the feid townfchyppe.

	£.	s.	d.
All rekeneth, & pd. remaynyth in the Towne boxe, —	11	15	8

Some of the Churche-Wardens receipts in different years.

Anno Regni Henrici fexti poft Conqueftum 29.

	£.	s.	d.
1451. Rec. of Thomas Comber 2500 full heryns, 200 fchotyn Allec. in Moneta, — — — —	0	1	0
Barca *Thome Buck* un. *John Glover* eft Magift. 1100 fperlings, for the Kyng's heryngs * — — — —	0	13	4
1453. Sexto die Maii at a *Cherche Ale*, — ——	0	13	4
Item de uno *Cherche Ale* in Fefto *omnium Sanctorum*,	0	16	0
At a gaderyng on the *Sonday* next aforn the fefte of the Poftel *Seynt Barnebe*, Apoftal the 31 zer of the Kyng yat now is,	0	1	8
1458. For the foule of Syr *Harry Barbour*, ———	0	6	8
Of *Richard Cokk*, for the fchoppe at the chyrche-yate,	0	3	8
1459. Of *Cha. Browne*, for the gylde of *Seynt Barbara*, —	0	9	11
For the gylde *Sanctæ Mariæ Virginis*, — —	0	7	0

* The town of Walberfwick had a floriſhing fifhery on its own coaft from 1450 to the beginning of the laft century.

		£.	s.	d.
1463.	Of *Alson Kocks*, for the gylde of *Seynt Andrew*, —	0	3	9
	For the gylde of *Seynt Johannis* — —	0	9	2
1466.	For *Seynt Johannys Schoppe*, — —	0	1	0
	Of Syrre *John Kock*, — —	0	0	4
1481.	Of *John Norton*, for a net, — — —	0	12	0
	Of *Cutberd Eyer*, for the Queth word of *Tym Chawmbyr*,	2	0	0
1498.	For a peyre of bedys that were *Marg. Middleton's*, —	0	4	4
	Of *Pecke* for ſtanding in *Seynt Johnnys* hows —	0	2	6
1499.	Of *John Wolward*, that he took for keyage, —	0	4	2
	Of the baly of *Blabur* *, for the hows in *Blabur*, —	0	6	8
	Of *Thomas Browne*, for ferme of the land at *Blaknes*,	0	1	0
	Of *Ceſyly Peggot*, for ferme of the town lands for the laſt yeer, — — — —	0	3	0
	Of *Thomas Draper*, for his chamber for a zeer, —	0	6	8

Some of the Church-Wardens Diſburſements in different Years on the old church which ſtood South of the town near the marſhes, the ſite ſtill known by the name of the *Church Land*, and was taken down 1473: the windows of St. Chriſtopher and St. Wolſtane ſeem to have been removed from it, with the tables of St. George and King Harry, to the preſent church. This was built 1493 on an eminence three furlongs to the North. A North aile was added 1507, " whoſe adjoyning is very obvious by both ends of the old ſtanding wall. By the alteration thereof for the conveniency of the additional aile, ſhews the likelyhood that the aſcent to the candlebeam was demoliſhed; for a hole was cut through the South wall, and a *pair of ſtairs*, ſtill remaining, made and caſed with free-ſtone erected therein. The North aile fell firſt into decay," and wanted ſcrewing up 1678.

1451.	Payd for ſkoring of the cherche ger, — —	0	0	8
	For waſhyng of the cherche clothes, — —	0	3	0
	For offring *Feſt. Trinitatis* at *Blibro*, for the taper,	0	6	8
	For *Romeſcot* in Feſt. *Paſchae*, — —	0	0	11½
	For watching of candel eſtorne nytis, — —	0	0	7
	For halyng up of the ferme-tre, and other labor, —	0	0	8
	For cloth for amyts and girdelys, — —	0	1	4
1451.	Payd for making of a ſurplys, — —	0	1	8
	For new bynding 2 bokes, — — —	0	3	2
	For wax azens Eſtern, and filling the rowel, —	0	4	6
	Apud *Southwalde* at a chirche ale, — —	0	0	6
	For a cloth aforn the hey auter of black bokeram,	0	0	6

* *Blithborough.*

1451.

		£.	s.	d.
1451.	To *Rob. Sammes*, pro 1 cade of hering for the King,	0	4	4
	To *Will Amrigale*, for the dyner of my Mayſter *Hopton*,	0	7	1
	To *Ric. Breton*, for the ton land, and the ſchereuys torn,	0	1	7
	For a rop to the paſkil,	0	0	1
1452.	For clay wark to the cherche houſes, and ſtraw,	0	2	0
	For redyng and thakyng of the cherche logge, for ſhetis and byndyngs,	0	2	2
	For frakencens 2 lb.	0	0	8
	For makyng the hoſys afore the rode,	0	0	4
	At *Blibro*, for halwyng of the pyx, auter clothis, and a tonych, an aube, an amyte, and expens,	0	1	8
	For a kerchef of ſylc,	0	1	0
	To *Herri Terri*, clarke, at Myghelmes,	0	3	6
1454.	To the queſt men for the ton,	0	1	0
	To the clarke, for kepyng of the candells de Sepulchris,	0	0	6
1458.	To *Jenkyne Joll*, elder, for gate to *Londone*,	0	1	4
	At *Southwold*, for ſendyng to my Lord *Roos*,	0	1	0
	For makyng of a welle,	0	2	10
	To *Will. Roper*, when he went to the norre contre for the Kyng's viage,	0	6	8
1458.	To *Water Perſe*, for rydyng to the Kyng,	0	6	8
	To *Will. Alcock*, for cleanſynge of the ymages,	0	3	3
1463.	To Syrre *John Engelyſſche*,	1	6	8
1466.	To *Nyc. Byrd*, for mony that he payd to Syrre *John Howard* for the town,	2	0	6
1472.	For a kade of heryngs to Ser *John Haveningham*,	0	7	4
1476.	To *John Waller*, for rydyng to *Newcaſteel* and *London*, 5 noblys.			
	To *Rob. Gardynyer*, for rydyng to my Lady *Brandon*,	0	0	4
1478.	To Maſtyr *Nicholas*, 5 noblys.			
1485.	To my Lady *Brandon*, 10 marks.			
	To *Thomas Brown*, for fiſche that went to Syr *John Henyngham*,	0	1	0
1488.	To a dyner for Maſtyr *Hopton*,	0	11	4
1490.	To the ſexteyne, for his rewar for ryngyng the day-belle,	0	0	11
1491.	To the ſexteyne, for ryngyng of the kerfow-belle,	0	3	4
1493.	For a beſſume of pekoks fethers,	0	0	4
1496.	To *Dunwyche*, for the ſute of the ſtal bots for a full payment 5 noblys.			
1499.	For dreſſynge of the haly watyr ſtoppe,	0	3	4

1450.

		£.	s.	d.
1450.	Solutio eſt pro uno candelabro coram Sancto *Andrea*,	0	10	0
	To a redern mending of the cherche, ——	0	0	6
1451.	———— mending and thacking the cherche logge,	0	2	2
	To makyng hoſys to the cloth aforn the rood, ——	0	0	4
	To a board in the windone afore our Lady, ——	0	0	4
1452.	For ſtonnys in *Saint Andrew's* Foot and *Seynt Johnnys*,	0	2	6
1453.	For peyntyng the image of our Lady, — —	0	5	0
	payd for nettys for the low awters, ——	0	0	6
1454.	For mending of the canope at the hey awter, —	0	0	1
1466.	Payd a man for amendynge of the orgeyns, ——	0	1	2½
1473.	Rec'd on the Monday when they brokyn down the cherche *,	0	1	6

1472. Payd *Wylliam Alcock*, for *Seynt Johnnys* tabernakyll, 5 noblys.
For a cloth to the awter of *Seynt Nicholas*, — 0 4 4
For organs makyng, 5 noblos.

1474. *T. M.* I will that my executors do peynte and gylde the tabernakyll of our Lady of Pity at my coſt, according to the forme of the image of *Seynt Mary of Pity* of Southwold.

1476. Payd for the ſheylle on *Seynt Nicholas* awtyr, — 0 1 4

1478. *Waiyyer Alward* left to the cherche, 5 nobylls.

1479. Payd for brokyng down the walle where *Seynt George* ſtandyth, — — — — — 0 0 6

For a cloth of *Seynt George*, and a halbe, — 0 2 6

For irennys and wyer to the tabal of *Seynt George*, 0 0 6

1482. Payd *Edmund Wryte*, for makyng of the cwrynge owyr *Seynt Andrew* and *Seynt John*, — — — — 0 1 0

1483. Payd for peyntyng of *Seynt Johnnys* awter, — 0 0 8

1486. *T. Johannis Wyiward*, Nov. 6, by will proved at Southwold, April 2, 1487, gave to adorn the cherche of *Seynt Andrew* in *Walburiſwick*, 8 marks.

1487. Payd the glaſwryzte for mendyinc *Seynt Kryſteferys* windown, — — — — — 0 8 4

for mendyng *Seynt Walſteneys* wyndown. 0 0 9

1489. *T. Rob. Dolſynby*, I will have made *Seynt John Evangeliſt* and the tabernakyll thereto, according to the makyng of *Seynt John Baptiſt*; and I will that both be peynted at my coſt.

1491. Payd for peynting of our Lady, — — — 0 13 4

1492. Payd to *Iſbel Paſchelew*, for makyng of the clothys to *Seynt John*, —— —— —— 0 1 8

1493. Payn for mendyng of *Seynt Thomas*, and *Seynt Johnys* tabernaclys, — — — — — 0 0 10

* Walberſwick Account Book.

	£.	s.	d.
1493. Payd for halwyng of the cherche of all coſts, —	6	18	0
To *Rebard Byrd*, for makyng of the trone, —	0	9	8
1496. Payd for bryngyng hom of the *Crwſyfix*, mete and drynk,	0	1	5
for ſetting up the *Crwſyfix*, mete and drynk, —	0	1	0
1497. Payd to *Edmund Wryte*, for remeving of King *Herey's* tabell, &c. — — — — —	0	3	6
1498. Rec'd by a gatheryng in the towne, to peyntyng of the falyng, — — — — —	3	5	0
Payd *William Rede* and *William Sharſt*, for peynting the cruſyfix, and the ſelyng, — — — —	11	10	0
1503. *T. Kat. Brown*, I will that my executors doo peynt and gylde the tabernkyll of our *Lady of Pity*, at my coſt.			
1507. *T. Will. Ferry*, I will that my wyfe doo make an image of *Seynt James*, in the aforeſaid church, both peynted and gylded, to the value of — — — —	1	0	0
1518. *T. Will. Ryſche* (alias *Ferryman)*, I bequeath to the image of our Lady in the North ele, a tabernakyll, to be made like unto the tabernakyl of *Seynt John Baptiſt* on the South ſide.			
1496. By a gaderyng of the wyvys in the towne for a glas-wyndown. — — — —	0	9	0
Ameys Arnold gaff nets to the cherche, —	0	8	6
1498. *Aleyn Weſtmer* gaff to the cherch qweche money he had lent the Kynge, — — —	1	10	6
1500. *John Almyngham*, by will, 7 Oct. gave to the church twenty pounds. Ten pounds which was to be boute a peyer of orgonys. Item, with the reſidue of the ſaid ſume I will, a canope over the hygh awter, welle done with oure Lady, and 4 aungelys, and the Holy Ghoſt, goyng upp and down with a cheyme *. And yf there be no ſpace that the ſaid canope may not be made ther, I will that *Seynt Andrew* have a tabernakyl with the ſame money. And to a new ele, — — —	10	0	0
1506. In the will of *Tho. Kelot*, 24 Feb. I bequethe toward the makynge a new ele of the ſeid cherche, — —	0	3	4
1507. Of *Will. Ferry*, 18 April, to the makyng a newe ele of the North ſyd of the ſeid cherche, — —	0	6	8
1509. Of *Margaret Pynne*, 6 Jan. to the ſame on the North ſyd of *Seynt Andrews* in Walburſwick, — —	1	0	0
Of *Johan Bliburgh*, 27 Aug. to the ſame on the North ſyd of the ſeid cherche, — — —	0	1	0

* Q. *Chain* or *chime*.

	£.	s.	d.
1511. Of *Alex. Richardſon*, 16 July, to the ſame of the foreſaid cherche of *Seynt Andrew*	1	13	4
Of *Johan. Cooper*, 16 December, Itm, I bequeth unto the ſame,	0	6	8
1512. Of *Thomas Chapell*, 22 April, to the ſame in the paryche cherche of *Walberſwick*,	0	3	4
of *Tho. Kerych*, 6 Jan. to the ſame of the North ſeyd of the ſeid cherche,	1	0	0
1499. Payd *Tho. Cuttyng*, for makyng of the vyſe * unto the candelbem,	1	8	10
Tho. Cuttyng, for ſteppys of the vyſe on to the kandylbem, &c.	0	4	8
Tho. Cuttyng, for bordyng of the maſonys for making of the vyſe on the beam,	0	14	8
1678. Paid *Ed. Barker*, for ſkrewing up the wall the North iſle of the church,	0	5	0
for planck and work,	0	5	6
more,	0	3	6
1483. Payd to *Pays*, for the porche † makyng,	9	0	0
for flint to the porche,	0	2	6
for iryn to the porche,	0	0	9
for glaſſyng of the porche wyndonys,	0	4	0
Nicholas Melle gaff to the porche, 5 marks.			
Margerie Palmer, to the porche,	1	2	0
1450. Solutio eſt for dityng of the belles	0	5	0
for eight fanes to the ſtepil	0	4	9
for gilding eight fanes to the ſtepil	0	10	0
1451. Payd to the clock-maker,	0	0	11
1452. to the clock-maker,	0	12	8
1466. Payd the foundyr of the bellis for full payment of three bellis,	12	0	0
1467. to the bell-makerre for a full payment,	5	0	0
the foundry of the bellis for a full payment for the laſte belle,	7	0	0
for the bryngyn hom of the belle,	0	3	8
to *Munde Wryght*, for tymbur to the lytyl bell, and warkemanſheppe and hanging,	0	0	0
for makyng of the gos,	0	13	0

* Q. Stair caſe.

† "The porch is indifferently well built, with a chamber over it. On the beam is an inſcription in gold letters, through age grown illegible and almoſt obliterated."

1486.

		£.	s.	d.
1468.	Payde to *Jonne Maggys*, in party of payment of a belle,	2	0	0
1469.	Payde for mendynge of the goose, — —	0	1	0
1471.	for the belles hallweyng, — — —	1	5	8
	Alyson Kock gaff to the belles hallweyng, —	0	10	0
	Rob. Dolphynby, to the same, — —	0	4	4
	Tho. Nunn, the the bellis of zyft, —	0	6	8
	Alice Welymote, to the same, — — —	0	0	8
	Margerie Fuller, to the same, — —	2	0	0
	Payd *Edmund Wryzth*, for the chyme, — —	1	0	0
	for 18 pounds of weer for the chymys, —	0	4	7
1495.	Payd *John Payn* of *Southwold*, the smyth, for a new cloke,	0	6	8
1499.	Payd to *Nycholas Schrebbys*, for the cloke, —	1	13	4
	more, — —	0	6	8
	more, — —	1	2	0
	more, — —	0	13	4

The Covenant for building Walberſwick Steeple.

" This bill endentyd witneſſith, that on Teweſday next after the Feſte of Seynt Mathie Apoſtle; the fourte zeer of King Henry the Sexte, a comenaunt was maked betwyn Thomas Baugot, Thomas Wolfard, William Ambrynghale, and Thomas Pellyng, of the town of Walbureſwyk, on the one partye; and Richard Ruſſel, of Donewich, and Adam Powle, of Blythtburgh, maſons, on the other partye, that is to ſeyne. That the fornſeid Richard and Adam ſchal make, or do make, a Stepel joyned to the cherche of Walbureſwyk fornſeid; with foure betraas, and one vice, and tirwelfe foote wyde, and ſexe foote thikke; the walles, the wallyng, the tabellyng, and the orbyng ſewtly, after the ſtepil of Dunſtale, well, and trewely, and competently; a dore in the Weſt alſo good, as the dore in the Stepel of Haleſworth, and a wyndowe of foure dayes above the dore, ſewtly after the wyndowe of thre dayes of Haleſworth. And thre wyndows atte nethir ſoler; and eche wyndowe of two days, and foure wyndowes atte onerer ſoler, the wyndowe of thre dayes ſewtly after Haleſworth. The fornſeid Richard and Adam ſhal werke, or doo werke, on the ſtepel fornſeid, two termes in the zeer, ſaf the ferſte zeer zeerly, in the tyme of werkyng, of ſettyng, and leying; that is to ſey, bitwixen the feſtes of the Annuncyacion of our Lady, and Seint Mychel Archaungel: but if it be other maner conſentyd on bothe partyes, and the fornſeid Thomâs Baugot, Thomas, William, and Thomas, ſhal fynde alle maner of mateer to the ſtepel fornſaid; that is to ſay, freſtoon, lyme, and Calyan wat, and ſond; and alle maner thyngge that nedith to ſtagyng, and wyndyng, and ſchouellis, and alle maner veſſel that is nedefull to the ſtepel fornſeid. And an hows to werke inne, to ere, and drynke, and to lygge inne, and to make mete inne; and that be hadde by the place of werkyng. The fornſeid Richard and Adam ſchal take of the fornſaid Thomas Baugot, Thomas, William, and Thomas, for the zarde werkyng, 40

 ſcheelynggs,

fcheelynggs, of laughfull money of Inglond. And a cade of full herynge eche zeer, in tyme of werkyng. And eche of hem a gowne of lenore ones, in the tyme of werkyng; fo that they fcholden be gode men and trewe to the werk fornfaid."

An Account of Utenfils in Walberfwick Church.

Anno Dm MCCCC,IX,II, viz. 1492.

In the Lofte over the Veftry.

Imprimis, a cope, red velvet.
It. one cope, blacke vellet.
It. one cope, whighte fufthian.
It. eight diap. towellys.
It. three aulter cloathes diap.
It. two playne albes, and a greate flevid furples.
It. a peynted aulter clothe.
It. two fteyned lanper clothes.
It. a pair of chalice of filver for the communion.

In the Veftry.

It. five furpluffes.
It. two alter clothes.
It. two hempuling towells.
It. two corporace cappes, one with a cerchief, another without.

In the Loft over the Porch.

It. one cope, whight damafke, with prieft Decoy and Subdecoy *; four the fame; one cope, whight fufthian.
It. one cope, blacke wurfted.
It. a veftment, with mones.
It. a veftment, whight fufthoon.
It. a veftment, blew wufted, with a grene.
It. the herce clothe of faten brigge, with a red croffe of fylke.
It. two pix cloths of fylke.
It. a carde clothe.
It. two cufshinx of fylke.
It. the lamide † for the fepulture.
It. eleven coparace cappes.
The cloth for the fepulture fteyned.
It. all the wax appurteyning to and for the fepulture remayned.

There were, befides the utenfils mentioned in the foregoing account, cenfors and candlefticks, both of filver and lattin; and difhes wherein the candlefticks ftood before the altars.

* Q. deacon and fubdeacon.

† *Ch*lamide or Lami*ne*.

1645.

	£.	s.	d.
1465. Payd for ſkoryng of the canſtelys, and of the ſenſyrs,	0	5	0
1483. Payd for menyng* of ſylvyr canſteks ten pence, and lattin croſſes one penny, — — — —	0	0	11
1492. Payd for changyng of a chalys, — —	0	13	10
1496. Payd for changyng of a ſylvyr ſenſer, ——	1	10	4
Payd *Edmund Wryte*, for makyng a kaas for the ſylvyr canſtekys, &c. — — — — —	0	1	8
1499. Payd to a man of Beclys, for ſkoryng of canſteks, and the lawmpe, — — — — —	0	1	8
1585. The great bell was ſold for 31 ſhillings per cent. the weight 1707 lb. amounting to —— ——	26	8	9
1596. Payd unto the paynter for writing of the Ten Commandments, and makyng of the Queen's Arms, — —	0	14	4
1633. A rate was made by the inhabitants for glazing the church and running the great bell, — —	11	12	6
1604. Paid in parte of the King's Arms, — —	0	5	8
1644. April 8th, paid to Maſter *Dowſon* † that came with the troopers to our church, about the taking down of images, and braſſes off ſtones, — — — —	0	6	0
1644. Paid that day to others for taking up the braſſes of graveſtones befor the officer *Dowſon* came, — —	0	1	0
and the next day to *Edwards* and *Pretty*, taking down 26 Rheils ‡, —— —— —— ——	0	6	10
April 26, Rec. of *John Trappit*, with the conſent of the paryſhners, for 2 bellows, and wooden ſtofe from the Orgens,	0	6	8
Rec. this 6th of January, 1644, from out of the church, 40 pounds weyght of braſſe, at three-pence halfpenny per pound	0	11	8
1650. March 7, paid to *John Prety*, for raſhing § out the King's Arms in our church, —— ——	0	1	0
1653. Laid out about the rofe of the meeting-houſe ‖,	0	4	0
1656. Receved upon the ſilver cup of *Elezebeth Chayman*,	1	10	0
of *Goodman Picher*, for ihorn that came out of the windows, —— ——	0	7	6
1661. Payd for ſwaring the church-wardens at Cort, and expenc,	0	1	4
for a paper that was brought to towne concerning miniſters ſeats, and to the cleark, and *Hum'frey Harne* at the ſpiritual court, —— ——	0	0	10

* Men*d*yng.

† *Dowſing*; whoſe ravages in Suffolk ſee in "The Journal of William Dowſing, of Stratford, "Parliamentary Viſitor, appointed under a Warrant from the Earl of Mancheſter, for demo- "liſhing ſuperſtitious Pictures and Ornaments of Churches," &c. 1786, 4to.

‡ This word is not intelligible.

§ Q. eraſing.

‖ Into which the church was now converted.

1661. To

	£.	s.	d.
To *Humfrey Harre*, for an order that was read concerning praying for the King, —	0	0	4
Payd to *Andrew Lilly*, mason, for the church-yard walls mending — —	6	10	0
more —	1	15	0
To *John Roberts*, for houckes and nailles for the church-yard gate, — —	0	1	0
1662. Given to a briefe, having no minister, therefore could not be collected in the church, as is the usual manner, —	0	0	10
Given more to a considerable briefe for the reason afore,	0	2	6
Payd at three courts at Yoxford, for not having things convenient at our church, — —	0	9	6
Payd for charges at the Bishop's Visitation Court at Bungay,	0	16	4
Payd for the Book of Articles, —	0	4	8
Payd at the court at Blyburgh, —	0	4	8
For the Book of Common Prayer at Blyburgh,	0	10	0
Payd to *Goodman Kell*, the plumber, for mending of the leads of the church, — —	2	12	0
To *Goodman Prety*, for wood for the use of the plumber,	0	5	6
To *John Roberts*, for a key to the church chest,	0	0	6
1663. Payd, for glaseing the church, to *John Eade*,	5	0	0
For drink with the glasers, —	0	1	0
For coonles * and broume for the gtasers, —	0	2	3
For lime and heare for the church, —	0	3	8
For irons, to *John Roberts*, for the church, —	0	5	6
1663. Paid at Bungay, at a court there howllon, 23 Sept.	0	13	0
1674. Paid for the King's Arms with a freame, bringing home, and setting up, — —	1	0	6

The town was visited by the bishop, his suffragan, and the archdeacon 1480.

	£.	s.	d.
1695. The lessening of the church by taking down what was decayed, and making a new one, cost —	291	8	9
The three bells, lead, and timbre, sold for —	303	1	11
Difference due to the town, — —	11	13	2
1480. The Suffragan, his dinner cost, —	0	1	6
1481. His dinner and other charges, —	1	10	0
1483. His dinner, — —	0	8	6
1485. The same, — —	0	8	4

* Meaning unknown.

1486.

		£.	s.	d.
1486.	The ſame, — —	0	2	6
1487.	The ſame, — —	0	6	0
1488.	The Biſhop's dinner, —	0	4	10
	The Biſhop's dinner, and one gallon of wine,	0	7	7
	The Arch-deacon's dinner and wine, —	0	3	4
1491.	The Biſhop's dinner, — —	0	1	5
1492.	The ſame, — —	0	11	0
1493.	This year the church was hallowed.			
	Biſhop's dinner, wine, and horſe-meat,	0	11	2
1494.	The ſame, — —	0	13	0
1495.	The ſame, — —	0	13	8
1496.	The ſame, — —	0	9	9
1497.	The ſame, — —	0	9	10
1584.	The Archbiſhop of Canterbury's viſitors coſt,	0	2	0

1586. July 23, Theſe viſitors enjoined the Churchwardens to repair the Paraphraſes of Eraſmus; to provide "Muſculus' Common-places, or the Apologies;" to provide a cover for the Communion-cup; to amend the church-yard fences, gates, and grate; to provide a new ſurplice. All to be done before Allhollantide following.

1451.	Maſter *Robert* was chaplain.			
1452.	Sir *Edmund* made the Manuel for —	0	6	8
1468.	Payd to Syr *John Walter* for one of the bokys, 8 marks.			
1473.	Payd to Sowr *John Wilkinſon*, for a book klepyd a Pye,	0	2	0
1485.	Payd to Syr *Alexſawnder*, for hys chyld at Eſtoryn,	0	10	0
1503.	*Bartholowew Middleton*, prieſt.			
1603.	Payd to Mr. *Ody*, the preacher, —	0	4	0
1603.	Maſter *Vaken*, Miniſter.			
1618.	*John Faſtleft*, miniſter.			
1671.	*John Bull*, clericus.			
1683.	*James Dier*, miniſter.			
1696.	*John Skoalding*, curate.			

Extracts

Extracts from the Churchwardens Accompts of BROCKDISH, Norfolk.

From the Old Town Book of Brockdiſh.

1553, 1 Queen Mary. Paid for a book called a Manuel,	0	2	6
For two days making the altar and the holy-water ſtope, and for a lock for the lock,	. . . .		
1559. Paid for the rood,	0	0	9
1554. Paid for painting the rood-loft,	0	1	2
At the viſitation of my Lord Legate,	0	1	4
To the organ maker,	0	0	4
For the chalice,	1	6	0
1557. Paid for carriage of the Bible to Bocnam *,	0	1	0
For delivering account of the ſmall books at Harlſtone,	0	1	3

The Engliſh Bibles and religious Proteſtant Tracts uſually at this time left in the churches for the information and inſtruction of the common people, were now called in by the Papiſt Queen.

Paid for images making,	0	5	0
For painting them,	0	1	4
For irons for them,	0	0	8

But in 1558, as ſoon as Queen Elizabeth aſcended the throne, all theſe Popiſh inſcriptions, &c. were removed out of the church.

Paid for ſinking the altar,	0	0	4
Carrying out the altar,	0	0	5
Mending the communion table,	0	0	3
1561. Paid for the Ten Commandments,	0	1	6
For pulling down the rood-loft,	0	1	2
Paid *Roger Colby*, for repairing the croſſe in the ſtreet,	1	6	8
For a lock to the croſſe houſe, &c.	. . . .		
1565. For digging the ground and levelling the low altar, viz. in the South chapel, and mending the pavement,	. . . .		
For makyng the communion cup of Harlſton, besides 6s. 2d. of ſilver more than the old chalice weyed.	0	5	4
1569. Paid to *Belward* the dean for certifying there is no cover to the cup,	0	0	8
1657. Layd out for the relief of Attleburgh viſited with the plague,	0	19	4
Laid out for the repair of the Brockdiſh part of Sileham bridge leading over the river to Sileham church,	0	17	0

This bridge is now down, through the negligence of both the pariſhes, though it was of equal ſervice to both, and half of it is repaired by each of them.

In 1618 the church was wholly new-paved and repaired; and in 1619 the pulpit and deſk new made, new books, pulpit cloth, altar-cloth, &c. bought.

Blomefield's Norfolk, vol. III. p. 228.

* Buckenham.

Church-

Churchwardens Accompts of WIGTOFT, Lincolnſhire.

(Continued from p. 84.)

Lambt Worme & *Johannes Frankysche*, electi ſu't[1] poſitores eccleſiæ de *Wygtofte*, xii die Maii, anno Dm̄ MCCCC nonageſimo nono. Thyes be the reſcaytts of the ſayd *lambrt worme*[2] and *Joh Frankyſche*.

	£.	s.	d.
It. rec. of *lambrt Worme*, ———	6	1	11½
Itm. reſeyd of *Willm Magelyn*, ———	1	0	0
Itm. reſevyd of *John Brygg*, ſern.[3] ———	0	19	1
Itm. reſevyd of *Agnes Brygg*, ———	0	1	8
Itm. reſevyd of *labt*[4] *Worme*, —	0	17	4
Itm. reſeyd of maſt. *Bale*, — —	0	3	4

M^d^ y^t^ *Joh Brygg* eld. made hs Accounte before ye parech in chych of Pet^r^ and Paule, of *Wygtofte*, at ye feſte of ye perificati' of o^r^ lady y^t^ was in the yere of o^r^ lorde MCCCCLXXXXIX. of ye xx marks, y^t^ y^e^ ſayd *John Brygg* reſeived of ye execut^s^ of *Robt Collynſon*, of weſt miles, at y^w^ recevyng y^e^ ſaid *Joh Bryg*, hath yſpent & payd be divs tymes xvi marks xi^s^ iiii^d^, and the ſayd *Joh bryg* eyh[5] of y^e^ ſayd xx marks xlii^s^ iiii^d^.

	£.	s.	d.
It. payd for bording of y ſayd *Joh harvy*, ———	0	0	3
It. pay'd to *ed. ſmyth*, for yne[6] warke to ye bels, —	0	0	5
It. payd to *Joh Frankyſh*, for ii days helpyng y^e^ ſecond bell for warkman ſhyppe & bordyng, ———	0	0	7
It. payd to *ed. ſmyth*, for a gudyon and kays, ———	0	0	6½
It. payd to *Joh harve*, for helpe agayne ye greete bell,	0	0	6
It. payd for bordyng of y^e^ ſayd *Joh harve*, ———	0	0	3
It. payd to *Joh frankyſh* for i day di. to helpe *Joh harve*, About the bells for warkemanſhyppe & bordyng, ———	0	0	6
It. ſpent for rydyng[7] to *John wryght* at ii tym^s^, ———	0	0	6
It. ſpent for ye towne matt^r^ at *Joh brygg*[8], ———	0	0	3
It. payd for weſhyng at ii tim^s^ ye kyrke cloyhys, —	0	0	8

[1] *Sunt*, or *fuerunt*.
[2] They are quite unobſervant of the due place of capitals.
[3] Senior.
[4] As they do not note ſeparate dates, we are to ſuppoſe this a ſecond payment.
[5] Hath.
[6] Q. *y'ne*, iron.
[7] They paid this to John Wright for journeys.
[8] John Brigg might keep a public-houſe.

A promys

A promys is mad be at ye Piſhon [1] when a kyrk greive [2] is choſyn, he ſhall cheſs hym a felow, and he wyll not agre ther to, he ſhall pay to the kyrk maiſter xx^{d}. Wryttyn the xvi yerr of the Reyn of kyng herry the vii. aronzo [3] de ffryday, the ſame day *lambert worme* ſtandyng kyrk grieve, and at hys choſs to cheſs hym lot felow *Joh Snell*, and ſo ewyrr aftyr to contenew.

M^{d} off all ye Recets y^{t} *John Allynſon*, *John ffrankyſh*, ye kyrkgraves off Wygtoft, hath reciev'd ſen ye laſt countt y^{t} was at ſen mykaelys day, In ye yere off o^{r} lord MCCCCC.

	£.	s.	d.
It. Inpmys recey'd of *John Alynſon*, ——	0	11	10
It. receyd off g adryd [4] W^{t}yn ye towne of Wygtoft, —	0	7	0
It. recevyd off *Tho. howſon*, ffor the kyrke howſe, —	0	2	0
It. recevyd off *Will'm Brygthe*, for the chauntre, ——	0	6	8
It. recevyd off *Ryc. Newman* at ii tim^{s} — —	0	10	10
It. recevyd off *Willm proctor*, for the chauntre, ——	0	6	0
It. recevyd of *John Lawyn*, *John hogeſon*, off the ſepulkyr [5] lyght,	0	4	8
It. recevyd of ſed *John lawyn* for a rvsh [6], ——	0	1	3
It. recevyd of *John Brege*, — —	0	3	0
It. recevyd off *Wyllm Magellyn*, h^{s} hante [7] Bureall, ——	0	2	6
It. recevyd off ye gadryng yn ye kyrk, ——	0	2	8
It. recevyd of *Willm Brege* xii^{d}. It. off ye Wykar [8] ii^{s}. —	0	3	0
It. recevyd off *Rob. ffeylld*, ffor ye chauntre moone, —	0	4	0
It. recevyd off *Wyllm Dorbay* off Donynton [9], ——	0	1	0
It. recevyd of *Wyllm proctor*, — ——	0	1	0
It. recevyd off *Secelle ffrankys*, ffor ye kyrk warke, —	0	1	0

Sm̄ to. off ye Rec^{s} —— [10] 3^{l} 13^{s}.

Theys ys the Receytt off Mony that *John Allynſon* and *John Frankys*, ye cheyrche mayſters off ye pyiche cheyrche off Wygtoft, hath recevyd ſen ye laſte chownte In ye yeyr off our lord MCCCCC. ſen our lady day Natyvitate.

	£.	s.	d.
Inprymys, It. recevyd off ye yomen leyght, ——	0	6	8
It. recevyd *Ryc. Leynze*, ffor led ffor *ſteven Farrad*, —	0	3	4
It. recevyd *John Faarad*, off Bykyr [11], ffor *John Boman*,	0	3	4
It. *John Brandon*, — — —	0	1	0
It. recevyd off a homan [12] off quadreyn, ——	0	1	8

[1] I cannot exactly ſay what this word is, but imagine it to mean at the veſtry or pariſh meeting in the church. [2] *Church-reeve*, or warden.

[3] I cannot decypher this obſcure word, or its meaning. [4] Gathering within the town.

[5] A light to burn before the holy ſepulchre in the North ſide of the chancel: of which ſee inſtances in the preceding pages. [6] Q. ruſhes to ſtrew the floor of the church.

[7] His Aunt's burial. [8] Vicar. [9] Donington, four miles diſtant.

[10] Here is a miſtake; I can make the ſum no more than 3l. 7s. 5d.

[11] Biker, two miles diſtant.

[12] A woman, or perhaps yeoman, of Quadryng, a village in the neighbourhood.

It. for

	£.	s.	d.
It. for byyng[1] off ye tyell[2] xxd. and ffor beyryng[3] off of ye xxd,	0	3	4
It. for mete and dreynke,	0	0	5
It. for shoynyng[4] of ye Browkyn[5] Tyell, and for beyryng hovr ye haven[6],	0	1	0
It. for makyng of ye Gavinbpe[7] and makyng of the locke,	0	1	0
It. for ye olvttæ[8] of ye comyssary,	0	0	8
It. for feycheynf of ye saunde[9]	0	1	6
It. for mete & dreynke,	0	0	1½
It. for ye yomen leyght,	0	1	3
It. *John Nwman*, *John Alynson*, *lamb. Worme*, each 1*s*.	0	3	0
It. *John lawyn*, *Tho. Westfelld*, *Ryc. Brandon*, each 1*s*.	0	3	0
It *Wyll'm cheyswright*, *John Snell*, *John Breg*, each 1*s*.	0	3	0
It. *John frankys*, *John Frever*, *Ryc. Nwman*, each 1*s*.	0	3	0
It. of *Thomas Westfelld* hovygng[10] of olld,	0	2	4
It. *Thomas howson* old rente of ye keyrke howse,	0	3	0
It. *Agnes Brregge*,	0	6	8
It. [11] pmys for yryn Warke of the bellys,	0	1	2
It. for ye hyngylls[12] of ye chyrche dor,	0	1	0
It. for takyng off ye olde & settyng on the nw,	0	0	2
It. payd to *harve*[13] for hys warke abowtte bellys and nayllys,	0	1	1
It. for wood to make ye ptycion[14] scholl house,	0	0	3
Also aboutte ye bellys,	0	0	3
It. for my labor, 6 dayes mett & drynke,	0	2	0
It. payd to make upe ye wayte for the chaylys[15],	0	2	0
Itm. payd to ye makyng of ye chalys,	0	18	7
Itm. to ye olde challys mendyng,	0	2	7
It. for expens for horse mete and manys mete att lyncon,	0	1	3
It. for ye clapr of ye grett beyll,	0	2	0
It. to *Wyllm Wyllyamson*, for willyng[16],	0	0	5½
It. *Margarytt Farrad*, for bordyng of *harve*,	0	0	5½
It. for hoks and hyngyll for bothe dorys of ye scoll house,	0	0	8

[1] Probably *beryng* or carrying. [2] Flooring tiles or pavings.
[3] Carrying. [4] Joining or mending. [5] Broken.
[6] Carrying over the Haven which was a considerable branch from the Welland, and went to Horfleet, Bicker, &c.
[7] Cannot decyper this word. [8] Nor this. [9] Perhaps sand.
[10] Owing. [11] *Pynys*, pins. [12] Hinges.
[13] A surname, *Harvey*. [14] Partition of the school-house.
[15] The sacramental cup might have been exchanged for a new one.
[16] I am not clear as to the meaning of this word.

	£.	s.	d.
It. for brokyn ſyln[1] to ye ollde chaylys,	0	1	10
It. payd for tylle,	0	10	0
Itm. payd for beyryn[2] and expenſys that tyme,	0	0	8
It. payd for ſhotyng[3] of the ſainctys[4] belle,	0	0	10
It. payd for aylle[5],	0	0	2
It. payd for bying 12^{lb} nw mettyll,	0	0	4
It. payd for yryn warke,	0	0	4
It. payd to *Tho. houſeſon*, for hellpyng of the bellys,	0	1	0
It. payd to *J. franckyſhe*, for 4 days warke aboutte ye Sanctys bell,	0	1	3
It. payd for nayllys 1^{d}, for beylls roppes 4^{d},	0	0	5
It. payd for ſtray[6],	0	0	2
It. payd for mendyng of ye clapur,	0	1	0
It. payd for Fyrdylls[7],	0	0	1
It. payd for wheychyng[8],	0	0	4
It. payd hallowyng[9] of ye challys,	0	2	8

Here follows a liſt of 70 inhabitants, with their contributions; none higher than 8*d.* or leſs than 1*d.*; but moſt of them 2*d.* or 3*d.* Whether this was by aſſeſſment or voluntary does not appear, but moſt probably the latter.

	£.	s.	d.
It. payd for 3 tray of lyem,	0	3	0
It. payd for beyryng & fecheyng fro *John Bouttre*,	0	0	4
It. payd for a trey of lyem and a hallfe,	0	0	5[10]
It. payd for a trey of Maſt. *Baudre*, beyryng and fecheyng,	0	0	6
It. payd for mette or dreynke,	0	0	3
It. payd for mette And dreynke At howme,	0	0	2
It. payd to *Ryc. Nwman* for dryvyng,	0	0	2
It. payd for iiii cccc[11] tyyll,	0	1	4
It. payd for pathyng[12] of ye floure,	0	3	6
It. payd to *John frankys* for pathyng of ye keyrke fluor, And hellpyng to ley tyyll And levyllyng of ye floure,	0	3	4
It. payd to *Tho. Goſe*, for a day mett and dreynke,	0	0	3
It. payd to *Ryc. moore*, for a day's mett and dreynke,	0	0	3

[1] Sylv or broken ſilver.
[2] Carriage of the tiles.
[3] New caſting. So the bell *ſhottar*, p. 203.
[4] Saints' bell.
[5] Ale.
[6] Perhaps ſtraw.
[7] Q. faggots or bundles of wood, or *fir deals*.
[8] Waſhing the albes, &c.
[9] Conſecrating.
[10] Here ſeems an inconſiſtency with the former price; perhaps for carriage only, as in th next article.
[11] 400 of paving tiles.
[12] Paving.

It.

	£.	s.	d.
It. payd to *Agnes Wryght*, for bordyng,	0	3	0
It. payd for a li.[1] waxe,	0	0	6
It. payd to ye Glacyars[2],	0	7	10
It. payd for deyr[3] bourd,	0	2	0
It. payd to ye tylar,	0	2	10
It. pay'd for vi ſtreke lyem,	0	1	0
It. payd to *J. frankes*, for ſcolyng[4] y^t^ was behynd,	0	1	8
It. payd to *John Frankys*, for v days,	0	1	8
It. payd to *John Crece*,	0	0	1
It. payd to *Agnes Wryght*, for burding,	0	3	0
It. payd for iii[5] peyns for ye kandyllſtckytt,	0	0	3
It. payd for bell ſtreyns[6],	0	0	4

Sm̃ $1^l\ 17^s\ 8^d$.

Theſe byn y^e^ receypts of mony that *John Alynſon* and *John frankes*, y^e^ churche-maſters of y^e^ peche churche of *Wygtoft*, have recevyd ſen y^e^ laſt cownts In the yer of owr lord god MCCCCCV.

(Here follows a liſt of 80 inhabitants in the ſame manner as before, with their contributions.)

It. recayved rent for ye kyrke howſe of *Thomas howſon*,	0	2	0
It. recevyd of *Ric. Newman*,	0	3	4
Itm. of holflytt[7] may[8] lyght,	0	3	0
Itm. rec. of *Robart Bull*, for leede,	0	1	3
Itm. rec. of *labart Worme*,	0	3	4
Itm. recevyd of ye may lygthe of *Eſtthorppe*[9],	0	3	3
Itm. rec. for ye Wytword of *Willm Brygthe*,	0	1	0
Itm. rec. of *Ric. N—an*, ye elder,	0	1	8
Itm. rec. of ye vic' for tymbur of ye footte[10],	0	1	4
Itm. rec. for y^e^ ſame tymbur of *Ric. branden*,	0	1	0

[1] Pound of wax, probably for lights. [2] Glaziers. [3] Their board.
[4] Scouring, or ſchooling money owing to him, now paid.
[5] Three pins for the candleſtick. [6] Bell-ſtrings or ropes.
[7] I conjecture this may be Horfleet, a hamlet to Wigtoft, one mile diſtant; or *Holfleet*, a proper name of a perſon.
[8] Quære, a light burnt at his obit or month's mind.
[9] A man's name. [10] Q. by the foot meaſure.

 Theys

	£.	s.	d.
Theys Be ye Receitys of *John frankys*, *Ric. Newman*, cheyrchemaſteyrs of ye paryſche cheyrche of *Wigtoft*, feſt of ye Reliques, In ye yerre of oWre God MCCCCCVIIth.			
Receyd In p'mys of *John Nwman*, for ys yſſon [1] Wytword,	0	1	0
It. for *Wyllm hawdall*, for ys Wytword,	0	1	0
It. *John Brandon*,	0	1	0
It. *Agnes looke* Wytword,	0	2	0
It. recevyd *Tho. howſeſon*,	0	0	3
It. recevyd *Tho. Weſtfelld*,	0	3	0
It. recevyd of *Alys Sheppard* Wytword,	0	0	2
It. recevyd of *John hogeſon*, *Ric. Barlayman*, of ſepaullcor [2] lyght,	0	7	4
It. recevyd of *John OWrey*,	0	6	8
It. rec. of *Thomas feld*, for Aſhys [3],	0	0	4
It. rec. of *Ric. Waryngton*, for a Wytword of he [4] fadr,	0	0	4
It. Rec. of *John frankyſch*, of the Goodys of *Agnes looke* to the Repacon of ye chyrche,	1	0	0
It. payd to *Ryc. Nwman*, *John frankes*, ye fowndacion of ye orgounes [5],	0	1	1
It. payd for Nayllys and teymber,	0	0	4½
It. payd for iii ſtavys for ye Weyll,	0	0	4½
It. payd for bellroppes,	0	0	5
Itm. payd for Iyern Warke,	0	0	7
Itm. payd for heyngyng [6] of ye ſecond bell,	0	0	6
Itm. for naylls and for ye mendyng of ye cheyrche waull,	0	0	1½
It. payd for paper and for maund [7],	0	0	2½
It. payd for teymber for ye ſtepowll [8],	0	9	0
It. payd to the ſed men for mette and dreynke,	0	0	8
It. payd for exſpenſys for byyng of ye ſed teymber,	0	0	3
It. payd to ye warkeman at ye feſtyng [9] of ye grett bell,	0	0	4
It. payd for feſchyng of lyem And ſand to *Ric. Nwman*,	0	0	6
It. payd for Wheſyng,	0	0	8
It. payd for expencys for ye Orgounpllayar [10],	0	0	2½
It. payd to ye pllowmar [11],	0	12	2
It. payd to *Ryc. mychell*, for mett, dreynk, And hyyr,	0	1	8
It. payd to *John frankyſche*, for viii days Warke,	0	3	0

[1] His ſons obit or month's mind.
[2] Light to burn before the holy ſepulchre.
[3] Probably wood aſhes.
[4] His father.
[5] It appears they erected an organ in 1507. There has been none in living memory.
[6] Hanging.
[7] A baſket hamper, or ſieve.
[8] Steeple or ſpire.
[9] Perhaps fixing, or it might have been a feaſt at the putting up of the great bell?
[10] A modern organiſt would think this a poor reward.
[11] The plumber.

4 It.

	£.	s.	d.
It. payd mett and dreynke to ye sed *John*, ——	0	1	1½
It. to *Ryc. Nwman*, iii days for hyyr, mett and dreynke, —	0	0	10
It. payd for naylls for ye teymber warke to ye pllowmar, —	0	1	4
It. payd to the men tht halld up ye teymber In to stepowll, mett And dreynke, —— —— ——	0	0	6
It. payd to *John Freve* for ire[1], —— ——	0	0	3
It. payd for bellroppys, —— —— —	0	0	11
It. payd to the sawar[2], —— —— ——	0	3	6
It. payd to *John frankys*, for breykyng[3] of ye wod, ——	0	2	0
Md that Mayst. Wykar yave them ther Bowrd, ——	. . .	. . .	. . .
It. payd for mett And dreynke, —— ——	0	0	10
It. for expenssys for ye Comyssary, —— ——	0	0	5
It. in expens upon *John Wryght*, —— ——	0	0	4
Itm. for Wayshyng of Awtr clothys, —— ——	0	0	4

Sm tot. 18s 3½d.

	£.	s.	d.
It recevyd of *John frankes* to ye fersayd warke of goodds of *agnes loocke*, execr to ye yayd *agn*s, —— ——	1	4	0
Md yt *John frankysch* and *Ric. Newman*, kyrkgreves of *Wygtoft*, have made Account of all be ym Resevyd on ye v day of marche, the xxiii yere of kyng *herry* the vii. And All thyngs acountyd and Reconyd, ye forseyd kyrkgreves as owyng clerly, ——	0	0	9
Itm. recevyd of *Ric. lamsa'* for ye berryall of his brodur, —	0	6	8
Itm. Recevyd of ye executurs of *Xtofur*[4] *hormslay*, ——	0	6	8
Itm. Recevyd of *Any bryg*, ye beryall of hyr husband, ——	0	6	8
Itm. Recevyd of *John Abar*, for ye Wytword of *harry loke*,	0	3	4
Itm. Recevyd of *Ric. newman*, for *Rob. may*, ——	0	6	8
Itm. *Wyllm Magellyn*, —— —— ——	0	2	4
Itm. recevyd of *Ryc. Brandon*, for dryvyng of ye mares[5],	0	1	8
Itm. for beryyng of a chylde of his wolm[6], ——	0	3	4

Sm̃ 1l 18s 1d.

	£.	s.	d.
Itm. payd to *Willm Spensar*, for warkkyng of ye stepull, —	0	8	6
Itm. payd to *Thomas Weddbe 7s. 4d.* To *John frankys 8s. 8d.*	0	16	0
Itm. payd for naylys 16*d*. Itm. payd for naylys 11*d*. ——	0	2	3
Itm. payd for bordyng into blakamor wyff, — —	0	12	0
Itm. payd to *Ryc. Mour*, mendyng of ye kyrke walle, —	0	0	1

1 Iron.
2 Sawyer.
3 Hewing into proper pieces.
4 Christopher.
5 I am not clear in this word; but it appears most like mare or mares.
6 Woman.

Itm.

	£.	s.	d.
Itm. payd to *Ryc. Nwman*, for ys belſtrenys [1],	0	1	6
Itm. payd to *Wyllm Rycſon*, for v days,	0	1	3
Itm. payd to *John franckyſch*, for iii days,	0	9	0
Itm. payd to y^{e} ſed *John*, for ſecund bell hyngyng,	0	0	4
Itm. payd to ye ploumar, for the ſteppoull,	0	13	4
Itm. payd to *John Breythe*, for teymbyr,	0	0	11
Itm. payd to *Wyllm Tollar*, for y^{e} ſteppull warkyng,	0	1	0
Itm. payd to ye Orgunpllayar,	0	2	0
Itm. payd to *John Blacmour*,	0	1	0
Itm. payd to ye plowmar day di. [2]	0	1	0
Itm. payd for Sawdur,	0	0	6
Itm. payd to *Jenet Brandun*, for bordyng,	0	2	4
Itm. payd to *Wyllm tollar*, for day And di.	0	0	3
Itm. payd to ye gllacyar [3],	0	0	4

Sm̄ 3^{l} 13^{s} 7^{d}.

Continuation of Wigtoft Pariſh Book.

Md. y^{t} *John ffrankyſeh* & *Ric. Numan*, kyrkgreves, has acowntyd off al Recyſſetts be y^{em} Res. the xv day off Jly,[4] A° r. h. vii. xxiii°. And all thyngs acowntyd, And ſo nothyng reſt in ther hands.

It. recevyd of *Go copy* [5], And of *John Wood*,	0	0	2
It. recevyd of *Pet. thowrke*, for howre [6] of *John Snell*,	0	7	0

Md. y^{t} *Ryc. Nwman*, *John Lawys*, kyrkgrevys of *Wygtoft* choyn, In the yerre of howre lord God MCCCCCIX.

It. recevyd of *John frankys*, Cow [7] And A ſtage,	0	11	0
It. recevyd of *John gacſon* [8], of bykyr,	0	5	0
It. recevyd of *Roger Snell*, A Cow,	0	7	8
It. recevyd *John franckys* lam [9],	0	0	10
It. recevyd *John Nwman*,	0	1	8
It. recevyd for *John Balle*,	0	6	8
It. recevyd *John Nwman*, kyrkwarke,	0	1	0
It. rec. for *Rob. Feyld* 4*d.* *Ryc. Tyllnay* 2*d.* Itm. *Thos Snell* 2*s.*	0	2	6

Sm̄ 1^{l} 16^{s} 4^{d}.

[1] I imagine this to mean bell-ſtrings or ropes. [2] Day and half. [3] Glazier.
[4] July, anno regni Hen. VII. [5] I am not clear whether this is John Copy.
[6] This, though written plain, I cannot tell its meaning.
[7] It appears they contributed animals, and here liberally a cow and ſtag, value 11*s*.
[8] Jackſon. [9] A lamb.

It.

	£.	s.	d.
It. payd for ye Grett beyll clappur, ——	0	2	4
It· payd for ye Grett beyll yoke, — —	0	1	4
It. payd to ye bell shottar [1] for Rydyng heder, ——	0	0	10
Itm. payd to *Tho. Beall*, for ledyng [2] of ye beyll, ——	0	5	0
It. payd for hors mett, —— ——	0	2	0
It. payd to hever, — —	. . .	. . .	. . .
It. spent In ye way Rydyng deder [3] and legyng theyr to swyllys ye beyll Washe shotyng, — —	0	1	11
It. payd for hors mett, — —	0	2	0
It. payd for yockyng of ye beyll, — —	0	4	4
It. payd for ys bowrdyng, — —	0	1	0
It. payd yryn Warke, — —	0	0	6
It. payd *Rob. Blancnay*, hangyng of ye beyll And yryn Warke,	0	2	4
It. spent wen ye beyll sholar Washeyr [4], ——	0	0	4
It. payd to ye beyll shotar Wan he Was heyr In Auttamffs [5],	0	0	2
It. payd for yryn Warke to the Sams beyll, —	0	1	0
It. payd for mendyng of ye secund beyll, ——	0	0	3
It. payd to *Rob. Adnell* 1*d*. *Tho. howson* 1*d*. —	0	0	2
It. [6] payd for hyngyng and strycyng of ye beyll drynke, —	0	0	4
It. payd to ye Glacyars for Sauyur And Warkemanship,	0	2	4
It. payd for mett And drynke, — —	0	1	0
It. payd for to [7] ston seymull for beyll Roppus, —	0	1	0
It. payd for makyng of the Roppus, — —	0	0	8
It. payd to ye *John* [8] carvar, — —	0	3	4
It. payd for thackyng [9] to *John hawyt*, —	0	4	0
It. payd for Suffpendyng [10], — —	0	0	9
It. payd for Answeyryn for ye town, —	0	0	5
It. payd for Weysyng of ye Awtor clouth, —	0	0	1
It. payd for Wesheyng [11] 1*d*. It. payd for weyshyng 2*d*. —	0	0	3
It. payd to *John patlar* 6*d*. It. payd for Rosherop [12] 2*d*.	0	0	8
It. payd to *Wyllm Spensar*, for the beyll, —	0	0	10
It. payd to *Thos Weysfeld* xiii scor [13] reyd the pryce, —	0	2	2

[1] Probably bell-founder. See note [3], p. 198. [2] Carrying.

[3] Riding hither, and lying or lodging there while the bell was casting.

[4] Was here. [5] I suppose autumn.

[6] This item was for drink to the assistants in hanging, and what they term striking the bell.

[7] It appears the price of femble was now raised from 5d. to 6d. per stone, since the first accounts.

[8] I conjecture this to be paid to John the Carver.

[9] Thatching. [10] What fault had caused this suspension does not appear.

[11] How different the orthography of the same word even in immediate succession.

[12] Rush rope for thatching.

[13] Thirteen score sheaves of reed for thatching; the usual price of reed at this day is from 10s. to 12s. a 100 sheaves.

	£.	s.	d.
It. payd to *John Lawys* for vii fcor reyd, —	0	0	10
It. payd for a peefe of Tymb' for a yokke, —	0	0	2
It. payd for wefchyng off Auter clothys, —	0	0	3

Sm 2^l 15^s 7^d.

M^d. that *John Lawys* & *Ric. Numan*, kyrkegravys of *Wygtoft*, have made a cownt of All recet^s & bequefts be them recevyd, the vi day of Ap'l, the feconde yere of kynge *herry* the viii^th, And all thyngs reeonyd and a countyd, the forfayd kyrkgrevys ar owyng *5d.*

And the fayd *John lawys* hath chofyn to hym *Wyllm Proct*^r, a cordyng to ye olde ordynans, Inpymis a that We have reconyd of a Wolm for the bareall of *Ifb. Carva*[1], — 0 3 4

It. recevyd of ye wyff of *Churufkowe* for the legac^s of hyr hufband,	0	0	2
It. recevyd of *petur Thurke*, for ye rent of hys howfe, —	c	2	0
It. recevyd of *Thos kynge*, for rent of hys fchoppe[2], —	0	1	0

Theys byn the expens and payment that *John lawys* and *Willm proct*^r, Chyrche maftrs of ye piffche chyrche of *Wygtoft*, have payd fro ye vi day of Ap'le, in the yere of owre lord Millæ CCCCC and XI.[3] unto the fefte of ye Afcenfon of owr lord in the yer next foloing aft^r that.

In ye fyrfte, payd for ye makyng of a gudgeon to ye grete beell,	0	1	8
It. payd for a nod^r gudgyn to ye fame beell, —	0	0	3
It. payd to *Willm Spens*, for warkeman fchepe, —	0	0	5
Itm. paid for ther mete & drynke, — —	0	0	8
Itm. paid to *Willm Richardfon*, for dreffing of ye grete beell,	0	0	2
I m. paid for i ftone of finll[4] for bell ftryngs, —	0	0	6
I . paid for makyng of ye fame bell ftryngs, —	0	0	4
It. paid for fkowryng & makyng of i per of fenfs[5], —	0	0	4
Itm. paid for a fyre pane, — —	0	0	6
Itm. paid for ye forbell clapur fchotyng[6], —	0	1	6
Itm. paid for carege of ye fame clapp^r, —	0	0	2
It. paid for a ryng of yron a bowte ye tabernakull of Saynt Paul[7], and for ryngs to ye fame, — —	0	0	3
Itm. paid for i ftone femull for bell ftryngs, —	0	0	6

[1] This almoft mocks conjecture: it may be the burial of Ifabel Carver.
[2] Shop. We have had no mention of the falt-pan for fome time paft.
[3] Date 1511.
[4] An abbreviation of Femble.
[5] Pair of cenfers.
[6] Cafting.
[7] The church was dedicated to St. Peter and Paul.

It.

	£.	s.	d.
It. paid for di. ſtone ſemull,	0	0	3
Itm. paid for i lyne for ye clocke,	0	0	3
It. paid to *Thoms kyngge*, for the locke,	0	0	5
Itm. paid to ye wyff of *Thoms Betts*, for makyng of bellſtryngs,	0	0	4

Md. that *John lawys* & *Willm proct*^{r}, churche Maſt^{s} of the churche of *Wygtoft*, have made ther acownt of all thyngs before namyd, the xx day of May, that is to ſay, the feſte of ye Aſcencon of our lord, In the yere of our lord god Millm. CCCCC XII. And y^{e} ſame tyme the ſaid *Willm proct*^{r} hathe electe to hym *Thomas Beell*.

Md. y^{t} ye eayrke [1] mayſters of *Wygtoft* has Reſaved.

	£.	s.	d.
It. payd to the plummar,	0	2	8
It. payd to *John ſmyght*, of kyrton,	0	1	1
It. payd to *John ſpyrman*, for ye yate dryſſyng,	0	0	4
It. payd for nayls 6*d*. It. to *Jeſſe Wyſe*, for Wyſſyng of cloſe,	0	0	3
It. payd to *John Jeſſe*, for dreſſyng of ye kyrke Wale,	0	0	1
It. payd for to kyng [2] gyrdyl,	0	0	2
It. ſpynte at Spawldyng [3] for gat for gryſe mone,	0	0	10
It. payd to *ſpnſer* & hys mane, to mete, & drynke, & Wagys,	0	5	4
It. payd for a ſanctys [4] belſtring 4*d*. for fyre, & borde, & nayls, 3*d*.	0	0	6
It. payd for a ſtone of ſembulle 8*d*. makyng of ſame ſtone 4*d*.	0	1	0
It. payd for Wyree [5] y^{t} was ſpente 1*d*. A ſanctys bellſtryng 4*d*.	0	0	5
It. payd to *John grayſe*, for mayndyng of ye chaſſe [6],	0	0	4
It. payd to *lennard pynſbyke* Wyfe for bowldur [7],	0	5	6
It. payd to *John caruſe* & hys man,	0	3	8
It. payd to *Rob*^{t} *haddenelle*, for ſtoppyng of caudows [8] owte,	0	0	4
It. payd to *halſome Jeſſe* [9], for Wyſſyng of hawter clowſe,	0	0	2
It. ſpaynte of halle [10] Whan ye bellſe Waſe wone downe at kyrk & at kyton,	0	0	6
It. payd to *John Smyghte*, of kyrton, for hyrum [11] warke,	0	1	4
It. ſpaynt for rydyng for *John caruſe*, at kyme [12] 2*d*. for naylles 2*d*.	0	0	4
It. payd to *Jenyt* of brandon, for mete and drynke y^{t} was ſpente,	0	4	0
It. for Alſim' me for Wigtword [13] to cayke Wark,	0	0	6

[1] This is the moſt curious way of ſpelling kyrk I have yet met with. This line ſeems the ſum total of receipts, and a freſh account of payments immediately follows.

[2] I cannot explain this item. [3] Spalding. The reſt of the line I cannot decypher.

[4] Saints' Bell. [5] What can *wyree* mean?

[6] Q. chaſte, i. e. cheſte, as hereafter, p. 212, the chyſt.

[7] What can *bowldur* ſignify? [8] Daws, or jack-daws. [9] A waſher woman's name.

[10] Id eſt, the whole expence when the bells were taken down at the church and at Kirton.

[11] Iron. [12] *Kyme*, a town's name.

[13] The *wight word* or commemoration of Alice Mee. See p. 207 and 208, where we have both *wight* word and *quethe* word.

 It.

	£.	s.	d.
It. for rydyng to boſton 4*d*. for ſcholyng ye bell clapure 6*s*. 8*d*.	0	7	0
It. payd for a ſtone of fembulle, — —	0	0	8
It. ſpaynte Wan ye belle Was truſt [1] hup, — —	0	0	4
It. payd to *Alſom Jeſſé*, for Weſſyng, — —	0	0	4
It. payd to *badnelle* for ye kyr Walle, — —	0	0	1
It. payd for makyng of ye bellſtrynks, — —	0	0	4
It. payd to *John Spermane*, for dreſſyng abowte ye chirche, —	0	1	8
It. payd for a hoke [2] and a thymbull, — —	0	0	7

Sm̄ [3] 39^s. 9^d.

Md that in ye yer of owr lord god Mill CCCCCXIX.[4] the feſte of co'pore xp̄i [5] fell upon mydſom^r evyn, ye Which evyn Was faſtyd uppon co'perxp̄i evyn, & not uppon ye daye.

M^d y^t ye kyrgrevs of *Wygtoft* chyrche have recevyd of maſt^r *Wollm*^r fo beyryng of *barre davit* w^t In Wygtoft chyrche[6].

And alſo of *thorylſto* Wyfe of fenhourſe [7], —	0	0	2
And alſo y^d ledhowte[8] for makyng of A gudgytt [9] to ye greytt bell,	0	1	8
And alſo for Anodyr gudgytt to the ſame bell, —	0	0	3
And alſo to *Wyllm ſpenſar* & hys man for warkmanchyp,	0	0	5
And alſo for y^r meyt And drynke y^t had abowte the hyngyng of the bell — — —	0	0	8
And alſo to *Wyllm Rychardſon*, for dreſſyng of ye gret bell,	0	0	2
And alſo for a ſtone of fembull to ye belſtryngs, ye pryce,	0	0	6
And alſo for makyng of y^e ſame belſtryngs, —	0	0	4
And alſo for ſkoweryng and makyng of A payr of ſenſars,	0	0	4
And alſo for A fyar pan to the chyrche, —	0	0	6
And alſo for the forbell clapeyr ſchowtyng [10], —	0	1	6
And alſo for caryge of y^e ſame clapeyr, —	0	0	2
And alſo for A yorn [11] makyng afore ſen *John*, and ryngs to the ſame, — — —	0	0	3

M^d y^t *John lawes* & *Willm proctur* have reſevyd of *petur thyrke* [12],	0	2	0
It. for one ſtone of fembull for belle ſtryngs of *J. lawes*,	....		

[1] Got up into the ſteeple again. [2] Perhaps the irons to hang the gate with.

[3] This is caſt up wrong: I make it 2l. 0s. 4d.

[4] 1519. This appears a memorandum inſerted out of proper place, as we have earlier dates after this. [5] Corpus Chriſti.

[6] This Henry Davit might be a child: the uſual price of interment in the church was 6s. 8d.

[7] This is a hamlet belonging to the town, called the Fen-houſes. Thorylſto is a very uncommon name. [8] Laid out or paid.

[9] Or *gudgeon*. [10] See before, p. 204. note 6.

[11] This may intend iron. [12] I ſuppoſe this was the rent of the kirk-houſe.

It,

	£.	s.	d.
It. for halfe a ſtone of ſembull of *Wyllm proctur,*	. . .	. . .	. . .
It. for one lyne for ye cloke pcii [1],	0	0	3
It. reſavyd of *Thomas kyng,*	0	1	0
It. payd to y^{e} ſame *thomas* [2] for one loke,	0	0	5
It. to Wyffe off *thomas bett,* for one ſtone of hempe makyng for ye belleſtryngs,	0	0	4

Theys ys the Reſceyte of mony y^{t} *Wyllm procter* & *Thomas beell,* kyrke mayſters of *Wygtoft,* has Reſayvyd.

	£.	s.	d.
It. Reſavyd of *Thomas ſnaylle,*	0	6	8
It. Reſavyd of *John gryſſe,*	0	4	8
It. Reſavyd of *John crece,*	0	0	2
It. Reſavyd of *Thomas Weſtfelde,*	0	2	0
It. Reſavyd of che monay y^{t} we gadur [3],	0	1	3
It. Reſaved of *peter thyrke,*	0	3	4
It. Reſavyd of *Thomas kynge,* for y^{e} ſchope,	0	1	0
It. Reſavyd of *John grayſe* iis. of *peter thyrke* iiis.	0	5	0
It. Reſavyd for maye [4],	0	0	8
It. Reſavyd for *John numane* of *John hogynſon,*	0	6	8
It. Reſavyd of *Thomas kynge,*	0	1	0
It. rec. ye Wytworde of *Alſe mee* [5],	0	0	6
It. rec. of *Robt. yngulby* harygns [6] Wytword,	0	2	0

Theis is the Reſceite of money that *Robt. Brygg* and *Thos Beell,* chyrche maiſters of the p'iſhe chirche of *Wigtoft,* hathe Recevyd from the feſt of Saynt pet^r, callyd Ad vincla Sci pet^r, In the yer of owr lord god M^l CCCCCXIIII. unto the next Acownt.

	£.	s.	d.
In the firſt Reſcevyd of *John Greve* powndage for the ſchep [7] of ten men,	0	1	8
It. rec. of *Thos Snell* and of *Nicholas Thurke,* for the quethe Word of *Als Snelle,*	0	1	8
It. Rec. of *Nicholas* for the quethe Word of *Rog^r Snelle,*	0	0	4
It. Rec. of *Pet^r Thurke,* for rent of ys howſe,	0	2	0
It Rec. of *Willm Tollar,* for oon yer rent of y^{e} ſchoppe,	0	2	0
It. Rec. of *Robt yngulby,* for the quethe Word of *Nicholas hagworthynggam* [8],	0	1	4

[1] This may be an abbreviation of *Pretium.*

[2] This one of the moſt imperfect accounts I have yet copied, the receipts and payments being promiſcuouſly together. I have divided them by a line where I properly could.

[3] Money that we gathered.

[4] It is not clear whether this is a ſurname or not.

[5] See before, p. 205.

[6] It appears to be wrote *harygns,* I imagine a cognomen ill ſpent.

[7] Impounding ſheep.

[8] This is an uncommon ſurname; but there is a village in the northern part of the county called Hagworthingham. It is afterwards written *Hagrynggam,* p. 209.

It.

	£.	s.	d.
It. rec. of *John lawys* & *Robt lambeſon*, for the powndage of Quadryng ſchepe[1],	0	2	0
It. Rec. of *Thos Weſtfyld*, for 2 yers rent of oon ſalt panne,	0	3	0
It Rec. of *Ric. Numan*, the quethe Word of *Robt Bayly*,	0	1	0
It Rec. of *Thomas kyng*, for the ſchoppe,	0	1	0
It. Rec. of *Ric. Numan*, for the quethe Word of *Numan*,	0	6	8
It. Rec. of *John Lawys*, for the quethe Word of *Robt lawys*,	0	0	6
It. Rec. of *Edmunde howſon*, for the quethe Word of hys fadr,	0	0	6
It. Rec. of *Thoms hume*, for ye bereall of Ceall[2] Numã,	0	6	8
It. Rec. of *John Baſton*, for hys ſchepe pynded of ye marſche,	0	1	0
It. Rec. of *Robt. Snelle* aftr ye ſame manr,	0	0	4
It Rec. of *Thos Edwarde*, for hys kye[3] pyndyd of ye marſche,	0	0	4
It. Rec. of *Willm hogſon* 4d. & of *henr Edwarde* in like manr 3d.	0	0	7
It. Rec. of *Petr Thurke*, for rent,	0	2	0
It. Rec. of *Thomas Weſtfyld*, for rent of a ſalt panne,	0	2	0
It. Rec. of *Willm Tollar*, for rent,	0	1	0
It. Rec. of *Robt. Sneller* & *Adam* & *lambt peveſonne*, for ye catell,	0	0	8

Theis bene the coſts, expenſes, and payments, of *Robt. Brygg* & *Thomas Beell*, chirche maiſters aforſayd, done & payd in the yere Aforeſayd.

	£.	s.	d.
In the firſt payd to *John Roock*, for 2 bell clapurs ſhotyng,	0	2	1
It. paide to the plũbars[4], for 3 dais & di.	0	5	3
It. paide for ſawder the ſame tyme,	0	9	8
It. paide to *petr Thurke*, for repacon[5] of hys howſe,	0	3	0
It. paide for *Robt. Brygg* & *Thoms Beell* Bordyng,	0	0	6
It. paide for Nayles 1d. for 1 Stone of ſemull 6d.	0	0	7
It. paide for ye makyng of ye ſame 4d. It. for the bell clapur 1s.	0	1	4
It. paide for ye helpyng of yehe polegate[6],	0	0	8
It. paide for Ale when ye grete bell was ſtryckyn,	0	0	4
It. paide for a thymbull & for nayles,	0	0	3½
It. paide for mendyng of ye kyrke yeate,	0	0	2
It. paide for ye grette bell whele to *Robt. hungyng*,	0	5	4
It. paide for bowſtryng of the grete bell,	0	0	4
It. paid to *John Spereman*, for pavyng,	0	1	8
It. paide to *Robt. hungyng*, for helpyng of oon borde in the Roode loft,	0	0	2

[1] It ſeems the poundage of cattle was applied to the uſe of the church. At this day this generally belongs to the lord of the manor.

[2] Probably Cecil.

[3] Cow, or kine.

[4] Plumbers.

[5] Reparation.

[6] This ſeems to be the mending (here termed *helping*) of a gate, here called the Polegate.

It.

	£.	s.	d.
It. payd for 3 Store of ſemull 18d. It. for makyng of the ſame 1s.	0	2	6
It. payd to *John ſeely*, for bottyng[1] of 2 bell clapurs,	0	2	4
It. payd to *John Rooch*, for ſchootyng of ye bell clapur,	0	2	5
It. payd to the ſame *John* for y^{e} ſame bell clapur,	0	1	0
It. payd to *Willm deene*, for ye makyng of 1 ſtone & di. of ſemull,	0	0	6
It. payd to *Robt. Ardnell*, for helpyng of the chyrche Wall,	0	0	3
It. payd for ſoope to Waſche clothis,	0	0	2
It. payd for ye holy Wat^{r} fatte mendyng[2],	0	0	2
It. payd to *John Agarth*, for yron Waike to ye grete bell,	0	1	10
It. payd to *Robt. hunyngam*, for truſſyng of ye grete bell,	0	0	8
It. payd for naylys & borde[3],	0	0	2
It. payd for *Robt. hunyngam* ys bordyng,	0	0	8
It. payd to A thacker & to hys men 4 days & di.	0	1	6
It. payd for y^{er} bordyng y^{e} ſame days,	0	1	0
It. payd to *Thomas Cartar*, for Reede,	0	0	4
It. payd for Ruſche roope,	0	0	2
It. payd to ye plūbers, and for drynke,	0	4	2
It. payd to *Thoms*, for ledd to ye helpyng[4] of ye organys,	0	0	4
It. payd for helpyng of ye hande bell,	0	1	1
It. payd to *John Agarth*, for ye forlock[5] to ye grete bell,	0	0	5
It. payd for Ale when ye grete bell was ſtrykyn,	0	0	3½

Theis is the receyte of money that *Robt. brygg* And *Ric. Numan*, chyrche maſters of ye Piſhe Chirch of *Wygtoft*, have receyvyd frome the laſt Acownts made there as hyt is before wrytton unto the xv day of Aprle, in the yere of owre lord god A thowſand CCCCCXX.

Inpmis, reſceyved of *pet^{r} Thurke*, for hys howſe,	0	1	8
It. reſceyved the legacy of *John Blakem^{r}*[6],	0	1	8
It. reſceyved of *pet^{r} Thurke*, for hys howſe rent,	0	2	4
It. receyved of *Robt. yngulbe*, for the legacy of *Nicholas hagrynggam*,	0	4	0

Sm 9s. 8d.

Theis bene ye coſtys, Expens, & payment, of *Robt. Brygg* & *Richard Numan*, chyrche maiſters aforeſayd, done and payd in the yerys aforeſayd.

Inpmis, payd to A glaſyar for oon pane & od^{r} Wyndows helpin above in ye clereſtory,	0	1	3

[1] I am not clear what *bottyng* means. Q. bo*l*tyng, *ſhotyng*, as before, and p. 212.

[2] Mending the holy water veſſel or piſcina.

[3] From the ſmallneſs of the ſum, and being joined with nails, it probably means deal or wood.

[4] Some repairs done to the organ, as in the next article to the hand-bell and windows.

[5] I am not clear what the *forlock* intends.

[6] Blakemoor.

	£.	s.	d.
It. payd for the bere[1] mendyng, —	0	0	1
It. payd for hangyng of the poclay[2] 2d. and naylys to the ſame 1d.	0	0	3
It. payd for payntyng of ye rowndell[3], —	0	1	0
It. payd for femull to make belſtryngs, —	0	0	8
I payd for makyng of y^e^ ſame, — —	0	0	4
It. payd for makyng of ye grete bell clapur, —	0	1	8
It. payd for helpyng of ye baner[4] clothys, —	0	0	4
It. payd for mendyng of an od^r^ bell clapur, —	0	1	10
It. payd for on lyne y^t^ ye roundell hangs by, —	0	0	3
It. payd for clothys waſchyng, — —	0	0	5
It. payd for a bockell to ye forbell, — —	0	0	1
It. payd to *Robt. hunnyngam*, for ye rowndell mendyng, —	0	1	6
It. payd for bordys and nayles to ye yeate, —	0	0	8
It. payd for bell ſtryngys to *Willm Chaters*, —	0	1	0
It. payd for clothys Waſchyng on od^r^ tyme, —	0	0	3
It. payd to *Robt. hunyngam*, for makyng of ye churche yeates,	0	1	0

Sm̄ 12^s^. 7^d^.

Thys ys ye receyte of money y^t^ *Robt Brygg* and *Robt yngulby*, chyrch maſtrs of ye Piſhe church of *Wygtoft*, have receyvyd from ye laſt acownt made there ye xv day of Ap'le, in ye yere of owre lorde god A thowſand fyve hundrith xx, unto the laſt day of Junii A^o^ dm̄. millmo quingenteſimo xxi.

In pmis Reſcevyd of ye exec^s^ of *Ric. Waryngton*, —	0	0	4
It. Rec. of ye exec. of *John howſon* Wytword, —	0	1	0
It. Rec. of *M. Wolm*, of money y^t^ he had before Receyvyd, and was laſte of ye frame[5] money, — —	0	1	6
It. Rec. of *pet^r^ Thurke*, for hys howce rent, —	0	1	8
It. Rec. of *Thoms Beel*, — —	0	0	6

(Here follows a liſt of 65 inhabitants, with their contributions, as the former liſts, from 1d. to 8d.)

Sm̄ 5^s^.

[1] Bier, or frame, to carry or reſt dead bodies on, when going to be interred.
[2] I cannot ſay what the *poolay* was, unleſs the *polegate* mentioned p. 208.
[3] Nor am I clear as to the rowndell. [4] Cloths for banners or flags.
[5] I am not certain whether this is *frame* or *ſame*.

It.

Theis bene ye payment and expenses That *Robt Brygg* and *Robt yngulby*, chirch mastrs of ye Pishe chirche of *Wygtoft*, have payd from the last acownt made there the day of ye moneth & yere before namyd, unto the last day of Junii A° dm̄. Millmo quingentesimo xxi.

	£.	s.	d.
In pmis, payd to *Robt. hunyngam*, for helpyng of the chirch yeate,	o	1	o
It. payd to *Robt. hunyngam*, for the forbell mendyng, —	o	o	4
It. payd for hys bordyng, ——— ———	o	o	4
It. payd for a locke & a stapull, —— ——	o	o	6
It. payd to *Robt. Ardnell*, for ye chyrch Wall mendyng,	o	o	4
It. payd to *John Agarth*, for ye chyst mendyng, ——	o	4	o
It. payd to *Thomus*, for helpyng ye revestry gutt [1], —	o	o	4
It. payd for mendyng of a glas Wyndowe, ———	o	o	8
It. payd to *Robt. hunyngam*, for a trestyll [2] makyng, —	o	o	6
It. payd to *John Agarth*, for mendyng of the stapull of ye chawnsell and ye Revestry dorys, — — —	o	o	10
It. payd to *Thoms leeke* & *Thoms dekynson*, for pavyng, glasyng, & plumbyng, — — —	o	1	8

Sm 10^s. 6^d.

	£.	s.	d.
It. payd to *Robt. hunyngam*, for a ledd^r [3] makyng, —	o	1	o
It. payd for 2 buckull tongys [4] for the bells, ———	o	o	2
It. payd for Whitledd^r [5] to ye same, —— ——	o	o	1
It. payd for a locke & gemals [6] for ye frame, ———	o	3	4
It. payd to *John Agarth*, —— ——	o	o	6
It. payd th *Thoms*, for helpyng of a glas windowe, —	o	o	2
It. payd for nayles 5d. & for ye bowett [7] mendyng 10d. —	o	1	3
It. payd to *Robt. hunyngam*, —— ——	o	o	2
It. payd for makyng of ye dore & Wyndowys, ———	o	o	5
It. payd for A ston & A halff of semull, ———	o	1	o
It. payd for makyng of ye same, — —	o	o	6
It. payd for clothys Wasshyng at dyvs [8] tymys, —	o	o	5
It. payd for schotyng of ye bell clapur, ———	o	1	4
It. payd for naylys, —— ——	o	o	1

Sm 1^l. 0^s. 11^d.

[1] Q. gutter. [2] Tressel. [3] A ladder.
[4] Buckle tongues. [5] Witleather, or the strong white leather used by tanners.
[6] Unknown. [7] Bolt, or bowelt. [8] Divers times.

M^d. that

Md. that at ye laſt Acownts of *Robt. Brygg* And *Robt. yngulby*, there remayned in there handys, all thyns Acownted & Allowed, 3s. 7d.

Md. that we *Thoms*[1] *Brygg* & *Robt. yngulby*, churche wardens[2], have Reſſavyd of the towne,

	£.	s.	d.
In fyrſt leſte of ye ſeſment[3] In owre hands,	0	3	7
It. Reſavyd of *John Knrchener* for Wytword,	0	1	0
It. of *John thomſon*,	0	0	8
It. *Roger holland* for ye ſchope,	0	2	0
It. of *Ryc. collynſon*, for ye ſchope,	0	1	1

Sm 8s. 4d.

Theis bene ye payments and expenſes done be *thoms Brygg* & *Robt. yngulby*, chirche wardens.

	£.	s.	d.
It. for ſchottyng 3 gudgyngs & kayes to ye bells,	0	1	9
It. for a Wryght[4] for ye ſpas of 3 days, Mete and Wage,	0	1	6
It. for a Newe gudgyng,	0	0	11
It. for ſcottyng of A nolde gudgyng,	0	0	7
It. for mendyng of ye ſcollhows[5] dor & nayllys,	0	0	8

Sm. 5s. 5d.

	£.	s.	d.
It. for mendyng of the kyrke wall,	0	0	1
It. for hyngyng of ye ſecond bell 4d. & of the for bell 2d.	0	0	6
It. for thakyg[6] don of ye bells & hangyng of ym A tyme, bred[7] & All,	0	0	3
It. to *Wyllyam ſpens* & *Robt. Adnell*, 2 dayes,	0	1	2
It. for claſpys to ye pides[8] to ſet candyls in,	0	3	0
It. for dreſſyng A bell Whele, mett & Wages,	0	0	6
It. pd for A ſton & A half ſemble,	0	0	9

Sm. 9s. 8d.

Md. yt yes ben ye coſts & charg don By *thomas Brygg* & *Robt. lamſon*, cherch Wardynys, in ye yere of our lord god MCCCCCXXIII.

	£.	s.	d.
Fyrſt for ye bell gudyon ſchottyng,	0	1	2

[1] Probably the brother of Robert Brygg.
[2] I think this is the firſt time I meet with "Church-*wardens*."
[3] Nor do I remember to have met with "ſeſment" for aſſeſſment before.
[4] A workman for 3 days.
[5] School-houſe door.
[6] Taking down of the bells.
[7] Bread and ale.
[8] It is uncertain what this word is.

It.

	£.	s.	d.
It. payd to *Robt. Wright*, for mendyng ye fayd bell, ——	o	o	6
Itm. payd for A ftone fembull & A halfe, ——	o	o	9
Itm. payd for makyng of ye fayd hempe, ——	o	o	6
Itm. payd to ye beke [1] bynder Wen he was hyryd, —	o	o	6
Itm. payd for helpyng of a bell Welle [2], ——	o	1	5
Itm. to *John Butler*, for yryne Wark to ye fayd Welle and nalys,	o	o	2½
Itm. payd for caryge of ye kyrk boke to furfled for ledyng & fetchyng, —— —— ——	o	o	4
Itm. payd for A ftone hempe, a halfe w^t^ ye makyng, ——	o	1	3

Sm 6^s^. 7½^d^.

Theys is ye Receyte of *Thomas Brygg* & *Robt. lamfon*, chyrch mayfters of ye fayd chyrch of *Wygtoft*, by us reconyd [3] ye yer of o^r^ lord a thoufand V^C^XXIII.

	£.	s.	d.
In pmis, Recevyd of *Wyllm Tollar*, — —	o	1	o
It. Recevyd for dryvyng fcheppe of ye mche [4], ——	o	o	6
It. Recevyd of ye fayd *Wyllm tollar*, —— —	o	1	2
It. Recevyd of *Ric. colynfon*, for rentt, ——	o	1	o

Sm 3^s^. 8^d^.

Theys ys ye Receyt of *Robt. lambefon* And *John atkynfon*, cherch mayfters of ye chirche of *Wygtoft*, In ye yere of o^r^ lord MCCCCCXXIIII.

	£.	s.	d.
In pmis, Receyved of ye abbat [5] of dorr, ——	o	1	o
Itm. of *agnes morley*, for rent of on howfs, ——	o	1	o
Itm. for hold bell ropys, —— ——	o	o	6
Itm. Receyvyd of *Thomas leyke*, for ye Wytword of *Ric. Newman*,	o	6	8
Itm. of *Jenyt lawes* Receyvyd, —— ——	o	o	2
Itm. Receyved of *Willm Pakey*, for ye Wytword of *Ric. Newman* [6],	o	13	4
Itm. Recevid for ye Wytword of *John lawes* theld^r^, —	o	3	4
It. Received for the beqweft of *Ric. Tilney*, theld^r^, ——	o	o	2

[Sm̄ 1^l^. 6^s^. 2*d*.

[1] This is a charge fomewhat curious. By a fubfequent article it feems the book-binder lived at Surfleet, about four miles diftant.

[2] Bell wheel. [3] Recognized or acknowledged, [4] Driving fheep of the marfh.

[5] John de la Warre lord of Ewyas gave to Dore abbey in Herefordfhire an acre of land in Wygtoft, with the advowfon of the church, 4 Edward III. (Mon. Angl. I. 864.) The church was appropriated to that abbey 27 Edward III. (Pat. 27 Edward III. p. 2. m. 20, 21, vel 22.)

[6] The firft of thefe fums is a half, the fecond a whole year's payment of R. Newman's anniverfary, by different perfons. There was a perfon of the name of *Pakey* in this parifh untill very lately. The *Wytword* is the fame with the *queythe word*, p. 77, where and in other places it fhould have been explained as here.

Md. that thys is the afcefmet of ye money Afceffyd to ye church of *Wygtoft*, be *John lawes*, fenior, And *Robt lambefon*, Wardens of ye feyd chyrch, MmoCCCCCXXIIII.

(Here follows a lift of 103 names of the inhabitants, with their affeffments, none higher than 12d. or under 1d.)

Thys is the Receyte of mony that *John lawes* and *Robt lambefon*, chyrch mayftrs of ye P'ifch church of *Wygtoft*, have receyved for ye afcefmēt yt afceffed be them And the P'ifche in ye moneth of decembr A° dm. millmo quingent° XXIIII.

	£.	s.	d.
Inpmis, Recevyd of pt. of ye fyrft paymet, —	0	10	6
It. Recevyd for fellyng of old belle ropis, —	0	0	4
It. Recevyd of *Ric. collynfon*, for hys howfe, —	0	1	0
Itm. refevid of *m. bralyh*, for ye beryall of on chyld in ye chyrch,	0	3	4
It. refevid of ye legacy of *Thomas hunne*, — —	0	3	4

Sm 18s. 6d.

Theis bene ye expens & payments of *Robt lambefon* & *John atkynfon*, church maifters of ye fayd chirch, done & payd yt be d'ves perfones.

	£.	s.	d.
Inpmis, payd to ye plommer in pt. of paymet, —	0	6	8
Itm. for i ftone hempe and di. for to make belropys and makyng of ym, — — — —	0	1	3
Itm. payd to *John lawes*, for woode, — —	0	0	6
Itm. to *John butler*, for clafpis makyng, — —	0	0	4
Itm. payd to *Alexand' mchand*,[1] for woode, — —	0	1	3
Itm. payd to ye plommer at ii payments, — —	0	1	8
Itm. payd to the cloke[2] maker, — —	0	1	0
Itm. to *Robt lambefon*, iiii s. Itm. to ye feid *Robt lambefon*, ii s.	0	6	0

Sm̄ 18s 8d.

Thyes bene ye cofts, Expenfis, and payments, of *John lawes*, fenior, And *Robt lambefon*, chyrche maftrs of ye fayd chyrch, done & payd yr be dyvers perfonas.

	£.	s.	d.
Inpmis, payd at bofton for halowed[3] of autr clothes, and makyng of ye chalys, — — — —	0	3	10
It. to *marget hoggefon*, for weffyng, — — —	0	0	4

[1] *Merchand*, his furname.

[2] Clock-maker.

[3] I fuppofe hallow*ing* the altar clothes.

It.

	£.	s.	d.
It. payd for ye coneng[1] of ye hy autr, — —	0	1	6
It. to *John Butler*, for makyng A lock, — —	0	0	3
It. payd to *colynson* & *John coke*, for making of ye chyrch walle,	0	0	2
It. payd to *Robt hunyngam*, — —	0	0	3
It. payd to a glaſſer of boſton for glaſyng of ye chyrch Wyndowes, & and for hys bordyng to *Thomas dekonson*, —	0	3	8
It. to *Miles chesbrouth*, for makyng erth to ye glaſſers, and his bord,	0	0	3
It. payd to *John Butler*, for makyng of iii bell clapers, —	0	6	8
It. payd at boſton for makyng of the gret claper, —	0	6	8
It. payd to *Willm chaters*, for makyng of i ſtone & di. hempe,	0	0	6
It. payd to *Willm manne*, for ye litell belſtryng, —	0	0	4
It. to *Robt ardnell*, for makyng ye cyrch walle, —	0	0	1
It. to *John buttelar*, for a Wyndyng to ye forebell, & for nayles,	0	0	6
It. to *Robt honynggam*, for helpyng ye forbell Whele, and hyngyng hyt, — — — —	0	0	7
It. payd for drynke about ye ſeyd bell, — —	0	0	3
It. payd to *Willm chaters*, for bell ropys, — —	0	1	3
It. payd to *John creſſey*, for mendyng the chyrch wall, —	0	0	1
It. to *John butler*, for mendyng ye grett bell claper, —	0	2	8
It. payd for ye haly bred ſteppe[2], — —	0	0	2
It. to *Margaret hoggeson*, for wiſchyng, — —	0	0	1

Sm̄ 1l. 13s. 5d.

The Aſceſment of ye P'iche of *Wygtoft* then aſſeſſyd for the Repac̄on of the chirch, An° MCCCCCXXV.

(Here follows a liſt of 86 inhabitants with their aſſeſſments from 1d. to 3s. 4d.)

Thyes bene the expence & paymēt of *Robt lambeson* & *John atkynson*, chirch maiſtrs of ye ſeid chirch, done & payd be dyvēs perſons, An° ſalut.

Inpmis, payd to *James Sougar*, plommer for Workyng abowte ye chirch, — — — — —	0	6	8
Itm. payd for i ſtonne hempe & di. for bell ropis, & for makyng,	0	1	3
Itm. payd to *John lawes*, for Woode, — —	0	0	6
Itm. payd to *John butler*, for makyng claſpis to ye bellis, —	0	0	4
Itm. payd to *Alexand' marchand*, for Woode, — —	0	1	3

[1] Compleating the pinnacles of the high altar, or it may be coveng, i. e. covering.
[2] This was a ſtep or paten on which the holy bread was laid.

	£.	s.	d.
Itm. payd to ye plomer at ii payments, —— ——	1	0	0
Itm. payd to the cloke maker 5 s. Payd to *Robt lambeſon* 4 s.	0	9	0
Itm. to ye plommer afforſeyd, — ——	0	3	4
Itm. payd to ye afforſeid *Robt lambeſon*, for pewt^{r}, ——	0	2	0
Itm. payd to *Thomas Dekonſon*, for w^{t} ſpent at ſwynneſhed baume [1],	0	3	4
Itm. payd to y^{e} ſeid *Thomas Dekonſon*, for bordyng of *Ric. cany*, of Swynneſhed, & his mane, — — —	0	1	8
Itm. to *John*, for Wood, 6d. Itm. to the ſeid *James* [2], 20s.	1	0	6
Itm. to *Robt lambeſon*, 12d. Itm. to *John atkynſon*, 2d. —	0	1	2
Itm. payd to *frankes*, for i ſtryke wheyt [3], — —	0	0	8
Itm. payd for nayles 2d. Itm. for Clok meynddyng, 4s. —	0	4	2
Itm. for Clowys wyeſſyng, 7d. Itm. for ii obb [4] Syrpleys Wyeſſyng, 3d. —— —— — —	0	0	10
Itm. for byelſtryngs, 3s. 2d. Itm. payd to *John Cryſſe*, 7d.	0	3	9
It. payed to *ſtybyerd plaver*, 2s. 2d. It. payed to *John Cryſſe*, 13d.	0	3	3
It. for neylls to ye chyrch, 5½d. It. payeng [5] in ye chyrch, 8d.	0	1	1½
It. for ii pound pewt^{r} [6], — — —	....		
Itm. owyng to *John atkynſon*, for ii pownd pewd^{r} & iii treys lyme.			
Itm. owyng to *Robert lamſon*, for ii pownd pewder.			
Itm. owyng to *Robt lamſon*, for makyng of ye belſtryngs, 4d.			
Itm. owyng to y^{e} ſayd *Robt*, 4d.			

Sm 4^{l}. 4^{s}. 8^{d}.

Thes be ye reſaytts that we *Robt* & *John* reſevyd.

	£.	s.	d.
In pmis, of Maſt^{r} *Wolmer*, 5s. 8d. Itm. of *John Lawys*, 6s. 8d.	0	7	4
Itm. of *nicholes thurk*, 3s. 8d. Itm. of *amos morlay*, 12d.	0	4	8
It. Reſewyd of *John hartly* & *John bayker*, executors of *Rychard laborn*, for a ſ'tyn [7] legace, gyven & beqwethed to ye cherch Wark of *Wygtoft*, — — — —	0	5	0
It. Reſayved of ye aforſayd *John hartly* & *John bayker*, for on other legaſe, gyven to pare [8] w^{t} in *Wygtoft*, — —	0	10	0

Wytnes to this, *gorge atkynſon*, *Ric. Wallgat.*

Sm 1^{l}. 12^{s}.

[1] This is an obſcure word: we have Spaldyng ba*unne*, p. 221. Is it Swineſhead and Spaldyng *feaſt* or *wake*?

[2] John *Lawes* for wood: James *Sougar*, plumber, is the laſt *James* mentioned.

[3] Did they buy wheat to make the holy bread with?

[4] I imagine two odd or old ſurplices.

[5] Probably paving.

[6] It does not appear what the pewter was uſed for. By the laſt 4 items being owing for, one might ſuppoſe the aſſeſſment, &c. money exhauſted:—indeed this was a very expenſive year.

[7] This is an abbreviation of *certain*.

[8] I imagine this an abbreviation of "to repair with in Wigtoft."

3 M^{d}.

	£.	s.	d.
Md. yt *Robert Brygg* and *Jhon atkynson*, chyrch Wardons of *Wygtoft*, hayth payd to *John Butler*, for schotyng ye gret bell claper, & for gudgyons makyng, — — —	0	5	0
Itm. payd to *Robert hunynggam*, for trusyng of ye gret bell, & for mendyng of ye same bell Weyll, — —	0	1	4
Itm. payd to *Robt shepperd*, for a ston to make a holy Water fat.	0	1	4
Itm. payd for Wassyng clothys, — —	0	0	8
Itm. payd to *John Butler*, for mendyng a chyste, —	0	1	1
It. payd for Wysson [1] of closses, — —	0	0	4
Payd to a plomar for mendyng of de stepel, — —	0	3	1
It. payd to ser *John*, for a sorples [2], — —	0	5	0
It. payd for A ston & half of sembel for belys strengs, —	0	1	0
It. payd for makyn of dem, — —	0	0	6
It. payd for Wesyn closes, — — —	0	0	3
It. payd At nottyngg [3] for ye forbell schottyng, —	1	6	0
It. for expẽsis to & fro, & for ye bell clap. schottyng, —	1	6	0
Itm. for takyng downe ye seyd bell, & hangyng up again, to costs & charg yt dosota [4] to *Ric. caney*, to mette & Wag	. . .	. . .	. . .
It. payd to *John Wallgate*, for clothys Wassyng, —	0	0	6
Itm. payd to *Ric. collynson*, for A stone sembull & makyng,	0	1	2
Itm. for barnar clothys sewng, 4d. Itm. for nalys, 2½*d*.	0	0	6½
Itm. payd for clothys Wasschyng, — —	0	0	6

Sm 2l. 13s. 4d.

Md. yt We *Robert Brygg* & *Jhon atkynson*, ye chyrch Wardons of *Wygtoft*, hayth resavyd of *Jennet yngulbey*, for hyr husband beryall,	0	4	0
It. of *Robt mason*, for hys house, — — —	0	2	0
It. *Wyllm Collynson*, for *roberd lamson* Witword, —	0	3	0
It. *John Stell* for hys house, — —	0	2	0
Thoms helton, for hys Wyfe berealle, — —	0	5	0
Itm. Resavyd of *Robert mason*, for hys howse, —	0	2	0
Itm. of *Robt Adnell*, for ye same, — —	0	2	0
It. Resavyd by ye byll [5] made by ye town schepe of *Wygtoft*,	1	0	0

[1] However extraordinary the orthography, this means washing of clothes. [2] Surplice.

[3] Nottingham. By the charge I suppose *schottyng* means new-*casting* the fore or great bell. See p. 78.

[4] I can make nothing of this word: whatever the expence was, it seems to have related to the bell, and is omitted in the book.

[5] It does not appear of what charges this bill of the township consisted: this part of the church revenue might arise from the salt-pan, impounding cattle, &c.

An°

An^{o} XXXI [1].

	£.	s.	d.
Md. that we *Robt breg* And *John Atkynſon*, the chyrche Wardons of *Wygtoft*, have Reſavyd off *Jenyt yngulbe*, ffor hyr huſband's Wyt Worde [2],	2	0	0
Itm. Reſavyd off mr. vycar [3], ffor pamet' to the bell,	0	3	4
Itm. Reſavyd of *margaret Wyllamſon*, for hur hous,	0	2	0
Itm. Receyvyd of *Ric^{d} clarke*, for his chamb^{r},	0	0	6
Itm. receivd of maſter *Thomas robſon* Witword,	0	10	0
Itm. reſeived of *roberd maſon*, for *roberd badmed* houſe,	0	3	0
Itm. in mony y^{t} remaned at the laſt cownt,	0	4	0

Sm totalis 3^{l}. 2^{s}. 10^{d}.

	£.	s.	d.
M^{d}. that we *Robt bryg* And *John Atkynſon*, ye chyrch Wardons off *Wygtoffth*, haffe payd to ye bell fouud^{r},	1	13	4
Itm. payd to *Simon mone*,	2	0	0
Itm. payd for on ſtone off ffēbyll ffor the bell ſtrynkys,	0	0	10
Itm. payd for the makyng off the ſayd bellſtrynys,	0	0	4
Itm. payd to *John ffulsflove*, for ye chyrche yatte,	0	0	2
Itm. payd to *ric. cane*, for de bell Well [4] menden,	0	1	2
Itm. payd to *Jon creſſe*, for menden of de chamber,	0	0	3
Itm. payd to ..... *tamworte*, for ye merſement [5]. P^{d} for nelles 1d.	0	0	8
Itm. payd for on ſton & haff of ſembell for bellſtreens,	0	1	0
Itm. payd for maken of dem,	0	0	6
Itm. payd for A ſton of ſembell,	0	0	7
Itm. for makyn of y^{t} & for clot [6] lens makyn,	0	0	6
Itm. for clos Wyſſen,	0	0	4
Itm. payd to *Symon moyn*, of ye chantre money,	0	13	4
Itm. payd to ye afforſeyd *Symon*, borowed of *M. Wolmer*.	2	6	8
Itm. payd to *John botler*, for menden of the bell Well,	0	0	7
Itm. payd to de ſed *John*, for A bokell [7],	0	0	1
Itm. paid for ii hopes for a polped [8],	0	0	3
Itm. payd for cloſſe Weſſen,	0	0	2
It. payd for A ſton of ſembel for belſtres̃ 8d. for makyng of dem 4d.	0	1	0

[1] An abbreviation of 1531.

[2] Forty ſhillings was a conſiderable legacy.

[3] The Vicar contributed 3s. 4d. to the bell, probably a new one, or new caſt.

[4] Bell wheel.

[5] The pariſh was amerſed or fined 7d. on ſome account.

[6] Clock-lines making.

[7] Buckle.

[8] Two hoops for the pulpit, which gives one ſome idea of the ſimilarity of tubs and pulpits.

It.

	£.	s.	d.
It. payd for a beer [1], ——— ———	0	3	4
It. payd for a ſtabel eten [2] yn defoute, ——— ———	0	0	6
It. payd for cloſe Weſſen 2d. It. payd for bellitrens makyn 6d.	0	0	8
Itm. for menddyng of ye churche Walle, — —	0	0	3

Sm 7^l^. 6^s^. 6^d^.

The Account of *John Atkynſon* And *Robt Brygg*, churche Wardons of ye church of *Wygtoft*, maid y^r^ the xix daye of ye monythe of m'che, Wych was then Good fryday, in the yer of o^r^ lorde god M^le^CCCCCXXXII. Whereas then the afforſeyd *John* & *Robt*, church Wardons, hath mayd A full accountt byfore ye Piche of all Man^r^ of recetts & paymet^s^, done, had, and writton, in y^s^ boke in y^s^ thyme, And has eleċt as now to be church Wardons *Robt Brygg* afforſaid, And *John Redway*, Into whos hands was delivred of ye church goodds, — — — — — 0 12 4

Recept p me *John redway*.

fyrſt recevid of *John atkynſon* And *Robt Shepperd*, for the plowght [3] lyght, — — — — 1 6 8

Itm. recevyd of *John howſon*, for grenpote [4] lyght, ——— 0 13 4

[1] A bier. [2] I cannot decypher this. Is it a ſtaple conſumed by ruſt through neglect ?

[3] The plough light; Q. on Plough Monday. Theſe different lights were lighted on certain feſtivals. The Romiſh church dealt much in waxen tapers, and it ſeems they took much ſupporting. The names of theſe different lights are obſcure.—"The ſeveral altars in churches had lights burning before them, which, with other expences attending, were provided for by the legacies of 4d. or 8d. in general by each pariſhioner to each light in their pariſh church, and by bequeſts of land to them. Thus to St. Margaret's light at Boughton under Blean was given one or two acres of land, called *St. Margaret gafel*, and to this day the *Margaret acre*. For the lights of the other altars was given a ſtock of cows and ewes bought with the above legacies of money. Theſe cows and ewes were let out by the churchwardens, who were truſtees of them for the pariſhioners, at 1s. and 1s. 8d. year each cow, whoſe value was computed at 10s. and every perſon who had one was obliged to find ſureties for the forth coming of it. The yearly rent of an ewe was 3d. and its whole value 2s. The rent of theſe cows and ewes is ſtyled in the churchwardens' accounts the *mole* or *moll* of the kyne or ewes. It appears by the churchwardens' accounts, who were then four in number, there were no fewer than 20 cows and 120 ewes, producing a yearly rent of 2l. 10s. which would purchaſe at leaſt as much as 20l. would now. Beſides the lights before the altar of particular ſaints, there was in every church a *rood light*, or that which was burnt before the crucifix in the rood loft; and the *hearſe light*, which burnt before the bier or hearſe of thoſe which were carried to be buried. For the finding of theſe lights here there was the intereſt of a ſtock of 5l. in money, which was then at leaſt 10s. By the injunctions of Edward VI. 1547, it was ordered that the profit of cattle or money given to the finding of lights, lamps, &c. ſhould be put into the poor cheſt, and diſtributed to the poor and needy of the pariſh." Lewis's Hiſt. of Faverſham, p. 86; Haſted's Kent, III. 8. *(s)*. In Whitſtaple church there was the *Strode* light, and the *Tankerton* light, ſo called from lords or manors there. Haſted, lb. 559. *(f)*.

[4] *Grenpote* may be a proper name.

Itm.

	£.	s.	d.
Itm. of *rog^r maye*, for ye fame lyght, — —	0	6	8
Itm. of *Nicholas thurke*, for ye fame, — —	0	6	8
Itm. of M.[1] *Wyllm lyncolne*, for kyr chowffe may lyght[2], —	0	13	4
Itm. of *John greve*, of hys owne gyffte, — —	0	3	4
Itm. of *Willm Bawnne*, for Wormeflande[3], — —	0	13	4
Itm. of *Edmond howfon*, for ye hogn[4] lyght, — —	0	6	8
Itm. of *rec. Deconfon*, for all Souls[5] lyght, — —	0	13	4

5^l. 3^s. 4^d.

recetts Recevyd by *Edmond howfon* And *John redway*, church wardons (An^o dm.) 1532.[6])

	£.	s.	d.
fyrft Recevyd of M. *rychard Wolm^r*, for land holde to him Wych Was gyvon to ye church by *Robt lambefon* Wyll at ye thyme of his depting[7] & deth, — — — —	2	0	0
Itm. recevyd of *John lawes* of ye fepulc^r[8] lyght, ——	0	6	8
Itm. of *Robt Mayfon*, for *Robt ardenell* howffe, —	0	3	0
Itm. of *Ric. Arley* & *John meferr*, for *i thorpe*[9], ——	.....	.....	.....
Itm. Recevyd of *Willm mafon*, Wever, for bord[10], ——	0	0	4
Itm. receyvyd of *Edmond howfon*, of eftthorppe lyght, —	0	0	4
Itm. receyvyd of *Thomas Sharforth*, for i part of the fparrs and borde y^t Warr of ye noth yld[11], —— ——	0	2	10
Itm. recevyd of *margaret brygg*, for ye quethword of *Robt Brygg*, hir hofband, — — ——	0	1	0
Itm. of ye feyd *m^rgaret* for his beryall, —	0	6	8
Itm. recevyd in ye church ftik[12] y^t was offord y^r of *John collyfon*, *Cecely feft*, and *Robt mayfon*, — — —	0	0	2
Itm. recevyd of *katyn*[13] *frankefh*, for ye beqweft of hir hufband's Wyll, — — — — —	0	0	8
Itm. recevyd of ye feyd *katyn* for rent of land of *lambt Wormes*, gyvon to ye towne, — — — —	0	4	0

4^l. 4^s. 8^d.

[1] This is a capital M. and is fynonymous with our Mr.

[2] Q. The church houfe May light.

[3] This might be land fo called left to the church.

[4] Q. *high*, i. e. before the high altar.

[5] On All Souls day.

[6] This is the firft time I find the date in figures: before it was always in Roman numerals.

[7] Departing. They frequently ufe the *p*, with a line through the tail, in the midft of words, as an abbreviation for *per*, or *par*.

[8] Light to burn before the holy fepulchre. See before, p. 200.

[9] If this is a furname, it feems to be *J. Thorpe*; but I am not clear in it.

[10] Board and lodging at Mafon's houfe.

[11] North ifle.

[12] Q. ftock.

[13] Abbreviation for Catherine.

Thies

	£.	s.	d.
Thies folowyng be paymēt payd by *Robt Brygg* and *John redwarre*, Church Wardons, An° dm. 1532.			
fyrst, payd to *Thomas Wedby*, Wryght [1], for Workyng abowte ye roodloft i day for meytt & Wayg [2] 6d. Itm. for i bordd 4d.	0	0	10
Itm. payd to *Petr ynghold* & *Wyllm feddr*, plommēs, for v days & di. Workyng, to meitt & Wayg, — —	0	5	10
Itm. payd to ye said *Petr* & *Wyllm*, for xxvi li. saudr, —	0	8	8
Itm. payd to *gorge matsey* & *henry dayles*, for Workyng aboutt ye churche Wayles i day to mett and Wayg, — —	0	0	8
Itm. to *matsey* for layng Wood togedr, — —	0	0	2
Itm. payd to the plommēs for xxvi li. saudr, — —	0	8	8
Itm. payd to the same plommēs, for iiii dayes Workyng, —	0	4	0
Itm. payd to *Alexandr payther* & his man, for i day Workyng & mendyng the ston Warke of ye churche, — —	0	0	6
Itm. payd to *John lytster* Wyffe of boston, for i tray of lyme,	0	2	0
Itm. payd to *Simon Moon*, of Swyneshed, Wryght, —	0	1	8
Itm. payd to *Thomas Sorthey*, of boston, for i Ml threpeny nayles [3], And i Ml of thopeny nayles, — —	0	4	2

Sm 1l. 17s. 2d.

Itm. payd to *marteyn*, the gyldr, — —	0	13	4
Itm. to the seyd *marteyn*, an angell nobyll, —	0	7	6
Itm. payd to *John Cresey*, *Robt Whaytt*, & his sone, for beym [4] sellyng ye church & mendyng ye churche Wall, —	0	0	10
Itm. to *katyn deconson*, for ii days yr [5] borde, — —	0	1	0
Itm. payd to *George matsey*, for makyg i bell roppe, —	0	0	2
Itm. payd to *Simon moon*, at his last paymet, —	0	10	0
Itm. payd to *petr ynghold* & *Wyllm feddr*, plommers, for layng the ledes, for viii dayes to mett and Wayg [6], — —	0	8	0
Itm. payd to ye seyd plommers xxiiii li. Sawdr, —	0	8	0
Itm. payd to ye seyd plommers In rewardd [7], — —	0	1	8
Itm. payd to *Saundr payther* and his man, for paytyng [8] and casting the churche Wallys, iii days di. — —	0	1	9
Itm. payd to *marteyn*, the gyldr, for his warke, —	0	10	0
Itm. payd at boston for halffe a seme lyme, — —	0	0	8
Itm. payd to *petr yngkold* and *Wyllm feddr*, plommēs, for ii dayes Wyrkyng and for Sawdr, — — — —	0	4	3

[1] Carpenters are sometimes called wrights, as now in Scotland. [2] Wages.

[3] 1000 of three-penny, and 1000 of two-penny nails.

[4] Beam cieling or putting up a roof where there was no ceiling to cover the beams, as is the case in a great many parish churches at this day. [5] Their.

[6] Meat and wages. [7] Over and above the agreement.

[8] Saunder the painter. Painting and rough casting or plaistering the church walls.

Itm.

	£.	s.	d.
Itm. payd to *Sand*r and his man for ii days, — —	o	1	o
Itm. payd to *Marteyn Scrosborgarre* [1], gyldr, ——	o	10	6
Itm. payd to ye same *marteyn*, for Wyerre, — —	o	o	3
Itm. payd to ye seid *marteyn*, for mendyng ye domme [2] and paynteng itt mor yan his cownnand [3] was to, —— ——	o	6	8
Itm. payd to *John hockynson*, of boston, for i trey of lyme,	o	1	9
Itm. payd to *Gorge matsey*, for ledd pewr [4], ——	o	o	2½
Itm. payd to *Alexand*r *holnell* and his hand [5], to yr Waygs for kestyng [6] the church, v days di. —— ——	o	2	9
Itm. payd to *Robt Wayethe*, for mendyng deskys in ye churche, And erthyng [7] ye bellofft, — — —	o	o	9

Sm 4l. 9s.

	£.	s.	d.
Itm. to *katyn deconson*, for drynke and bredd at ye creyeng of Spauldyng Baunne [8], — — — —	o	o	9
Itm. payd to ye seid *katyn*, for drynke, — —	o	o	1
Itm. payd to *Thomas Cart*r Wyffe, for bordyng *Alexand*r *hollnell* And his hand xii days, — — —	o	4	8
Itm. payd for the cryeng of Spauldyng bayn, ——	o	6	8
Itm. payd to *Edmond howson*, for a borde, — —	o	o	4
Itm. payd to *John harcastill*, of boston, for glass, ——	o	o	11
Itm. payd to *ferm*r, the smythe, of boston, for makyng barrs to the glas wyndows, and ii bokyls to ye bells, — —	o	1	6
Itm. payd to *Robt.* [9] glassynr, for Workyng And glasyng xvi dayes to his Wags, —— —— ——	o	5	4
Itm. to ye same *Robt.* for holde [10] glasse, — ——	o	1	o
Itm. payd to *thomas Deconson*, for his bord, — —	o	3	5

[1] This Marteyn, the gilder, we might take for a Dutchman by his surname; or he may have been of Scrosbesbyrrig or Shrewsbury. He appears to have been a capital workman.

[2] Q. if a painting of the general *doom* or judgement? Such a painting made the altar-piece of Enfield church before the Reformation; and on the late repair, 1789, was found fastened up over the West face of the arch dividing the nave from the chancel concealed by the altar-piece of 1665, which had been hoisted up like its predecessor out of the way, when the liberality of Gascoigne Nightingale, Esq; the impropriator, smothered a handsome East window with a heavy Grecian pediment and pillars, which the present parishioners with difficulty submitted to have lightened by inserting the Decalogue and its accompaniments into the blank pannels.

[3] More than his agreement came to.

[4] Probably lead and pewter.

[5] A man or assistant is not uncommonly called a *hand*.

[6] Rough casting or plaistering.

[7] New laying the earthen floor of the bell-tower or loft.

[8] Whether this baunne or bayn was a statute for hiring servants, or what else I cannot say. The same article has been charged before. See p. 216. *Banns* is a *proclamation*, as for marriages and the arriere *ban* in France.

[9] Here the surname is omitted.

[10] Old.

	£.	s.	d.
Itm. to *cart*^{r} Wyffe for di.[1] Weeke bord, —— —	0	0	8
Itm. payd for drynke to Warkmen, — ——	0	0	3
Itm. payd to *Deconſon*, for bredd & halle[2] at the dreſſyng of ye grett bell, — — — —	0	0	4
Itm. payd for mendyng & ſtaying ye Roodlofte in hale, —	0	0	2
Itm. payd to *Ric. Cony*, for truſſyng ye forebell[3], ——	0	0	6
Itm. payd to *Robt. Browne*, for hale[4], —— —	0	0	0½
Itm. payd to *John butler*, for makyng thymbles & hoks for mary and John, & for ye Angells[5], —— ——	0	0	6
Itm to y^{e} ſame *John*, for ſhotyng ye forbell clapper & truſſyng ye grett bell, —— —— ——	0	2	0
Itm. payd to *fermer*, of boſton, for makyng purlls[6] & kayes,	0	0	2
Itm. payd to *Agnes bawne*, for Wesſhyng of Aut^{r} clothys, —	0	0	4
Itm. payd to *Rog*^{r} *May*, for ii ſtonne of ſemble to bellropis,	0	1	2
Itm. payd to *John ſharppe*, for makyng belroppys, ——	0	0	9
Itm. payd to *Alyxand*^{r} *m'chand*, for ye cloth y^{t} cov^{s}ys ye rood & the donne[7], —— ——	0	11	3
Itm. payd to *fermer*, of boſton, Smythe, for the makyng ii ſtryngs[8] of hyeren, ii thymbles And renggs, — — —	0	4	8
Itm. payd to *Wyllm brown*, for canvys and lopys, ——	0	0	5
Itm. payd to *Wylm Toleye*, for makyng ye cortynes, ——	0	0	8
Itm. payd to *John Sharppe*, for makyng the curtyng ſtryngs,	0	0	4
Itm. payd to *Alyxand*^{r} *hollnett*, of Donyngton, for ſettyng on the hyern Warke, & cov^{s}yng[9] of ye cruſifyxe & ye dome, to mett & Wayg^{s}, —— —— ——	0	0	6
Itm. payd to *John butler*, for makyng hyern pymys to ſett candylſtycks on, & for ſtayis, —— —— ——	0	1	4
Itm. to *Alyſon Randall*, for ſcoweryng ye candylſtyks, ——	0	0	4
Itm. for bred And halle, And for nayles, ——	0	0	2½
Itm. payd to *Ric. Rygatt*, for iiii^{c} redd[10], ——	0	4	4
Itm. payd to *Thomas Deconſon*, for ii^{c} rede, ——	0	2	0
Itm. payd to *Edmond howſon*, for ii^{c} redd, —— —	0	2	0

[1] Half a week. [2] Ale. [3] Q. *Great* bell.

[4] Though we find the liquor ale ſo frequently mentioned, no quantity being noted, we cannot aſcertain its price at that time.

[5] To ſupport their ſeveral images.

[6] Q. pullies and keys; *purlles* is placed with a lock, p. 225.

[7] See p. 221, note [2]. [8] Strings of iron probably mean the curtain rods or iron wires.

[9] Q. *doom* or judgement. See before, p. 222, note [2]. Theſe ſacred images and paintings perhaps were only exhibited on the more ſolemn occaſions: we find charges for curtains, which probably concealed them in common, as was the caſe with the paintings on the walls of Hungerford chapel at Saliſbury, in Lent time. (Dugd. Bar. vol. II. p. 209.)

[10] 400 ſheaves of reed for thatching. The preſent price of reed per 100 is from 10s. to 12s.

	£.	s.	d.
Itm. payd to *Edmond leche*, the thakkar, of Donyngton, And his ii men, for thakyng viii days, to y^{r} Wagg, — —	0	5	1
Itm. to *margarett cartar*, for y^{r} bord, — —	0	5	1
Itm. payd to *Rog^{r} margband*, for makyng herth [1], & drawyng it to the howse, — — — —	0	0	4
Itm. payd for the thacke roppe [2], —— ——	0	0	9
Itm. payd to *John Cressey*, for daubyng and Walyng, ——	0	0	4
Itm. payd to *Antony*, for drawyng erth, — —	0	0	1
Itm. payd to *Agnes bawnne*, for Wesshyng of Awt^{r} clowys to Well [3] & od^{r} of ye churchis, — — — —	0	0	3

paymēts An^{o} dm̄. 1533.

	£.	s.	d.
first payd to *Agnes Bawnne*, for Wesshyng, ——	0	0	2
Itm. payd to *Bryan*, the plomar, for mendyng the Brocke, A kestyng [4] Webbes of ledd to ye makyng of the Bell Wyndows, & cov'yng part of the northe hylde, & Workyng ye same, —	1	14	4
Itm. payd to the seyd *Bryan*, for iii^{l} di. Saud^{r}, ——	0	1	2
Itm. payd to the same *Bryan*, for Sawdyng the leeds of ye revestry And od^{r} plac^{s} of ye rooffe, And hyld of the churche, ——	0	0	6
Itm. payd to my lord [5] of Swynneshed abbe, for fewell toward the shottyng [6] of ye leed Webbys, —— ——	0	2	8
Itm. payd to *Thomas Dekonson*, in pt. of his Waigs all ye mony that We recevyd of M. *Wolm^{r}* to say, ——	2	3	4
Itm. payd for Nayles to ye bell Wyndos, ——	0	1	2
Itm. payd to *Agnes bawnne*, for Weshyng, — —	0	0	1
Itm. payd to *Robt.* for glasyng, to his Wayg and bord, —	0	4	0
Itm. payd to *Symon moyn*, for hangyng ye Saintts bell, to meytt and Waygs, —— ——	0	0	8
Itm. payd to *John Butler*, for makyng Wark to ye grett bell and for makyng i hespe and staple to ye north dore, ——	0	0	7
Itm. payd to *Agnes bawne*, fo Weshyng, —— —	0	0	3
Itm. payd to *John Sharppe*, for makyng belstryngs, ——	0	0	5

Sum 4^{l}. 9^{s}. 4^{d}.

[1] Making common walling mortar for the walls, and ridge of, perhaps, the vicarage house.

[2] Thatching string.

[3] Washing altar clothes belonging to the church of *Well* and other churches.

[4] Casting sheets of lead, &c.

[5] My Lord Abbot; it seems Swineshead abbey had fire-wood to spare for sale.

[6] Shotting the bells or lead, I find, is synonymous with casting. See before *passim*. Or, when applied to bell strings, as in the next page, it may mean simply *making*.

An^{o}

An° dm̄ 1534 paymēts.

	£.	s.	d.
ffyrst payd to *Symon moyn*, for makyng ye church yatte ye same meddyng,	0	2	8
Itm. payd for his bord & to his Wayge,	0	0	8
Itm. payd to *John butler*, for mēdyng ye yern Warke 1d. Itm. for nayles 2d.	0	0	3
Itm. to *gorge mattsey*, for medyng ye church Walle,	0	0	1
Itm. to *Agnes bawne*, for Wesshyng,	0	0	2
Itm. payd to *John Sharppe*, for makyng ye lytel belstryngs,	0	0	1
Itm. payd to *Thorppe* And *Thom^s^*, both of Swynneshed, for Wat[1] rett hemp,	0	5	2
Itm. payd to *John Dekynne*, for makyng ye seid hempe,	0	2	6
Itm. payd to *John Sharpe*, for makyng the lytyll belstryngs,	0	0	3
Itm. to *Agnes bawne*, for Wesshyng,	0	0	3
Itm. payd to *Willm hulle*, carvar, for makyng the gorge[2] & the dragonne,	0	8	8
Itm. payd for nayles And yern warke to ye gorges,	0	1	4½
Itm. payd for the beyne[3] to the same,	0	1	4
Itm. payd at the erlis[4] gywyng of ye gorges,	0	1	8
Itm. payd to *harye Dayles*, for shottyng belstryngs,	0	0	1
Itm. payd to ye Smythe of Swynneshed, for on Sneke[5] to ye churche dour,	0	0	6
Itm. for a lokk and purlis to the bell,	0	0	1
Itm. payd to *John Cressey*, for makyng ye Indiffe[6],	0	0	3

Sum 1^l^. 6^s^. 0½^d^.

The Account of *John Redwarre* Xrest And *Edmond howson*, Churche Wardons of *Wygtoft*, mayd ye xxvi day of marche, Wyche Was than good fryday, in the yer of o^r^ lord god M^l^CCCCCXXXV. When as then ye afforseyd *John* and *Edmond*, before namyd church Wardons, hath mayde a full Countt by for ye Pyche, of all man^r^ of receytts and paymēts done, had, And Wrytton in y^is^ boke in o^r^ tyme: And has elect As now at y^is^ Account to be churche Wardons *Edmond howson* And *Rog^r^ Maye*, Into whose hands ys delyv'ed ye churche goods.

	£.	s.	d.
M^d^. y^t^ all thyngs Accountyd at ye seyd Account y^r^ is owyng unto *John* And *Edmond howson*,	0	5	0

[1] Here must have been a considerable quantity of hempe; it is called watrett or watered hemp from being soaked in water a proper time before it will properly peel, or rett, as they call it.

[2] The St. George and the Dragon.

[3] This is probably bey*me* or *beam*.

[4] Q. at the Earl's giving of the George: though what earl was the donor I cannot tell.

[5] Hinge or some iron plating to ornament the door.

[6] I cannot conjecture what this word means.

Receyts receyved by *Edmond howson* And *Rog^{r} maye*, church Wardons, An^{o} 1535.

(Here follows a list of ninety-three inhabitants, with their contributions, from 1d. to 30s.)

	£.	s.	d.
Itm. recevyd of ye plowght lyght, — —	1	6	8
Itm. of Esthorpe lyght, — — —	0	13	4
Itm. kyrchowse maylyght, — —	0	13	4
Itm. of the hoggnes lyght, — —	1	6	8
Itm. of the yongmenis lyght, — — —	0	10	0
Itm. of *Symon Straiker*, for rent, — —	0	2	4
Itm. receyved of m^{r}is [1] *kyme*, — —	0	8	4
Itm. of the seyd maist^{r}es *kyme*, for his beriall, —	0	6	8
Itm. of *agnes maye*, for ye beriall of hir hosband, —	0	6	8
Itm. of *Symon Straiker*, for his howsse, — —	0	2	4
Itm. Borowed of *Robart park*, — — —	1	0	0

Sum Recvyd wth ye Contribut^{s} 22^{l}. 13^{s}. 10^{d}.

Paymēts layd forth for ye churche Warke by *Edmond howson*, and *Roger maye*, churche Wardons.

	£.	s.	d.
First, payd to ꝑ *John Redwarre* and *Edmond howson*, that they War howyng [2] at ye last account, —	0	5	0
Itm. payd to *Robt.* the plome' of Spalding, —	0	2	4
Itm. to *Ric. Robynson*, for h'yng [3] hym, —	0	1	3
Itm. to *Robt. Cony*, of Swynneshed, carn' for mendyng ye grett bell Wele & the second, —	0	1	9
Itm. payd for nayles 2*d*. Itm. payd for a replevy [4] 2*s*. 4*d*.	0	2	6
Itm. for ye mett of ye catell 4*d*. Itm. payd to M. *irbye* [5] 3*s*. 4*d*.	0	3	8
Itm. payd to *Robt. Robynson*, ye plomm^{r}, —	0	1	2
Itm. paid for a M. ot 2 peny nayles to ye stepull, —	0	1	2
Itm. to *Wm. Gybson*, wryght, for makyng the Creidyll [6] to mett and wayg, —	0	1	0
Itm. for bord [7] to ye same creidyll, —	0	1	1
Itm. for Expens don on *Jaymes*, ye plomm', & of *Thos Wyttyne*, Wryght, — —	0	0	4

[1] Of Mrs. Kyme for her husband's burial.

[2] Were owing or indebted. Money they had expended above their receipts.

[3] I conjecture this may be hiring hym.

[4] Was this replevin for the release of cattle in the fold or pound? one might think the cattle were common property: if private, why in this account?

[5] A surname: Irbye.

[6] I know not what the "Creidyll" means, unless it be that machine in which workmen are drawn up to repair churches.

[7] Deal or wood.

Itm.

	£.	s.	d.
Itm. Expendd at lyncoln in byeng clappall borde[1] for the ſtepull,	0	0	8
Itm. in Expens & caryeng the leed from lynwood unto Swynneſhed,	0	0	10
Itm. for 2 ⊖[2] of 2 peny & di. nails, ——	0	0	5
Itm. payd to *Raynold*, the charſe[3], of boſton, for ii m[l] of 2 peny nayles, —— ——	0	2	4
Itm. to maiſt'es *heyſſell*, for i m[l] nayles. —	0	1	6
Itm. for 2 m[l] of 2 peny nailes, bought at Sleyforth[4],	0	2	2
Itm. for vi peny neyles, ——	0	0	4
Itm. for a i thowſand of 2 peny nailes, ——	0	1	4
Itm. paid for clappall borde, ——	0	10	0
Itm. for Carryeng the ſame borde to y[e] Wat[r] ſyde, And for tolle and for y[e] caryage to langrake[5] & home, —	0	3	3
Itm. paid to *Symon moon*, to his Waigs, & his nands for iiii days,	0	5	4
Itm. paid to *Thomas Whyttney*, to his Waigs, and his nand for iii days, —— ——	0	3	4
Itm. paid to *Thomas Cart'* Wyffe for all y[s] borde, —	0	6	3
Itm. paid for y[e] dyn[r] of *Jamys*, y[e] plomm', & *Thomrs Wyttney*,	0	0	4
Itm. paid to *Robt.* the plommer, to his Waigs, ——	0	10	0
Itm. to *Ric. Robynſon*, for fnyng y[e] ſeid plomm[r],	0	2	0
Itm. to *Robt. poſtler*, ——	0	1	0
Itm. to *Alexand[r] Devy*, Smythe, for makyng yherne Warke to y[e] bells, —— ——	0	0	6
Itm. payd to *Thomas Cart'* Wyffe, for the Wryght's bord,	0	13	2
Itm. for caryeng ſand, And beryng ſand And leed up of y[e] ſtepull,	0	0	6
Itm. paid to *Tho[s] Whyttney*, for xv days his ſelffe, And his nand vi dais for y[r] Waygs, ——	0	10	0
Itm. to *Symon moon*, and his nands for y[r] Waygs for xv days,	0	12	0
Itm. for caryeng the leed frome lynwood to Swynneſhed,	0	7	8
Itm. payd for i Wynddyng[6] roppe, ——	0	2	4
Itm. payd to *Jaymes*, y[e] pomm[r], iiii mk[s][7], ——	2	13	4
Itm. to *Nicholas betts*, for mẽdyng the Wyndow, And Workyng about y[e] ſtepull for ii days to mett and Waige, ——	0	1	2
Itm. paid to *Rog[r] Maye*, for byeng And carryeng iii lood of ſand,	0	6	0
Itm. paid to *John Walgat*, for his howſe, ——	0	4	4
Itm. to *Thomas Dekonſon* Wyff, for makyng of i rogytt[8],	0	0	4
Itm. for drawyng up leed unto y[e] church rooffe, —	0	0	4
Itm. paid to *Stayker* for Warke, ——	0	0	8

[1] Clapboard. [2] This is the character for C. or centum, 200 and half of nails.
[3] Probably an ironmonger or nailer. [4] Sleaford, about 12 miles diſtant.
[5] Now Lanrick Ferry over the Witham, about 10 miles diſtant. It ſeems the "clappall "borde" was bought at Lincoln; they paid for it carrying to the water ſide there with the uſual toll. I imagine it came by water to the ferry, and then by land carriage.
[6] This was probably to wind up the lead for covering the roof. [7] Four marks.
[8] Q. *rochet*, part of the prieſt's habit.

	£.	s.	d.
Itm. paid to M.[1] *Robt buſſye*, knyght, for ii food'[2] of leed,	9	6	8
Itm. paid to *Jaymes*, the plommr, for ſhottyng[3] ye leed of ye medill ild, —— ——	1	6	8
Itm. for puryeng[4] the leed to met & Waig, ——	0	11	10
Itm. to *Robt. Cony*, of Swynneſhed for makyng ye ſecond bell Whele, —— ——	0	2	4
Itm. to *John Tyler*, for caryeng the ſecond bell Whele to Swynneſhed, & *Agnes baune*, for weſshyng, —	0	0	4
Itm. to *Jaymes*, the plommr, ——	0	13	4
Itm. to *Agnes bawne*, for Weſshyng, ——	0	0	3
Itm. paid to *Rogr maie*, for tyng[5] Waige yt he payd,	1	4	0
Itm. paid to *Robt. park* yt we borowed, —	1	0	0
Itm. payd to *Symon moon*, Wryght, for makyng of ye grete bell Whele, — —	0	5	8

Sm.[6] ſolut. 24l. 15s. 9d.

The expenc And payment layd forth by *John aliſon*, church maiſtr, for the bell ſchottyng at Nottynggam.

Firſt, for ye bell clapper, ——	0	0	6
Itm. for the ſhoyng[7] of vi horſes, and for removis, —	0	1	8
Itm. payd at Bottysforth for ſope'[8] And brekfaſt, —	0	0	10
Itm. payd for the gryſſe[9] of 9 horſis, —	0	0	8
Itm. at Notyngham for the mett of ye ſaid horſis from Wedonſdaye at none unto Thurſdaye at none, ——	0	1	6
Itm. for theer dyn'es, — —	0	0	6
Itm. for drynk to ye hands at caſtyng ye bell, —	0	0	4
Itm. for theer ſopper at night, & dyn' at thurſday at none,	0	1	0
Itm. for makyng of ye obligacon[10], —	0	0	4
Itm. for theer drynkyng by ye Way, to Ward And fro Ward,	0	0	4
Itm. at thurſday at nyght at potysforth[11] for yr Sopper,	0	0	6
Itm. for yr horſis mett 8*d*. for *John Sna'd* breakfaſt 2*d*.	0	0	10
Itm. for bryngyng ye bell Wele from boſton, —	0	0	2

9s. 2d.

[1] I think they mean this for Mr. though improperly applied to a knight. This Sir Robert Huſſye, it ſeems, was a merchant; whether he lived at Lincoln or Boſton does not appear.

[2] A fodder of lead differs in weight in different places. In London it is 19 hundred and an half; at Newcaſtle 21; in Derbyſhire 24.

[3] Caſting the lead for covering the high roof over the middle aile.

[4] I cannot ſay what this means, unleſs it be putting or adjuſting it on.

[5] Qu.

[6] *Summum ſolutum.* Total paid 24l. 15s. 9d. It appears they had done ſome heavy repairs this year; perhaps in great part new leaded the church.

[7] Shoeing, and removing the ſhoes.

[8] Supper.

[9] Graſs for nine horſes.

[10] The agreement with the bell-founder.

[11] *Botſford*, as before, p. 228.

Theys

	£.	s.	d.
Theys be ye refeytts Receyd by me *Alane lawys*, church Wardons of ye chyrche of wygtoft, wt *John Proct'*, In ye yere of our lord god M CCCCC XLIII.			
Thys ys ye Cownt maide by us *John Proct'* & *Alane lawys*, Chyrch Wardons of the chyrche of Wygtoft, ye xxiii day of marche, ye yere of or lord god M CCCCC XLIII.			
In pmis, received of *agnes lufbery*, for ye beqwech [1] of *John tuly* & Wyff, — ——	0	13	4
Itm. of *fimon ftraker*, fugft [2] redd' ——	0	4	8
Itm. for ye beqwech of *Richard ftork*, ——	0	1	0
Sum 19s.			
Thes be ye expenfes layd forth by us *John Proctr* & *Alayn laws*, chyrch Wardons.			
In pmis, for weefyng of ye chyrche Cloyffe, ——	0	0	4
Itm. for a ftone & a halffe of femull for ye bell ftryngs,	0	0	8
Itm. for makyng off ym to *Willm deyn*, ——	0	0	7
Itm. to *ftephin Smyth*, for mendyng ye loke of ye chyrche dore,	0	0	7
Itm. for Wefchyng of ye chyrche Cloffe Agunffe [3] eft,	0	1	0
Itm. for iiii yards of fayr [4] clothe, ——	0	1	7
Itm. to *Wyllm mafon*, for mendyng of ye gudgons, & for nayles,	0	0	1½
Summ total 4s. 10d. ob.			
Alane lawes, ye chyrche Wardon of ye chyrche of Wygtoft, ye yaer of or lord god M CCCCC XLIII. And takyn to hym *John atkinfon*.			
In p̃mis deliv'ed to ye faid *John atkynfon* & *Alane lawis*,	0	13	0
It. Receved of *Rychard perfe*, for rent, ——	0	2	4
Itm. Refeived of *gorge Roftle*, for the buryng of *John tomfon*, & for ye beqwefte of ye fame *John* to ye chyrche, —	1	6	7
Sum 2l. 1s. 11d.			
Expenfes payd by us *John atkynfon* & *Alane lawys*, chyrche wardons of wygtoft,			
In p̃mis, to *Wyllm mafon*, for mendyng of ye holy water ftoke [5],	0	0	4
Itm. to *herre dale*, for cov'yng of ye gravis befor ye chanfell dore, And for mendyng of ye chyrche Waall, ——	0	2	4
Itm. paid to *John vebyll*, of ye inventorye of ye veftre,	0	0	3

[1] Bequeft. [2] I am at a lofs here.

[3] For wafhing the church clothes or linen againft Eafter.

[4] This probably means cerecloth.

[5] The veffel containing the holy water, before called *vatte*, p. 209.

Itm.

	£.	s.	d.
Itm. yt *John atkynſon* ſpent at boſton, ———	0	0	8
Itm. paid for A cytacon [1] for *John hulle*, ———	0	0	4
Itm. paide for brede & Ale yt we dranke at ye yicarige Wan we maide or boke, ——— ———	0	0	1½
Itm. paid for drynke Wan We Were at Swynſhed to change ye bell, — —	0	0	2
Itm. to *ſtevyn Smythe*, for ye bell Clapper, & for other yrne Warke, — —	0	0	7
Itm. to *nicoles bell*, for hengyng ye bell, and for Ale & brede at yt tyme, ——— ———	0	0	5
Itm. to *henri dayl*, for caryng ye bell to ye abbay, & bryngyng ye other home, ——— ———	0	0	2
Itm. paid to *Wyllm bown*, for A lyne to ye fontt [2],	0	0	7
Itm. to *thoms*, ye Wryght, for A pulle & for dryvyng of ym,	0	0	2
Itm. to *ſtephin ſmythe*, for a boltt of erne 1*d.* for Weſchyng cloſſe 2*d.* — —	0	0	3
Itm. to ye Seyd *ſtephin*, for mendyng ye herne Warke in ye Rode loft, — —	0	0	4
It. paid payd the brotherer [3] of boſton, for makyng of one cope and ii veſtments 20*s.* Itm. paid for a lanthorne 6*d.* —	1	0	6
Itm. paid to the ſeym brotherer for ii hokes for ye ſeym veſtments,	0	8	0
Itm. to *nicolas bell*, for dreſſyng ye rode lofte, and for nayls,	0	0	2½
Itm. to *herre dayl*, for pavyng ye graffe [4] of *John tomſon*, & for mendyng ye chyrche wall & ye yayt, ———	0	0	3½
Itm. to *thom.* Wryght, for mendyng ye chyrche yayte, & for nayls,	0	0	7½
Itm. for Wode to ye chyrche yayte, ———	0	0	5
Itm. paid to *Agnes Sayler*, for Weſhyng ye chyrche clothes,	0	1	1
Sum tot. laid out 1l. 18s. 3d.			
[5] Et ſic comput' computand' et Alloc Allocand' adhuc in manibus . . . . ——— —	1	4	9
Of the whiche ſeid 1*l.* 4*s.* 9*d.* *Alan laws* haith rec. 3*s.* 4*d.* & *John Atkynſon* for money yt he lent to ye Town when ye ſteeple was ſnyled [6], ——— ———	1	0	0

[1] Citation.

[2] Line and pully to draw up the cover of the font.

[3] The broiderer, or rather the embroiderer.

[4] Grave.

[5] i. e. All accounts thus made up and allowances allowed, remains in hand the ſum of 1l. 4s. 9d.

[6] It is not clear what *ſnyled* means.

EXPENCES of the BARRIERS in WEST-SMITHFIELD, 1524.

THE following record in the Exchequer afcertains the curious combat alluded to by Shakefpear, and mentioned by our Chroniclers, between an armourer and his fervant, 25 Henry VI. in which the armourer was overcome and killed, as related by feveral of our Chroniclers.

Fabian does not mention it under this year, though he gives the fame fheriffs as in the record; nor is it in Hall: but Grafton fays, "This yere an armourer's fervaunte of London appeled his mafter of treafon, which offered to be tried by battaile. At the day affigned the friends of the mafter brought him malmefye and aquavite to comfort him withall, but it was the caufe of his and their difcomfort: for he poured in fo much, that when he came into the place in Smithfelde where he fhould fight, both his witte and ftrength fayled him; and fo he being a tall and hardie perfonage, overladed with hotte drinkes, was vanquifhed of his fervaunt, being but a cowarde and wretch, whofe body was drawen to Tyborne, and there hanged and behedded." P. 594.

"In the fame yeare alfo a certeine armourer was appeached of treafon by a fervaunte of his owne. For profe whereof a daie was given them to fight in Smithfield, infomuch that in conflict the faid armourer was overcome and flaine, but yet by mifgoverning of himfelf; for on the morow, when he fhould come to the field frefh and fafting, his neighbours came to him, and gave him wine and ftrong drinke in fuch exceffive fort, that he was therewith diftempered and reeled as he went, and fo was flain without guilt. As for his falfe fervant, he lived not long unpunifhed, for being convict of felonie in court of affife, he was judged to be hanged, and fo was at Tiburne." Holinfhed, II. 626.

"John David appeached his mafter, William Catur, an armourer, dwelling in St. Dunfton's parifh, in Fleteftrete, of treafon; and a day being affigned them to fight in Smitfield, the mafter being well beloved, was fo cherifhed by his friends, and plied fo in wine, that, being therewith overcome, was alfo unluckily flaine by his fervant; but that falfe fervant (for he falfely accufed his mafter) lived not long unpunifhed; for he was after hanged at Tyborne for felony. Let fuch falfe accufers note this example, and looke for no better end, without fpeedie repentance. Myfelfe have had the like fervant, that likewife accufed me of many articles: he liveth yet; but hath hardly efcaped hanging fince. God make him penitent." Stowe's Annals, p. 383.

Shakefpeare does not adhere to hiftorical verity: (Second Part of K. Henry VI. Act I. Sc. III. p. 320. Ed. Johnfon and Steevens, 1786.)

Peter. Againft my mafter, Thomas Horner, for faying, That the duke of York was rightful heir to the crown.

Q. Mar. What fay'ft thou? Did the duke of York fay, he was rightful heir to the crown?

E e *Peter.*

Peter. That my miſtreſs was? No, forſooth: my maſter ſaid, That he was; and that the king was an uſurper.

Suf. Who is there?—Take this fellow in, and ſend for his maſter with a purſuivant preſently:—we'll hear more of your matter before the king.

[*Exit Peter, guarded.*

Enter Horner the armourer, and his man Peter, guarded.

Suf. Becauſe here is a man accus'd of treaſon:
Pray God, the duke of York excuſe himſelf!

York. Doth any one accuſe York for a traitor?

K. Henry. What mean'ſt thou, Suffolk? tell me: What are theſe?

Suf. Pleaſe it your majeſty, this is the man
That doth accuſe his maſter of high treaſon:
His words were theſe:—"That Richard, duke of York,
"Was rightful heir unto the Engliſh crown;
"And that your majeſty was an uſurper."

K. Henry. Say, man, were theſe thy words?

Arm. An't ſhall pleaſe your majeſty, I never ſaid nor thought any ſuch matter: God is my witneſs, I am falſely accus'd by the villain.

Peter. By theſe ten bones, my lords, [*holding up his hands*] he did ſpeak them to me in the garret one night, as we were ſcouring my lord of York's armour.

York. Baſe dunghill villain, and mechanical,
I'll have thy head for this thy traitor's ſpeech:—
I do beſeech your royal majeſty,
Let him have all the rigour of the law.

Arm. Alas, my lord, hang me, if ever I ſpake the words. My accuſer is my prentice; and when I did correct him for his fault the other day, he did vow upon his knees he would be even with me: I have good witneſs of this; therefore, I beſeech your majeſty, do not caſt away an honeſt man for a villain's accuſation.

K. Henry. Uncle, what ſhall we ſay to this in law?

Glo. This doom, my lord, if I may judge.
Let Somerſet be regent o'er the French,
Becauſe in York this breeds ſuſpicion:
And let theſe have a day appointed them
For ſingle combat, in convenient place;
For he hath witneſs of his ſervant's malice:
This is the law, and this duke Humphrey's doom.

K. Henry. Then be it ſo. My lord of Somerſet,
We make your grace lord regent o'er the French.

Som. I humbly thank your royal majeſty.

Arm. And I accept the combat willingly.

Peter. Alas, my lord, I cannot fight; for God's ſake, pity my caſe! the ſpight of a man prevaileth againſt me. O, Lord have mercy upon me! I ſhall never be able to fight a blow: O Lord, my heart!—

Glo. Sirrah, or you muſt fight, or elſe be hanged.

K. Henry.

K. Henry. Away with them to priſon: and the day
Of combat ſhall be the laſt of the next month.—
Come, Somerſet, we'll ſee thee ſent away.

[*Flouriſh. Exeunt.*

Act II. Scene III. p. 347.

York. Lords, let him go.—Pleaſe it your majeſty,
This is the day appointed for the combat;
And ready are the appellant and defendant,
The armourer and his man, to enter the liſts,
So pleaſe your highneſs to behold the fight.
Q. Margaret. Ay, good my lord; for purpoſely therefore
Left I the court, to ſee this quarrel try'd.
K. Henry. O'God's name, ſee the liſts and all things fit;
Here let them end it, and God defend the right!
York. I never ſaw a fellow worſe beſted,
Or more afraid to fight, than is the appellant,
The ſervant of this armourer, my lords.

Enter at one door the armourer and his neighbours, drinking to him ſo much that he is drunk; and he enters with a drum before him, and his ſtaff with a ſand-bag faſtened to it; and at the other door enters his man, with a drum and a ſand-bag, and prentices drinking to him.

1 *Neigh.* Here, neighbour Horner, I drink to you in a cup of ſack; And fear not, neighbour, you ſhall do well enough.

2 *Neigh.* And here, neighbour, here's a cup of charneco *.

3 *Neigh.* And here's a pot of good double beer, neighbour: drink and fear not your man.

Arm. Let it come, i'faith, and I'll pledge you all; and a fig for Peter!

1 *Pren.* Here, Peter, I drink to thee; and be not afraid.

2 *Pren.* Be merry, Peter, and fear not thy maſter: fight for credit of the prentices.

Peter. I thank you all: drink, and pray for me, I pray you; for, I think, I have taken my laſt draught in this world.—Here, Robin, an if I die, I give thee my apron;—and, Will, thou ſhalt have my hammer:—and here, Tom, take all the money that I have.—O Lord, bleſs me, I pray God! for I am never able to deal with my maſter, he hath learnt ſo much fence already.

Sal. Come, leave your drinking, and fall to blows.—Sirrah, what's thy name?

Peter. Peter, forſooth.

Sal. Peter! what more?

Peter. Thump.

Sal. Thump! then ſee thou thump thy maſter well.

* A Spaniſh ſweet wine.

Arm. Mafters, I am come hither, as it were, upon my man's inftigation, to prove him a knave, and myfelf an honeft man: and touching the duke of York,—I will take my death, I never meant him any ill, nor the king, nor the queen; And therefore, Peter, have at thee with a downright blow, as Bevis of Southampton fell upon Afcapart.

York. Difpatch:—this knave's tongue begins to double.
Sound trumpets, alarum to the combatants.

[*They fight, and Peter ftrikes him down.*

Arm. Hold, Peter, hold! I confefs, I confefs treafon. [*Dies.*

York. Take away his weapon:—Fellow, thank God, and the good wine in thy mafter's way.

Peter. O God! have I overcome mine enemy in this prefence?
O Peter, thou haft prevailed in right!

K. Henry. Go, take hence that traitor from our fight;
For, by his death we do perceive his guilt:
And God, in juftice, hath revealed to us
The truth and innocence of this poor fellow,
Which he had thought to have murder'd wrongfully.—
Come fellow, follow us for thy reward. [*Exeunt.*

HENRICUS

HENRICUS Dei gracia Rex Angl' & Franc' & dñs Hibn' Thes' & Baronbs suis de sccio saltm. Cum Johes Davy nup appelat' in cur' nrã militari coram constabulario & marescall Angl' Willm Catour de London armerer de quibusdam pdictionibus p ipsum Willm erga personam nostram fact' & imaginat' unde partes predicte in duellum coram pfat' constabulario & marescall' in eadem cur' se posuerunt, ac tricesimus primus dies Januarii prox' futur' ad duellum illud in loco de Westsmythfeld in suburbiis civitatis nostre London dirimend' & pficiend' p cur' pdictam datus sit & assignatus, & p bre nostrum pcepim' vicecomitibus, civitatis predicte & com' Middx quod quasdam listas & barruras de maeremio satisfortes & in omnibus sufficientes in loco pdicto ad diem pdictam ex causa pdicta nostris sumptibus & expensis, videlicet, de primis denariis de firma civitatis & com' pdictorum ac de exitibus, pficuis, revencionibus, & aliis commoditatibus de eisdem pvenientibus erigi, construi & fieri ac humũ sive aream infra listas pdictas cum zabulo & arena plene & competent' cooperiri facient; Ita quod impedimentum sive offendiculum aliquod p lapides seu alit' infra easdem listas ad diem pdictum non eveniat nec contingat quovis modo. Et ultius locum nob competentem & statui nostro regio convenientem ibidem erga diem pdictum nostris sumptibus & expensis pdictis de dictis primis denariis de firma, exitibus pficuis revencionibus & aliis commoditatibus pdictis p avisamentum carissimi consanguinei nostri Johannis ducis Norff, marescalli Angl' construi, erigi, & pparari facient nos de omnibus & singulis pecuniarum summis quas circa pmissa exponi & expendi facient eisdem vicecomitibus in compoto suo de officio suo vicecomitum civitatis & com' pdictorum ac secundum nostram debitam allocacionem habere facient statuto de laboratoribus in contrarium edito non obstant' vob mandamus quod viso mandato nostro pdicto omnes pecuniarum summas quas vob p sacrum eorumdem vicecomitum aut deputatorum suorum rationabilit' constare potit eosdem vicecomites circa pmissa ptextu mandati nostri pdicti solvisse et applicasse eisdem vicecomitibus de dictis primis denariis de firma exitibus pficuis revencionibus & aliis comoditatibus in compoto suo de officio vicecomitum civitatis & com' pdictorum nobis ad sum nostram pdictum reddend' debite allocetis statuto de laboratoribus incontra edito aut aliquibus donis concessionibus annuitatibus sive assignacionibus p nos seu aliquem pgenitorum de firma, exitibus, pficuis, revencionibus, & commoditatibus pdictis pcipiend' alicui persone pantea factis sive concessis in aliquo non obstant'. T. meipso apud Westm' 25 die Novemb' anno r. n. 25°.

p breve de privato sigillo, STURGEON.

London'

London' } Particule comp' Roberti Horn & Galfr. Boleyn nuper vic' London' &
Midd' } Midd' de denar' p̱ ipſos ſolut' ſuper factur' conſtruct' & erect' liſtarum & barrur' in loco de Weſtſmythfeld, London', ad duellum ibidem inter Johannem Davy, appellatorē, & Willm̄ Catour, armerer London' de diverſis p̱diccionibus p̱ ipſum Willm̄ factis, dirimend' & p̃ficiend' p̱ breve R. de magno ſig' noſtro dat 25° die Nov' a. 25. eiſdem nuper vic' direct' & pen' has particulas rem' ut infra.

Theſe ben ye parcell and ye coſtes aftyr wretyid ya was don in Smythfield for the Barreres, and for the makyng of the feld, the whiche parcell and coſtis was don and payde from ye .... day of .... in ye 25th yer of Kyng Henri ye Sexte, into ye .... day of .... in ye ſaid yer, by *Robert Horne* and *Geffray Boleyn*, ſchrevys of ye cite of London, at ye comaundement of oure Sov'aygne Lord ye Kyng.

Wednyſday. £. s. d.

Inprimis, paid to 28 laboreres for to feche ye barrers from Weſtmynſter, for 1 day ev'y laborer 4*d.* a day, ſum 9*s.* 4*d.*

Alſo paid to 12 laborers for 1 day to dygge holys in Smythfeld, ev'y laborer per day 5*d.* ſum 5*s.*

Alſo paid to 2 carpenters for 1 day in Smythfeld, ev'y man 8½*d.* ſum 17*d.*

Alſo paid for 9 cartys for to carie the barrers from Weſtmynſter, ſum 3*s.*

Alſo paid for ye hyryng of 4 barres of iron to make holys in the grownd, 4*d.*

Alſo paid for the hyryng of 2 barwes 1 day in Smythfield, 3*d.*

Alſo paid for pakthred yat ſame day, 1*d.*

} 0 19 5

Thurſday.

Alſo paid 16 laborers for 1 day to labor in Smythfelde, ev'y pec' 5*d.* ſum 6*s.* 8*d.*

Alſo paid for a carte to carye away ye ſnowe owte of ye feld for 1 day 12*d.*

Alſo paid to 7 carpenteres for 1 day, to ſette up ye barrers, ev'y man 8½*d.* ſum 4*s.* 11½*d.*

} 0 12 7½

Fryday.

Alſo paid to 14 laborers for 1 day to labor in Smythfeld, ev'y man 5*d.* ſum 5*s.* 10*d.*

Alſo paid to 7 carpenters for 1 day to ſette up ye barrers, ev'y man 8½*d.* ſum 4*s.* 11½*d.*

Alſo paid for 21 barrys, ſum 6*s.* 8*d.*

} 0 17 5½

Sa'tday.

	£.	s.	d.
Sat'day. Alſo paid to 4 laboreres in Smythfeld for a day, ev'y laborer 5*d*. ſum 20*d*. Alſo paid to 4 carpenters in Smythfeld for one day, ev'y man 8½*d*. ſum 2*s*. 10*d*. Alſo paid for 300 fete of elmyn bord, per le 100 2*s*. 6*d*. ſum 7*s*. 6*d*. Alſo paid for 100 nayles of 5 penny nayle, ſum 5*d*. Alſo paid for 100 nayles of 6 penny nayle, ſum 6*d*. Alſo paid for a penyworth of 10 penny nayle, ſum 1*d*. Alſo paid for a penyworth of 9 peny nayle, ſum 1*d*. Alſo paid for 2 barres of tymber, per ye ped 4*d*. ſum 8*d*. Alſo paid for 2 ſmale pecis of tymbyr, p'd ye ped 2*d*. ſum 4*d*. Alſo paid for ye cariage of ye ſame borde and tymbar, ſum 4*d*.	0	14	4
Monday. Alſo paid to 4 carpenteres for 1 day labor, ev'y man 8½*d*. ſum 2*s*. 10*d*. Alſo paid to 6 laborers for a daye's labor, ev'y man 4*d*. ſum 2*s*. Alſo paid for 100 naylles, per C. 6*d*. ſum 6*d*. Alſo paid for 5 pecis tymber, per C. ſum 8*d*. Alſo paid for ye carriage of poſtis, raylis, and tymber, 4*d*. ſum 4*d*.	0	6	4
Teweſday. Alſo paid to 7 carpenters for 1 day labor, ev'y man 8½*d*. ſum 4*s*. 11½*d*. Alſo paid to 6 laborers for 1 day labor, ev'y man 4*d*. ſum 2*s*. Alſo paid for 6 rafteris, per le pec' 3*d*. ſum 18*d*. Alſo paid for 300 fote of elmyn bord, per le C. 2*s*. 6*d*. ſum 7*s*. 6*d*. Alſo paid for 4 rafters, per ye pec' 2*d*. ſum 8*d*. Alſo paid for 100 five peny nayll, per C. 5*d*. ſum 5*d*. Alſo paid for 100 nayllys, per C. 6*d*. ſum 6*d*. Alſo paid for 3 pen'worth of 10 peny naylle, 3*d*. ſum 3*d*. Alſo paid for ye cariage of bordys and of rafteris 4*d*. ſum 4*d*. Alſo paid for ye cariage of poſtes and rayles 4*d*. ſum 4*d*.	0	18	5½

Thurſday

		£.	s.	d.
Thurſday.				
Alſo paid to 6 carpenters for a daye's labor, ev'y man 8½*d.*	ſum 4*s.* 3*d.*			
Alſo paid to 6 laboreres for a daye's labor, ev'y man 4*d.*	ſum 2*s.*			
Alſo paid for CC. nayles, 11*d.*	ſum 11*d.*			
Alſo paid for 2 penyworth of 10 peny nayll, 2*d.*	ſum 2*d.*			
Alſo paid for 3 rayles 12*d.*	ſum 12*d.*			
Alſo paid for 17 poſtes, per le poſt 15*d.*	ſum 21*s.* 3*d.*			
Alſo paid for 24 copyll barres, per le copyll 8*d.*	ſum 16*s.*	3	1	4
Alſo paid for 13 peces of oke tymber, per le pece 7½*d.*	ſum 8*s.* 1½*d.*			
Alſo paid for 2 peces of elmyn tymber, per le pece 12*d.*	ſum 2*s.*			
Alſo paid for C. of elmyn bordes, pec' 2*s.* 6*d.*	ſum 2*s.* 6*d.*			
Alſo paid for tymber to make of ſteppes 20*d.*	ſum 20*d.*			
Alſo paid for C. di. of latthes, 10*d.*	ſum 10*d.*			
Alſo paid for 100 lathe nayll, 7½*d.*	ſum 7½*d.*			
Friday.				
Alſo paid to 6 carpenters for a daye's labor, ev'y man 8½*d.*	ſum 4*s.* 3*d.*			
Alſo paid to a tyler,	ſum 4*d.*	0	5	6
Alſo paid for reſhes,	ſum 3*d.*			
Alſo paid for 4 rakes,	ſum 8*d.*			
Monday.				
Alſo paid to 6 laborers for a day's labor, ev'y man 4*d.*	ſum 2*s.*			
Alſo paid to 1 carpenter for a day's labor,	ſum 8½*d.*			
Alſo paid for a di. C. of 6 peny nayll,	ſum 3*d.*	0	3	6½
Alſo paid for 2 bordes,	ſum 5*d.*			
Alſo paid for traſsl',	ſum 2*d.*			
Tewyſday.				
Alſo paid to 18 laborers for di. a daye's labor, ev'y man 2*d.*	ſum 3*s.*			
Alſo paid to 2 carpenters for their labor,	ſum 8*d.*			
Alſo paid for naylles,	ſum 1*d.*			
Alſo paid for 168 lode of ſonde and gravell, the lode 4*d.*	ſum 56*s.*	2	19	9
Alſo paid for ye borde of *John Straunge*, ſergeaunt, and of *William Cok*, and *Nicholas Ybery*, yemen, for 14 days,				
Alſo paid to ye ſaid *John Straunge*, and to ye ſaid *William* and *Nicholas*, for their labor, and for kepping of ye feld on halidayes,				
*Alſo paid to officeres for watchyng of ye ded man in Smythfelde ye ſame daye and ye nyghte aftyr that ye bataill was doon, and for hors hyre for ye officeres at ye execution doying, and for the hangman's labor,	ſum 11*s.* 6*d.*	0	12	7
Alſo paid for ye cloth yat lay upon ye ded man in Smythfelde, 8*d.*				
Alſo paid for 1 pole and nayllis, and for ſettyng up of ye ſaid mannys hed on London-brigge,	8*d.*			
Sum total of yeſe forſaid ꝑcell		10	18	9

* The original of this curious article has lines croſſed over with a pen, becauſe not allowed by the barons of the Exchequer, as an expence allowed by the ſheriff.

Extracts from the Books of the Stationers' Company, between December 1554, and July 1557.

The chargis layde oute for our Corporation.

	£.	s.	d.
FYRSTE, for two tymes wrytinge of our boke before yt was ſygned be the Kynge and the Quene's Majeſtie's Highnes,	0	18	0
Item, for the ſyngned and the prevy ſeale,	6	6	8
Item, for the great ſeale,	8	9	0
Item, for the wrytynge and inrolynge,	3	0	0
Item, for wax, lace, and examenacion,	0	3	4
Item, to the clerkes for expedycion,	0	10	0
Item, for lymnynge and for the ſkyn,	1	0	0
The charges of our denner as foloweth, that is to ſaye:			
Item, payd for 18 doſyn of breade,	0	18	2
Item, payd for a barrell of ſtronge bere,	0	9	0
Item, payd for a barrel of dubble bere,	0	5	4
Item, payd for a ſtande of ale,	0	3	0
Item, payd for 20 galons of wyne,	1	0	0
Item, payd for 11 galons of Frenſhe wyne,	0	11	0
Item, payd 37 lb. of beffe,	0	4	7
Item, payd for 4 loynes of vele,	0	4	8
Item, payd for a quarter of vele,	0	2	0
Item, payd for 11 neckes of motton,	0	6	6
Item, payd for 2 loynes of motton,	0	2	0
Item, payd for 9 mary-bones,	0	2	4
Item, payd for 25 lb. of ſuette,	0	4	2
Item, payd for 38 punde of butter,	0	9	8
Item, payd for 2 freſhe ſamons,	1	3	2
Item, payd for 4 doſyn of chekyns,	1	0	1
Item, payd for 3 busſhells 3 peckes of flowre,	0	17	4
Item, payd for 20 pounde of cherys,	0	3	4
Item, payd for 20 capons of grayſe,	2	13	4
Item, payde for 20 capons to boyle,	1	6	8
Item, three capons of greſe,	0	9	0
Item, payd for 18 geſe,	1	4	0
Item payd for 3 geſe,	0	4	6
Item, payd for 3 doſyn of rabbetts,	0	10	6
Item, payd for 6 rabbetts,	0	1	10
Item, payd for 2 galons of creme,	0	2	8
Item, payd for bakynge of 20 paſtyes of venyſon,	0	1	8
Item, payd for bakynge of 16 chekyn pyes,	0	1	4

	£.	s.	d.
Item, payd for falte, — — —	0	1	0
Item, payd for venyger, — — —	0	1	0
Item, payd for vergis, — — —	0	1	1
Item, payd for mufterde, — — —	0	0	4
Item, payd for gofe buryes, — — —	0	0	10
Item, payd for a bafkett, — — — —	0	0	3
Item, payd for 10 dofyn of trenchers, — —	0	1	9
Item, three dofyn of ftone crufys, — —	0	3	0
Item, payd for tappes, — — — —	0	0	1
Item, payd for a pottle pycher, — —	0	0	2
Item, payd for 2 ftone potts, — —	0	0	2
Item, payd for packe thyrde, — — —	0	0	1
Item, payd for a hundreth of fagotts, — —	0	4	4
Item, payd halfe a thoufand of belletts, — —	0	4	4
Item, payd for 12 fackes of coles, — — —	0	7	6
Item, payd for flowres and bowes, — —	0	1	3
Item, payd for garlands, — — —	0	1	0
Item, payd for the carver, — — —	0	2	0
Item, payd to the minftrelles, — —	0	10	0
Item, payd to the buttlers, — —	0	6	8
Item, payd to the coke, — —	1	3	4
Item, payd to the under cokes to drink, —	0	0	3
Item, payd to the water berer, — —	0	3	10
Item, for 3 porters that caryed over meate, —	0	0	6
Item, payd to the fmythe, — —	0	0	2
Item, payd for the hyre of 3 garnefhe of veffell, —	0	2	0
Item, payd for a hundreth and 24 eggs, —	0	4	0
Item, payd for 2 ftrayners, — — —	0	0	8
The fpyfe as folowthe:			
Item, payd for 2 lb. and a quarter of pepper, —	0	6	0
Item, payd for a quarte of pounde cloves, —	0	1	4
Item, payd for 4 pounde of datts, — —	0	4	0
Item, payd for 5 punde of currans, — —	0	1	8
Item, payd for 24 pounde of prunys *, — —	0	3	8
Item, payd for fafferon, — — —	0	0	9
Item, payd for fynimon and gynger, — —	0	3	8
Item, payd for a pounde of greate reafons, —	0	0	2
Item, payd for 10 lb. of curfe fuger, — —	0	8	4
Item, payd for 8 lb. of whyte fuger, — —	0	8	0

* This and fome other articles will account for the following entry made on the fame books in the year 1560: "Item, payde for makyng clene the *prevye*, by Mr. Jugge and Mr. Judfon, "which conteyned 12 tonne, the 28th day of December, £1. 6*s*. 8*d*."

Item,

	£.	s.	d.
Item, payd for learge mayſe, ——— ———	0	1	8
Item, payd for ſmale mayſe, —— —— ——	0	1	8
Item, payd for a punde of beſketts and carywayes, ———	0	1	6
Item, a rewarde for bryngynge of a ſyde of venyſon, —	0	0	9
Item, payd for p'ſcance, ——— ——— ———	0	0	8
Item, payd for wafers, —— —— ——	0	5	0
Item, payd for epycryſe 4 galons, ——— ———	1	0	8

The chargis for ſettynge forthe of 4 men the 13 day of July, 1557.

Item, payd for 4 cotts of wacket coller, —— ——	1	0	6
Item, payd for 2 newe billes, —— —— —	0	2	8
Item, payd to every one of them 5*s.* and 2*d.* le pece, which ys in the hole, —— ——— ———	1	0	8
Item, payd for the barge hyre, ——— ———	0	1	0

The firſt copy enter'd on the books of the Stationers' Company is,

To *William Pekerynge*, a ballett, called a Ryſe and Wake,	0	0	4

Mony ſpent on 3 quarters' denners at the hall about neceſſarye buſynes.

Item, a loyne of vele, ——— ——— ———	0	1	4
Item, a pece of beffe, ——— ——— ——	0	0	8
Item, for breade, —— —— —— ——	0	0	6
Item, paid for bere and ale, —— —— ——	0	0	10
Item, payd for wyne, —— —— ——	0	0	6
Item, payd for a capon, —— —— ——	0	2	8
Item, payd for 2 conyes, ——— —— ——	0	0	8
Item, payd for nother denner, —— —— ——	0	4	4

The chargis of ſettynge fourthe of men to ſerve the Quene accordynge to our commyſſion.

Item, for preſt monye for 8 men, ——— ———	0	8	0
Item, for preſte monye for 8 men more, at 6*d.* le pece, —	0	4	0
Item, payd for 4 cappes, —— ——	0	3	0
Item, payde for thayre meate that daye whan thay went fourthe,	0	4	4
Item, monye delyvered to them for thayre neceſſaryes, ——	0	13	4
Item, payd for gonne powther and matche, ——	0	0	7
Item, payd for thayre cundett monye at 18*d.* le pece, ——	0	6	0
Item, for ſettynge of 2 bowes, —— ——	0	0	8
Item, payd for 2 doſyn of poynts, ——— ———	0	0	4
Item, payd to the taylor for makyng of yoelet hooles in the jackes,	0	0	4
Item, payd for bowe ſtrynges, —— ———	0	0	2

	£.	s.	d.
Item, payd for 3 jackes, — — —	0	1	8
Item, payd for 4 ſwords, — —	0	11	0
Item, payd for 4 dagors, — — —	0	8	0
Item, payd for a bowe and a ſhaffe of arrowes, —	0	4	8
Item, payd for 2 jackes, — — —	1	1	4
Item, payd for 6 gyrdelles, — — —	0	0	6
Item, payd for 2 hornes for gonne powther with chargis,	0	3	0
Item, payd for 6 gorgetts, — — —	0	8	0
Item, payd for 2 pounde of gonne powther, —	0	2	0
Item, payd for 2 rolles of matche, — —	0	0	2
Item, payd for a hande gonne, — —	0	6	0
Item, payd for 4 cappes, — — —	0	3	0
Item, payd for 5 payre of ſpynts, — —	0	13	8
Item, payd to the armerer for mendynge of a harnes and a hed pece,	0	1	0
Item, payd for 6 doſyn of poynts, — —	0	1	0
Item, payd for 24 yards of whyte cotton for ſouldiours cotts, at *7d.* le yarde, — — —	0	14	0
Item, payd for 2 yardes of grene carſaye for to garde the ſayde cotts, at *22d.* le yarde, — —	0	3	8
Item, payd for makyng of the ſame cotts, and red clothe for the croſſes, — —	0	6	4
Item, payd for mendynge of a gonne, —	0	0	6
Item, payd for mendynge of 2 dagors, —	0	1	0
Item, payd for a bracer and a ſhowtynge glove, —	0	0	10
Item, payd for 2 freyſe jerkyns for the gonners, —	0	12	0
Item, payd for a payre of hoſe, — —	0	2	0
Item, payd for 4 payre of ſhoyes, — —	0	8	0
Item, payd money to them by commandmente, —	0	13	4
Item, payd for meate and drynke for them that daye, —	0	2	8
Item, payd for lede to make pellets, — —	0	0	2
Item, payd for bowe ſtrynges, — — —	0	0	2
Item, payd to them for cundett monye, accordynge to comandemente, — — — — —	0	14	0
Item, payd for 2 purſis for thayre pelletts, — —	0	0	8
Item, payd for a lynke for to leade them from Leadenhall to the Towre, — — — —	0	0	8
Item, payd for 2 blacke bylles, — — —	0	2	4
Item, payd for 2 newe keyes with one new locke, and mendynge of the old lockes, — — — —	0	4	0

Here-

Hereafter foloweth the chargis of the denner at the chufynge of the Mafter and Wardyns, the v daye of July, in a° 1558.

	£.	s.	d.
Fyrfte, for 12 capons, — — —	1	6	0
Item, for 7 geffe, — — — —	0	9	4
Item, payd for a dofyn of rabbetts, — —	0	4	4
Item, payd for 2 dofyn of chekyns, — —	0	9	4
Item, payd for 2 rounds of fturgion, — — —	0	8	0
Itam, payd for 2 breafts of veele, — — —	0	2	8
Item, payd for a furloyne pece of beffe, — —	0	2	2
Item, payd for egges, — — — —	0	0	5
Item, payd for 13 pounde of butter, — —	0	3	4
Item, payd for flowres and rofys, — —	0	1	5
Item, payd for orrynges, — — —	0	0	4
Item, payd for 6 mary bones, — — —	0	1	4
Item, payd for goffe buryes, — — —	0	0	4
Item, payd for mary golds, — — —	0	0	1
Item, payd for lavynder, — — — —	0	0	1
Item, payd for parfylly, — — — —	0	0	1½
Item, payde for 2 neckes of motton, — —	0	1	0
Item, payd for 4 rabbetts, — —	0	1	4
Item, payd for a loyne of vele, — —	0	1	0
Item, payd for 6 fackes of colys, — — —	0	4	0
Item, payd for a quartron of bylletts, —	0	2	5
Item, payd for a quartron of fagottes, — —	0	1	0
Item, payd for a ftonde of ale, — —	0	2	0
Item, payd for 2 dofyn of breade, — —	0	2	0
Item, payd for falte, — —	0	0	2
Item, payd for a barrell of bere, — —	0	4	8
Item, payd for 20 pounde of cheres, — —	0	1	8
Item, payd for 3 pynts of whyte venyger, — —	0	0	6
Item, payd for 3 quarts of vyrgis, — —	0	0	5
Item, payd for a pottle of mufkedele, — —	0	1	4
Item, payd for 12 galons of wine, — —	0	16	0
Item, payd for 4 pound of fuete, — —	0	1	0
Item, payd for 16 pounde and an once of fuger, —	0	18	0
Item, payd for fynomon one pounde 6 onz and a halfe, —	0	16	0
Item, payd for gynger 5 onz 3 quatrons, —	0	4	7
Item, payde for halfe pounde of pepper, — —	0	1	4
Item, payd for an onz of mayfe, — — —	0	1	4
Item, payd for cloves and mayfe one onz. —	0	0	7
Item, payd for 6 pounde of currance, — —	0	2	0
Item, payd for 4 pounde of dates, — —	0	2	8
Item, payd for 5 pounde of prunes, —	0	0	10

Item,

	£.	s.	d.
Item, payd for nuttmegges half a pounde, ——	0	3	4
Item, payd for water, —— ——	0	1	3
Item, payd for 5 peckes of flowre, — —	0	1	5½
Item, payd for bakynge of pyes, — —	0	1	10
Item, payd to the coke and his man for dreſſynge of the denner,	0	5	0
Item, payd to the buttler for his attendaunce at the denner,	0	4	0
Item, payd for waffers, — — —	0	4	0
Item, payd to the ſcrevener for wrytinge of the indentures of the ſurrender for the feffers of truſte unto the maſter and wardyns of this companye and thayre ſucceſſors, —— ——	0	14	0

This ys the inventory of all ſuche ſtuffe, with other thyngs, as dothe appertayne to this howſe as foloweth, that ys to ſaye:

In the hall.

In the hall joined with vayneſcott playne pannelles, with creſtes and benches.

Item, a ſkrene with a deſke for plate.

Item, the hall payſſe over the hygh bourde.

Item, a deale table of 5 yardes and a halfe longe, with 3 treſſelles.

Item, 2 ſyde tables paynted red and blacke, one of them with a leafe and a ſtaye of ireon, with 6 treſſelles to them.

Item, 6 new joyned formes.

Item, all the wyndowes glayſed.

Item, one banner.

Item, 3 ſcutcheons.

In the great plour.

Item, a joyned table, with a frame of 4 yards longe.

Item, a joyned table, with a frame of 3 yardes longe.

Item, 12 joyned ſtowles.

Item, 2 olde formes.

Item, a joyned cubberte, with a hall payſe, and a deſke for plate.

Item, all the plour joyned with wayneſkott with playne pannells and creſts.

Item, a dornexe carpett.

Item, an iron plate for the chymne.

In the counſell plour.

Item, a table of the names of the Auncients.

Item, a newe joyned drawyng table, with a frame.

Item, one vyſſer and 2 whippis for reformacyon.

Item, 2 new joyned formes.

Item, a cheſte with 3 lockes 3 keyes.

Item, a box with 2 lockes and 2 keyes.

Item, a joyned box with a locke and a key, for the herſe clothe.

6 Item,

Item, all the plour joyned with waynefkott new playne pannell and crefts, with benches alonge the table.

Item, all the wyndowes glayfed, with 6 cafements of iron.

Item, 9 paynted ftoryes ftandynge above the vaynefkott in the fayde plour.

Item, a courte cubberte, with 2 ftayes of iron.

Item, a grene carpett of 2 yardes and 3 quarters longe.

Item, one herfe-clothe of the gift of Mr. *Cawood.*

In the cappell.

Item, a table with 3 treffelles in 2 peces.

Item, 2 jackes.

Item, 3 gonnes.

Item, a bowe and a fhaffe of arrowes.

Item, 8 alman revetts.

Item, 5 hed peces.

Item, 3 fkulles with 2 cappes.

Item, 7 payre of fpents and one fpente.

Item, 9 gorgetts.

Item, 4 fwordes

Item, 4 cotts.

Item, a bore fpere.

Item, 8 blacke bylles.

Item, 5 blacke gyrdelles.

Item, one pyke.

Item, 3 gyrdelles.

Item, 4 dagors.

In the buttrye.

Item, a great chefte bought of Mr. *Seres.*

Item, a horne garnesfhed with a leppe, and the toppe fylver and gylte, and the foote coper and gylte.

Item, 3 olde playne table clothes.

Item, 3 olde playne towelles.

Item, 4 ftone crufys covered with pewther.

Item, 28 ftone potts.

Item, 12 dofyn of trenchers.

Item, 2 fhelves

Item, a gefte for ale and bere.

Item, a new tabull cloth for one old by *Toye.*

Item, 1 dofyn of napkyns gyven by Mrs. *Toy*, pleyne.

In the Kytchen.

Item, a dreffynge bourde 4 yardes and a halfe longe.

Item, 2 fhelves.

Item,

Item, a payre of iron roſtynge rackes.
Item, an iron barre in the chemne.
Item, 3 tramelles to hange potts on.
Item, 3 ſpytts.
Item, a braſſe potte, and a braſſe panne.
Item, a ſtone morter and a peſtell,
Item, 4 creſſetts with ſtaves.
Item, 46 platters.
Item, 44 deſhes.
Item, 48 ſawcers.
Item, one olde deſke beſyde.

On the Seller.

Item, a geſte for bere and ale.
Item, in olde lede contaynynge in wayghte 2 hundreth lacken 5 pounde.
Item, of a thouſande of tyle.

Remaynynge in the cheſte with 3 lockes and 3 keyes, which ſtandeth in the counſell chamber.

Inprimis, one longe caſe with locke and keye, covered with lether.

Item, the Corporacyon of Stacyoners under the greate ſeale of Englande, made in anno Phil. & Marie 3° & 4°.

Item, one box of evydence conteynyng 8 pieces for the purchaſe of our hall.

Item, one leaze betwene the Company and *John Poynt*, concernynge the howſe he dwellyth yn for the terme of 31 yeres to his oblygacyon for performance of covenants.

Item, one oblygacyon made by *Adam Bland* to the Company in parte that he ſhould doo no injury to the hall.

Item, one oblygacyon that *Hugh Singleton* ſtandyth bound to *William Seres* in 20 nobills for payment of £4. 10*s.* whereof 26*s.* 8*d.* is payde, and ſo remayneth £3. 3*s.* 4*d.* which oblygacyon is gyven to the hall.

Item, another boxe with a patent given by harolds to the Company of Stacyoners, concernynge their armes, with charges, a gyfte of Mr. *Cawood.*

Item, one ſpone of ſylver parcell gylt, of the gyft of Mr. *Dockray.*

Item, a ſpone all gylt, of the gift of Mr. *Cawood.*

Item, a ſpone of ſylver all gylte, of the gyft of Mr. *Walye*, &c.

Extracted

Extracts from a File of Records of *Hamlet Clarke*, an Attorney, &c. being an Inventory of the Stock in Trade and Furniture of a Tavern in Bishopsgate-Street, in 1612. (First published in the Gent. Mag. LVIII. p. 581.)

In the cellar of the defendante George Hitchecocke's dwellinge-house, called by the name of *The Mouthe Tavern* *, without Bishoppsgate.

	£.	s.	d.
Imprimis, fower pipes of white wine, — —	20	0	0
Item, two hogsheades of old Graves wine, —	2	0	0
Item, seaven hogsheads of Orliance wine, — —	17	10	0
Item, one butte of Malligo wine, — —	17	0	0
Item, one ranlett of sherry sacke, contayning sixteene gallande,	1	12	0
Item, 3 quarters of a pipe of old Malmsley, —	1	10	0
Item, one third of a butte of Malmsley, — —	5	0	0
Item, 3 gallande of Alligante, at 3 sh, per gallande, —	0	9	0
Item, halfe a pipe of Malligo wine, — —	6	0	0
Item, one hogsheade of old clarrett, — —	0	16	0
Item, one hogsheade of Graves wine, —	3	0	0
Item, half a hogsheade of Orliance white wine, —	2	10	0
Item halfe a hogshead of Graves clarrett, — —	0	10	0
Item, one thyrd part of a hogsheade of red wyne, —	1	10	0
Item, 3 tunne and a half of emptye hogsheads, at 6s. per tunne,	1	1	0
Item, 3 Rochell pipes, emptye, — —	0	9	0
Item, one Alligant pipe, emptye, — —	0	3	0
Item, two dusson and eight bottles of ale, — —	0	5	8
Item, one cane and a funnell for wyne, —	0	1	8
In the roome called *The Percullis*, of the same howse.			
Item, one longe table of waynscote, with a fforme, —	0	13	4
Item, one oyster table with a fforme, — —	0	3	4
Item, one little cubbord table, and one court cubbord, —	0	7	0
Item, one olde wyne stoole, and a payre of playinge tables,	0	1	0
In the roome called *The Pomgrannatt*, of the same howse.			
Item, an olde table, with a fforme, — —	0	3	4
In the roome called *The Three Tuns*, of the same howse.			
Item, one little standynge .... carpenter's table, with two stooles,	0	2	0
In the roome called *The Crosse Keys*, of the same howse.			
Item, one standynge table, with two benches, —	0	2	0
In the roome called *The Vyne*, of the same howse.			
Item, one olde table, wlth one old fforme, and two benches,	0	2	0

* The correspondent who communicated this inventory to Mr. Urban asks if this was the present *White Hart* Tavern, which bears the date 1480 on its front, but for what reason has not been ascertained, nor where this other tavern was situate. All that Stowe says of the first of these is, that it " is a famous inne for the receipt of travellers." Of the sign of *The Bull and Mouth*, see Gent. Mag. LVIII. 671; Survey, p. 173. ed. 1720.

	£.	s.	d.
In the roome called *The King's Head*, of the fame howfe.			
Item, an old table, with a forme and three benches, and an old oyfter-table, with a child's ftoole, — —	0	6	8
Item, the boorded partitions of and belonging to the drinkinge roomes aforefaid, — — — —	1	0	0
In the chamber over *The Percullis* of the fame howfes			
Item, one preffe cubbord of waynfcote, — —	0	13	4
Item, one waynfcott cheftt, — —	0	5	0
Item, two downe pillowes, in the fame cheftt, and one ffeather pillow, — — — —	0	8	0
Item, fix payre of olde flaxen fheets, — —	2	0	0
Item, one olde canvas table-cloth, — —	0	5	0
Item, one duffon and a halfe of napkyns, of feveral fortes, in the faid cheftt, — — — —	0	3	0
Item, one other napkyn, — — —	0	0	2
Item, one coverlette of tapeftree, — —	1	6	8
Item, one wainfcott cheftt, — — —	0	3	4
Item, two duffon of drinkynge-towells, in the fame cheftt, —	0	12	0
Item, five table-clothes, — — — —	0	5	0
Item, 3 payre and one odd fheete, — — —	0	18	0
Item, one other olde diaper table-clothe, and fix olde diaper napkyns, — — — —	0	6	0
Item, one duffon of napkyns, wroughte with Coventree blew thredde, — — — —	0	8	0
Item, one olde damafke table-clothe, and a duffon and a half olde napkyns, — — — —	0	6	0
Item, one carpette of greene ftrype ftuffe, with fix green cufheons,	0	14	0
Item, 3 payre of pillowberes, — — —	0	6	0
Item, fix olde haunde towells and a table clothe, —	0	1	0
Item, an olde bedfteade, in the fame chamber, with two old darnid curtens and two curten roddes, — — —	0	10	0
Item, one olde ffeather-bedde, one bolfter, one pillowe with pillowbere, and a mattreffe, — — —	0	18	0
Item, one olde payre of fheets, two old blankets, and an olde coverlidde, — — — — —	0	10	0
Item, two olde little chairs, — — —	0	3	4
Item, one olde valance, with a ffafke, — —	0	1	0
In the garratte of the fame howfe.			
Item, three flock-bedds, with fowre olde bolfters, —	0	13	4
Item, two olde half-headed bedfteades, — —	0	5	0
Item, two payre of fheetes, one old blankette, with an olde grene rugge, and an olde coverlette — — — —	1	0	0

Item,

	£.	s.	d.
Item, one olde peftle, with a payre of creepers*, two curten-roddes, with fome olde endes of iron, — — —	0	2	6
Item, one olde tike, — — — —	0	2	0
Item, nyne olde cufhens of feveral fortes, — —	0	3	0
Item, fix olde broken chefts, — —	0	6	0
Item, two oaken boordes and old lumber in the garrett, —	0	6	0
In the lodging-chamber over the kitchen of the fame howfe.			
Item, one payre of iron andirons, with fowre braffe knobbs and two payre of tounges, and one payre of creepers, —	0	10	0
Item, one wicker chaire, two payre of playinge-tables †, one table-boorde, — — — —	0	6	0
Item, one bedfteade, with fine curtens and vallence of greene fay, with 3 curten-roddes, — — —	2	0	0
Item, two ffeather-beddes, two bolfters, one pillow, one mattreffe, three blanketts, one coverlette, and a payre of fheets, —	3	0	0
Item, one trundle-bedde, with a flocke-bedde, one bolfter, a payre of fheets, two blankettes, and a matte, — —	0	10	0
Item, one warmynge-panne, — —	0	3	0
Item, three table-cloths of canvas, diaper towels, one towel wroughte with blewe, and two drinkynge-cloths, —	1	0	0
Item, two lether trunks and one cheft, — —	0	10	0
In Plate.			
Item, fifteen fmalle drinkynge bowles of filver, one brode bowle and 2 beakers, one greate faulte, a trencher faulte, and two filver fpoones, waighing 154 ounces, at 3*s.* and 10*d.* per ounce, —	37	4	4
Pewter and braffe in the kitchen of the fame howfe.			
Item, fourteene greate pewter difhes, — —	1	8	0
Item, fowre leffer difhes, — — —	0	6	0
Item, feaven leffer than thofe, — — —	0	4	8
Item, nyne plate trenchers, — —	0	2	3
Item, fix fallet difhes, — — —	0	2	0
Item, nine pottengers, — — —	0	2	3
Item, one bafon and ewre, — — —	0	2	4
Item, five pewter candlefticks, — — —	0	2	4
Item, two pye-plates, — — —	0	3	4
Item, three pewter chamber-pots, — —	0	4	0
Item, one baking coffen, — — —	0	2	4
Item, fowre pewter faultes, — — —	0	2	0
Item, two haunde-peeces, — —	0	1	8

* Our dictionary-makers call thefe *Andirons*, probably of a form fomewhat different from the things commonly known by that name, in the form of the hand, and probably are what we now call firecats. Gent. Mag. LVIII. 672. Dr. Johnfon defcribes them as "an iron ufed to flide "in kitchens;" and fo another correfpondent of Gent. Mag. ubi fup. 848, defines them the moveable iron fides of kitchen or range grates, the convenience of which are to contract or enlarge the fire occafionally, and not improperly called *Creepers*.

† Dice boards.

Item,

	£.	s.	d.
Item, one ale pint potte, — — — —	0	0	8
Item, three greate braſſe pottes, — —	3	0	0
Item, two leſſer braſſe pottes, — —	0	15	0
Item, one greate braſſe kettle, — —	0	7	0
Item, two ſmale braſſe kettles, —	0	7	6
Item, ono copper kettle, —	0	13	4
Item, three braſs ſkillets, —	0	2	6
Item, foure braſſe chafen diſhes, —	0	4	0
Item, one braſſe cullender, — — —	0	1	0
Item, one ſmalle braſſe kettle, and a braſſe panne, —	0	2	0
Item, foure braſſe ſkimers, — —	0	4	0
Item, one braſſe candleſticke plate, — —	0	1	8
Item, one braſſe ladle, — —	0	0	6
Item, two braſſe candleſtickes, — —	0	2	0
Item, two iron drippynge-pannes, — — —	0	5	0
Item, eighte ſpittes, — — —	0	8	0
Item, one jacke, with a waighte, — —	0	10	0
Item, one payre of iron racks, a payre of potte-hangers, a barre of iron in the chimney, two fier-ſhovells, one pair of tounges, a fier-fforke and an iron plate before the fier, an iron band for a kettle,	0	10	0
Item, two ffryinge-pannes and two gridirons, — —	0	3	0
Item, one ctſterne of lead with a cocke, —	1	4	0
Item, one braſſe potte with a handle to it, —	0	5	0
Item, one buckinge-tubbe * and a three-legged tubbe, with two ſtooles and a chaire, — — —	0	2	6
Item, one cheeſe-knife and a choppinge-knife, —	0	0	4
Item, one muſtard-querne †, with a greene mortar and peſtle,	0	2	6
Item, one earthen Turkey baſon, with painted diſhes, —	0	1	6
Item, one iron-bande paile, two payre of belloes, —	0	1	0
Item, two fformes, with the dreſſers and ſhelves in the kitchen,	0	3	4
In *The Crowne.*			
Item, two tables, two fformes, and two benches, and a greate wooden chaire, — — — —	0	7	0
In *The Dolphin and the Bell.*			
Item, two tables with ſeates and partitions belongi2g thereunzo, with a breade-bynne, — — —	0	5	0
In *The Barre.*			
Item, two gallon-pottes, five pottle-pottes, nyne quarte-pottes, eight pynte-pottes, one halfe-pynte-potte, and a gille-potte,	1	6	8
Item, one braſſe baſon for a candle, and 1 candle plate, —	0	2	6
Item, one payre of ſhovinge-tables, — —	0	1	0

* Waſhing or rincing-tub. *Buck*, in Shakeſpeare, is ſynonymous with waſhing.
† Q. hand-mill to grind muſtard.

The inventory of all the Goodes of Sir Peter Fretheville, Knight[1], deceaſed[2], late of Staveley, in the Countie of Darby, praiſed by Robert Sitwell, Henry Oxley, and Anker Rycharde, at Staley, the 25th of Novembre, 1559[3].

Imprimis, fyve fate oxen, —		
Itm. viii fate[4] kyne, — —		
Itm. xviii draught oxen, —		
Itm. xvi mylk kyne, — —		
Itm. xii young ſtears, —	xcl.	
Itm. xxii yerelings, — —		
Itm. viii wayninge calves, —		
Itm. one bulle, — —		
Itm. ii ſtonede horſes, —		
Itm. ix naggs and geldings, —		
Itm. vii mares, — —	xxvil.	
Itm. iv coltes, — —		
Itm. v foles, — —		
Itm. corne in the barnes and alſo on the grounde, —	lxxxl.	
Itm. xii ſwyne, — —		xls.
Itm. waynes, plowes, and yokes, —		xls.
Itm. xc doſen of iren[5], at vis. the doſen, —	xxviil.	
Itm. fyve ſcore and x ſhepe, —	xiil.	
Itm. one ſilver ſalt[6] parcell gilte, beinge xii ownces, after iv s. the ownce, and ii playne drinkinge bolles, —	iiil.	ivs.
Itm. one ſilver cup with a cover parcell gilte, —	il.	xs.
Itm. one gilted ſpone, —		
Itm. vi other ſilver ſpones with knappes[7], —	ivl.	
Itm. xiii playne ſilver ſpones without knoppes, in all xx ownces, after ivs. the ownce, — —		
Itm. x fether beddes, — —	vl.	
Itm. xii mattreſſes, — —		xlvis. viiid.
Itm. xi bolſteres, — —		xxs.
Itm. viii pelowes, — —		viiis.
Itm. vi peire of blanketts —		xxvis. viiid.
Itm. xxiv coverlettes, — —	ivl.	
Itm. iv counterpeyntes, — —	iiil.	xs.
Itm. a praſs[8], a foldinge table, ii cheares, and a coffer,		xxvis. viiid.

[1] Knighted for his valour at Muſcleborough, temp. Edw. VI. Dugd. Baron. II. p. 482.
[2] He died November 6, 4 Mary, at Staveley. [3] Obſerve a mixture of Arabic with Roman figures.
[4] Fat. [5] Iron. [6] For middle of the table.
[7] Knobbs. Spoons were often ornamented at top, and ſometimes with images, as of the Twelve Apoſtles, thence called *Apoſtle ſpoons*. [8] A preſs.

H h

Itm.

Itm. iiii trusebeddes with teasteres and hangyngs, — iiil. xs.
Itm. a bedsteade, a trundelbede, a longe coffer, ii cheares, curteynes, and teastures, —— —— xxs.
Itm. ix spittes, a peire of caiwlots[8], a girde iren[9], a fleshe axe, ii drypping pannes, one fryinge panne, with all other iren gerre[10], xxxs.
Itm. brass potts and posnets, with a chaufer[11], — xlvis. viiid.
Itm. pannes and a keytle, —— xxvis. viiid.
Itm. pewter vessell, —— —— iiil.
Itm. xx peyre of lynnen sheets —— } vl.
Itm. xx peir of canvas shetts and harden[12], —— }
Itm. xii candilstickes, —— —— xxs.
Itm. sixe playne quisshenes[13], — — viiis.
Itm. ix wrought quisshenes, — — xxviiis. viiid.
Itm. a carpet of grene clothe, — — xiiis. iiiid.
Itm. a table, a frame, certein cheares and stoles[14], with all the tables, cheares and stoles, not before remembrede, — xxxs.
Itm. iiii launde irens[15], with a peire of tonges, — xiiis. ivd.
Itm. kymnell, with all other implementes thereto belonginge, vs.
Itm. in the brue howse a kule[16], with other stuffe, — vs.
Itm. ii beddes, —— —— liiis. ivd.
Itm. a fate, ii tubbes, with cuppes and cannes, and all thuscylmentes[17] therto belonginge, — — xs.
Itm. iii bassens and ewers, — — xvs.
Itm. whole timbre xx^{ti} gnungs[18], with xii peire of mathews[19] and other, —— — — xxxiiis. ivd.
Itm. money in his purse and within the howse, — xxiil. xiiis. iiiid.
Itm. money that was owinge to hym of George Burley, Esquier, cl.
Itm. owinge of Nicolas Cadman, —— viil. xvis.
Itm. his apparell appertenynge to his bodie, —— xl.

Sum̄a totalis hujus — — ccccxxxvil. iid.

Extractum erat hocce inventorium per Petrum Fretchvill, armigerum, Ag^{tris}[20] pro pleno Inventario, &c. xvii^{mo} Junii, a° 1559.

THO. ARGALL.

[8] Quære. [9] Gridiron. [10] Gear, i. e. utensils. [11] Chafing-dish.
[12] *Hards* are the coarse part or refuse of flax. Littleton's Dict. [13] Cushions.
[14] Stools. [15] Landirons. [16] A kyle or a cooler.
[17] Thuscylments. The huscylments, the *hushelment*, as in the last line of the other inventory; a word corrupted of housholdment, meaning houshold-stuff of all kinds, and commonly called husselments in Derbyshire.
[18] Perhaps *gang*, i. e. set. [19] Naves or nathes. [20] Quære, the meaning.

An

An Inventorye off the Godes of Peter Fretevile, of Staveley[1], Esquire[2], late discceased, taken and prysed the 17th of February, 1581, by Robert Setwell, George Pole, Thomas Turnar, George Savage, Henry Browne, and Robert Lilly.

The Great Chamber.

Imprimis, a long table, —	
Itm. iii square tables, — —	
Itm. iii fowroms, — —	
It. ii wrought cheyres and one turned cheyre[3], —	
It. one covered stole, — —	
It. vi quishings[4], — —	xl.
It. one stand bedd with vallance and curteyns, —	
It. ii fetherbeds, ii bolsters, ii pillowes, —	
It. one matteres, on paire of blankets, —	
It. one coverlett, one Arras[5] coveringe, —	
It. one mattrees, ii fetherbeds, one boulster, —	
It. one coverlett, and one paire of blankets, —	
It. in the farr chamber, one stand bed with vallins and courteyns,	
It. ii matterasss, one downe bedd, one white rugge,	
It. one payre of blankets, one coverlett, —	
It. one Arras coveringe, — —	
It. one mattres, ii fether beds, ii coverletts, —	xl.
It. one payer of blankets, one boulster, —	
It. one cubbart, ii chayres, one covered stole, —	
It. one longe pillow, and one grene cubbart clothe, —	
It. ii boulsters, ii pillows, and one cheist, —	
It. one stand bed, with vallance and courtaynes, —	
It. one fetherbed, one matteres, one coverlett, —	
It. one paire of blankets, ii boulsters, ii pillowes, —	
It. one Arras coveringe, — —	
It. ii fetherbeds, one matteres, ii boulsters, —	vl.
It. one paire of blanketts, and ii coverletts, —	
It. one cubbart, and one greene cubbard clothe, —	
It. one longe pillow, and ii turned cheyrs, —	

[1] Com. Derb.

[2] Dr. Thoroton, p. 55, calls him a knight; but I suppose he is mistaken in that.

[3] Made by the turner, as now they are seen in country barbers shops.

[4] Vide note 13 on the former inventory.

[5] A kind of stuff made at *Arras* in *Artois*.

It. one

It. one ſtand bed, with vallance and curtayns,
It. ii fetherbeds, one mattres, ii pillowes, one boulſter,
It. one blankett, one white rugge, one coveringe,
It. on trindle bed, one matteres, ii fether beds, — vi l. xiii s. iiii d.
It. one boulſter, ii pillowes, one payer of blankets,
It. ii coverletts, and one coveringe, one long pillow,
It. one table, one fowrem, one table clothe,

It. one ſtand bed and one trindle bed,
It. iii fetherbeds, iii mattereſs, iii boulſters,
It. one pillow, ii payer of blanketts, — iiii l.
It. v coverletts, and one clothe coveringe,
It. one cubbart and cubbart cloth, iii quiſhing, iii cheyers,

It. ii featherbeds, one mattres, iv boulſters,
It. one ſtand bed, one trindle bed, — xxx s.
It. ii payer of blanketts, iv coverletts, one coveringe,

It. ii ſtand bedds, iii fetherbeds, iii boulſters,
It. one payer of blanketts, vi coverletts, — xx s.

It. one ſtand bed, with vallance and curteyns,
It. one trindle bed, ii mattres, ii fetherbeds, — iii l.
It. ii bolſters, iii pillowes, iii coverletts,

It. one cubbart, one cubbart cloth, ii quiſhings,
It. one cheyre, one baſket ſtole, iii cheyſts,

It. one ſtand bed, one fetherbed, one mattreſs,
It. one boulſter, one pillow, on cheyre, on quiſhing, — xx s.
It. one payer of blanketts, ii coverletts, one coveringe,

It. ii preſſes, ii cheſts, — xxx s.

It. iv ſtand beds, iii matterefe, iv fetherbeds,
It. vi boulſters, ii pillowes, ii coverings, — lii s.
It. iii payer of blanketts, vi coverletts, one table,

It. iv coverletts, and viii plate [6] coats, — viii l.
It. x bells, ii calevers, — xxx s.
It. viii ſculls and ſalletts [7], one drum, iii long pikes, — xiii s. iiii d.
It. one tent, — iiii l.

It. one baſen and euer, ii lyveray potts,
It. ii juggs parcell gilt, one jugg dubble gilt,
It. one garniſht pott, one ſalt dubble gilt,
It. vi tunns [8], a ſalt, a peper box, one oud ſalt, — L l.
It. iii boulles parcell gilt, ii boules dubble gilt,
It. ii white boules, and ii gilt ſpones,
It. one doſen great ſpones parcell gilt, one doſen of litle ſpones,
It. one ſugar box, and a litle ſpone, on peper box dubble gilt,

[6] Probably not rightly read.

[7] Scull-caps and helmets. Archæologia, vol. I. p. 249. Brit. *Saled.*

[8] These are plainly the letters; yet it cannot be right.

It. his

It. his apparel and cheyne, — — —	L l.
It. his purse, dagger, and girdle, — — —	vii l. xii s. iiii d.
It. in the great parlor, ii large tables and cloths, ii table clothes,	
It. iiii short fowremes, and one longe fowrem, —	
It. one great table, ii cubbarts, and cubbart cloths, —	4 0 0
It. vi buffett stoles, iiii cheyres, and one covered stole, —	
It. ii longe pillowes, and ii dosen of quisshings, —	
It. in the Hall, one longe table, ii long fowrems, —	x s.
It. xlvi payer of sheets, — — —	xii l.
It. xx long table clothes, — —	iii l. xviii s.
It. xii square table clothes, — —	xxx s.
It. xii dosen of napkins, — — —	iii l.
It. xii towels, — — —	xx s.
It. xii cubbard clothes, — — —	xiii s. iiii d.
It. xxiiii pillow bears, — — —	xx s.
It. iiii garnish[9] of vessell, — — —	v l.
It. v basings and euers, — — —	xx s.
It. vii liveray potts, — — — —	x s.
It. ii dosen of candlesticks, — —	xxvi s. viii d.
It. xii chamber potts, — — —	x s.
It. x spitts, 5 payer of pott hookes, —	
It. ii ranges, — — —	
It. xiii brase potts, ii fryinge panns, — —	ix l. xiii s. iiii d.
It. ii payer of standing racks, — —	
It. v panns, 4 dripping pans, — — —	
It. ii brasen morters and pestels, — —	
It. ii leads, — —	iiii l.
It. iii great panns, with other vessels of wood, —	
It. corne and hey in the barne and stacks, — —	L l.
It. hard corne on the ground, — —	L l.
It. iii bulls, — — — —	iiii l.
It. xx steares, — — —	xxii l.
It. xxi steares, — — —	xxvi l.
It. xi steares, — — —	xvii l.
It. iiii kyne, — — —	v l. x s.
It. xx kyne, — — —	xxvii l.
It. xviii draught oxen, — — —	xxxvi l.
It. xi other runt oxen, — —	xxvii l.
It. xiii hoggs, — — —	viii l.
It. cxlv ould shepe, — — —	xxxii l.
It. iiii geldings, — — —	xvi l.

[9] It seems to mean here *a set.*

It. one ſtone horſe, — — — iiii l.
It. xx horſes and mares, — — — xxvi l.
It. xi foales and fillyes, — — — ix l.
It. xxvii ſwyne, — — — — v l.
It. fleſh on the balks [10], — — — vii l.
It. inſtruments of huſbandry, as waynes, ploughs, teames, and ſuch like, — — — — viii l.
It. other huſtelments[11] in the howſe, — — ii l.

Exhibit. apud Lychfeld, 11mo die menſis Maii, anno Dñi 1582.

RICHARDUS COLE, deputat.
MARGARET FRICHEVYLLE [12], uxoris.

[10] Flicks, &c. of bacon, put up on high to dry on frames of wood.

[11] Vide note [17] on the former inventory.

[12] This was Margaret Kaye, daughter of Arth. Kaye, of Woodſome, co. Ebor, and ſecond wife of the deceaſed.

Extract from the Inventory of the Goods, Chattels, &c. of THOMAS KEBLE *, Esq. Serjeant at Law, appraised by VALENTINE MASON, General Appraiser to the most Reverend Father in GOD the Lord Cardinal and Archbishop of Canterbury, 6° Julij, 15° HEN. VII. 1500. (From Gent. Mag. vol. XXXVIII. p. 257.)

IN THE PARLOUR.

	£.	s.	d.
A compleat hanging of broad Alexander, containing in length 60 yards, and in breath 3 yards—six score yards, at 2*d.* *per* yd. —	1	0	0
One dozen of cushions of verders stuffed with feathers —	1	13	4
A sperver of broad Alexander — — —	0	13	4
A feather bed and bolster — — — —	1	0	0
A pair of old fustians — — — — —	0	8	0
A pair of blankets — — — — —	0	2	0
A pair of flaxen sheets of 3 breadths, containing 21 yards at 6*d.* each	0	10	6
A counterpane of tapestry work, *sore worn* — —	0	5	0
A table, two christalls, two forms, two chairs, and a cupboard	0	2	0
An old cupboard-cloth of green say — — —	0	0	6

IN THE CHAMBER OVER THE PARLOUR.

	£.	s.	d.
A compleat hanging of green say — — —	0	6	8
Two carpets — — — — —	0	10	0
A sperver of broad Alexander — — — —	0	10	0
An old feather bed and bolster — —	0	8	0
An old counterpane of tapestry-work — —	0	3	4
A counterpane of imagery-work — —	0	10	0
A counterpane of verders with birds — —	3	0	0
A cupboard — — —	0	2	0
A counterpane of red damask, *sore worn*, 34 yards —	5	0	0
A sperver of red damask, with curtains of coarse red sarcenet	3	6	8
A pillow and two cushions, covered with ray-sattin from Burges, stuffed with feathers — — —	0	13	4
A pair of new fustians — —	0	13	4
Six hangings of tapestry-work, containing 90 yards, at 12*d. per* yd.	4	10	0
One remnant of black double sattin, containing 3 yards, at 8*s. per* yd.	1	4	0
Three doublet-cloaths of tawney sattin, 8 yards and a half, at 8*s.* yd.	3	8	0
A remnant of tawney sattin, containing 2 yards and half, at 6*s.* yd.	0	15	0
A remnant of black stamyn, containing 2 yards and half, at 2*s.* yd.	0	5	0
A pair of great old amber beads of twelve stones —	0	10	0
A pair of beads ten stones, cassidens, &c. jasper, partly cover'd with gold	4	0	0
A book written in French on parchment, called *La Abuse in Court*	0	10	0
An old harness-girdle, with divers little buckles —	1	6	8
An altar-cloth of arras, containing in length three yards, in breadth one yard, at 1*l.* 6*s.* 8*d. per* yard — —	4	0	0
Two remnants of black velvet, containing 10 yards, at 12*s. per* yard	6	0	0
A piece of tawney velvet, containing 3 yards, at 12*s. per* yard	1	16	0

* Of Humberston in Leicestershire; where a monument was placed for him and his two wives, which Mr. Burton by mistake ascribes to *Walter* Keble. His whole-length figure was on it, dress'd in serjeant's scarlet robes and coif.

	£.	s.	d.
Eight pieces and half of new broad Alexander, at 8*s*. *per* piece	3	8	0
Five chefts, of divers forts —— ——	0	10	0
Two remnants of black velvet, containing 4 yards and half, at 12*s*.	2	14	0
A book, in French, of the Chronicles, on parchment ——	2	13	4
A book imprinted, called *Ludovicus de Vita Chrifti* ——	0	10	0
A doublet cloth of black ftamyn, containing 4 yards, at 2*s*. *per* yd.	0	8	0
A little velvet pouch, with a fingle ring, filver, and gilt —	1	0	0
A little fperver of ray-filk, with curtains of green ——	4	0	0
In the Kitchen.			
Three garnifh of pewter veffels, little occupied, at 21*s*. *per* garnifh	3	3	0
Three dozen of platters, 5 great chargers, 2 dozen and three porringers, and 2 dozen and four fawcers ——	3	6	8
A great brafs pot —— ——	0	12	0
Two brafs pots of 3 gallons each ——	0	10	0
Four little poffnets, at 12*d*. each poffnet ——	0	4	0
Three great pans, of 5 gallons each pan ——	0	15	0
Three other little pans —— ——	0	6	0
A little mortar of brafs, and a peftle — —	0	4	0
Two pair of racks —— ——	0	6	8
A little pair of racks —— ——	0	2	0
Two pair of broches fquare —— ——	0	11	4
Two great round broches —— ——	0	6	0
Two little round broches —— ——	0	1	8
Two bird broches —— ——	0	1	0
Two chaffing-difhes —— —— —	0	2	0
A great pewter chaffour, fomewhat broken ——	0	2	8
Three pair of pot-hooks, and four hanging-irons —	0	0	10
A frying-pan —— —— ——	0	0	6
Two cullenders —— ——	0	0	4
Two fkimmers, two ladles, and a gridiron ——	0	1	8
A great kettle —— ——	0	2	0
A cleaving knife, and three flicing (carving) knives —	0	0	8
And in lumber and trafh —— ——	0	0	6
Plate.			
Two bafons and two ewers, part gilt, weighing 117 oz. at 3*s*. 4*d*. oz.	19	10	0
Three ftanding cups with covers, two chafed and one plain, a goblet with a cover, and two little falts with covers, all gilt, weighing 96 oz. at 3*s*. 6*d*. *per* oz. —— ——	16	16	0
Six great bowls, with a cover gilt, and two little falts with a cover (wrethyn) wrought and enamelled, 208 oz. at 3*s*. 8*d*. *per* oz.	38	2	8
Two little goblets with two little covers gilt, four old goblets pounfed, two pieces chafed, 22 fpoons, and a flat piece, 100 oz. at 3*s*. *per* oz.	15	0	0
Six pieces, chafed, with a cover partly gilt, 165 oz. at 3*s*. 4*d*.	37	10	0
Two pots (of filver double-gilt) weight 94 oz. at 4*s*. *per* oz.	20	7	4
Two great bafons, with two ewers, partly gilt, 183 oz. at 3*s*. 4*d*.	30	10	0

2

Six

	£.	s.	d.
Six goblets with two covers gilt, 110 oz. at 4s. *per* oz. —	22	0	0
Six goblets with two covers, part gilt, 100 oz. at 3s. 4d. *per* oz.	16	13	4
Four great falts with a cover chafed and gilt, 52 oz. at 4s. *per* oz.	10	8	0
Twelve great fpoons with knobs, wrought and gilt, 24 oz. at 4s.	4	16	0
A dozen of fpoons not gilt, 14 oz. at 3s. 2d. *per* oz. —	3	4	4
A little fpoon of working gold, 1 oz. 3-4ths —	3	1	8
A fignet of fine gold, with an eagle difplayed, 2 oz. except 30 dwts. at 3l.	3	17	6
A little piece with a cover gilt, 12 oz. ½, at 4s. *per* oz. —	2	10	0
A little pot not gilt—*pax bread*—two cruets, and a facrying bell, 25 oz. at 3s. 2d. *per* oz. — —	3	19	2
Two pottle pots, 63 oz. at 3s. *per* oz. —	9	10	6
A wafer with a bofs broken — —	1	0	0
A little falt, of gold, with a cover chafed with oak-leaves, 2½ oz. at 3l. *per* oz.	7	10	0
A ftanding wafer with a cover gilt —	1	10	0
A chalice, with a patten and cover, with round knobs, 16 oz. at 3s. 4d.	2	13	4

Wearing Geere.

	£.	s.	d.
A fingle gown of fcarlet, *fore worn*, with a hood of the fame	0	10	0
A crimfon gown (fingle) with a hood of the fame —	1	0	0
A night-gown of worfted-ftuff, furr'd with coarfe black lawn	0	12	0
A fingle gown, of violet colour, with a hood —	0	13	4
Three fingle gowns of blue ray, with two hoods, *fore worn*, at 8s. each	1	4	0
Two fingle gowns of green ray, with two hoods —	0	16	0
A gown, cloth of new blue ray and worfted —	0	13	4
A new gown, cloth of blue ray and tawney —	0	13	4
A gown, cloth of green ray and violet —	0	13	4
An old cloak, of violet — —	0	5	0
A red mantle, *fore worn* — —	0	3	4
A brown tawney gown, furred with fox-fkins —	0	13	4
A brown tawney gown, furred with black lamb —	1	0	0
A fhort riding gown, lined with black cotton —	0	10	0
A coarfe fingle gown of mufter — —	0	8	0
A fingle gown, with a hood of murray in grain —	1	3	4
A violet gown, fingle, with a hood —	1	2	0
A doublet of black velvet — —	1	6	8
A doublet of tawney fattin — —	0	12	0
A jacket of black velvet, furred with martin-fkins —	1	6	8
A book, in French, wrote on parchment —	1	0	0
An old fcarlet gown of his firft wife's, unfurred, with an old purfull, quarter deep, with lettyce — —	2	0	0
A woman's gown with violet in grain, unfurred, with a purfull of mynkes, quarter deep — — —	2	0	0
A chyrtle of ruffet camblet — —	0	13	4
An old gown of his firft wife's, unfurred, with a purfull of white lettyce, quarter deep — —	1	6	8

A gown,

	£.	s.	d.
A gown, cloth of new green ray	0	13	4
The two compleat veſtments of green broad Alexander	2	0	0
A frontell for an altar of green ſilk fringed	0	12	4
An altar-cloth of green Alexander	0	5	0
In the Chapel.			
Two altar-cloths of Alexander, plain	0	3	0
A crucifix of wood	0	1	8
Two images, one of our Lady, another of St. John	0	2	8
Two curtains for the altar, of changeable Tartian	0	6	8
A veſtment, *ſore worn*	0	13	4
A corporas, and the caſe, of old black velvet	0	1	0
A pax, a ſacrying bell, two cruets of latyn (horn)	0	0	8
In the Barn.			
A little ſtack of wheat, containing, by eſtimation, 4 quarters, at 3*s*. 4*d*. the qr.	0	13	4
In the Granary.			
Fifty quarters of malt, at 3*s*. 4*d*. *per* quarter	8	6	8
Corn in the Fields.			
A ryck of peaſe, containing, by eſtimation, 15 quarters, at 2*s*. qr.	1	10	0
Eighteen acres of barley, at 1*s*. 6*d*. *per* acre	1	10	0
Eighty loads of timber (hewn), at 4*s*. *per* load	0	16	0
Two mill-ſtones, for a windmill, of Engliſh make	0	18	0
One fodder of lead	0	5	4
Three waynes ſhod with iron	10	0	0
Two plows, with the harneſs	0	6	8
Cattle, &c.			
Twelve ſcore ſheep, wethers, unclipped, at 1*s*. 8*d*. apiece	20	0	0
Eight ſcore ewes, unclipped, at 13*d*. apiece	8	13	4
Eight ſcore lambs, at 6*d*. apiece	4	0	0
Twenty-ſeven bullocks, at 7*s*. apiece	9	16	0
A couple of oxen, at	1	3	4
439 wethers of young and old (6 ſcore to the hundred), at 9*l*. *per* hund.	38	3	6
379 fleeces of wool, at 4*d*. *per* fleece	6	19	8
Six ſcore hogs (ſheep ſo called) that were ſhorn, at 12*d*. each	6	0	0
Fifty-three ſteers and heifers, at 9*s*. one with another	23	10	6
Eighteen kine (cows), at 8*s*. a-piece	7	4	0
A grey trotting gelding, at	1	0	0
A black ambling hobby, at	1	6	8
A grey ambling gelding, at	1	3	4
A little dunn ambling horſe, at	1	0	0
A great black trotting gelding, at	10	0	0
And, an old grey gelding, at	0	10	0
Three ſwans	0	10	0
Three cranes	0	5	0
Two geeſe	0	3	4

ANNOTATIONS ON THE PRECEDING COLLECTION OF ACCOMPTS, By the late REV. SAMUEL PEGGE, LL. D. 1791.

ST. MARGARET'S, WESTMINSTER.

P. 1. l. 2. *Anno . . . . anno*] dele the firft *anno*; and for *menfo'* r. *menf'*.

Sti.] This feems to fhew that the firft, and fome of the following articles, were copied into the prefent book from loofe papers (fee p. 85); fince Henry VI. would not have had the title of *Sanctus* in the fecond of Edward IV.

5. *Braddines.*] See p. 5. l. 18.

6. *iiij Tor.*] Little was done in thefe ages of grofs Popery without lights. Thefe torches coft 1*s*. 8*d*. apiece; but we find them of various prices, according, as we may fuppofe, to their fize. The churchwardens appear to have provided them; and confequently they were an article of profit to the church *.

7. *Ancrefe.*] The *anchorefs*. See p. 2. l. 26; p. 5. l. 32; p. 10. l. penult.

8. *deliv'at'.*] i. e. *deliberat'* (whence our word to *deliver)*, ufed in that fenfe in the bafe Latinity.

predict',] not mentioned before in this accompt.

pro guerris,] not long before the battle of Towton field.

1464. *perfonar',*] mif-written, or mif-read, for *prifonar'*; for which laft fee Du Frefne, & infra, l. 33.

12. *Chayryng,*] *Charing* (whence we have *Charing-crofs)* was then a hamlet.

13. *ejufdem,*] f. *cujufdam*, for fhe has not been mentioned before.

16. *Charyng.*] We are not to fuppofe the hermit was interred there, but that he was of that place, and lived there.

19. *Abbate.*] Edmund Kirton was then Abbot of Weftminfter. Willis, Mitred Abbeys, vol. I. p. 206. In l. 31. r. *Edmundi.*

21. *Reginaldi.*] Q. whether this daughter of Reginald Lord Grey (here written Graa) of Wilton occurs any where elfe; or if the time of his death be elfewhere mentioned? Compare Dugdale, Bar. vol. I. p. 714.

22. *Germyn.*] This anchorite was no nobleman, but an ecclefiaftic.

25. *Stapulæ,*] *ftaple* (Spelman's Gloffary), there being a wool-ftaple here. See p. 5. l. 11.

30. *Capellâ,*] potius *capella'*, i. e. *capellam.*

31. *Edwardi.*] Q. *Edmundi*; for fee on lin. 19.

33. *Cuft',*] *Cuftode.*

2. 1. *Imprimis.*] Here begin the expences.

infra,] f. *inter.*

* Thefe torches, it is conceived, were made of wax, which in ordinary cafes were let out by the church, and charged to the party according to the confumption at the moment. This appears in the York Churchwardens' Accompts, where wax is charged. Edit.

P. 2. l. 2 *Comptacōis,*] *computationis,* which occurs not in Spelman or Du Fresne.
3. *Mut,*] *mutton.*
7. *Randolf's.*] Q. *Randal's* alley?
12. *Chales,*] a *chalice*; so p. 9. l. 28.
Sr R^d *Wydevile,*] probably youngest son of Richard Earl Rivers. Dugdale, Bar. vol. II. p. 231—233.
14. *Antiphoners,*] books used in the Romish service, containing the Antiphonæ (*i. e.* chanting, or responsive singing). Spelman. See *Antiphonarius.*
20. *Sistern,*] members of some female *gild*, or sisterhood, in the management of these churchwardens; see p. 3. l. 20; perhaps St. Mary; see p. 4. l. 41; p. 5. l. 20; p. 6. l. 23. 36; many gilds here; p. 7. l. 26. 28. 32. 34; p. 8. l. 5.
21. A priory of Black monks in Berkshire.
28. *John Fogge, knight,*] of Repton, parish of Ashford, Kent. Hasted's History of Kent, vol. III. p. 260. Philpot, p. 56.
30. *Caxton,*] our famous old printer. See p. 3. l. 24. 43; p. 5. l. 15.
33. *Pik,*] *Pitt,* grave *. *Pytte* in next line, *& alibi.* So in the English Psalms. 6*s.* 8*d.* was the customary fee.
34. Wm *Alyne.*] See p. 3. l. 12.
35. *Church-yard.*] Preaching in church-yards was common now; witness St. Paul's cross.
37. St *Erasmus,*] bishop and martyr; a saint in great request here. See p. 3. l. 42. There is (or was) St. Erasmus's chapel in the abbey. See Crull's History of the Abbey. The altar seems to have been without the church.
41. *Convicte house,*] for such perhaps as had been in arms against the King. See p. 7. l. 18.

3. 4. St *Marg' and* St *Kat',*] images in the church. St. Margaret was the patron saint; the image of whom was to be in every church. Lyndwood, p. 253, ed. Oxon. See p. 10. l. 9. So on restoration of Popery, in the reign of Queen Mary, it was put up again; p. 14. l. ult.
7. *Stoner.*] See p. 5. l. 13.
12. *Alyn.*] Newcourt, vol. I. p. 608. There seems to be some mistake in calling him *Daniel*; perhaps *Dane*, as p. 6. l. 15. See before, p. 2. l. 34.
17. *Feretre isle.*] Q. can it mean where the *bier* or *biers* were kept? or where the shrine stood †?
21. *Harry Sharp.*] He occurs not in Newcourt, vol. I. p. 747.
24. *Caxton.*] See p. 2. l. 30.
St *Gregory.*] Gregory the Great, whose image, we may suppose, was in the church; see line 30, where it is written *Pety.* A *Piety* was a bank, or box, for the poor.

* *Pits* and *knells* continue to this day customary articles in the churchwardens accompts of St. Bride's. Edit. † Most probably the *shrine*, which, presumably, was inclosed by iron rails, commonly called *ferretres.* Edit.

P. 3.

P. 3. l. 28. *Dragon,*] uſed probably in pageants.

30. *St Gregory's Pety.*] See line 24.

31. *Abington.*] See l. 40; alſo p. 5. l. 28.

33. *Rynſyvale,*] *Roncefvalle*, in Navarre. See the geographers. Where this gild or brotherhood was is not known *. *Ronncydevall*, p. 7. l. 24. A place near St. Margaret's, with a chapel, p. 11. l. 30. 32.

40. *Abyngdon.*] See l. 31.

42. *St Eraſmus.*] See p. 2. l. 37.

43. *Caxton.*] See p. 2. l. 30.

ult. *St Cornelius.*] There was a fraternity of St. *Cornelius* in St. Margaret's church at Weſtminſter. See a pardon granted to them, Brit. Top. vol. I. p. 772, 773. The word *licence*, p. 4. l. 10, 11, alibi, may mean *permiſſion* or *leave* to lend them.

4. 1. *Grey of Wilton.*] If this were Lady Grey, ſhe occurs not in Dugdale.

2. *Lady Billing.*] For this great benefactreſs to the church of St. Margaret, ſee Newcourt, p. 721.

3. *De Word,*] relatives of Wynken, the printer. Ames, Typographical Antiquities, p. 79.

5. *Mr. Lacy.*] Lady Billing married a Mr. Lacy to her third huſband; and if you will ſuppoſe ſhe erected that monument for her three huſbands (Weever, p. 493. Newcourt, p. 721.) in Lacy's life-time, no improbable ſuppoſition, this may be the perſon.

Lord of Dudley.] John Sutton. Dugdale, Bar. vol. II. p. 216; and ſee below, p. 5. l. 23.

12. *Edmund.*] The child dying at a year old, this probably was ſome diſtribution of money at his birth or death.

19. *Owen Tudor,*] third ſon of Owen Tudor and Queen Katharine, a monk of Weſtminſter. Sandford, p. 285. 293. This is a very curious article. He was buried probably in the abbey.

21. *Faulks Hall,*] now *Vaux Hall.*

23. *Mendyne,*] the pronunciation of *mending*.

24. *Flour,*] *floor.*

Rents,] f. *Abyngdon rents.*

25. *for four*] *torches.*

26. *Amner,*] *almoner.* This perhaps was ſome diſtribution of money, on occaſion of Prince Arthur's wedding.

28. *College money.*] The ſum being ſo large, it ſhould mean *collected* money.

29. *Dragons,*] enſigns of the family of Tudor, then on the throne.

30. *Kelby,*] a prieſt probably.

40. *Pynſon.*] Ames's Typographical Antiquities, p. 111.

5. 1. *Simeon.*] Q. whether he occurs elſewhere?

4. *Clifton.*] Ob. 28 H. VII. 1506. Thoroton, p. 55.

6. *Selerer,*] *celarer.*

* Northumberland-houſe ſtands on the ſite of a cell of St. Mary de Ronceval, diſſolved by Henry VIII. Edit.

P. 5. l. 6. *Weſtminſter,*] i. e. monaſtery.
11. *Wolſtapler.*] See p. 1. l. 25.
13. *Stoner.*] See p. 3. l. 7.
18. *Bradding*] See p. 1. l. 5.
26. *Place,*] f. private chapel.
27. *Wm Balard.*] See p. 8. l. 19.
32. *Ancres.*] See p. 1. l. 7.
42. *Said church.*] It is difficult to ſay by what title our churchwardens received this money.

6. 4. *Curate,*] nominated by the abbey of Weſtminſter.
6. *Vampage,*] See below, l. 20; and p. 10. l. 33.
15. *Buckfaſt,*] the Ciſtertian abbey of Buckfaſtre, Devon. Tanner, Not. p. 91. infra, p. 7. l. 13.
20. *A pax,*] called by Archbiſhop Winchelſea *oſculatorium* (Lyndwood, p. 252. ed. Oxon.), a crucifix ſubſtituted to be kiſſed at maſs, in lieu of the antient *oſculum pacis.*
21. St *Margaret finger.*] This muſt be a valuable acquiſition to this church. St. Margaret was Queen of Scotland, died 1093, and her feſtival was 10 June.
24. *Brethren.*] See p. 2. l. 20.
25. *Feſtfull,*] feſtival.
28. *Aynſworth,*] Dr. Henry, who died 1537. Newcourt, vol. I. p. 502. infra p. 7. l. 7. 20.
29. *Rys ap Thomas,*] knight of the Garter. Fuller's Worthies, in Carmarthen, p. 27.
31. *Juxſon,*] probably grandfather of the Archbiſhop William Juxon. Wood, Athen. vol. II. col. 1144.
33. *Ld Cardinal*] Wolſey.
34. *Lord's place,*] York-houſe, or Whitehall.
36. *Lady lands.*] See p. 2. l. 20. ad infra, l. 38.
40. *Ruſhes,*] uſed in ſummer for coolneſs*, both in churches and great houſes. See p. 12. l. 10.
ult. *Boyling alley.*] Q. *Bowling* alley, by Dean's yard? Survey of London and Weſtminſter by Pariſh Clerks, p. 271.

7. 2. *Box money.*] Q. if of the gilds? See l. 16. & p. 8. l. 5.
7. *Aynſworth.*] See p. 6. l. 28.
13. *Morley,*] infra, p. 33. & ſupra, p. 6. l. 8. She appears to have died in 1524, p. 9. l. 17.
19. *Legh,*] infra, l. 42.
20. *Aynſworth.*] See p. 6. l. 28.
21. *Biſhop.*] See p. 8. l. 3.
24. *Rouncycevall.*] See p. 3. l. 33.
30. *St. Cornelius.*] See p. 3. l. *ult.* and p. 9. l. 21.
33. *Morley.*] See line 13.

* Rather uſed both for warmth and ornament in *winter*, both in churches, and in halls of entertainment in palaces, and great houſes. Edit.

P. 7.

P. 7. l. 34. *Watir,*] the pronunciation of *Walter*.
35. *Rode loft.*] This, I think, was commonly placed between the choir and chancel; perhaps there might be two here.
43. *Legh,*] fupra, l. 19. *Mr.* here is rather a tautology.
8. 3. *Bifhop.*] See p. 7. l. 21.
7. *Barnefton,*] for the fteeple. See l. 10.
11. *Pylage,*] perhaps piling or ftowing the ftones in the barge.
13. *St Katryn port,*] probably St. Catharine's wharf.
14. *Crifpanyan day,*] Crifpinus & Crifpinianus day, 25 October.
15. *Scala celi,*] in imitation of the *fcala celi* at St. Peter's, Rome.
17. *May game.*] The fports ended, the children, we may fuppofe, collected money from the fpectators, and made this offering to the church out of it.
18. *Borough.*] Thomas Lord Borough, knight of the Garter, married Margaret, daughter of Thomas Lord Roos of Kendal, and died before 29 May, 1495. Dugdale, Baronage, vol. II. p. 288.
19. *Balard.*] See p. 5. l. 27.
20. *Pitt.*] The charging 17*s.* 4*d.* is very high. See p. 3. l. 33.
26. *Lord Rede,*] perhaps Sir Robert Read, chief juftice of the Common Pleas. Kimber, Baronage, vol. II. p. 179.
28. *Monftre,*] a *fhew*-glafs. Cotgrave, French Dictionary.
29. *Pondre,*] weight.
42. *Rys ap Thomas,*] See p. 6. l. 29.
9. 4. *Man,*] fervant.
7. *Herft clothe,*] hearfe cloth.
10. *Hallowed.*] Q. the occafion of this new confecration; perhaps in the repairs mentioned in line 15?
13. *Morley.*] See p. 7. l. 13.
19. *Judacis,*] i. e. Judafes, for fome pageant or interlude.
21. *Cornellis-houfe,*] belonging probably to the gild of St. Cornelius. See p. 7. l. 30.
22. *Condett,*] conduit.
23. *Pales-gate,*] palace at Weftminfter.
28. *Chales.*] See p. 2. l. 12.
36. *Skelton.*] John Skelton the poet. See the editor's preface to his works, edit. 1736. He was then in fanctuary at the abbey.
ult. *Wykers for the quere,*] *wiekers,* or rufhes, for the choir, or quire.
10. 3. *Parden,*] i. e. pardoner.
6. *Hay Crofe.*] Q. where this place was? V. infra, p. 11. l. 23. Q. *High* Crofs.
7. *Hencheman,*] an attendant, or rather a page.
8. *Mette,*] meat. *Thef,*] thief. *Stalle,*] ftole. *Pyx,*] in this the hoft was placed when carried to a diftance.
10. *St Margarett's tabernacle.*] See p. 3. l. 4.
16. *Almfhoufe,*] founded by Margaret, mother of Henry VII. Newcourt, vol. I. p. 721. Stowe, by Strype, vol. II. p. 634. 641. 642.
18. *Iflype.*] John Iflip. See Newcourt, vol. I. p. 717.
19. *Wynkefeld,*] wife perhaps of Sir Anthony Wingfield.

P. 10.

P. 10. l. 22. Surplices for pariſh clerks (ſo I underſtand it), and the ſexton is extraordinary *.

25. *Totehill,*] where there was a burying-ground. Newcourt, vol. I. p. 722.

30. *Monyth mynde,*] the trental.

30. *Elizabeth.*] Dugdale, Bar. vol. I. p. 198.

33. *Dane,*] f. dame.

Vampage.] See p. 6. l. 20. and below here, l. 37.

37. *Dawbneis,*] of the Scotch family of *Stewart* †. Crawford, p. 257.

38. *Chalis.*] As chalices were often preſents to churches, in great churches they had many of them, and could let them out to hire.

39. *To regiſtre.*] This was the firſt regiſter ordered by Cromwell, Vicar General.

43. *Lady Ancreſs.*] See p. 1. l. 7. As the corporas cloths for the covering of the hoſts were ſacred linen, it was very proper to put them to be waſhed into the hands of an *anchoreſs*, or religious woman, who was paid for it.

11. 2. *Injunction.*] Burnet, Reform. p. 249. They paid for it, it ſeems, at twice. So below, p. 13. l. 16.

4. *King's arms.*] This was the firſt time they were put up in churches. The King's arms, which are generally placed over the entrance of the chancel from the body of the church (or choir) are ſuppoſed to have ſuperceded the *rood.*

Privy ſeals] of Thomas Cromwell, Earl of Eſſex.

6. *Chapelle*] within the pariſh of St. Margaret's, as line 12.

7. *Viſitors.*] Q. of this viſitation?

10. *Old place,*] or palace, perhaps Weſtminſter, the King being removed to Whitehall.

18. *Mr. Chidley,*] made ſerjeant at law 32 H. VIII. Dugdale, Chron. Ser. p. 85.

23. *Eye Croſs.*] Q. High Croſs? See p. 10. l. 6. if the ſame place.

30. *Rouncyvall.*] See p. 3. l. 33.

34. *Creping to the croſs.*] For this act of devotion, ſee Strype, Life of Cranmer, p. 135, 136. and his Memoirs, vol. II. p. 256. More may be ſeen in the Northumberland Houſehold Book.

41. *Kitchen.*] Dr. Ant. Kitchen, Biſhop of Landaff. Wood, Faſti, vol. I. p. 62. Strype, Cranmer, p. 137. Memoirs, vol. II. p. 67. See Godwin de Præſul.

12. 9. *Cage,*] a temporary priſon for ſmall offenders. Many of theſe have exiſted very lately; and others perhaps are now in being. They were generally in the market-place.

10. *Dedication day,*] i. e. of the church; a grand feſtival in all churches.

16. *Conception*] of the Bleſſed Virgin, a picture.

Barnard.] Perhaps Theod. Bernardi. Walpole on Painting, vol. I. p. 174, ed. 8vo.

* Might not both the clerks and the ſexton (i. e. ſacriſtan) be then eccleſiaſtics? EDIT.

† The preſent Duke of Richmond is Duke D'Aubigny in France; and his title was acknowledged before the French Revolution, and regiſtered. EDIT.

P. 12.

P. 12. l. 26. *Knightſbridge.*] This is within the liberty of Weſtminſter.

35. *Viſitours.*] Strype, Memoirs, vol. II. p. 46. Names occur, p. 47.

39. *Commandments.*] This was a new thing; and query, whether this be not the firſt inſtance? Taken away anno 1557, p. 15. l. 6.

41. *Purcyvaunte,*] purſuivant.

42. *Brothered,*] brotherhoods, or gilds, which were given to the King this year by parliament. Strype, Memoirs, vol. II. p. 63. 135.

13. 1. *Images.*] Then ſold. Strype, Memoirs, vol. II. p. 9. 49.

3. *Said.*] Not mentioned before.

4. *viii a clock,*] ringing the bell then.

7. *Harneſſes,*] men's defenſive armour.

16. *Paraphraſe of Eraſmus.*] Strype, Memoirs, vol. II. p. 28. V. infra, p. 15. l. 11.

20. *Commiſſioners.*] See p. 12. l. 35.

26. *Lattymer.*] The martyr, Hugh Latimer.

27. *Books.*] Common Prayer Books. Strype, Memoirs, vol. II. p. 84.

37. *vi chapter of St. John.*] This and the following article is very ſingular; and query, whether we have any other inſtance of writing this chapter on a table in chancels? They certainly applied the words to the Sacrament of the Lord's Supper. See p. 15. l. 15.

14. 1. *Richard Sycell.*] This was the father of the great Lord Treaſurer; the name being very variouſly written in theſe times, as Cicell, Sitſilt, Cecil, &c.; and yet, as he died 35 H. VIII. it is ſtrange the grave ſhould not be paid for till 1552.

2. *S*[r] *John Arundel,*] of the family of Treryſe. Dugdale, Bar. vol. II. p. 483.

6. *Recreation.*] repaſt, or entertainment.

11. *Commiſſioners.*] See p. 12. l. 35.

14. *Communion Books.*] Strype, Memoirs, vol. II. p. 214.

15. *Pulpit,*] reading-deſk. See p. 21. l. 9.

20. *Wyat.*] Sir Thomas Wyat of Kent.
The Queen] Mary.

24. *Scripture.*] Perhaps the 6th chapter of John, before-mentioned, p. 13. l. 37.

27. *Viſitation*] to the ſick.

28. *Reconciliation*] to Romiſh religion again, which Cardinal Pole was to do. Strype, Memoirs, vol. III. p. 156.

28. *Biſhop's dinner.*] Edmund Bonner.

30. *Veil,*] *veal*, calf.

36. *M*[r] *Deane*] of Weſtminſter, Hugh Weſton.

40. *Sheffe,*] ſheaves.

44. *Yeorle of Suſſex,*] Thomas Ratcliffe. See p. 20. l. 2.

15. 2. *Abbot,*] John Fekenham. Le Neve, Faſti, p. 364.

6. *Serplys,*] ſurplices of this cloth. See p. 12. l. 39.

9. *Portriſmarthe,*] Portſmouth. Strype, Annals, p. 22.

11. *Parafrawſe,*] paraphraſe of Eraſmus. See p. 13. l. 16.

12. *Communion Book.*] Strype, Annals, vol. I. p. 80. ſeq.

P. 15. l. 14. *Mary and John.*] These images had, it seems, been restored by Queen Mary. See line 17.

15. *Tabil.*] See p. 13. l. 37.

18. *Visitors.*] For them and the visitation, see Strype, Annals, vol. I. p. 165. 167. infra, p. 18. l. 11.

33. *Jane Semer,*] daughter of the late Protector Seymour, Duke of Somerset. Brooke, p. 218.

16. 2. *Concealed lands.*] See Strype, Annals, vol. II. p. 209. III. p. 404. 468. &c.

12. *Coorse,*] coarse.

21. *Skochyns,*] escutcheons.

22. *Bawdkyn,*] a rich stuff. Leland, Collectanea, vol. IV. p. 324. Barnes, Edw. III. p. 632.

29. *Patent,*] rectiùs *Paten*, i. e. *Patina*.

33. *Almen Rvelette.*] I have met with the word *Almaine rivets*, but cannot recollect where. These are *German* somethings; q. what?

38. *Newhaven.*] See p. 17. l. 17. This is now *Havre de Grace*. Strype, Annals, vol. I. p. 367.

17. 5. *Song books,*] music books.

9. *Mantells,*] r. *manuels*, i. e. exercises.

12. *Privy purse*] of Mr. More, who seems to have had the management of the *Privy purse* of this church. See p. 16. l. 37.

16. *Easing of warrs.*] See this prayer, or *service*, as here it is called, in Strype's Annals, vol. I. p. 293.

17. *Newhaven.*] See p. 16. l. 38.

20. *Prest money,*] enlisting or retaining money. Blount.

24. *Dogs,*] being supposed to spread the plague, when it once broke out; the dogs were killed both abroad and here. Volney's Travels, vol. II. V. infra, p. 23. l. 26. seq. p. 27. l. 15. Of this plague, see Ascham's English works, p. 191; Strype, Life of Parker, p. 131. 140; Life of Grindal, p. 70.

31. *Sr Wm Sentlow,*] captain of the guard, and third husband of Elizabeth Hardwick, Countess of Shrewsbury. Kennet, Memoirs of Cavendish, p. 66.

33. *Verdyte,*] of the sidemen, p. 18. l. 14.

18. 1. *Book of praises.*] See Strype, Life of Parker, p. 232. infra, p. 35.

5. *Scotland.*] See Stowe, by Strype, vol. II, p. 578.

7. *Coat armour,*] f. Queen's arms.

9. *Stonagers*] See Strype, Annals, vol. I. p. 554; particularly, p. 556.

11. *Visitors.*] See p. 15. l. 18.

21. *North parts.*] Q. whether any thing unusual in this?

26. *Injunctions.*] Sparrow's Collection, p. 65.

31. *Aulter stone*;] a table was now used. Many of these altar stones, so *defaced* and *laid down*, may be seen in our churches, as at Peterborough minster, on the floor, St. Albans, and Bridlington, on a tomb.

35. *Turk.*] V. supra, l. 1.

19. 3. *Ld Wharton.*] The second Lord Wharton. Dugdale, Bar. vol. II. p. 389.

P. 19. l. 4. *College*] of Weftminfter.

9. *Havering*,] in Effex, where there was a royal manfion. Mr. Gough, in his fine edition of Camden, p. 52. Of the Queen's being here at this time, fee Mr. Nichols's Progreffes of this Queen, preface, p. vii.

10. *Bifhops*.] Q. how four of thefe Common Prayer Books coft but 6*d*.?

12. *Vifitacion*.] See p. 15. l. 18.

20. *Maundy*,] diftribution of alms on Thurfday before Good Friday.

21. To *liquor*,] to greafe.

24. St *Ann's chapel*.] Newcourt, vol. I. p. 721. V. infra, l. 28. Stowe, by Strype, vol. II. p. 634. 643.

30. *Calyvers*,] guns. Littleton, and Johnfon's Dictionary.

38. *Soiers*,] q. foldiers? *Anfyant*,] antient, i. e. enfign or colours. *Drome*,] i. e. drum.

43. *Vifitation*.] However it came to pafs, the charge is exceffive.

44. *Abridgement of the Statutes*;] probably *Raftal's Abridgement* in Englifh, for which fee Mr. Ames's Typographical Antiquities, p. 143.

20. 2. *Lady Suffex*.] See p. 14. l. 44.

5. *Payne*,] *pane*, or *panel*, whole light, or compartment, in a large window.

11. *Conduit*.] Stowe, p. 634.

18. *Otelande*,] a royal palace in Surrey.

21. Ld *Windfor*,] Frederick. Dugdale, Bar. vol. II. p. 309.

30. *Cornellis*,] perhaps Cornelius Van Dun. Stowe, by Strype, vol. II. p. 624. 634.

36. *Parliament*.] Strype, Annals, vol. III. p. 293.

37. Ld *Admiral*,] Charles Howard, Lord Effingham, afterwards Earl of Nottingham.

39. *Sir Edw. Sutton*, &c.] Dugdale, Bar. II. p. 217.

41. *Blacks*, &c.] Thefe black cloths, perquifites to the church, were redeemed with money.

21. 6. *Books of Prayers*.] Strype's Life of Whitgift, p. 269.

8. *Taking the traytors*.] Strype, Annals, vol. III. lib. ii. c. 5.

9. *Lector pulpit*,] reading defk. See p. 14. l. 15.

15. Ld *Bourghes*,] Lord Borough. See p. 25. l. 7.

21. *Sarrizons*,] Saracens.

24. L^y^ *Stafford's clofes*,] a clofe pew. She was a lady of quality, and died in 1604. Stowe, by Strype, vol. II. p. 621.

26. *Actor*.] Q. the lector? V. fupra, l. 9.

31. *Canterbury's*.] I find nothing of this vifit of the Queen's in Strype's Life of Whitgift.

38. *Servante*.] See p. 23. l. 11.

ult. *Dinner*.] Nothing of this dinner is found in Mr. Strype's Life of this great prelate.

22. 7. *Prayer Books*.] Strype, Annals, vol. III. p. 517.

19. *College church*] of Weftminfter.

P. 22. l. 21. *Baron Southerton,*] John Sotherton, Baron of Exchequer. Dugdale, Chron. Series, p. 94.
23. *Nonsuche,*] a royal palace in Surrey.
25. *Mr Secretary's,*] Sir Francis Walsingham's; but query?
34. *Somerset House,*] which then belonged to the crown, and was one of her occasional residences.
23. 1. *Feckenham.*] He died 1585. Fuller, Worthies, in Worcestershire.
11. *Servante.*] See p. 21. l. 38.
14. *Lord Chancellor's.*] Sir Christopher Hatton.
24. *Cromwell.*] Henry Lord Cromwell, buried at *Laund* abbey *, co. Leicester. Dugdale, Bar.
26. *Dogs.*] See p. 17. l. 24. Of this plague, see Fuller's Church History, vol. IX. p. 219.
32. *Mr Dean*] of Westminster.
35. *Chapell,*] St. Magdalen. Newcourt, vol. I. p. 722. query, of this Mr. Palmer?
24. 6. 313 *poor people*] dead; probably of the plague.
11. *Hospital,*] For Lady Dacre's hospital, see Stowe, by Strype, vol. II. p. 644.
32. *Dere time.*] See p. 25. l. 11.
25. 4. *Spaniards*] at Cadiz. Rapin, vol. II. p. 145.
5. *Prayer Book,*] Thanksgiving Prayer on taking Cadiz. Strype, Annals, vol. IV. p. 262.
7. *Ld Borrowes.*] See p. 21. l. 5.
11. *Great scarcity.*] See p. 24. l. 32.
20. *Sanctuary.*] Stowe, by Strype, vol. II. p. 613, 614.
22. *Raynolde.*] Ibid. p. 622.
24. *First letter,*] called *Blooming letter.*
27. *Marmaduke.*] His surname was *Servante.* See p. 21. l. 38.
28. *Ldy Burghley,*] Mildred, second wife of Lord Burleigh, and daughter of Sir Anthony Cook.
26. 2. *Great wind.*] See Baker's Chronicle, p. 408.
5. *Masters.*] These, I presume, are called *worshipfulls,* p. 11. alibi.
7. *Said.*] See p. 25. l. 44.
14. *Towels for the comunicants.*] Q. V. infra, p. 31. l. 31.
16. *Brigs,*] bridges; perhaps over the ditch mentioned p. 25. l. 37.
17. *To,*] i. e. total.
34. *Hospital.*] Q. infra, l. 40. and p. 27. l. 2. &c.
27. 4. *Plague.*] Stowe, Hist. p. 857.
13. 14*th March*;] perhaps on account of Tir-Oen.
20. *The King*] James.
24. *Folks,*] dead, probably of the plague.
31. *Utter,*] outer.

* His monument still remains there, and is engraved in Mr. Nichols's History of Leicestershire.

P. 27.

P. 27. l. 34. *5th of August,*] anniverſary of his arrival. See l. 20.
35. *Canons.*] Sparrow, Coll. p. 263.
39. *Daughter,*] Princeſs Mary. Sandford ſays ſhe was born . . . March.
28. 12. *King's child,* Princeſs Sophia, born 21 June.
13. *K. of Denmark,*] Chriſtian, the Queen's brother.
31. *Gowre's day,*] on account of Gowry's conſpiracy. Rapin, vol. II. p. 151. 163.
36. *Royſton,*] part in the county of Cambridge, part in Hertfordſhire. He had probably been hunting there. See p. 29. l. 25.
29. 14. *Prince of Wales,*] Prince Henry, created 30 May. Sandford, p. 557. Salmon, Chron. Hiſt. p. 97.
15. *Fire works.*] Q. whether the firſt in England?
19. *5th Aug.*] Gowry's conſpiracy. See p. 28. l. 32.
26. *Fleſh.*] This ordinance was for the purpoſe of encouraging the fiſhery.
28. *Birth day.*] Sandford, p. 564, ſays, Princeſs Elizabeth was born 19 Auguſt. Q. whether he or the churchwardens are miſtaken?
29. *Map-roller*;] perhaps of the Sewers. See p. 26. l. 6; or of the pariſh eſtates, if ſuch ſurveys were of ſo early date.
30. 2. *Richard*] Neile.
7. *Dunbar,*] George Hume. Crawford, p. 113.
20. *Orris-powder,*] Iris.
26. *Queen of Scots,*] whoſe body was removed from Peterborough. See Stowe, p. 601.
28. *Elizabeth,*] the King's eldeſt daughter. She was married to the Count Palatine of the Rhine. Sandford, p. 564. V. infra, p. 56.
36. *Elizabeth.*] Vide ſupra, l. 28.
38. *D^r^ Maſters,*] probably *commiſſary*.
40. *King of Denmark.*] This was his ſecond viſit. See p. 28. l. 13.
31. 27. *Prince, his creation.*] Charles, on the death of Prince Henry, was created Prince of Wales.
33. *Her grace's child.*] Charles Ludovick, commonly called *The Palſgrave.*
34. *Towelling.*] V. ſupra, p. 26. 14.
32. 5. *Stone door*;] perhaps *door-caſe*, as below, l. 23.
7. *Correction houſe.*] This, I preſume, is now in being, under the name of *Tothil-Fields Bridewell.*
30. *Mills*;] probably for the people to work with.
33. 19. *Spaniſh ambaſſador.*] Q. Gondamor?
29. *Iſſues,*] fines. Johnſon's Dictionary.
31. *Muckenders,*] handkerchiefs. Ibid. Called *muckingers* in the North at this day.
34. 8. *Braſs*;] perhaps for badges.
30. *George,*] George Mountaigne.
35. *Viſited,*] i. e. with the plague. Stowe's Hiſtory, p. 1041. Salmon, Chron. Hiſt. vol. I. p. 106.
41. *Dr Bargrave,*] Dr. Iſaac Bargrave, made Dean of Canterbury 1625.
35. 6. *Coronation day,*] 2 Feb. 1625.

P. 35. l. 8. *Elsinge,*] clerk of parliament.
11. 1447 *poor*] dead of the plague.
18. *Vault*] in the chapel there.
37. *Fast.*] Q. if this fast, and those, p. 37. l. 30 and 40, and p. 38. l. 22. be noticed any where else?
ult. Coronation;] a mistake, 27 March was the *accession*. So again, p. 37. l. 6. p. 37. l. 39. p. 43. l. 19.
37. 6. *Coronation day.*] See p. 35. l. *ult.*
14. *William,*] William Cecil.
15. *Eight pounds.*] Money was then at 8 *per cent.*
21. *Edgelie*] was of Cambridge. See Wood, Fasti, vol. II. col. 40. A loyalist, and a person of good note. Ibid.
23. *Rd Goodwin,*] probably of Cambridge.
2. *Winchester.*] Dr. Richard Neile.
18. *Rd Busby.*] Afterwards the famous master of Westminster school. Infra, p. 41. l. 15.
27. *Buckingham,*] stabbed 23 Aug. 1728.
37. *With child,*] miscarried of a son. Salmon, p. 112.
39. 6. *Voltelins,*] Valtelins; allies of the Swiss, and Protestants.
18. *Brenford Bridge,*] a county business. See p. 40. l. 19. seq. p. 4. l. 3.
37. *Ld Paget.*] He died 1628. Dugdale, Bar. vol. II.
40. 12. *Sr Jno Corbet.*] Stowe, p. 622.
25. *Dr Vinc. Peirs.*] See p. 41. l. 2.
30. *Charles his birth,*] 29 May, 1630.
35. *From Spain,*] in the reign of James I.
36. *Jno Martin.*] Nothing more is known of him.
41. 2. *Dr Peirs.*] See p. 40. l. 25.
14. *Visited houses*] with the plague. See Mr. Nichols's Bibl. Top. Brit. No XV. p. 70.
20. *Lady Marie,*] afterwards Princess of Orange.
32. *Theobalds,*] a royal palace, co. Hert.
34. *Visc. Dorchester,*] Anne Charlton, whose husband died 1631. Dugd. Bar
42. 10. *Verge,*] The jurisdiction of the Lord steward of the household.
18. *King Charles' hospital.*] Q. what is become of this? See l. 32. seq.
43. 3. *Keimoul,*] Kirnoul.
13. *Ship money,*] now first imposed.
17. *St Paul's.*] It had been burnt anno 1561. Newcourt, p. 3.
26. *Childbed.*] Princess Elizabeth was then born.
44. 3. *Ldy Mary.*] See p. 41. l. 20.
4 *Ldy Anne,*] born 1.. March, 1626; ob. 1640.
11. *Said Mr Glynne.*] He has not been named before; but see p. 45. l. 15.
27. *Chersey Bridge,*] in Surrey. See p. 45. l. 6.
35. *Spain.*] Temp. Jac. I. See p. 40. l. 35.
45. 15. *Mr Jno Glynne and Mr Maynard.*] See p. 44. l. 11. *Maynard* perhaps was afterwards the famous old serjeant Maynard.

P. 45.

P. 45. l. 23. *5th of Octcber.*] See p. 40. l. 34. it is 6th of October.
25. *Queen Mother,*] Mary de Medicis.
28. *Dr Eden,*] Dr. Thomas Eden, a very eminent civilian. Ward's Lives of Gresham Professors, p. 240.
32. *Delivery*] of Henrietta Maria. Sandford, p. 608, says she was born 16 June, 1644. Q.
33. *Declaration.*] For this and the following, see a collection about ecclesiastical affairs in Scotland, 1638, printed anno 1639, small folio.
46. 2. *Innocents,*] idiots. Infra, l. 39.
7. *Said Tho. Kirke;*] not mentioned before. He was high constable. Infra, l. 35.
13. *Pollet,*] John Lord Poulet, of Hinton St. George. Dugdale, Bar. vol. II. p. 375.
16. *Richmond,*] Frances, relict of Lodowick Stuart, Duke of Richmond. Dugdale, Bar. vol. II. p. 426.
21. *Barwick.*] Rapin, vol. II. p. 308; see also below, l. 36.
24. *St Martin's,*] incorporated with St. Margaret's in this. See p. 58. l. 17.
41. *Canons.*] Sparrow, Collect. p. 335.
47. 1. *Heywood.*] He was stabbed by a Papist, but not mortally, in Westminster Hall. Salmon, p. 122.
3. *Triennial Parliament,*] 16 Feb. Rapin, vol. II. p. 355.
6. *Protestation.*] Rapin, vol. II. p. 369.
7. *Articles,*] perhaps against Lord Strafford. Rapin, p. 374.
39. *Tho. Gawen.*] See p. 48. l. 9.
ult. *Fasts.*] Rapin, vol. II. p. 35. See below, p. 48. l. 23.
48. 9. *Tho. Gawen.*] See p. 47. l. 39.
12. *Birth-day,*] not easily to be found elsewhere.
15. *Return from Scotland.*] Salmon, p. 126. Rapin, p. 388.
23. *Fast-day.*] See p. 47. l. ult.
49. 3. *A fast.*] This fast is not in common histories.
6. *Braintford.*] Salmon, p. 132. Rapin, p. 465.
9. *New chapel.*] Stowe, by Strype, p. 643.
15. *Black chest.*] See p. 25. l. 38. p. 54. l. 11.
17. *Dr Wimberley,*] Dr. Gilbert Wimberley. Wood, Fasti, vol. II. p. 215. Infra, p. 55. l. 35. Dead 1653; p. 62. l. 38.
21. *Ld General,*] Earl of Essex.
26. *Fast-day.*] The Commons ordered these so frequently, that we need take no farther notice of them. See p. 54. l. 31. seq.
30. *Boatheyer,*] boat-hire.
32. *Ireland.*] The parliament borrowed money for this purpose (Rapin, p. 456.); but applied it against the King. Salmon, p. 530.
50. 26. *Covenant,*] Scotch covenant, introduced here to be taken by all the Parliamentarians. Rapin, p. 483. V. infra, p. 36; p. 52. l. 3.
51. 14. *Toombe stones.*] These brasses were not stolen; but allowed to be taken from the grave-stones; and it is well known what *Dowsing* did by authority. See his Journal, 1786, 4to. *passim*.

P. 52.

P. 52. l. 18. *Directorie,*] Form of Prayer to be ufed inftead of Common Prayer Book.
19. *Mr Gibfon;*] perhaps the minifter, or curate.
20. *Lady Spotfwood,*] an Irifh lady, written Spotfworth, p. 55. l. 30.
29. *Market.*] Stowe, by Strype, p. 641.
38. *Colledge,*] Weftminfter abbey.
42. *Streets.*] This was the way of lighting the ftreets then; as now, I prefume, it is at *Paris*.
ult. The chaines.] See p. 50. l. 8.

53. 1. *Captain White,*] a brafier, or pewterer, of which rank of people the officers of the parliament army often confifted.
2. *Dartmouth and Hereford.*] Salmon, p. 141.
23. *Earl of Effex,*] The Lord General once, but now fet afide. He died 14 September.
37. *At Chriftmas.*] This cuftom ftill continues in moft places.
42. *Chriftmas Day*] abolifhed, with other feftivals, by the Puritans.

54. 10. *Rd Willis, Efq.*] created a baronet 11 June, 1646, afterwards a parliamentary fpy.
11. *Black cheft.*] See p. 49. l. 15.
13. *Manley,*] juftice of peace.

55. 14. *Goring Houfe,*] of Lord Goring, which had been feized by the parliament.
28. *Ofoulfton hundred,*] in Middlefex.
30. *Spotfworth.*] See p. 52. l. 20.

56. 1. *George Hare,*] clerk of the veftry. See p. 63. l. 24.
4. *Gurney Houfe.*] Infra, p. 61. l. 44.
6. *Dean and Chapter lands,*] diffolved 1640. Rapin, p. 380.
10. *Lord Mayor's fine,*] Sir Abraham Reynardfon (Salmon, p. 152.), lord mayor of London 1649, fined 2000*l.* for refufing to proclaim the act abolifhing kingly power in England, which fine was levied by fale of his goods. Hiftory and Antiquities of Tottenham, p. 99.
36. *Broken Crofs.*] Q. where was this?

58. 20. *Counfill of ftate,*] erected 1649. Rapin, p. 574.
22. *Scotifh prifoners,*] taken probably at Worcefter.
26. *Long woolftaple.*] See p. 59. l. 3. Survey of Parifh Clerks, p. 278.
27. *Lady Abbey.*] V. infra, p. 62. l. 31. in King-ftreet, Weftminfter.
40. *State's arms,*] in lieu of the King's.

59. 17. *Genl Ireton.*] He died 26 Nov. 1651, and was buried with great funeral pomp; infra, l. 39.

60. 6. *5l.*] read 25.
10. *Anchorift's,*] i. e. Anchorite's. So again, p. 63. l. 37.
18. *Albury,*] in Surrey.

62. 17. *Inftalled*] 16 Dec. 1653.
26. *Genl Deane.*] Salmon, p. 156.
27. *Mr Scobell,*] clerk of the Houfe of Commons.
40. *Birkhead,*] ferjeant at arms. Salmon, p. 158.

P. 63.

P. 63. l. 11. *Waldenses,*] Protestants of Piedmont. Salmon, p. 163.
14. *Primate of Ireland,*] James Usher, whom the Protector buried. Salmon, p. 163.
16. *Bp of Glocester,*] Godfrey Goodman, who died 19 Jan. 1655-6.
33. *Protector's funeral.*] He died 12 Aug. 1658, and buried 23 Nov.

64. 22. *Mr Phelps,*] clerk of the committee that sat on the King (Trial of Regic. p. 48.), and at the trial (Black Tribunal, p. . .); so that he was executed afterwards, on the King's return, 29 Aug. 1660, as a most obnoxious man.
34. *Duke of Glocester.*] He died of the small pox, 13 Sept. 1660.
Princesse Royal,] Mary Princess of Orange, died of the small-pox, 24 Dec. 1660.

65. 2. *To Parliament,*] 29 Aug. 1660.
5. *Queen's return,*] 2 Nov. 1660.
13. *Coronation,*] 23 Apr. 1661.
18. *Dr Gifford,*] probably rector of St. Michael Bassishaw. Newcourt, p. 478.
38. *Queen's landing,*] 14 May, 1662.
42. *Dr Tucker.*] He seems to have been the curate. See p. 66. l. 15,

66. 5. *Dr Bolton,*] Dr. Samuel Bolton. Le Neve's Fasti, p. 373.
11. *Sr Wm Scrogg,*] serjeant at law, or King's serjeant. Dugdale, Chron. Series, p. 117. Afterwards Lord Chief Justice.
15. *Dr Tucker.*] See p. 65. l. 42.
19. *Damage*] by the coronation.
28. *Mrs Hambden.*] V. infra, p. 69. l. 32.
31. *New church.*] Q. New chapel?
Fast;] perhaps 5 April, for success against the Dutch. Salmon, p. 187.
40. *Duchess of York,*] Lady Anne Hyde.

67. 3. *Victory,*] 3 June.
6. *Thanksgiving day,*] 30 June.
10. *Monthly fast,*] on account of the plague. Salmon, p. 187.
14. *Ld Ruthen.*] V. infra, l. 42.
28. *Victory,*] 25 and 26 July. Salmon, p. 190.
40. *Sr Robt Pye.*] Newcourt, p. 923.

68. 5. *Dr Wm Outrim.*] Newcourt, p. 463. Below, p. 69. l. 28. ubi rectiùs *Outram.*
7. *Lady Wheeler.*] See p. 72. l. 22. Stowe, by Strype, vol. II. p. 623.
16. *Peace*] with the Dutch.
24. *Dr Exton,*] commissary. See p. 69. l. 21.

69. 38. *Sr Wm Doyly,*] teller of the exchequer, l. 43.
41. *Mr Hanwell.*] See p. 71. l. 4.

70. 29. *Duke's funeral,*] General Monk, Duke of Albemarle, interred with great public funeral solemnity. Salmon, p. 196.
30. *Doctor,*] Dr. Outram, the minister of St. Margaret's.

71. 1. *Union of both houses.*] Rapin, p. 655.

P. 71. l. 3. *Dr Twisse,*] minister of the new chapel. Newcourt, p. 923.
4. *Good Friday.*] See p. 69. l. 42.
Hanwell.] Ibid, and Stowe, by Strype, p. 625.
30. *Osestrey,*] Osulston. See p. 55. l. 28.
36. *Mrs Barnett.*] See p. 22. l. 40.
43. *Prince of Orange,*] 30 Oct.
72. 1. *Dolben,*] afterwards Sir Gilbert, for whom see Kimber, Baronetage, vol. III. p. 10.
9. *Plymouth.*] Salmon, p. 197.
40. *Mrs Barnett.*] See p. 71. l. 38.
12. *Peace*] with Holland. Salmon, p. 202.
74. 23. *Prince of Orange,*] contracted to the lady *Mary.* These were afterwards King William and Queen Mary.
75. 6. *The plot,*] Rye House plot. Salmon, p. 227.
7. *Prince George*] of Denmark, whose marriage with Lady Anne, daughter of James Duke of York by his first wife, was solemnized 28 July following.
11. *Coronation day*] of James II. 23 Apr. 1785.
24. *Time* ;] perhaps *fine.*
Stanes,] in Middlesex.
27. *Cloath*] used at the coronation for walking upon. See l. 30.
76. 7. *Sr Thomas Rowe,*] probably the famous traveller Sir Thomas *Roe.* See p. 76. l. 37.
11. *French Protestants.*] Rapin, p. 760. See also below, l. 25.

W I G T O F T.

77. 6. *Cathedra Petri,*] 18 Jan. See p. 78. l. 30.
10. *Algarkirk,*] now Alderkirk, or Alderchurch, co. Linc.
16. *Houston.*] How very small the legacies are! shewing the scarcity, and great value of money, in 1484. See l. 30.
25. *Alsowell.*] Q. if not mis-read for *Alsewell*; *als* ocurring for *as*, in Forme of Cury, p. 124, and in other old authors?
27. *Kirk-house,*] an alehouse near the church, belonging to the church or parish. See p. 80. l. 3. p. 84. l. 11.
30. *Strik,*] a strike is a bushel, or four pecks, in many Northern parts.
78. 2. *A strik of barley,*] the increase of measure in malting.
12. *Brd* ;] perhaps for bord.
17. *Chantr',*] chantry. Q. if not now founded by some gild; the contributions being large?
33. *Yat aftr,*] *y* is here for *th*, and *that after* is *thereafter* *.
38. *Femble,*] a kind of hemp. Littleton writes *fimble.*
43. *New casting.*] Clappers were not *cast*; it seems therefore to mean *forging.* See p. 79. l. 1. 9.

* *At after* (meaning *afterwards*) is common in Yorkshire to this day, and most probably in the Northern parts of Lincolnshire. EDIT.

P. 79. l. 7. *Bordyng,*] entertainment.
15. *Fatte.*] Dugdale, Mon. vol. III. p. 276.
38. *For his noble*;] perhaps inftead of his 6*s*. 8*d*. the common due for burying in a church.
80. 24. *Awbes,*] *Alba* in Latin. *Alb*, Northumberland Houfehold Book, p. 431.; but ufually *Awbe*, as p. 97. l. 33. p. 99. l. 4.
81. 21. *Hill the hye road,*] cover the high rood or crofs. See *Heal*, in Ray's words.
22. *Mary's Autr.*] The church of Wigtoft is dedicated to St. Peter and St. Paul; fo that this was another altar within the church, appropriate to the chantry mentioned p. 78. l. 17.
82. 9. *Eleys,*] nearer to the *ailes*, and a better one confequently than *ifles*.
13. *Heyning,*] covering the walls with hay, or ftraw, perhaps, if they were of mud. Or this may mean *healing*, the fame as *hill*, p. 81. l. 21.
30. *Eny,*] *ev'y*, i. e. *every*. See again, p. 83. l. 14.
36. *Sutterton,*] a plaufible conjecture, were there not two Suttons in the neighbourhood.
83. 5. *Hangles,*] the parts of hinges that reft upon hooks. We call them now *riders*. Both are proper.
12. *Shefe.*] Q. if this fhould not be *fhete*, i. e. *fheet?*
19. *Well,*] benefit, as above, p. 80. l. 33.

ST. MARY HILL, BILLINGSGATE.

85. 20. *W*^th^ *criftal.*] See p. 93. l. 7.
ult. *The bell,*] Q. an alehoufe?
Sr *S. Cornwallis.*] Dugdale, Bar. vol. II. p. 480. again, p. 91.
86. 24. *Natural*;] it means *legitimate*, contrary to its prefent fenfe.
87. 6. *Powle,*] *Paul.*
5. *Contaryn.*] *Contarini*, a Venetian merchant. See p. 118. l. 1.
93. 8. *Paxes.*] Q. was the *pax* intended for this ufe?
16. *ij tapers.*] The churchwardens provided the tapers; but how the wafte of two fhould come to 1*l*. 5*s*. 4*d*. is ftrange. But fee note on p. 243.
94. 1. *Chayne.*] It was ufual in thofe times, and long after, to chain books with a fmall chain in churches, and in the public libraries, that they might not be ftolen, or carried away *.
2. *Bawdryk* †, *&c.*] a belt and buckle. Gloffary to Chaucer.
ult. *Tukkyn girdles.*] Q. if *ticken* ‡? ftill what could they be for?
96. 5. *Sepulchre*] of Chrift. V. infra, p. 98. l. 19.

* Almoft every volume in the public library at Leicefter is ftill fo chained. EDIT.

† The common term for the ftrap and buckle, by which the clappers of bells were fufpended. See Phillips's World of Words *in voce*. EDIT.

‡ Or it may be ftraps ufed to *bind*, or *tuck*, in oppofition to thofe ufed for *fufpenfion*. EDIT.

P. 96. l. 8. *Paſcall**.] It cannot mean *a rood or croſs* as conjectured in the note; for a *pewter diſh* †, as line 11, has no relation to a croſs. Q. if not to receive the Eaſter offerings in? See p. 102. l. 21.

15. *Stalls.*] For the ſtalls in chancels, ſee Mr. Thorpe's Regiſtrum Roffenſe, p. 60. Haſted's Hiſtory of Kent, vol. I. p. 537. vol. II. p. 45. Archæologia. vol. XI. p. 317—394.

97. 8. *Eſtrich,*] See p. 118. l. 6. a *rick*; I take to be *ric*, or kingdom, and ſo to be equivalent to Eaſt land. See p. 123. l. 30.

21. *Valuenge,*] amending. See p. 90. l. 4. *l* and *n* are often confounded.

27. *Church Hawe,*] church yard.

33. *Amys,*] *Amices*, ſurplices.

34. *Keying, &c.*] This article not intelligible.

98. 9. *Poleſis* ;] it ſeems to mean *pullies*; the veil was uſed in Lent to conceal the altar, &c. See p. 109. l. 27.

10. *Rayl,*] parting church and chancel.

23. *Pynning,*] ſupporting ‡. In *Kent* they call the bottom part of a wall the *underpinning*, which is a general term for brick foundations under timber.

99. 5. *Evangeliſts,*] images of them.

100. 13. *Teyſe* ;] perhaps Fr. *toiſe*, our fathom.

19. *Antiphoner.*] a liturgical book. Palmer was, we muſt ſuppoſe, an eccleſiaſtic that wrote well.

26. *Hallowing,*] all the veſtments, I think, were hallowed.

30. *Clouting,*] new covering at the toes, or patching in general.

35. *Baſtard.*] Leland, Itin. vol. VI. p. xviii.

101. 12. *May,*] f. *May-day.*

15. *Suffragan,*] *ſuffragan biſhop*, Thomas Epiſc. Pavadenſis. Bibliotheca Topographica Britannica, N° XXVIII. p. 40.

18. *Super alterys,*] linen cloths to be laid upon the altars §.

19. *Bokſkynne,*] buck ſkin.

22. *Fabyan,*] probably the author of the Chronicle.

28. *Cou̅nants,*] covenants.

102. 7. *Sprigge,*] nails. See p. 104. l. 15.

23. *Sarpe lathe,*] f. *ſap*, as oppoſed to heart laths.

34. *Note,*] article, or covenant.

* The *Paſcal*, a term which occurs independently in p. 96, and p. 259, and elſewhere, ſeems to mean the large TAPER, or *conſecrated* CANDLE, placed on or before the high altar at Eaſter. *Paſcal* TAPERS are expreſſly mentioned, p. 140. l. 8. and l. 15. In Batteley's edition of Somner's Antiquities of Canterbury, the *Paſcal* TAPER is deſcribed to have weighed 300lbs.; and at Weſtminſter abbey, A. D. 1557, its weight was the ſame. [See Strype's Memorials, vol. III. p. 445.] When, therefore, the *Paſcal* is mentioned in theſe accompts, the word *taper* or *candle* was an implication well known. To ſupport this *candle*, one may eaſily believe that *timber*, &c. as in p. 96, were neceſſary. EDIT.

† See p. 190. l. pen. where we read of *diſhes* whereon the *candleſticks* ſtood before the altars. EDIT.

‡ Or may not this mean what is now called pointing? EDIT.

§ Perhaps the corporax which covered the hoſt. The altar-cloth was not, however, the ſame as the corporax. EDIT.

P. 103.

P. 103. l. 17. *Songes,*] hymns or anthems. See p. 110. l. 16.
28. *Shoreham*] in Kent, in Sutton Lathe.
104. 8. *Pere,*] pears. See p. 106. l. 27. p. 108. l. 18.
15. *Sprigg,*] See p. 102. l. 7.
21. *Cressemes for the pallys.*] Can this mean *Chrisoms for the bells,* at their consecration? See Lewis's History of Thanet, p. 145.; Leland's Collectanea, vol. IV. p. 253.
22. *In,*] inn.
23. *Valtom,*] Waltham, as l. 30.
26. *Lentty clothe,*] to cover the altar with in Lent.
32. *A nask.*] Q. if there be a crasis; yet what is *an ask?*
36. *Tyning ...... garnets,*] for the garnets, see p. 98. *Tyning* seems to mean *tinning* *.
38. *Of reede,*] for preserving and securing the window, instead of modern wire.
39. *Reddyng,*] reading.
105. 4. *Byrche.*] See p. 111. l. 29.
6. *Pesyng,*] pieceing.
Antiphones,] antiphoners, as p. 100.
7. *Polomes,*] are psalters? Symnols, p. 110. l. 22.
9. *Bederolle,*] list of those that were to be specially prayed for. Maister Darby was probably a scribe, or writer.
22. *The Vyse.*] See p. 107. l. 6.
35. *Strake,*] took down. So to *strike the colours* at sea.
ult. *Transfiguration,*] 6 August.
106. 6. *A waynscot,*] a board.
24. *Pulpit,*] reading desk.
107. 1. *Pargetour,*] a pargeter, Dr. Littleton tells us, is a *plasterer*; and *pargetting* is still the term for the coarser sorts of plaster †, particularly what is applied to the inside of chimnies.
3. *Pastal.*] Q. *Paschal?* as p. 96, meaning the shew of the Passion; perhaps acted at Easter.
5. *Therewe,*] thorough.
6. *Vyse.*] See p. 105. l. 22.
9. *Sepulchre,*] part of the Easter exhibition, erected on the occasion, and then taken down ‡.
11. *Stopp.*] This was not of lead, as suggested in the note; for lead was not then 6*d.* a pound, but, on the contrary, cheap. See p. 121. l. 24.
31. *Romeland.*] See p. 111. l. 7.
108. *ult.* *Francis I.*] add, by Charles V. Emperor, our Queen's relation.
109. 1. *Greyes,*] badgers.
22. *Hay.*] Q. for what purpose?
27. *Lent.*] See p. 98. l. 9.

* Perhaps *setting*, or *re-setting*, from A. S. Tynan, to *enclose*. Edit.

† *Parget*, plaster. Phillips's World of Words.

‡ It seems to mean the *hearse*, mentioned afterwards, p. 140. l. 8. Edit.

P. 109. l. 29. *Drying,*] f. cleaning.

30. *Pekrell,*] a young or ſmall pike. There is a public houſe at Cambridge with this fiſh for its ſign, called the *Pickerel* inn. It is in the ſtreet leading to the bridge.

31. *Naſyng,*] John Naſing, founder of a chantry here. Newcourt, vol. I. p. 449.

110. 2. *Edward,*] afterwards King Edward VI.

22. *Symnols.*] See p. 105. l. 7.

31. *Biſhop's myter,*] f. the boy biſhop, as St. Nicholas occurs in the next line, when this paſtime began. See p. 114. l. 5.

41. *Biſhop,*] the cruel Edmund Bonner.

111. 3. *Regalles.*] See Gent. Mag. vol. XXXVII. p. 206. LIII. p. 636. Strype, Memoirs, vol. III. p. 35. Archæologia, vol. VI. p. 394.

4. *Poles,*] St. Paul's.

7. *Romeland.*] See p. 107. l. 2. Queen Elizabeth we muſt ſuppoſe to have acceded. Rome-land, however, ſeems to have been peculiar to Waltham Abbey.

25. *Obleys,*] Forme of Cury, p. 21.; it means a wafer, or cake.

29. *Birchbowes.*] See p. 105. l. 4.

35. *Browderer,*] embroiderer.

38. *Dekoy,*] a dekon; i. e. deacon.

113. 4. *Ault,*] alſo *awlt*; perhaps *awbe*; ſed Q.

114. 6. *Anelyd,*] f. enamelled.

15. *Flakon,*] flagon.

115. 6. *Imbered,*] embroidered.

116. 42. *Sr Joh' Colyns,*] perhaps an eccleſiaſtic.

43. *Well'm Weld,*] William Wild, inducted 18 Aug. 1467. Newcourt, p. 454.

117. 3. *Farmings,*] f. Ermines.

4. *Mylyngs.*] See line 27.

5. *On,*] *un*, i. e. *not*, as again, l. 8.

17. *Seer,*] withered, decayed. Gloſſary to Chaucer. Shakſpeare, Macbeth. *Dry.* Milton, Lycidas, l. 2. Ivy never *ſere*. Idem. Pſ. II. l. 27. fuel *ſere*.

19. *Woon,*] one.

25. *Trew loves,*] knots uſually ſo called.

27. *Mylyd.*] See line 4.

34. *Ihs,*] the uſual abbreviation of Jeſus; the Greek Ι Η Σ, perverted by taking the letters for Roman, and ſo interpreted *Jeſus Hominum Salvator.*

39. *For men,*] becauſe ſome were for boys.

118. 3. *Place in Botolph-lane.*] This is plainly a private houſe in the pariſh; but perhaps belonging *to* the pariſh or the church.

10. *Covvey,*] covered. Beds' teſters being often then made of wainſcot.

16. *Spere,*] it ſeems to mean a ſkreen.

P. 119.

P. 119. l. 17. *Bethe myne,*] are tolerably.
21. *Jn° Port.*] This appears alfo to be a private houfe let by the parifh.
30. *Dovell,*] f. double.
31. *Stakyd,*] fixed.
120. 2. *Ofter.*] Q. *Eafter*, from *Efterych*, i. e. *wainfcot.*
6. *Beam of Laton,*] f. a kind of creffet, made of tin.
8. *Choffell,*] fhovel. *Schoffell*, p. 121. l. 21. Pronunciation governed with an abfolute fway, before our orthography was a little better fettled.
25. *Polakes,*] pole-axes.
122. 3. *Valate.*] Q. on velvet?
123. 15. *Slyffe,*] fleeves.
125. 2. *Fowks,*] f. fox-fkin.
12. *Callyvan and myntes.*] Q. l. 30. caleyvan.
126. 4. *Pyllor,*] pillows; for fee line 7. and 8.
10. Q. the meaning of this line?
23. *Lymmed,*] f. lymned.

SIR WILLIAM BRUGES' WILL.

132. 11. *Mean,*] advocate, mediator.
17. *Scoppe,*] r. ftoppe, a ftoop.
20. 1 *fpone,*] one fpoon.
25. *A coupe.*] This is a pyx.
133. 1. *Nourt,*] not, i. e. nouȝt. So is mifread.
10. *Corver,*] called a *couple*, l. 12.
20. *Byll,*] f. hook.
23. *Samyn,*] think.
24. *Ye,*] they.

GREAT MARLOW.

135. 6. *Bifham,*] in Berks. The Queen went to Lady Ruffell's. Mr. Nichols's Progreffes of Queen Elizabeth, vol. II. 1593. *Byffome*, l. 18. *Buftleham*, l. 21.
8. St *Hugh's day,*] 17 Nov. Hugh, the Burgundian, was Bifhop of Lincoln; and Marlow is in that diocefe.
10. *Leofte,*] loft or gallery. It feems ftrange that players fhould pay any thing.
12. *Morrys coats,*] for the morris dancers. See line 39.
16. *Parritor,*] apparitor, as l. 42.
25. *Garters of bells,*] called bawdrick, p. 130. l. 32.
31. *Bridge wardens,*] over the Thames.
32. *In the church.*] Q. the occafion?
43. *Amtill,*] Ampthill, Bedfordfhire.

ELY

ELY INVENTORY.

P. 136. l. *ult.* *Garters.*] Q. the uſe?
137. 3. *Offers,*] f. *Orphreys.* See l. 27.; p. 139. l. 4.
12. *Apparels,*] alibi, *parures.* Again, l. 32. 33.
20. *Bp West,*] Nicholas Weſt, Biſhop of Ely, ob. 1533.
27. *Offers and,*] f. of, as line 3.
38. *Strakes,*] in ſtripes, or ſtreaks; *ſtraks* in the North being uſed for ſtripes. White *ſtrakes.* Gen. xxx. 37. Ring*ſtraked.* Ib. 35. 39. 40.
138. 1. *Weſt.*] See p. 137. l. 20.
8. *Alcok,*] John Alcock, Biſhop of Ely, and founder of Jeſus College, Cambridge, ob. 1500.
11. *Gilted,*] gilded.
26. *Pall,*] from Latin *pallium,* a *covering.*
27. *Lecture,*] reading-deſk.
29. *Redmann,*] Richard Redman, Biſhop of Ely, the immediate ſucceſſor of John Alcock in that ſee, died in 1505.
39. *Tinſon,*] f. tinſel.

ABINGTON.

140. 8. *Herſe lights*] for the pageant of the ſepulchre at Eaſter, for which ſee p. 145.; ſee here alſo, l. 16.; collected from the pariſhioners, p. 142. l. 5.
23. *Of the paryſhes,*] ſo that a collection ſeems to have been made for the purpoſe.
25. *Of ye clarke for ye holy lofte.*] Q. How the clarke comes to pay this money? the *holy loft* ſeems to be the rood loft. P. 141. l. 17. it is *loft.* See p. 142. l. 12. 13.
30. *Paule.*] This pail, to be uſed at funerals, was totally different from that at the altar, mentioned p. 138. l. 26.
39. *Quater dirges.*] Can it mean *quatuor?* or *quarter,* i. e. once a quarter?
141. 8. *Suffragan,*] Thomas Bickley, alias Motley, Epiſc. Marlebergenſis. Nichols, Bibl. Top. Brit. N° XXVIII. p. 43.
10. *Paſcall,*] the light. See l. 16. p. 96. 102. theſe were very large.
15. *Thenſe.*] See p. 145. l. 19.
Holyeyoyle,] Chriſm.
142. 15. *Monument,*] i. e. mind; *monument* here means remembrance. Again, l. 17. 19. See p. 145. l. 24.
28. *Morres bells.*] for the Morrice dancers. See p. 135. l. 39.
33. *For ye maſſe.*] This is ſtrange, anno 1561, and muſt be owing to cuſtomary language and expreſſion.
36. *For ye rood lofte*] to be taken down, as in the next article.
143. 5. *Omellies,*] homilies.

P. 143.

P. 143. l. 9 *Agaynst,*] relative to, or in order to, as it is now used in the North.
11. *Robin Hood's bower.*] for encouragement of archery.
13. *General Sermons*] See p. 147.
21. *Articles.*] See p. 147.
144. 9. *Burn,*] not to burn it, for that was the use of the censer, but to keep it in.
147. 9. *First instance.*] It may well be so as in former times, when Popery prevailed, there was not much preaching.

GREAT WIGSTON.

148. 27. 12 *communions,*] i. e. wine.
31. *Lenton fair,*] co. Nott. a great fair formerly. Or, read Len*ten*.
36. *Admiral's licence,*] Charles Howard, Earl of Nottingham.
38. *Willoughby,*] co. Leicester.
149. 22. *Enderby,*] Leicestershire.
25. *Brooke-rushes,*] bullrushes.
150. 26. *K. and Queen,*] in their progress to the North. Salmon.

HEYBRIDGE.

151. 6. *Strykynge.*] So, l. 30. 36.
21. *Ladye,*] the Annunciation.
31. *Betynge,*] again, l. 34.
152. 21. *Knepitt.*] Q. l. 23. it is *Knepill,* in next page *napyll,* p. 154. *knappell.*
153. 12. *Shyngler,*] *shingles* are wooden tiles, as we may call them, which our times have seen succeeded by *paper* ones.
antepen. Strykynge,] i. e. wax. See p. 151. l. 6.
155. 35. *Chirche holidaye,*] wake, or dedication-feast.
24. *Seme,*] quarter.
156. 10. *Ledde n ile*] for the leads of the church.
13. *Solare,*] gallery.
17. *Bileigh,*] Premonstratensian abbey in Essex.
157. 11. *Battilments,*] payments. There is some doubt of the origin of a *batteler* at Oxford. Perhaps he is one, who, not being upon the foundation, and consequently having no account kept regularly for him, *pays* daily, and instantly, for what he eats and drinks.
21. *Graunte.*] Q. what the nature of this grant?
158. 20. *Basen of our Lady.*] Q. see l. 21. 29. This seems to relate to the rood-loft.
161. 18. *Campyng sporte**.] See p. 162.
162. 12. *Cheyz,*] cheese.
15. *Agrette*] f. by agreement, i. e by the *great,* as we now express it.
21. *Campyng **.] See p. 161. l. 18.

* Q. *Campaign?* and whether these entries do not relate to Hock-tide? EDIT.

P. 162. l. 23. *Cape,*] cope.
165. 19. *Moche Totham,*] Great Totham.
171. 16. *Ld Abbot*] of Bilegh, perhaps.
30. *Setting a Saynte,*] placing him in his tabernacle or niche.
36. *For pale*] of churchyard. See p. 172. l. 3.
ult. *Stylle,*] ſtile.
176. 35. *Andrewe,*] patron of the church.
177. 13. *Sherpolys,*] ſurplice.
179. 2. *Ower playe.*] See p. 180. ſeq.
181. 20. *Folle,*] fool.
34. *Baſterer,*] *baſter* *, that baſted the meat when roaſting.
182. 9. *Gydde,*] guide or manage.
14. *Stoke,*] perhaps value of it.

W I G T O F T.

195. 1. *Poſitores,*] i. e. *prepoſitores*, written, or ſhould be written, *p̃poſitores. Prepoſitours*, 22 Edw. IV. at North Wingfield, co. Derby, and 29 H. VI.
8. *Sern.*] This is interpreted in the note *ſenior*; and he was probably the elder; but, as the ſcribe was aware of the diſtinctive expreſſion of *elder*, ſee line 12, I ſhould think it rather means *fermer*, agricola.
11. *Maſter Bale.*] Could this be the famous *John Bale?* The title *maſter* denotes pre-eminence; and the date 1449 accords very well.
18. *Eyh,*] i. e. *eth*, which may be *hath*, or perhaps *oweth*.
20. *Said.*] He is not mentioned before.
196. 3. *Ay on gode ffryday,*] perhaps *as on Good Friday*.
7. *Countt,*] account. *Chaunte*, l. 38.
16. *A ruſh,*] ruſhes, a part for the whole. See the price.
21. *Moone,*] money.
30. *Yomen leyght,*] given by the yeomen; or perhaps young men, batchelors. Again, p. 197.
197. 7. *Byyng,*] buying.
37. *Lyncon,*] Lincoln.
199. 21. *May lyght.*] Again, l. 24. perhaps for *May-day*.
200. 2. *Whesyng,*] perhaps waſhing, as p. 203.
201. 31. *Zayd,*] ſaid.
202. 22. *Choyn,*] joint. See p. 197.
24. *Stage,*] ſ. a young thing of the colt kind.
203. 14. *Sholar,*] ſ. *ſhotar*, i. e. belfounder; to *ſhote* is to caſt.
20. *Sauyier,*] ſeems to mean *ſolder*.
204. 11. *Awolm.*] This is a ſurname in the pariſh. See p. 210.

* See p. 181, where the baſterer is immediately mentioned after the perſon who turned the ſpit. EDIT.

P. 205.

P. 205. l. 12. *Kyrton,*] in Holland, Lincolnſhire.
32. *Cayke wark,*] f. kirk or church work. See l. 10.
206. 11. *Co' per xp̄i even,*] Corpus Chriſti is Thurſday after Trinity-Sunday; ſo that, if Midſummer-day fell upon Friday, the even or feaſt would be on Corpus Chriſti day, a great feſtival; ſo the faſt of Midſummer-day was kept on Wedneſday, and not on Corpus Chriſti day.
207. 21. *Harygus,*] perhaps a proper name, *Hary Gus.*
24. *Ad vincula St[i] Petri,*] 1 Auguſt.
208. 12. *Kye.*] The plural of *cow*, often uſed in Derbyſhire.
28. *Helpyng,*] mending, as l. 35. and p. 209. l. 6. 18. *& alibi ſæpè.*
antepen. Bowſtryng,] bolſtering. Q. what is bolſtering a bell? q. if the ſame as truſſing?
209. 2. *Bettyng,*] ſame as *ſcholyng*, p. 106. l. 1. but, q. what that means?
210. 2. *Pooley,*] perhaps pulley.
211. 23. *Gemals,*] hinges, called *jimmers* in Yorkſhire.
212. 12. *Wryght,*] a carpenter.
215. 1. *Coneng,*] f. cov'eng, covering; probably in Lent.
216. 4. *Pewter,*] probably *ſodder*, as below.
217. 21. *Barner,*] f. banner.
32. *Byll,*] perhaps aſſeſſment.

STATIONERS COMPANY.

221. 4. *Boke,*] charter of incorporation. See p. 228. l. 19.
11. *Lymnyng,*] f. illuminating initial and other letters.
222. *Stone Cruſys.*] See p. 227. l. 33. perhaps *crewets.* See *cruſe* of water, 1 Sam. xxvi. 11, 12. Φακος, LXX; *ſcyphus*, Vulg.; *honey*, 1 Kings, xiv. 3. Σταμνος, LXX; *vas*, Vulg.; *oil*, 1 Kings, xvii. 12. 14. Καψακη, LXX; *lecythus*, Vulg.; *water*, 1 Kings, xix. 6. Καψακη, LXX; *vas*, Vulg.; *water for ſalt*, 2 Kings, ii. 20. Υδρισκη, LXX; *vas*, Vulg.
223. 7. *Epycriſe,*] Hippocras.
15. *A Ryſe,*] i. e. *Ariſe.* The firſt words of the ballad, now probably loſt. William Pickering was a member of the Stationers company, who printed only ballads himſelf, and was fined 16*d.* for printing one without licence 1567. See Herbert's Ames, p. 1315.
16. They dined in the hall once in a quarter.
224. 13. *Spynts.*] Q. ſee p. 227. l. 16.
18. *Carſaye,*] Kerſey.
To garde,] to bind, ornamentally.
21. *Croſſes,*] badges, to diſtinguiſh the ſeveral companies.
antepen. Blacke bylles.] Strype, Life of Parker, p. 275.
226. 14. *Creſtes.*] So again, p. 227. l. 1.
16. *Hall payſſe.*] So again, l. 29. Q. the *haut pas*, where the upper table ſtood, or the canopy over the upper table?
227. l. 5. *Courte cubberte.*] So again, p. 227. l. 1. Q. a *low*, or ſhort cupboard?

P. 227. l. 16. *Spents.*] Q. *ſpynts*. See p. 224. l. 13.
28. *Leppe,*] perhaps a *lip*, as it was for drinking.
36. *A geſte.*] So p. 228. l. 13. ſeems to mean a *thrall*, or frame of wood, a *joiſt*, or ſtand.

INVENTORY OF A TAVERN, A. D. 1612.

229. 7. *Graves wine.*] Q. alſo, l. 16. and 18. Perhaps *vin de Grave*, a French wine.
18. *Alligante,*] Alicant, a city in Spain.
28. *Court cubbord,*] a cupboard, anſwering to what was ſince called a *beaufet*. The *court-cupboard* is mentioned in Romeo and Juliet, act I. ſcene 4. See the note in the edition by Johnſon and Steevens. It was a moveable piece of furniture. See p. 227. l. 5.
230. 18. *Drinking towels.*] Q. mufflers?
231. 1. *Creepers.*] Theſe were of this form ⌐¬ to lay the fuel or wood on. See Gent. Mag. vol. LVIII. p. 687. 791. 848. vol. LIX. p. 108. When theſe creepers had ornamental fronts they were called *dogs*, from reſembling thoſe animals in a ſtanding poſture; and it is believed are ſtill ſo termed in Kent, and elſewhere, when wood is uſed for fuel in gentlemen's houſes.
32. *Pottengers,*] porringers, I ſuppoſe. Surely, *pottengers* is beſt, a corruption of *pottagers*.
37. *Coffen,*] any thing to receive meat, &c. to be baked. Gloſſary to *Forme of Cury*, p. 131.
232. 12. *Candleſticke plate,*] a plate whereon the candleſtick ſtood. See before, p. 260. This interpretation agrees alſo with l. *penult*. It was uſually made of pewter.
ult. *Shovinge-tables.*] They had formerly at inns a very long table, called *a ſhovel-board*, on which the players were to ſlide braſs weights of two or three ounces (the parties having each three of them); and no bad exerciſe it was in rainy weather. (See Walton's Angler.) They had the *ſhovel-board* alſo in the great halls of private houſes; and I have played on them often; but theſe being in the *barre* could not be of that kind, unleſs we may ſuppoſe them to have been of ſmaller dimenſions.

S. P.

⁂ Dr. Pegge obſerves, that "the receipts and diſburſements in theſe pariſh-accompts (and he believes in moſt others) ſhew that it muſt be difficult at the paſſing them to ſtrike a balance. We diſcover in them many clergy and other perſons of note not to be found elſewhere; and more particulars of ſome that are already known. In the firſt of theſe accompts (thoſe of *St. Margaret's, Weſtminſter*), *æ* perpetually occurs in the Latin page, where we may be ſure, it was always *e*. The language and orthography of the following pages alſo are by no means thoſe of the reign of Henry IV. but have been modernized, if not tranſlated, by the tranſcriber. The ſums of money too are all in Arabic figures, which were but little then in uſe; whereas the numerals in the body of the reſpective articles are all Roman."

A Bill

A Bill of Fare for Fifty Members of the Worſhipful COMPANY of SALTERS, LONDON, Anno Domini 1506.

	£.	s.	d.
36 CHICKENS	0	4	5
1 Swan and 4 geeſe	0	7	0
9 Rabbits	0	1	4
4 Breaſts of veal	0	1	5
2 Rumps of beef tails	0	0	2
6 Quails	0	1	6
2 Ounces of pepper	0	0	2
2 Ounces of cloves and mace	0	0	4
1½ Ounce of ſaffron	0	0	6
3 Pounds of ſugar	0	0	8
2 Pounds of raiſins	0	0	4
1 Pound of dates	0	0	4
1½ Pound of comfits	0	0	2
½ Hundred eggs	0	0	2½
1 Gallon curds	0	0	4
1 Gallon gooſeberries	0	0	2
Bread	0	1	0
1 Kilderkin of ale	0	2	3
Herbs	0	1	0
2 Diſhes of butter	0	0	4
Bacon	0	0	6
¼ Load of coals	0	0	4
Faggots	0	0	2
3½ Gallons of Gaſcoine wine	0	2	4
1 Bottle Muſcovadine wine *	0	0	8
Cherries and tarts	0	0	8
Salt	0	0	1
Verjuice and vinegar	0	0	2
Paid the cook	0	3	4
Perfume	0	0	2
1½ Buſhel of flour	0	0	8
Water	0	0	3
Garniſhing the veſſels	0	0	3
Total	1	13	2½

* Muſcadine or Muſcadel wine, made from a grape the produce of Candia. It had the ſmell of muſk. PHILIPS.

It is preſumed to have been a rich ſweet wine; and taken as a grace-cup, from the ſmall quantity here provided.

EXTRACTS FROM THE CHURCHWARDENS' ACCOMPTS OF SAINT MARTIN OUTWICH, LONDON.

PARISH expences from the ffeste of Thadnunciacion of oure Lady Saint Mary Virgynt 1509, unto the same feast 1510:

Also, receyved of the gyfte of our late sovaigne lorde Kyng Henry the vij[th], two torches, and in redy money, ——— ——— xxs̄.

Also, paid to Randolf Merchunt, wexchandiller, for the Pascall *, the taps affore the Rode, the Cross candelles, and Judas candelles, — ixs̄. iiijd̄.

1510—1511.

First, paid for palme, boxfloures, and cakes, ——— iiijd̄.

Also, to s̄ William, for playing atte organs iij q[ut]ers, — vs̄.

1511.

Paid to William Wright, morowe masse preste †, for his wages for halfe a yere, ended at Midsomer, ——— ——— xxxiijs̄. ivd̄.

Also, to the same Sir William, for kepyng of thorgans the same half yere, vjs̄. viijd̄.

Also, paid to Sir Thomas Bedellesdale, morow masse preste, for a q̄, ended at Mighelmes, for his wages, ——— ——— xvjs̄. viijd̄.

Also, paid to M[r] Doctor, that he leyde oute atte Guyldehall, to John Hale, of the mayers courte, for forche of the evidences concerning the foundacion of the the chaunterye, for half the morowe masse prests salary — xijd̄.

Also, delivēd to M[r] Baret, for the suyt of the same matier iiijd.

Also, paid for the carriage of viij lodes of erth oute of the chirche yeard to Saint Mary Spytell, the lode iijd̄. Sum̄ ——— ijs̄.

1515.

An enventorye of all the howrnaments that pteynythe to the churche of S[t] Marten's Otewiche, wytthe in byschoppys gatte strette, in London, the xxvij[th] daye of Zenever', in the yeere of ow[r] Lorde God A. mv[c]xv[th], that tyme beyng cyrche wardennys Mathye Pemberton, m̄chant, and Stewyn Londe, ffuller:

* By the Churchwardens Accompts of the parish of St. Martin at Leicester (printed in the History of that County) it appears, that in 1547 the Sepulchre light then weighed 75 lb. at 3½*d.* per lb. and cost 21*s.* 10½*d.*—Payments also frequently occur for "charcoal, to make the "hallowed fire."

† *Morrow-mass* priest may perhaps mean a junior priest, or a supernumerary, whose office it was to perform the service on the *morrow* of a festival, and perhaps on the *eve* and the *octave* to ease the officiating priest.—The *morrows* and *octaves* of certain days are still spoken of in law-language.—In an antient list of trades of London, amongst Stowe's Collections, in Harl. MS. 541. fol. 229. is "holy wat' clerkys." Q. what was their office?—A *holy water stoup* is mentioned in the accompts of St. Mary at Hill, p. 98; and in Baker's Cambridge Collections, Harl. MS. 7048. at fol. 44. mention is made of "It' an haliwater stop," in an inventory of plate, &c. belonging to the chapel of Queen's college, Cambridge, taken 1544.

Jewells

Jewells and platte of felver.

Itm, in pmys, a chales, w^{t} the patten of fylver and geyltte, w^{t} a Trynyte in the patten anameld, pons xxixth unc' off Troye.

Itm, a chales off felver and geylt, wythe a vernakyl yn the paten, enamelde, pons xxvijth unc' of Troye.

Itm, a chales of felver, and geylt wythe a varnakyll * yn the paten, pons xix unc' of Troye.

Itm, a chales, pfell geylte, wythe a ffotte madde lyke a flower and a fcrypture, pons xxth unc' off Troye.

Itm, a chales, pfell geylte, wythe a fkerypture abowte the ffotte, pons xvij unc' off Troye.

Itm, a pexe off fylver ffor the fakerment, pons xvth unc' di. off Troye.

Itm, a boxe off felver ffor the fakerment, in veffitaciones, w^{t} Ihs en ye cower-yng, and armys on the feid, inamelde, pons ijth unc' di. & qr. off Troye.

Itm, the faid box of fylv' was put ynto the pyx when it was new made and gyldyd yn anno 1522 †.

Itm, a croffe of fylver and gylt, wythe owr Laddye and Seint John off Evan-geleyfte ‡, of the gyfte off my Lady of Burgayne §, fome tyme before y^{e} wyffe of Richard Naylore, mchant off London, pons $\overset{xx}{vj}$ unc' and xiijth of Troye.

Itm, a croffe off fylver, and geylt and anamylde, off the gyfte of Maft^{r} Warde, fometyme alderman and grocer off London, pons xlvth unc' of Troye.

Itm, a croffe of felver, and geylte, w^{t} a bace || on the ffotte, to putte yn rellyks, pons iijth unc' & di. off Troye.

Itm, a payer off candellfteks off felver, pcell gylt, off y^{e} gyfte of Maft^{r} Hewe Pemberton **, fome tyme alderman of London, $\overset{xx}{iij}$xjth unc'.

Itm, a fenffore of felver, pcell geylt, pons xxxix unc', with the yoryne in the bottome and all.

Itm, a crefmetorye †† off felver, pcell geylt, pons xviij unc' di. off Troye, wheroff

* *Vernicle* in the gloffary of the Royal Wills, where it is explained a *Veronica*.

† This laft entry in another hand.

‡ Our Lady and St. John always formed part of the rood when complete; and fometimes the patron-faint of the church was added.

§ Elizabeth Lady Abergavenny (often written Bergavenny). See Collins's Peerage, where fhe is faid to have re-married Richard Naylor; but her maiden-name is not mentioned.

|| Written *box* in the next page.

** Againft the North wall of St. Martin Outwich new church, under a triple ftone canopy with nich-work over the arches, and a cornice of oak-leaves, is an altar-tomb, with three fhields in quatrefoils in front: on the front and end edge whereof, when in the old church, was,

" —— Aldermannus ejusdem civitatis et Katerina uxor ejus qui quidem Hugo obiit vij^{o} die mensis Septembris anno d'ni mill'imo vc^{o} quorum a'i'abus propicietur Deus. Amen."

This was erected to the memory of Hugh Pemberton.

In re-building the church, that part of the infcription on the end edge, from vc^{o} to the end, has been loft. What remains of the former part will, when the church is finifhed, be re-placed. The whole tomb, when cleanfed from the different coats of paint with which it has been co-vered, appears to be of beautiful fhell marble.

†† Chrifmatory.

was

was geyffyn by Margret Erle a pece of felver, w^t ertayne fpowynys; the reft, wythe makyng, and more fylver, it cofte the chyrche boxe xxxs. ft. A° 1515.

Itm, a paxe of fylver and geylt, pons iiij unc' & di. qr. off Troye.

Itm, a payer of crewetts off fylver, pcell gylte, pons vij owyncs.

Itm, a boxe off ewery *, garnyfhede w^t filver, pons iij unc' di. off Troye.

Itm, a boxe, with diverfe rellyks thereyn to the nomber off a xj, w^t fcrypturs on them.

Cowpper.

Itm, a croffe of cowper and geylte, wythe Marye and John.

1517.

Payd on Seynt Marten's day, for bred and drynke for the fyngers, vs.

1518.

Itm, a cloth called a vayle of whyte lynneyn, to draw affor the awter in Lent tyme.

In an inventory of ornaments, 1522, we have,

Itm, a croffe of fylv' and gilt, w^t a box ov' the ffote to put theryn relycks, waiying . . . . . , w^ch *was luftated and made a monftrans as after aperith* †.

Itm, a box of yvory, garnifhed wyth fylv', and another box wth xj relyks theryn. Itm, a monftrans, w^t a relike of Sent Marten, the fote fylv' and gilt, and the flat edge about the relik fylv', and all the refidue cop and gilt.

1524.

Itm, for mendyng of the hovell on Sent Marten ‡,		—	vjd.
Itm, for rofe garlands on on Corpus Xpi day,		—	vjd.
Itm, for byrche at Midfomer,	—	—	ijd.
Itm, for rofe garlands, brede, wyne, and ale, on ij Sent Marten's days,			xvd. ob.
Itm, for holy and ivy at Chryftmas,	—	—	ijd. ob.
Itm, for red wyne on Relik Sonday,	—	—	jd.

Mafboks and other Boks.

Itm, iiij mafboks, a pyftyll boke, ij manvells, and an ordinall §.

Itm, iij antyffonere ||, a legend **, and ij porteffys ††.

Itm, a boke of the lyf of Seynt Marten.

Itm, iij new queyre of the iij newe feaftys, and iij old feryall books.

Itm, iiij Proceffyoners, a boke called a Pye ‡‡, and a boke called a Martylage.

* Ivory. † In another hand.

‡ Perhaps the canopy of the tabernacle of Wiche, wherein the image of St. Martin, the patron-faint, ftood.

§ A book of rules and orders to direct the manner of performing the fervice. Staveley, 185.

|| Antiphoner.

** The legend contained the leffons to be read in the morning-fervice. Staveley, 184.

†† The portefs was a breviary. Johnfon's Dictionary.

‡‡ The pye (Latin, *pica*) was a fervice-book, fo called from the different colours of the text, and the rubrick. Johnfon's Dictionary.

1525.

1525.

Paments made by John Hasilwood and John Amynton, wardens of the pysshe church, yn the yere of our Lord m5^{c}xxv as folowith:

Paid to the morowe masse pst for his quart' wags dew at our Lady-day abovesseid, — — — xvjs. viijd.

Paid to the same pst, by way of reward, dewe the yere afore past, granted by the pysshons, — — vjs. viijd.

Paid for palme on Palme Sunday, — ijd. ob.

Paid for kaks, flowers, and yow, — ijd.

Paid to Symon Jenyngs, clarke, for his wags, for owr Lady-day quart', xxiijs. iiijd.

Paid to the clark's wiff, for wasshing of the churche's gere xijd.

Paid for brome ageynst Ester — — jd.

Paid to the smyth, for a key to the locke in the vestry, — iiijd.

Payd for a quart' of colys on Est' evyn, — iiijd.

Payd for bred and ale, and wachyng of the sepulc^{r}, — xijd.

Payd to Thomas Vauce, waxchandler, for makyng and renewyng of the beme lyght, and for makyng of the paskall, w^{t} the tenabur candell, and crosse candell, xxs.; and for waste of the same pascall a pounde and halfe qrt', viijd.

Payd to the sayd Thomas Vauce, for viij taps brynnyng befor the rode, at vijd. ob. the pownde, vs.; and vj taps, at viijd. the pownd — iiijs.

Payd for rosse garlonds on Corp' Xpi daye — vjd.

Payd for byrche and bromys at Mydsom' — iijd.

Payd for brede, ale, and wyne, and garlonds, on Seynt Marten's day *, ye t^{r}nslacyon. — — — xvjd.

Payd to the organmakers svant, for skoryng † of the pypes of the organs, iiijd.

Payd for holy and ivye at Crystmas, — ijd.

Payd to the wryter of thys accounte, — iiijd.

1527.

Item, rescayved of the wardens of the fullers, for the gyft and bequest of Steven Lond, for the pascall light, and for the standarts at his obit, the time of dirge and masse amount, — — viijs.

Item, monay rescayved for the obitt of Mr. Clerke, xijd.; and for the obit of John Carpent^{r}, xxd.; amont, — — ijs. viijd.

John Amanton and Rouland Goodman, cherchwardens, ys dewe to have, for monay by thayme paid to Sir John Thoms, pst, singing for M^{r} ‡ Owtwich, for a whole yere, endit at Cristimas last past, iijl. vjs. viijd.; and for a reward gyven hym by the consent of the paresh, vjs. viijd.; amonts, — vil.§ xiijs. iiijd.

* The 4th of July. † Q. *Cleaning? scouring?*

‡ As this church, according to Stowe, was founded by *four* persons of the name of Outwich (or Otewich), one of whom had the Christian name of *Martin*; perhaps the *M* here may designate the plural number; unless *Martin* Outwich is emphatically commemorated on account of his Christian name.

§ So in the original, but should be iijl.

1539.

To Syr Thoms Bellow, morrow masse prist, for his wags, qrtly xxxvs. amts his wags for ij yeres, —— —— xiijl.

To the Masters of Pappe*, for the porchase of the churche yrde, in the presence of Mr Hamon, —— —— ijl. xiijs. iiijd.

1540.

Recd of the wardens of Clothwarkers, for the pascall lyght, viijs.

The following entries, in the years 1544 and 1545, appear to concern a suit instituted against one of the mass priests:

1544.

Itm, paid for vj newe boks, yn Ynglishe, for the p'cession, js. vjd.

Itm, paid to Mr Doctor Wilson, for the sute and expence of owr morowmas pryst salary, as aperth by a bill of his pcells, —— ijl. xvjs. xjd.

Itm, paid for bote hyre to and from Westmynstr iiij tymes, yn folowyng the sute agt Pady and Joyn', vd.; and unto the sgeant of the corte of the Kingswarde, for somonyng of the said Roger Pady ij tymes, for payment of the morowms pste salary and wagis, iijs.; amountyth, —— iijs. vd.

1545.

Item, for money r' of Roger Padye, by the hand of Maister Hallyley, for the averageis of the sallarye of the morowe mase pste, for foure hole yers, endid at Mydesomer laste paste, after iijl. vjs. viijd by the yere, amontithe, xiijl. vjs. viijd.

Item, more r' of the same Roger Paddye, by the hands of Mr. Halliley, for the costs in the sewete of the same, —— xxs.

An order takin for the parishe clerk, for pitts, knyell, ande peyll, to take effecte imediatly after the decease of Symonde Jennyns, late parishe clerk.

Item, for eny pitt or grave at or churcheyarde at Pappe, being no innocentt, the some of eight pense.

Item, for eny pitt or grave for innocentts, ether in the little churcheyarde at home, or at Pappe, the some of foure pense stirling.

In the presens of Mr Doctor Willsone, parsone, Sr John Mordan, Knight, &c. &c. &c.

Tayllowres Hall, in Seynt Martyn's pysh, next ye well wt ij boketts, ffast by Seint Antonyis †.

* The hospital belonging to the fraternity of St. Charity and St. John the Evangelist, near the church of St. Augustine in the Wall, for poor impotent priests of the Papey, founded, 1480, by William Owen, William Barneby, and John Stafford, chantry priests, in London. The foundation and statutes, and the names of the masters and wardens, from 1442 to 1548, are in the Cott. Lib. Vitell. F. xvi. 2. 3. Tanner, p. 325. The church of St. Augustine "de *Pappey* infra Bishopsgate" stood in Camomile-street, and was destroyed in the great fire. The burial-ground purchased of this fraternity still remains in use in Camomile-street. "In some languages priest are called *Papes*." Stowe, p. 156. *Papa* is the appellation of patriarchs and bishops in the Eastern church (Du Fresne); and in Russia the term is still applied to priests.

† Harl. MS. 541. being the fifth volume of Stowe's Historical and Topographical Tracts, f. 225. b.

RECEIPTS

RECEIPTS AND DISBURSEMENTS OF THE CANONS OF THE PRIORY OF ST. MARY IN HUNTINGDON, FROM MICHAELMAS 1517 TO MIDSUMMER 1518.

(Tranfcribed from the Original at BUCKDEN, by the Rev. Mr. MANNING, vicar of Godelming. Communicated by Mr. GOUGH.)

[EUSTACE DE LOVETOT, about the year 1140, as in Tanner's Notitia Monaftica, built here a priory of Black Canons, to the honour of St. Mary; it was endowed at the Suppreffion with revenues of 187*l.* 13*s.* 8*d.* as in Dugdale; and 232*l.* 7*s.* as in Speed; though in another valuation, according to Dugdale, with 241*l.* 11*s.* 4*d.*; and, according to Speed, with 256*l.* 1*s.* 3*d.* It confifted of a prior, eleven canons, and thirty-four fervants. Henry VIII. in 1592, granted the fite to Sir Richard Cromwell, alias Williams, as he did alfo the fmall convent of Hinchingbrook, which Sir Richard converted into a feat for his family, who dwelt there till they fold Hinchingbrook to Montague, the firft Earl of Sandwich, in the reign of Charles II. I fuppofe before 1660.

Thomas Forte, Bifhop of St. Chad in Ireland, held this priorfhip *in commendam* with his bifhoprick, 1492; and voided it by death, 1503, when

Gregory Norwich, prior of Rifhemead, or Rufshmede, co. Bedford, was chofen prior 1503. His fucceffor, about the year 1528, was

William Gidding, on whofe refignation, on April 13, 1532,

Hugh Whitwick, the laft prior, was admitted.

In a manufcript in the Cotton Library is the following account of the names of the religious, and inventory of the goods of this convent:

Hugh Whitwick, prior, to whom was allotted, on the furrender, July 17, 1539, a penfion for life of 26*l.* 16*s.* 4*d.* which he received anno 1553, being then living, and unprovided for. William Gidding, late prior, on his refignation had an allowance of 6*l.* 13*s.* 4*d.* *per annum*, and meat and drink, and fuel for his chamber. He was living at the furrender anno 1639, and aged 60. The other monks then were, Michael Broughton, aged 70; John Willingham, aged 59; Thomas Southowe, aged 54; Nicholas Allington, aged 43; Robert Huntingdon; John Rufhington; William Wardboys; John Streetham, aged 33; James Huntingdon, aged 29; William Ramfey, aged 30; who were returned to be all of them priefts of good confideration and report, defirous to continue in their religion.

 The

The inventory of the goods was then returned as follows:

Lead and bells.

Webbs of lede, 972.

Item, fix bells of a tune, and a clock bell, whereof the deepnefs and bredth appeareth by the inventory.

	£.	s.	d.
The houfe is merely well repaired.			
Stuff and ornaments, to the value of —	96	2	4
Plate, worth — —	33	3	8
Corne fowed, appraifed at —	28	16	7
Corne unfowed, appraifed at —	33	9	0
Horfes, kine, &c. appraifed at —	58	5	8
Debts owing by the houfe, —	244	19	9
Debts owing to the houfe, —	103	0	4
Rental of the houfe, valued at —	217	6	11

Befides the four prefent parifhes in Huntingdon, viz. St. Mary, All Saints, St. John Baptift, and St. Benedict's, of which the churches of the two firft are only ftanding, there were thefe other churches, St. Martin, St. Edmund, St. Andrew, St. Peter, St. Botolph, St. George. St. Botolph, St. Martin, St. Edmund, and St. Andrew, occur in Henry the Third's time. St. Peter's was pulled down about the beginning of Queen Elizabeth's reign. Q. if not alfo churches of St. Nicholas and St. German? BROWNE WILLIS.]

Compotus Frm Robti Broughton, Supprioris, & Johis Godmycheft, Sacriftæ, receptorum Prioratûs Canonicorum Ecclefiæ btæ Mariæ de Huntingdon; à fefto Sci Michis Archi, anno regni Regis Henrici VIII. poft Conqueftum nono, ufq; ad feftum Nativitatis Sci Johis Baptiftæ anno predicti Regis decimo.

	£.	s.	d.
Arreragia.—In primis de arreragiis ultimi computûs de anno proximo precedente — —			3¾di.
Huntingdon.—Item, de Johe Claryvans collectore ibidem, hoc anno pro terminis Sci Michis Archi, Natalis Domini, & Annunciationis Beatæ Mariæ —	6	19	0
Offic' Elemof'.—Item, de eodem collectore pro terris & tenementis pertinentibus offic' elemof' infra burgum prædictum, ad feft' predict' — —		28	4

Offic'

	£.	s.	d.
Offic' Sacristæ.—Item, de eodem collectore pro decimis molendinorum aquaticorum de Huntingdon prædict', p annum, ad festum Sancti Michaelis Archangeli		10	0
Item, de eodem collectore pro firmâ decimarum garbarum & feni in parochiâ Sc̄i Edmundi, ad festa predicta — —		5	0
Item, de eodem collectore pro firmâ unius tenementi infra precinctus monasterii sic dimissi Joh̄i Benet hoc anno — —		10	0
Summa —	9	12	4
Godmychestr.—Item, de Thome Styvecley, pro firmâ unius prati vocati Cawceholme, pro terminis Sc̄i Mich̄is Arch̄i & Annunciat' Beatæ Mariæ —		20	0
Herford.—Item, de Joh̄e Pope, collectore ibidem, pro redditibus tenentium pro predictis tribus terminis, æquis portionibus solvenda —	10	8	3¾
Item, de Joh̄e Pope, pro firma rector' ibidem, pro termino Purificationis Beatæ Mariæ —	4	6	8
Item, de Joh̄e Pope, collectore, pro vesturâ & herbagio unius prati vocati over the Ree —		45	0
Item, de eodem collectore, pro vesturâ & herbagio unius prati vocati Est-medowe —		47	8
Item, de eodem collectore, pro vesturâ & herbagio unius prati vocati Short-medow, cum una aqua vocat' Goreaqua — —		6	2
Item, de eodem collectore, pro vesturâ & herbagio novem solucionum ibidem jacentium friscorum —		0	18
Item, de eodem collectore, pro firmâ molendinorum aquaticor' cum separali aquâ ibidem pro predictis tribus terminis — —		40	0
Item, de Joh̄e Byrt, pro firmâ manerii ibidem, pro fest' & termino Purificationis Beatæ Mariæ —		40	0
Offic' Elemos'.—Item, de predicto collectore, pro firmâ certa terræ jacentis in campis de Hertford predicto, pro terminis Sc̄i Mich̄is Arch̄i & Paschæ, pertinent' offic' elemos'		27	0
Summa —	25	2	3¾

	£.	s.	d.
Styvecle Magna.—Item, de Thoma Hylle, collectore ibidem, pro redditu diversorum tenentium, pro terminis Sc̃i Michis Archi & Paschæ ——	6	15	0
Item, de Johe Hedyngley, pro firmâ rectoriæ ibidem, pro termino Purificationis Beatæ Mariæ	10	0	0
Summa —	16	15	0
Gydding Magna.—Item, de Thomas Clerke, pro firmâ rectoriæ ibidem, pro terminis Natalis Domini, Paschæ, & Sc̃i Johis Baptistæ ——	14	12	6
Item, de Roberto Tufte, pro firmâ unius molendini ven-triticis, pro terminis Sc̃i Michis Archi, Natal' D'ni, & Paschæ —— ——		7	6
Item, de Robto Button, collectore, pro redditu liber' tenent' & customariorum ad duos anni terminos	15	4	11
Summa —	30	4	11
Hillington.—Item, de Robto Button, collectore, pro reddit' liber' ten' & customariorum, ad duos anni terminos solvendis	4	15	8½
Wynnewycke.—Item, de Robto Button, collectore, pro reddit' tenent' ibidem ad festum Sc̃i Michis Archi tm		47	1
Item, de Johe Bucke, firmar' rector' ibidem, pro termino Purificationis Beatæ Mariæ Virginis —		110	0
Summa —	7	17	1
Hemyngford.—Item, de Thoma Asheman, firmario rectoriæ ibidm, pro termino Purificationis Beatæ Mariæ Virginis	8	0	0
Brampton.—Item, de ballivis de Hunt' pro unâ clausâ vocatâ Bromholme per annum, ad fest' Sc̃i Michis Archi terminandum —— ——		23	4
Item, de Johe Henson, pro firma decem acrarum terræ arabilis in campis ibidem, ad festum Sc̃i Michis Archi tm ——		5	0
Summa —		28	4
Stoughton.—Item, de Edmundo Parell, collectore, pro reddit' liber' tenentium & customar' ad fest' Sc̃i Michis Archi tm		20	4

Sowtho.

		£.	s.	d.
Sowtho.	—Item, de Joħe Stowghton, pro firmâ unius croft & unius virgatæ terræ per annum ad feſta Sc̄i Michis Archi & Paſchæ —		8	0
Hayleweſton cum Lytlay.	Item, de Roƀto Offe, pro uno tenemento & octo acris terræ per annum ad feſta Sc̄i Michis Archi & Paſchæ		8	0
	Item, de Olivero Leder, pro firmâ decimarum garbarum & feni conjunctim, pro terminis Conceptionis Beatæ Mariæ, Annunciacionis ejuſdem, & Aſcenſionis D'ni		100	0
	Item, de dicto Olivero Leder, pro quadam paſturâ inclusâ, vocatâ Lytlay, pro terminis Sc̄i Michis Archi, & Paſchæ — —		20	0
	Summa —	6	8	0
Groſſham.	—Item, de Joħe Hacocke, pro uno tenemento & dimidiâ virgatâ terræ, ad feſtum Michis Archi t^{m} —		8	0
	Item, de Wiltmo Carter, pro uno tenemento & dimidiâ virgatâ terræ, ad feſtum Sc̄i Michis Archi t^{m}		6	8
	Summa —		14	8
Offord Dacy.	—Item, de Joħe Reynold, pro firmâ unius tofti & viginti acris terræ, pro termino Sc̄i Michis Archi t^{m}		5	0
Conyngton.	—Item, de Joħe Hopkyn, pro firmâ unius tenementi, ad feſtum Sc̄i Michis Archi t^{m} —		5	0
Copmanford.	—Item, de Joħe Jordan, pro firma unius virgatæ terræ & unâ clauſâ, pro termino Sc̄i Michis Archi, t^{m} —		2	0
Caldecote.	—Item, de Wiltmo Smyth, pro firmâ unius virgatæ terræ, pro termino Sc̄i Michis Archi —		2	0
Catworth.	—Item, de abbate de Sawtre, pro quieto redditu unius acræ terræ arabilis ibidem, ad feſtum Sc̄i Michis Archi		0	2
Stylton.	—Item, de Thomâ Smyth, pro firmâ unius toft, & dimidiâ virgatâ terræ ibidem, per annum, ad feſtum Sc̄i Michis Archi — —		2	0
Alkunbury Weſton.	—Item, de Thoma Hylle, collectore, pro redditu liberorum tenentium & cuſtomariorum ibidem, per annum, ad feſtum Sc̄i Michis Archi —		37	11

Papworth.

	£.	s	d.
Papworth.—Item, de Thoma Hylle, collectore, pro reddit' liber' tenent' cust' ibidem, ad festa Sci Michis Archi & Paschæ ——— ———		116	8
Gyllyng.—Item, de Thoma More, pro firmâ suâ ibidem, ad festa Sci Michis Archi & Paschæ ———		40	0
Item, de Johe Lutte, pro firmâ unius tenementi cum certâ terrâ, per annum, ad festa predicta —		8	0
Summa —		48	0
Croxton.—Item, de Johe Sawnder, pro firmâ sua, pro termino Purificationis Beatæ Mariæ ———		26	0
Item, de Johe Ratford, pro firmâ sua, pro termino predicto ——— ———		13	4
Summa —		39	4
Drayton.—Item, de Johe Pollard, pro quieto redditu ad festum Sci Michis ——— ———		13	4
Bernewell.—Item, de Johe Lete, pro firmâ certæ terræ ibidem, ad festum Sci Michis ———		20	0
Cantabr'.—Item, de Willmo Nores, pro firmâ certæ terræ in campis de Cantabr', ad festa Sci Michis Archi, & Paschæ		20	0
Bennewick.—Item, de Willmo Claypole, pro firma unius gurgitis aquæ, ad festa Sci Michis Archi & Paschæ —		6	0
Dene. ——Item, de Simone Halle, collectore, pro redditibus tam liberorum tenentium quam customar' ibidem, per annum, ad festa Sci Nicholai & Scæ Crucis —		68	3
Item, de Thoma Eston, firmario manerii ibidem, ad festa predicta ——— ———	4	13	4
Summa —	8	1	7
Swyneshed.—Item, de Johe Henson, pro firmâ certæ terræ ibidem, pro termino Annunciationis Beatæ Mariæ —		15	0
Sowthwycke.—Item, de Humfrido Ros, firmario nostræ rectoriæ, per annum, ad festum Annunciationis Beatæ Mariæ		100	0

Rushton.

	£.	s.	d.
Rushton.—Item, de Johe Sprot, pro firmâ suâ ibidem, ad festa Sci Michis Archi, & Paschæ ——		26	8
Harodon.—Item, de Richardo Yong, pro quieto redditu unius tenementi & certæ terræ ibidem, ad festum Sci Michis Archi —— ——		2	0
Item, de vicario ibidem, pro firmâ unius clausæ, ad fest' predictum ——		0	16
Summa —		3	4
Evenley.—Item, de Richardo Wayneman, firmario nostræ rectoriæ ibidem, per annum, ad festum Sci Michis Archi		20	0
Stamford.—Item, de præpositis ecclesiæ Sci Petri in le Westgate, pro firmâ unius tenementi, ad festum Sci Michis Archi		2	0
Stoke.——Item, de Johe Raskall, collectore, pro redditibus tam liberorum quam aliorum tenentium, ad festum Sci Michis Archi —— —		50	7
Pensiones.——Item, de priore de Shene, pro pensione in Roddeston, per ann' —— ——		14	0
Item, de rectore de Hardgrave, pro pensione suâ hoc anno —— ——		6	8
Item, de rectore de Offord Dacy, pro pencione suâ hoc anno —— ——		30	0
Item, de magistro hospitalis Sci Johis in Hunt', pro pens' hoc a° ——		13	4
Item, de rectore Omnium Scorum in Hunt', pro pensione suâ hoc a° ——		10	0
Item, de rectore ecclesiæ Sci Benedicti in Hunt', pro pensione suâ —— ——		6	8
Item, de rectore ecclesiæ Sci Johis in Hunt', pro pensione suâ —— ——		6	8
Summa —	4	7	4
Porciones.——Item, de rectore de Gyllyng, pro porcione nostrâ ibidem hoc anno —— ——		20	0
Item, de rectore de Grofsham, pro porcione nostrâ ibidem hoc anno —— ——		6	8
Item, de rectore de Mollesworth, pro porcione nostrâ ibidem hoc anno —— ——		10	0

Item,

		£.	s.	d.
	Item, de rectore de Polbrocke, pro porcione nostrâ ibdem hoc anno —— ——		13	4
	Item, de rectore de Stylton, pro porcione nostrâ ibidem hoc anno —— ——		10	0
	Item, de rectore de Thyrnynge, pro porcione nostrâ ibidem hoc anno —— ——		6	8
	Summa —		66	8
Oblaciones Capelle.	Item, de oblacionibus capellæ Beatæ Mariæ a festo Sc̃i Michis Archi usq; ad vigilias Sc̃i Johis Baptistæ, prout patet per billam de parcellis ejusdem		59	5
Dona & Legat'.	—Item, de Richardo Viryle de Godmychestr, pro quadam legatione exeunte de redditu tenementi sui hoc anno —— ——		6	8
Vendit' Lanæ.	—Item, de Willmo Towselond, de Alkunbury, pro 12 petris lanæ, pretium cujuslibet petræ, 4s. —		48	0
Perquisit' Curiarũ.	—Item, de collectore ville de Herford, pro communi fine ad curiam tentam ibidem ad festa Sc̃i Michis & Paschæ ——		13	4
	Item, de eodem collectore, pro fine unius cotagii Johis Pope —— ——			3
	Item, de eodem collectore, pro fine unius cotagii Willi Broke —— ——			4
	Item, de eodem collectore, pro fine unius teñti Roberti Willson —— ——			18
	Item, de eodem collectore, pro fine unius rodæ terræ Willmi Thorley ——			3¼
	Summa —		15	8¼
Exitus Grangiarum.	—Item, de Robto Rowley de Hunt', pro pascuâ & pasturâ pro omnibus suis pascendis tempore yëmali		8	6
	Item, de Richardo Gorwode, pro consimili —		5	0
	Item, de eodem Richardo, pro quodam parvo horreo tempore yëmali —— ——			12
	Item, de Willmo Flawen, pro agestamento equorum in pratis —— ——			7
	Item, de Agnete Cranefeld, pro agestamento ovium suarum tempore yëmali ——			16

	£.	s.	d.
Item, de Thoma Wyng, pro agestamento sui equi in grovagio * —— ——			4
Item, de Rob̄to More, pro agestamento sui equi in grovagio —— ——			6
Item, de Rowland Holdon, pro agestamento suorum equorum in grovagio ——			16
Item, de Joh̄e Harrys, pro agestamento suorum equorum in grovagio —— ——			4
Item, de Joh̄e Baker, pro herbagio unius clausæ juxta Sappley, à festo Natalis Domini usque ad Annunciationem Dominicam ——		3	4
Summa —		22	3
Exit' Coquine.—Item, de Joh̄e Magot, pro 19 corriis crudis de mactacione vaccarum à festo Sc̄i Mich̄is usque ad Quadragesimam; pretium cujuslibet 2*s.* 4*d.* ——		44	4
Item, de eodem Joh̄e, pro uno corrio crudo —		2	4
Item, de eodem Joh̄e, pro uno corrio crudo de mactatione unius bovis ——		3	4
Item, de eodem Joh̄e, pro 2 corriis crudis de mactatione 2 boviculorum, pretium cujuslibet corrii 2*s.* 8*d.*		5	4
Item, de Joh̄e Motte, pro 6 pellibus pellectis de mactatione à festo Sc̄i Mich̄is Arch̄i usque ad festum Sc̄i Dionysii; pret' cujuslibet dd †, 2*s.* 5*d.* —			14½
Item, de eodem Joh̄e, pro 2 duodecim & 4 pellibus lanatis de mactatione ovium à festo Sc̄i Dionysii usque ad Quadrages' pr' cujuslibet dd. 5*s.* ——		11	8
Item, de eodem Joh̄e pro 3 pellibus lanatis de mactatione ovium à festo Paschæ usque ad tonsionem; pretium cujuslibet pellis, 8*d.* ——		2	0
Item, de magistro cancellario, pro allec' alb' in Quadragesimâ —— ——			5
Item, de Rogero Heynes, pro 24 petris cepii; pret' cujuslibet petr' 12*d.* ——		24	0
Item, de Joh̄e Monyment, pro 12 petris & 11 lb̄. de flottesse *; pret' cujuslibet petræ, 14*d.* ——		14	1
Summa —		109	6¼

* These words are not in the Glossaries. † Duodecim.

		£.	s	d.
Exit' Piſtrin.—Item, de Johe Mermyon, pro 7 quarteriis & 2 buſh' de furfure; pretium cujuſlibet quarterii, 16*d*.			9	8
Receptus forenſici.	Item, de Richardo Newcom de Leyceſter, pro una campana fracta in pondere 20 c. & 9 lb.; pret' cujuſlibet lb. 2*d*. $\frac{1}{3}$ — —	19	18	2
	Item, pro uno pare cultellorum, venientium vel captorum per eſcheatam, infra præcinctus monaſterii			6
	Item, pro uno pare percarum, captarum ſimili modo; vendit' pro — —			6
	Item, pro uno pileo rubeo, de eâdem capturâ; vendito pro — — —			12
	Item, pro uno manitergio, per conſimile —			2
	Item, pro uno naperio de bokeram, ſimil' capt' & vendito pro — —			6
	Item, pro una avelana mortua, vendita apud Papworth			4
	Item, pro 5 capitibus ſalicinis, venditis Johi Stone, creſcent' in Long-mede — —			6
	Summa —	20	0	20
Receptus debitorum.—Item, de rectore eccleſiæ de Offord, pro medietate pencionis ſuæ à retro exiſtentis anni precedentis — —			15	0
Denar' mutuat'.—Item, de Doctore Taylard, in denariis mutuatis		30	0	0

Summa totalis receptuum cum arrerag' — 220*l*. 5*s*. 5¾*d*. dim.

N. B. The ſum of the receipts in the original MS is 219*l*. 11*s*. 5¾*d*. dim. which differs from this copy 14*s*.; and ariſes from the writer of that having omitted 15*s*. in the article of Hillington, and inſerted 1*s*. too much in caſting up the particulars of Herford.

Reſolutio

	£.	s.	d.
Reſolutio reddit'.—In primis, to the Kyng, by the hands of the ſhereff of Hunt', for the fee-ferm of Herford —		106	8
Item, to Maſt[r] Huddleſton, for the ſame —	6	13	4
Item, to the Kyng, by the hands of the ſhereff, for the manors of Gydding, Wynnewycke, and Wodeweſton — —		21	4
Item, to the Kyng, for the aſſart in Wodweſton and Sappley — —		4	0
Item, to the Kyng, for the honor of the caſtell in Hunt'		6	0
Item, to the abbot of Sawtre —		13	4
Item, to the prior of Bernewell —		4	0
Item, to the lord of Brampton —		7	0
Item, to the lord of Copmamford —			4
Item, to the Kyng, and the lord of Gyllyng —			13½
Item, to the lord of Alkunbury —			4¼
Item, to the ballyves of Hunt', for the hagable rent		33	11
Item, to the lord of Engayne's fee in Gydding		2	0½
Item, to the lord of Saint John's in J'zalem in Englond			6
Item, to the conſtables of Herford, for the comon fyne			8
Item, to the abbot of Peterborowe, for rent and amerciments — —			19½
Item, to the baylyves of Hunt', for amercyment			8
Summa —	16	16	10¾
Penciones.——Item, to the prior of Hatfeld —		60	0
Item, to the prior of Newnham —		53	4
Summa —		113	4
Augmentac[ns].—Item, to the vicar of Sowthwycke —	4	0	0
Item, to the vicar of Hemyngford —		66	8
Item, to the vicar of Wynnewycke —		40	0
Summa —	9	6	8
Denar' per Dn̄m Priorem recept'.} Item, rec[d] by owr beyond the ſtynt of his veſture — —		6	8

 Procurac'

		£.	s.	d.
Procurac' & Synodal'.	Item, to the Pope's collector ———		7	0
	Item, to my Lord of Lyncoln, for Sowtho chyrch		20	0
	Item, to Mr Commyſſary, for the locacion of Wynnewycke parſonage ———		6	8
	Item, to my Lord of Lyncoln, at his viſitacion, for our churches that bene imppred * ———		24	4
	Item, to the priors of Lawnde and Newnham, at their viſitacion, for their procurations ———		20	0
	Summa —		78	0
Xmæ & XVmæ, cum aliis oneribus.	Item, to the prior of Saynt Neots, collector of the firſt half dyme † in the archdeaconry of Hunt'		63	9½
	Item, to the collector of Ely dioceſe ———		13	3
	Item, to the collector of Bedfordſhyre ———		7	2½
	Item, to the collector of Northamptonſhyre —		6	0
	Item, to the collector of Lyncolnſhyre ———		2	9
	Item, to the prior of Newnham, collector of certain money, graunted to the reparacion of the college for ſcolers of our religion in Oxenford —		40	0
	Item, to the collectors of Normancros hondrede, for the 15th peny of Cannon-ſtrete ———		3	4
	Item, to the collectors of the 15th peny in Hunt', for owr tenement there ——— —		4	0
	Item, to the Duke of Bokyngham, to the knyghtyng of his ſon and eyre, for our londes holden of hym		27	1
	Summa —	8	7	5
Onus Capelle.	—Item, for 6 lb. of brochis; price of every lb. *5d.*		2	6
	Item, to William, keper of the chapell, for a hole yere's wages ——— ———		6	8
	Summa —		9	2
Veſturæ Prioris & Convent'.	Item, to owre maſter prior ‡, for three quarters of a yere — —		40	0

* Impropriated. † Tenth.

‡ Gregory Norwich, prior of Buſhmede, elected to this anno 1503, and continued to about 1528; then ſucceeded by William Gydding, to whom he reſigned.

Item,

	£.	s.	d.
Item, to the fupprior *, for 3 quarters —		20	0
Item, to ß † John Bury, for 3 quarters —		20	0
Item, to ß Willm Gyddyng, for 3 quarters —		20	0
Item, to ß Thoms Sowtho *, for 3 quarters —		20	0
Item, to ß John Godmycheft, 3 quarters —		20	0
Item, to ß Edward Hemyngford, for 3 quarters		20	0
Item, to ß Hugh Afteley, for 3 quarters —		20	0
Item, to ß Robert Huntyngdon *, for 3 quarters		20	0
Item, to John Rufhton *, noviciate, for 3 quarters		10	0
Item, to John Papworth, noviciate, for 3 quarters		10	0
Item, to ß Nicholas Elyngton *, fcolar, for a hole yere		53	4
Summa —	13	13	4

	s.	d.
Expenf' Prioris & Convent'. Item, in expenfe of the covent, in keping the anniverfary of Alice Shenyngton, at the chyrch of St. John, in Hunt' — —		8
Item, to 8 of the brethren, priefts, and to 2 noviciates, for kepying of the anniverfary William Clerke; to every prieft, 4*d.*; and every noviciate, 2*d.*; and to the fexten, for waft of wex, 1*d.* —	3	1
Item, to 8 of the brethren, priefts, for the chauntry of Sir John Sutton, every weke, 12*d.* for 38 wekes	38	0
Summa —	41	9

	s.	d.
Feod' Generof'.—Item, to maftr Wynd, ftyward, in part of his fee	26	8
Item, to maftr auditor, for his fee —	26	8
Item, to maftr Richard Halom, our paritor, to appere for us in vifitacion and ‡ for Michelmas terme		20
Summa —	55	0

	s.	d.
Feod' Ballivorum.—Item, Robto Button, baylyff of Moche Gydding	26	8
Item, to Symon Halle, baylyff of Dene —	13	4
Item, to John Rafkall, baylyff of Stoke —	3	4
Item, to Edmond Parell, baylyff of Stowghton —	2	0
Item, to the bayly of Herford, for fellyng of the medow	3	0
Summa —	48	4

* Members at the time of the furrender, anno 1539, July 11.

† This mark ufed for S throughout the original; where it evidently ftands for *Syr*, the ufual appellation of a prieft. On the academical ufe of this title at the feveral Univerfities, fee Gent. Mag. vol. L. p. 376; and vol. LI. pp. 120. 175.

‡ Penes. *Orig.*

Stipend'

		£.	s.	d.
Stipend' famul' Dñi Prioris.	Item, to the barber, for the hole yere —		10	0
	Item, to Thomas Hylle, for a hole yere —		26	8
	Item, to Richard Stowghton, for half a yere —		10	0
	Item, to John Claryvans, for a hole yere —		20	0
	Item, to Lawrence Sherard, for a quarter of a yere		5	0
	Summa —		71	8

		£.	s.	d.
Stipend' famul' Husbandr'.	Item, to John Baylyff, for halfe a yere —		16	8
	Item, to Richard Stowghton, baylyff, for half a yere		13	4
	Item, to Richard Lawson, for a hole yere —		20	0
	Item, to Henry Large, shepherd, for a hole yere		20	0
	Item, to Ric. Butteler, hoggerd, for a hole yere		16	0
	Item, to John Paterson, bruar, for half a yere —		8	0
	Item, to William Barnaby, for 3 qrs. of a yere —		12	6
	Item, to John Mose, for half a yere, and half a quarter		11	4
	Item, to Robt Wryght, for a quarter of a yere —		6	8
	Item, to William Gonny, for a quarter of a yere		6	8
	Item, to James Aborow, for a hole yere —		16	0
	Item, to Symon Owndell, for halfe a yere —		8	6
	Item, to John Wylkynson, bruar, for half a yere		11	8
	Item, to Robt Ducheman, for a quarter of a yere		3	0
	Item, to Ric. Bartlot, for 3 quarters of a yere —		13	6
	Item, to Thomas Burton, for 3 quarters of a yere		15	0
	Item, to Robt Halle, for half a yere —		10	6
	Item, to Denyse More, for 3 qrs. of a yere —		12	9
	Item, to Thomas Ferror, for half a yere —		9	0
	Item, to William Pygot, for half a yere —		8	6
	Item, to Thomas Snowe, coke, for half a yere		10	0
	Item, to Thomas Williamson, for fourscore and 16 days werke, every day 1*d*. —		8	0
	Item, to Lawrens Gardyner, for 16 days werke, every day 1*d*. — —			16
	Item, to Edward Shepherde, for 3 wekes werke —			9
	Item, to Symon Owndell, for 10 days werke —			10
	Item, to Robt Wryght, for 11 days werke —			11
	Item, to Robt More, for 8 days werke —			8
	Item, to Willm Barnaby, for 6 days werke —			6
	Summa —	13	0	5

		£.	s.	d.
Custus Ecclīarum.	—Item, to Symon Plomer, werkyng upon the chyrche, the frayt *, and the grete chamber, 21 days and ½, takyng ev'ry day 3*d*. — —		5	4½

* Q. fratris?

Item,

		£.	s.	d.
	Item, payd to Barnaby, for ſervyng off hym —			14
	Item, payd for 6 lb. of ſowde —			15
	Item, for 2 c̃. nayles to the ſame —			5
	Item, to the glaſyer, for 22 fote of glaſs, for every fote 3*d.*		5	6
	Item, for 4 fother of lyme, for the grete chapell		5	2
	Item, to John Tylar, werkyng 11 days and ½ upon the ſame chapell of owr Lady, every day 4*d.* —		3	10
	Item, to John Wylkynſon, his ſervant, for 11 days and ½, takyng for every day 2*d.* —			23
	Item, to a glaſyer, for mendyng the chancell wyndowes at Hemyngford — —			14
	Item, for mendyng of the chauncell wyndow at Styvecley			1
	Summa —		25	10
Reparaciones infra precinct' Monaſterii.	Item, to Johan Gryg, for drawyng of ſtrawe, and ſerving the thacker in the bern-yerde, 49 days, taking every day 1*d.* — —		4	1
	Item, to Rob. Wryght, thacker, werkyng in the bern-yerde 15 days, takyng every day 2*d.* —		2	6
	Item, payd to John Pykard, of Wyſtow, for 18 c̃. and ½ of ſege, price of every c̃. 16*d.* —		24	8
	Item, to the glaſyer, for 8 fote of glaſſe for the wyndowes		2	0
	Item, for 6 fote of glaſſe for the chamber wyndowes			18
	Item, to John Tylar, werkyng upon the chamber 1 day			4
	Summa —		35	1
Huntgdon.	—Item, to Thomas Millar, for thackyng the lytyll hows in the angell, by grete —		2	0
	Item, to the ſame Thomas, for claying there 12 days, takyng every day 5*d.* to fynd hymſelf —		5	0
	Item, to Willm Stanny, carpenter, for 2 days werke and ½			12
	Item, for 2 fother of lyme to Bone's hows —		3	1
	Item, to John Tylar, for 6 days and ½ werkyng there, takyng every day 6*d.*; to fynd hymſelf —		3	3
	Item, to his ſervant, for 6 days and ½, every day 4*d.*		2	2
	Item, to Wyllm Fleetwoode, for ſcouring of the well there			4
	Item, to Thomas Barton, for laying in a newe beme in the backhows — —			5
	Item, to John Bone, for mendyng of 3 wyndowes there			6
	Item, for reparacions done at maſtr Styvecle's 2 tenauntres, in thackyng, claying, and wryght's werke, in grete — —		21	0

Item,

		£.	s.	d.
	Item, for 2 fother of lyme for Somerbe's hows		3	1
	Item, for a bonche of lathes ———			9
	Item, for a bz of tyle pynnes ———			4
	Item, to John Tylar, for 5 days werke, takyng every day *6d.*		2	6
	Item, to his servant, for 5 days, every day *4d.* —			20
	Item, for nayles to the same hows ———			1
	Item, for clayng of the same hows ———		2	1
	Item, for gatheryng of rede to the same hows —			18
	Item, to Thomas Barton, for settyng in of 5 studdes *			4
	Item, to Thomas Barton, for settyng in 3 studdes in Nottyngham's hows ———			3
	Item, to John Gryg, for clayng of the same, 3 bays			1
	Item, to Thos Barton, and his felow, for mendyng of the roffe of the tynkar's hows, in grete ——		2	4
	Item, to Thomas Barton, for basyng of the chamber			5
	Item, for basyng of the halle, in grete ———			9
	Item, to John Gryg, for clayng of the same hows			12
	Item, to Thos Barton, for gestyng and bording the solers		2	3
	Item, to Thos Barton, for makyng of dores and wyndowes			4
	Item, for 2 c̃. nayles to the same hows ———			9
	Item, to the thacker, for 14 days werke upon the same hows, takyng every day *2d.* ———		2	4
	Item, to Willm Barnaby, for servyng him 14 days			11
	Item, to Johan Grygge, drawyng strawe 14 days			14
	Summa —		63	8
Papworth.——	Item, for 10 lode of strawe to John Blackman		4	0
	Item, for thackyng and drawyng of strawe, in grete		2	8
	Summa —		6	8
Gydding.——	Item, to a carpenter werking 2 days upon John Bate's bern and kechyn ——— ———			6
	Item, for his borde the same 2 days ———			4
	Item, for 2 peces of tymber to the same werke			8
	Summa —			18
Styvecley.——	Item, for a c̃. nayles and ½ to the kylle and bern dores			6
	Item, for scowryng of the parsonage dycke there			12
	Item, for thackyng, and clayng, and splenting of Herry Freman's hows, in grete ———		10	0

* *Quarters* as they are now called in wooden partitions.

3 Item,

		£.	s.	d.
	Item, to Thomas Barton and his felow, for mendyng of Ric. Langle's bern, in grete		2	6
	Summa		14	0
Conyngton.—	Item, payd for ſtrawe, and thackyng, drawyng, and ſerving, in grete, for the ende of the hows there		4	1
Hemyngford.—	Item, for a fother of lyme to the ſame parſonage there		2	8
Gyllyng.—	Item, for 2 lode of ſtrawe, and thackyng of the ſame, in grete, of the grete bern there		6	8
Empt' & ſolut' neceſſar'.	Item, to John Andrew, for 5 days and ½ mowyng halme*, takyng for every day 5*d.* to find hymſelf		2	3
	Item, to John Baker, for 7 days and ½ mowyng halme alſo		3	1
	Item, to Andrew and Baker, for gatheryng and rakeying the ſame halme, in grete			14
	Item, for geldyng of 28 pygges			14
	Item, for geldyng of 3 calves			1½
	Item, for ſawyng of 3 waynſcott bordes			4
	Item, for an empty wyne veſſell called a butt, for to make 2 ale cubbes of			16
	Item, to Will. Woode, for ſcowryng the Kynge's dycke			19
	Item, to Elſabeth Bullocke, for threſhyng and dreſſyng of ye muſtard ſeede			2
	Item, for mendyng of tryce and ſtage at ye brewhows pond			6
	Item, to Will Bullocke's wyff, for mendyng ye botoms of 3 ſyves that wer broken			4
	Item, for a new boket to the well in the berne yard			2
	Item, for a mylke payle to the day hows			2½
	Item, to Thomas Barton and his felow, for hewyng and ſquaryng of 60 peces of rowgh tymber		2	2
	Item, to the belman, for crying of 2 ſtray pygges			2
	Item, for ſawyng of a bord logge of 7 ſcore fote bord			14
	Item, for ſawyng of the grete ladder pece			2
	Item, for ſtavyng and makyng of the ſame			4
	Item, for a chesfat † to the day ‡ hows			1
	Item, for a creme pott and a mylke pan			1
	Item, for mendyng of the old chyrn			4
	Item, to Thomas Barton, for mendyng of the hoggerd's carr			3
	Item, for a coverlet to the meyne's bed			12

* Q. Stubble, or the *hawn* of peaſe? † Cheeſe vat. ‡ Dairy.

		£.	s.	d.
	Item, for 4 elles of canvas to make them a ſhete of			16
	Item, for wrytyng of Doctor Taylard's indenture *		2	0
	Item, for 10 ſtone of lede and ½, price of a ſtone 5*d.*		4	4 †
	Item, for 6 lytyll hangyng lockes ——			9
	Item, for 5 elles of cloth for the table in the frayt			22
	Item, for treacle for 2 ſeke oxen ——			1½
	Item, for a botell for the neteherd ——			3
	Item, to Robt Wryght, hyred to ſett wyllowes 2 days			2
	Item, for 2 quayers of paper ——			4
	Item, for 4 ‡ pottes ayenſt my Lord of Lyncoln's comyng —— ——			2
	Item, to Thomas Barton and his felowe, hyred to make 5 newe ladders, and the baylyffe's brygge —			21
	Item, for a peyr of ſhetes ——		3	0
	Summa —		34	§ 2½
Expenſ' forenſic'.	Item, for Hille's coſtes to Stylton for owr rent —			2½
	Item, for Thomas Hylle's coſtes to Northampton for owr rent —— ——			9
	Item, for Will. Barnabe's coſtes with Joh. Paterſon, to ſett owr meres and foles from the fen —			2
	Item, for the ſexten's coſtes to S. Ives, to by malt			3
	Item, for the ſupprior's coſtes in Hunt', to ſpeke wt Joh' Garnet —— ——			1
	Item, for Tho. Hylle's coſtes to Stretham, to ſpeke wth ye parſon of Papworth ——			4
	Item, for Laurence Sherard's coſtes to Kynſton upon Temys, to ſpeke with my Lord of Lyncoln		4	4
	Item, for Tho. Hylle's coſtes to Sawceton —			4
	Item, for the ſupprior's coſtes to Sent Nedes, to ſpeke wth the prior — —			1
	Item, for Tho. Hylle's coſtes to Ely, after Ely fare			12
	Item, for Tho. Hylle's coſtes to Woburn, to bere my Lord of Lyncoln a letter — —		3	0
	Item, for the ſexten's coſtes to S. Ives to bye herrynges			2
	Item, for the ſupprior's coſtes in Hunt', to ſpeke wth maſtr Feldyng ——			1
	Item, for owr maſter's coſtes in Hunt', 2 Sondays in Lenton, after the ſermons, to drynke with the parichoners			8
	Item, for the ſexten's coſtes to Sent Ives, 5 Mondays in Lenton, to by freſh cates ‖ there ——			5
	Item, to Tho. Hylle's coſtes to Stamford, for owr rent			1

* Q. Bond, on his lending them the money? p. 284. † 3*d.* in orig.

‡ Hyney, orig. Q. Honey? § 1*d.* in orig. ‖ Proviſions.

4 Item,

	£.	s.	d.
Item, for the ſupprior's coſtes in Hunt', to ſpeke wth Doctor Taylard			2
Item, for owr maſter's expences in Hunt' upon the viſitors			6
Item, for Tho. Hylle's coſtes to Ruſton, for rent			4½
Item, for the ſupprior's coſtes at Salom fayr			11
Item, for the ſupprior's coſtes at Elſtow fayr			13½
Item, for maſt^{r} Tho. Sowtho's coſts at Conyngton, to put owr beſtes in the fen			2
Item, in expences of the covent at the ſpytell hows in the rogacion weeke			4
Item, for Tho. Hille's coſtes to Cambryge and to Stretam			8
Item, for Ric. Stowghton's coſtes to Sent Nedes upon th'Aſſencion even and day alſo			3
Item, for the ſexten's coſtes to Sent Yves, to by cheſe			2
Item, for Ric. Stowghton's coſtes to Sent Nedes, in die Corporis Xti			2
Item, to maſt^{r} Hugh Aſteley, for his coſtes to Leyceſter to the generall chapter		8	0
Summa		24	9½

	£.	s.	d.
Dona & Regarda.—Item, to maſt^{r} commyſſary, for to delay and put over the ſeanes of Michelmas and Eſter, for every time 6*s.* 8*d.*		13	4
Item, to maſt^{r} Ric. Halom, his ſcribe, for the ſame cawſe, every time 3*s.* 4*d.*		6	8
Item, for a pyke, 2 tenchys, and 2 elys, ſent to Bucden to my Lord of Lyncoln for a preſent		7	0
Item, gyven to a purſevant of the Kynge's, a reward			8
Item, gyven to oon of the Kynge's hunters that came with many of his howndes, a reward			8
Item, gyven to John Gray, maſt^{r} commyſſary's ſomoner, whan he browght my Lord of Lyncoln's letter			4
Item, gyven to a purſevant of the Kynge's, upon New-Yere's day			8
Item, gyven to the ſergeantes of Huntingdon, a reward			20
Item, gyven to the ſhereff of Huntingdon, his offryng		6	8
Item, gyven to the underſhereff, his offryng		3	4
Item, to maſt^{r} Tyſe, to have his frendſhypp		3	4
Item, gyven to Will. Radley, a reward			6
Item, gyven to the prior of Newnham's ſervant, whan he browght the mandat			4

Item,

	£.	s.	d.
Item, gyven to a gentylman goyng to Rome, by the deſyre of th' abbot of Petyrborow			12
Item, gyven to hym that browght my Lord of Lyncoln's mandat			12
Item, gyven to 12 pore men upon Shere-Thorſday		2	0
Item, gyven to 2 purſevants together upon Low-Sonday			12
Item, gyven to the fen reve of Conyngton, when we ſent owr beſtes thedyr to the fen			2
Item, gyven to Sent Antony's clerke			4
Item, gyven to the wyves of Herford, to the makyng of there May			12
Item, gyven to the belman in the rogacion weke			2
Item, gyven to maſt[r] auditor's ſervantes, a reward		2	8
Item, gyven to a purſevant the 10 day of Jun.			8
Item, gyven to maſt[r] Edward Watſon, to have his favor		6	8
Item, 3 rewards gyven to my Lord of Lyncoln's ſervantes, at the tyme of his viſitacion		23	0
Summa	4	4	10

Cuſtus Huſbondriæ.

	£.	s.	d.
Item, for 10 flaggen colers for horſes			9
Item, for 12 payr of plowgh traytes *			22
Item, for whyppcord			4
Item, for 4 lether halters			21
Item, for 7 hempen halters			7
Item, to the plowgh wryght for his werke, 7 days		2	4
Item, for 6 corlers of lether for horſes		3	8
Item, for 2 horſe lockes			9
Item, for pakthredd to ſewe ſakkes with			0½
Item, for a payr of fetters			4
Item, for 2 horſe ropes of here			5
Item, for a payr of whelys		4	7
Item, for a ſyth with a ſneth			14
Item, for ſewyng of the here cloth			1
Item, for letting owr horſes blede in Cryſtmaſſe weke			4
Item, for a hyde of whyte lether			16
Item, for lyne for the wombe ropes			4
Item, for 2 cart ſadell pannelles			8
Item, to Rob. Mortlake, for the hyer of 3 oxen a yere		6	0
Item, to the ſmyth for yron and yron werke, from Michelmas to Mydſomer		53	0½
Summa	4	0	4

* Traces.

Trituratoribus

		£.	s.	d.
Trituratoribus granorum.	Item, to Tho. Williamſon and Rob. More, for threſshyng of 19 qurt̃rs and 3 buſh. of whete —		6	5
	Item, to the ſame Thoˢ and Rob̃t, for threſshyng of 9 qrt̃rs and ½ of rye — —		3	2
	Item, to the ſame Thoˢ and Rob̃t, for threſshyng of 9 ſcore and 1 quarters of barly, price of every quarter 2*d*.		30	0
	Item, to the ſame Thoˢ and Rob̃t, for threſshyng of 3 q̃rters of otes — —			6
	Summa —		40	1
Empt' Panis.—	Item, for brede, ayenſt the com̃yng of m̃. comyſſary			2
	Item, for brede, ayenſt the com̃yng of m̃ Wynd —			1
	Item, for brede, ayenſt the com̃yng of the prior of Buſshmede — — —			1
	Item, for brede, ayenſt the com̃yng of m̃. chaunceller, at 2 tymes — —			5½
	Item, for brede, upon Shere-Thorſday, for the Maundy			2
	Item, for brede, ayenſt the com̃yng of the viſitors of owr religion — —			9
	Item, for brede, ayenſt the com̃yng of my Lord of Lyncoln to his viſitacion, 10 doz. and ½ —		10	6
	Summa —		12	2½
Empt' Vini.—	Item, for a potell of wyne at the com̃yng of mʳ archdeacon — — —			4
	Item, for a potell of Malveſey, and 2 gallons of red wyne, and claret, at dyverſe tymes, to maſtʳ chaunceller — — —		2	0
	Item, for a quart of Malveſey and ſugre to the viſitors of owr religion — — —			5
	Item, for 3 gallons of wyne and ½, in tyme of my Lord of Lyncoln's viſitacion — —		2	4
	Summa —		5	1
Empt' ſerviſſ'.—	Item, for a doz. and a half of good ale, ayenſt the com̃yng of the viſitors of owr religion —		2	3
	Item, for 10 doz. and ½ of good ale, ayenſt the viſitation of my Lord of Lyncoln — —		15	9
	Summa —		18	0

Empt'

	£.	s.	d.
Empt' focal'.—Item, payd to Thomas Barton, for fellyng of wood in Thomas Hylle's closs 7 days —			7
Item, to Thoˢ Barton, for fellyng of wood in yᵉ Swan close 2 days — — —			2
Item, to Symon Plomer, for loppyng of 6 c̃. hedes of wyllows, by yᵉ grete — —		4	4
Item, to Will. Stanton and his felow, for fellyng of 2 acres and a rode in Alkunbury wood —		16	3
Item, to John Baker and his felow, for making 2 mill. and 2 c̃ faggotes — —		39	0
Item, for ernest of 13 trees in Geyne's parke —			13
Item, for fellyng of the same trees — —			13
Item, to Thoˢ Barton, for toppyng and loppyng of the same trees 4 days and ½ — —			9
Item, to John Stowghton, for caryeng of 4 of yᵉ same trees — — —		3	4
Summa —		66	7
Empt. candel'.—Item, payd for 12 doz. and 8 lb. of candell, price of every lb. 1½*d.* — —		19	0
Empt' granorum.—Item, payd to John Bucke, of Wynnewycke, for eight quarters of whete, price of every quarter 8*s*.		64	0
Item, to Thoˢ Clerke, of Moche Gyddyngg, for 20 quarters of barly, price of every quarter 4*s*. —	4	0	0
Item, to Thoˢ Assheman, for 20 quarters of barley	4	0	0
Item to John Bucke, for 10 quarters of barley —		40	0
Item, for 3 quarters of malt, bowght at Sent Yves, in the market holden there the 26th day of October		14	5
Item, to Ric. Butteler, for 3 combes of barley —		5	6
Summa —	14	3	11
Empt' staur'.—Item, payd to father Bayly, for a cowe for the store		10	0
Item, for 2 kyen for the store, bowght at Spynney feld		22	0
Item, payd to John Maryet, for 2 kyen for the store, and for 2 calves of a yere old — —		26	8
Item, to John Claryvans, for 2 heeforths for the store		10	0
Item, for 2 steres for the plowgh, bowght at the pasture		22	4
Item, for 4 steres for the plowgh, bowght at Browghton of Richard Cockes — —		45	0
Item, to John Baker, for a yeryng for store —		3	0

Item,

		£.	s.	d.
	Item, payd for 3 horſes bowght at Salom fayr for the plowgh, and carte, and huſbandry —	4	3	10
	Summa —	11	2	10
Cuſt^s coquinæ.—	Item, for half a garnyſh of pewtyr veſſel —		7	5
	Item, for a pan of braſſe —			22
	Item, for 2 ladelles — —			1
	Item, for a ſtreynor — —			1½
	Item, for mendyng of the fornays in the kechyn —			2
	Item, for peckyng of the muſtard quern —			1
	Summa —		9	8½
Cuſt^s molend'.—	Item, payd for mendyng of the malt mylle at 2 tymes			6
Cuſt^s piſtrin'.—	Item, for a newe boltell — —			4
	Item, to father Willm, for mendyng of the oven —			1
	Summa —			5
Cuſtus pandoxatorii.	Item, for mendyng of the fornays of the grete lede			10
	Item, for makyng of the botom of the maſshe fatte			5
	Item, for barme for 46 bruynges, every bruyng ½*d.*			23
	Summa —		3	2
Cuſtus ſepimentorum.	Item, to Rob. Wryght, for hedgyng 2 days —			4
	Item, to John Baker, for fellyng of 22 lode of hedgyng thornys — —		3	8
	Summa —		4	0
Cuſt^s Faldæ.—	Item, payd for 4 doz. fold hardelles, price of a doz. 21*d.*		7	0
	Item, for caryage of the ſame from Moche Gyddyng			16
	Item, for 12 lb. of pytche for brondyng —			12
	Item, for waſshyng of 6 ſcore ſhepe —			6
	Item, for clyppyng of the ſame —			12
	Item, for wyndyng of the wolle —			4
	Summa —		11	2

Placita

	£.	s.	d.
Placita cum Brev'.—Item, for a wrytte of *scire facias* ayenst Doctor Taylard, for witholdyng owr pencyon —		6	3
Item, to the shereff, for grene wex ——		6	8
Item, to the same, for yssues ——			12
Summa —		13	11
Expens' Hospitii.—Item, payd for expenses of the howshold from Myhelmas unto Mydsomer, as appereth by ye kechyn boke —— ——	41	14	4½
Debita soluta.—Item, payd to master Richard Blom, de London	20	0	0
Item, to master Parcell ——		20	0
Item, to Thomas Manby —— —		6	8
Item, to Thomas Basse —— ——		20	0
Item, to master Wynd —— ——		33	4
Item, to the wydow of Howghton ——		40	0
Item, to John Benet —— ——		2	0
Item, to John Coryar —— ——	4	0	3
Item, to the baylyff of Alkunbury ——		60	0
Item, to Doctor Halle —— ——		11	3
Item, to Symon Halle ——		2	8
Item, to Agnes Clerke —— ——		13	0
Item, to the baylyff of Hemyngford ——			8
Item, to Gronger of Godmychest^r ——	6	13	4
Item, to the sexton —— ——			9
Item, to Robt Rowley —— ——		8	6
Item, to the baylyff of Copmanford ——			12
Item, to Roger Heynes —— ——		11	8
Summa —	42	5	1
Summa omnium solutionum —	221	3	0¼

THE YEARELY ORDYNARY EXPENCES OF SAVOYE*, WITH THE REVENUES CERTAYNE AND ORDYNARIE.

(From the Cotton MSS. Vefpafian C. XIV. fol. 538.)

Rents within the fyte of the Savoye	xxxixl.
In St. Clemens parrifhe	xxxixl. xs.
In Effex —	xliiil.
In Yorkefhire	cviiil. iis. xid.
In Lyncolnefhire	viiil. xiiis. vid. ob.
In Leycefterfhire	vil. xvs. vid. ob.
In Northamptonfhire	xvl. vis. viiid.
In Durham —	xxs.
In Lancafter —	xivl. viiis.
Summa totalis	ccliiil. vis. viiid.

The mafter's wages — — —	xxxl.
The wages of three chaplines for a yeare, and a fourth for a quarter	xiiil.
The wages of three fifters — — — —	xiil.
The mafter's two fervaunts — — —	iiiil.
To the porter, butler, cook, undercook, clearkof the kitchen, laundreffe, &c.	xxl. xs.
To the parfon of St. Clemens for tyth — —	xxvis. viiid.
To the pettie canons of Paules for their yeares fee —	xls.
To the collector of rents in the North — —	xls.
To the co-brother of the hofpital of St. DD's † — —	xxs.
For collecting of rents in Northamptonfhire — —	xxs.
To the minifter of St. DD's † — — —	xxxs.

To the furgeon ‡ for his yeares fee iiiil.—To the auditor for the like vl.

* This houfe, originally built as a palace for Peter Earl of Savoy on his coming into England to vifit his niece the Queen of Henry III, became afterwards part of the poffeffions of the dukes of Lancafter. In the rebellion of 1381, under Jack Straw, the tumultuous populace, from hatred to John of Gaunt, burnt the palace, then efteemed to be the faireft ftructure in the nation, with much rich furniture, and other things of value, particularly charters, evidences, and MSS. After which, the whole of this magnificent building lay long in afhes and rubbifh, till the time of King Henry VII; who, by his laft will, directed it to be re-built, not now for an houfe to be inhabited by nobility as it was before, but for a charitable foundation, to harbour 100 poor people, fick or lame, or travellers, to be furnifhed with lodging, food, firing, and attendance, for a certain time, dedicating it to St. John Baptift, and endowing it royally. All this was duly performed by King Henry VIII. who caufed this infcription to be placed over the gate:

" Hofpitium hoc inopi turbe Sauoia vocatum,
Septimus Henricus fundavit ab imo folo!"

The letters patent for the foundation were dated 5 July, 4 Henry VIII; and the ftatutes for its regulation June 20, 15 Henry VIII. The firft mafter was William Holgyll, prieft, who had fuperintended the building of the houfe; the four firft chaplains, John Sutton, *doctor in decretis*, who was appointed vice-mafter; Thomas Thornegh, who was facrift; Alexander Palmer, LL. B was confeffor; and John Hoode, M. A. hofpitaller. Under thefe, were four affiftant chaplains, called *altariftæ*; and, among other lay officers, an *ortulanus*, or keeper of the garden, who was to be a fingle man, of difcreet life, and at leaft thirty years old.

† This was the hofpital of St. David's, at Kingfthorp, near Northampton, founded in 1200, for the reception of pilgrims, and poor and indigent fick perfons. The fite and lands of this hofpital were granted, 4 and 5 Philip and Mary, to the Hofpital of the Savoy. See Tanner; and Bridges, Hiftory of Northamptonfhire, vol. I. p. 416.

‡ The furgeon was to be *fufficienter auditus*; and of good practice within the city of London.

For

For rent resolute iil. viis.—To the scavenger vis. viiid.

Expensæ pauperum & consimilium	—	xliil. xvs. iid. ob.
Lyveries for the master, chaplyns, and servants	—	xivl. xs.
Expensæ hospitii hoc anno	— —	cclxiil. ixs. vid.
Summa totalis	— — —	ccccxviil. xs. viid. ob.

Reparations xviil. xiiiis.—Expensæ in Lege xiiiil. xviiis.

Arrerages cxxxil. viis. viiid.—Fines xxixl. xiiis. iiiid.—
Expensæ in Donis, Legationibus, Eleemosinâ, lxxiiil. xiiiis. } ccxxxiiiil. xiiiis.

The state of this house, as it was reported to the king and his council, 5 Edw. VI.

"The value and issues of the lordships, manors, lands, &c. the last year, amounted to 541*l.* 5*s.* 5*d.* ob.—Reprizals, fees, payments, expences, reparations, &c. 746*l.* 7*s.* 7*d.* ob. q.—So that the expences exceeded the revenue by 205*l.* 4*s.* 2*d.*

"*Numerus Pauperum Ægrotantium.*

"The numbers of the poor refreshed within the said hospital, from Michaelmas, anno 4 Edward VI. to the 24th of September, anno 5 Edward VI. of sick and impotent people, besides others nightly lodged there, 8339.

"The yearly fees and salaries briefly stood thus: to the master of the hospital, 30*l.*; to the four chaplains, 16*l.*; two conducts, 6*l.* 13*s.* 4*d.*; thirteen sisters, 52*l.* 6*s.* 8*d.*; ten servants, 22*l.* 6*s.* 8*d.*; other officers, as physician, surgeon, auditor, and steward, 28*l.*; expences upon poor people, 133*l.* 6*s.* 4*d.* ob.

"Besides the damage this house received by the first master of all, the Savoy was become ruinous, and in a very declining condition; which inclined the King, upon a motion made to him by the city of London, to dissolve it; as he did; and granted the beds and furniture to the city, for the use and benefit of the poor, to be harboured at Bridewell; and settled much of the revenues of the said hospital upon it; so that the charity did not cease hereby, but was removed *."

* The revenues of this hospital were seized on by Edward VI. in 1547, as directed to superstitious uses; but it was founded anew in 1557 by Queen Mary, who incorporated and endowed it; all the court ladies and maids of honour, in imitation of the Queen's charity, contributing their parts and shares towards it, by sending sufficient stores of beds and bedding, and other things necessary, for furniture of the rooms where the poor were to be harboured. In Queen Elizabeth's time, a great many rogues and idle beggars sheltered themselves here, upon pretence of being needy, or lame, or sick, and to want relief, according to the order of the foundation; which was to receive *Claudicantes, Ægrotantes, & Peregrinantes* In the reign of King Charles II. it was made use of in good part as a garrison; and soldiers were here lodged; their beds being placed as they usually are in hospitals. In 1702 it was finally dissolved. See Bibl. Top. Brit. p. 238; Cotton MSS. Cleopatra, C. V. 1.; and Strype's Stowe, vol. I. p. 211.

EXPENCES

EXPENCES OF SIR HENRY UNTON'S EMBASSY TO FRANCE, 1591.

(From a contemporary MS.)

Her Maties Paſporte, dated the 21ſt of July, 1591.

ELIZABETH R.

WHERAS we have apoynted our truſtye and wel-beloved ſervant Sir Henry Unton, knyght, to make his repayre into France, ther to be our ambaſſador reſident with our good brother the French king: we ſtraightly chardge and commaund you, and every of you, not only to ſuffer him, with his company and trayne, and all his and ther horſes and geldings, monye, juells, plate, males, cofers, bagge, and baggages, and all his neceſſary and houſhould proviſions and furniture whatſoever, at all tymes quietly to paſſe by you, withowte any manner your ſtay, let, or interruption; but alſo, that all you, and every of you, ſee him and his ſayd trayne furniſhed, from place to place, to the ſea-ſyde, both of ſufficient and able horſes, and of any other cariages alſo which he may need, at reaſonable pryſes. And farther, that ye be alſo ayding and aſſiſting unto the ſayd Sir Henry Unton, for providing him of convenient ſhipping, for the ſuer and ſaffe tranſportation of him and his trayne, and this likewiſe at pryſes reaſonable; not fayling heerof, as you tender our diſpleaſure, and will anſwer for the contrarye at your perill. And thes our letters ſhall be your ſufficient warrant and diſchardge in this behalffe. Geven under our ſignet, at our mannor of Greenwich, the xxth of July, in the XXXIII yeare of our raigne.

To all juſtices, mayors, ſhrieffes, bayliffes, conſtables, cuſtomers, controlers, and ſearchers, and to all other officers, miniſters, and ſubjects, to whome in this caſe it may appartayne, and to every of them. ED. LAKE.

The note of indenture of the Queen's plate, delivered to my Lo. owte of the juelle houſe, 25 July, 1591.

This indenture, made the XXVth day of July, anno XXXIII° Regine Elizabethe, witneſſethe, that John Aſteley, eſquier, maſter and thr̃er of her Maties juells and plate, hath delivered unto Sir Henry Unton, knight, legier ambaſſador ſent unto Fraunce, thes p̧cells of ſilver veſſels following:

First, two great platters, p̧ oz. —— —— $^{xx}_{iiii}$VI oz. di. q̃r.
Itm, fower demy platters, p̧ oz. —— CXIX oz. III q̃r.
Itm, ſix leſſer platters, p̧ oz. —— CXLI oz. q̃r.
Itm, eight diſhes, p̧ oz. —— —— CXVIII oz.
Itm, nyne demy diſhes, p̧ oz. —— —— CX oz.
Itm, ſix leſſer diſhes, p̧ oz. —— LVIII oz. & q̃r.
Itm, one baſſin and ewer of ſilver, whete, p̧ oz. —— LXII oz. di. q̃r.
Itm, ſix ſawcers, p̧ oz. —— —— XXIX oz.

In wittnes wheroff, the p̧ties aboveſayd have to thes p̃ſent indentures interchangeably ſet ther hands, the day and yeare above written.

Subſc. J. ASTELEY. Teſt. N. PIGEON.

A note of the charges Sir Edward Stafford demaunded, every 3 monethes, for intelligence monie; and the words of his warrant were these, as followeth, subscribed under his owne hand, to Mr. Secretarie Walsingham:

For so muche monies by me disborsed, for three monthes, as namely, Aprill, May, and June, for necessarie and especiall causes, for her Matie's s̃vice in Fraunce, subscribed by me for iij monethes before receited, untill the . . . of this instant moneth —— —— cxxxviii.

This rate he demaunded at his goinge out of service.

And he demaunded at his first enterance to the service but $^{xx}_{IIII}$ l.

Wares were the causes for thre moneths: by the same reason you may set down more then he did for his iij monethes.

Wheras I receaved now lately of the Queene's Matie monie by impresse the som of cc$^{xx}_{IIII}$ l. by vertue of her Ma^ts privie seale, bearinge date the xxiith day of July, in the xxxiiith yeare of her Highnesse raigne; the said som is to be defaulked in allowance of my diet, after the rate of iij l. vj s̃. viij đ. the day, which is now expired, the xxth day of March, in manner and forme followinge, and allowinge xxviij daies to the moneth:

For my diet of xj daies in December, beinge on the xxth daie therof, the said daye beinge inclusive.

For xxxj daies in Januarie.

In xxix daies in Februarie.

For xiij daies in Marche.

Mr. Petters, I praie you deliver to this bearer my s̃vant, Nicholas Payne, the som of ccLxxxl. monie nowe dewe to me by imprest by vertue of the Queene's Matie's privie seale, bearinge date the xxth daie of July, in the xxxiijth yeare of her Highnesse's raigne, for allowance of my diet, from the xxth daie of March exclusive, untill iij monethes next followinge be expired. Dated at the Camp, the xxth daie of March, 1591. Your verie lovinge frend.

To his verie lovinge frend Mr. Robert Peters, esquier,
auditor of her Matie's excheq^r.

The particular chardges of Sir Henry Unton, knight, her Matie's ambassador into Fraunce, for his transportations, cariages, and other ordynarye chardges, since his departure, from the 23th of Julye, untill the 20th of December, in the same yeare, 1591.

	£.	s.	d.
Item, for cariage of some of my stuffe from London to Dover	20	0	0
For 46 post-horses from London to Dover ——	24	0	0
For the transportation of my horses, stuffe, and servants, from London, wher thei weer shipped, and of myselff and my companye, and other chardges, from Dover to Diepe, with pillotage ther dew	81	0	0

For

	£.	s.	d.
For carying my ſtuffe from Deipe to Rawnye, beinge 56 leagues	48	0	0
For my horſes from Diep to Rawnye	60	0	0
For the chardges of ſuch as weer with me to convoy me untill comming to the K. and rewarde to them	60	0	0
Sum totall	293	0	0

Wheras I received now laſtlye of the Queene's Matie's monye, by impreſſe, the ſomme of 500l. by vertue of her Matie's privye ſeale, bearing date the 22th day of Julye, in the 33th yeare of her Matie's raigne: The ſayde ſome is to be defalked in allowaunce of my dyet, after the rate of 3l. 6s. 8d. the day, which is nowe expyred, the 20th day of December, in manner and forme followinge, and allowing 28 dayes the month:

For my dyet of 8 dayes in July, beginning in the 23 day therof, the ſayd day being incluſive	26	13	4
For 31 daies of Auguſt	103	6	8
For 30 daies in September	100	0	0
For 31 in October	103	6	8
For 30 daies in November	100	0	0
For 20 daies in December	66	13	4
Sum	500	0	0

Mr. Peeters, I pray you to deliver to this bearer my ſervant, Nicolas Payne, the ſome of 280l. mony now dew to me by impreſſe, by vertue of the Queen's Matie's privie ſeale, bearing date the 22th of July, in the 33 yeare of her Highnes raigne, for allowaunce of my dyet, from the 20th day of December, till 3 monthes next followinge be expyred. Dated at the Campe before Roan, the 20th day of December, 1591. Your verye loving frend, HENRY UNTON.

To his verye loving frend Mr. Auditor Peeter, eſqu^r, of her Matie's exchequer.

Wheras I received, &c. *ut ſupra:*

For my dyet of 11 daies in December, being on the 20 day therof, the ſayd daye being incluſive	36	13	4
For 30 dayes in Januarye	103	6	8
For 29 dayes in Feabruarye	96	13	4
For 19 daies in March	63	6	8
Sum totall	300	0	0

Mr. Peteers, I pray you deliver to this bearer, &c. *ut ſupra.* Dated the 29th of March, 1591, at Deipe.

The

The perticular chardges of tranſportations, and other ordinarye chardges, in retourning home to the Courte, the 17th of June, 1592.

	£.	s.	d.
Imprimis, for my tranſportation, with ſervants, and myſelff, from Fere in Tartanoys in Diepe, being 60 leagues ———	60	0	0
For chardges of 120 horſe, which went with me for convoy, and reward to them ——— ———	60	0	0
For tranſportations from Diep to Dover, of myſelff and 22 ſervants	20	0	0
For tranſportation of my ſtuffe, horſes, and 26 ſervants, from Diep to London ——— ——— ———	50	0	0
For 23 poſt-horſes from Dover to London ———	11	10	0
Sum totall ——— ———	210	10	0

The firſt bill for intelligence monyes.

It may pleaſe your Lo. I have ſent a bill for ſuch monies as been diſburſed by me in eſpeciall and neceſſarie cauſes of her Matie's ſervice, amounting to the ſomme of 285l. which I humblye beſech your Lo. to ſubſcrybe. In like manner, I have layd owte, for conveyaunce of letters for her Highnes' eſpeciall cauſes, the ſome alſo under-written, which are incloſed in the ſame bill:

		£.	s.	d.
20 Decem. 1591.	For eſpialle and intelligences ———	200	0	0
	For ſending of letters in Auguſt, at ſevrall tymes, to Noyon to the French K. and Grymſton, by her Matie's ſpeciall order, and your Lo.	20	0	0
	For ſending of letters in September and October, to her Matie and your Lo. and for her ſpeciall ſervice ——— ———	20	0	0
	Sum of the total by me diſburſed, from 23 of July until the 20 of Decembr then next following, amounteth to the ſome of	220	0	0
27 June, 1592.	For eſpyall monye and intelligences, and for ſending of letters in April, May, and June, for her Matie's ſervice ——— ———	160	0	0
	More, for ſo much monyes by me diſburſed, for 3 monthes, as namely, Januarye, February, and March ——— ———	100	0	0
	Sum ——— ———	260	0	0

EXTRACTS

EXTRACTS FROM THE HOUSEHOLD BOOK OF THE REV. JOHN BOWLE, D. D. DEAN OF SALISBURY 1621—1629 *.

(From PECK's Defiderata Curiofa, Book XV.)

1621,	Jan. 18.	1000 laths for playfter, 6*s*. 8*d*.
	Feb. 1.	2 labourers 4 days to caft earth, [8 pence *per* day,] 5*s*. 4*d*.; 2 labourers 2 days, 2*s*. 8*d*.
	16.	Lime 18 bufhels, 6*s*.
1622,	Dec. 7.	Bufhel of oats, 1*s*. 8*d*.
	Jan. 13.	Ditto 3 bufhels, 5*s*.
1623,	July 11.	2 bufhels of wheat, 12*s*. 6*d*.
	15.	3 bufhels of oats, 6*s*.; fack of malt, 13*s*. 4*d*.; a pound of butter, 3*d*.; quire of paper, 4*d*.
	19.	3 dozen $\frac{1}{2}$ butter, at 2*s*. 8*d*. 10*s*.; beef, mutton, and veal, 140 lb. 2$\frac{1}{2}$*d*. *per* pound, 1*l*. 9*s*.
	29.	2 pound butter, 8*d*.; 2 bufhels wheat, 13*s*.
	Aug. 2.	Beef, fuet, and veal, 220 lb. 2$\frac{1}{2}$*d*. 2*l*. 5*s*. 10*d*.; 27 barrels of beer, at 2*s*. 6*d*. the barrel, 3*l*. 7*s*. 6*d*.
		For 12 dozen of trenchars, 13*s*.
		For 21 quarters of malt, 1*l*. 4*s*.; grinding do. 8*d*.
		To the wood-cleaver 1 day and $\frac{1}{2}$, 12*d*.; to a labourer 3 days, 2*s*.
1624,	May 13.	4 capons, 4*s*. 8*d*.; 12 chickens, 4*s*. 8*d*.; ditto, 2*s*.
		Wheat, 2 bufhels, and grinding, 10*s*. 3*d*.
1625,	Apr. 12.	2 bufhels wheat, 12*s*.; 4 bufhels oats, 7*s*. 4*d*.
	15.	Butter, 6 pound, 3*s*. 6*d*.; beef, mutton, and veal, 160 pd. at 3*d*.
	18.	Pound of hard fugar, 16*d*.; of powder do. 14*d*.
	21.	Bufhel of wheat, 6*s*.; 12 pigeons, 2*s*. 3*d*.; meat 135 pd. at 3*d*.
	26.	6 pd. butter, 3*s*.; 12 pigeons, 20*d*.
	Sept. 4.	7 couple of chickens, at 9*d*. *per* couple; 2 pullets, 14*d*.; 3 capons, 3*s*. 9*d*.; 4 bufhels of wheat, 1*l*. 0*s*. 4*d*.; 8 bufhels of oats, 12*s*.

* He was dean of Salifbury in June 1620; and fubfcribes his laft account, with his trufty fervant Johnfon, 15 Jan. 1629, *John Bowle, Dec. Sarum, Roffenf. Elect.* He was confecrated Bifhop of Rochefter Feb. 7 following. What particular fervices he did to Ralph Winterton, fellow of King's college, do not appear: but his dedication to him of his tranflation of Gerard's Meditations, printed at Cambridge in 1631, feems to have arifen from the overflowings of gratitude. In this, among other matters, he fays, "What Vefpafian profeffed in word to Apollonius, the late Reverend Dean of Salifbury hath performed in deed to me; the gates of his liberality and hofpitality have never been barred againft fcholars and ftrangers." He died Oct. 9, 1637; and was buried, as appears from the entry in the College of Arms, in St. Paul's cathedral.

1625, Oct. 8. Meat, 154 pd. at 2½*d.*
28. Item, for mending the pump the second time when the queene was here, 12*d.*
Nov. 10. For washing your ruffs when you came from Plymouth.
16. For borde borrowed to make a partition, while the queene was here, 1*s.*
22. For borde to make a dore between you and Sir Lawrence Hyde, 1*s.*
Feb. 20. To Mr. Robert Hyde, upon my master his bill of exchange, 55*l.*
1626, Mar. 27. Sope, 2 pds. 6*d.*
Apr. 1. Oats, quarter, 15*s.* 4*d.*
6. Butter, 8 pd. 3*s.* 8*d.*
8. For a black *goddard*, 2*d.*; candles, 6 pd. 2*s.* 2*d.*; meat, 168, 2¾*d.* 2*l.*; white wine, 3 pints, 12*d.*; peck of salt, 8*d.*
15. Meat, 140 pds. 2½*d.*: bushel wheat, 5*s* 4*d.*; 10 pigeons, 2*s.* 6*d.*
21. Pigeons, 12, 2*s.* 6*d.*; wheat, 2 bushels, 11*s.*
22. Meat, 150 pd. 2½*d.*
26. Pigeons, 2 dozen, 4*s.* 8*d.*; shoemaker, for shoe-strings, 8*d.*
28. 140 pd. meat 2½*d.*
Oct. 3. Bl. wheat, 4*s.* 6*d.*
12. Ditto, 4*s.* 8*d.*
Mar. 13. Quarter of oats, 11*s.*
17. Wheat, 2 bushels, 11*s.*
20. Meat, 165 pd. at 3*d.* 2*l.* 1*s.* 3*d.*
1627, Apr. 7. Do. 150, at do.
10. Oats, sack, 6*s.* 4*d.*; wheat, 2 bls, 10*s.*
1628, Jan. 16. 2 bls. wheat, 6*s.*; sack of oats, 4*s.* 8*d.*
Apr. 3. To the officer at church for laying of cushions in the consistory, 1*s.*
5. Wheat, 2 bushels, 6*s.* 2*d.*
12. Beef, mutton, and veal, 125 pd. at 3*d.* 1*l.* 11*s.* 3*d.*
15. Couple rabbits, 8*d.*; 8 chickens, 2*s.* 8*d.*; 6 pd. butter, 3*s.*
Sep. 20. 2 bls. wheat, 7*s.* 4*d.*; beef, 67 pd. at 2*d.*; butter, 8 dozen, 32*s.* 4*d.* pd.
Oct. 7. 2 bls. wheat, 6*s.* 6*d.*
1629, Apr. 7. Mr. Powel for a sermon on Easter day, 10*s.*
Meat, 90 pd. at 2¾*d.* 1*l.* 1*s.* 6*d.*; sugar, 1 pd. 1*s.* 3*d.*
Sep. 29. Butter, 4 pd. 1*s.* 6*d.*; bushel barley, 2*s.* 3*d.*; 18*s.* *per* q̄ter.
Jan. 9. Wheat, 2 bls. 7*s.*

EXTRACTS

EXTRACTS FROM THE CHURCHWARDENS' ACCOMPTS OF ST. MICHAEL SPURRIER-GATE, IN THE CITY OF YORK, (IN THE SIXTEENTH CENTURY.)

(From a Tranfcript made by the late Mr. THOMAS BECKWITH, of York, F. S. A.)

[Communicated, with Notes, by SAMUEL PEGGE, Efq. F. S. A.]

			£.	s.	d.
1518	(1)	A fack of Charkoll for Pafh Evyn' —	o	o	4
	(2)	Paid for writing of S[t] *Royke* Maffe —	o	o	9
	(3)	P[d] for making of 2 Tonykills & Frenges to the fame	o	o	9
	(4)	P[d] for making of the Tapytts agains Xtymaffe	o	o	4
	(5)	P[d] to the Pyner for 4 Days & Di. —	o	2	3
	(6)	to the Joyner for a hoylle Weyke —	o	2	9

(1) On Good Friday an interdiction enfued in the Romifh church, and all the fires were totally extinguifhed. The *charcoal* here mentioned was therefore provided on Eafter-eve, for renewing the fires on Eafter day; when, however, they were kindled again, it was done by pure elemental fire produced by a flint and fteel, and not from unhallowed embers. From this fire the *Pafcal-taper* was alfo lighted.

Thus Hofpinian de Feftis Chriftianorum, p. 88, edit. 1674: "Ignem veterem omnem in templis extinguunt, & novum ex chalybe eliciunt ac confecrant. Deinde candelam ceream magnam, quam cereum Pafchalem nominant, in templa hoc die ferunt, eumque benedicunt, & de igne illo novo accendunt."

(2) St. Royk, St. *Roch* (Aug. 16). Q. why commemorated in particular? There is *Roche* abbey in the Weft riding of the county of York, which does not take its name from the faint, but from its fituation on a rock, and is dedicated to the Virgin Mary. Tanner.—The writing probably means making a new copy of the mufic appropriated to the day.

(3) Tonykils, *tunicles*. The *tunica* was a garment worn by the fub-deacon affifting the prieft at a mafs. Staveley on Churches, 187.—The price here mentioned extends no farther than the workmanfhip in making them up, and adding the fringes.

(4) Tapitts, *tapers*; for every candle, be its fize what it would, was then called a *taper:* even the ALTAR-*candle* at Canterbury, though its weight was 300 lb. was termed the Pafchal-*taper*. See before, p. 260, in note *.—N. B. that this charge of 4 pence is for *making* the tapers when the church provided the wax, whereas the price of a fingle new taper (as in art. 19) was 5 pence.

(5) The church was then under fome repair, as farther appears below in article 16. The *pyner* feems to mean the bricklayer, or mafon, who was employed in this work. *Pynning* has been mentioned before, p. 98. Here, however, it moft probably means what we now call *pointing* walls.

(6) This and the preceding article fhew the price of labour at the time. The difference between the proportionate pay of the *pyner* and the *joyner* (in conjunction with the articles 9, 10, and 11), feems to arife from the circumftance of the *nails* (in the latter cafe) having been provided by the parifh, and which bore a much higher price than *plafter*, as appears from art. 34.

			£.	s.	d.
1518	(7)	Pd for 5 Hundreth of Walle Teylle —	0	2	1
	(8)	for a Payr of Jontters to a Ambre —	0	0	2
	(9)	for 2 hundreth Sharplings —	0	1	4
	(10)	for 2 M. Skotfym' (or Skafyme) Stotfeyme	0	2	0
	(11)	for 2 M. Stonebrod — —	0	2	0
1519	(12)	Recd of Maft' *Gegs* Wyffe that hyr Hufband whyttyd to owr Kyrke Warke — —	0	3	4
1520	(13)	Recd of Sr *Robt Berker* for ftruyng of ye Kyrk	0	4	0
	(14)	Recd for 3 Kyrchoys yt was gyffyn to ye Kyrk Wark	0	5	0
	(15)	Pd for haloying of 2 chalyffys & 3 Patans, a Corporax & 5 Auterclothes — —	0	4	0
	(16)	Pd for helping of 2 Hemeches —	0	0	4
	(17)	Pd for 2 Strynkylls —	0	0	1

(7) Walle Teylle, that is *wall-tile*. *Tile* was the generical term, and prevails in Yorkfhire to this day, meaning *bricks*, in contra-diftinction to our fpecific word *tile* for the roofs of houfes, which is there alfo ftill called *thack-tile*. In the Anglo Saxon, *theac-tigil* is a *roof tile*. Somner.

(8) Jontters, *joints*, i. e. *hinges*.

Ambre, *ambry*; a cup-board in general, as well for keeping veffels as provifions. Bailey.

(9) (10) (11) Thefe feem all to be terms ufed for *nails* of different forts. *Sharplings* one would fuppofe to mean *brads* or *fprigs*. The *ftotfeyme*, art. 52, are there expreffly called *nails*; and *fkafyme* appears again in article 49.

(12) For the term *whitted*, we refer to article (53).

(13) *Sir* is well known to have then been the title ufually given to a prieft. The receipt of 4*s*. paid by Sir Robert, for ftrewing the church, we can hardly fuppofe to have been his own perfonal expence; bnt rather, that the money (which was then a confiderable fum) paffed, through his hands to the churchwardens, from the patron, which at that time (1520) was the rich abbey of St. Mary at York.

(14) Kyrchoys, *kerchiefs*, to be fold, and the value applied to the repair of the church. The *kerchiefs* were then very large (perhaps as long and wide as a woman's hood now worn at funerals), and poffibly often embroidered, or highly ornamented. We meet with a fimilar article below (35), but more decidedly expreffed, relating to a girdle given by a woman, which either was fold for, or redeemed at, the price of 6*s*.

(15) The 4*s*. here paid for hallowing (or confecrating) the chalices, &c. might partly confift of incidental travelling charges, and of fees given to the officers of the bifhop's chapel. Expences, in general terms, are charged on a like occafion in the accompts of Walberfwick, p. 185.—In the accompts of the churchwardens of St. Mary's at Cambridge, is a charge of 8*d*. *ob*. "for the new hallowing or reconcyling of our church, being interdicted at the buryall of Mr. Bucer, and the charge therunto belonging, frankincens, and fweet perfumes for the facrament, and herbes, &c. Baker, in Harl. MSS. 7044. p. 184.—The corporax (*corporal* or *corporas*, and in Latin called *corporale* five *dominicale*) was a cloth of the fineft linen, in which the hoft was laid upon the altar, in remembrance that Chrift's body was wrapped in fine linen. Staveley on Churches, p. 194.

(16) Hemeches, *images*. *Helping* is a common term for *mending* or *repairing* any thing, at this day, in feveral counties of the Northern parts of England.

(17) Strynkills; little whifks ufed to fprinkle the holy water. To *ftrinkil* means to *fprinkle* in the Scotifh language. Gloffary to Gawen Douglas's Virgil.—" Strinkling light." Milton.—In the parifh accompts of Lambeth (1523) is a payment for " a holy-water fprynkill." Lyfons.

			£.	s.	d.
1520	(18)	Pd for a Baldrege to the Second Bell —	0	0	6
	(19)	Pd for 3 Tapitts — —	0	1	3
	(20)	Pd to Sr *Robert* for D' Beyd Roylle —	0	2	0
	(21)	Pd to the Pyshe for Lady Mess — —	0	6	8
	(22)	Pd for Dry Ferme — —	0	2	6
1521	(23)	Re'd for *Mylys Robynson* Beriall a Tone of Plaster.			
	(24)	Pd for a Cord to the Sthyme — —	0	0	1
	(25)	Pd for helping of the Pyke — —	0	0	4
	(26)	Pd to Sr *Herry* for the Beide Roylle —	0	2	0
	(27)	Pd for kilting Belts — — —	0	0	1
	(28)	Pd for a Pair of Mosfits for to wase the Corporax	0	0	2

1521

(18) Baldrege, *baldrick* (or *bawdrick)*, signifies a *belt* or *strap*, in general; but here it means the thong by which, fastened by a buckle, the clapper of a bell is suspended. See Bailey's Dictionary, and Phillips's World of Words; in both which this particular use of the term is pointed at. See also before, p. 259.

(19) See article (4).

(20) The bead-rolls seem to have been let out for hire to the parish by the priest at *two* shillings *per annum* each; for, we find below, in the year 1533, that Sir Harry received *four* shillings for the use of one for *two* years. See a similar payment before, in p. 105. l. 9. The difficulty in this item seems to rest on the abbreviation D', which, from the proportion, appears to mean half the usual payment, viz. for *one* year (as was practised afterwards in article (26) and (36); though, in article (58), it was again paid only at the end of *two* years, according to the common practice.

(21) This payment to the *parish* (for so the abbreviation *Pyshe* seems to mean) for Lady-mess, or the mass on the 25th of March, one would suppose, means alms given to the poor parishioners on that high festival.

(22) Ferme, for *fern*; called also *bracken* in Yorkshire, and in the South *brakes*. The use of it seems to have been for strewing the church in lieu of rushes, which probably bore a greater price.

(23) Such a specific fee for a burial is rather singular: but the church was in a state of reparation; and perhaps the deceased was a plasterer, and otherwise insolvent. It was an actual church *due*, and not a *bequest*.

(24) Sthyme. Q.

(25) Pyke, the *pix*. The vessel in which the host was carried when the priest visited the sick to administer the Sacrament to them.

(26) See article (20).

(27) Kilting belts. The same words occur again in article (38), and seem to mean no more than some ordinary coarse bandages, used for the purpose of *tying* things together. We meet with the term also in the Wigtoft accompts, p. 205, under the name of a *tucking* girdle, there written *to king*, as if it were two words; and in p. 94. l. ult. it is more explicitly written *tukkin* girdles.

The verb *kilter* in the Danish language signifies to *bind*; and the substantive *kilting* means a *girding* or *tucking* up. See Wolff's Danish Dictionary.—Douglas's Virgil has *kiltit* for *tucked up*. See the Glossary.—The large wrapping plaid of the Scots is called the *kilting* plaid.

(28) Mosfits, perhaps a corrupt spelling of *mostick*; though we are left very open to conjecture. A *mostick*, according to our lexicographers, means a stick, about a yard long, on which a painter leans his arm to steady it when at work. Hence it may be applied to any stick of similar dimensions, and the use be carried to other purposes.

			£.	s.	d.
1521	(29)	Pd for makyn of 3 Tapytt for the hye Alt' —	0	0	2
	(30)	Pd for a Bowdregſe — —	0	1	4
	(31)	Pd for Bords to a Greſſe — —	0	0	5
1525	(32)	Pd for 2 Bukkylls to the Bawdrygyes —	0	0	2
	(33)	Pd for Two Bawdrygyes — —	0	1	10
	(34)	Pd for a Wenyon' of Plaſter — —	0	0	1½
1526	(35)	Rec'd for a gyrdyll that *John Strynger* wyff gaffe to Seynt Myghell — — —	0	6	0
	(36)	Pd to Sr *Herre* for the Beid Royll —	0	2	0
	(37)	Pd for dyghtyng of the Stawyll — —	0	0	2
	(38)	Pd for a Kyltyng Beltt — —	0	0	2
	(39)	Pd for Gyrs to a Say — —	0	0	1

In the inſtance before us it is expreſſly ſaid to have been uſed in waſhing the corporas, a linen cloth. The mode of waſhing at that time was by *bucking*, in which proceſs ſticks (and poles) were employed to ſtir about the linen in the *bucking-tub*. The *corporas* was an hallowed appendage to the altar, all of which were prohibited from being touched by any but the officiating miniſters; and particularly by the hands of women. Platina, in the Life of Pope Sixtus I.—As theſe ſticks were provided by the church, we may conclude that the waſhing, under the above reſtriction, was confined to ſome ſubordinate officer of the church, and moſt probably to the *ſacriſtan*, who had the care of all the utenſils belonging to the church.

The *corporas* was ſo ſacred that it was kept in a *caſe* appropriated to itſelf. See before, p. 242, in the Inventory of the Goods, &c. of Serjeant Keble. We may alſo refer to the Royal Wills, &c. publiſhed by Mr. Nichols; and to the Will of King Henry VII. printed 1775. Anonymous.

It is true, that in the accompts of St. Margaret's, Weſtminſter, p. 10, the *corporas*, &c. appear to have been waſhed by a *lady anchoreſs* (as ſhe is called) 1538; but ſhe muſt be looked upon as a conſecrated perſon, perhaps an ejected abbeſs from ſome diſſolved monaſtery, who might be glad to undertake the office for a ſmall ſum, in aid of her other pittances.

(29) See article (4).

(30) See article (18). By the price, this baldrick muſt have been uſed for one of the larger bells.

(31) Greſſe (written, by various authors, *greece*, *grieze*, *griſe*, and *grice*,) means ſometimes a flight of ſteps, or a ſtair-caſe; and at others ſimply a ſtep. Compare with article (62).

(32) (33) See article (18).

(34) From the ſmall price of the plaſter (1½*d.*) one is led to ſuppoſe that a *wanyon*, the diminution of *wain*, might mean a wheel-barrow, or ſome ſuch vehicle.

(35) See article (14).

(36) See article (20) (26).

(37) *Dighting* ſometimes implies ornamenting, and at other times cleaning, to which latter we here incline; and by the *ſtawyll* (the ſtall), that the *reading-deſk* is meant; for, at this time (1526) there was not much preaching.

(38) See article (27).

(39) *Gyrs* is ſuſpected to mean *greate*; for, in Yorkſhire, the letter *r* and its vowel are very frequently tranſpoſed, as they uſe *girn* for *grin*, *brid* for *bird*, *brun* for *burn*, &c. A *grid*-iron, in the Inventory of Sir Peter Frechevile's Chattels, is called, p. 234, a *girde*-iron. *Say*, it is apprehended, implies a *ſaw*, which occurs again in article (56). This is the pronunciation in Derbyſhire; where alſo the common people uſe the word *dray* for *draw*. See the Wigtoft accompts, p. 198, where *ſtraw* is written *ſtray*. Or the meaning may be *geers* to a *ſaw*, in general terms, ſuch as are ſpecified in article (56); and the price accords with it.

			£.	s.	d.
1526	(40)	Pd for a Glaſſe for a Ymage to ſett in ys Breſt	0	0	1
	(41)	Pd to a Frerer for wryttyng off a ſequens —	0	4	0
	(42)	Pd for a Leyge & Trenctylls — —	0	0	1½
	(43)	Pd for the Holy Watt' fawtt —	0	2	8
	(44)	Item, paid for Pawper to mak 2 Regenall Boks; the on for the Royd Lyght and Seynent Lyght, the oyr for to writt or hympyllmentt of or howſit in —	0	0	2
	(45)	A Pottel of Maveſey & Mayne Brede —	0	0	7
		N. B. Sonnyng the Veſtments occurs twice.			

1528

(40) To replace ſome ſuppoſed jewel that had been ſet in the breaſt of an image. We may reaſonably conjecture that the *image* was that of St. Michael, the patron ſaint; and that, though the value of the piece of glaſs was no more than 1*d*. it was intended to ſupply the place of ſome original characteriſtic device, perhaps St. Michael and the devil, as uſually repreſented.

(41) Frerer, a *friar*. Sequens, a *ſequence*, which was an antiphonal ſervice ſung chant-wiſe between the prieſt and the people alternately. Sir John Hawkins, in his Hiſtory of Muſick, vol. II. p. 248, ſays that the *ſequence* was ſung after the epiſtle had been read. In the Gloſſary to X Scriptores, it is confined to certain high feſtivals, viz Eaſter, Whitſuntide, and Corpus Chriſti day. Hence, from the price here mentioned (4*s*.), one is induced to ſuppoſe that the charge is for a *ſet* of *ſequences* for the whole year, which Staveley on Churches, p. 185, calls *Liber Sequentiarum*.

(42) Leyge, *legend*. A table of the leſſons to be read in the Morning Service. Staveley, p. 184.—Trenctylls, *trentals*, from the French *trente*; a ſervice of *thirty* maſſes ſaid or ſung for the dead, or a ſervice performed thirty days after their death. Staveley's Romiſh Horſe-leech, p. 201. But Proteſtant writers do not perfectly decide whether they were all ſaid together on the thirtieth day after the death of the party, or one on each day for thirty days in ſucceſſion. This, however, poſſibly was governed by the direction of the perſon who left the ſtipend for the performance of them. See Burn's Eccleſiaſtical Law; and Sir John Cullum's Hiſtory of Hawſted, p. 16.

(43) Fawt, the *vat*, or veſſel which contained the holy water. It is called a *ſtoup* in p. 98; and in the Churchwardens' Accompts at Wigtoft it is again termed a *fat* (i. e. *vat)*, and expreſſly ſaid to have been made of ſtone, through which no part of the water could exude. Many of theſe receptacles for holy water are yet to be ſeen, projecting from the walls, at the entrance, and in other parts, of ſeveral old country churches.

(44) The beſt comment that we can make upon the firſt part of this obſcure article is, that it ſeems to imply two *original* (or *new)* accompt-books, in which might be entered ſums of money, or other donations, bequeathed or contributed toward furniſhing the lights which were uſed on ſolemn occaſions in the rood-loft, and before the image of the patron ſaint, &c. That there were ſuch funds appears from articles (69), (70), (75), and (76), whence the collective body of the church ſometimes drew money for particular public purpoſes.

What follows is ſo very unintelligible, that one has hardly courage enough to hazard a conjecture. Nevertheleſs, in theſe accompts, p. 190, among the utenſils, &c. in the veſtry of the church of Walberſwick, among other towels of a finer ſort (viz. diaper), we meet with *hempuling towels*. If then we may be at liberty to ſuppoſe that by theſe are meant towels of a coarſer ſort, wherein various things were promiſcuouſly collected together occaſionally, a *hympylment*, or *hemplement*, may, without much force, be interpreted an *inventory*. This idea will lead us to another bold conjecture, and to imagine that the word *howſit* (which, in ſuch caſe, muſt be conſidered as a plural, of which the common people in the North generally leave out the ſign) may be a very corrupt ſpelling of the word *effects*, comprehending the veſſels, veſtments, linen, &c. appertaining to the church of St. Michael.

(45) Maveſey, *Malmſey*. This ſpelling comes nearer to orthography than our name of Malm-

ſey;

			£.	s.	d.
1528	(46)	Pd for 4 Holly Watt' Strynkylls —	0	0	4
	(47)	Pd for a Candyll of 1 lb. for Laydy Mafe —	0	0	6
	(48)	Pd for a loyfer — — —	0	0	8
	(49)	Pd for 3 Thoufand Skafyme — —	0	3	0
	(50)	Rec'd off Thos Appylyerd for a God's Penne of ys Houfe	0	3	4
1530	(51)	Pd for 2 Styks of 7 Nyks ———	0	0	1½
	(52)	Pd for 1000 Stotfeyme Naylls ———	0	0	11
1531	(53)	Rec'd for *John Wyrall* Beryall & ys Wytword.			

fey; for, Phillips (in his World of Words) tells us, that Malmfey "is a lufcious wine, brought from *Arvifium*, in the ifland of Chio, now called *Malvafia*." It is written *Malvefey* in the Receipts, &c. of the Priory of Huntingdon, p. 295. By *mayne brede* (without going into the more antient diftinctions of *manchet*, &c.) we may underftand *mean* or *middle* bread, between the *brown* and the *white*, which is now known in the North by the name of *whity-brown*, called in Kent *ravel*-bread. There are the fame terms for paper refpectively, viz. *whity-brown* paper, and *ravel* paper.

N. B. *Sonnyng* the veftments occurs twice in thefe accompts; but, as no charge is made, it may be fuppofed that fome very trifling gratuity was given; and that by *fonnyng* is meant *airing* thofe veftments not in conftant ufe, when they were occafionally brought forward on the high feftivals.

(46) See article (17).

(47) The candle for this folemnity feems to have been fomething larger than thofe before mentioned in article (19), as it exceeds each of them by the price of 1*d*. We here fee the value of wax at the time.

(48) Loyfer; probably a *lever*, as the church was repairing.

(49) See article (9), (10), (11).

(50) A God's penny is an *earneft* paid to confirm an agreement or bargain, ftill known in Yorkfhire, on ordinary occafions, though the term might be originally derived from concerns of the kind which were purely ecclefiaftical. See before, p. 106, and the note. In Yorkfhire it is alfo called, in common cafes, the *fefting*-penny, i. e. the *faftening*-penny, by which a bargain is ftruck, and the parties mutually bound. The word *fefting*, as a corruption of *fafteniug*, occurs in the preceding Wigtoft accompts, p. 200, l. 29.

(51) It is not eafy to guefs at the meaning of "2 ftyks of 7 nyks," unlefs they may be fuppofed to imply two very narrow boards of feven inches in length or breadth, for the purpofe of repairing fome fmall matter. The charge is but 1½*d*.

(52) See article (9), (10), (11).

(53) A *wit*-word, and a *queythe*-word, both which occur more than once in p. 77, and elfewhere, in the preceding accompts, feem to have the fame meaning, and to imply a *dictum*, or verbal requifition of the dying party, that fomething fhould be given to the church after death*. The terms themfelves import that the gift was of a nuncupative kind, and that it differed from a teftamentary bequeft. This diftinction is very clear by what we meet with in p. 77, and p. 213, among the Wigtoft accompts, where the entry of the *witword* of one man is immediately followed by the *legacy* of another, in exprefs terms of difcrimination; the latter being given decidedly under the formality of a will. The purport of thefe *vivâ voce* donations was, to atone for tithes and oblations omitted, and were generally directed to be given to the high altar; but fometimes for particular purpofes, as in article (12).

* Thefe terms are both of Saxon derivation; the former from the old defective verb *weet*, *wit*, or *wet*, to *know*, or to make known; and the latter from *qeyth*, fince written *quoth*, another old defective verb. Whence we have preferved *to wit*, and *quoth he*. See Gill's Logonomia Anglica, 2d edit. 4to, 1621, p. 64; and Bifhop Lowth's Introduction to Englifh Grammar, p. 105.

1533

			£.	s.	d.
1533	(54)	Rec'd at *Mr. Roger* eghtyn day 5 lb. Candylls.			
	(55)	It', rec'd at his thowlmothe day 5 lb. Candylls.			
	(56)	Pd for a Gyrthe & a Neyre to a Saye —	0	0	1
	(57)	Pd for a Rope to the Rowyll —	0	0	11
	(58)	Pd to Sr *Herry* for the Beidrowyll for 2 Yeres	0	4	0
1534	(59)	Pd *Maſtris Hardſon* for helping 2 Albys —	0	0	4
	(60)	Pd to Sr *John Baitman* for ſyngyng in ye Churche	0	3	4
	(61)	Pd for 2 Pare of Gloves for ſyngyng A mynd of me	0	0	4
	(62)	Pd for a Steyk of 6 Nyks for Stapys to A Greſe	0	0	2
	(63)	Pd for 6 Wayne Loid of fyer Erth —	0	2	0
	(64)	Pd for ledyng away of Ramell — —	0	0	4

(54) (55) Something like this has appeared before, in the Wigtoft accompts, p. 213, but not ſo diſtinctly; for, here the *month's mind* is expreſſly divided into *two* celebrations, with a payment of five pounds of candles about the *half-month* day, and five more at the *whole-month* day. Theſe inſtalments there is reaſon to believe were not uncommon, and have given riſe to an expreſſion ſtill uſed in the Northern parts of England, where they not only ſay, " I have a *month's mind* to do ſo or ſo ;" but alſo, " I have *half a mind* to do ſuch a thing."

(56) A *ſaye* we have preſumed, in article (39), to mean a *ſaw*. We therefore imagine that the *girth* expreſſes the handle, faſtened to the blade of the ſaw by a ſcrew with a nut, or ſome ſuch ſecurity here called a *neyre*. A *knur* is a knot of hard ſubſtance often found in timber. The word is *teutonic*. See Kilian in voce *knorre*. It may not, therefore, be improperly applied to the *nut* by which a ſcrew is ſecured.

(57) By the *rowyll* is moſt probably meant the bead-*roll* or roſary, which conſiſted of a certain number of *beads* ſtrung upon a *rope*, in common caſes, every tenth of which beads was larger than the reſt, and called a *gaude*. By theſe they could reckon the number of their invocations. The common *beads* were for *Ave-Marias*, and the *gaudes* for *Pater-Noſters*. Sir John Cullum's Hiſtory of Hawſted, pp. 16 and 17.

(58) See article (20), (26), (36), referring to this article.

(59) The word *helping* has been accounted for in article (16). The *albe* (as its name imports) was a long *white* garment, not unlike our ſurplice; but cloſed at the wriſts. It was not only worn by the prieſts, but by the children belonging to the choir, as appears hereafter in article (83). As a remanent of this, our choriſters wear ſurplices; as do the ſchool-boys, on moſt of the royal foundations, upon Sundays, and other particular days.

(60) It is probable that this prieſt was famous for his ſkill in ſinging, and that he was retained for ſome particular occaſion, though he might belong to another eſtabliſhment; or rather, perhaps, for a certain ſeaſon, as his pay was ſo conſiderable.

(61) This preſent of a pair of gloves could not be a perſonal compliment to Sir John Baitman from the churchwarden who inſerted it, becauſe it is charged to the pariſh; and *of me* ſhould ſeem to mean *by me*, who made the payment, and preſented the gloves officially. A ſimilar caſe occurs in the ſame words, article (77).

(62) See article (51). Here *greſſe* evidently means a ſtair-caſe; or at leaſt a flight of a few ſteps.

(63) Fire-earth muſt mean either *turf* or *peat*, both which are ſtill uſed as a cheap fuel in various parts of the North of England.

(64) Ledyng, *leading*, a general term for fetching, or carrying away, in Yorkſhire. *Ramell* poſſibly means rubbiſh.

1535

			£.	s.	d.
1535	(65)	P[d] for helpying of the Paxe and the Lattron —	0	0	2
	(66)	P[d] to *Rob*[t] when he browght the Clothes frome the Byshope y[t] was Halowyd — —	0	0	2
	(67)	P[d] for a Gods Penny y[t] was gyffyn to y[e] Paryshe Clark	0	0	1
1536	(68)	Rec'd off the Stok in the Churche to helpe to pay for the Orgons.			
	(69)	Rec'd of the Roid Lyght — —	4	0	0
	(70)	Rec'd of Seynt *Seyth* Lyght ——	4	0	0
	(71)	Paid for a Pare of Orgons — —	8	0	0
	(72)	P[d] to *Mr. Watson* for a Payre of Splents —	0	1	8

(65) The *pax* was a figure of Chrift, moft probably a crucifix, painted or carved, and fixed to a piece of wood or metal, which, after the mafs, was tendered to all the people prefent to kifs. It was a fubftitute for the *ofculum pacis* (which ufed to be perfonally given in token of peace), and called in Latin *ofculatorium*. The cuftom, no doubt, was founded on the words of St. Paul, "Greet one another with *an holy kifs*."

By the *lattron* we fuppofe is meant a *lanthorn*, which was furnifhed with lights at vefpers.

[We here take the liberty of remarking, that the term *bowet*, which has occurred in p. 211, l. 26, is ufed in fome parts of Yorkfhire to fignify a *lanthorn*, as it is likewife in Cumberland.]

(66) This confirms what has been faid on article (15), that the fum there paid for halowing feveral parts of the furniture of the church was compounded of fome incidental charges.

(67) See article (50). The God's penny we collect from a note on p. 106 (on the authority of Du Cange, in voc. *Denarius Dei*) was the property of the church, and probably diftributed according to the cuftom of each particular eftablifhment.

(68) (69) (70) Thefe three items ought to be taken together, being receipts for money drawn from two funds for one purpofe, and fhould be read thus: received "from the *roid*-light 4*l.*; and "from Seynt *Seyth*-light 4*l.*; to help to pay for the orgons." The price of the organs tallies with the fum received, viz. 8*l.* The extra charge of carriage, &c. might be paid from the ordinary fund belonging to the church.

The *roid* doubtlefs means the *rood*. As to St. *Seyth*, or *Syth*, it has been fuppofed that St. *Ofyth*, the patronefs of the monaftery of Chich (afterwards called by her name), was intended; but we do not, at prefent, difcover the leaft connection between that religious houfe and the monaftery of St. Mary at York, or any of its members. There was a St. *Sethrid*, who appears in fome calendars, though fhe was ftill more remote, having been abbefs of a fmall foundation in France. We leave it therefore undecided; though this faint, whoever it was, muft have been held in much reverence, to have had an image lighted from a fund of its own.

(71) A *pair* of organs was the term at that time, when there were two kinds of organs, the one fixed, and the other portable, adapted perhaps to the fize of the church, or to its revenues. See Sir John Hawkins's Hiftory of Mufic, vol. II. p. 447.—The laft were probably divifible into two parts, and thence obtained the name of a *pair*. This continued to be the term in the reign of King James I. at the leaft, and had not increafed in price, as appears from the Diary of Edward Allen, founder of Dulwich-college; which may be feen, under his article, in the "Biographia "Britannica."

(72) By fplents (or *fplints*) we are inclined to fuppofe are meant *fpars*, or, in general terms, *bars* of wood. Hence our word *fplinter*, a fraction of a *fplint*. To diftinguifh *fpars*, or *fplints*, from *bars*, it is probable, that, when they were ufed as uprights they were termed *fplints*, and when they were placed horizontally they were called *bars*.

			£.	s.	d.
1536	(73)	P[d] for 2 Doſſ. Ponts — —	0	0	2
	(74)	P[d] for helping 2 Pars of Splentts —	0	0	4
1537	(75)	Rec'd of the Keepers of Seint *Syth* Lyght to pay to the Chawmer of York to help bring yt out of Dett	0	13	4
1538	(76)	Rec'd of Seint *Sythe* Stok what tyme that we ſhuld have bowght wax wyth itt to have mayd Seint Sythe Lyght fyve Doſſen Wax compleyt — —	0	13	4
	(77)	P[d] for a Pare of Gloves for playing of A mynd of me	0	0	2
1539	(78)	P[d] for a Paxe to the hye Alter —	0	0	2
	(79)	P[d] for Pake thred to Seynt Palcure Candylls	0	0	0
1540	(80)	P[d] for helpyng off 2 Bawtrys off the Bells —	0	0	7
	(81)	P[d] for Talbys for the Amyſſes —	0	0	2
	(82)	P[d] for a Holy Watter Strynkyll —	0	0	1

(73) Ponts, perhaps *points*, or large nails, what are now called *holdfaſts*, to fix the *ſplints*; as the price 1*d.* *per* dozen differs ſo very much from any nails before mentioned.

(74) See article (72).

(75) By the keepers of this *light* we are inclined to underſtand the perſons who had the charge of the money, &c. given to this particular *light*; for each light ſeems to have had its ſeparate fund.

This ſum was borrowed to aſſiſt the chamber of York, moſt probably in common with other churches, and was only a contribution of its quota; for, it is ſtated to have been given in aid, viz. *to help it out of debt.* The number of illuminations in the Romiſh church which were annually made, was very great, and occaſioned a vaſt conſumption of wax; while the contributions to ſupport them were equally conſiderable, according to the value of money in thoſe times. See the Wigtoft accompts of the year 1532, p. 219, 220, 226.

(76) This ſeems to have been a ſimilar affair, and happened in the following year, 1538, at a time when the money had been previouſly deſtined to complete the uſual and appropriated number of wax candles for a certain ſeaſon.

N. B. The abbey and its dependencies had not fallen into the hands of the crown; for, it was not diſſolved till 1540.

(77) Having now purchaſed an *organ*, the ſervices were probably performed in a more ſolemn and ſtriking manner, and thoſe for the dead became particularly attended to. The gratuity to the perſon who played the organ was (as before, in the caſe of a celebrated ſinger) a *pair of gloves.* The wording of this article is to be underſtood in the ſame manner as article (61), being likewiſe charged as a pariſh-payment.

(78) See article (65). The revenues of this church muſt have been very ſmall, or the ſacred appendages very mean, when a *pax* for the high altar coſt but 2*d.* One is charitably inclined to believe there is an error in the entry, and that the charge ſhould have been for *repairing* the pax.

(79) We refer this to article (85), (86), and (87).

(80) Baldreges (or baldricks) firſt appear in article (18); to which this, and other intervening mention of them, is referred.

(81) The amis (*amictus*, which ſee in the Latin Gloſſaries) was one of the veſtments worn by the officiating prieſts, which was faſtened about the neck in front by ſmall cords, or in ſome other manner. If we underſtand this article right, it looks as if they were (in the caſe before us) faſtened by a button, and a ſhort ſtrap called a *tab*, which contained a button-hole.

(82) See article (17).

			£.	s.	d.
1542	(83)	P^d for helpyng of ye Chyldren Albis —	0	0	5
	(84)	P^d for 2 Boks of the new Proceſſion & Kyreleſons	0	0	10
1546	(85)	P^d for Pake thred for bynding of St Pulcur Candylls	0	0	0½
	(86)	P^d for whyt Thred to the Paryſh Clark for ſewyng of Seynt Pulcure Howſe & the Veſtements —	0	0	1
	(87)	P^d to *John Carver* for a Day & Di. mendyng of Seynt Pulcure Houſe & for helping of ye Angells Wyngys & the Stawylls in the churche, & for di. Day helping of the Hamerrys in the Church — —	0	1	0

(83) See article (59).

(84) The abbey of St. Mary had been diſſolved in the year 1540, and this article occurs two years after that, and about ſix years after the commencement of the Reformation, when proceſſions, as ſuperſtiious parades of the Romiſh church, except a very few, were aboliſhed. What remained ſhould ſeem to have been regiſtered, as ceremonials, in the books here ſpecified; though they might rather have been termed *new books* of proceſſions, than *books* of *new* proceſſions. Such books were called *proceſſioners*. See St. Martin Outwich, p. 272.

The *kyreleſons* mean thoſe ſhort ejaculatory verſicles, "Lord have mercy upon us;"—"Chriſt "have mercy upon us;"—which were called by the antients a ſhort Litany, and in ſome liturgical books ſtill retain the Greek terms of *Kyrie Eleeſon*, and *Chriſte Eleeſon*. See Sparrow's Rationale, p. 45, edit. 1722.—It is poſſible that in this little church, where they uſed only to be *ſaid*, they might now be accompanied by the organ, and that this charge was for copying the *muſic* into their books; for, in the old rubricks, they are directed to be *ſaid* or *ſung*. Wheatly, 273.

(85) (86) (87) To render theſe articles more compact, it may be obſerved, that by *hamerrys*, in the laſt line, are meant *ambries*, cupboards, as in article (8), or cloſets, in which various things belonging to the church were depoſited.

The principal object is the "*pulcure houſe*" (which has been mentioned before in various places in this Collection), and ſeems to have been intended as a repreſentation of *the holy ſepulchre* at Jeruſalem. This pageant was an annual exhibition in the Romiſh churches between Good Friday and Eaſter-day; and ſeems, in this caſe, to have been a temporary frame of wood (covered moſt probably with black), and furniſhed on the outſide with tapers, ſometimes called in theſe accompts *ſepulchral-lights*, and at other times *hearſe-lights*. This *ſepulchre* was watched, in imitation of the ſoldiers, for two nights. See the Abingdon accompts, p. 141, and the note. And it appears from article (87), now before us, that there was the figure of an *angel*, which, we may preſume, was ſuppoſed to announce the reſurrection on Eaſter-day.

It is in the memory of many now living, that, after the death of perſons of high rank, a *hearſe*, adorned with armorial enſigns, bannerols, penons, &c. was often placed over or near the grave, for a certain ſeaſon. In the concluding article of the preſent volume "the tymber hearſe for an Earle" is delineated.

That this *hearſe* was intended to repreſent *the holy ſepulchre*, we may refer to Dugdale's Baronage, vol. II p. 244, for a clauſe in the will of Thomas (Fienes) Lord Dacre, dated 1531. He directs that a tomb ſhould be erected in the pariſh church of Hurſt-Monceaux, on the North ſide of the high altar, whereupon ſhould be placed *the ſepulchre of our Lord*; and alſo, that, to furniſh lights for the ſame *ſepulchre*, an hundred pounds ſhould be employed in tapers of ten pounds weight apiece, to burn about it, when an honeſt prieſt ſhould ſing there for his ſoul, by the ſpace of ſeven years.

A COLLECTION, to explain divers old WORDS, TERMS, and CUSTOMS, neceſſary to be underſtood by all thoſe who deſire knowledge, and the true grounds of ſundry USAGES and ANTIQUITIES, chiefly relating to the ENGLISH CHURCH and NATION. Gathered, and obſerved in reading, by F. PECK, M. A. (From the original MS.)

THE ROOD

was an image of our Saviour crucified, carved in wood, and generally as big as life, ſet up in churches over the ſcreen which parted the nave, or middle aile, from the choir or chancel; and, in many places, are yet to be ſeen the ſtairs which went up to the rood-loft, or gallery, over the ſaid ſcreen. In the ſaid gallery ſtood, alſo, two other images, as big as the life, the one repreſenting the Bleſſed Virgin Mary, the other the beloved diſciple St. John. Before all theſe, in ſervice-time, and in ſome places conſtantly night and day, were burned divers lamps; and, in many places, the images had divers ſuits of veſtments, which were put on them, and varied *pro tempore*, as the day was ferial, or a high day. "On the 17th of Nov. 1547, was begun to be pulled down the roode in Paul's church, with Mary and John; and the like was afterwards done in other churches *." Theſe images at St. Paul's ſtood in the old church, partly where the organ now ſtands in the new: for they were every where placed full over againſt the weſt door, ſo as to be immediately ſeen as ſoon as you entered the church. When ſervice was done, there was generally a veil, or curtain, let down before them. "Doctor Storie, and other, were appointed by cardinal Pole, 2 Mary, to viſit every pariſh church in Middleſex, to ſee their rood-lofts repaired, and the images of the crucifix, with Mary and John, thereon to be fixed †." Images were firſt removed out of churches in 1538, by command of Henry VIII; and about 1559, queen Elizabeth took them away ‡.

TEXTS OF SCRIPTURE ON CHURCH-WALLS.

Texts of Scripture were firſt written upon church-walls, in Engliſh, the ſame day that roods were taken down, Nov. 17, 1547; and thoſe texts were at firſt chiefly ſuch as condemned images. "Nov. 17, was begun to be pulled down the rood, &c. and textes of Scriptures were written upon the walls of churches, againſt images ‖."

ALTAR.

When ſtone altars and raiſed altar-pieces were taken down, veils were beſtowed on ſome great churches. Thus, "June 11, 1551, the altar in Paule's church was pulled down, and a table ſett where the altar ſtoode, with a vayle drawne beneathe, and ſtepps. And, on the Sunday next, a communion was ſung at the ſame table. And, ſhortlie after, all the altars in London were taken downe, and tables placed in their roomes §."

"In all the churches which ever I ſaw, belonging to the church of Rome, in France, Spain, Italy, and the Low Countries, and alſo in Rome itſelf, the high altar, where the ſacrament is kept and delivered, is encompaſſed with rails; which

* Stowe's Chron. Lond. 1615, p. 595, a. 10. † Ibid. p. 627. ‡ Leyceſter, p. 360.
‖ Stowe, p. 595. a. § Ibid. p. 604. b.

rails

rails are commonly placed above the ſteps by which they aſcend to the high altar; within which rails, the prieſt only and he that ſerveth at maſs do abide, except in the ſinging of high-maſſes, when he is accompanied with the deacon, ſub-deacon, maſter of ceremonies, and two acolythi *."

FONTS.

Baptiſm being a ſacrament, it is very unſeemly to thruſt the font into a corner, as is generally done: it is moſtly placed near the church door, and ſometimes behind it. In cathedrals it is not received into the choir, but uſually ſtands in the nave.

CROSSES AND COPES.

The Proteſtant biſhops had their croſſes borne before them, and wore copes, till the 1ſt of Nov. 1552, 6 Edw. VI. Then came out the new ſervice-book, called the 2d book of king Edward VI. whereby they were forbidden. They were forbidden becauſe the hungry courtiers had an eye upon them. "Nov. 1, the new ſervice-book beganne in Paule's, the biſhop of London, Ridley, executing the ſervice in the forenoon, in his rochet onely, [&] without coape or veſtment, preached in the quire. At afternoone he preached at Paul's-Croſſe, to the ſetting forth the ſaid late-made booke. By this booke, all coapes and veſtments were forbidden through England, and [the] prebends of Paul's left off their hoods, the biſhoppes left their croſſes, &c. as by act of parliament more at large is ſet out †. In April and May following, commiſſioners were directed through England, for all the church-goods remaining in cathedral and pariſh-churches, that is to ſay, jewells of golde and ſilver, croſſes, candleſticks, cenſors, chalices ‡, and all other ſuch like, with their ready mony, to be delivered to the maſter of the king's jewels in the Tower; as alſo all copes and veſtments of cloth of gold, tiſſue, and ſilver, to the maſter of the king's wardrobe; the other coapes and ornaments to be ſold, and the money delivered to the king's treaſurer, Sir Edm. Peacham; reſerving to every church one chalice, with table-clothes for the communion, at the commiſſioner's diſcretion §."

THE LITANY

was antiently ſung alternately, as the Pſalms are now chaunted in cathedral churches, one part by them who kneeled on one ſide of the quire, and the other part by them who kneeled on the other. Thus, "Sept. 8, 1547, the letanie was ſung in Engliſh, in Paules church, London, in the place between the quire and the high altar; the ſingers kneeling, halfe on the one ſide, and halfe on the other ſide ||."

CANDLEMAS-DAY

is ſo called, from the people's bearing candles and lighted tapers in their hands upon that day, as they walked in proceſſion; or at high maſs. "On the 2d of Feb. 1547-8, the bearing of candles in the church was left off throughout the whole cittie of London **."

* Richard Carpenter, Experience, Hiſtory, and Divinity, p. 125. † Stowe, p. 608. b.
‡ So early as 1139, almoſt all the chalices in England being ſold to redeem Richard king thereof taken by the duke of Auſtria coming from the holy land, and detained by the emperor. Camden's Annals, Ireland. § Stowe, p. 609. b. || Ib. p. 594, b. 50. ** Ib. p. 595. a. 38.

ASH-WEDNESDAY, *Dies Cinerum*,

was ſo called, from the prieſt's giving aſhes to the people as they went into the church, for which end he ſtood ready in the church-porch to preſent them to the pariſhioners as they went in to hear ſervice; thereby inſinuating, that, Lent being now begun, they ſhould, like good penitents, humble themſelves with faſting and prayer; and with putting ſackcloth on their bodies, and aſhes on their heads, as was antiently the cuſtom of the Jews, in times of any great calamity, or devotion. " On Feb. 14, 1547-8, the uſe of giving aſhes in the church was left [off] *."

PALM-SUNDAY

is ſo called, from the people's antient cuſtom in bearing palms (which they received of the prieſt, after he had firſt bleſſed the ſame), and walking in proceſſion with them in their hands, in imitation of the Jews, who ſtrewed them in the way when our Bleſſed Lord made his public entrance into Jeruſalem. Paſſion-Sunday, or the Sunday next before Eaſter, is the true Palm-Sunday; though ſome, by reaſon of the Goſpel, and the picture of our Saviour's riding into Jeruſalem there placed over againſt it, in their Common-prayer books, are apt to miſtake the Firſt Sunday in Advent for it. " Anno 1547-8, the ceremonie of bearing of palmes on Palme-Sunday was left off †." Dr. Hickes, in his Devotions, has two collects, &c. the one for Palm-Sunday, the other for Paſſion-Sunday. The firſt, I preſume, is intended for the Firſt Sunday in Advent. It is yet the cuſtom at King's Cliffe, in Northamptonſhire, to ſtick the church with palms on Paſſion-Sunday.

LIBRARIES

" were firſt heard of in Egypt; and the titles they bore on the front inſpired the reader with a longing to penetrate the myſteries reſerved in them. They were called *the offices for the diſeaſes of the ſoul*, ψυχῆς ἰατρεῖον; and with great juſtice, becauſe the ſoul was there cured of ignorance, the moſt dangerous, and the parent of all her maladies ‡."

EMBALMING.

" Many hands were employed in this ceremony. Some, with inſtruments purpoſely made, began with emptying the body of every thing which was ſuſceptible of corruption, the brain, the entrails, and the inteſtines. As this evacuation (neceſſarily attended with ſome diſſections) ſeemed to have ſomething in it inhuman and cruel, the perſons employed fled as ſoon as the operation was over, and were purſued with ſtones by the ſtanders-by. Thoſe who embalmed the body were honourably treated. They filled it with myrrhe, cinnamon, and all ſorts of ſpices. After a certain time, the body was wrapped in folds of the fineſt linen, which they paſted on with the thineſt gum, and then chafed over with the moſt exquiſite perfumes.

* Stowe, p. 595. a. 48. † Ibid. p. 595. a. 58.
‡ Rollin's Antient Hiſtory, vol. I. p. 54.

By this means, it is ſaid, that the entire figure of the body, the very lines of the face, and the hairs on the lids and eye-brows, were preſerved in their natural perfection *."

POLYGAMY

"was allowed in Egypt, excepting to prieſts, who could marry but one woman †."

CHARON.

"It is a comfort to a dying man to leave a good name behind him; and this is the ſingle human bleſſing which death cannot raviſh from us. But it was by no means ſuffered by the Egyptians, that praiſe ſhould be beſtowed indifferently on all the dead: this honor was to be had from the public voice. The aſſembly of the judges met on the other ſide of a lake, which they croſſed in a boat. He who ſat at the helm was called Charon, in the Egyptian language; and this gave the hint to Orpheus, who had been in Egypt, and through him to the other Greeks, to invent their fable of Charon's boat. As ſoon as a man was dead, he was brought to his trial. The public accuſer was heard. If he proved, that the life of the deceaſed perſon had been ſcandalous, his memory was condemned, and he was deprived of ſepulture. Thus the people were ſtruck with laws which extended even beyond death; and every one, touched with the diſgrace inflicted on the dead perſon, was afraid to leave diſhonour on his memory and family. But, if the dead was convicted of no crime, he was honourably buried ‡."

APIS, THE OX.

"The Egyptians worſhiped the Ox, whom they called *Apis*. And it is eaſie to ſee the golden calf ſet up near Mount Sinai, by Aaron, was the effect of their abode in Egypt, as well as thoſe which were afterwards ſet up by Jeroboam §. Our author ſhould have added here, Jeroboam fled into Egypt ‖."

SWINES-FLESH.

"Hog-herds had a general ill-name throughout Egypt, as they had the care of ſo impure an animal. Herodotus, lib. ii. cap. 47. tells us, that they were not permitted to enter the Egyptian temples, nor would any man give them his daughter in marriage **."

* Rollin's Antient Hiſtory, vol. I. p. 48, 49. † Ibid. p. 37. ‡ Ibid. p. 49, 50. § Ibid. p. 42. ‖ 1 Kings, ii. 40. ** Anonymous, in a note ad imum p. 59. ib.

DE REGISTRIS PAROCHIALIBUS; an unfiniſhed Sketch. In a Letter, from the Rev. GEORGE NORTH, of Codicote, Herts, to Mr. Profeſſor WARD, of Greſham College.

WORTHY SIR, *Dec.* 7, 1748.

IN a late accidental converſation concerning Pariſh Regiſters, you expreſſed your opinion, that it was a ſubject very well worth the pains and enquiry of ſome member of our Society, and was pleaſed to recommend it particularly to my conſideration. I could not be wanting in any thing which could ſpeak my regard to you or your opinion, and therefore with pleaſure ſet about the taſk; preſuming to promiſe myſelf this ſatisfaction and advantage, that you would, with your uſual candour, excuſe, correct, and ſupply, whatever errors and deficiencies you ſhall meet with in this attempt.

The original of Pariſh Regiſters (as far as I can gather) is ſo very recent, that it naturally excited my reflections how the want of them was ſupplied in preceding ages, as ſomething ſimilar ſeems to have been always neceſſary; having never met with any attempt (though ſuch there may be) to clear up this queſtion, nor any thing like a clue to lead one through the mazes of more remote time.

A conſideration of what uſes are principally intended and ſerved by our preſent Regiſters is moſt likely to lead us to a diſcovery by what methods the want of them was formerly ſupplied. The chief, if not only, uſes intended were, I ſhould apprehend, the aſcertaining deſcents and kindreds, and theſe purely for the ſake of property: titles to honours have indeed been concerned in them; but, as honours were always in ſome proportion to property, or, at leaſt, never ſo much ſevered from it as to ſubſiſt alone, the proof of a title to property always aſcertained the ſame of its appendages. Few men need be told that times have been when property in general was very ſmall, and that too very unequally divided. In the time of our anceſtors the Saxons, the number of thanes in each ſhire was but ſmall, and theſe alone ſeem to have had any independent property or conſiderable poſſeſſions. In the laws of King Athelſtan, no other titles or diſtinction of honour are enumerated than Earl, Earldoram, Heregeraſſa, and Thane. None of theſe were hereditary, or ſucceſſively appendant to any quantity of poſſeſſion, but the laſt; all the reſt being offices and appointments merely perſonal. As to land, indeed, the poſſeſſion of it was almoſt all ſtrictly hereditary, and not deviſable to any one elſe than the next heir in blood, as is enacted by the 37th law of Alfred, and by ſome more antient law likewiſe, as is plain from his own will or teſtament; and as no alienation could be made even of what was allowed to be aliened, nor poſſeſſion upon a deviſe by will taken, but at a county court, there was little poſſibility of a right of inheritance being defeated. In the times when commerce was little or none, and every man lived, as we may ſay, within his own hedge, when no man could leave the lordſhip he belonged to without leave of his lord [Lex X Ed[i] ſen'], nor out of his ſhire without leave of the ealderman of it [Lex 33 Alfredi], and by the 2d of Athelſtan every man was to belong to ſome lord, on penalty of being conſidered as a fugitive, or thief; under theſe circumſtances every man's birth and lineage muſt be known. The arts of fraud, in theſe ages of poverty and ſimplicity, were hardly known; and, if we farther conſider how frequent and public their courts of juſtice were, it was next to impoſſible that any man's deſcent and claim could be forgotten, or admit of much diſpute. Theſe methods rendered Regiſters almoſt needleſs: accordingly we do not find any remains of ſuch among the Saxons. They were needleſs in reſpect of the common people, who were nailed, as it were, by the foot to one place, whoſe families were inſignificant, and whoſe ſmall dependent properties were protected by their lords; and the inheritors of the thanes were regiſtered, and tranſmitted in the memories of the whole ſhire, ſo often meeting in the county courts; and, when any diſpute happened, and was determined there, to give it a more laſting remembrance and ſecurity it was entered in a conciſe manner in ſome ſacred books of an adjacent monaſtery, of which ſort of entries are divers inſtances in Dr. Hickes's *Diſſertatio Epiſtolaris*. Beſides, as very few among the Saxons had any more than one name (or, if they had, it was no more than barely a patronymic, as *Putting* for *Puttoc ſuna* or *Puttoc filius*), no *nomina gentilitia*, or family name from thence; it was impoſſible to form a regiſter to ſerve ſuch purpoſes as our preſent ones do, *i. e.* to tranſmit and aſcertain a lineage and kindred.

I muſt beg leave here to obſerve, though I may ſeem to wander from my main point, that Sir Henry Spelman, as quoted by Dr. Hickes, p. 28, in his letters to Ptoloemon Roſcantz, ſays, "Nullus quod ſciam occurrit Saxo vel Danus gentili "fretus cognomine, nec ejuſmodi quempiam repperi inter Gallos veteres apud Gre"gorium Turonenſem, nec ſub mediis ſeculis apud Aimonum, nec inter Longobar"dos apud Paulum Warnefridum ſeu Diaconum." This will not hold true of all the Northern nations of Gothic originals; for, in Caſſiodorus, is mention of *Stirps Amalorum*, of which family were Amal Afrida, Thedoricus Germana, and Amalaſuintha, and Amala Freda, his two daughters; and I well remember, though I cannot at preſent find it, mention in Ammianus Marcellinus of a Goth, with two names, one of them a *nomen Gentile*.

Upon the whole, I apprehend, the Saxons had nothing like our preſent Regiſters; and, what little ſcraps of pedigrees of any particular great men among them have come down to us, they were preſerved in the annals of ſome neighbouring monaſtery, to which they had in ſome manner been protectors or benefactors.

Servius Tullius, to aſcertain the number of births and burials, ordered, when a child was born, that its kindred ſhould bring a piece of money into the Ærarium of Juno Lucina; and when any died, into that of Venus Libitina.

This cuſtom being afterwards aboliſhed, was revived by Auguſtus Cæſar at the birth of children. See Lipſius in Tacitum.

In the Code Louis, publiſhed at Paris 1667, are ordinances for the regiſtering of chriſtenings, marriages, and burials, in each pariſh. See title XX. art. 8, 9, 10, 11, 12, 13, 14, from p. 107 to 112.

Though there are ſome few Parochial Regiſters as old as the firſt original of them, by injunction from Lord T. Cromwell*, in Sept. 1538, 30 H. VIII. (renewed and inferred by the Injunctions of Edward VI. in 1547); likewiſe by Cardinal Pole, by his articles of viſitation, dated Lambeth, 4 Feb. 1556; yet the regiſter of this pariſh [Codicote] going no farther back than the beginning of Queen Elizabeth's reign, muſt be ſuppoſed to have been begun to be kept in obedience to the Injunctions relating thereto, in her firſt year. But, as in thoſe times they were uſually written on paper, it was, for the better preſervation of them, ſtrictly enjoined by the laſt of the Conſtitutions made in the ſynod of the clergy of the province of Canterbury, begun 25 Oct. 1597;

" Ut libri ad hunc uſum diſtincti quo tutius reſervari & ad poſteritatis memoriam " propagari poſſint, ex pergameno ſumptibus parochianorum in poſterum conficiantur, iiſque non modo ex veteribus libris chartaceis tranſumpta, nomina earum " qui, regnante Dominâ noſtrâ Elizabethâ, aut baptiſmatis aqua allui, aut matrimo- " nio copulati, aut eccleſiaſticæ ſepulturæ beneficio affecti ſint, ſuo ordine inſcri- " bantur, ſed eorum etiam qui in poſterum baptizati vel matrimonio conjuncti, aut " ſepulti fuerint."

With regard to the copying of the old regiſter, it was ordered in the ſame Conſtitution,

" Poſtquam autem paginam aliquam integram nomina inſcripta compleverint ex " veteribus libris cartaceis tum miniſtri tum gardianorum ipſius parochiæ ſubſcrip- " tionibus volumus eam communiri, ſed diligente ac fideli prius adhibitâ collatione."

By this laſt particular is explained why the names of the ſame miniſter and churchwardens ſo generally occur at the bottom of the page, from the beginning to the year 1598; viz. as witneſſes only of the faithful copying of the regiſter till that time; the ſame reaſon is to be given for their being generally written in one and the ſame hand to the ſame year.

* " This moſt wiſe and beneficial regulation is ſaid to have been firſt introduced in the year 1538, by the direction of Cromwell, then vicar-general; before which time, probably, the parochial clergy were not often ſufficient penmen to keep ſuch regiſters, nor were there at this period exciſe-officers who could be employed as *amanuenſes*. The great convenience ariſing from this ordinance of Cromwell's, occaſioned its being enjoined during the reigns of Edward VI. Queen Elizabeth, and James I. I take this from Biſhop Gibſon's Codex, though in Sparrow's Collection of Injunctions, printed in 1684, in 4to, I do not find any mention of this regulation during the reign of Queen Elizabeth. The keeping, however, a regiſter was enjoined by Edward VI. A. D. 1547; and for neglect in ſo doing, the miniſter is mulcted 3*s*. 4*d*. to the poor's box; whilſt in the ſame year it makes one of Cranmer's articles of viſitation to the province of Canterbury." Mr. Barrington, in the Preface to " a propoſed Form of Regiſters for Baptiſms and Burials, 1781."

 Moreover,

Moreover, becauſe they had been before very negligently and irregularly kept, it was by the ſame conſtitution ordered,

" Ut exemplar quotannis cujuſque anni auctæ nominum inſcriptionis ad epiſcopi " dioceſani regiſtrum per gardianos infra menſem poſt feſtum Paſchalis tranſmitta- " tur, & ſine feodo ullo recipiatur, atque in archivis epiſcopi fideliter cuſtodiatur."

This has ſince been regularly obſerved at the archdeacon's viſitations*; and to this we owe the preſervation and excellent order of parochial regiſters throughout the kingdom.—In Thoreſby's Leeds, p. 162, there is a good model for a Pariſh Regiſter.

" A Bill for a Treaſure-Houſe in every ſhire for keeping of the Records," was read the firſt time in the Houſe of Commons Nov. 15, 1547, 1 Edw. VI. †

Extract from King Edward's Injunctions ‡.

ALSO, that the parſon, vicar, or curat, and pariſhioners of evry parriſhe within this realm, ſhall, in their churches and chapels, kepe one booke or regeſter, wherein they ſhall write the daye and yere of everye wedding, chriſtening, and burial, made in their pariſhe for their tyme, and ſo every man ſucceeding them likewiſe. And alſo therein ſhall write every parſone's name that ſhall be ſo wedded, regiſtered, or buried; and for the ſauſe keaping of the ſame booke, the parriſhe ſhall be bound to provide, of their common charges, one ſure coffer, with two locks and keyes, whereof thone to remain with the parſon, vicar, or curate, and thother with the wardeynes of every parriſhe churche or chapell wherein the ſaide booke ſhall be layde up, whiche booke they ſhall every Sonday take furthe, and, in the preſence of the ſaide wardeyns, or one of them, write and recorde in the ſame all the weddings, chriſtenyngs, and burialles, made the hole weeke before, and that doon, to lay up the booke in the ſaid cofer as afore, and for every tyme that the ſame ſhall be omitted, the partye that ſhall be in the faulte thereof, ſhall forfait to the ſaid churche 3 s. 4 d. to be employed to the poore men's box of that parriſhe.

Signd at top, at beginning, with the King's own hand; *ad finem* with hands of Archbiſhop Cranmer, Lord Protector, and other privy councell.

In the preface:

——— whereof parte were geven unto them heretofore by thautoritie of his mooſte deerely beloved father King Henry the Eight, of mooſte famouſe memory, and parte are nowe m . . . . ., and gevyn by his Majeſtie.

The articles of Feb. 5, 1562, are ſigned by David Kempe de Sc̄o Albano §.

* One of Mr. Urban's correſpondents (vol. LXIII. p. 703.) obſerves, " that this injunction has not been regularly complied with, as well becauſe churchwardens are not always willing to defray the charge of making the tranſcripts, as that they are to be received at the office without a fee. Such a reſtriction does not ſeem to have been calculated to induce regiſters and their deputies to preſs for a return of theſe certificates; nor, conſidering the little chance there is of any emolument likely to accrue from the cuſtody of the papers, was it to be expected that they would be duly arranged, and carefully preſerved."

† Journals of the Houſe of Commons, vol. I. p. 1.

‡ Miſcell. III. p. 498. in the MS. Library at Ben'et College, Cambridge.

§ David Kempe was collated to the archdeaconry of St. Alban's July 17, 1560, and reſigned the ſame in 1580 Le Neve, Faſti, p. 198.

A Bill

A Bill to autoriſe every Archbiſhop and Biſhop to erect one office of regiſterſhip of all the church books, in due order, to be kept in every dioceſe, 15 Eliz. Written by Thomas Boweſey, and preſented to Archbiſhop Parker for his approbation †.

Whereas a laudable, good, and univerſal ordre was taken throughout this realme, in the 30th yere of the reign of the late K. of famous memory, Henry theight, that the parſons, vicars, curates, and chaplain, of every pariſh church and chappell, for the time being, ſhould keepe a booke of remembrance of the times of the birth, chriſtening, buriall, and marriage, of every perſon or perſons fortuning to be born, chriſtened, buried, or married, in the ſame town or pariſh, for that oftentimes there happened much controverſy, ſuit, and contention, as well upon the privitie of birthes, and in triall of the titles of ſome of the perſons ſo borne, divers times of the former marriage of any perſon happening to be twyes married, or happening to marry two wives both living at one time, otherwhiles upon the full age of any perſon or perſons meaning to avoid his or their owne deeds or bonds, being of full age, upon pretence of minoritie, or be to ſue their liverie, or to be out of ward, or having nede for any other cauſes to know his or their owne ages, as alſo upon an infinite nombre of other occaſions (ſithence partly well cut off and deciſed), by the more ſpedy, due, and true triall thereof, in ſome places where the ſame bookes be duely kept and mainteyned by force of the ſame good ordre, to the relief and redres of many injuries or oppreſſion that otherwiſe that would have been offered and done, if ſuch teſtimony had not been apparent and verified by the ſame church book, and to the ſtaying of a great numbre of contentions, ſuits, and ſtrifes, which otherwiſe would have unconcionably been ſtirred up and rayſed by the occaſions aforeſaid. Yet the ſame of late time hath been much and greatly abuſed in moſt places, partly by reaſon of the multitude of curates and miniſters that have of late been changed in divers of the ſaid churches, and thereby the more negligently kepe the ſame bookes, notes, and titles, and remembrance, and partly through the little regard taken to the ſame, for want of one overſeer, whereby the ſame once made be not only ſafe kept, but alſo omitted, and not entred at all into the ſaid booke, writinge, titeling, and remembrance; and that, foraſmuch as no pain hath been appointed by the magiſtrate before time, for the not entring, or evilkeping, or entring of the ſame, but moſt chiefly, and the rather, inſomuch that it oftentimes fortinith, that the ſame perſons, vicars, curates, miniſters, or other the kepers thereof been not able to anſwer the harmes of diſenheriſon, damages, and other troubles, that might chance, and dayly doo and may enſue, by the evil uſage and corrupt keping of the ſame booke, the lack whereof hath already not only been much felt and perceived in the ſame places of defect, to the great hindrance in trialls of verities, and to the

* Miſcell. III. p. 365. in Bene't College Library.—This bill was read the firſt time in the Houſe of Commons March 9, 1562-3. Journals, vol. I. p. 68. But it does not appear from any other minute that it was ever read a ſecond time, or why it was not proceeded in.

diſinheritance

disenheritance of a great numbre of freholders, coppiholders, and custumary tenants, as also to the great incommoditie of others, and to the great increase of perjurie, and just provocation of God's wrath and high displeasure, but very like hereafter to turne to unspeakable inconvenience, damages, and enormities, if better ordre be not herein spedely provided. Be it therefore enacted, by the Queen's most excellent Majesty, our sovereign lady, the lords spiritual and temporal, and the commons of this present parliament assembled, and by the auctoritie of the same, that at all times for henceforth it shall and may be lawfull, as well to the most reverend fathers in God the Archbishops of Canterbury and York, and either of them, as to all other bishops and ordinaries in this our realm of England, and to their successors, and to every one of them, to erect, establish, and make, within his or their several diocese and jurisdiction, by his or their several graunt under his or their authentick and usual seal, one office of registership and register, to survey, safe kepe, and streightly looke to the said church book, and the same truly from henceforth to register in some decent book of parchment, for a perpetual memory and testimony of the premisses, as well for thavoyding of thenormite aforesaid, as also to the entent that, from time to time, upon any serch to be made by any hir grace's subjects for the veritie, true triall, and perfect knowledge of the certente of the premisses, there may be written and made out of the said register book, so to be kept in every one of the said offices, a true record, or certificate, of the certainty of the premisses, to any person or persons hereafter serching or requesting the same, under the usual seal of the said office, to have, hold, exercise, and enjoy the said office or offices of registership, to every such person and persons, or their sufficient deputies, from the day of the date of every his and their said grant and graunts to him or them as aforesaid, to be made for and during the natural life or lives of the same register or registers. And moreover be it enacted, by the auctoritie aforesaid, that all and every the said persons, vicars, curates, ministers, and every of them, for the time being, from time to time, yerely hereafter, not only truly, distinctly, perfectly, and plainly enter, wright, note, and entitle, into their several church book, all and every the births, christenings, marriages, and burialls, of all and every person and persons happening to be born, christened, married, or buried, in the whole weeke precedent, with the just days and yeares of the same, in such manner and form as by the same registers and officers, or their sufficient deputies, or any of them, shall be prescribed or appointed, but also shall shew forthe the same so entred and written every Sonday after the evening prayer, in the presence of the churchwardens, or two honest men of the same parish. And still further, at thende of every yere hereafter successively ensuing, immediately upon commaundement to them, or any of them, given by or from the bishop or ordinaries, or their successors, or any of them, safely deliver, or cause to be delivered, to the said register or registers, their assistants or deputies, all and every the same their church booke, notes, and remembraunce, as well heretofore taken, entred, and written, by virtue of the saide good laudable ordre, or otherwise, as hereafter to be taken, entred, and written, by virtue of this present acte, by them, or any of them, in forme aforesaid, of the yeare precedent, to be registred, recorded, laid up, and safe kept, for a perpetuall memorye, record, and testimony,

as

as aforefaid, at fuch time and place as by the faid archbifhops, bifhops, ordinaries, or their fucceffors, or any of them, fhall be, from time to time, limited and appointed, upon pain that every fuch perfon, vicar, curat, minifter, or any of them, fo offending, fhall, for every one offence and default in the premiffes, or any of them fo to be made, upon due proof thereof had, forfeit the fum of 10 s. to be levied or taken of the revenues and profits of his and their fpiritual promotions, perfonages, vicarages, ftipends, or otherwife, by feifure of his goods, or diftres to be taken of the fame, by the faid churchwardens or regifters for the time being, or any of them, thone moietie thereof to be to the ufe of the poore people's common boxe within the fame parifh, and thother moytie to thufe of the regifter or regifters, or their fufficient deputy or deputies, for the time being. And be it alfo further enacted, by the authority aforefaid, that, from and after the prorogation or diffolution of this prefent parliament, the parent or parents of every child chriftened in any parifh church or chappell within this realme of England, having lands, tenements, or hereditaments, to him or his heires in fee fimple, or fee tayle, to the yearly value of 40 s. or having goods and cattals to the value of 5 l. fhall from henceforth pay at the chriftening of every child 1 d.; and every perfon or perfons hereafter efpowfing or marrying any wife, to pay at their marriage 1 d.; and every man having landes or goods of the value aforefaid, at the buriall of his wife, to pay 2 d.; and every woman having lands or goods of the faid value, at the buriall of hir hufband, to pay 1 d.; and every fuch man or woman to pay, at the burial of his or their fone and daughter, and his or their houfhold fervant, 1 d. to the churchwardens of the faid parifh or chapell for the time being, or, in their abfence, to the perfan, vicar, curat, or minifter, chriftening, marrying, or burying, any of the faid perfon or perfons, in forme aforefaid, to the ufe of the faid churchwardens being abfent; and by them fo receiving the fame feveral fummes of money at the end of every yeare fucceffively enfuing, to be repayd to the faid regifter or regifters, or his or their fufficient deputy or deputies, in that behalf, in confideration that every one of the fame regifters, or their fufficient deputies, fhall, at their great coft or chardge, within the fpace of fix years next enfuing the dates of his or their graunt or graunts, to be made and graunted as aforefaid, well and truly regifter, or caufe to be regiftred, as well all and every the faid former church books, titles, notes, and remembraunce, of 24 yeeres continuance alredy paffed, or therabouts, as allfo all and every the faid church bookes, title, notes, and remembraunce, yerely hereafter to be regiftered, as well of all and every perfon and perfons not having any lands or goods of the value aforefaid, or of every perfon or perfons fo having into great deacent books of parchment in forme before declared, and towards their yearely travell and chardges in gathering up the fame church books into every one of his or their faid office or office. And furthermore be it enacted, by the authority aforefaid, that if it fhall happen any the aforementioned feveral fomes of money at any time hereafter to be behynd and unpayed by any perfon or perfons who by force of this acte ought or been charged to pay the fame, in manner and forme before declared, that then, and at all times after, it fhall and may be lawfull to and for all and every fuch perfon or perfons, regifter or regifters, or or their aſſigns and deputies, and the executors of any of them, to whom any the aforeſaid ſeveral ſumes of money, from time to time hereafter, be due and payable, in forme aforeſaid, to diſtrain the goods and cattalls of all and every ſuch perſon or perſons, or executors of any of them, ſo refuſing or denying to pay any the ſaid ſeveral ſomes of money before ſpecified, and due, to be paid, by force of this preſent acte, as is before declared; and the ſame diſtreſs or diſtreſſes, ſo taken, to leade, drive, and carry away, and deteyne untill the ſame be fully ſatisfied and payed. And further, be it alſo enacted, that all officials and commiſſaries of any ſuch dioceſe or juriſdiction, and all mayors, ſheriffs, bayliffs of towns corporat, and juſtice of peace of the ſhires, wherein the ſaid perſons, vicars, curats, miniſters, and ſervitors, bene at all time and times requiſite, ſhall aide, aſſiſt, help, mayntein, and defend, the ſaid regiſter or regiſters, their aſſigns and deputies, and every of them, in and about the due exerciſe of their office or offices aforeſaid, and in every point, according to the tenor, effect, and true meaning of this acte; and further, by their diſcretions, condignely to puniſh thoffenders and hinderers of the execution of the ſame in any point. And furthermore, for the due ordre and aſſignment of reaſonable fees hereafter to be taken by the ſaid regiſter, for the perpetuall maintenance and continuance of the ſame ſeveral offices in forme aforeſaid, be it enacted, by the authority aforeſaid, that every perſon or perſons hereafter requeſting any ſerche to be made in any of the ſaid regiſter bookes and offices, ſhall pay to the regiſter or regiſters, or their deputies, for every ſuch ſerch ſo to be had the ſome of 4 d.; for every certificate, made and written on parchment out of the ſaid record, to any perſon requeſting the ſame under the ſeal of the office, 12 d.; and for every ſeale of office put to any ſuch certificate or record 4 d.

In Strype's Annals, vol. IV. p. 45. is the following outline of a Project, addreſſed in 1590 to the Lord Treaſurer Burghley, for an Office for a general Regiſter * of all the Chriſtenings, Marriages, and Burials, &c. [A patent for this was ſent from the Lord Treaſurer to the Archbiſhop of Canterbury for his judgement.]

"The benefit that will grow to her Majeſty and her ſucceſſors thereby: 1. An annual rent of 100*l.* by year to her Majeſty and her ſucceſſors for ever. 2. That it

* By another article in the ſame volume it appears that in or about the year 1590 ſome one had endeavoured to obtain an office to appoint all Pariſh Clerks; the inconveniences of which are thus ſtated to the Lord Treaſurer by Archbiſhop Whitgift's ſecretary: "1. Law and cuſtom hath in all pariſhes eſtabliſhed the appointing of the pariſh-clerk and ſexton, in the miniſter and pariſhioners. 2. Their ſervice is to the miniſter in church matters, for the uſe of all the pariſhioners; therefore fitteſt to be choſen by them; as it is obſerved every where. 3. They receive their fees and accuſtomed wages of the pariſhioners; therefore a ſtranger cannot be obtruded well upon them; for, if any of another's appointment be their clerk, they will think it hard meaſure that they ſhould be forced to maintain him. 4. He that is no way beholden either to the miniſter or pariſhioners, nor in any awe of them for his office, will neither perform duty nor diligence. 5. If the grantee ſhall do the office in his own perſon, then can he have but the employment of one pariſh; for he muſt be attendant thereon upon all occaſions, early and late. If by a deputy, ſuch one will hardly leave his wages, when their common ſervant is appointed by another: beſides, the grantee will for his own commodity reſerve ſome part for himſelf; and ſo the ſervice will be either

it will be much profit to her Majesty, for explaining of the ages of her wards, being now greatly abused by escheators and feodaries, in the benefits and commodities which may thereby grow to her subjects. 3. That it shall tend to the great good of many which shall have occasion for certificates, either for lawful copplement in matrimony, or in case of bastardy. 4. That it shall clearly avoid all cosinages made by those under age, either in levying of fines, suffering recoveries, acknowledging statutes or recognizances, or doing any other matter of record. 5. That the entrance of the baptisms, as it shall be provided for, will be a clear deciphering of all half-bloods, or controversies daily happening under colour of half or whole blood. 6. That it will be a curb for those who pretend to be sundry times married. 7. That it shall much tend to the deciding of many controversies, which daily grow by reason of the life or death of persons. 8. There shall be also yearly delivered unto your honour, and unto every Lord-Treasurer, from the time being, a summary of the whole. Whereby it shall appear unto you and them how many christnings, weddings, and burials, be every year within England and Wales, and every county particularly by itself, and how many men, children, and women, children in either of them severally set down by themselves."

Mr. Barrington informs us *, that a canon of 1603 directs registers to be made up from *the law's first taking place*, i. e. A. D 1538, and more particularly so from the first year of Queen Elizabeth †; which last injunction seems to shew that before that period they were either neglected, or slovenly kept.

The Civil Wars during the next reign often prevented the parish ministers from executing regularly this part of their duty, which seems also to have been greatly neglected during the Common-wealth; though in the year 1653 an ordinance passed, directing, that the parishioners, contributing to the relief of the poor, should provide a book of vellum or parchment, which was to be kept by a person chosen by the said parishioners ‡ every three years, and who was to make the proper entries of marriages, births, and burials.

either performed by an insufficient man, or at least be very greatly neglected. 6. The office of surveying all parish-clerks is but a shift to pick out money from the poor men, and in no respect requisite or needful; for, the reformation of them being negligent or faulty, is by law already settled in the ordinaries. 7. These and such like grants, as they are very extraordinary, so are they burthensome to the Queen's subjects, and unprofitable for the commonwealth, and serve only for the private gain of private persons; which nevertheless prosper not when they have them. By the copy of the patent which your Lordship sent unto me, there is granted the buying of books, clappers of bells, and other necessaries for the use of the church, at the parishioners cost and charges. A matter most unreasonable. For so he may still poll them, and make what accounts he list, and they have no remedy. 9. Besides, the laws and her Majesty's injunctions lay this trust upon the churchwardens of the parish, being of the substantialest men, whom the rest think good to trust; and therefore do make choice of, to disburse their money in that behalf."

* In the Preface already quoted.

† Every minister, at visitations, was, amongst other things, to subscribe to this protestation: "I shall keep the Register-boke according to the Queene's Majestie's injunction."

‡ Extract from the register of burials in Maidstone:

"The 29th of September, 1653. Henry Pierce, of the town of Maidstone, in the countie of Kent, being chosen by the parishioners to bee register for the said towne and parish, was this day sworne before me John Sanders, maior of the same towne and parish, and justice of the peace there. And I doe approve of him to be register accordinge to an act of this present parliament, intituled, An Act touching Marriages and registring thereof; and also touching Births and Burials."

C Upon

Upon the Reſtoration, regiſters ſeem to have been again attended to, and poſſibly by the injunctions of the biſhops at their viſitations.

During the reign of King William, the firſt parliamentary notice is taken of them; though the object of the legiſlature is not to encourage this moſt uſeful evidence, but to raiſe ſupplies for carrying on the war with France.

By 6 and 7 William III. c. 6. ſ. xxiv. every clergyman is to keep a regiſter of births, burials, and baptiſms, under a penalty of 100*l.* *

By 7 and 8 William III. c. 35. ſ. v. every parent is to give notice of the birth of their child within five days, under a penalty of 40*s.*; and the penalty is extended to the miniſter, not making an entry of the child thus born and not chriſtened.

By 4 Anne, c. 12. ſ. x. the clergyman is indemnified from the penalty of 100*l.* impoſed by 6 and 7 William III. in caſe the duties upon chriſtenings, births, and burials, ſhall have been really paid.

At Lady-day 1754, by 27 Geo. II. a new regulation took place reſpecting the entries of banns and marriages.

Laſtly, in 1784, by 24 Geo. III. a farther regulation was attempted, by laying a tax of 3*d.* on every entry either of chriſtening, marriage, or burial. But this tax, having been found both inconvenient † and inefficient ‡, was repealed in 1793.

Mr. North's Remarks on the Regiſters of ſome Churches in Hertfordſhire.

The regiſter-booke of the pariſh church of Bengeo, conteyning all ſutch chriſtnings, marriags, and burials, as have bin from the yeere of our Lord 1539 unto this preſent year of our Lord 1600.—Continued only to Oct. (incluſive) 1597.

Baptiſms begin Nov. 2, 1539. Eliz. daught. of Robt North of Rickners, bapt. 1542.—They end May 7, 1553, and diſcontinue to Oct. 10, 1562.

Tranſcript of baptiſms from old book end 28 Aug. 1597, and quite diſcontinued to May 3, 1601.

Marriages omitted from 28 Oct. 1545 to 9 Sept. 1548.

This entry—from the 26 Jan. 1553, aforeſaid, untill 8th day of Nov. 1562, aboveſaid, the beginning of Richard Hailies entrance into the vicaridge of Bengeo, their is not any mention made of any marriage.—Omiſſions of ſeveral other years.

Among the burials is this memorandum: The ould regiſter paſſeth from this 28 of February, 1553, unto the 18 Oct. 1562, the beginning of Richard Hailies entrance into the vicaridge of Bengeo; all the burials of 1556 omitted.

Charles, the ſon of John Grac, 1661, 03 deſen.

Nomina præſertim connubia funera poſſim
Hic ſimul inſerta continet iſte liber. Wm. Tr, ſcripſit, cler.

* In the regiſter of Stockerſton in Leiceſterſhire, notice is taken of the tax laid by act of parliament, which began May 1, 1695. This tax is explained in Gent. Mag. vol. LXII. p. 716.

† See Gent. Mag. vol. LXII. pp. 596. 716.; vol. LXIV. p. 895.

‡ Mr. Throſby, in his "Excurſions in Leiceſterſhire," met with one pariſh (p. 69) where the Regiſter was kept by a Farmer; who, to ſave the tax, or not underſtanding it, put no name down for two years; and another (p. 370), where no entry had been made ſince the act took place.

The

The church-regifter belonging to the parifh church of St. Peter's, in the borough of St. Albane's, conteining the name of fuch as were baptized, maried, and buried, there, from the beginning of the reign of our foveraigne Ladie Elizabeth, by the grace of God, &c. which is from the 17 daye of November, in the yere of our Lord 1558; tranfcript out of the ould regifter belonging to the fame church, according to a canon in that behalfe made and agreed upon, at a fynode houlden at London, anno Dom. 1597, and in the yere of the raigne of our faid foveraigne ladie 39.

Braintfield regifter begins 15 Jan. 1559 to Aug. 27, 1598, in the fame hand. The preface to it is as follows:

The regifter book of all the chriftnings, marriages, and burials, fince the year of our Lord 1559 untill this year 1598, and fo continue hereafter as followeth.

Mem. That Francis Greene did bring to mee a certificate of the confent of the inhabitants of the parifh of Braintfield, in the choofing of the regifter of the faid parifh, upon the 28th of March, 1654; and that, according to the late act of marriages, he did take his oath, and was approved by me, ISAAC PULTER.

June this 4th, 1666. This regifter book of chriftnings, and burials, and marriages, was brought and delivered to me Edward Boughton, rector of Braintfeild, by Francis Greene of Braintfeild, in the prefence of Thomas Love, conftable of the faid Braintfeild.

All Saints Regifter.

The regifter-book of chriftnings, marriages, and burials, for the parifh of All Saints, in the town of Hertford, and archdeaconry of Hunt', wherein is written all that was to be found in the old book; made the 25 Oct. An° D'ni 1598.

Written in this book from the beginning thereof unto the yere of our Lord God one thoufand five hundred fowerfcore and eightene, by me, Peter Rylande, of St. Alban's, Sec'.

Mem. It appears (by an ordre, made 8th Feb. 1600, to prevent it for the future) that all rates for repair of the church, and fupport, and for the gayle, ufed to be made in the church during common prayer. Ordered, and agreed, that each fhould fend his money to the churchwardens feats.

Publications and marriages, according to the act of parliament, made the 29th of Sept. 1653:

Sept. 6, 1656. William Cooper, of Gilfton, yeoman, and Anne Cramphorne, of Sabridgeworth, fpinfter, thrice publifhed in the market-place, in Hertford.

Jan. 30. Richard Ladd, of Hoddefdon, yeoman, and Anne Norris, of this parifh, three feveral Lord's days publifhed in the church.

Dec. 5, 1657. Richard Walfey, butcher, and Mary Weblie, both of Codicote, three feverall market days publifhed in the market place.

N. B. The laft inftance is of a publication on the 10, 17, and 24, of Dec. 1659.

M. H. 25 Sept. 1709, bap. Oct. 3.

Pariſh of St. Peter's within the borough of St. Alban's. 10 Sept. 1653.

Be it remembred, that at a veſtry houlden by us the pariſhioners of the pariſh aforeſaid, whoſe names are hereunto ſubſcribed, William Retchford, miniſter of the goſpel, there was choſen by us regiſter, accordinge to the tenor of a late acte, intitled, "An Act touchinge Marriadges, and the regiſtringe thereof; and alſo, touchinge Birthes and Burialls."

I William Foxwiſt, eſquier, one of the juſtices of the peace for the burrough aforeſaid, and one of the inhabitants of the pariſh aforeſaid, do hereby approve of the choyſe of the ſaid Willm Retchford to be regiſter as aforeſaid; and for the execution of his place have ſworne hym according to the tennor of the act aforeſaid. In witneſs whereof I have ſubſcribed my name. W. FOXWIST.

January 15, 22, 29, Lord's days, 1653.

The publication of contract of marriage between Haſledine, labourer, of the pariſh of St. Peter's, and Jane Dowſell, of Clerkenwell, London, was made on the ſeveral Lord's days abovementioned, in the church of St. Peter aboveſayd.

Jan. 30, 1653.

Wm Haſeldine and Jane Dowſell aforeſayd were then married, according to the tenor of an act of parliament in that behalf, by Wm Foxwiſt, eſq. one of the juſtices of the peace for the borough of St. Alban's, and county of Hartford, and dwelling within the pariſh of St. Peter's aforeſayd. W. FOXWIST.

Notes relative to ST. ALBAN'S ABBEY, written on the ſame Paper, by Mr. NORTH.

Had quidam homo nobilis & Chriſtiana uxor ejus dederunt St. Albano, pro animarum ſalute, Newenham & Beandiſch.

Hardewynus de Scaliers dedit nobis villam de Brantefeld cum eccleſia ejuſdem villæ.

Roger de Hertford dedit nobis decimam ſuam de Boxa.

Willielmus filius Simonis dedit huic eccleſiæ quaſdam decimas in villa de Hatfeld ad officium Scriptoria.

Rodbertus Cementarius tempore Pauli Abbatis circa re-edificationem hujus eccleſiæ laboravit, & ſing' annis quamdiu vixit dedit x ſolid' Sancto Albano. Vide Chron. Sax. ad 1116.

Edwardus de Cantebrigia, & mater ejus, dederunt Sancto Albano eccleſiam Sancti Benedicti que eſt in Cantebrigia.

Magiſter Reginaldus de Sancto Albano affectus penes eundem martyrem ſpecialiter & iſtud monaſterium, conſtruxit capellam glorioſæ virginis in Orientale parte eccleſiæ ubi quotidie miſſa per notam in honorem ejuſdem virginis celebratur.

D'nus Joh' Roulonde, rector eccleſiæ de Todynton.

Magiſter Willielmus Burtoun, juriſperitus, & clericus archidiaconi hujus monaſterii.

Rob' de la Chaumbre & Agnes uxor ejus contulerunt ad officium eleemoſynar' tenementum ſuum cum duabus acris terræ & aliis pertinentiis quod in vicario Sancti Petri villæ Sancti Albani ſituatum eſt, viz. ex oppoſito illius eccleſiæ.

Concerning the reſervation to the King (Henry III.) of the promoting to the abbies of St. Alban's, when his Queen Alianora was regent here, while he went into Gaſcony, ſee Madox, p. 476.

Farther Remarks on Regifters. By the Rev. S. Denne, M. A. F. S. A.

WHILST the memorial courts, leet and baron, were regularly kept every year, and oftener, as, it is believed, in fome places, the ages of the refiants muft have been pretty well known. In the courts leet the jurors would not have been ignorant what young men were from their years liable to be called upon to perform offices and fervices; and thofe who could certainly would plead to be difcharged from them when they had attained to an advanced period of life.

The homage of the court-baron muft always have prefented the deaths of tenants of every degree, and have fpecified whether the heirs were of a competent age to be admitted, and to take the oath of fealty to the lord.

In a feries of years, when, by the increafe of money, the reduced comparative value of the quit-rents, reliefs, and other emoluments, were not fufficient to pay the expence of holding courts, they would be difcontinued, and this mode of evidence would ceafe. Very many men are there now known only by name, and many, many, more would probably have been relinquifhed, had not the lordly Nimrods been anxious to afcertain the boundaries, that they might have for their fport plenty of game.

At the courts leet the women were not bound to attend; nor at the courts baron, if they had brothers to inherit their father's property; and one confequence was, that the jurors were not in duty bound to afk how old they were; and perhaps the females might not in thofe days be forry that there was not any recorded minute touching their ages, at leaft not till after they had dropped their maiden names.

Regifters and ledgers of monafteries perpetuated only the obits of benefactors. It was truly obferved, by Mr. Carte *, that they did not feem to have been interefted in baptifms; and though, in the opinion of the monks, marriage was a facrament, they from principle encouraged celibacy; for which reafon thefe lines of Chaucer muft be confidered as almoft folely applicable to parochial churches:

"She was a worthy woman all her live,
Hufbands at the *church door* fhe had five †."

Such a publicity was expedient, indeed requifite, when it was not the practice to record a wedding by a fpecific entry: it fhould feem that it had its origin from this confideration. A wedding, fo celebrated, muft have had for witneffes every perfon that might be paffing by at the time; and he or fhe muft have been an incurious or inattentive fpectator, who did not enquire and remember the names of the bridegroom and of the bride, who received her dowry at the church-door— *Dos ad oftium ecclefiæ.* At the Reformation, that part of the ceremony (and it was the greateft part), which ufed to be performed at the church-door, was directed to be performed in the body of the church, and at the time of divine fervice, that the congregation might be witneffes. The *body* of the church occurs in the rubric of our prefent form; and when I was a ftripling I recollect this rule being ftrictly followed in Lambeth church. Haffocks were placed in the middle aile below the reading-defk; the fervice to the conclufion of the firft bleffing being there read, there was a remove to the communion-rails to finifh the reft of the office.

* Archæologia, vol. X. p. 214.

† Wife of Bath.

Cromwell

Cromwell (Earl of Eſſex) has the beſt title to the merit of introducing Parochial Regiſters. That they had not a more early commencement, ſtrong evidence of the negative kind may be deduced from there not being before 1538 any injunctions to the clergy to attend to regiſters, either in epiſcopal regiſters, or in acts conſiſtorial or viſitatorial of biſhops and archdeacons.

From the great change in the religious tenets and habits of the people of England, and many of them before the 16th century, the advantages of regiſters, with reſpect to the public and to individuals, were not ſo great as Cromwell probably imagined might have enſued from his politic plan. But it may reaſonably be preſumed, that in 1538 he had not a notion that there would ere long be many perſons to whoſe baptiſms the clergyman of the pariſh muſt be an abſolute ſtranger, and many detached cemeteries for the interment of diſſenters from the Eſtabliſhed Church; and he muſt have been gifted with a wonderful degree of ſecond-ſight to have foreſeen, that in the middle of the 18th century there would be a ſet of Chriſtians, who, as to the mode of recording the marriages of the members of their community, would be allowed the like indulgence that was reſerved for the royal family. In juſtice, however, to the Quakers, it may be obſerved, that their weddings are publicly celebrated; and that they deem it a compliment if the ſpectators, whoever they may be, will be ſubſcribing witneſſes to the nuptial union of the young friends.

There have been attempts, from time to time, to render the plan of Cromwell more extenſive, more correct, and more beneficial; and the failure of them is to be regretted. Of theſe attempts one was the bill written by Boweſey*; not noticed, I ſuſpect, by either Burnet or Collier in their General Hiſtories, nor by Strype, either in his Annals, or in Life of Parker; but in which there were capabilities that might have been perfected by the wiſdom of parliament.

In the original directions in the reign of King Henry VIII. birth, as well as baptiſm, was to be regiſtered; in the directions in the reigns of Edward VI. and Elizabeth, and by the canon of 1603, the baptiſms only are mentioned; but it is obſervable, that, in the bill compiled by Boweſey, the time of birth was to be kept in the Book of Remembrance, and for this ſubſtantial reaſons are aſſigned, to which more might be added. There is not a day-labourer to whom ſuch a memorial may not be of uſe; as, after the death of parents, and of perſons preſent at a birth, very difficult is it to meet with ſatisfactory evidence of the fact. And yet it will frequently happen that there is ſo great an interval between the days of birth and baptiſm, that, could the former be aſcertained, a man might be proved to be paſt the age in which he is liable to be balloted for a militia-man. From a conviction of the expediency of recording births, I have for ſeveral years paſt been in the habit of acquiring the needful information; and, though for a time I perceived, with ſome ſurprize, that it was a matter of indifference to the parents, I now find that they have altered their minds. It is, however, my wiſh to have my intelligence from mothers and nurſes rather than from fathers, becauſe I have often occaſion to obſerve, that days of the month are not apt to make an impreſſion on the memories of the latter; *e. g.* I am not unfrequently told by a father that Jack or

* See p. 5.

Dick

Dick was born a day or two before, or a day or two after, or Chriftmas, or Lady-tide, or Midfummer, or Milemas; or he takes his date from the fair of W. (St. George's day), or the fair of D. (May-day); or when the increafe of family was at a diftance from fuch noted æra, the anfwer is perhaps to this purport, that the child was born on laft Thurfday fortnight, or laft Friday three weeks; however, with this *datum*, and the aid of an almanack, the point can be eafily adjufted; and I beg leave to repeat, that, as the pooreft man may be interefted by having his birth minuted, it ought not to be omitted.

A lawyer has more than once hinted to me, that, as it is founded upon hearfay evidence, it may not be deemed admiffible in Weftminfter-hall; however, *valeat quantum*, when better evidence is wanting; and I am fure that this confideration ought to have its weight, that neither parent nor paftor can have any finifter motive for making an incorrect entry.

On the regiftering of burials I fhall only obferve, that it may be advifable, when an opportunity offers, to fpecify the place of birth of the deceafed, and of the maiden name of the woman, in cafe of her being married; and why not notice her age, as that particular may be the means of identifying the perfon!

Formerly, as it fhould feem, the keepers of regifters were expofed to actions of damages for neglect of duty*; it being declared in Bowefey's bill, p. 5, "that it oftentimes

* Of the carelefs keeping of regifters, fee Gent. Mag. vol. LXIV. p. 1166.

Dr. Burnaby, the prefent Archdeacon of Leicefter, in a late excellent Charge to his Clergy, very forcibly recommends the ftricteft attention and regard to the keeping of parifh regifters, and to the making out and preferving of full and faithful accounts of parochial charities. "The former, he fays, is of great confequence to the civil and temporal interefts of mankind, that perhaps no one regulation is pregnant with more various or more weighty confequences; for, upon accurate accounts of the births, the marriages, and the deaths, of individuals, the order of fucceffion, of inheritance, and, in fhort, the entire property and fortune of families frequently depends.—It is well known in our courts of judicature how much confufion and what infuperable difficulties have arifen from the want or neglect of them Indeed, too much care and attention cannot be paid to this article: and where, by procefs or length of time, regifters are in danger of perifhing or becoming illegible, it would be highly commendable, I think, were the minifters and churchwardens of parifhes, while the meafure is yet practicable, to have accurate and faithful copies made of them; to have them properly witneffed and authenticated; and afterwards depofited, together with their originals, in the ufual places of cuftody. Such copies, I apprehend, would be admitted and received in our courts of law as evidence or authority: but be this as it may, they certainly would be very ufeful; and might in many inftances facilitate the difcovery of facts, highly neceffary to be known, in the afcertainment and adjudication of property. I am forry to obferve, that many of the old regifters, which I have examined, are in a very mutilated and imperfect ftate. Some indeed have been irrecoverably loft: others have no binding; have had feveral leaves torn out; and in every refpect appear to have been moft fhamefully neglected. At one place, where I enquired if they had no regifter prior to the prefent century, I received the following curious anfwer: They had at this time no other regifter, they faid, except the one produced. They had had another fome time ago; but it was very old; was quite out of date; of no manner of ufe, for none of the neighbours could read it; and it had been toffed about in the church, till either fome workmen or fome children had carried it away, or elfe torn it in pieces. In fhort, it was irrecoverably loft."

The late Mr. Bigland alfo, in his ufeful "Obfervations on Marriages, Baptifms, and Burials, as preferved in Parochial Regifters," publifhed in 1764, notices fome ftriking inftances of neglect; and oftentimes fortinith, that the same persons, vicars, curates, &c. had not been able to answer the harmes of disenherison," &c.

Mr. North's observation, p. 4. l. 6. is not well founded; copies of registers not being regularly delivered at visitations, and, instead of being preserved and kept in excellent order throughout the kingdom, they are in divers offices *indigesta moles* *, covered with dust, decaying by mould, and food for worms. The cause is plain; they were to be received *sine ullo feodo*, without hardly a chance of receiving a fee for a search. It was doubtless in order effectually to obviate this objection, that, by the bill to authorize the erecting one office of registership of all the church-books to be kept in every diocese, a provision was made, that the churchwardens should collect money, from persons in circumstances to pay it, for every entry in a register, which was to be transmitted to the register-general, though it may puzzle a man of a moderate capacity to assign a plausible reason, why a widow on the burial of her husband was to contribute 1*d*. only, and a man at the interment of his wife is to pay 2*d*.

In Gent. Mag. vol. LXVI. pp. 985, 986, are noticed the advantages that would arise from an Index to Parish-registers. This meritorious service has actually been done by the Rev. John Pridden, M. A. F. A. S. to a considerable part of the extensive register of St. Bride's parish, where he was several years curate; and to a great portion of the register of Maidstone parish an index has in like manner been made by the present minister of that parish.

"Mr. John Antram (vicar of Helton, Dorsetshire) has entered a memorandum in the register 1660, that, in the time of the Civil Wars, he was by the power of the sword violently kept out of his living, from Michaelmas 1646 till Michaelmas 1660, when he was by law restored; so that, in that compass of time, the register has been kept very imperfect." Hutchins's History, vol. II. p. 420.

"Bishopweremouth register begins—" Si quis registrum hoc mutilare in ulla parte, vel nomen aliquod delere, addere, aut in falsum immutare, vel quovis alio modo violare audeat, pro sacrilego habeatur à Domino. Tho. Broughton, curatus."

"The above Mr. Broughton has kept all the registers in a most exact manner; and they are continued to the present time in the best form of any Parochial registers in the county: the births are inserted as well as the baptisms." Mr. Allan's Notes, in Hutchinson's History and Antiquities of Durham, vol. II. p. 512.

and one case where the clerk, being a tailor, had applied sixteen leaves, and part of another, out of a Register which consisted originally only of eighteen, to the use of slips for measuring his customers.—Two parishes in Leicestershire, it may be added, owe the preservation of their Registers to the writer of this note; who rescued one of them from the shop of a bookseller; the other from (a much worse situation) the corner-cupboard of a working blacksmith, where it had lain perishing and unheard-of for more than 30 years.

* Mr. Bigland informs us, that under the stair-case of a certain Cathedral, in a place on the North side of the North aile, on the damp ground, without the security of a door, free for any one to go to, he found a promiscuous heap of extracts of registers, some very fairly transcribed, from the different parishes of the diocese. These, by reason of the damps, were exposed to depredations equally destructive as those said to be committed by the tailor; and probably are, if not since removed to some securer place, either lost or become illegible.

IN-

INSTRUCTIONS FOR MY LORD PRIVEY SEALL (CROMWELL), CONCERNING THE BISHOP OF LINCOLNE, AND HIS ARCHD', TOUCHING THE BISHOP HIS DEMAND OF PRESTATIONS.

(From a MS. in Bibl. Cotton Cleopatra F. I. 4.)

WHAT apperteyneth to th'office of an archdeacon, and whereupon his revenewſe, and what heretofore hath thereunto appertayned:

Procurations.
Synodals.
Peter-Pens.
Penſions or indemnities.
Fines of teſtaments.
Vacations of benefices.
Inſtallations of abbots.

Procurations be dewe for viſitation. Th'archdeacon is bownde yerely to viſite all his archdeaconry thoroweoute; then to enquire of all crimes and miſgovernance of the people, as well the clergie as the laitee, by churchwardens and other; and to reforme whatſoever they finde otherwiſe than well, other committede haynouſly againſt the lawes of God, or th' ordinance of the prince for a quiet commonwele, diſſonant to God's lawes, to man's lawes, and politique order of the worlde; to reforme the ſame, other by godly perſuaſion and good advice, by commination, or by paynes and penaltyes, according to the humility and umble ſubjection of the offender, and repentans of the offens. For this his viſitation he hath procurations.

Synodalls be dewe for the fene *, kept at Eſter by th'archdeacon, or his officers; calling together the parſons, the vicars, and pariſh prieſts, diligently enquiring if every of the ſame doe and have done their dewties according to the lawes of God, lawes of the prince eſtabliſhed, and th'ordinance of the churche accuſtomede; and have godely and diligently miniſterede all ſacraments and ſacramentals to their pariſhioners at Eſter then paſt, and ſoe the yere before. For this kind of viſitation ſinodals be dewe to the archdeacon, wiche the biſhope wolde now in any wiſe have, becauſe of a decretale that ſaith *quod epiſcopo debentur ſynodalia*; and for that text now wolde the biſhope turne from his Peter-pens, calling them Preſtations or penſions, and wolde have now dewe for ſynodalls, wiche the archdeacons have had and enjoyed this . . . hundrethe yeeres, without let, interruption, or contradiction, of any biſhope. My ſynodals be not 19*l.* by yere, and yet muſt I give to my official 5 marks fee yerely, and as much to my regiſter; and alſo bere their coſts yearly in riding to the ſene 4 or 5*l.* ſo have I not 10*l.* clear for my ſynodalls. But put the caſe that theſe ſynodals were the biſhop's, yet wherefore ſhould I be bounde to gather his ſynodalls? or why ſhould I give 20 nobles to my officers to ſerve him, and to be his collector? *Dicat Apollo.*

* *Synod.* A payment made by the clergy when they met the biſhop in ſynod, and claimed by the archdeacon, or any other ſpiritual perſon, only on the foot of compoſition or preſcription. Burn.

All archdeacons of England gathered *Peter-pens* of every fyer-houſhold within every pariſhe one penye, which were granted eight hundred yers paſt by King Hyvo, and aftir confyrmed by Inas, then by Offa Rex Merciorum, by Arnulphus, and other moe following, and by John for his time. Aftir ſome antique authors, they were granted for a yerely preſt, or a perpetuall yerely ſubſidy. *Epiſcopo Romano præſtabantur in ſubſidium*, ſaith divers authors. Others ſay they were given to a ſcole in Rome, to the mayntenance of Engliſh ſcolars there, as Fabian and Guido, with other; but now th'archdeacons, after thes pens gathered, paid the ſame in part, or all, to the collector of Rome, ſaving the archdeacon of Lincolne and Sarum; theſe payd the pens gathered to the biſhope, the biſhope payd to the collector, and had his acquitance by the name of Peter-pens. Th'archdeacons had their acquitance of the biſhope by the name of preſtation-money; ſo the biſhope of Lincolne payd, but he gathered none: th'archdeacon gathered and payd, not to the collector, but onely to the biſhope. Soe, finally, ſeeing the biſhope never gathered Peter-pens, and yet payd them to the collectors every yere, and th'archdeacons gathered them yerely, and none to the collector, but only to the biſhope; what ſhould the biſhop his demaunde be other than Peter-pens?

To prove that this word *Preſtation* is very Peter-pens, it is ſo manifeſtly declared in the biſhope of Rome his own lawe, in an epiſtle-decretall, ſent *epiſcopo Cantuar' & ſuffraganeis ſuis*. The biſhope of Lincolne is one of his ſuffragans; and perchance it was meant for him that was then biſhope of Lincolne, if he were as nigh ſcrapyng as the biſhope that now ys at this preſent time. *Textus eſt in capitulo de cenſibus*, in the decretals, *ea quæ de avaritia verba ſunt hæc. Ne gravetis parochias & eccleſias veſtras propter viſitationem beati Petri, cum feceritis collectam denariorum*. Gloſſator Bernardus, one of the biſhope of Rome his ſecretaryes, expoundeth *hoc verbum Collectum. Collecta, inquit, eſt præſtatio quædam quam Anglici ſolvunt eccleſiæ Romanæ; & debet eſſe moderata, &c.* Soe the Preſtation is taken for Peter-pens in the biſhope of Rome his own lawe.

Penſions, or *indemnityes*, be theſe. When a church is improprede to an abbeye or college, then the archdeacon for ever loſyth his induction-money; and in recompence of that, he ſhall have yerely, out of the ſaid benefice ſoe improprede, 12*d*. or 2*s*. for a yerely penſion, more or leſſe, as hit is agreed at the tyme of the impropriation. And this money is called penſions, or indemnityes. And like as the archdeacon *conſervatur indempnis* by this his yerely penſion, payd in the liew of the induction; even ſoe *epiſcopus conſervatur indempnis*, and hath a like penſion for his indemnitye, in the liew of his inſtitution, which he likewiſe calleth his penſion.

The title of *Archdeacon* is of no leſs antiquity than the primitive times of Chriſtianity; the uſe then being, that the deacons did elect out of themſelves one whom they knew to be moſt eminent for his induſtry, and gave him that title, to ſuperintend the clergy, by making viſitations.

DE

DE OFFICIO ARCHI[DIACO]NORUM, ET EORUM PRÆEMINENTIA, ET JURAMENTO, ET CENSU ANNUO.

ARCHI[DIACO]NORUM orta in ecclesiâ poteſtas & officium in exteriori juriſdictione conſiſtit ut ſubcitorum curas gerant, eorum cauſas juſto libramine dirigentes, mores reformantes & exceſſus corrigentes juxta qualitates delinquentium & exceſſuum quantitatem. Sane, contemplatione dignitatis ſuæ intra eccleſiam, in voce, ceſſione, & proceſſione & aliis hujuſmodi, præeminentiam ante alios ſimplices canonicos eos ſortiri volumus, dumtamen fuerint præbendati & pariter inſtallati; quorum major ſit Lincoln, poſt eum Northampton, tertio Leiceſtr', quarto Buckingham, quinto Oxon', ſexto Huntingdon, ſeptimo Bedford, octavo Stow.

Præſtant archidiaconi predicti epiſcopo obedientiæ & fidelitatis juramentum ratione exterioris adminiſtrationis; pro quo, & pro cathedralis ſynodalicis & denariis beati Petri per archidiaconos ipſos in ſynodis quas vice epiſcopi celebrant receptis, ac aliis juribus epiſcopalibus, ſunt eidem epiſcopo cenſuales in ſummis ſequentibus, ad terminos Sancti Michaelis Archidiaconi & Paſchæ per equales portiones ſolvend'.

Archidiaconus Lincoln (ut prefertur) reſpondet de annuo cenſu	c marc'.
De quibus reſpondet ad manus epiſcopi ad predictos terminos —	XLIIII l.
Item, prebendar' præbendæ Decem librarum de burſo epiſcopi in ecclesiâ Lincoln — — — —	X l.
Item, præbendar' præbendæ de Karelton Kyme, in eadem eccleſiâ Lincoln — — — — —	L s.
Item, quatuor virgariis in eccleſiâ Lincoln percipientibus ſtipendia ſua de epiſcopo ad eoſdem terminos æqualiter —	LVIII s.
Item, in pretio balſami quam idem archidiaconus propriis expenſis annuatim miniſtrabit epiſcopo die Cenæ ad criſma conſecrand'	X l.
Archidiaconus Northampton — — —	LIIII l. X s.
Archidiaconus Leiceſtr' — — —	XXIX l. VI s. VIII d.
Archidiaconus Buckingham — — —	XX l.
Archidiaconus Oxon' — — — —	XX l.
Archidiaconus Bedford — — — —	XIIII l.
Archidiaconus Huntingdon — — —	XXVIII l.
Archidiaconus Stow — — — —	XX l.
De quibus reſpondet ad manus epiſcopi ad prefatos terminos equaliter	VII l.
Item, magiſtro hoſpitalitis Sanctæ Mariæ Magdalenæ de la Malandrye ex Lincoln — — — —	XIIII l.

This is a true copy, taken out of the regiſtry of the dean and chapter of Lincoln, faithfully examined, the 16th day of May, 1733, by us,

MOSES TERRY, regiſtrar. JOHN BRADLEY, N. P.

Extractum ex Regiſtro Novo Eccl' Cathedralis Beatæ Mariæ Lincoln, quod compilatum fuit anno Domini milleſimo quadringenteſimo quadrageſimo, tempore ſcilicet preſulatûs Gulielmi Alnwick tunc dictæ eccleſiæ epiſcopi.

ENDOWMENTS OF VICARAGES.

" THE method purſued in allotting vicars their portions was this. An inquiſition was made, in the chapters of the rural deans *, into the value of the rectories, and the competent portions to be aſſigned to the vicarages; regard being always had, in proportioning the laſt to the nature and ſize of the cure. A return was then made to the biſhop, who was to approve and confirm the acts of the chapters, and had power withal to make any neceſſary alteration in them; after which, the allotment was to be entered in the biſhop's regiſter, he, in effect, having the whole management of the buſineſs in his hand †.

The quota uſually apportioned to vicars comes next to be conſidered. At *Stodham*, [Herts], the vicar was to have the whole *altaragium* except one mark, the tythe of lambs, and a croft, which contained about ſeven acres. The rectory was judged to be worth 20 marks, and the profits of the vicarage ſix, ſo that the vicar enjoyed ſomething leſs than a third part of the value of the living. *Huſſeburne* was eſtimated at twelve marks, and the vicar was to have five marks and four ſhillings, to ariſe from the altarage, a houſe, a croft, and a croft and meadow on the ſouth. By *altaragium* in theſe caſes is evidently meant *all ſmall tithes and dues*; and it is as clear, that the rule obſerved in providing for a vicar was to inveſt him with a revenue of five or ſix marks, ſix at the moſt, and five at the leaſt ‡; theſe ſums being eſteemed a competent maintenance at the time for a ſingle perſon, and even to enable him to maintain ſome degree of hoſpitality ||. It appears again, that the vicar's portion conſiſted of manſe, glebe, and ſome ſhare of the profits of the living; and that in the ſmaller livings his part was proportionably the greateſt.

As to the *onera*, as they were called, incident to eccleſiaſtical livings, the vicars were generally to bear ſome part of them. Thus the priory of Dunſtable, in conſideration of the large ſhare it enjoyed of the profits of the above livings, was to entertain the archdeacon in his parochial viſitation, to find books, veſtments, utenſils, to repair the chancels, and to pay the ſubſidies §; and the vicars were to take all other burthens upon them **."

Thus far from the Life of Biſhop Groſſeteſte by the late very learned Dr. Pegge; who, in the courſe of his enquiries on this ſubject, received from Mr. Fardell, Regiſtrar of the dioceſe of Lincoln, the following remarks on Bp. Wells's Roll.

" Mr. Johnſon's account, in the Archæologia ††, of Biſhop Wells's book of endowments, is not correct. He aſſerts, it contains the endowments of *all* the vicarages

* Theſe were epiſcopal officers, employed by, and under the archdeacons. They were uſually concerned in eſtimating the value of livings, &c. † Sir Henry Chauncy, p. 37

‡ The refectory of Mickleover, in the county of Derby, was rated in 1154, at twenty ſhillings for a tenth, and therefore was worth ten pounds *per annum*, and the vicar anſwered for a third part, 3*l.* 6*s.* 8*d.* or five marks. || Burton's Deſcription of Leiceſterſhire, p. 185.

§ Vicars, however, often paid tenths, &c. Thorne, inter X Script. col. 2162, 2170, ſeq. This, therefore, depended entirely on the particular terms and covenants of the ordinations.

** " Et ſciendum, quod prior ſuſtinebit *onera* quod hoſpicium archidiaconi, et ſuſtentationem in libris, et cancellis, et veſtimentis, utenſilibus, et talligiis, pro ſua portione, alia onera ſuſtinebit vicarius." Annal. Dunſtap. ibidem. The uſual *onera* of vicars in M. Paris, in Vit. Abb. p. 131. are " Parochialia, ſynodalia, archidiaconalia, ordinaria et conſueta;" which ſhews, that theſe things varied in different places, according as the agreements were made. †† Vol. I. p. 30.

carages in the diocefe; whereas it contains only an account of the endowments of fuch vicarages as were endowed by, or previous to the time of, Bifhop Wells. Great numbers of vicarages were afterwards endowed; and the endowments are interfperfed in the feveral Regifter-books of the Bifhops of Lincoln till the Reformation, when the bifhop's power to ordain vicarages ceafed.

The book you refer to is a thin quarto, containing 32 leaves of vellum or parchment. The feveral years in which the refpective ordinations were made are not afcertained, the only diftinctions being—" auctoritate concilii ordinata"—" ex dudum ordinata"—" ab antiquo ordinata"—I therefore cannot point out with certainty fuch vicarages as were endowed prior to the year 1219; but rather think the greater part of thofe entered in this book were ordained before that time, becaufe Bifhop Wells, immediately upon fucceeding to the fee of Lincoln, fet about carrying into execution the canon; and one made in the council at London in the year 1200, relative to the procuring of a better maintenance for the fecular clergy. One endowment occurs in the firft year of his prefiding over the fee.

I will give you a fhort account of this book, which I have in the autograph of my worthy and much-efteemed friend, the late Mr. Bradley; who defcribes it thus:

" The general title of the book is, *Liber antiquus de Ordinationibus Vicariarum tempore Hugonis Wells*; by which title it has been known for fome hundred years; and therein are regiftered the endowments of fome hundreds of vicarages between the years 1209 and 1235, when the bifhop died; the diocefe then extending over the counties of Lincoln, Leicefter, Northampton, Rutland, Oxford, Bucks, Huntingdon, and Bedfordfhire, with part of Hertfordfhire. The endowments are arranged under their feveral counties." Mr. Bradley accounts for the neceffity of the canon in 1200, for the better maintenance of the fecular clergy, thus: " Before the year 1200, the fuperftitious Normans, as an atonement for their oppreffions, exactions, plundering, difpoffeffing, and flaughter, of the Saxon and Englifh noblemen and gentlemen, were perfuaded by the priefts of that age of the neceffity of good works, and of founding and endowing religious houfes, and beftowing benefactions to monks and friars, to pray for their fouls, and the fouls of their anceftors: for this purpofe, and by this means, it was, that fo many religious houfes were erected; and parfonages or rectories, and perpetual advowfons, with the whole tithes and profits, were appropriated to abbeys and monafteries, referving only a fcanty allowance for the fervice of the cure by a fecular prieft, in fome of them no more than what the monks thought proper to allow, and in others the cure was ferved by a friar of the monaftery having epifcopal ordination. In order to remedy this evil, and to make fome provifion for the fecular clergy, at a general council held at London in the year 1200, a canon was enacted in thefe words: 'Decernimus ut in qualibet ecclefiâ monachorum, vel quorumlibet religioforum, fui ufibus canonicè appropriatâ, vicarius inftituatur provifione epifcopi, honeftam & fufficientem fuftentationem *de bonis ecclefiæ percepturus*.' It was under the fanction of this canon that Bifhop Wells took into confideration the ftate of the appropriate rectories in his diocefe, and endowed fo many vicarages, the vicars whereof being not otherwife fufficiently provided for before his time; and this accounts for the words, *auctoritate concilii*, in the many endowments made by him during his incumbency on the bifhoprick.

The

The late Dr. Ducarel took an account of the endowments in this book, which he considered as containing the endowments of *all* the vicarages in the diocese of Lincoln, when, in fact, it contains only a part of them; and I have reason to believe some clergymen were prevented from searching the office and finding their endowments, having been informed by Dr. Ducarel they were not recorded.

I hope to compleat an accurate Repertory of the Endowments of all the Vicarages in this diocese; which will certainly be of use to the Clergy of it."

In the course of the correspondence on this subject, Dr. Pegge thus explained some terms, which occasionally occur in those endowments.

"*Lætare* is Midlent-Sunday *, when the *Introit* to the mass begins *Lætare Jerusalem*, as may be seen in the Missals. It is referred to in the Annals of Burton, p. 372, as an epoch, or day, well known, in these words, "Die dominicâ post dominicum quâ cantatur *Lætare Jerusalem*, in capitulo Westmonasteriensi, coram prælatis, &c." This was in 1256.—*Procurations* may be here intended; and masses, it seems, were to be on Midlent Sunday in this singular instance; or a *pension*, as, in cases of appropriating rectories to monasteries, archdeacons had a pension from the rectories oftentimes, in recompence of the loss of their rights.

There was a *Legatum Principale* for a vicar, at Wimeswold, in Leicestershire †, to receive 'omnes proventus illius ecclesiæ, exceptis decimis tam garbarum quam minoribus & principalibus legatis;' and of consequence the *Legatum Secundum* had a reference to that; and therefore, on translating this term, it may be expressed, I think, by saying, *a mortuary of the second value*, as mortuaries differed much in value, according to the rank and quality of the person deceased. It can never be supposed that two mortuaries were paid for one person, though there was such a thing, as you well know, as a *corps present*. I do not imagine that *Legatum Secundum*, a mere ecclesiastical expression, had any relation to the lord's heriot."

This produced from Mr. Fardell a farther elucidation of the same terms.

"The information you have given me respecting the term *Lætare* has enabled me to trace the origin of it more minutely than I had done before; and I am now certain it is not synonymous with *Procurations*, as I had first imagined; for, upon looking into the endowment of Erdete, in the county of Huntingdon, recorded in Bp. Sutton's Register-Book of Institutions, fol. 85. in which, after enumerating what particular species of tithe the vicar should receive, is added, "Onera autem ecclesiæ predictæ incumbentia sunt hæc, sustentatio vicarii & unius clerici, procurationes archid', synodalia, & Lætare, quibus modò onerandus sit vicarius." This evidently shews that the *Lætare* is a payment of a different nature from *Procurations*; and, upon looking into Cowel's Interpreter, I find he thus explains the word:

'*Lætare Jerusalem*, the old duty of Quadragesimals, or the customary oblations made on Midlent-Sunday (when the proper hymn was *Lætare Jerusalem*, &c.) by the inhabitants within a diocese, to the mother cathedral church; which old custom of procession and oblation at that time was the beginning of the practice, which is still retained among us, of mothering, or going to visit parents on Midlent-Sunday.

* A paper of Dr. Pegge's, on the subject of *Lætare Jerusalem*, communicated to the Society of Antiquaries, was controverted by Sir H. C. Englefield, bart. and both suppressed together.

† Burton, p. 310.

These

Thefe voluntary offerings on that Sunday were by degrees fettled into an annual compofition, or pecuniary payment, charged on the parochial prieft, who was prefumed to receive them from his people, and obliged to return them to the cathedral church.'

Under the word *Quadragefimalia*, Cowel fays, ' It was the cuftom for people to vifit their mother-church on Midlent Sunday, and to make their offerings at the high altar, as the like devotion was to be obferved in Whitfun-week; but, as the proceffions and oblations at Whitfuntide were fometimes commuted into a rated payment of Pentecoftals or Whitfun-farthings, fo likewife the Lent devotion was changed into a cuftomary rate, called *Quadragefimalia* and *Denarii Quadragefimales*, and fometimes *Lætare Jerufalem*, becaufe that hymn was fung on Midlent Sunday.'

This fully confirms your conjecture, and fhews whence the payment derived its name and origin. And, in Bp. Gravefend's Roll of Inftitutions, anno 12. I find the endowment of Bilfby, where it is faid, the impropriators fhall bear all burthens incumbent upon the rectory, ' fynodalibus & *Lætare Jerufalem* duntaxat exceptis;" and to this day the impropriator there pays the Procurations, and the vicar the Synodals. This, I think, farther corroborates the conjecture, and evinces that the *Lætare* was a payment, or cuftomary offering, different from Procurations, but fomewhat fimilar to Pentecoftals, ufually paid by the parifh-prieft to the mother-church of the diocefe; and was probably paid to the archdeacon, for the ufe of the mother-church. At this time the archdeacon of Lincoln pays annually to the dean and chapter, at Whitfunday, 1*l.* 9*s.* 8*d.* under the denomination of Pentecoftals. I prefume, the archdeacon might alfo receive the *Lætare* for the dean and chapter; and probably the two payments of *Lætare*, or Pentecoftals, being due nearly at the fame time, might afterwards be confidered as one, and accounted for under the name of Pentecoftals only.

In looking into fome old endowments, I meet with the term " principali legato;" as, " vicar' in eccl'a de Bramfeud habebit nomine ppet' vic' totum altaragium, cum *principali legato*."—Lyndwood, de Decimis in cap. Quoniam propter, verb. *Legati Principalis*, fays, " Iftud dicitur mortuarium, & vocatur principale legatum, quia decedentes folebant, & in quibufdam partibus adhuc folent, optimum vel fecundum optimum fuum animal primo & ante cetera legata Deo & Ecclefiæ pro animâ fuâ legare." And the fame author, De Confuetudine, cap. *Statutum*, fays, if the deceafed had three or more animals, the beft fhall be given to him to whom it is due, and the fecond beft be referved for the church. As the cuftoms of places varied very much with refpect to the value of mortuaries, it feems not improbable that, when the cuftom prevailed for the minifter to have the principal animal, or firft choice of the deceafed goods, it was called *Principale Legatum*; and when by cuftom he was to take the fecond beft animal, or fecond choice of the goods of the deceafed, it was called *Secundum Legatum*; and I think the text of the firft abovementioned Legatine Conftitution feems rather to favour this conjecture; for it fays, ' In petitione autem principalis legati volumus quod confuetudo provinciæ, cum poffeffione Ecclefiæ, obfervetur.'—Your tranflation of the words *Secundum Legatum*, ' a mortuary of the fecond value,' I conceive to be the moft proper that can be made ufe of.

I have

I have in my poſſeſſion a parchment roll, containing the names of the mayors and bailiffs of the city of Lincoln, beginning in the 34th year of Edward III; and, when any very remarkable event has happened, the writer has noted it briefly; as, in the 11th year of Richard, he ſays, "This year the archbiſhop of York, with others, was empeched of trayſon." The following words frequently occur, "Ludus de Pater noſter hoc anno;" and there is alſo mentioned, "Ludus Sc̃i Laurencii," "Ludus Sc̃e Suſanne," "Ludus de Sc̃o Jacobo," "Ludus Corpus Xp̃i, &c."

I applied to a ſenſible Roman Catholic prieſt, for an explanation of the *Ludus Pater Noſter, Ludus Sc'i Laurencii, &c.*; but he could not give me any information upon the ſubject. May I requeſt the favour of your explanation of theſe terms?

To which Dr. Pegge thus replied:

"It was cuſtomary in the Romiſh times to have proceſſions, ſports, ſacred interludes, or plays, on various feſtivals, thoſe particularly of the ſaints to whom the reſpective gilds or fraternities were ſacred, and whom we may call their patron ſaints. Hence came the extraordinary celebrities of Corpus Chriſti * day, which is met with ſo often in authors prior to the Reformation. Thus, I conceive, there might be a gild of *Pater Noſter* at Lincoln; of which the members in certain years, not every year, exhibited a grand and extraordinary ſhow, for the entertainment of the people, and to induce them to become members of their ſociety. *Pater Noſters*, I confeſs, are no Church holyday in thoſe times. This, however, does not hinder but there might be a gild or fraternity of that denomination at Lincoln. This is certain, that a fraternity of the *Roſary* † occurs in Du Freſne, in v. and that is very near akin to it. This is the moſt probable explanation I can give of thoſe paſſages. Indeed, if *Pater Noſter* can ſignify the *Chapel*, or *Roſary*, as I ſuppoſe it may (ſee Du Freſne, v. *Pater Noſter*); then *Ludus de Pater Noſter* and *Ludus Roſarii* will be the ſame. But you will aſk, how happens it that it is called by one name in one place, and by a different one in another ‡? I anſwer, becauſe the paſſages were written in different times, and by different perſons probably. Now theſe *Pageants*, as they were commonly called, conſiſted chiefly of repreſentations of the legends or ſtories of the reſpective ſaints, as of St. Lawrence, St. Suſanna, &c. But, as this was not the caſe with the *Roſary*, we know not now in what manner the gild celebrated this feſtival."

* Among the guilds at Leiceſter, that of Corpus Chriſti appears to have been the principal one. The others were called Trinity guild, St George's guild, and St. Margaret's guild.

† The fraternity of the Roſary was inſtituted againſt the Saracen pirates, or againſt the Albigenſes, by St. Dominic; for authors differ about it. Du Freſne in v. The prayer of the Roſary, invented by St. Dominic, was addreſſed to the Virgin Mary, with meditations, containing a ſhort recapitulation of the life of Chriſt. As no *Ludus* or pageant belonged to this fraternity, neither does the acceptation of *Pater Noſter*, as ſynonymous with *Roſarians*, a ſtring of beads, at all apply to it R. G.

‡ In France they had formerly an holyday, called, the Feaſt of Fools. "The prieſts and clerks went maſqued to church, and, at their return from thence, went about the ſtreets, and, mounted on ſtages, performing all the moſt impudent poſtures and buffoonries, with which watermen are wont to divert the fooliſh mob. That feſtival continued in France above 150 years, fom the 12th to the 15th century. See Critical Dictionary, vol. III. p. 115.

Annis Regnorum PHILIPPI & MARIE, Regis & Regine, &c. tercio & quarto.

Newe Yere's Guiftes geuon to the Quenis Maieſtie, by theſe Perſones whoſe Names hereafter enſue, the firſt of January, the Yeres abouesaide.

(From an original Roll, formerly belonging to Sir WILLIAM HERRICK, of BEAUMANOR; and ſtill in the poſſeſſion of his immediate Deſcendant, WILLIAM HERRICK, Eſq.)

Marye the quene

BY the Lorde Cardenall his grace, a faulte, with a couer of ſiluer and guilt, having a ſtone in the ſame, and muche enamyled therin of the ſtorye of Job, weing, 48 oz. in compō R. Willbram.
Delyverid into the office of the Quein's Maieſtie's jewells and plate.

By the Ladie *Elizabeth* her grace, the fore part of a kyrtell, and a peire of ſleves of cloth of ſilv', richly enbraudered all ouer with Venice ſilver, and rayzed with ſilu' and blake ſilke.
Delyverid to Thomas Hobbes, yeoman of the reobes.

By the Lady *Anne of Cleve*, in haulf ſoueraignes — 20 0 0
With the Quein's Majeſtie.

By the Lady *Margarett Strainge*, in golde and ſiluer — 6 13 4
With the Quein's Majeſtie.

By the Duke of *Norff'*, a cup of chriſtall, with two eares, garniſshed with ſiluer and guilt, weing 35 oz. in compō R. Willbram.
Geven to Jacob Royoſon, eodem die.

By the Marques of *Wincheſter*, in half ſoueraignes — 20 0 0
With the Quein's Majeſtie.

EARLES.

By the Earle of *Arundell*, lorde ſtewarde, in a ruſſet purſe, in hauf foueraignes — —	30	0	0
By the Earle of *Shrewiſburye*, in haulf foueraignes —	20	0	0
By the Earle of *Darby*, in Frenche crownes, and two haulf foueraignes	20	0	0
By the Earle of *Huntingdon*, in piſtoletts —	15	0	0
By the Earle of *Weſtmorlande*, in golde —	10	0	0
By the Earle of *Oxfurde*, lorde great chamberlen, in haulf foueraignes	10	0	0
By the Earle of *Rutlande*, in haulf foueraignes —	8	0	0
By the Earle of *Penbroke*, in a purſe of golde, ſilu', and ſilke, knyt, in haulf foueraignes — —	30	0	0
By the Earle of *Bath*, in a purſe of cloth of ſilver, in angelles	10	0	0

With the Quein's Maieſtie.

By the Earle of *Suſſex*, a guilt cup, with a couer, weing 24 oz. di. in compō R. Willbram.

Gevon to the Buſshoppe of *Bath*, eodem die.

VICOUNTE.

By the Vicounte *Montigue*, in French crownes —	13	6	8

With the Quein's Maieſtie.

BUSSHOPPES.

By the Archebuſshop of *Yorke*, lorde chaunclour, in angelles	40	0	0
By the Buſshop of *Elie*, in haulf foueraignes —	40	0	0
By the Buſshop of *Durkum*, in a tawny vellat purſe in haulf foueraignes — —	50	0	0
By the Buſshop of *Wincheſter*, in Frenche crownes —	50	0	8
By the Buſshop of *Saliſbury*, in Frenche crownes —	13	10	0
By the Buſshop of *Exetor*, in haulf foueraignes —	10	0	0
By the Buſshop of *Chitcheſter* elect, *Chriſtopherſon*, a booke written, couered with crymſon vellat.			
By the Buſshop of *London*, in French crownes and haulf foueraignes	20	0	0
By the Buſshop of *Lichfelde and Couentrye*, in Frenche crownes	13	6	0
By the Buſshop of *Norwiche*, in golde —	20	0	0
By the Buſshop of *Oxfourde*, in angelles —	10	0	0
By the Buſshop of *Worceſter*, in Frenche crownes —	20	0	4
By the Buſshop of *Bath*, in French crownes and two foueraignes	20	0	0

By

By the Bufshop of *St. Davye's*, in a litell red purfe, in French crownes	13	6	8
By the Bufshop of *Rochifter*, in a purfe, in haulf foueraignes	10	0	0
By the Bufshop of *Briftowe*, in haulf foueraignes —	10	0	0
By the Bufshop of *Glocefter*, in haulf foueraignes —	10	0	0
By the Bufshop of *Chefter*, in golde — —	10	0	0

With the Quein's Maieftie.

DUCHESSES, MARQUESSES, and COUNTESSES.

By the Dowches of *Norff'*, dowager, a cufshen-cloth, frenged and taffelled with golde.
Delyvered to Mrs. Babington.

By the Duches of *Norff'*, a falte of filuer and guilt, weing 15 oz. qr. in compo R. Willbram.
Gevon to the Vicountes *Mountague*, eodem die.

By the Duches of *Somerfet*, a fmoke, wrought all ou' with filke, and collor and ruffes of damafke golde, purle, and filuer.
Delyvered to the fame Mrs. Babington.

By the Lady Marquys of *Exetor*, in a litell purfe of tyncell, in angelles	10	0	0
By the Lady Marques of *Winchefter*, in haulf foueraignes —	10	0	0
By the Countes of *Surrye*, in angelles ——	5	0	0
By the Countes of *Arundell*, in haulf foueraignes ——	15	0	0
By the Countes of *Penbrouke*, in a litell purfe of grene filke and filu', in haulf foueraignes —— —	15	0	0
By the Countes of *Bedfurde*, dowager, in French crownes and thre piftoletts — — —	20	0	0
By the Countes of *Bedfurde*, in French crownes ——	10	0	0

With the Quein's Maieftie.

By the Countes of *Oxfourde*, dowager, one guilte falte, with a peper box, per oz. 10 oz. qr.

By the Countes of *Oxfourde*, in haulf foueraignes —	5	0	0
By the Countes of *Huntington*, in a red purfe, in Frenche crownes	10	0	0
By the Countes of *Shrewifbury*, dowager, in a purfe of red filke and golde, in angelles ——	10	0	0
By the Countes of *Shrewifbury*, in piftoletts, Frenche crownes, and filuer	10	0	0
By the Countes of *Darby*, in haulf foueraignes —	10	0	0
By the Countes of *Rutlande*, in haulf foueraignes ——	10	0	0
By the Countes of *Bath*, in a purfe of red filke and golde, in angelles	10	0	0

With the Quein's Maieftie.

VICOUNTES.

By the Vicountes *Herfourde*, five handkercheves, wrought with golde and red ſilke.
By the Vicountes *Mountagu*, in golde — 6 13 4

LORDES.

By the Lorde *Paget*, lorde preuie ſeale, in a purſe of grene ſilke and ſiluer, in ſoueraignes — — 20 0 0
By the Lorde *William Howarde*, lorde admyrall, in Frenche crownes 10 0 0
By the Lorde *Williams*, lorde chamberlen to the king, 28 Frenche crownes and a haulf, and fourtene piſtoletts — 13 7 2
By the Lorde *Clynton*, in angelles — — 10 0 0
By the Lorde *Cobham*, in a purſe of blake vellat and golde, in haulf ſoueraignes — — 10 0 0
By the Lorde *Riche*, in a paper, in haulf ſoueraignes — 10 0 0
By the Lorde *Darcye*, in a purſe of vellat and golde, in haulf ſoueraignes 20 0 0
By the Lorde *Stafforde*, in haulf ſoueraignes — 10 0 0
By the Lorde *Burgavennye*, in a blake ſilke purſe, in haulf ſoueraignes 5 0 0
With the Quein's Maieſtie.

By the Lorde *Windeſour*, two cruetts of chriſtall, garniſhed with ſiluer and guilt, per oz. 15 oz. qr. in compo R. Wilbrams.
By the Lorde *John Gray*, ſixe handkercheues, wrought with golde and ſiluer.
Delyverid into the office of the juells and plate.

By the Lorde *Sandewic*, in dymy ſoueraignes — 10 0 0
By the Lorde *Northe*, in a purſe of blewe ſilke and golde, in haulf ſoueraignes — — 20 0 0
By the Lorde *Robert Dudley*, a faire purſe, in haulf ſoueraignes 10 0 0
With the Quein's Maieſtie.

LADYES.

By the Lady *Pagett*, in a purſe of blewe ſilke and golde, in haulf ſoueraigns — — 10 0 0
By the Lady *Burgauenny*, in a blake ſatten purſe, in haulf ſoueraignes 5 0 0
With the Quein's Maieſtie.

By the Lady *Clynton*, a faire ſmocke, wrought with golde and blake ſilke.
Delyverid to the ſaid Mrs. Babington.

By

By the Lady *Howarde*, in piftoletts — 5 0 0
With the Quein's Maieftie.

By the Lady *Bray*, thelder, two fmockes, wrought with blake worke.
By the Lady *Grey*, the Lorde John Graye's wif, two peire of working gloues of filke, knit.
Delyverid to the faid Mrs. Babington.

By the Lady *Anne Grey*, in a filuer purfe, thre olde ryalles 45 0 0
By the Lady *Awdley*, in a litell purfe of golde, in haulf foueraignes 4 0 0
By the Lady *Sandowes*, in Frenche crownes, and filuer — 5 0 0
With the Quein's Maieftie.

By the Lady *Butler*, two faire fmockes, wrought with filke and golde.
Delyverid to Mrs. Babington aforefaid.

By the Lady *Manxwell*, in a blake purfe, in French crownes and pyftellats — — 5 0 0
By the Lady *Peter*, fome olde foueraignes — 6 0 0
By the Lady *Jernegaen*, in haulf foueraignes — 5 0 0
By the Lady *Wharton*, in a litell red purfe, in haulf foueraignes 10 0 0
By the Lady *Walgraue*, in haulf foueraignes — 5 0 0
With the Quein's Maieftie.

By the Lady *Hubblethorne*, fixe handkercheiues of white worke.
By the Lady *Shelton*, a cufshion cloth, edgid with filuer and filke, buttonned and taffelled likewife.
Delyverid to the faid Mrs. Babington.

By the Lady *Kempe*, in a faire purfe of filke and golde, in haulf foueraignes — — — 10 0 0
By the Lady *Freefton*, in a paper, in haulf foueraignes — 5 0 0
With the Quein's Maieftie.

By the Lady *Joflen*, two fmockes and foure handkercheues, edged with filke and golde.
By the Lady *Ratlyff*, a combecafe, furnifshed with ebonett and a faire chriftall glafe.
Delyverid to the faid Mrs. Babington.

By the Lady *Browne*, Juftice Browne's wif, in a purfe of red fatten, in monye of diuers coynes — — 2 19 6
By the Lady *Capell*, a purfe of golde and red filke.
With the Quein's Maieftie.

By the Lady *Mafon*, a partelett and ruffes, wrought al ou' with filuer.
By the Lady *Greye* of the Moate, a facrament cloth, frenged and taffelled richlye with golde and pearle.
Delyverid to the faid Mrs. Babington.

By

By the Lady *Yorke*, divers frutes, as 6 ſuger loues, ſixe tapnetts of figges, foure barrelles of ſucketts and oringe water, &c.
Delyverid to Mrs. Edeth Brydeman.

By the Lady *Vmpton*, a waſtecoate of white ſatten, embraudered with ſiluer.
Delyverid to the ſaid Mrs. Babington.

By the Lady *Gyfforde*, a cuſshion of nedleworke, frenged and taſſelled with golde and grene ſilke, the backſide of grene vellat.
Delyverid into the office of the removing guarderobe of beddis.

By the Lady *Jane Seymour*, a faire ſmoke of whiteworke, Flaunders making.
Delyverid to the ſaid Mrs. Babington.

By the Lady *Mordaunt*, in haulf ſoueraignes — 5 0 0
By the Lady *Shirley*, in a red ſatten purſe, in haulf ſoueraignes 4 0 0
With the Quein's Maieſtie.

By the Lady *Tyrrell*, a loking glaſſe of chriſtall, couerid with crymſon vellat, enbrauderid with golde and ſiluer.
Delyverid to the ſaid Mrs. Babington.

By the Lady *Barcklei*, in haulf ſoueraignes — 5 0 0
With the Quein's Maieſtie.

By the Lady *Dyer*, a corporas caſe of crymſon ſatten, embrauderid.
By the Lady *Cateſbye*, a combecaſe, furniſshed with combes of ebonet.
Delyverid to the ſaid Mrs. Babington.

KNIGHTS.

By Sir *Thomas Cheyny*, threaſourer, in haulf ſoueraignes — 20 0 0
By Sir *Robert Rocheſter*, comptrouler, in angelles — 66 15 0
By Sir *Henry Jarnegam*, vicechamberlen, in Frenche crownes 10 0 0
By Sir *Edwarde Haſting*, maiſter of the horſe, in piſtellettes 13 6 8
By Sir *William Peter*, ſecretary, in olde ſoueraignes — 10 0 0
By Sir *John Bowrne*, ſecretary, in gold and ſiluer — 10 0 0
With the Quene.

By Sir *Fraunces Englefilde*, maiſter of the wardes, a ſpice box of ſiluer, and guilt, with a ſpone in it, guilt, weing 31 oz. di. in compo R. Wilbram.
Delyverid into the ſaid office of juels and plate.

By Sir *Edward Walgraue*, mr of the greate warderobe, in ſoueraignes and haulf a ſoueraigne — — 10 0 0

By

By Sir *Edmunde Peckham*, threafouror of the mynt, in foueraignes	12	0	0
By Sir *Richard Sowthwell*, maifter of the armery, in angelles —	6	0	0
By Sir *John Baker*, in haulf foueraignes ——	10	0	0
By Sir *John Hurlefton*, in angelles ——	6	0	0
By Sir *Dauie Browke*, in a red purfe, in angelles ——	10	0	0
By Sir *Richarde Sackevyle*, in foueraignes ——	13	0	0
By Sir *John Yorke*, in a litell purfe, in angelles ——	8	0	0
By Sir *Walter Myldmay*, in a vellat purfe, in angelles ——	5	0	0

With the Quene.

By Sir *William Raynfourde*, twelve handkercheiues, edged with gold.
Delyverid to the faid Mrs. Babington.

By Sir *Thomas Joflen*, in angells ——	8	0	0
By Sir *William Drury*, in a purfe of red filke and golde, knyt, in haulf foueraignes —— —— ——	10	0	0

With the Quene's Maieftie.

By Sir *Leonard Chamberlen*, foure waftcoates, four peire of flevys, and foure peire of hoofen, of Garnefey making.
Delyverid to the faid Mrs. Babington.

By Sir *Phillip Parryce*, in a paper, in angelles ——	5	0	0

By Sir *John Mordaunte*, in a red purfe ——

By Sir *Henry Neuell*, a lute in a cafe, couerid with blake filke and golde, with two litell rounde blak tables, thone of the phifnamy of the emperour and the king's maieftie, thother of the king of Boheme and his wif.

By Sir *John Mafon*, a mappe of Englande, ftayned vpon cloth of filuer, in a frame of woode, having a drawing cou', painted with the king's and quein's armes, and a booke of Spanifh, couered with blake vellat.

By Sir *Richard Frefton*, coferer, in a purfe, in haulf foueraignes.	5	0	0
By Sir *Anthony Saintleger*, thre portagues ——	10	10	0

With the Quein's Maieftie.

By Sir *John Ales*, a prymer, couerid with purple vellat, and garnifshed with damofkyn worke.
Delyverid in chardge to Edward Shefilde, keper of the howfe at Grenewiche.

CHAPLAYNES.

By Doctour *Weftone*, deane of Windfour, in French crownes	10	0	0
By *Peter Vann*, deane of Salifbury, fourtie piftoletts —	12	6	8

With the Queine.

By

By *Rycardes*, clerk of the closet, a superaltary of blake stone, garnisshed with siluer and guilt.
Delyvered to the same Ricardes, to the Quein's vse.

By persone *Lewyn*, a table, with the passion, embrauderid.
By *Knight*, a booke of prayers, couerid with crymson and vellat, and garnisshed with siluer and guilt.
With the Quene her Maiestie.

By Doctor *Mallet*, junier, a faire salter, couerid with purple vellat, and garnisshed with siluer and guilt.
Delyvered to the said Rycards.

And in a red purse, in angelles — — 5 0 0
With the Quene her Maiestie.

By *Baker*, confessor, foure peire of gloues, two of them furred, and thother two lined.
Delyverid to the said Mrs. Babington.

GENTLEWOMEN.

By Maistres *Clarentius*, in a litell chery bagge of crymson satten, 21 French crownes — — 6 13 0
By Mrs. *Finche*, in a red satten purse, in haulf soueraignes 6 0 0
By Mrs. *Russell*, in a litell red purse, in haulf soueraignes — 4 0 0
By Mrs. *Sturly*, in a litell red purse, in haulf soueraignes, French crownes, and two grotes — — 6 13 4
With the Quene.

By Mrs. *Ryce*, a partelet and ruffes of blake silke.
By Mrs. *Barbara Hawke*, sixe frowes kircheues, playne.
By Mrs. *Babbington* thelder, a smocke, faire wrought with blake silke and golde.
Deliuerid to the said Mrs. Babington thyong'.

By Mrs. *Babington* the yonger, in a litell purse, in angelles 4 0 0
By Mrs. *Basset*, in siluer — — 3 6 8
With the Quene.

By Mrs. *Scurlok*, a partelett lining and ruffes, wrought with blake silke.
Delyuerid to the said Mrs. Babington.

By Mrs. *Bacon*, in haulf soueraignes — 4 0 0
By Mrs. *Mary Tomew*, in a purse of red silke and gold, in haulf soueraignes — — 5 0 0
With the Quene her Maiestie.

By Mrs. *Frankewell*, two greate bagges, and twentie and foure ſwete bagge of ſilke.

By Mrs. *Penne*, his wif of Codyton, in a wodden boxe, ſixe handkercheues, edged with paſſamayne of golde.

By Mrs. *Penne*, that was King Edwarde's nurſe, ſixe handkercheues, edged with paſſamayne of golde and ſilke.

By Mrs. *Hunnynges*, ſixe handkercheues, and two ſwete bagges.

By Mrs. *Levyna Terling*, a ſmale picture of the Trynite.

By Mrs. *Ball*, ſilkewoman, twelve handkercheves, edgid with gold.

Delyverid to the ſaid Mrs. Babington.

By Mrs. *Vincent*, a ſtowle of wallnuttre, ſet with boneworke, couered with cloth of golde, and fringed with golde.

Delyverid to Thomas Mayneman, keper of the ſtanding guarderobe at Grenew[h].

By Mrs. *Wilkenſon*, ſilkewoman, a faire purſe of golde and ſiluer cawleworke, buttoned and taſſelled, and ſome regeſters, garniſshed with golde and peerle.

With the Quene her Maieſtie.

By Mrs. *Cicyly Barnes*, thre guilt ſpones, weing 4 oz. di. in compo R. Wilbram.

Gevon to the Lady Wharton the ſame daye.

By Mrs. *Amy Shelton*, in a boxe of tyncell, ſixe handkercheves.

Delyuerid to the ſaid Mrs. Babington.

By Mrs. *Stanton*, eight Turquey-hennes.

Delyuered into the kytchen.

By Mrs. *Pawne*, ſixe handkercheves, edged with golde paſſamayne.

By Mrs. *Caveley*, a partelet, and a peire of ruffes of blake ſilke.

By Mrs. *Dannet* thelder, a combecaſe couered with vellat, and embrauderid with damaſke purle of damaſke golde, garniſshed, and a cheyne of ſiluer and guilt, with two combes in it.

Deliverid to the ſaid Mrs. Babington.

By Mrs. *Brydemay*, a holy water and ſprinkell of ſiluer and guilt.

In the pryvy chamber.

By Mrs. *Welſhe*, ſixe handkercheues of white worke, in a red box.

Delyverid to the ſaid Mrs. Babington.

By Mrs. *Mary Mychaell*, twelve piſtyllatts —— 3 14 0

With the Quene.

By Mrs. *Clyfton*, a ſmocke, wrought with blake worke.

By Mrs. *Sturley*, of London, a partelett, and a peire of ruffes, wrought with golde and blewe ſilke.
Delyverid to the ſaid Mrs. Babington.

By Mrs. *Preſton*, a fatte gooſe and a capon.
By Mrs. *Reymounde*, two ſwannes and capons.
Delyverid into the kytchen.

By Mrs. *Zyzans*, a peire of gloues, wrought with ſilke.
Delyverid to the ſaid Mrs. Babington.

By *Henrye Mynk's* wif, pomegranettes, oringes, lemans, and a table with the King's picture in it.
The table with the Quene; the fruete delivered to the ſaid Mrs. Edeth.

By *Gent*, two Gynny-cokks ſcalded.
Delyvered into the kytchen.

By *Avys Byllyard*, ſmale marchepannes, oringes, and a baſket of Frenche pypins.
Delyverid to Mrs. Edeth aforeſaid.

By Mrs. *Donn*, a ſmocke, wrought with blake ſilke.
By Mrs. *Morchows*, two night-ſmockes, wrought with blake ſilke.
By Mrs. *Woddall*, a doſſon of handkercheues, trymed with golde and ſilke.
By Mrs. *Hollande*, two handkercheues, edged with paſſamayne of golde and ſiluer.
By Mrs. *White*, two handkercheves, faire wrough with ſilu'.
Delyverid to the ſaid Mrs. Babington.

GENTELMEN.

By Maiſter *Cordall*, ſoliſter, two portagues —— 7 0 0
With the Quene her Maieſtie.

By Mr. Doctor *Owen*, two pottes of conſervas.
By Mr. Doctor *Wendy*, two potts of conſervas.
By Mr. Doctor *Hughes*, two pottes of conſervas.
Delyverid to the ſaid Mrs. Edeth.

By Mr. *Rowlande Scurlok*, a peire of knives of damoſken-worke.
Delyverid to the ſaid Mrs. Babington.

By Mr. *Mychaell Wentworth*, two fat oxen.
Delyverid into the catrye.

By

By Mr. *Thomas Myldmaye*, foure olde ſoueraignes —	6	0	0
By *Barthelmew Compayne*, tenne double ducketts —	6	13	4
By Mr. *Thomas Stanley*, in haulf ſoueraignes —	6	0	0

With the Quene.

By *White*, ſewer, a ſtanding cup of maſſer, with a couer, ſlightly garniſshed with ſiluer, with fourtene peces of ſtrainge coynes of ſilu'; the cuppe in compo R. Wilbram.
The ſtrainge coynes with the Quene; the cup delyverid to the ſaid office of the juells and plate.

By *Shefelde*, keper of Grenewich houſe, ſixe pomegranetts.
Delyverid to the ſaid Mrs. Edeth.

By *Nicholas Luzer*, a table painted with the Maundy.
With the Quene her Maieſtie.

By *Cawodde* *, printer, a book in Laten, entitelid, "Vita Chriſti, by Ludlphus Carthagienſis †," and a litell booke of an Exhortacion to yonge men.
The Exortacōn with the Quene; thother booke delyverid to the ſaid Shefild.

By *Smalwodde Croſſer*, in a boxe, nutmeggs and gynger, and long ſtawlke of cinamon electe.
Delyverid to the ſaid Mrs. Edeth.

By *Keyme*, lokeſmyth, an irone to hange the ſacrament ouer the aulter.
Delyuerid to the ſaid Rycards.

By *Nicholas Vrſin*, a faire cloke in a caſe, couerid with blake vellat.
By *John Grene*, a cofer, couerid with crymſon vellat, edged with paſſamayn of golde.
With the Quene.

By *Reyn'd Wolf* ‡, a booke, called, "Georgius Agricola de re metallicâ §."
Delyverid to the ſaid Shefilde.

By *Chapell*, bedmaker, a faire cuſshion of purple vellat, alou' embrauderid with golde.
Delyverid to the foreſaid Thomas Maynemā.

By *Thomas Kent*, ſixe handkercheves, frenged and taſſelled with gold.
Delyverid to the ſaid Mrs. Babington.

By *Knevet Skaunte*, porter, a purſe, wrought with golde.
With the Quene her Maieſtie.

* Of John Cawood, who was printer to the Queen, ſee Herbert's edition of Ames, vol. II. p. 785.
† See Maittaire, vol. V. p. 35. ‡ Of Reynard Wolf, ſee Herbert's Ames, vol. I. p. 535.
§ See Maittaire, vol. V. p. 14.

By *William St. Barbe*, a faire crosbow.
By *Allen Bandeson*, another like crosbowe.
Delyverid to John Hedde, footeman.

By *Henry Mylles*, grosser, a bottell of roose water, a lof of suger, sinamon, gynger, and nutmegges, in papers.
Delyverid to the foresaid Mrs. Edeth.

By *Nicholas Andrewe*, *Anthony Mary*, *Edwarde Devne*, and *John Pecok*, the saggbuttes, seuen fannes, to kepe of the heate of the fyer, of strawe, thon of white silke.
Delyvered to Mrs. Babington.

By Mr. *Babington*, a boke in French, couerid with grene vellat, wrytten howe a kinge shulde chose his counsaile.
With the Quene her Maiestie.

By Mr. *Norres*, twelve handkercheves, edged with siluer.
Delyverid to the said Mrs. Babington.

By Mr. *Thomewe*, in a purse of red silke and golde, in haulf soueraignes 6 0 0
With the Quene.

By Mr. *Frankewell*, a peire of perfumed gloves.
Delyverid to the said Mrs. Babington.

By Mr. *Walter Earle*, a booke, couerid with blake vellat, of the Comentary of Warre, in Englishe.
With the Quene.

By *John Soda*, sixe boxes of marmalade and cordyall.
By *Keiley*, plasterer, a cake of spice brede.
By *Boddye*, clerke of the grene cloth, a pot of grene gynger and synamon.
By *Bouett*, gardener of Richmonde, a dishe of peches and a basket of aples.
Delyverid to the foresaid Mrs. Edeth.

By *Pascall*, a peire of gloues, ꝑfumed, and cuffed with golde and siluer.
By *Thomas Gresham*, a bolte of fine Hollande, in a case of blake lether.
Delyverid to the said Mrs. Babington.

By *Thomas Northe*, tenne live partriges, in a basket.
Delyverid into the kytchen.

By *Burrage*, m^r^ cooke, a marchpane, and two dishes of jelley.
By *Bettes*, sergaunt of the pastrye, a quince pye.

By *Harrys*, fruterer, a basket of pomegranetts, cheryes, apples, oringes, and lemans.
Delyverid to the said Mrs. Edeth.

By

By *Browne*, hoſeyere, thre peire of hoſen.
Delyverid to the ſaid Mrs. Babington.

By *Foſter*, fyſhmonger, a caſting bottell of ſilu' and guilt, weing 11 oz. 3 qr. in compo R. Wilbram.
Delyverid into the ſaid office of the juells and plate.

By *Myles Huggard*, a booke written.
With the Quene her Maieſtie.

By *Phillip Manwaring*, two peire of gloues.
By *Fraunc is Euerarde*, two peire of gloues.
By *Jones*, taylor, a waſtcoate of white lynen, quylted.
Delyverid to the ſaid Mrs. Babington.

By *Hunyngs*, a deske couerid with crymſon vellat.
By *John Demolyn*, a cloke with a lambe on it of copper, guilt.
By *John Baſſon* and his bretherne, one faire cytterne.
By *Marke Barnarde*, a rounde perfume of damaske worke, with a box of perfumes in it.
By *Armygell Wade*, a glaſſe of aqua compoſſata.
By *Holforde*, ſewer, a purſe of grene ſilke and ſiluer.
With the Quene her Maieſtie.

By the Henchemen, a peire of gloues.
By *Anthony Anthony*, a peire of gloues, with lowpes of golde, lyned with crymſon vellat, in a boxe.
By *Anthony Lambortyne*, a peire of gloues.
Delyverid to the ſaid Mrs. Babington.

By *Egidius Beraldus*, a booke of the Paſſion, written.
With the Quene her Maieſtie.

By *Hannyball*, a peire of perfume gloues.
Delyverid to Mrs. Babington aforeſaid.

By *Guilham Smyth*, a fier ſhouell and a fier forke.
Delyverid to the foreſaid Mrs. Edeth.

By *Alexander Zynzan*, a boxe, with the picture of Chriſt.
By *Zenzan's* two ſonnes, two peire of gloves.
Delyverid to the ſaid Mrs. Babington.

By *Richarde Baker*, a table painted, of the woman of Samarya.
With the Quene her Maieſtie.

By *Laurence Brodſhaw*, two boltes of cambryke.
Delyverid to the ſaid Mrs. Babington.

By

By the *Secretary to the Frenche Ambaſſator*, foure Frenche books bounde in parchement, and two bookes couered with red lether, in French.
Delyverid to the ſaid Edwarde Shefilde.

By *Haynes*, a table, with the picture of Chriſt and his mother.
With the Quein's Maieſtie.

By *Childe*, a litell loking glaſſe.
Delyverid to Mrs. Babington aforeſaid.

By *Spylman*, groſſer, a caſtell of ſuger plate.

By *Robert Raynes*, a cup of chriſtall, garniſshed with ſilu' and guilt, and a couer, 25 oz. in compo R. Wilbram.
Delyverid into the ſaid office of the juells and plate.

By *Guilham*, treaſourer, a peire of virge milles.

By *Curtes*, a table of nedleworke of the Maundy.
With the Quene her Maieſtie.

By *Edwarde Nevell*, two perfumes of ſilu', with perfumes in them, weing 3 oz. di. and two purſes of grene vellat to them.
Delyverid to the ſaid Mrs. Babington.

By *Suete*, painter, a table painted of the Quein's Maieſtie's maryage.
With the Quein's Maieſtie.

By *Jacob Ragoſon*, a Italien, a faire cheire of ebonett, couered with crymſen vellat, and frenged with ſilke and golde; a carpett of Turquey making; a basket of ſilu', with tenne caſes of ſilu' and nedells in them.
The basket, with caſes and nedles, with the Quene; the cheyre and carpett delyverid into the ſaid removing guarderobe.

By *Sebaſtian*, ſcolemaiſter of Powles, a booke of dities, written.
With the Quein's Maieſtie.

By *Guilham*, bytmaker, two byttes.
Delyverid to the mr of the horſe.

By Mr. *Sturton*, a deske to write on, with divers diviſes, and a peire of tables, and cheſſebourde, with a pece of ſiluer, thre ſiluer boxes for compters, ſande, and inke, and fourtie compters; all the ſilu' weing 9 oz. di.
With the Quein's Maieſtie.

By *Sheparde*, of the chapell, thre rolles of ſonges.
Delyverid into the chapell.

By *Richarde Edwardes*, of the chapell, certeigne verſes.

By

By *Lynnell*, porter of the Tower, a handkercheve, wrought with ſilke and golde.

By *Dauncy*, marchaunte, a pece of fine Hollande.
    Delyverid to Mrs. Babington.

By *Binſtede* and his fellowes, boweyers, fiftie bowes.

By *George Starkey* and his fellowes, ſtringers, 2 groſe and 4 doſſen ſtrenges.
    Twentye and foure bowes and one groſſe of ſtrengs delyvered to m[r] vicechamberlen; the reſt of the bowes and ſtrengs deſtributed, by the Quein's com̄andement, to the m[r] of thoffice.

By *John Smyth* and his fellowes, fletchers, 5 doſſen of croſbow arrowes.
    Two doſſen delyverid to the ſaid John Hedde; the reſt diſtributed as aforeſaid.

By *John Coates*, oone doſſen of ſhafts.

By *Thomas Leye* and two mo', 3 doſſen of arrowes.
    Gevon and deſtrebuted as aforeſaide.

By *Browne*, inſtrument-maker, a faire lute, edged with paſſamayne of golde and ſilke.
    With the Quene her Maieſtie.

Marye the quene

Annis

Annis Regnorum PHILIPPI & MARIE, Regis & Regine, &c. tercio & quarto.

Newe Yere's Guiftes geuon by the Quenis Maieſtie, to thoſe Perſones whoſe Names hereafter enſue, the firſt of Januarye.

(From an original Roll, formerly belonging to Sir WILLIAM HERRICK, of BEAUMANOR; and ſtill in the poſſeſſion of his immediate Deſcendant, WILLIAM HERRICK, Eſq.)

Marye the quene

TO the Lorde Cardenall his grace, a peire of guilte pottes, Raynes, weing 118 oz. and a guilt cup, Raynes, weing 25 oz. 3 qr. di. ——— ———	143 oz. 3 qr. di.
Too the Lady *Elizabeth* her grace, thre guilte bolles, with a couer, Raynes, weing 63 ounces; a guilt cup, Raynes, per oz. 25 oz. 3 qr.; another cup, Raynes, weing 21 oz. qr.; and a guilte jugge, Raynes, per oz. 21 oz. qr. di. In toto,	132 oz. qr. di.
To the Lady *Anne of Cleeve*, a bolle, with a couer, Raynes, weing 27 oz. qr.; a guilte cup, Raynes, per oz. 22 oz. qr. di.; and a guilt cruſe, Raynes, per oz. 14 oz. 3 qr. In toto,	64 oz. qr. di.
To the Lady *Margerett Strainge*, oone guilt jug, Raynes, weing	18 oz. di.
To the Duke of *Norff'*, a guilt cup, Raynes, weing —	26 oz. di. qr.
To the Marques of *Wincheſter*, a guilte bolle, with a couer, Johnſon, weing ——— ———	38 oz. di.

EARLES.

To the Earle of *Arundell*, lorde ſtewarde, oone guilt cup, Raynes, weing ——— ——— ———	56 oz. 3 qr.
To the Earle of *Shrewiſbury*, a guilt bolle, Raynes, weing	30 oz.

To

To the Earle of *Darby*, oone guilt bolle, Raynes, weing — 31 oz. qr.
To the Earle of *Huntingdon*, oone guilt cup, Raynes, per oz. — 22 oz. 3 qr. di.
To the Earle of *Westmerlande*, a guilte cruse, Rayns, per oz. — 17 oz. qr. di.
To the Earle of *Oxfourde*, lorde great chamberlen, a guilt cup, Raynes, per oz. — 18 oz. di. di. qr.
To the Earle of *Rutlande*, a guilte cup, Raynes, per oz. — 16 oz. qr.
To the Earle of *Penbrouke*, oone guilte cup, Raynes, per oz. — 57 oz. qr.
To the Earle of *Bath*, a guilte cup, Raynes, per oz. — 21 oz. 3 qr.
To the Earle of *Suffex*, a guilte cup, Raynes, per oz. — 22 oz. 3 qr.

VICOUNTE.

To the Vicounte *Mountague*, oone guilt cup, Raynes, per oz. — 19 oz. di.

BUSSHOPPES.

Too the Archebusshop of *Yorke*, lorde chauncellour, a guilte cup, Raynes, per oz. 23 oz. quarter, di.; and a guilt cruse, Raynes, per oz. 17 oz. 3 qr. In toto, — 44 oz. qr. di.
To the Busshop of *Elye*, a guilt cup, Raynes, per oz. 26 oz. 3 qr.; and a guilt jugge, Raynes, per oz. 19 oz. 3 qr. di. In toto, — 36 oz. di. di. qr.
To the Busshop of *Durham*, a guilte bolle, Raynes, per oz. — 36 oz. qr.
To the Busshop of *Winchester*, a guilt cup, Raynes, per oz. 15 oz. 3 qrs.; and a guilte bolle, Raynes, per oz. 16 oz. di.; and a guilte salte, Raynes, per oz. 4 oz. qr. In toto, — 36 oz. di.
To the Busshop of *Salisbury*, a jug, Raynes, per oz. 18 oz. qr.; and a cruse, Raynes, weing 13 oz. qr. In toto, — 31 oz. di.
To the Busshop of *Exetor*, a guilt jug, Raynes, per oz. — 15 oz. qr.
To the Busshop of *Chitchester* elect, a guilt cruse, Raynes, per oz. — 14 oz. di.
To the Busshop of *London*, a guilte bolle, Raynes, per oz. — 27 oz. 3 qr. di.
To the Busshop of *Lichfelde and Couen'*, oone guilt jug, Raynes, per oz. — 21 oz. di. qr.
To the Busshop of *Norwich*, a guilt cup, Raynes, per oz. — 25 oz. qr.
To the Busshop of *Oxfourde*, a guilt jug, Johnson, per oz. — 18 oz.
To the Busshop of *Worceter*, a guilt cup, Raynes, weing — 24 oz. qr.
To the Busshop of *Bath*, oone guilte cup, gevon this daye and yere by the Earle of Suffex, weing — 24 oz. di.
To the Busshop of *St. Davie's*, a guilt jug, Raynes, per oz. — 17 oz.
To the Busshop of *Rochester*, a guilt jug, Raynes, per oz. — 15 oz. di.
To the Busshop of *Bristow*, a guilt jug, Raynes, per oz. — 15 oz. qr. di.

To the Bufshop of *Glocefter*, a guilt jug, Raynes, per oz. 18 oz. qr. di.
To the Bufshop of *Chefter*, a guilt boll, Raynes, per oz. 16 oz. qr.; and a guilt fpone, per oz. 2 oz. 3 qr. di. In toto, — 19 oz. di. qr.

DUCHESSES, MARQUESSES, and COUNTESSES.

To the Duches of *Norff'*, dowager, a guilt cup, Raynes, per oz. 11 oz. di.
To the Duches of *Norff'*, a guilt jug, Raynes, per oz. — 17 oz. 3 qr.
To the Duches of *Somerfet*, a guilte falte, Raynes, per oz. 8 oz. di.; and a guilt jug, Raynes, per oz. 13 oz. di. di. qr. In toto, — — — 22 oz. di. qr.
To the Lady Marques of *Exetor*, a guilt jug, Raynes, per oz. 16 oz.; and a guilte falte, Raynes, per oz. 13 oz. di. In toto, 29 oz. di.
To the Lady Marques of *Winchefter*, oone guilt bolle, Raynes, per oz. — — 24 oz. qr.
To the Countes of *Surry*, a guilt jug, Johnfon, per oz. 14 oz. di. qr.
To the Countes of *Arundell*, a guilt cup, Raynes, per oz. 26 oz. qr.
To the Countes of *Penbrouke*, a guilt cup, Raynes, per oz. 25 oz. di.
To the Countes of *Bedfourde*, dowager, a guilt cup, Raynes, per oz. 16 oz. qr.; and a guilt jug, Raynes, per oz. 15 oz. di. In toto — — — 31 oz. 3 qr.
To the Countes of *Bedfourde*, a guilt cup, Raynes, per oz. 22 oz. di. qr.
To the Countes of *Oxfourde*, dowager, a guilte crufe, Raynes, per oz. — — 9 oz. 3 qr.
To the Countes of *Oxfourde*, a guilt crufe, Raynes, per oz. 13 oz.
To the Countes of *Huntingdon*, a guilt cup, Raynes, per oz. 18 oz. qr.
To the Countes of *Shrewifbury*, dowager, a guilt cup, Raynes, per oz. — — 21 oz. di.
To the Countes of *Shrewifbury*, a guilt cup, Raynes, per oz. 21 oz. di.
To the Countes of *Darbye*, oone guilt cup, Raynes, per oz. 21 oz. di. di. qr.
To the Countes of *Rutlande*, a guilt jug, Raynes, per oz. 15 oz. qr. di.
To the Countes of *Bath*, a guilt jug, Raynes, per oz. 18 oz. qr.

VICOUNTES.

To the Vicountes *Herefourde*, oone guilte crufe, Raynes, per oz. 9 oz. di. di. qr.
To the Vicountes *Mountague*, oone guilte falte, gevon to the Quene by the Duches of Norff' eod' die & ãis, &c. per oz. 15 oz. qr.

LORDES.

LORDES.

To the Lorde *Pagett*, lorde preuie feale, a guilt cup, Raynes, per oz. — — —	33 oz. qr.
To the Lorde *William Howarde*, lorde admyrall, oone guilt cup, Rayns, per oz. — — —	21 oz. 3 qr.
To the Lorde *Williams*, lorde chamberlen to the King, oone guilte boll, Raynes, per oz. 27 oz. qr.; and a guilte crufe, Raynes, per oz. 10 oz. 3 qr. di. In toto, — —	38 oz. qr. di.
To the Lorde *Clynton*, oone guilte cup, Raynes, per oz.	21 oz. qr. di.
To the Lorde *Cobham*, a guilt cup, Raynes, per oz. —	21 oz. di. di. qr.
To the Lorde *Riche*, a guilte cup, Raynes, per oz. —	18 oz. qr. di.
To the Lorde *Darcye*, a guilt boll, Raynes, per oz. —	27 oz. di.
To the Lorde *Stafforde*, a guilt crufe, Raynes, per oz.	12 oz. 3 qr.
To the Lorde *Burgauenny*, a guilt crufe, Raynes, per oz.	13 oz.
To the Lorde *Windfour*, oone guilte crufe, Raynes, per oz.	12 oz. di. qr.
To the Lorde *John Greye*, a guilt crufe, Raynes, per oz.	9 oz. qr.
To the Lorde *Sandowis*, a guilte jug, Raynes, per oz. —	18 oz. qr. di.
To the Lorde *North*, a guilte boll, Raynes, per oz. —	28 oz.
To the Lorde *Robert Dudley*, a guilte cup, Raynes, per oz.	20 oz. di.

LADYES.

To the Ladye *Pagett*, oone guilte boll, Raynes, per oz.	21 oz. qr.
To the Lady *Burgavenny*, a guilt crufe, Raynes, per oz.	12 oz. di.
To the Lady *Clynton*, a guilt crufe, Raynes, per oz. —	13 oz. di. qr.
To the Lady *Howarde*, a guilt crufe, Raynes, per oz. —	14 oz. di.
To the Lady *Bray* thelder, a guilt crufe, Raynes, per oz.	10 oz. di. di. qr.
To the Lady *Graye*, Lorde John Graye's wif, a guilt crufe, Raynes, per oz. — — —	18 oz. 3 qr. di.
To the Lady *Anne Graye Walfingham*, a guilt crufe, Raynes, per oz. — — —	13 oz. di. qr.
To the Lady *Awdley*, a guilt crufe, Raynes, per oz. —	10 oz. di. qr.
To the Lady *Shandowis*, a guilt jug, Raynes, per oz. —	13 oz. qr.
To the Lady *Butler*, a bolle with a cou' guilt, Raynes, per oz. 14 oz.; and a cafting bottell guilt, Raynes, per oz. 7 oz. In toto, — — —	21 oz.
To the Lady *Manxwell*, a guilt cup, Raynes, per oz. —	18 oz.
To the Lady *Peter*, a guilte jug, Raynes, per oz. —	17 oz. di. di. qr.
To the Lady *Jarningam*, a guilt jug, Raynes, per oz.	17 oz. di.

To the Lady *Wharton*, a guilt jug, Raynes, per oz. 19 oz.; and thre guilte ſpones, gevon by Cnelly Barnes this daye and yere, per oz. 4 oz. di. In toto, —— ——	23 oz. di.
To the Lady *Waldgraue*, nyne guilt ſpones, percell of 12, Raynes, per oz. — — —	18 oz. qr. di.
To the Lady *Hubblethorne*, a guilt cruſe, Raynes, per oz.	10 oz. 3 qr.
To the Lady *Shelton*, a guilte cruſe, Raynes, per oz. —	10 oz. qr.
To the Lady *Kempe*, a guilte bolle, Raynes, per oz. 16 oz 3 qr.; and a guilt caſting bottell, Raynes, per oz. 7 oz. di. qr. In toto, —— ——	23 oz. 3 qr. di.
To the Lady *Freſton*, a guilte cruſe, Raynes, per oz. —	12 oz. qr. di.
To the Lady *Joſlyn*, a guilt cruſe, Johnſon, per oz. —	11 oz. qr. di.
To the Lady *Ratlyff*, a guilt jug, Raynes, per oz. —	13 oz. 3 qr.
To the Lady *Browne*, Juſtice Browne's wif, a guilt cruſe, Johnſon, per oz. —— —— —	11 oz. 3 qr. di.
To the Lady *Capell*, a guilte cruſe, Raynes, per oz. —	8 oz. 3 qr. di.
To the Lady *Maſon*, a guilt cup, Raynes, per oz. —	15 oz. di.
To the Lady *Grey* of the Moate, a guilt cup, Raynes, per oz.	10 oz. qr.
To the Lady *Yorke*, a guilt cruſe, Johnſon, per oz. —	9 oz. di.
To the Lady *Vmpton*, a guilt jug, Johnſon, per oz. —	13 oz. 3 qr.
To the Lady *Gyffourde*, a cup with a cou' guilt, Raynes, per oz.	17 oz.
To the Lady *Mordaunt*, oone guilt cruſe, Raynes, per oz.	11 oz.
To the Lady *Shirly*, parte of a guilt jug, Raynes, 17 oz. therof	16 oz. qr.
To the Lady *Tyrrell*, a guilt caſting bottle, Rayns, per oz.	7 oz. di. qr.
To the Lady *Buckler*, parte of a guilte jug, Raynes, per oz.	11 oz.
To the Lady *Dyer*, oone guilt ſalt, Raynes, per oz. —	11 oz. di. qr.
To the Lady *Catyſbye*, oone guilt ſalt, Raynes, per oz. —	6 oz.

KNIGHTS.

Too Sir *Thomas Chayne*, treaſouror, a guilt cup, Raynes, per oz.	33 oz. 3 qr.
To Sir *Robert Rocheſter*, comptrouler, a peire of guilt pottes, Raynes, per oz. 56 oz. di. di. qr.; and a guilt cruſe, Johnſon, per oz. 11 oz. qr. di. In toto, ——	78 oz.
To Sir *Henry Jarnegam*, vicechamberlen, oone guilt cup, Raynes, per oz. —— —— —	34 oz. di.
To Sir *Edwarde Haſting*, m^r of the horſe, a guilt boll, Raynes, per oz. —— —— ——	26 oz. 3 qr.
To Sir *William Peter*, ſecretary, a guilt cup, Raynes, per oz.	23 oz. qr.
To Sir *John Bourne*, ſecretary, a guilt cup, Raynes, per oz.	21 oz. 3 qr. di.
To Sir *Fraunces Englefelde*, m^r of the wardes, a guilt cup, Raynes, per oz. —— —— —	28 oz. di.

To

To Sir *Edward Waldgraue*, m^r of the greate guarderobe, a guilt cup, Raynes — — 26 oz.
To Sir *Edmunde Pekham*, threasouror of the mynt, a guilt boll, Rayns, per oz. — — 27 oz. qr. di.
To Sir *Richard Sowthwell*, m^r of the armyre, a guilt cup, Raynes, per oz. — — — 23 oz. qr.
To Sir *John Baker*, a guilt cup, Raynes, per oz. 21 oz. di. di. qr.; and a guilt salte, Raynes, per oz. 2 oz. 3 qr. In toto, 24 oz. qr. di.
To Sir *John Hurleston*, a guilt cup, Raynes, per oz. — 15 oz. qr. di.
To Sir *Davy Browke*, a guilt bolle, Raynes, per oz. — 20 oz. 3 qr. di.
To Sir *Richard Sackvyle*, a guilt cup, Raynes, per oz. 24 oz. 3 qr. di.
To Sir *John Yorke*, a guilt cup, Raynes, per oz. — 15 oz. qr.
To Sir *Walter Myldemaye*, a guilte cup, Raynes, per oz. 14 oz. 3 qr.
To Sir *William Raynfourde*, a guilt cruse, Raynes, per oz. 11 oz.
To Sir *Thomas Joslyn*, a guilt jug, Raynes, per oz. — 16 oz. qr.
To Sir *William Drewery*, a guilt cup, Raynes, per oz. 22 oz.
To Sir *Leonarde Chamberlen*, a guilt cruse, Raynes, per oz. 13 oz.
To Sir *Philip Parrys*, a guilt cruse, Raynes, per oz. — 12 oz. 3 qr. di.
To Sir *John Mordaunte*, a guilt cruse, Raynes, per oz. — 11 oz. di.
To Sir *Henry Neueil*, oone guilt jug, Raynes, per oz. — 14 oz. qr. di.
To Sir *John Mason*, oone guilt cup, Raynes, per oz. — 22 oz. di. di. qr.
To Sir *Richard Freston*, a guilt cruse, Rayns, per oz. 13 oz. qr.
To Sir *Anthony St leger*, a guilt cup, Raynes, per oz. — 17 oz. di. di. qr.
To Sir *John Ales*, oone guilt jug, Raynes, per oz. — 15 oz.

CHAPLAYNES.

Too Doctour *Westone*, deane of Windsor, a guilt cup with a couer, Raynes, per oz. — — 19 oz.
To *Peter Vann*, deane of Salisbury, oone guilt boll withowte a cou', Johnson, per oz. — — 17 oz. di.
To *Ricardes*, clerke of the closet, a guilt salt, Johnson, per oz. 11 oz. di.
To parsone *Lewyn*, oone guilt cruse, Raynes, per oz. — 9 oz.
To *Knight*, oone guilt cruse, Raynes, per oz. — 7 oz. qr.
To *Mallet*, am̄n', a guilt bolle, Raynes, per oz. — 20 oz. di. di. qr.
To *Baker*, confessor, oone guilt salte, Raynes, per oz. — 3 oz.

GENTLEWOMEN.

Too Maisteris *Clarentius*, parte of a guilte cup, Raynes, per oz. 32 oz. therof — — — 22 oz.

To

To Mrs. *Finche*, a guilte bolle withowte a couer, Johnſon, per oz. 18 oz. qr.; and a guilte ſpone, Raynes, per oz. 2 oz. In toto,	20 oz. qr.
To Mrs. *Ruſſell*, parte of a guilte cup, Raynes, per oz. 26 oz. di. di. qr. therof, 18 oz. di. di. qr.; and a guilt ſpone, Raynes, per oz. 2 oz. In toto, — —	20 oz. di. di. qr.
To Mrs. *Sturly*, parte of oone guilt boll, Johnſon, per oz. 24 oz. 3 qr. therof to her —	18 oz 3 qr. di.
To Mrs. *Babington* the yonger, a chamberer, a guilt jug, Raynes, per oz. — — —	15 oz. di. qr.
To Mrs. *Ryce*, chamberer, parte of a guilt cup, Raynes, per oz. 34 oz. 3 qr. therof — —	14 oz. 3 qr.
To *Edeth Brydeman*, a chamberer, pte of oone guilt ſalte, Raynes, per oz. 19 oz. di. therof — —	14 oz. di.
To *Barbara Hawke*, a guilt jug, Raynes, per oz. —	14 oz. qr.
To Mrs. *Babington* thelder, a guilt jug, Raynes, per oz.	10 oz. 3 qr.
To Mrs. *Baſſet*, oone guilt jug, Raynes, per oz. 16 oz. di. qr.; and parte of a guilt ſalte, Raynes, per oz. 19 oz. 3 qr. therof, deliverid di. oz. — — —	16 oz. di. di. qr.
To Mrs. *Bacon*, a guilt jug, Raynes, per oz. —	15 oz. 3 qr. di.
To Mrs. *Mary Thomewe*, oone guilt jug, Raynes, per oz.	16 oz.
To Mrs. *Frankewell*, oone guilt cruſe, Raynes, per oz. 14 oz. and parte of another cruſe, Raynes, per oz. 13 oz. di. di. qr. thereof oone oz. di. di. qr. In toto, — —	15 oz. di. qr.
To Mrs. *Penne*, his wif of Codycote, oone guilt jug, Raynes, per oz.	18 oz.
To Mrs. *Penne*, that was King Edwarde's nurſe, parte of a guilt cruſe, Rayns, per oz. 16 oz. di. therof —	13 oz. di.
To Mrs. *Hunyngs*, a guilt cruſe, Raynes, per oz. —	7 oz.
To Mrs. *Levyna Terling*, a guilt ſalte, Rayns, per oz. —	6 oz. qr. di.
To Mrs. *Ball*, ſilkewoman, a guilt ſalte, Raynes, per oz.	6 oz. 3 qr.
To Mrs. *Vincent*, oone guilt jug, Johnſon, per oz. —	18 oz.
To Mrs. *Wilkenſon*, ſilkewoman, oone guilt cruſe, Raynes, per oz.	10 oz. di.
To Mrs. *Cicely Barnes*, oone of the previe chamber, oone guilt cruſe, Rayns, per oz. 11 oz.; and a guilt ſpone, Raynes, per oz. oone oz. di. di. qr. In toto, —	17 oz. di. di. qr.
To Mrs. *Amy Shelton*, a guilt cruſe, Raynes, per oz. —	9 oz.
To Mrs. *Pawne*, a guilt ſalt, Raynes, per oz. —	7 oz. qr.
To Mrs. *Caverley*, a guilt ſalt, Raynes, per oz. —	14 oz. 3 qr. di.
To Mrs. *Dannet* thelder, a guilt cruſe, Raynes, per oz. —	9 oz. di. qr.
To Mrs. *Welſh*, a guilt ſalt, Raynes, per oz. —	3 oz. 3 qr.
To Mrs. *Mary Mychall*, a guilt jug, Raynes, per oz. —	13 oz. 3 qr.
To Mrs. *Stanton*, oone guilt ſalte, Rayns, per oz. —	10 oz. di. di. qr.
To Mrs. *Clyfton*, a caſting bottle, Raynes, per oz. —	7 oz.
To Mrs. *Sturley*, of London, a guilt cruſe, Raynes, per oz.	7 oz. di. qr.
To *Preſton* his wif, a parcell guilt ſpone, Raynes, per oz.	1 oz. di.

To

To Mrs. *Reymounde*, oone guilt ſalte, Raynes, per oz. —	6 oz. qr.
To *Henry Mynk's* wif, oone guilt ſalte, Raynes, per oz.	6 oz.
To Mrs. *Gente*, oone guilt cruſe, Raynes, per oz. —	7 oz.
To *Alys Byllyarde*, oone guilt ſalt, Raynes, per oz. —	4 oz. di. di. qr.
Te Mrs. *Dorm'*, oone guilt cup, Raynes, per oz. ——	16 oz. qr.
To Mrs. *Morchous*, oone guilt jug, Raynes, per oz. —	10 oz. 3 qr. di.
To Mrs. *Woddall*, one guilt jug, Raynes, per oz. —	13 oz. 3 qr. di.
To Mrs. *White*, a guilt ſalt, Raynes, per oz. —	20 oz. di. qr.
To Mrs. *Scurlok*, a chamberer, a guilt jug, Johnſon, per oz.	14 oz. 3 qr.

FREE GUIFTES.

To the Lady *Anne Somerſet*, oone of the maydes, oone guilt cruſe, Johnſon, per oz. —— ——	9 oz. 3 qr.
To the Lady *Jane Seymor*, another of the maydes, oone guilt cruſe, Johnſon, per oz. —— —	9 oz. di.
To *Mary Howarde*, another of the maids, a guilt cruſe, Raynes, per oz. ——— ——	9 oz. di. qr.
To *Mary Manxwell*, another of the mayds, oone guilt cruſe, Raynes, per oz. ——— —	9 oz.
To *Cycelly Arundell*, another of the maids, oone guilt cruſe, Raynes, per oz. — —	9 oz.
To *Margerit Cooke*, another of the mayds, oone guilt cruſe, Raynes, per oz. — ——	9 oz.
To *Dorothy Broughton*, mother of the maydes, oone guilt cruſe, Raynes, per oz. — —	11 oz. 3 qr. di.
To *Betterys*, laundrys, oone guilt ſalt, Raynes, per oz.	10 oz. qr.

GENTELMEN.

To Maiſter *Cordall*, ſoliſter, oone guilt cup with a cou', Raynes, per oz. — — —	23 oz. di. qr.
To Doctor *Owen*, oone guilt jug, Raynes, per oz. —	14 oz.
To Doctor *Wendy*, a guilt cruſe, Raynes, per oz. —	14 oz. 3 qr.
To Doctor *Hughes*, oone guilt jug, Raynes, per oz. —	14 oz.
To *Rowlande Scurlok*, oone guilt cruſe, Raynes, per oz.	12 oz. di.
To *Mychaell Wentworth*, m[r] of the houſholde, oone guilt jug, Johnſon, per oz. — —	18 oz. di.
To Mr. *Thomas Myldmay*, a cup with a couer, Raynes, per oz.	16 oz. di.
To *Barthelmewe Compaine*, a guilt jug, Raynes, per oz.	15 oz.
To Mr. *Thomas Stanley*, oone guilt ſalt, Raynes, per oz.	13 oz. di. qr.

To *White*, sewer, oone guilte cruse, Raynes, per oz. — 9 oz.
To *Nicholas Luzarde*, oone guilt cruse, Raynes, per oz. 12 oz. 3 qr. di.
To *Cawodde*, the Quein's printer, oone guilt cruse, Raynes, per oz. 11 oz.
To *Smallwodd*, grosser, a guilt cruse, Raynes, per oz. 9 oz. 3 qr.
To *Keyme*, lokesmyth, parte of a guilt cup, Raynes, per oz. 21 oz. qr. di. therof — — 11 oz. di. qr.
To *Nicholas Vrsine*, oone guilt salte, Raynes, per oz. — 12 oz. 3 qr. di.
To *John Grene*, oone guilt salte, Johnson, per oz. — 13 oz. 3 qr.
To *Reyne Wolf*, oone guilt cruse, Raynes, per oz. — 13 oz.
To *Chapell*, oone guilt cruse, Raynes, per oz. —— 11 oz. qr.
To *Thomas Kent*, oone guilt salte, Raynes, per oz. 8 oz. 3 qrs; and parte of another guilt salte, Raynes, per oz. 5 oz. di. therof, 4 oz. qr. In toto, —— 13 oz.
To *Knevet S'gent*, porter, oone guilt cruse, Raynes, per oz. 10 oz. di. di qr.
To *William St. Barbe*, oone guilt jug, Raynes, per oz. — 18 oz. 3 qr.
To *Allen Bawdeson*, oone guilt salte, Raynes, per oz. — 13 oz. di.
To *Henry Myles*, grosser, oone guilt salt, Raynes, per oz. 9 oz. 3 qr. di.
To *Nicholas Andrewe*, *Anthony Mary*, *Edwarde Device*, and *John Pecok*, sagbut, oone guilt cruse, Raynes, per oz. — 11 oz. qr.
To Mr. *Babington*, oone guilt cruse, Raynes, per oz. 10 oz. 3 qr. di.
To Mr. *Norres*, oone guilt jug, Raynes, per oz. —— 19 oz.
To Mr. *Thomewe*, oone guilt cruse, Raynes, per oz. —— 12 oz. qr. di.
To Mr. *Frankewell*, parte of a guilt cruse, Raynes, per oz. 13 oz. di. di. qr. therof — — 12 oz. di.
To *Walter Earle*, oone guilt cruse, Raynes, per oz. — 9 oz. qr.
To *John Soda*, oone guilt salte, Raynes, per oz. — 9 oz. qr.
To *Pascall*, parte of a guilt salte, Raynes, per oz. 15 oz. 3 qr. therof — — 9 oz. qr.
To Mr. *Thomas Gresham*, oone guilt jug, Raynes, per oz. 16 oz. di.
To *Harryes*, fruterer, oone guilte cruse, Raynes, per oz. 12 oz. di.
To *Browne*, hoseyer, oone guilt salte, Raynes, per oz. — 6 oz. di. qr.
To *Foster*, fyshmonger, oone guilt salte, Raynes, per oz. 12 oz. di. qr.
To *Myles Huggard*, oone guilte salte, Raynes, per oz. — 5 oz. di.
To *Phillip Manwarring*, oone guilt salte, Johnson, per oz. 12 oz. qr.
To *Fraunces Evered*, oone guilt salte, Raynes, per oz. 5 oz. di. di. qr.; and a guilt salte, Raynes, per oz. 6 oz. qr. di. In toto, 12 oz.
To *Jones*, taylor, oone guilt cruse, Raynes, per oz. — 7 oz. di. di. qr.
To Mr. *Hunnyngs*, oone guilt cruse, Raynes, per oz. — 11 oz.
To *John Demoloney*, oone guilt cruse, Raynes, per oz. — 13 oz. qr.
To *Anthony Basson* and his brytherne, oone guilt cruse, Raynes, per oz. —— — — 11 oz di. qr.
To *Mark Barnarde*, oone guilt jug, Raynes, per oz. — 15 oz. qr.
To *Armygell Wade*, oone guilt salte, Johnson, per oz. — 13 oz. qr. di.
To *Anthony Anthony*, oone guilt cruse, Johnson, per oz. 14 oz.

To

To *Hannyball*, oone guilt falte, Raynes, per oz. — 4 oz.
To *Guilham Smyth*, oone guilt falte, Raynes, per oz. — 5 oz. 3 qr. di.
To *Alexander Zynzan* and his wif and two fonnes, a guilt crufe, Johnfon, per oz. — — 9 oz. 3 qr.
To *Laurence Brodfhaw*, furveyor of the works, oone guilt jug, Raynes, per oz. — — 13 oz. di.
To *Robart Raynes*, oone guilt cup, R. per oz. — 13 oz.
To *Guilham*, threafourour, oone guilt falte, Johnfon, per oz. 13 oz. 3 qr.
To *Curtes*, alderman of London, oone guilt jugg, Raynes, per oz. 18 oz. qr.
To *Edwarde Nevell*, oone guilte falte, Raynes, per oz. 10 oz. qr.
To *Jacob Ragofon*, oone cup of chriftall, garnifshed with filuer and guilt, with two eares and a couer, gevon by the Duk of Norff' eodem die, per oz. — — 35 oz. di.
To *Sebaftian*, fcolem' of Powles, oone guilt crufe, Raynes, per oz. 9 oz.
To *Guilham*, bytmaker, oone guilt falte, Raynes, per oz. 8 oz. di.
To *Sturton*, oone guilt crufe, Raynes, per oz. — 11 oz.
To *Dauncye*, marchaunte, oone guilt crufe, Raynes, per oz. 16 oz. di. qr.

FREE GUIFTES.

To Mr. *Wilbram*, mr of the juelhoufe, oone guilt cup, Raynes, per oz. ——— ——— 18 oz. 3 qr.
To Mr. *Ryte*, parte of a guilt cup, Raynes, per oz. 34 oz. 3 qr. therof for his guift — — 18 oz.
To Mr. *Baffet*, parte of oone guilt falte, Raynes, per oz. 19 oz. 3 qr. therof ——— ——— 14 oz. qr.
To Mr. *Kemp*, oone guilt falte, Raynes, per oz. — 10 oz. 3 qr.
And more thre parcell guilt fpones, per oz. — 4 oz. di.
To Mr. *Ligons*, parte of a guilt jug, Raynes, per oz. 27 oz. therof for his guift — — 13 oz.
To Mr. *Tyrrell*, oone guilt crufe, Raynes, per oz. — 11 oz. di.
To Mr. *Dauncye*, oone guilte crufe, Raynes, per oz. 11 oz. 3 qr. di.
To Mr. *Grene*, oone guilt crufe, Raynes, per oz. — 11 oz. qr. di.
To Mr. *Smyth*, a guilt crufe, Raynes, per oz. ——— 11 oz.
To *Burrage*, mr cook, oone guilt falt, Raynes, per oz. — 9 oz.
To Mr. *Briftowe*, clerke of the juelhoufe, pte of a guilt crufe, Raynes, per oz. 11 oz. 3 qr. di. therof for his guift 10 oz. 3 qr. di.
To Mr. *Halile*, yoman of the faid juelhoufe, parte of a guilt crufe, Raynes, per oz. 12 oz. 3 qr. therof for his guift 10 oz. 3 qr. di.
To Mr. *Kyrkeby*, alfo yoman of the faide office, parte of a guilt crufe, Raynes, per oz. 13 oz. 3 qr. di. therof for his guift 10 oz. 3 qr. di.
To *Edmunde Pigeon*, grome of the fame office, a guilt crufe, Raynes, per oz. — — 10 oz. di.

To *Dodde*, ſergante of the ſeller, parte of a guilt cruſe, Johnſon, per oz. 8 oz. 3 qr. therof for his guift — 7 oz. 3 qr.
To *Bettes*, ſergante of the paſtrey, parte of a guilt cruſe, Raynes, per oz. 9 oz. 3 qr. di. therof for his guift — 6 oz. qr. di.
To *Chriſtopher Morchous*, grome of the previe chamber, parte of a guilt cruſe, Johnſon, per oz. 8 oz. di. for his guift 5 oz. di.
To *George Brydeman*, another grome, parte of a guilt ſalte, Raynes, per oz. 19 oz. therof for his guift — 5 oz.
To *Stephen Sadnall*, parte of a caſting bottle guilt, Raynes, per oz. 7 oz. qr. therof for his guift — 5 oz. di. qr.
To *Thomas Large*, a guilt ſalte, Raynes, per oz. — 5 oz.
To *Thomas Hobbes*, yoman of the roobes, a guilt ſalt, Raynes, per oz. — — 11 oz. 3 qr.

DELIUERED by the Quein's Maieſtie's comaundement, the 8th of Febr', ãis ſecundo et tertio regnorum Philippi et Marie, to *Robart Raynes*, her highnes' goldeſmyth, threſcore and ſixe ounces and a haulf of golde, being parte of Saint George's heade of golde, of the chardge of the ſaid office of the juelles and plate, recevid from Windſour, to make a cheyne; wherof was a cheyne made with fourtene ouncs quarter of the Quein's owne golde, being angelles received owte of her handes, putt therto; and the ſame cheyne, being ſo made, was deliuerid to the Quein's owne handes ——— 66 oz. di.
Item, geuon by the Quein's Maieſtie to the *Fryers at Grenewich*, the 12th of February, oone pixe, parceil guilt, bought of the faide Raynes, and paide for by warraunte emongs the mending ſtuff, per oz. — — 6 oz. 3 qr.
Item, deliverid to the Quein's Maieſtie's owne handes, thre guilt bolles with a couer, Raynes — 57 oz. di.
Item, deliuerid to the Quein's owne handes, oone guilt cruſe with a cou', Raynes, per oz. — 8 oz. di.
Item, deliverid by the Quein's comaundement, the 16th of Marche, annis pred', to the ſaid Robert Raynes in broken golde, to make crampe rings, being parte of a George hedde of golde received from Windſor, of the chardge of the office of the juelles and plate, hauing enamell and other rubyſhe in it, deliverid for fyftie and five ounces, the ſame being tryed and clerly melted, and retournid by him into golde jemewes, weing — — 53 oz.
Item, more deliuerid the ſame tyme to the ſaide Raynes, to make cramp ringes, in broke plate of ſilu' theiſe parcelles: a baſone

and a lyre of ſilu', late the Earle of Bedfourde's, and of the chardge of the ſaide office, per oz 85 oz. di.; item, two chaundllors of ſilver, late the ſaide Earles, and of the ſaid chardge, per oz. 42 oz. qr.; and a cryſmetory box of ſilu', of the plate received from churches, per oz. 12 oz.; all weing togethers oone hundreth thirtie-nyne ounces thre quarters, whiche was ret' by hym in ſiluer jemewes — 34 oz. 3 qr.

All whiche golde and ſiluer, being made into cramp rings, were halowed by the Quein's Maieſtie on Good Frydaye, and ſo geuon by her Highnes awaye, as hath bene accuſtomed.

Item, deliuerid by the Quein's comaundement, the 10th of Maye, ãis pred', to the ſaid Robt Raynes, oone Magdalyne cup of golde with a couer, late Duke of Northumberland's, of the chardge of the ſaid office, per oz. 12 oz. di.; itm, oone ſmall coller of garters with a George, of the chardge of the ſaide office, late Duk of Northumberlande's, per oz. 8 oz. di.; itm, parcell of the couer of a cuppe of golde, made againſt the Quein's coronacon, for a guift to the Earle of Arundell for his fee, thereof oone ounce di.; and in broken golde, being parte of the ſaide George hedde of golde, 11 oz. di.; all weing 34 oz. therof waſted in melting oone qrter of an ounce, ſo remayneth in tough golde 33 oz. 3 qr. wherof was made a cheyne, deliverid to the Quein's Maieſtie's owne handes 34 oz.

Item, more gevon by the Quein's Maieſtie, the 20th of Maye, to *Clerk,* oone of the yomen of her Highnes' chamber, to his maryage, oone guilt ſalte with a couer, bought of the ſaide Robt Raynes, and paide for by the ſaide warraunte of mending ſtuff, weing — — 8 oz.

Item, more gevon by the Quein's Maieſtie, the 24th of Auguſt, ãis tertio & quarto regnor' Philippi et Marie, at the chriſtening of the Earle of Lynnex' childe, oone guilt cup with a couer, parcell of the plate prouided by Willm Danſell in Flaunders, and of the charge of the ſaide office of the juelles and plate, per oz. —— —— 63 oz. di.

Item, more gevon by the Quein's Maieſtie, the 12th of November, ãie pred', at the chriſtening of Sir Nicholas Sturlye, knight, his childe, oone guilt cup with a couer, chaſed with longe bullions, and with a parmey enamelid vpon a plate in the buſshell, parcell of the chardge of the ſaide office, per oz. — 26 oz. di. qr.

Item, more gevon by the Quein's Maieſtie, the 5th of December, to a woman dwelling at Burye, for healing Jane the foole her eye, oone guilt ſalte with a couer, prouided and paide for by warraunte

warraunte emongs new yer's guiftes, ãis tertio et quarto ſupradičs, per oz. — — 10 oz. 3 qr.

Item, more gevon the ſame time, to Maiſtres *Ayer*, for keping the ſaide Jane during the tyme of the healing of her eye, two guilt ſalts with a couer, provided and paide for by warraunte emongs new yer's guifts, as aforeſaide, per oz. — 18 oz. di.

Item, more gevon by the Quein's Maieſtie, the 3d of January, ãis pred', at the chriſtening of Sir Henry Tyrrell, knight, his childe, oone guilt cup, prouided of Raynes, and paid for emongs new yer's guifts, ãis pred', per oz. — 21 oz. 3 qr.

Item, deliverid to the Quein's Maieſtie's owne handes, the 20th of Marche, annis ſecundo et tertio laſt paſt, and by her Highnes gevon the ſame tyme to the Lorde Cardenall his grace, thenne beinge made Archebuſshop of Caunterbury, oone miter, garniſshed with ſiluer and guilt, and ſome golde ſette with ſmalle ſeede peerle and other ſtones, of the chardge of the ſaide office of juelles and plate, per oz. all togethers — 97 oz. di.

Item, more deliverid to her Highnes, and likewiſe gevon the ſame tyme to the ſaide Lorde Cardenall, oone croſyer ſtaff of ſiluer and guilt, plated vpon a ſtaff of wodde, newe made of plate received from churches, and of the chardge of the ſaide office of juelles and plate, per oz. — 83 oz.

Item, deliverid to her Maieſtie's owne handes, the 10th of February, ãis tertio et quarto pred', and by her Highnes gevon to . . . . ambaſſator of Venice, oone faire ſtanding cup, guilt, with a cou', having vpon the foote a chriſtall, of the chardge of the ſaid office of juells and plate, per oz. 122 oz.

Marye the quene

Ex^r p Ric' WILBRAM.

A Warrant of Queen Mary.

Marye the quene

OUR will and pleaſure is, that you ſhall have, and preſently take to your owne uſe, as of our gift, theiſe parcelles of hanginges of verders of the brode blome, with birdes having apples beneth and above at the corners of the borders, lyned with canvas paned; that is to ſay, one pece, contayning, in Flemiſh elles, 27 di. another pece, contayning 22 di.; another pece, cont' 29 di. di. quarter, and one naile; another pece, cont' 15 qr. di. and one naile; another pece, cont' 16 di. di. qr.; and alſo theis parcelles or peces of hanginges of verders, with water flowers and birdes, having pomgranets at the upper corners, and apples with roſes at the neither cornors, lined with canvas paned; one pece, contayning, in Flemiſh elles, 23 di. qr.; another 26 di. di. qr. and one naile di.; another pece 30^{ti} 3 qr. di.; another pece 22 di.; another 17 di.; and one other, contayning 19 di.; being together 11 peces. And further our pleaſure is, that you take to your owne uſe alſo, as of our gift, foure window peces of verders of the brode blome, lyned with canvas, paned, viz. one pece, contayning, in Flemiſhe elles, 6 di. qr. and one naile; another pece, contayning 6 di. qr. and one naile; another 4 qr. di. and one naile di.; and another, contayning 5 di. di. qr. All which percelles or peces of hanging and windowe peces remayne, and be now in your own cuſtody. And theis our l̃res, ſigned with our ſigne manuel, ſhal be your ſufficient warraunt and diſcharge in that behalf. Geven at our mannor of Saint James, the 16 of October, the fiſt yeare of our raigne.

To our truſtie and welbeloved ſervant George Brodiman, one of the gromes of our privie chamber, and keeper of our Palace at Weſtm'.

A Letter

A Letter from the Princess ELIZABETH whilst at Hatfield.

MR. AUCHER, My cofferer hath well declared unto me your good will and readiness in your dispatche and delyvery of my plate, which I have received of hym, amounting to one thowsand threescore and two ounces. This your towardnes will I so remember, that whensoever occasion may serve, I woll requite it, desiring youe, that when, for thexchanginge of any plate, I shall have nede of your like gentlenes, ye woll therin no lesse extend it towards me, then in this my cause you have bene both prest and forwarde to further it. And this faire you well. At Hatfelde, the 9th of December. Your frende, *ELIZABETH.*

To my good freende Sir Anthonie Aucher, Knighte.

A Warraunte to the Greate Wardrobe for your Majestie's Mawndye.

ELIZABETH R.

WEE woll and comaund you, that, imediatelye upon the sight hereof, ye doe lyver, or cause to be delyvered, to our welbeloved servaunt Rauf Hope, yeoman of our warderobe of robes, for thuse of our Mawndye, and our said warderobe, theyse percelles of stuff followinge, that is to say, first, one hundreth thirtye and fyve yerdes of russet cloth, to make fourety and thre gownes for fourtye and fyve poore women; and fourety and fyve peire of single soled showes for them. Item, two hundrethe fyvetye and eight elles of lynen cloth, aswell to make smockes for the said poore women, as also to be employed in the service of our said Mawndye. Item, twentie and sixe peire of bearinge and trussinge sheetes of two bredthes and a half of Hollande cloth, and two elles thre quarters longe the pere. Item, thirtye elles of diaper of elle quarter brode; and eighteene napkyns, cont' one elle longe the pere, for thuse of our said warderobe. Item, one peire of presse sheetes, of fower bredthes of Hollande cloth, and nyne elles longe the pere. Item, one curten for a presse, of lynen cloth, cont' seven bredthes and two elles longe. Item, thirtye elles of canvas, and the boultes of stronge rope to trusse the said stuff in. And that ye content and paye for making of the premisses; and also for cariadge of the same from our greate warderobe to the place wheare, God willing, we shall make our said Maundye. And theyse our lres, signed with our owne hande, shal be your sufficient warraunte and dischardge in this behalf annempst us, our heires, and successors. Geoven under our signett, at our pallaise at Westm', the 12th daye of Marche, the 21st yeare of our reigne. Jo. SARU'.

To our trustie and welbeloved servaunte John Forteskewe, esquier, maister of our greate warderobe. Ex' p N. PIGEON.

Lettre

By the QUEENE.

A PROCLAMATION, with certayne Clauses of diuers Statutes, and other neceſſary additions, firſt publiſhed in the xix yeere * of the Queenes Maieſties reigne, and now reuiued by her Highnes commandement to be put in execution, upon the penalties in the ſame conteined.

WHEREAS the Queenes Maieſtie hath by ſundry former Proclamations notified vnto her louing Subiectes of this Realme the great inconuenience and miſchief that hath growen to the ſame, by the great exceſſe of apparell in all ſtates and degrees, but ſpecially in the inferiour ſort, contrarie to divers Lawes and Statutes of the Realme, whereof notwithſtanding there hath folowed no redreſſe, or very litle at al; whereby hath appeared no leſſe contempt in the offendours, than lacke of ductifull care in thoſe to whome the authoritie to ſee due execution of the lawes and orders prouided in that behalfe was committed; which thing might give her Maieſtie iuſt cauſe (were it not that of her own gracious diſpoſition ſhe is naturally inclyned rather to clemencie then ſeveritie, ſo long as there is any hope of redreſſe otherwayes) to commit the execution of the ſaid lawes to ſuch perſons as would have proceeded therein with all extremitie. Notwithſtanding, her Maieſty meaning to make ſome further tryall, before ſhe have recourſe to extreme remedies, and finding upon conference had with the Lordes and others of her pryuie counſayle, for the redreſſe of ſo greeuous and pernicious a ſore in this commonwealth, the chief remedies for the ſame, to be example, and correction: Her Maieſtie therefore for the firſt, whiche is example, thynketh it very meete and expedient, that the due execution in her Maieſties moſt honourable houſe, of ſuch orders and articles as are annexed to this Proclamation, ſhoulde ſerve for a paterne throughout the whole Realme, and therefore her Maieſtie hath already giuen, and by theſe preſentes doth giue ſpeciall charge to all thoſe that beare office within the ſayde houſe, to ſee due obſeruation of the ſame, which ſhe truſteth wil be duely obſerued. And further her Maieſtie doth generally charge all Noblemen, of what eſtate or degree ſo euer they be, and all and every perſons of her Priuie Counſaile, all Archbiſhoppes and Biſhops, and the reſt of the Clergie, and all other perſons, according to theyr degrees, that they doo reſpectiuely ſee the ſame ſpeedily and duely executed in their

* And printed in that yeere by Richard Jugge.

priuate houſeholde and families: and likewiſe doeth charge all Maiors and other head officers of Cities and Townes Corporate, the Chancellours of both the Uniuerſities, Gouernours of Colledges, Readers, Aucientes & Benchers in euery the Innes of Court and Chauncerie, and generally all that haue any ſuperioritie or gouernement ouer and upon any ſocietie or feloweſhip, and eche man in his owne houſeholde for theyr children and ſeruantes, that they likewiſe doo cauſe the ſayde orders to be ſtraightly kept by all lawfull meanes that they can.

And for the ſeconde, which is correction, her Maieſtie hath cauſe to thinke, that if there had bene that ſeueritie vſed by thoſe to whom the ouerſight of the due execution of the lawes prouided in that behalfe was committed, as to them in duetie appertained, both this ſore had bene cured, and this Proclamation not needefull to haue bene publiſhed at this preſent.

For the better reformation whereof, her Maieſties will and pleaſure is, and ſo doth ſtraightly charge and commaunde, not onely al Juſtices of peace, and euerye of them, to make inquirie of the defaultes and breaking of the ſayde orders, at euery their Quarter Seſſions, and alſo the Juſtices of Aſſiſe in ther circuites, and to ſee ſuch examples made, and due puniſhments extended upon the offendours, as by the Statutes of this Realme, with ſuch qualifications as in this preſent Proclamation are conteyned, is provided in that behalfe: but alſo, that aſwell the ſayde Juſtices, as all Maiors, Shirifes, and other head officers, in Cities, Townes, and Boroughes, ſhall at any other time cauſe all ſuch perſons as ſhall be founde faultie, and tranſgreſſing agaynſt this proclamation, after the laſt day of Marche next enſuyng, to be apprehended and brought before them; and finding them culpable, to commit them to pryſon, there to remayne without bayle or mayneprife by the ſpace of one moneth, unleſſe the ſaid parties ſo found culpable, or charged as culpable, ſhal enter into bonde to appeare before the Juſtices at the next Quarter Seſſions of the peace, or of the Aſſiſes to be holden within the ſame Shyre, Citie, Borough, Towne Corporate, Fraunchiſe, or libertie, and there to be anſwerable for al ſuch offences as ſhal be prooued that they have committed contrary to the true intent and meaning of this Proclamation.

And whereas it is appointed by the Statutes of this Realme, what every perſon ſhall or may weare in theyr apparell, according to the ſeveral rates of theyr lyuings in landes or fees, over and above all charges, and in ſome caſes, of goodes, foraſmuch as the lacke of the true and common underſtandyng of every mans eſtate and liuing, in ſort before expreſſed, hath been (as it ſeemeth) heretofore ſome principal cauſe of the lacke of the true execution of the ſayde Statutes, and that it doeth manifeſtly appeare, that the ſame cauſe will alſo in time to come worke the like effect, for that there is no conuenient meanes to make the ſtates of mens liuings and values, in ſuch ſort as is expreſſed in the ſeuerall ſtatutes, to be commonly knowen, to ſuch perſons as ought to haue ſpeciall care of the execution of the lawes and orders now preſcribed: Her Maieſtie, being deſirous for the great benefite of al her Highneſſe Subiectes, to haue theſe orders more duely executed than they haue beene, and finding that it is very harde for any mans ſtate of liuing and value to be truely underſtoode by other perſons, if before proofe made they ſhoulde

ſeeme

feme to take knowledge of any other values and rates than of fuch as be, or ought to be, for the greateft nomber expreffed in the Subfidie booke, and fo for lacke of the knowledge of the true rates and values mentioned in the faide ftatutes, the due execution of thefe orders may be defrauded; doeth therefore, for the auoyding of the inconuenience that may enfue, order and commaunde, that all perfons, that by this Proclamation be appointed to have care of the execution of thefe orders, fhall for the firft calling, arrefting, committing, or any other purfuing of any perfon, for any offence committed againft thefe orders, take knowledge of the rates and values, whereby fuch perfons are feffed in the Subfidie bookes, and fhall accordingly proceede, upon fuch knowledge of their values, to impeach fuch as will in their apparel offend to the contrary thereof. Neverthelefle, if any perfon fhall finde hymfelf greeued to be impeached therewith, and for the juftifying of the wearing of his apparell, fhall upon any arreft or inditement founde agaynft hym, auowe, and offer to prooue his lyuing to be fuch, and fo great, as by the rates expreffed in the ftatutes he may be warranted to weare the apparel for the which he is or fhall be impeached; Her Maiefties meaning and pleafure is, that euery fuch perfon fhalbe admitted to make fuch proofe, and thereupon fhall receyue iudgement of condemnation, or acquittal, according to the rates expreffed in the ftatutes, and not otherwife, without impeaching any officer, or other perfon, that did arreft, chalenge, or proceed againft him for fuch matter, though in the Subfidie book his values were not fufficient to warrant the values mentioned in the actes of Parliament: Not doubting, but that all fuch perfons as, for the maintenance of their fond vanitie in apparell, will feeke to make their liuings to be knowen and prooued to be greater, than they were before in feffementes of Subfidies taken to be, whereof her Maieftie had the loffe, fhalbe thought meet by fuch Commiffioners as hereafter fhall have authoritie to rate men upon the graut of any Subfidie, to be feffed in the Subfidie bookes, according to fuch values as themfelves will auowe to have for defence of wearing of fuch kinde of apparell, and alfo will be content to be anfwerable to the charge of other neceffarie fervices for the Realme, as caufes fhall require.

And becaufe there are many perfons, that percafe fhalbe founde in outwarde apparance more fumptuous in their appareil, than by common intendement the values of their poffeffions or goodes may warrant, and yet they are not affeffed in any Subfidie booke, partly for that they are dwelling in fuch places of the Realme as are not chargeable to payments of Subfidies, or that percafe they have efcaped to be affeffed, or otherwife not affeffed, whereupon fuch perfons may thinke to continue their diforder, without reformation by the maner here next before prefcribed: Her Maieftie, for remedie hereof, commaundeth al maner of officers, that where they fhall fee any fuch perfons in outwarde appearance fo offendyng, and not having knowledge of their values by bookes of Subfidies, as afore is expreffed, that neuerthelefle they fhall ftay fuch perfons, and challenge them for fuch pretended offence, and deteyne them, as before by this Proclamation is limited, vntill they fhall enter into bond, to make good proofe that they can difpende fo much in lande and fees, or be fo much woorth in goodes, as by the lawes they be thereby warranted to weare ſuch apparell: And that no publique officer ſhalbe at any tyme impeached for ſuch ſtay and deteynor of any ſuch perſon, ſo apparantly ſeeming to have offended.

Provided alwayes notwithſtanding, that the ſayd publique officer ſhall not at any time, under the colour of the execution of this preſent Proclamation, arreſt any perſon or perſons, whom either they themſelves ſhalbe knowen and proued to malice, or els ſhalbe procured thereto by others, in reſpect of ſome particular quarell, upon payne of her Maieſties diſpleaſure, and ſuche puniſhment as ſhall be thought meete by the Lordes and others of her Maieſties priuie Counſayle.

Given at our Palace of Weſtminſter, the xii of Februarie, in the xxii yeere of our raigne.

God ſave the Queene.

A briefe Content of certaine Clauſes of the Statutes of King Henrie the Eyght, and Queene Marie, with ſome moderation thereof, and other prouiſions to be obſerued according to her Maieſties Proclamation above mentioned.

Mens Apparell.

<table>
<tr><td rowspan="2">None ſhal weare in his apparel</td><td>Sylke of the colour Purple cloth of Golde, or Silver Tiſſued, nor Furre of Sables.</td><td>Under the degree of an Earl.</td></tr>
<tr><td>Cloth of Golde, Silver, or Tinſell Satten.

Sylke, Cloth, Canvas, or any ſtuffe in any apparell, that ſhalbe mixed or imbrodered with any Gold or Silver.</td><td>Under the degree of a Baron.</td></tr>
</table>

Woollen

None ſhal wear in his apparel

- Woollen clothe made out of the Realme, ſauing in Cappes only.
- Veluet: Crymſon, Carnation, or Blewe.
- Scarlet cloth.
- Furres of: Blacke Jenets, or Luſernes.
- Imbroderie, or Taylors worke, having Golde, or Siluer, or Pearle therin. Nor any Enamiell, Muſke, Ambergrece, Agate, or any other precious Stone, in Chayne, Button, or Aglet. Nor any Dublet, Jerkin, or other apparel of any ſtuffe perfumed.

Under the degree of: A Knight of the order, one of the Privie Counſel, or a Gentleman of the Priuie Chamber.

- Gowns, Clokes, Capes, or other uppermoſt garments: of Veluet
- Furres of Libardes.
- Imbroderie, or Taylors woorke like to imbroderie, with Sylke, Bugle, or any other like thing.
- Nor any Cappes, Hats, Hatbandes, Capbands, Garters, Bootehoſe trymmed with: Golde or Syluer.
- Or Sylke neather Stockes.
- Shertes, Shertbandes: garniſhed, mixte, or wrought with Golde.
- Ruffes made or wrought out of Englande, commonly called Cutworke.

Under the degree of: A Barons ſonne, a Knight, and Gentleman in ordinarie office, attending upon her Maieſties perſon, or perſons that are aſſeſſed in the laſt ſubſidy books at CC li. lands, or fees.

7 Spurres,

<table>
<tr><td rowspan="3">None shal weare</td><td rowspan="3">Spurres,
Swordes,
Rapiers,
Skaynes,
Woodknyues,
or Hangers,
Buckles of
Gyrdles,</td><td>Damasked,</td><td>under the degree of</td><td>A Knight of the order.
One of the Priuie Counsell.
A Gentleman of the priui chamber.</td></tr>
<tr><td>Guylte,</td><td colspan="2">under the degree of a Knight.</td></tr>
<tr><td>Syluered,</td><td colspan="2">under the degreees and persons before mentioned.</td></tr>
</table>

<table>
<tr><td rowspan="3">None shal weare</td><td rowspan="3">In trappings, or Harnesse for any their Horses,</td><td>Studdes, Buckles, or other garniture, being</td><td>Gilte, Siluered, or damasked.</td><td rowspan="3">except</td><td rowspan="3">The degrees before mentioned, & al other Gentlemen onely in the furniture of their great Horses meete for service.</td></tr>
<tr><td colspan="2">Nor Stirrops Gilt, siluered, or damasked,</td></tr>
<tr><td colspan="2">Nor any veluet in Saddles, or Horse trappings,</td></tr>
</table>

<table>
<tr><td rowspan="6">None shal wear</td><td>Veluet in</td><td colspan="2">any kind of hose, or in garding of any garment, or in Slippers, Shooes, or Pantophles.</td><td rowspan="3">except</td><td rowspan="3">Men that be of the degree, & persons above mentioned, and men that may dispende one hundred Marks in lands or fees by the yere, and valued in the subsidy bookes, or valued at five hundred pounds in goods, or such person as shall continually keep a horse, furnished for service in warre.</td></tr>
<tr><td>Gowne or Hose of</td><td colspan="2">Satten,
Damaske,
Sylke Chamlet,
Taffata, or
tuffed Taffata, or
Hose made of Sylke Lace,</td></tr>
<tr><td colspan="3">Furre, whereof the like kinde groweth not within the Queenes Dominions, excepte Foynes, gray Jenets, Calaber, Budge, outlandish Hare, or Foxe.</td></tr>
<tr><td>any</td><td>Bonnet,
Batte,
Girdle, or
Scaberdies of Swordes, or Rapiers</td><td>of Veluet.</td><td rowspan="3">except</td><td rowspan="3">The persons and degrees above mentioned, the sonne of a knight, or of any man that may dispend three hundred Markes, and the eldest sonne of him that may dispend one hundred pounds by the yere, and is so assessed, *vt sup.* And men that may dispend twenti pound land and fees by the yere, *vt sup.* or valued at one hundred pounds in goods, or a Gentleman attending in ordinarie office upon any peere of the realme, or Lorde of the Parliament, or upon the wyddow of any peere, or upon a knight of the order, or upon any of the priuie Counsell.</td></tr>
<tr><td>any</td><td>Satten,
Damaske,
Taffata, or
Chamlet,</td><td>in Jackettes,
Coates,
Jerkyns,
Dublets,
or any silk in any kind,
in lynynges of Hose,</td></tr>
<tr><td>any Furre of</td><td colspan="2">Foynes, grave Jennettes, or other, whereof the kinde groweth not within the Queenes Dominions,</td></tr>
</table>

Note

Note that the Lorde
- Chauncellor,
- Treaſurer,
- Preſident of the Counſel,
- Priuie Seale, and the other like great officers of the Realme,

may weare in their apparel, and upon their Horſes, Mules, and Geldinges, as they might have done before by the prouiſion of former Statutes of this Realme.

Note that the
- Biſhops, and other of the Cleargie,
- Juſtices of eyther Benche,
- Barons of the Exchequer,
- Maſter of the Rolles.
- Sergeants at Lawe,
- The Queenes Learned Counſell, and the Queenes Phiſitions,
- and all other Graduats in the two Vniuerſities,
- Maſters of the Chauncerie,
- Apprentices of the Lawe,
- Maiors,
- Aldermen,
- Sheriffes,
- and al other head officers of Cities and Townes corporate, and Wardens of occupations, during the continuance of their offices,
- Barons of the Five Portes,

may weare in their apparell, and vpon their Mules, and Horſes, as they have done before by the proviſions of former Statutes.

Womens Apparel.

No woman ſhal wear any

- Sylke of the colour Purple. except ſuch perſons of great eſtate as are expreſſed in the Statute of 24 Henry VIII.
- Cloth of Golde or Silver tiſſue, Nor Furre of Sables. vnder the degree of A Counteſſe.
- Cloth of Golde, Syluer, Tynſelled Satten, Sylke, or Cloth, mixed or imbrodered with Gold, or Silver, or Pearle, ſaving Silke mixed with Golde or Siluer, in lining of Caules, Part-lettes, or Sleeves, vnder the degree of A Baronneſſe.

Velvet

No woman ſhall wear any

Velvet { Crimſon, Carnatiou, Blewe, Furres of { Blacke Jenets, Luſernes. Imbroderie, Wreath Lace, or Pacement Lace of, { Gold, or Silver,	except	All degrees above mentioned. The wyues of { knightes of the order, and of the priuie Counſell. The Laydes and Gentlewomen of { The privie Chamber, Bedde Chamber, and Maydes of honor.
Gownes or Clokes of Velvet, Satten, or tuffe Taffata, Furres of Libardes, Imbroiderie of any Sylke, nor Taylers woorke like to imbroderie, nor Caules, Sleeves, Ruffes, Partlets or linings trymed with { Pearle, Spangles, or Purles of gold or Silver,	except	The degrees and perſons above mentioned. And wyues of { Barons ſonnes, and alſo the daughters of Barons, and the wyues of knightes, or of perſons that may diſpend and be ſeſſed at two hundred poundlandes in the ſubſidie booke.
Hattes, Cappes, Hatbandes, Capbandes, { Garniſhed or Imbrodered with Gold or Silver, White woorkes, alias Cutwoorkes, made beyonde the Seas, Sylke hoſe,		Vnder the degrees and perſons aboue mentioned.
Gownes, Cloakes, or other vpper garments of { Damaske, Sylke Grograine, or Taffata, Kirtles of { Veluet, or Satten, Furres, whereof the kinde groweth not within the Queenes Dominions, except Foynes, gray Jenettes, Budge, and Woolfe, Caules of Gold or Siluer, or Caules mixed with Gold or Syluer, Veluet in gardes of Gownes,	except	The degrees and perſons above mentioned, or the wives of thoſe that may diſpend one hundred pounde landes by the yeere, and ſo valued in the Subſidie booke, and daughters of any knight, and ſuch as be ſworne the Queenes women, or the wyues of thoſe that ſhall keepe continually one great Horſe, with ſufficient furniture for her Maieſties ſeruice in the warres.

Gownes

None shal weare any

Gownes of	Taffata, Sylke Grograine, Chamlet,	except	The degrees and perſons before mentioned, the wife of the ſonne and heyre apparant of him that may diſpend one hundred poundes *vt ſupra*, and the wiues of thoſe that may diſpend one hundred markes by the yeere *vt ſupra*.
Kirtles of	Satten, or Damaske,		

Gentlewomen ordinarilye attendaunt upon	Dutcheſſes, Marqueſſes, Counteſſes,	May weare as the wyues of thoſe that may diſpend one hundred pounde by the yeere, and are valued *vt ſupra*.
Gentlewomen ordinarilye attendaunt upon	Viſcounts wyues, Barons wyues, the wyues of knyghtes of the order, and of the priuie Counſel,	May weare as the wyues of thoſe that may diſpend one hundred Markes, valued *vt ſupra*. And may alſo weare their liuerie Gownes garded with Velvet.

None ſhal weare any

Petticoates of Velvet, nor any Golde or Sylver upon any Peticoate,	Under the degree of a Baronneſſe.		
Peticoates of Sylke, Veluet, Taffata, Satten, or any Golde or Syluer in any	Cloake or Sauegarde,	under the degree of	A wyfe of a knight of the Order, or of the priuie Counſell, or any Gentlewoman attending on the Queenes Maieſtie in her Chamber, or the Maydes of Honour.

No perſon under the degrees aboue ſpecified ſhall weare any garde or welt of Sylke, upon any Cloake or Sauegarde.

Neceſſarie Additions.

1. Inprimis, that all officers of her Maieſties houſholde, and other her ſeruaunte in ordinarie, not conteyned within the rates limited and ſet forth by the Procla mation, ſhall obſerve ſuch orders for their apparel, as ſhalbe from tyme to tym ſet downe in wryting by the Lord Chamberlaine, the Maſter of the Horſe, and othe her Maieſties principal officers of her houſholde.

2. Item, if any perſon ſhal, in contempt and defrauding of this Proclamation deuiſe any newe kynde or fourme of apparell, and for garniſhyng thereof, and thereby ſhalbe at greater charge than appertayneth to his degree and qualite, and is

B here

here aboue mentioned and entended: Then the ſayde perſon to ſuſteyne the lyke puniſhment for his contempt, as if the ſayde garment or garniſhying had been eſpecially prohibited.

3. Item, that it ſhalbe lawfull for all Juſtices of Peace, and Sheriffes of Shires, to wear Veluet or other Silkes in their Coates or Caſockes, at ſuch tymes as they ſhall attende upon the Queenes Maieſties perſon, or when they ſhall reſort to places of Aſſiſes and Seſſions, and other generall aſſemblies for the Queenes ſervice.

4. Item, that no perſon under the degree of a Baron, a Knight of the Order, one of the Priuie Counſel, a Gentleman of her Maieſties priuie Chamber, or any other Gentleman ordinarily attendant upon her Maieſties perſon, ſhall weare any gardes of Veluet upon any one garment, exceedyng in the whole in Velvet the breadth of ſixe inches.

5. Item, that it ſhalbe lawfull for the Lordes of Parliament, to give for their lyueries, Coates, or Cloakes, garded with Veluet or any other Silke, the gardes in the whole not exceedying in breadth aboue foure inches.

6. Item, that it ſhalbe lawfull for the ſonnes of thoſe that may diſpende xl l. by the yeere, being ſo rated at the laſt Subſidie, and for wardes whoſe land is xl l. by the yeere, to weare Sarcenet in the lyning of their Hoſe, Dublets, Hattes, or Cappes.

7. Item, that it ſhalbe lawful to weare in liueries, Silke Buttons, and Taffata, Grograyne, Veluet, or other Silke in the facing of Coates, as is commonly uſed.

8. Item, that all inferior perſons, under the degrees aboue ſpecified, not otherwyſe prouyded for, or limited by this Proclamation, ſhall confourme themſelues in their apparel, in all thynges, according to the Statute made and prouided in anno 24 Henrici VIII. and in anno 1, 2, Philippi & Marie. Or els to ſuſteyne ſuch puniſhment as by the ſayd Statute is prouided.

9. Item, that all Apprentices at the lawe, and vtter barriſters of the Innes of Court, and all Merchauntes of any ſocietie, and al that keepe houſhold in Citie or Towne *, and ſuch as may diſpend xx l. by the yeere, may weare a welt of Veluet in their Gownes, Jackets, or Coates.

That no perſon ſhalbe impeached for wearyng of any cloth made within the Realme, ſo long as he ſhal obſerue the Order and Rates by this preſent Proclamation limited. But if any perſon ſhall willingly breake the tenor and effect of this Proclamation, then her Highneſſe pleaſure is, that every ſuch offender ſhall haue the penalties of the lawes extended againſt them to the vttermoſt, without any toleration or fauour.

* I find the following entry, dated September 4, 26 Eliz. in a book belonging to the Corporation of Wincheſter: "Item, that no citizen of this citie, that hath been elected bayliff of the ſame, or to anie office above that degree, ſhall from henceforth were, in the ſtrete within this citie, anie hoſe or ſtockings of white, grene, yellow, redde, blewe, weggett, or oringe color; neither ſhall were, at anie aſſemble bourowghmote, or ſeſſions, or at any ſermon to be preached uppon the ſundaies or hollidaies, anie white, grene, yellowe, or red doublet, uppon payne to forfayte and looſe, for everie tyme wherin anie perſon or perſons ſhall offend herein, IIs. VId. to be levied by diſtreſſe uppon everie offender or offenders, by the maiors ſergant for the tyme being, to thuſe of the poore people of the ſame citie."

 A Com-

A Commandment giuen by the Queenes most excellent Maiestie, the twelfth of Februarie, and xxii of her Highnesse Reigne, and declared by the Lord Chauncellor of Englande, and other the Lordes of her Maiesties most honourable Priuie Counsel in the Starre Chamber, concerning clokes and ruffes of excessiue length and depth.

IT is alſo to be underſtoode, that the ſaide xii day of Februarie, in this preſent yeere 1579, by the Queenes Maieſties expreſſe commaundement, it was declared and publiſhed by the Lord Chauncellor, and other the Lords of her Maieſties Councell in the Starre Chamber, that her Maieſties pleaſure was, by aduiſe of her ſaide Councell, that from the one and twentieth of this moneth, no perſon ſhall vſe or weare ſuch exceſſiue long clokes, being in common ſight monſtrous, as nowe of late are begonne to be vſed, and before two yeeres paſt hath not bene uſed in this Realme. Neither alſo ſhoulde any perſon uſe or weare ſuch great and exceſſiue ruffes in or about the vppermoſt part of their neckes, as had not been uſed before two yeeres paſt; but that all perſons ſhoulde in modeſt and comely ſort leave off ſuch fonde diſguiſed and monſtrous manner of attyring themſelves, as both was unſupportable for charges, and undecent to be worne.

And this her Maieſte commanded to be obſerved, upon paine of her high indignation, and the paines thereto due; and willed all officers to ſee to the reformation and redreſſe thereof, to the puniſhment of any offending in theſe caſes, as perſons wilfully diſobeying or contemning her Maieſties commandement.

Geuen the xxii yeere of her Highneſſe reigne, as is before expreſſed.

God ſaue the Queene.

Imprinted at London by CHRISTOPHER BARKER,
Printer to the Queenes moſt excellent Maieſtie.

Cum priuilegio Regiæ Maieſtatis.

Anno Dom. 1579.

By

By the QUEENE.

A branche of a PROCLAMATION publiſhed the twelfth day of Februarie, in the eight yeere of the Queenes Maieſties reigne, concerning Swordes, Daggers, Rapiers, and Bucklers: commaunded by her Highneſſe to be put in execution, and of all her louing ſubiects to be obeyed and kept, vpon paine of her Maieſties high indignation, and the penaltie in the ſame conteyned.

The branche or clauſe of the ſaide Proclamation.

ITEM, her Maieſtie ordereth and alſo commandeth, that no perſon ſhall weare any Sworde, Rapier, or ſuch like weapon, that ſhall paſſe the length of one yarde and halfe a quarter of the blade, at the vttermoſt: nor any Dagger aboue the length of xii ynches in blade at the moſt: nor any Buckler with any point or pike above two ynches in length. And if any Cutler, or other artificer, ſhall ſell, make, or keepe in his houſe any Sworde, Rapier, Dagger, Buckler, or ſuch like, contrary thereunto, the ſame to be impriſoned, and to make fine at the Queenes Maieſties pleaſure, and the weapon to be forfayted. And if any ſuch perſon ſhall offende a ſeconde time, then the ſame to be baniſhed from the place and Towne of his dwelling.

Given at our pallace of Weſtminſter, the twelfth day of Februarie, in the two and twentieth yeere of our reigne.

God ſave the Queene.

Imprinted at London by CHRISTOPHER BARKER,
Printer to the Queenes moſt excellent Maieſtie.
Anno Dom. 1579.

A Particular of the Plate fold belonging to the great guilt Cubberd of Eftate, 1626, 2 CHARLES I.

(From an original Roll, formerly belonging to Sir WILLIAM HERRICK, of Beaumanor, Leicefterfhire; and now in the poffeffion of his immediate Defcendant WILLIAM HERRICK, Efq.)

THIS INDENTURE, made the fifteenth day of September, in the fecond yeare of the raigne of our Soueraigne Lord Charles, by the grace of God, Kinge of England, Scotland, Fraunce, and Ireland, Defender of the Faith, &c. Betweene Sir Henery Myldmay, knight, m^r and threr of his Majeftie's jewells and plate, on the one party, and John Acton, the King's gouldfmith, on the other party, witneffeth, that whereas the King's Majefty, by his tres pattents, vnder the great feale of England, dated the thirteenth day of September laft paft, directed vnto the faid Sir Henery Myldmay, knight, for the deliuery of twenty thoufand ounces, or thereabouts, of gilt plate, out of his Majeftye's great gilt cupboard of eftate, and other his guilt plate remaining in his the faid Sir Henery Myldmaye's charge and cuftody, vnto John Acton, his gouldfmith, takinge a bill indented betweene him and the faid gouldfmith for the receipt thereof, mencõning therin the particular peeces and theire iuft waights, as by the faid tres pattents more plainly appeareth. The faid Sir Henery Myldmay hath deliuered vnto the faid John Acton thefe feueral parcells of gilt plate hereafter mencõed, viz.

IMPRIMIS, two water-potts gilt, with couers, and two handles a peece, per oz. — —	621 oz.
Item, a paire of gilt potts chafed in bullions, with crownes imperiall on theire couers, per oz. —	803 oz.
A paire of gilt potts, with thiftles and marygolds, with crownes imperiall, per oz. — —	704 oz. di.
Two watter-potts gilt, chafed in flames, with fnake handles, per oz.	732 oz.
A paire of gilt potts chafed, with grapes, hauinge crownes, per oz. — — —	710 oz.
A paire of gilt potts chafed, with bullions, hauinge crownes, per oz. — —	1049 oz.
A paire of like pottes, with bullions and crownes, per oz.	1046 oz. di.
A paire of gilt potts chafed, with antique fifhes, hauinge crownes, per oz. — —	862 oz.
A paire of like gilt potts, with crayfifhes and crownes, per oz.	882 oz. 3 qr.
A paire of ftoope potts, with antique heads, per oz.	522 oz.
A paire of gilt potts, with longe necks, and graven with rabbafke worke, per oz. —	157 oz.

A paire

A paire of flatte gilt flaggons, with bullions, plaine fcutchions, and crownes, per oz. — 787 oz.
A paire of flatte gilt flaggons, with funbeames and crownes, per oz. — — 853 oz.
A paire of like gilt flaggons, without funbeames, hauinge crownes, per oz. — 852 oz.
A paire of gilt fpoute potts, made of a paire of flaggons, with boffes, per oz. — — 537 oz.
Two layers, with one handle apeece, chafed, with flower de luces, per oz. — — 812 oz.
A wild man of filuer, garnifhed with fondry beafts and leaves, per oz. — — 1210 oz.
Two leopards gilt and enameled, with chaines, per oz. 1184 oz.
One ftandinge cupp of filuer, with a couer, per oz. 210 oz.
One cuppe and cou', garnifhed with fondry braunches of diuers collors, per oz. — 157 oz. 3 qr.
A doble Portingall cupp, with boffes, enameled, per oz. 77 oz.
One doble Almaine cupp chafed, with bullions, and ftricken with the ĺre N, per oz. — — 70 oz. di.
A doble Almaine cup, with bullions, and ftricken with ĺre H, per oz. — — 55 oz. di.
A doble Almaine cupp, with bullions, and ĺre N, per oz. 58 oz.
A doble Almaine cupp, with bullions, and ĺre P, per oz. 57 oz.
A doble Almaine cupp, ftricken with ĺre M, per oz. 45 oz. di.
A doble Almaine cupp, in bullions, with ĺre A, per oz. 57 oz.
A doble Almaine cupp, in bullions, with ĺre G, per oz. 58 oz. di.
A doble Almaine cuppe, with leaues, Noremborowe makinge, per oz. — 49 oz. qr.
A doble Almaine cuppe, with heades, and ĺre N, touch, per oz. 45 oz.
A doble Almaine cupp, in bullions, ĺre B, per oz. 46 oz.
A doble Almaine cupp, in bullions, ĺre E, per oz. — 51 oz. 3 qr.
A doble Almaine cupp, in bullions, ĺre C, per oz. 52 oz. qr.
A doble Almaine cupp, Noremborowe makinge, per oz. 76 oz. di.
A doble Almaine cupp, with boffes, and ĺre N, touch, per oz. 137 oz.
A doble Almaine cupp, with bullions, per oz. — 84 oz. di.
A doble Almaine cupp, in bullions, armes in the bottome, per oz. 89 oz. di.
A doble Portingall cuppe, with boffes, enameled, per oz. 81 oz. di.
A doble Portingall cupp, with boffes, wantinge a foote, per oz. 38 oz. di.
A doble Almaine cupp, with bullions, ĺre K, per oz. 44 oz.
A doble Almaine cupp, with bullions, ĺre V, per oz. 46 oz.
Sixe boles or fpice-plates, without a couer, hauinge longe topps, per oz. — — 100 oz.
Sixe flatte boles or fpice-plates chafed, with martlets, hauinge one couer, per oz. — — 342 oz. di.

Three

Three flatte boles, with martlets, hauinge one couer, and lre G, per oz. — ——	146 oz. 3 qr.
Two antique ſtandinge cupps, with perſonages and ſcutchions, per oz. — —	292 oz. qr.
A Noremborowe cupp and couer, per oz. —	73 oz. qr.
A Noremborowe cupp and couer, per oz. —	50 oz. qr.
A Noremborowe cupp and couer, per oz. —	41 oz. 3 qr.
A Noremborowe cuppe and couer, per oz. —	43 oz. 3 qr.
A peare cuppe and couer, per oz. —	42 oz. di.
A Portingall cupp and couer, well chaſed, hauinge labells, per oz.	90 oz. di.
A Portingall cupp and couer, with an inſcription, hauinge martlets, per oz. — —	74 oz.
A Portingall cuppe and couer chaſed, with the rape of Proſerpina, per oz. — —	72 oz.
A Portingall cuppe and couer, with labells, chaſed, with the ſtory of Bacchus, per oz. —	73 oz. 3 qr.
A Portingall cuppe and couer, chaſed, with the ſtory of Neptune, per oz. —	108 oz. 3 qr.
A Portingall cuppe and couer, with pendants, per oz.	77 oz. qr.
A Portingall cuppe and couer, with two men wreſtling on the couer, per oz. ———	103 oz. qr.
A Portingall cuppe and couer chaſed, with camells, per oz.	89 oz. 3 qr.
A Portingall cuppe and couer, with labells, well chaſed, per oz.	112 oz. 3 qr.
A Portingall cuppe and couer, with olde pearle, hauinge had labells, per oz. — —	75 oz. qr.
A Portingall cuppe and couer, with labells, per oz.	91 oz.
A Portingall cuppe and couer, hauinge had labells, per oz.	97 oz. 3 qr.
A Portingall cuppe and couer, like a chalice, with rings, and an inſcription, per oz. ———	54 oz. di.
Two cuppes and couers, with antelope hornes; the one plaine, the other in bullions, per oz. ——	86 oz. 3 qr.
A gilt Portingall cupp and couer, like a ſalt, per oz.	81 oz.
A ſtandinge cuppe and couer gilt, per oz. —	36 oz.
A gilt Portingall cuppe, with collets of aggot and mother of pearle, per oz. —— ——	53 oz.
A gilt Portingall cuppe ſett with boſſes and emblemes, per oz.	78 oz.
Two faire gilt boles pincked and couers, per oz.	83 oz. di.
A gilt bole and couer, with a roſe in the topp of the couer, per oz.	40 oz.
A bole and cou' graven, and ſome bullyons, per oz.	12 oz.
A gilt bole and couer grauen, per oz. —	36 oz. qr.
A litle Noremborowe cupp and couer, per oz. ——	12 oz.
A litle porrenger and couer, per oz. ———	6 oz. 3 qr.
A gilt egge-diſhe and couer, per oz. ———	60 oz. 3 qr.

 Two

Two gilt porengers, the handles dragons, and angells on their couers, per oz. ———	46 oz.
Foure fmall gilt boxes, with B P on theire bottomes, per oz.	15 oz. qr.
Twelue odde couers of gilt boles and fondry broken peeces, per oz.	211 oz. di.
Foure gilt cupps or vaines of filuer, per oz. ———	53 oz. di.
Foure gilt pomells for a chaire, per oz. —	48 oz.
Two pomells of filuer parcell gilt, per oz. —	6 oz. di. di.
Fiue gilt cupps for a feild bed, per oz. ——	32 oz. di.
Three gilt pomells for a chaire, parcell of fower, per oz.	43 oz. di.

All which faid feuerall parcells of gilt plate the faid John Acton doth acknowledge by thefe pertl' to have rec[d] from the handes of the faid Sir Henery Myldmay, amountinge in all to the nomber of 20,021 oz. di. qr.; and the faid Sir Henery Myldmay witneffeth, that the glaffe, copper, and horne, that were found in the faid feuerall pcells of plate, wayed nyne oz. and a halfe; and fo the totall of the ounces of neate filuer amounteth to the nomber of 20,011 oz. di. di. gr. In wittnes whereof the partyes abouefayd to thefe prefent indentures interchangeably haue put theire hands and feales the day and yeare aboue written.

HENRY MYLDEMAY.

Expences of entertaining KING JAMES II. at COVENTRY, 1687.

(From the Corporation Books.)

ON the firft of September, 1687, King James II. came to Coventry. The mayor* and aldermen, having notice of his intention, provided a cup of maffy gold, weighing about 3 lbs. price 167*l.* 7*s.* 6*d.* (another MS fays 171*l.* 17*s.* 6*d.*) Alfo, fuppofing he would choofe to lodge at the White Friers, fent the conftable to warn all houfeholders between Spon-Bargates and Newgate to whiten their houfes, &c.; and alfo, the inhabitants of Crofs Cheaping, Baley-lane, and Hay-lane; alfo, they required all houfeholders between Spon-Bargates and Newgate to fand their ftreets, and drefs the fronts of their houfes with green boughes, which was done. But, the day before, the harbinger came and declared his Majefty would lodge at the houfe of Richard Hopkins, efq. in High-ftreet, near the drapery-door. The mayor ordered alfo the companies to meet that morning; and about noon the mayor and aldermen rode on horfeback from St. Mary's Hall to Spon-Bars, being attended by the feveral companies, with their ftreamers, and with drums, and with all manmer of mufic that could be got; befides which, about 200 citizens, moft Diffenters, went to meet his Majefty as far as Meriden, where his Majefty fhewed them great refpect. Alfo, the deputy-lieutenant met his Majefty at Guilford Ford, where Sir Thomas Norton made an excellent fpeech. About five at night his Majefty came to Spon-Bars, where the mayor prefented the gold cup; and the fteward made, or read, a fpeech to his Majefty, and the mayor delivered to the King the fword; after which the mayor and aldermen rode before his Majefty, the mayor carrying the fword; the fenior alderman, Nathaniel Harriman, the cap of maintenance; alderman Webfter, the great mace; and the next in feniority, the other mace; and fo rode before his Majefty to his lodgings; the companies ftanding on both fides Spon-ftreet till his Majefty was paffed, and then followed into the city. Next morning, the mayor and aldermen attended his Majefty from his lodgings to the Crofs, and thence through Trinity church unto St. Michael's, where he touched about 300 perfons for the evil; then had a ftately breakfaft and banquet at St. Mary's Hall at the city's charge, and was attended thence to his lodgings, where he took horfe, being attended by the mayor and aldermen on horfeback as far as Bagginton Bridge, the feveral companies, with their ftreamers, ftanding on both fides Much Park-ftreet at his Majefty's paffing by. Moft of the nobility and gentry of the county waited on the King when at Coventry; and fuch numbers of country people flocked in, that ftandings at the windows of front rooms let at 12*d.* each.

* Septimus Bott, an apothecary.

Spent by the Corporation of Coventry at the Entertainment of King James II. in his Progrefs through Coventry.

(Mr. Richard Haywood, Treafurer.)

	£.	s.	d.
Gave a gold cup — — — — —	171	17	6
Mr. Septimus Bott, mayor, for fweetmeats — —	27	17	0
Meat — — — — —	13	14	4
Wine — — — — —	21	12	6
Homage fee — — — — — —	41	6	8
King's cook — — — — — —	10	0	0
City cook — — — — —	9	8	6
Steward Fielding, for making a fpeech to his Majefty —	5	7	6
For linen fpoiled, borrowed of Mrs. Smith, Spon-ftreet —	2	12	6
The aldermen that went to Worcefter to invite him —	3	18	9
The feveral companies, for waiting on the King — —	27	9	4
Alderman Webfter, for meat — — — —	3	6	0
Alderman Bradney, for corn — — — —	3	5	6
His Majefty's clerk of the market — — — —	1	1	6
The King's trumpeters — — — —	2	0	0
Richard Howcott, for carrying the city ftreamer —	0	7	0
The city bailiff's bill for fifh, fowl, and wine = —	88	18	2
	434	2	9

CEREMONIALS OF VARIOUS FUNERALS.

The order of the Funerall of Edward Earle of Darby, who died at Latham Hall, on Friday the XXIIIIth of Octobber, about XII of the clocke, and was buried at Ormskirke, on Thursday the 4th of December following, Anno Domini 1572.

First, after his departure his body was well seared, wrapt in lead, and chested; then the chappell, the house, with the two courts, was hanged with blacke cloath, and garnished with escutcheons of his armes.

Upon Saturday before the funerall, the body was brought into the chappell, where it was covered with a paule of blacke velvet, garnished with escutcheons of his armes, and thereon was sett his coate of armes, healme, and creaste, sworde, and targett, and aboute him weare placed the standerd, great banner, and six banerolls.

And on the Sondaye in the morning, before the sermon, the Earle of Darby his sonne being present, with a greate nomber of esquires and gentlemen, and the three chiefe officers, viz. the steward, threasurer, and controuler, standing about the body with white staves in their handes; Clarenceux King of Armes, with his riche coate on his backe, published this thanksgiving and stile of the defunct, in forme following:

"All honour, laude, and prayse, to Almighty God, who through his deere mercy hath taken out of this transitory life to his eternall joy and blisse, the Right Honourable Edward Earle of Darby, Lord Stanley, Straunge, and of Man, one of the Queene's Majestie's most Honourable Privie Counsell, and knight and companion of the most noble order of the Garter."

And on Wensday, the day before the funerall, at the beginning of evening prayer, the same was published by Norroy King of Armes.

The order and manner of the hearse wherin the body lay during the service.

At Ormskirk, two myles from Latham, was a stately hearse erected, of 5 princi-palls, 13 foote of length and 9 foote of breadth, 21 foote high, dubble rayled, all garnished, in this order as followeth.

First, the topp part and the rayles covered with blacke cloath, the valence and the principalls covered with blacke velvet; to the valence a fringe of silke.

The majesty being of taffita lyned with buckram, had thereon, curiously wrought in gould and silver, an hatchment of his armes, with his healme, creaste, suppor-ters, and word; and fowre other buckram escutcheons in mettle, and six greate bu-riall past escutcheons at the fowre corners, and the uppermoste topp; the valence ſett forth with ſmall eſcutcheons of his armes on buckram, in mettall within the garter. The rayles and poſts alſo garniſhed with eſcutcheons of royall paper in mettle.

The which hearſe was placed betwene the quire and the body of the churche. The church was alſo hanged with black cloath, eſcutcheons alſo being ſett thereon, not only of his owne armes within the garter, but alſo impaled with the three countеſſes his wives; and this being finiſhed by Wedneſdaye at night before the buriall, the order and proceeding on Thurſday, being the appoynted day of the funerall, was in manner following.

Firſt, two yeomen conductors, with black ſtaves, to lead the way;	Morgan ap Robert, Thomas Bottle.
Then all poore men in gownes two and two, in nomber	100.
Then the quire and ſinging men in ſurpleſſes, in nomber	40.
Then an eſquire bearing the ſtanderd, with his hood on his head, and his horſe trapped to the ground, garniſhed with a ſhaffron of his armes within the garter on his forehead, with 4 eſcocheons on buckram in mettle on each ſyde;	Peter Stanley.
Then the defunct's gentlemen mounted on comley geldings, in their gownes, and hoods on theire ſhoulders, two and two, to the nomber of	80.
Then the two ſecretarys of the defunct ridyng together, as the gentlemen aforeſayd;	Gilbert Morton, Gabriel Maſon.
Then the eſquires and knights in like order two and two, to the nomber of	50.
Then the defuncts two chapleynes with hoods on theire ſhoulders according to theire degrees;	Chriſtopher Tomſon, M.A. John Shirborn, B. D.
Then the preacher, being the Deane of Cheſter, his horſe trapped, and a doctor's hood on his ſhoulder;	Doctor Langworth.
Then the defunct's three chiefeſt officers, viz. the ſteward, threaſurer, and comptroller, with white ſtaves in theire hands, and hoods on theire ſhoulders, theire horſes trapped;	William Maſſy, Sir Richard Shierborn, Knight, Henry Stanley.
Then an eſquire, bearing the greate banner of his armes, his hood on his head, his horſe trapped and garniſhed with eſcutcheons, in manner as afore;	Edward Norrys.
Then an heralde of armes with his hood on his head, his horſe trapped as is before mentioned, wearing the defunct's coat of armes, made of damaſke, who bare his healme, parcill gilt, with mantles of black velvet, the knopps guilt. On a wreath of his coulers ſtood his creaſt, curiouſly paynted, and wrought in gould and ſilver;	Lancaſter.

Then

Then a king of armes, his hood on his head, wearing his coate of armes richly imbroidered with the armes of England, his horfe trapt and garnifhed as aforefayd, bearing the fhield of armes of the defunct within the garter, and theron a coronett according to his degree; — Norroy.

Then another king of armes ryding in like order, bearing the defunct's fword with the pommell upward, the hilt and chape gilte, with a fcabbard of velvett; — Clarenceux.

After them another king of armes ryding as the other, bearing another of the defunct's coate of armes, being wrought as the other was; and on the left fyde of him roade a gentleman ufher with a white rodde in his hand, his horfe trapped as aforefayd, and his hood on his head; — George Leigh, gent. ufher, Sir Gilbert Dethicke, Garter King of Armes.

Then the chariot, wherein the body was layde, covered with black velvett, garnifhed with efcotcheons, drawne by four horfes trapped in blacke, on each horfe fowre efcutcheons placed, and a chaffron of his armes. On each horfe fatt a page in a black coate, and a hood on his head; on the fore feat of the fayd chariot fatt a gentleman ufher in his gowne, and hood on his head, with a white rodd in his hand; — Thomas Bradfhawe, Alexander Rigbye, Nicholas Rigbye, Ralphe Brockfeilde, pages. Edward Scarefbrick, gentleman ufher.

Next about the body fowre efquires, being affiftants to the fayd body, their hoods on their heads, and their horfes likewife trapped to the grounde; — Robert Barton, Robert Dolton, Roger Bradfhaw, Jofeph Prefton.

And on the outfyde of them aboute the chariot rode fix other efquires with their gownes, and hoods on theire heads, their horfes trapped, each of them bearing a banneroll, not only of the defunct's armes, but alfo of the armes of fuche noble armes whereof he was defcended, viz.

The firfte banneroll had the armes of Thomas firfte Earle of Derby of that name, Lord Stanly and of Man, empaled with the armes of Elenor his wife, daughter of Richard Nevill, Earle of Salifbury, and fifter to Richard Nevill, Earle of Warwick and Salifbury, caried by — Edward Tarbucke.

The fecond banneroll was the armes of John Lord Stanley and Straunge, the fonne and heire of the fayd Thomas, empaled with the armes of Jane his wife, daughter and heire of John Lord Straunge of Knocking, which was caried by — Edward Leigh.

The third armes or banneroll was of Thomas fecond Earle of Derby, of that name Lord Stanley, Straunge, and of Man, empaled with the armes of Anne, daughter of Edward Lord Haftings, and fifter to George Lord Haftings, and the firft Earle of Huntington of that name, carried by — William Stanley.

The

The fourth banneroll was the armes of the defunct, empaled with the armes of Dorathy his firste wife, daughter of Thomas Duke of Norffolke, Earle of Surrey, Earle Marshall of England, Lord Mowbray, Segrave Bruse, which was borne by } Charles Holte.

The fift banneroll was also of the defunct's armes, empaled with the armes of Margrett his second wife, daughter of Ellice Barlow, Esq. which banner was borne by } George Middleton.

The sixt banneroll was empaled with the armes of the defunct, and Mary his third wife, daughter of Sir George Cotton, Knight, vicechamberleyn to King Edward the Sixt; } Fraunscis Holte.

Next after the chariot proceeded the chiefe mourner, in the mourning roabes of an earle; on each syde of him rode a gentleman usher with white rodds in theire hands, theire hoods on theire heads, and theire horses trapped.

Richard Asheton. } Henry Earle of Darby. { Marmaduke Newton.

The trayne bearer, Mr. Warren.

On the left syde of him, and something behynde, rode the gentleman of the horse to the defunct, his hood on his head, and his horse trapped, leading in his hand the horse of estate, all covered and trapped with velvet; } John Ormeston.

Next after rode eight mourners, assistants to the chiefe mourner, theire hoods on their heads, and theire horses trapped with fine cloath downe to the grounde; { John Lord Sturton,
Sir Rowland Stanley,
Sir Peter Leigh,
—— Butler, Esq.
—— Ratcliffe, Esq.
Alexander Barlow, Esq.
Alexander Rigby, Esq.
William Stopforth, Esq.

Then a yeoman in a black coate, bareheaded; George Watson.

Then two sonnes of the principall mourner in gownes, and hoods on their shoulders, eyther of them having a gentleman to leade his horse; } William Stanley, Esq.
Fraunscis Stanley, Esq.

Then two yeomen ushers with white rodds, on foot.

Then the defunct's yeomen two and two, the nomber of 500.

Then all gentlemens' servants two and two.

And thus being whiffled all the way by certayne yeomen in black coates, on foote, with black staves in their hands, proceed to the church doore, where theire servants attended to receave theire horses; and there being dismounted, all the gentlemen that proceeded before the corps, entred into the church, and tooke their places, according to theire degrees, leaving the hundredth poore men without the churche, on eache syde the waye.

2 Then

Then the body was taken out of the chariott by eight gentlemen in gownes, theire hoods on theire heads, affifted by fowre yeomen in black coates, and foe borne into the hearfe, where he was orderly placed upon a table, being three foote high, covered with black cloath, and upon him was layd not only a paule of blacke velvet, but alfo his coate of armes, fword, fhielde, healme, and creafte.

The names of the eight gentlemen that caryed the corps:

William Orrell, Jafper Worth, Frances Banes, John Moore, Thomas Starkey, John Byrom, Edm. Winftonley, James Bradfhaw.

The names of the four yeomen affiftants:

Frauncis Hamlet, Edmond Parker, Thomas Wilfon, Roger Hilton.

And thus the body being placed, the principall mourner entred the hearfe, where was prepared for him, at the head of the defunct, a ftoole with a carpett and two cufhions of black velvett to leane and kneele upon.

Then entred the other eight mourners and tooke theire places within the uttermofte part of the hearfe on each fyde of the body, having eache of them a cufhion of blacke velvett to leane uppon, theire ftools covered with black cloath, and cufhions of the fame to kneele uppon.

At the feete of the defunct without the rayle ftood the two efquires holding the ftandard and great banner, and on each fyde the hearfe ftood the other fix efquires, with the banerolls, and behynde the principall mourner ftood the three kings of armes, and fowre gentlemen ufhers, and betweene the ftanderd and the great banner ftood Lancafter Herald, wearing the defunct's coate of armes.

And thus the body being placed, and every other eftate accordingly in theire degrees, Norroy King of Armes pronounced the ftyle of the defunct as before is mentioned; which ended, the Deane of Chefter * began his fermon, and after the fermon a pfalme being fung, the vicar began the commemoration, and after the epiftle the offering was commenced in manner and forme as it followeth, the quire finging all the tyme of the offering.

The offering in the churche.

Firfte, Henry Earle of Darby, being principall mourner, did offer for the defunct a peece of goulde, having before him, Garter, Clarenceux, and Norroy, Kings of Armes, and Lancafter Herald, and on each fyde of Garter a gentleman ufher, and an efquire to bear the chiefe mourner's trayne; prefently after did proceede the eight mourners two and two according to theire degrees; and in like order hee with the fayd eight retourned agayne to theire places, wheare ftaying a fmall tyme the chief mourner went to offer for himfelfe, having before him Clarenceux and Lancafter, and thus having offered, he ftayed betweene the vicar and Lancafter to receave the honourable hatchments of his father, which were offered up by the other eight mourners unto him, in manner and forme following.

The coate	Firft, the Lord Stourton and Sir Rowland Stanley offered up the coate of armes, having going before them.	Clarenceux King of Armes.
The fworde	Secondly, Sir Peter Leigh, knight, and Thomas Butler, Efq. offered the fword, the pommell upward, having before them	Norroy King of Armes.

* Dr. Richard Langworth.

The

The targ	Thirdly, John Ratcliff, and Alexander Barlow, Eſquires, the targ of his armes, and before them went agayne,	Clarenceux.
Healme and creſt	Fourthly, Alexander Rigby and William Stopforth, Eſquires, offered the healme and creaſt, having before them agayne	Norroy.

This being don, the principall mourner repayred agayne into his place, and on each ſyde of him a gentleman uſher, his trayne borne by an eſquire as aforeſayd, and before him Clarenceux King of Armes, where he remayned until the reſt of the offering was ended.

Then offered the other eight mourners, viz.

The Lord Sturton and Sir Rowland Stanley offered for themſelves, having to goe before them	Clarenceux.
Then Sir Peeter Leigh, knight, and Thomas Butler, Eſquire, having before them	Norroy.
Then John Radcliffe and Alexander Barlow, Eſquires, and before them went	Lancaſter herald of Armes.
Then Alexander Rigby and William Stopforth, Eſquires, and before them went	Blewmantle purſuivant of Armes.
Thus, when the principall mourner, the eight mourners aſſiſtants, had all offered and placed agayne as aforeſayd, then the four eſquires aſſiſtant to the body offered	Lancaſter.
Then the ſtanderd was offered by the eſquire that bare it, and before him went	Blewmantle.
Then the great banner was offered by the eſquire that bare it, and before him went	Blewmantle.

The ſayd ſtanderd and banner being offered, the eſquires that bare them, as ſoone as they had offered them, put of their hoods, and tooke theire places among the reſt of the gentlemen mourners.

Then offered the ſteward, threaſurer, and comptroller, with white ſtaves in theire hands, and before them	Lancaſter.

Then offered all other knights, eſquires, and gentlemen, wearing black, proceeding in order two and two, according to theire degrees.

Then offered the yeoman uſhers, and after them the defunct's yeomen two and two in order.

The offering thus ended, the 100 poore men weare placed to proceede in order homewards on foote, and after them the gentlemen, eſquires, and knights, on horſeback.

Then Garter principall King of Armes.

Then the principall mourner with the other eight mourners two and two.

And the yeomen on foot in order, two and two.

After whoſe departure, preſently the body was, by the eight gentlemen and four yeomen aforeſayd, caried to the grave, and before it went Clarenceux and Norroy, Kings

Kings of Armes, and Lancaſter herald of armes, and aboute the body went the four eſquires aſſiſtants, and the ſix other eſquires bearing the bannerolls, and after the body went the ſteward, threaſurer, and comptroller, with the four gentlemen uſhers, and two yeomen uſhers, who, when the body was buried, kneeling on theire knees, with weeping teares, brake their white ſtaves and rodds over theire heads, and threw the ſhivers of the ſame into the grave.

That don, the ſix eſquires delivered up the ſix bannerolls, which weare partly with the reſt of the hatchments placed accordingly and orderly over and about him, and ſoe the ſayd officers departed to Latham Hall, where, before dynner, they receaved theire offices and ſtaves agayne of the new Earle their lord and maſter.

The Procedinge to the Church for an Earle.

Two conductors.
Poore men in gownes.
Two conductors.
Servantes of { Gentlemen. Knightes. Lordes. Earles. }
Trumpetor.
The ſtandard.
Yeomen, ſervantes to the defunct, in cloaks.
The guidon.
Gentlemen, ſervantes to the defunct, in cloaks.
The horſe, led by a groome of the ſtable.
Gentlemen in gownes.
Chaplaines.
Counſellors at lawe.
Secreataries to the defunct.
Gentlemen of his kindred.
Sergeantes at lawe.
The high ſhreife of the ſhyre.
Knightes.
Steward, threſorer, comptroler.
The great banner, borne by a knight.
Helme and creaſt.
Sword and target.
Coate of armes.
Four knights aſſiſtance | The body. | to the body.
The horſe of eſtate, led by a gentleman.
Garter principall kinge of armes.
Eaight aſſiſtance, being noblemen.
Two gentlemen uſshers barehedded.
Noblemen on horſback.
Then all other yeomen in coates.

The Proceeding to the Church for a Counteſs.

Two conductors.
Poore weomen.
Two conductors.
Servantes of { Gentlemen. Knightes. Lordes. Earles. }
Servantes of the defunct.
Gentlemen ſervantes to the defunct.
Chaplains.
Other gentlemen.
Eſquiers.
Knightes.
Steward, threſorer, comptroler.
The preacher.
The great banner.
Officers of armes.
Fower aſſiſtance | The body. | to the body.

A gen-

A gentleman usher—Garter—a gentleman usher.
A lady, cheiffe mourner, assisted by two earles, and her traine borne by a gentlewoman.
Eight other ladyes assistance.
Two servantes in cloakes.
All other ladyes and gentleweomen.
Gentleweomen to the defunct.
Ladyes gentleweomen.
Yeomen in coates.
The parish and others.

The Proceeding to the Funerall of a Baron.

Two conductors.
Poore men.
Two conductors.
Servantes of { Gentlemen. Knites. Barones. Earles.
The standard.
Servantes of the defuncte, in cloakes.
Gentlemen servantes of the defuncte, in cloaks.
The apothecaries.
Chirurgions.
Phisitions.
Chaplaines.
Secreataries.
Gentlemen in gownes.
Steward, thresorer, comptroler,
Knightes.
Executors.
The greate banner.
Helme and creaste.
Sword and targett.
Coate of armes.
Flags.—[The body.]—Flags.
A gentleman usher—Garter—a gentleman usher.
The chiefe mourner.
Six assistance.
Two gentlemen ushers bareheaded.
Lordes on horsebackes.
Knightes on horsebackes.
Yeomen in coates.
Knightes and gentellmen beinge not in blackes.

The Proceedinge to the Funerall of a Baroness.

Two conductors.
Poore weomen.
Two conductors.
Servants of { Gentellmen. Esquiers. Knightes. Lordes and Ladyes.
Servantes of the defuncte.
The steward.
Doctors.
Preacher.
The greate banner.
Officer of armes.
Flags.—The body.—Flags.
Garter, a gentleman usher.
A lady, cheffe mourner, supported by two knightes, her trayne borne by a gentleweoman.
Six ladyes assistans.
Two yeomen.
Gentleweomen in blackes.
Two yeomen.
Ladyes gentleweomen.
Yeomen in coates.
The parish and others.

The

The Proceeding for a Knighte's Funeral.

Two conductors.
Poore men in gownes.
Yeomen in cloakes.
The ſtandard.
Servantes of gentlemen.
Servantes of knightes.
Servantes of lordes.
Servantes of the defunct.
Gentlemen ſervantes of the defunct.
Gentlemen, Eſquires, Knightes } in blackes.
The preacher.
The penon.
Helme and creſt.
Sword and targett.
Coate of armes.
The body.
Cheif mourner.
Four aſſiſtance.
Knightes, Lordes } on horſbackes.
Two yeomen.
Gentleweomen in blackes.
Yeomen in coates.
Gentleweomen without blackes.
The pariſh and others.

Fees belonging to the Officers of Armes for the Funerall of a Knighte.

	l.	s.	d.
For Mr. Clarenceux, his fee, or his deputy for him	6	13	4
For his blackes —	6	13	4
Blackes for two men —	3	0	0
Tranſportacōn outward and homeward at 12d. the myle, from London to any part in his province.			
The heralde for his fee	3	6	8
For his blackes —	3	6	8
Blacke for one ſeruant	1	10	0
Tranſportacōn outward and homeward at 6d. the myle,			
Allowance for the hearſe	3	6	8
For the paule —	1	0	0
The certifficate —	1	0	0
Mr. Clarenceux, his fee, if but only one officer doth ſerue	3	6	8

Hatchments for the Funerall of a Knight.

	l.	s.	d.
A ſtandard —	2	0	0
A penon —	1	6	8
A coate of armes —	1	6	8
A healme —	0	16	8
A creaſte —	0	13	4
Mantles of veluet —	1	0	0
A wreath —	0	5	0
A ſworde with a girdle	0	10	0
A targett —	0	10	0
Six eſcocheons in bukeram	0	12	0
One dozen in paper mettle	0	16	0
One dozen in paper colours	0	12	0
Three irons —	0	6	0
Conductors ſtaues, two	0	1	0
A ſtaffe for the ſtandard	0	1	0
A ſtaffe for the penon	0	1	0

The Proceedinge of a Citezen's Funerall.

Firſt, the childerin of the hoſpitall.
Two conductors.
Poore men in gownes.
Gentlemenes ſervantes in cloaks.
Gentlemen in cloakes.
Gentlemen in gownes.
Aldermen in blackes.
The preacher.
The penon.
Helme and creaſt.
Coate of armes.

A penon of the marchants. The body. A penon of the companey.

The chief mourner.
Two aſſiſtance.
Aldermen not in blackes.
Gentlewoemen in blackes.
The liverie of the company.
Maſters of the hoſpitall.
Gentlemen not in blackes.
The pariſh and others.

A Certifficate to be taken at the Funerall of an Eſquire.

George Stonehouſe, of Little Peckham in the county of Kent, Eſquire, one of the clearkes of the greenecloath in the Queene's houſe, deceaſed at his houſe in London, on Sunday the xijth daye of July, in the xvth yeare of the raigne of our Soveraigne Lady Queene Elizabeth, and was buried in the pariſh church of St. Andrew Underſhafte in London aforeſayd, on Monday the xxth daye of the ſame month. The ſayde George, married to his firſt wife, Elizabeth, daughter of —— Gybſon, of the county of Kent, gent. by whome he had iſſue Edward Stonehouſe his eldeſt ſonne, Thomas, ſecond ſonne, Roaſe, eldeſt daughter, wife to Robert Taylor, Eſquire, one of the tellers of the Exchequor, and Mary, wife to Thomas Reade, of Barton neare Allington in the county of Barkſhire, gent. and Suſan, third daughter. The ſayde George maried to his ſecond wife, Elizabeth, daughter of David Woodroofe, Eſquire, ſometyme alderman of London, by whome he had iſſue William Stonehouſe, third ſonne, Nicholas fourth ſonne, Walter 5th ſonne, and James ſixth ſonne and youngeſt, and Dioniſia a daughter, all living, as well ſonnes as daughters, at the tyme of the death of the ſayd George their father. Sole executrix and performer of the laſt will and teſtament of the ſayd George, is Elizabeth his ſecond wife; and overſeers thereof weare Nicholas Woodroofe, Eſquire, ſheriffe and alderman of London, and Robert Taylor aforeſayd his ſonne in lawe; mourners at the ſame funerall weare Edward Stonehouſe his eldeſt ſonne, Thomas Stonehouſe ſecond ſonne, and William Stonehouſe third ſonne. Somerſett and Rougecroix, officers of armes, weare preſent, and did direct and order the ſame funerall, by whome this certifficate was taken, to bee regiſtred and recorded in the office of armes in London, which certifficate is verefied for true by the ſubſcription of the ſeverall names of the mourners aforeſayd, the daye and yeare of the funerall within written.

EDWARD STONEHOUSE.
THOMAS STONEHOUSE.
WILLIAM STONEHOUSE.

The Tymber Hearſe for an Earle.

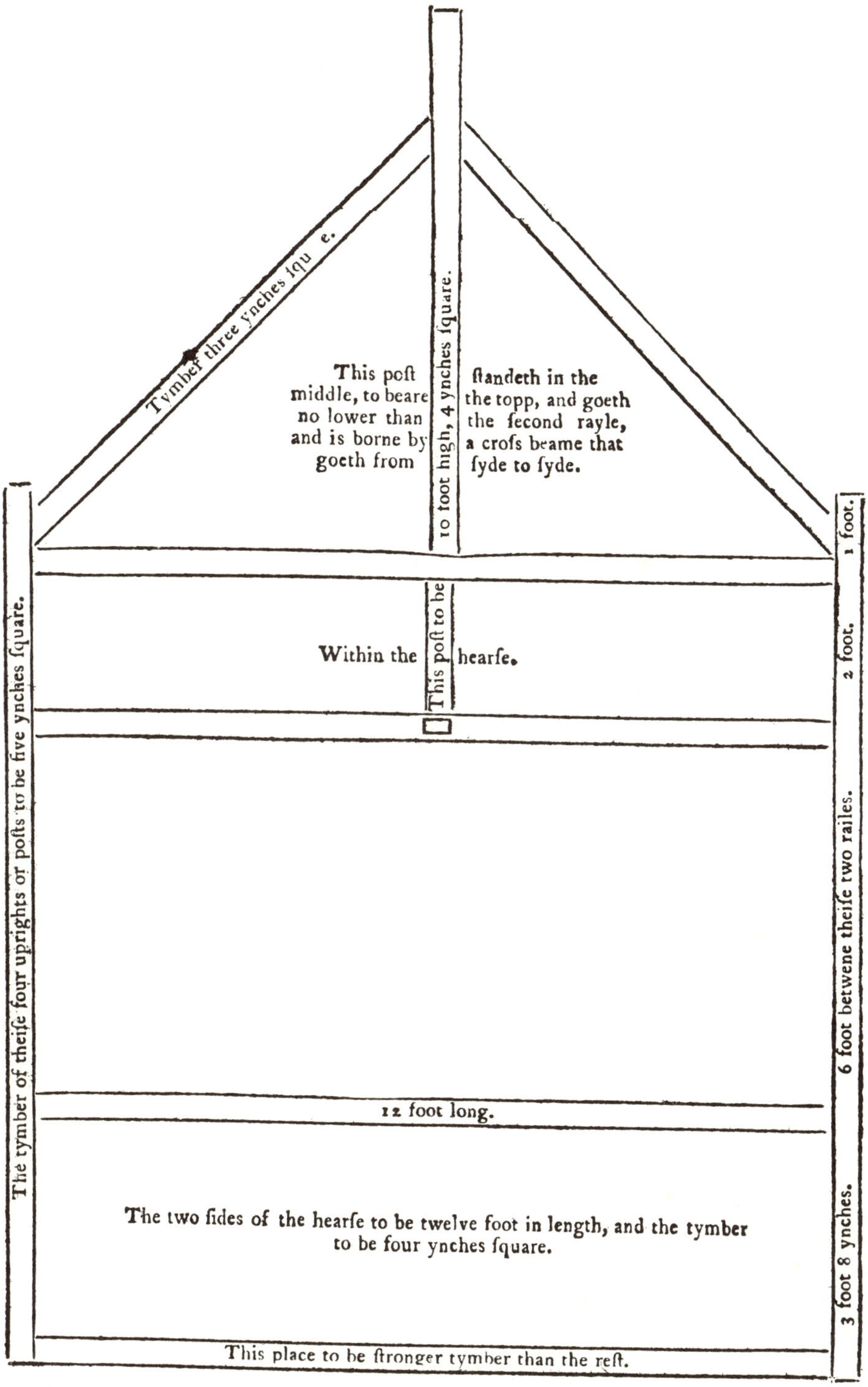

There muſt be an outward rayle of 22 foot in length, and 18 in the breadth, of tymber, about 4 inches ſquare.

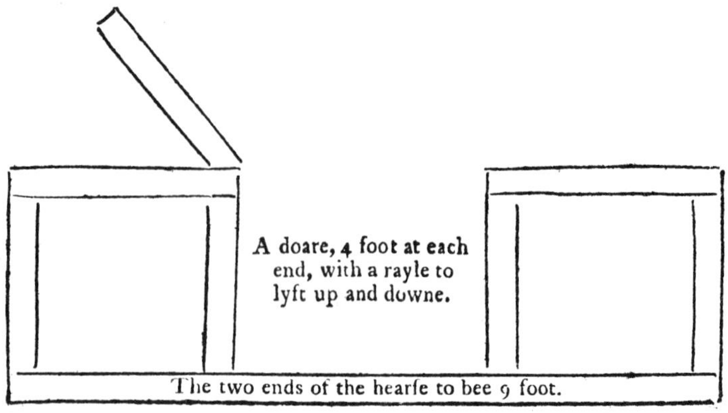
A doare, 4 foot at each
end, with a rayle to
lyft up and downe.
The two ends of the hearse to bee 9 foot.